HOT MUSIC, RAGMENTATION, AND THE BLUING OF AMERICAN LITERATURE

HOT MUSIC, RAGMENTATION, AND THE BLUING OF **AMERICAN LITERATURE**

STEVEN C. TRACY

THE UNIVERSITY OF ALABAMA PRESS

Tuscaloosa

The University of Alabama Press
Tuscaloosa, Alabama 35487-0380
uapress.ua.edu

Hardcover edition published 2015.
Paperback edition published 2016.
eBook edition published 2015.

Typeface: Caslon and Helvetica

Manufactured in the United States of America
Cover design: Mary-Frances Burt / Burt&Burt

∞

The paper on which this book is printed meets the minimum requirements of American National Standard for Information Science–Permanence of Paper for Printed Library Materials, ANSI Z39.48-1984.

Paperback ISBN: 978-0-8173-5896-9

A previous edition of this book has been catalogued by the Library of Congress as follows:

Library of Congress Cataloging-in-Publication Data
Tracy, Steven C. (Steven Carl), 1954–
Hot music, ragmentation, and the bluing of American literature / Steven C. Tracy.
pages cm
Includes bibliographical references and index.
ISBN 978-0-8173-1865-9 (cloth : alk. paper) — ISBN 978-0-8173-8813-3 (ebook)
1. American literature—African American authors—History and criticism. 2. African Americans—Music—Influence. 3. Blues (Music) in literature. 4. Jazz in literature. 5. Music in literature. I. Title.
PS153.N5T67 2015
810.9'896073—dc23

To Arnold Rampersad,
for his continued, unflagging, and invaluable support,
and his inspirational scholarship

Contents

Acknowledgments

So many people have been crucial to my work over the years, and this book is a culmination of so many aspects of my life, that it seems only fair that I try to gather them all together in one place for the thanks they deserve. When I was fifteen years old, I started listening to the blues, largely because of my exposure to the genre through the fantastic blues group Canned Heat. Not only did Alan Wilson, Bob Hite, Larry Taylor, Henry Vestine, and Fito de la Parra draw me in, but they were always concerned about giving others in the blues tradition their due. They led me to Big Bill Broonzy, Sonny Boy Williamson I, Charley Patton, Muddy Waters, Memphis Minnie, and others, thereby changing my life. I followed Al Wilson to a Son House recording, and Henry Vestine to an Albert Ayler recording, thereby opening myself up to Delta blues and jazz—and free jazz—in the process. And, of course, they helped put Albert Collins back on the front lines, and recorded with Sunnyland Slim, Little Richard, Ernest Lane, and John Lee Hooker as well.

Two other gentlemen, Mike Leadbitter and Simon Napier, who edited *Blues Unlimited* magazine, encouraged me to write and interview people for that greatest of blues magazines, leading me to interviews at the age of sixteen with blues song writer and A&R man Henry Glover and boogie woogie and blues powerhouse Amos Milburn. My increasing involvement in writing led me to do a story on Cincinnati blues for the other great blues magazine of the time, *Living Blues*, whose co-editors Jim and Amy O'Neal (now Amy van Singel) were always wonderful and supportive from the time I met them at the 1972 Ann Arbor Jazz and Blues Festival. Early works for these magazines, and *Jefferson* in Sweden, whetted my appetite to do more writing in the field. Of course, the only way I could write was to have the backgrounds and history explained to me through *Blues Unlimited* and *Living Blues*, and reading as much as I could as well. There were no better guides than the writings of the distinguished scholars Paul Oliver, William R. Ferris, Sterling Brown, Alan Lomax, Sam Charters, David Evans, Jeff Titon, John Broven, Tony Russell,

Paul Garon, and John Godrich and R.M.W. Dixon, along with poet Langston Hughes. I have, alas, not met most of them, though I had the great fortune of spending time with Paul Oliver on several occasions, which served to increase my admiration of him and his work.

Meanwhile, I had begun to perform the music I was writing about, leading to a victory in the Hohner Harmonica and Good and Plenty Candy sponsored National Harmonica contest (ages 13–18) in 1971. My appearance on the *The Tonight Show Starring Johnny Carson* playing Little Walter's "Off the Wall" with the Tonight Show Band—with Clark Terry in the trumpet section—made it impossible for a shy kid to remain quiet and withdrawn thereafter. Upon my return from New York, I appeared on the local TV shows hosted by Bob Braun and a number of times with the great gentleman Nick Clooney and his wife, Nina (yes, George's dad and mom, and two of the nicest people you will ever meet). From there, I went on to appear with the Cincinnati Pops Orchestra conducted by the great maestro Erich Kunzel, performing William Russo's *Three Pieces for Blues Band and Symphony Orchestra* alongside former Bengal Mike Reid, who was proving himself a world class musical performer (and person) at the time as well. I played and recorded with Kunzel and the orchestra several more times, including direction and support from the delightful Keith Lockhart. Perhaps most importantly, I began to write about and play with Albert Washington, Big Joe Duskin, Pigmeat Jarrett, James Mays, Phil Buscema, and Hudson Rivers III, the six deepest loves of my musical life. They inspired me to play more, to research more, and to write more, and we had the most exciting times performing together. They are indispensable to my life.

All this while I was becoming a record collector, too. There were not many outlets that carried the blues in 1970, so having J and F Southern Records, later Down Home Music, as an outlet was a great boon. The extremely friendly, committed, and knowledgeable proprietors John Harmer and Frank Scott (J and F) brought a lot of folks some outstanding music and helped lead to the blues boom. Of course, I also haunted local Salvation Army stores on Fridays and Saturday nights rather than dating—I was way too shy for that—and found some great seventy-eights at a quarter a pop. Prom night, I ran into some classmates at the Dairy Farmers while I was picking up some bread for my mother. They were all decked out for the prom; I was playing music with Albert at the Vet's Inn, which was, along with the Soul Lounge and Gus's Place, my favorite venue. My procurement of blues recordings helped make it possible for me to begin hosting, with the council of wonderful radio tutor Tom Knox, a radio show on the mighty WAIF-FM community radio, which provided crucial time for programming that other stations ignored. They also provided the opportunity to air interviews with and performances by local blues talent—H-Bomb Ferguson stopped by without Boo-Boo, his pet snake—as well as fundraising blues cruises that contributed very significantly to the popularity of the blues in Cincinnati. In the meantime, the combination of writing, performing, and hosting gave me the chance to play with Albert, Big Joe, Pigmeat, Phil, and Hudson in larger venues such as Al Porkolab's Bogart's, the only larger club booking blues at the time, and a club that began employing local blues groups as opening acts. Being an opening act is a significant and effective way to promote blues acts and the blues, and we had marvelous times opening for B. B. King, Muddy Waters, Sonny Terry and Brownie McGhee, James Cotton, Albert King, Bo Diddley, Johnny Winter, Paul Butterfield, Canned Heat, Roy Buchanan, Taj Mahal, Ray Charles, and many others, most of whom, especially B. B. King and Sonny and Brownie, were extremely gracious.

At the same time, I was in the process of earning three degrees at the University of Cincinnati. Having been discouraged from remaining in the Afro-American Studies department, I got a spot in the department of English (and some much-needed fellowship cash) with the help of an inspiring professor and mentor, Edgar Slotkin, leading to my discovery that I was passionate about all literature and changing the direction of my life. Once in the English department, I stayed, largely because of the friendship and brilliance of Professors Slotkin, Amy Elder, Wayne Miller, and Robert D. Arner. I continued my own study of blues music in connection with Professor Slotkin's knowledge of folklore, along with the guidance of my good friends and supporters Professors Angelene Jamison and Amy Elder in African American literature, and also specialized in nineteenth- and twentieth-century literature with professors Miller and Arner as my primary guides. I also clarified my aesthetic principles with courses from Professors Elizabeth Armstrong, Jon Kamholtz, and Bill Godschalk. Their most significant guidance in literary study helped me pull together my work on literature and the blues that was crucial for this book. Three Taft Fellowships during these years made it far more manageable to get this work done—they were a godsend.

When I submitted my doctoral dissertation for consideration by University of Illinois Press, the choice of the reader could not have been more felicitous. I have the utmost respect for the work of Arnold Rampersad, and I have come to know him as an outstanding mentor as well. I never took any classes with Professor Rampersad, and yet ever since I came on his radar, he has opened up opportunities for me and supported me FAR beyond the call of duty. Professor Rampersad is another of those teachers I have mentioned who exemplify the scholarship, teaching abilities, masterful writing, and demeanor that provides a template for me to follow. To paraphrase Wayne and

Garth, "I am not worthy!" This particular volume was suggested by Professor Rampersad when I finished the first book on Langston Hughes. Twenty years later, I still remember Professor Rampersad's recommendation. What did he see, or think he saw, in the unemployable and scared little boy before him? I don't know, but I am certainly glad he took the time to look—and ACT. All praises and honor to a great gentleman and scholar.

After I graduated I had difficulty finding a job at a university (ten years!), even after acceptance of my dissertation for publication by University of Illinois Press (thanks to Dick Wentworth and Carol Betts) and a post-doc to write a second one for the same press (thanks to Zane Miller). I spent several years with some wonderful students at Seven Hills Upper School, all the while continuing to perform and write for blues magazines. Steve Tracy and the Crawling Kingsnakes recorded a CD for Blue Shadow and toured the Netherlands behind its release. It was my first time out of the United States receiving hospitality and treatment that put many US club owners to shame. Ultimately, I despaired of getting a job in academia, putting away my diplomas on the shelf (literally the left back corner of the top shelf in my bedroom closet) and looking outside academia. In those years, I received continuing encouragement from Amy Elder and Angelene Jamison, and some unexpected but most kind support from Professor Cathy N. Davidson, who delivered some much-needed encouragement at a dark hour. Then my longtime friend, distinguished professor Joe Skerrett, helped put me together with Esther Terry, head of the Afro-American Studies department at the University of Massachusetts, and after a delay of two or three years, I was in Amherst. I would not be here without those two. I have been particularly fortunate in my colleagues here—John Bracey, Femi Richards, Richard Hall, Nelson Stevens, Bill Strickland, Jim Smethurst, and Tricia Loveland have been especially supportive and valuable to my endeavors, as Professor Skerrett has continued to be. Deans Lee Edwards, Joel Martin, and Julie Hayes provided support and funding beyond what I deserved. Support for this project also came from the TSRF Award subvention offered by Julie Hayes, Dean of Humanities and Fine Arts at the University of Massachusetts, Amherst.

Since I have been at UMass, I have been welcomed by a variety of presses—University of Massachusetts, Indiana University, University of Missouri, and Oxford University Press among them—that all provided me with excellent editors and opportunities for publication. I have been fortunate enough to work with the Department of Theater and the Department of Music and Dance while here. These interdepartmental collaborations led me to think even further about the interrelationships between various genres. My contacts with Alan Nadel and Robert J. Butler, and with Graham Lock, Professor Luo

Gong, Professor Roy Kedong Liu, and others, remind me of how collegial this profession can be. All of these people and events worked together to provide me with this mutifaceted perspective. I believe that they—and many more—have helped me see the complexities of the subject about which I am writing in this volume. I have been particularly revivified in my work by regular visits to China, where my colleagues and students have been so intelligent and delightful as to make me have to "take it up a notch" in my scholarship and teaching. I hope there is a long future of collaboration ahead of us.

Especially for this volume, I have received great support from four outstanding scholars. The great literary critic Professor Robert Butler stood beside the manuscript from its inception and gave great encouragement from a variety of different perspectives. Professor William R. Ferris is a giant in the blues world, of course, and having his approval and support meant a great deal to me. He is also a great gentleman and critic, and I have valued his works since I was a very young man. Professor David Evans lent his expertise and careful eye to the manuscript as well, and his books have always been among my inspirations. And Arnold Rampersad has been—well, Arnold Rampersad! Have I really had the luck to be associated with these scholars?

Additionally, I would like to extend my sincere gratitude to Professor Hank Lazer of the University of Alabama, who resurrected this project when it was dead and sitting on the shelf. Not only did Hank encourage me to dust off the manuscript, but he put me in touch with Dan Waterman at University of Alabama Press, who ushered the book through a very understanding and insightful book approval committee and helped save the book from oblivion. Special thanks also go to Dan Waterman and the professional and hard-working staff at University of Alabama Press, which dealt in a kindly fashion with a notoriously recalcitrant author. I have especially enjoyed working with Vanessa Rusch, whose patience and excellence was of great comfort in the production process. Special thanks also go to Cathy Tracy, Huan Zhou, and Zhu Fangfang for their invaluable, expert assistance with the index.

And especially to my wife and kids, who have always pleased me, entertained me, stuck with me, and made me proud. It has been a long road, and I could not have made it without Cathy, Michelle, and Michael. They are a life's work, and a lifetime of pleasure.

It is hard to explain how thrilling this book has been to write. Now, all books have their own special feeling. But this one. It felt like a culmination of my life's work as a musician, academic, writer, radio show host, collector, and aficionado. Sometimes it felt like, I swear, Whitmanian instant conductors were all over me, charging me ecstatically with thought and energy. Sometimes I felt as if I just needed to stay out of the way of whoever or whatever was writing this, inquiries and connections zipping into my head at too fast of a clip for me to manage. I wrote reminders at 3:32 a.m. on the pad by the side of my bed, recorded snippets of reminders on the tape recorder (it's been a good old wagon, but now it's done broke down), scribbled notes with a piece of chalk on a wrinkled and crumby Dunkin' Donuts bag on the passenger side floor of my car. And I repeated songs in my head endlessly so I could remember them when I got to my office to write them down. OCD is not always so bad.

Right now I am saying to myself, "Ok, Steve, this book isn't really that good. You are making a fool out of yourself. You'll be humiliated when it flops." I have always had that voice. Always. But this time, something is allowing me, not to ignore it—old habits die hard—but to resist it. If this doesn't work, if I have screwed something up, it is my fault, not the music's, nor the teachers', nor the musicians', nor the radio and TV hosts', nor anybody else's. Mine. But I have enough confidence in the muse who assisted me here, that I can still tentatively toss out a guardedly semi-confident comment. I am a custodian of this material. And as Walt Whitman, Langston Hughes, Carl Sandburg, Sterling Brown, and Allen Ginsberg all acknowledge, all of us workers have holy jobs. My father taught me that—how a man who works three jobs to support his family, one of them digging graves in an African American cemetery, laying out the artificial grass, and placing the flowers so everything looked nice for folks on their way to wherever, and the others at gas stations and pony kegs on nights and weekends, getting up the endless next mornings and going on to the same endless tasks—how that man has fought a dragon as big as any that have been fought on this earth, though you'll never read about him in a book. He belongs here. I wish I belonged here as much as he does.

He also taught me about how important music is. This man who dug graves for eight hours a day, then went to work pumping gas at night, and then worked the cash register at a pony keg on weekends. But *always* on Sunday nights, when he could have been sleeping, deserving that rest so much, up in a few short hours to start all over again, I say *always* on Sunday nights you could find him listening to Evangelist Little Abraham Swanson on the radio, followed by the most heavenly music I have ever heard. Dad would pull out his Echo harmonica, and "Church in the Wildwood," "Lady of Spain," "La Cucaracha," "How Great Thou Art," made the air there most rarefied. He could have been sleeping, escaping from the difficulty of his labors. But . . . that bit of musical beauty he could bring in the world, it was necessary, too. For him, for us, forever. The same cracked and calloused hands that wielded post-hole diggers and spades every day cradled that harmonica, handled those songs the way Langston Hughes said we should handle dreams, protecting and caressing them from all the ten-below-zero days in half-dug graves with only a fire in a rusty barrel pretending to fight with the frost. We didn't really argue or fight—Dad was too easygoing for that—but I still think of him when I read Robert Hayden's "Those Winter Sundays," and of the jobs for which he could never be sufficiently thanked.

My mother, of course, was always there when I needed her. And, maybe more importantly, not there when I didn't. She knew how to leave me alone when she knew she really couldn't do anything for me, because I had to do for myself. She trusted my instincts and my decisions, and she always supported me when I needed it. She was a Republican feminist, believe it or not. Oh, she would have balked at the feminist label, but nobody could ever tell her she couldn't do something because she was a woman. She always said she *wanted* to stay home and take care of her kids; if she had wanted to do something different, she would have done it. With everything I do since she has died, I have felt very acutely the wish that she were here so I could tell her about it. She always told me to learn broadly, and to exult in learning. I hope it shows that in all I do, I do for you, Mom.

Yes, the blues singers! I didn't have a real passion in my life before them. Then, my first black blues record purchase brought me Big Bill Broonzy, Charley Patton, and John Lee "Sonny Boy" Williamson, and I have never even blinked my eyes without syncopation since then. They have remained among my most treasured artists ever since, augmented by Blind Blake, Blind Lemon Jefferson, Ma Rainey, Memphis Minnie, Muddy Waters, Howlin' Wolf, Little Walter, Louis Jordan, Freddy King, B. B. King, Lightnin' Hopkins . . . well, you get the idea. But for me, the pinnacle is Elmore James. I remember the first time I heard that sublime recording of "Something Inside Me." Tom Knox played it on the radio one late afternoon while he was subbing on WEBN-FM, and I was transfixed. I stopped dead in the middle of the kitchen—and then I came back to life. The next day I sought out a copy of the recording, which I found on a forty-five. To my dismay, the forty-five was 1:01 shorter than the LP cut—and I couldn't miss even one second more of that sublimity. Elmore was fierce, tender, nuanced, and oh-so heartfelt. I think he taught me I could be those things, too, as a musician, and as a writer. I want to move people the way Elmore James does. I hope I never travel too far away from that. If you haven't heard these artists, especially Elmore, put down this book RIGHT NOW and go to the record store. When you have finished listening, pick up the book again. Check the discography in the back of this volume for CDs that contain some of the greatest music you will ever hear.

It is said that when the great blues singer Big Maybelle, riddled by the ravages of decades of addiction, moaned her last moan, she expired with a poignant "Thank God!" on her lips. I can't help but think that, even though I have never been to the bottom of *that* well, I can still go to it for inspiration. It was Maybelle's gift, and I hope it brought her some relief or brought her some relief knowing that others were relieved by it. Sometimes blues singers get a bad rap. To produce what Maybelle produced took suffering, inspiration, hope, and more hard work and practice than people could ever know. You don't just open your mouth and make that. It is a culmination of so many things. We need to offer all the praise and honor due to our blues singers. "Thank God" for the blues singers.

HOT MUSIC, RAGMENTATION, AND THE BLUING OF AMERICAN LITERATURE

Introduction

Upbeat

In October 1920, Leon Theremin invented his revolutionary electronic musical instrument, the theremin, also called the "aetherphone." Still an amazing, avant-garde electronic instrument today, baffling to the layperson, it makes music when manipulating hands control the space around two metal antennae in such a way as to alter pitch and volume to produce sounds without having to touch the instrument at all. Like the nineteenth-century Romantic metaphor the Aeolian harp, which made sound out of the air as it sat in currents of solitude in the branches of a tree—an instrument of "natural" composition, an exfoliating metaphor for the poet as creator—it too made music untouched by human hands. Unlike the Aeolian harp, the theremin was not a passive instrument. It needed human involvement, human movement, to play songs. Theremin's preference was a hand manipulator such as the great virtuoso Clara Rockmore. But Theremin also tried using five members of Eugene Von Grona's first American Negro Ballet group in the 1930s (one Theremin's future wife prima ballerina Lavinia Williams) to create the song with the movements of their bodies, and Langston Hughes referred to the theremin as commonly known among Harlem intellectual insiders in his story "Who's Passing for Who" (170). Rockmore was primarily a concert artist who performed classical music, but there is a video of Theremin from 1928 that features him playing along with a piano, which performs a light pop-ragtime tune with a stride bass figure associated with the ragtime idiom (Steven D. Martin). It depicts the Russian's intellectually progressive, avant-garde instrument, playing a popular version of music from the folk past, in the pop present, and pointing toward the cutting-edge future, the" hot" music of African Americans, for the edification of both the current-day masses and intellectuals in America and around the world. It appeared at the beginning of a decade of tremendous energy and activity in society and the arts, a culmination of social, musical, and literary developments in relation to African American society that gave the name "the Jazz Age" to the decade, manipulating the space between the white and black poles so as to produce pitches and sounds and volumes growing out of a vague familiar and solidify them into the sounds of America in a way that makes the 1920s a pivotal decade unto itself, worthy of separate discussion.

Interestingly, Rockmore shared the bill a number of times in the 1940s with the noted spiritual, folk song, and classical music performer Paul Robeson. She even recorded, alongside her interpretation of George Gershwin's "Summertime," a version of the black convict song that Avery Robinson helped popularize in a 1922 arrangement of "Water Boy," which had been sung in Robinson's arrangement by black performers Roland Hayes and Paul Robeson. That song, sprung from human interaction with the sweltering southern heat and other chained human bodies that seemed to intuit the sound and meaning of the words with every gasp of the thick, heavy air, was fundamental to Robeson's repertoire as well. Both Robeson and Rockmore could perform the traditional words proudly:

> Ain't no hammer
> In this mountain
> Ring like mine, boys
> Ring like mine (Robeson).

Sterling A. Brown used a variant of the song in his poem "Strong Men" (1931), which itself borrowed its refrain from Carl Sandburg's poem "Upstream," as well.

Small world.

Still, this notion of taking or making music out of the air is a metaphor that has been used by folk musicians from around the world who describe where their songs come from, carried and passed on by the breezes of tradition into the air they breathe. "I'm gonna write you a letter," Alabama bluesman Bo Weavil [*sic*] Jackson sang, "mail it in the air / Because the March wind blows, it blows news everywhere" ("You Can't Keep No Brown," 1927). While the theremin produces music electronically, some say artificially, many people describe the sound as other-worldly or heavenly, profoundly *real*. Georgia blues legend Ma Rainey took her songs out of the air, too. So did Texas bluesman Blind Lemon Jefferson; Russian-born pop-blues singing hot mama Sophie Tucker; white West Virginia country blues singer Frank Hutchison; New York pop, jazz, and blues orchestra leader Paul Whiteman; Davenport, Iowa, jazz trumpeter gone to Chicago Bix Beiderbecke; and radical classical composer from New Jersey George Antheil. They listened to the air as it blew them from rural and urban settings sounds and melodies from folk traditions, manipulated that air to produce exquisite new sounds that joined their precursors and blew/blue themselves into every corner of breathable air. In North Carolina professor-sociologist-folklorist Howard W. Odum's novel *Rainbow Round My Shoulder* (1928), hero Left Wing Gordon locates his joie de vivre in his "rockin' in the slime" (129) that permeated the air he breathed, while others such as Paul Whiteman took their pleasure at the 1924 Aeolian Hall concert that introduced George Gershwin's *Rhapsody in Blue*. Wherever Aeolus blows.

Describing a common African American post-slavery longing for geographical mobility in his June 1926 poem "Homesick Blues," Missouri-born Langston Hughes listened and wrote, "De railroad bridge's / A sad song in de air" (*Collected Poems* 72). His use of the bridge here, from one place to another, from one world to another, from one consciousness to another, demonstrates the utility of that bridge, and of those songs, in *moving* us in this large world. When Ezra Pound wrote that the first artist to explore elements of folk materials was nearly always successful, it was an acknowledgment that the folk environment, even if it became an industrial one, could still hearken to its past over the clangorous clamor of the assembly line buildings that sat heavily upon the earth. Obviously, the songs could travel far from the folk as well. But if we listen carefully, they *should* bring us all back to the same place, the place where folk materials began to formulate an identity that would always be a central, even if remote, part of urban and industrial identity.

Focal Point / Vocal Point

Since Word keeps contesting the words in the title of this book, I assume that they deserve an explanation and justification. The title actually encompasses the three major elements of African American hot music—a catch-all term for the overlapping nature of the genres of African American music bridging into the 1920s. For example, Fats Waller was a ragtime piano player who accompanied various blues singers such as Ada Brown, Rosa Henderson, Alberta Hunter, and Monette Moore; he also recorded jazz with Tom Morris, Red Allen, and white players Eddie Condon and Gene Krupa in the 1920s. One could make similar statements about Jelly Roll Morton and James P. Johnson; and jazz cornetist Johnny Dunn even employed all three piano players at two sessions in the space of thirteen days! Of course, we can see in work songs, spirituals, game songs, and field hollers some other, earlier, ancestors, but the sometimes undifferentiated reference to hot music frequently encompassed the genres of ragtime, blues, and jazz, frequently with reference to two or three of the genres, sometimes with negligible association to any. In one of his series of recorded interviews with Alan Lomax, "When the Hot Stuff Came In," Jelly Roll Morton, leader of the "Red Hot Peppers," asserts that "the hot stuff came in 19–2," qualifying that there was another style of hot music that came before—ragtime. Perhaps the etymology of the word "hot" with this meaning, combined with the stereotypical association of earthy or unbridled sexuality with African Americans, explains it: "hot," as a term meaning to act in a fashion that is passionate or sexually stimulating, goes back at least as far as Chaucer (Calt 128) and certainly draws on the popularity of Louis Armstrong's "Hot Five" and "Hot Seven." In his novel *Not Without Laughter* (1930), Langston Hughes has his Christian grandmother Aunt Hager call the music of her son-in-law Jimboy Rodgers "rag-time" (43), even though he plays a mixture of "blues, shouts, jingles, old hits" (66), as well as church songs, and a good many of the songs he plays in the chapter entitled "Guitar" are decidedly sexually suggestive blues (59–69). My book title arranges these three genres in a way that reflects not the chronology of their emergence, but the arc of influence based in attitudes toward the music and its creators, then transformations of artistic aesthetic, and finally incipient and continuing resolution of social and aesthetic problems in inter-orality and inter-textuality. The intent of this book is to focus as much as possible on the blues tradition, with the realization that the looseness with which this music overlappingly developed and the casual way that the terms for various genres were interchanged at the time mean that sometimes the discussion will veer toward hybrid mixes or ragtime or jazz genres to make relevant musical, social, political, and aesthetic points.

A title of a 1931 jazz recording by the Mills Blue Rhythm Band (named after the white Irving Mills, manager of Duke Ellington and others) captures the racial and aesthetic tensions and the spectrum of attitudes and possibilities for African American music at the time: "Futuristic Jungleism." Rooting jazz in the jungle experience exposes the often racist primitivism of attitudes among whites, and even some blacks, of the time. Often thinking of Africans as savage and backward, some people seeking basic and visceral thrills looked to jazz as an approximation of what it would be like to be earthy and impulsive. Rather than suppressing all of their desires as prescribed by the oppressive and empty society whose shortcomings had been exposed by industrialization and a war of a previously unimagined intensity and destructiveness, they partook in the vicarious thrill of pretending to be earthy and impulsive in the steamy "Negro" nights, while returning to their inhibitions in the chilly dawns. Getting back to the "real" person behind societally based pretensions brought many people, white and black, face-to-face with implications for African American society that not only swung ominously in that old direction, but also ripped a path to the future—art that progressively illuminated. If the jungle "past" and the urbanistic future are both frightening—"Jazz Frightens Bears" read a 1928 *New York Times* headline—they are also infinitely bewitching as well. If society becomes "new" by "regressing" to the jungle, then the jungle is not only contemporary, but futuristic for the avant-garde in terms of how they envision the "progress" of art. Futuristic Jungleism.

The sense of the break-up of contemporary society due to the fragmentation of ideas of morals, ethics, and art produced a feeling of vapidity and isolation that made the world seem hopeless and disordered to many —a "Lost Generation," as a garage owner fired off in a sally aimed at Gertrude Stein and her visionary friends. Of course, African Americans had faced such imposed conditions throughout their history of enslavement and exile in America, so their realization of these feelings in relation to America had come much earlier, and their capacity to deal with the changes artistically emerged in black music and other art before the twentieth century. I see the genre known as ragtime as taking the cultural fragmentation, the raggedness, the frequent dislocation of time, life, and art along with the corresponding sadness in the lives of African Americans, either as inherited from Africa or inherent in America, and "ragging" it. This means putting things back together again in a happier medium that takes the African-based stylistic alterations and discontinuities—the thrusting syncopation, the dialogue of call-and-response, the altered timbre and tone of buzzed, slid, and hollered notes—as a guide to resolution in approach and attitude. Typically ragtime playing combines the percussive rhythms of "patting juba" with syncopating melodies drawn from fiddle and banjo tunes, infusing the music with a heavy dose of traditional black folk culture, combining song, dance, and proud cultural difference into a rollicking attitude, aesthetic, and art. Perhaps even the galop, a lively country dance which was a forerunner to the polka in Prague, lurked in the raggish DNA. Even with its European form, melody, and harmony, it is still very much a folk-based product. Ma Rainey's "Southern Blues" (1923) includes a formula-type stanza that contains the lyric: "Let me be your rag doll, until your Chinee come / If she beats me raggin' she's got to rag it some." Here, the "China doll" clearly represents something precious of very great monetary value—and from another culture—but the singer introduces value of another kind, "raggin'" referring to vigorous sexual activity. The final line, beginning with the conditional "if," introduces doubt that the China can compete on this level with the rag doll, a confidence in the singer of her superior performance. The ragging is both an activity (noun) and a style (adjective) that reorients our values toward an appreciation of the validity, sometimes even superiority, of the rough and vigorous alongside the smooth and polished.

Ragtime is a rollicking, happy music, emerging from a signification upon the *American music without blacks*, that places African Americans at the center of society, creativity, and performance, expressing a cracked society in the process of uniting. This is the opposite of fragmentation—it is a ragtime augmentation. In author-performer Dan Burley's "The Jiver's Bible," to "rag out" meant "to dress up" (223), and "ragmentation" certainly was "stylin'." The piecing of these things together into a rollicking whole I would call the "ragmentation" of life, that which can reconcile all of the tensions, emotions, emptiness, fears, and hopes into a whole, a pastiche that allows us to laugh—even if only to keep from crying—while we shake, rattle, and roll with the risks upon which we must decide in our lives. Gamboling as we gamble, as fast as our gams will take us. Ragmentation is an augmentation. It increases the numbers of those recognizing the fragmentation and contributing their own loose abandon as response to the call of hard times. It grants us a coat of arms that identifies us with all those who suffer along with us—if only for the length of a song, but it is a beginning—and pushes the boundaries of those so-called perfect intervals by a semi-tone, like pushing back the circle of the crowd around a pair of dancers—and African and African American music is frequently found coupled with the dance—about to fly. Ragmentation.

What develops, then, is a white avant-garde and mainstream interest in African American music that results from an African American approach to life and artistic aesthetic, for its analogies to or expression of contemporary white fears and a desire to express them as well. What was perceived as shocking, angular, boundary challenging, and healing was just the prescription for the blues that the country needed:

> The focal base—rhythmic beat and percussive performance—,
> the need to piece together—the multi-themed collages of ragtime—,
> the quest to act impulsively—the improvisation of jazz and blues—,
> the need to effect changes in the old styles—tonal inflection and syncopation—,
> and the need to express the sorrows and the potential joys—blues—of a new era.

The process of imbuing the era and art with the spirit of hardship relieved by hope for the future is the feeling that "the sun gonna shine in my back door someday." The bluing of American literature.

Gershwin biographer Isaac Goldberg once called attention to the looseness and ambivalence with which American society dealt with jazz: "Jazz is all things to all ears. To the theological dogmatist it is a new guise of the ancient devil, to be fought as a satanic agency. To the pagan, if he is minded to interpret novelties in the language of social ethics, it is the symptom of a glorious release from the bonds of moral restraint. The musician, if he is one of the old school, looks upon it with mingled amusement and disgust; if he is of the modernist persuasion, he beholds in it rich possibilities of a new style." As for its racial implications, Goldberg continued, "Jazz was, literally and figuratively, a misalliance, an example of miscegenation that worked to the detriment of the superior race [*sic*]. It was a subtle triumph of black over white" (259–60). Jazz was everywhere, and conflicting opinions abounded about its beauty and significance. American culture was increasingly identifying with and employing its impressions of what African American culture was and meant. But the notion of victory of black over white is surely a paranoid falsity. To supplement is not to supplant; to augment is not to fragment. In an answer to a paraphrase of Hamlet's query "To blue or not to blue" comes the response "It bees dat way already. So move already." One tradition does not threaten the other; they expand each other.

Now if I could only get these infernal modern machines to quit pestering me that I've made a mistake.

The Inspiring Breath

Someone asked me once, "So what do you think—does the blues express emotion or produce emotion?" "Yes," I said. As a musician, the best way I can describe how I feel when I play is that it is as if something from very deep within me wells up, and at the best times takes over and tilts me toward some kind of heaven. Not some specific trouble or sadness, but the distillation of all my life's struggles just rises up from my gut and grit, wrenches my back, my elbows, and my shoulders as if I am making one last heartfelt plea to make it over just one more time, and dazzles me into another dimension. That accumulation of emotion is already there. Usually, as a harmonica player, the performance starts with me folded into myself, quiet and hunched, cradling the harmonica in my hands like I am protecting it from death itself. When it comes genesis time, generally I'll swing up with the upbeat, and wring the first note out of the harmonica with my hands still closed around the instrument, and the roof of my mouth depressed, which bends that note—that blues note—way below pitch as we prepare for the climb.

Slowly, I begin to draw in air through pursed lips, roof still descended, hands bent angularly around the harp, and strangle that harmonica note sensitively, carefully, even exquisitely, while with the muscles in my biceps and thighs flexed rigidly, as if I'm digging a grave, my hands slowly opening up the tomb for the harmonica to escape, the roof of my mouth rising, opening up with the opening of my hands, the music arises, and I arise, in an enthralling near-trance that transports to a place where all the ancestors, all their styles and notes and feelings, gather, prepared to help me through one more song, one more time, because without them I'm nothing until I contribute mine, and then I'll be one of us.

Playing the blues and hearing the blues, I think, work in similar ways. You start way inside yourself, and gradually emerge and open up to others through what you play and feel, offering them a way to live and think that is personal, communally personal, ancestral art out of yourself carried all the way over through performance to the audience itself. And thence to victory, the victory of artistic vision over mundane verisimilitude. The style and the subject matter match, they work together, crumbling the mere detritus of death into a mound of celebration. You always have to have the dirt there, the tangled roots, the slime, the worms, the sweat, and the rain falling sleekly and running over the brim of a long-worn-out Stetson of a weathered grave digger, dropping onto the cheeks and chin of a face in such a way that you can't tell, and never will be able to tell, whether there are tears coursing over that steadfast face, to be dried by the sun in this same place tomorrow, and for days too many to count, until the new man digs one for you.

With lips puckered, the roof of my mouth depressed, hands squeezing, and hunched in wait for the unfolding, with the upbeat over and the focal point set, I begin my rise.

1
Pro cess´, Pro´ cess
Shifting the Accents on the Way In

I

All of us have been touched by the blues. That statement, of course, can mean many things, experienced with various intensities and levels of feeling, from the wistful whish of wispy duckling fuzz to the shocking thump of a charging rhino's horn. What imprint it leaves on us is as important as the nature of the approach. If we think of "having the blues" as being synonymous with feelings of sadness, then its alpha to omega fingerprints are all over each of us, from helpless wail at birth to solemn tears at death. If we think of our exposure to the genre known as the blues in all of its various incarnations and formal and technical elements, then again its worldwide fame and reflections in a variety of other artistic genres makes its presence ubiquitous. If we think about the performance or recording of the blues, as understated as Leroy Carr or explosive as Big Maybelle might be, and how it has affected us emotionally, then many people will acknowledge the ability of the blues to describe and produce feelings of loss, isolation, loneliness, and yes, joy, and even indifference and ambivalence—a broad range of emotions. The ability of the blues to express for us and to us testifies to its power to unify through expression: "If you've ever been mistreated," Eddie Boyd sang in "Five Long Years," "you know what I'm talking about." This power to draw together local and international communities through its dramatic, performative spirit in its own very local, vernacular manner, obliterates arguments that deem it impossible for African American expression to be universal.

The efficacy of the blues for American literature became known to a number of artists in literature, music, and visual art soon after its presence became more broadly known through a variety of print, audio, and visual media around the turn of the twentieth century. Just a look at the career of one figure, Miguel Covarrubias, demonstrates the interconnections. Covarrubias was an ethnologist, caricaturist, painter, and art historian. His studies as an ethnologist led him to consider subject matter related to African American culture. He plied his trade as a caricaturist for *The New Yorker* and *Vanity Fair*. His work for those magazines also drew on his passion for the New Negro Renaissance scene in the 1920s, which was manifested in a variety of ways. Having befriended novelist and *bon vivant* Carl Van Vechten and playwright Eugene O'Neill, both of whom helped usher him around Harlem, he developed strong friendships with Langston Hughes and other black writers. He was set and costume designer for *La Revue Nègre* (1925) starring African American phenomenon Josephine Baker. He illustrated works by famed "Father of the Blues" W. C. Handy, as well as for masterful blues poet Langston Hughes and folklorist/writer Zora Neale Hurston. He worked with classical composer-avant gardist George Antheil (referenced by Hughes in his 1945 story "Who's Passing for Who" [170]), himself a close friend of and collaborator with Ezra Pound. From high-brow magazines to cabaret revues, book illustrations for musicians, poets, and folklorists to associations with the extreme cutting-edge classical music composers, Covarrubias demonstrated how widely the arms of the blues might reach, and the variety of disciplines they might embrace. This volume attempts to chart the emergence of the blues into a broad variety of arenas, especially American literature, attending to as many sources and examples as possible, and attempting to characterize the uses to which the blues have been put. It is frequently a very subjective and impressionistic exploration, especially given that "hot" music and "the Jazz Age" were frequent descriptors, likely because of the more sad and low-down connotations of the word "blues." I hope to pick up at 1930 with a second volume that will likely run about thirty years' worth of literature, and then follow with a third to bring things up to contemporary times. For now, a discussion ending at 1929 is plenty to cover.

Writing a volume dealing with the interactions of the blues with American literature is a daunting task. We live, after all, in a world where literary history is not viewed as a stable and continuous tradition where cause and effect relationships are easily determined and trusted, and chronology weaves a deceptive web that must be avoided by the critic who would fly in the face of old conventional notions of mechanical rather than the Bergsonian notion of a dramatic time, influenced by factors of the levels of interest and excitement. We live in an era that is distrustful of words like "meaning" and "influence," and perhaps quite rightly so, since determining such things out of the complicated welter of issues, influences, and modes of expression can be extremely difficult. Perhaps notions of the complementary nature of influence and intertextuality can assist in sorting through the dilemmas:

> Strictly, influence should refer to relations built on dyads of transmission from one unity (author, work, tradition) to another. More broadly, however, influence studies often stray into portraits of intellectual background, context . . . . The shape of intertextuality in turn depends on the shape of influence. One may see intertextuality either as the enlargement of a familiar idea or as an entirely new concept to replace the outmoded notion of influence. In the former case, intertextuality might be taken as a general term, working out from the broad definition of influence to encompass unconscious, socially prompted types of text formation (for example, by archetypes or popular culture); modes of conception (such as ideas "in the air"); styles (such as genres); and other prior constraints and opportunities for the writer. In the latter case, intertextuality might be used to oust and replace the kinds of issues that influence addresses, and in particular its central concern with the author and more or less conscious authorial intentions and skills. (Clayton and Rothstein 3)

In the case of the blues, we are dealing primarily with oral "texts," the authors of which are frequently indeterminate, and the transmission of which is frequently informal, undocumented, and variable in form—"tradition based communicative units informally exchanged in dynamic variation through space and time," as Barre Toelken articulates it (32). While I intend as much as possible to root ideas of influence and intertextuality in concrete and specific instances, those instances may in fact be individual examples of numerous variants that represent a more common occurrence in the tradition. The value of looking for them, or rather for the possibilities of them, by turning our world every which way but loose to try to approach understanding blues interactions with literature, should be clear.

I do not intend to fix anything pinned and wriggling on a specimen board. Surely that would violate the spirit and polyvocality of the blues. But I do intend to provide a backdrop against which I will discuss how various writers have been exposed to African American culture, either in itself or in its expression in white popular productions in a variety of media. In this way, the blues may provide examples of black art that are analogous to other techniques or ideas upon which writers (and other artists) of the 1920s were drawing. These blues may reinforce or extend analogous points, or reveal new possibilities for poetry, fiction, and drama that are directly connected with exposure to expressions of African American artistry.

My aim is to attempt to prepare a broad and specific social, cultural, aesthetic, cross-racial context that may render "evidence" that seems individually merely possible or even far-fetched more reasonable or convincing. Not everything will seem convincing to everybody. I will attempt to acknowledge significant possible alternatives to connecting points to the blues tradition. I hope, however, that the comprehensive details and close discussions that I provide will convince (yes, I know "con" is the first syllable of that word) readers that the perspective I am providing is viable and potentially illuminating, both about the era and the literature.

Most importantly, arguments or points about literary works that are sometimes individually unconvincing or seem far-fetched may, in combination with other observations about those literary works, help produce an aggregate argument that makes the blues a palpable presence. No, such things as loneliness and heartbreak are not exclusive to the blues. But given their ubiquitousness in the blues, to leave them out of a more extensive case for the presence of blues in a literary work would clearly be a mistake. Other blues elements, of course, *must* be there, but it makes no sense to leave out potential pieces of a puzzle.

Material from other genres that I will marshal in support will be drawn as much as possible from contemporary works and, preferably, works that antedate the era of the literature. My focus will be as concrete as the city streets on the soles/souls of the jobless, so that the likelihood of what I am saying about the uses to which the blues are put will stand out like calluses on the cracked outer edges of big toes. Is it problematic that author choices may have been limited by what they were exposed to that prevented them from making other choices? Certainly. Would it have been possible for them to explore other possibilities? Certainly again. Might there have been something about the time and place in which they lived that influenced those choices? Indeed. My intention is to get around to all of those issues and try to sift through the materials to make as intelligent a guess about the conscious or unconscious uses of the blues in their works as I can. Will someone disagree? Of course. Might they be right? Of course again. Can we discuss the possibilities? Indeed. And we should.

II

In "Gambler's Blues," B. B. King sang, "I don't know what love is, but let me tell you I must have it bad." Frequently it happens that we can identify feelings that are complex and quite discernible and clear to us, but can't articulate them definitionally. So with the blues. Some might think it odd that we compare the feelings of the blues with feelings of love, but that seems to be the result of an incomplete knowledge of the African American blues tradition—whence it comes, when it emerged, what it has gone through, how it functions, and, finally, what it represents. Viewed in such contexts, the blues is a multifaceted constellation of feelings, and a genre that has much in common with the nature and function of love. Although many people associate the word "blues" with sadness, the blues, as both music and feeling, actually express and evoke a variety of emotions. The primary subject matter of the blues deals with a variety of relationships between mates—overwhelmingly straight, sometimes gay, bisexual, or transgendered—experienced during the cycle of life, but mostly from the time of sexual maturity onward. Since the blues as a genre is frequently viewed as presenting honest emotions and scenarios rooted in real life, it makes sense that we would encounter a variety of emotions and subject matter associated with relationships, not just sadness, expressed in a variety of ways. And, indeed, we do.

The blues is rooted, rootless, loving, sensual, repulsive, combative, welcoming, yearning, hating, isolating, uniting, objectifying, idealizing, protesting, questioning, affirming, and more, and more. Robert Johnson declares, "I'm gonna beat my woman 'til I get satisfied" ("Me and the Devil Blues," 1937) and Jimmy Rushing gushes "I love my baby better than I do myself" ("Boogie Woogie Blues" 1937). Big Joe Turner celebrates fidelity with "My baby's my jockey she's teaching me how to ride" ("Roll 'Em Pete," 1938), while Texas Alexander laments unfaithfulness in "she cooks cornbread for her husband, biscuits for her back door man" ("Corn-Bread Blues," 1927). Bessie Smith sings the "Young Woman Blues" (1926) in the present, while Memphis Minnie reminisces about "In My Girlish Days" (1941). Lucille Bogan sings the lesbian "B.D. Woman's Blues" (1935), Charlie Manson his hyper-heterosexual "Nineteen Women Blues" (1936), which was based on Trixie Smith's "Sorrowful Blues" (1924). And then there is the almost paradoxical "compliment" offered in Georgia Tom Dorsey's "Pig Meat Blues" (1929), "folks may call you pigmeat, and you may be pigmeat, but you're built on an old hog frame." On the one hand Joe Pullum sang a smooth "Blues With Class" (1935), and on the other Curtis Jones barrelhoused his "Blues in the Alley" (1939) and "Down in the Gutter" (1939). Perhaps Memphis Minnie, miscredited under the pseudonym "The Yas Yas Girl," said it best in "Blues Everywhere" (1937), lamenting that the blues are ubiquitous—in her house, mailbox, bread box, meal barrel, and bed—since her "good man left town." As we will see, the blues were everywhere in several senses: in the racially delimited lives of African Americans and others of comparable class status; in a world rocked by war; in the aesthetics of the intelligentsia in America and Europe searching for a style adequate to their expression of ennui and irony on the one hand, and gayety with rollicking, syncopated abandon on the other; in those rejecting and rebelling against bourgeois values; and indeed all media from race records to pop culture to Broadway to art galleries to films to concert halls, and back again to the individual subconscious of the human mind. Indeed, the recent reissue *Black Europe*, a 44 CD set, contains 1,244 tracks recorded by people of African descent in Europe between 1890 and 1930, from rags, to coon songs, to spirituals, to pop songs, to African songs.

Saying that we have all been touched by the blues implies that we have an understanding of what the blues are, and by extension we ought to be able to define the blues. Problem: the oral and visceral nature of the origins of the African American blues tradition render definition too complicated for casual consideration. The blues come from obscure and mixed origins though clearly influenced by socio-political circumstances. They emerged at an indeterminate time. They were labeled with a term that implies one type of emotion that is inadequate to the breadth of experiences described. They encompass an array of formal patterns that are sometimes loosely employed but at other times entirely unnecessary to expressing the *elan vital* of the blues. And they evolved in combination with other elements over time, though maintaining their essential original nature. The moaning, groaning, cooing, and bellowing—the emotional vocalization of the blues—almost seems to necessitate a despondency of expression to match the frequently unhappy subject matter, or a rhapsodic effusion to express the cathartic feeling it evokes. The printed word is insufficient.

When Memphis Slim commented to Alan Lomax that "[t]he blues came from slavery" (*Blues in the Mississippi Night*, 1947)—echoed later by James Butch Cage in conversation with Paul Oliver (*Conversation* 22)—he was recognizing a unique and tragic set of historical circumstances to which was traceable a series of events that over centuries resulted in the emergence, after Reconstruction, of the musical genre called the blues. Had the greed and rapacity of the transatlantic slave trade not existed, violently disrupting the history and culture of two continents, the transnational and diasporic changes wrought by the economic enterprise would have not have existed in their present state. One of the darkest chapters in human history would not have been written, but neither would one of the most remarkable stories of human survival and transcendence have emerged from such horrors, nor would the blues genre have come into existence. Any attempt to understand African American culture, Slim is telling us, must take into account the manner of kidnapping and enslavement that characterized the arrival of most Africans to these shores up to the nineteenth century. And any attempt to understand and describe the lives of those captive Africans and their ancestors must confront the ways in which unique, syncretistic artistic production continually renegotiated the earliest and continuing legacies of African American chattel slavery. As David Evans has suggested, "through syncretism and reinterpretation, including consolidation, substitution, subversion, and accommodation, African musical characteristics have not remained static and frozen in time but live on vigorously in ever-changing, ever-adapting ways" ("Patterns of Reinterpretation" 214). These patterns extend to literary artists, both black and white, in the twentieth century.

The blues music genre, then, does not merely express instances of hardship and sorrow that characterize the etymological meaning of the term that predates the genre. Certainly blues can deal with those emotions, along with other shades of feeling along the gamut of emotions. The blues *is* a feeling. Further, though, the blues music genre is a cultural and historical mode of creation, expression, and survival that encompasses crucial elements embedded in the transnational diasporic experience that generated it—the African slave trade.

It is West African culture and aesthetics in syncretized fermentation with imposed Euro-American culture and aesthetics, slowly made manifest through a continuing development and interchange, that produced the work songs, game songs, spirituals, minstrel songs, ring shouts, and ragtime that preceded and sometimes overlapped in time the gradual emergence of blues music in the late nineteenth and early twentieth century. For example, Solomon Northup reports the following social song in his slave narrative *Twelve Years a Slave* (1853):

> Who's been here since I been gone?
> Pretty little gal wid a josey on. (220)

The lyrics are known to blues fans through non-blues recordings by Leadbelly from 1935:

> Who's been here since I've been gone?
> Pretty little girl with a red dress on.
> Pretty little girl with a red dress on.
>   Who's been here since I've been gone?
>   Great big man with a derby on
> Great big man with a derby on ("Po' Howard")

Plus blues from Bo Carter from 1938:

> Baby, who've been here since your daddy been gone?
> I don't know who the man was, daddy, had a derby on
>   ("Who's Been Here?")

and Howlin' Wolf in 1956, over one hundred years after Northup:

> Whoa-oo, who been here baby since
> I-I been gone?
> A little bitty boy, derby on.
> A-whoo-hooo, whoo-hooo
> Whooo ("Smokestack Lightnin'")

One can find many other lyric as well as musical carryovers from this music into the blues. The aesthetic results of this evolution of conflict and resolution are impossible to chart with absolute assurance or with absolute historical and chronological accuracy. The system of slavery viewed such developments in the realm of orality beneath the attention of historians—indeed, many commentators found the idea of African and African American culture by and large—beneath the realm of possibility.

But certain larger and more obvious differences between the cultures of the two continents do suggest that each contributed, one through continuity of particular West African cultures—though, as David Evans points out, "typical blues traits are quite widespread in Africa" ("African Elements" 10)—and one through the selection from imposed Euro-American ideas, something to the gumbo concocted by African American chefs. When imagist poet Amy Lowell wrote, in 1920, that "the complicated syncopation of the American negro has captivated the world under the vulgar and misleading name of ragtime," and that "[r]agtime must be instinct in the Negro race, a memory of the Congo, probably," she references such contemporary scientists as Franz Boas, European anthropologist (who taught, encouraged, and likely exchanged ideas with Zora Neale Hurston), as a way of trying to negotiate what she hears as great rhythmical complexity in their syncopation. This is a complexity, which most folks do not associate with "savage or semi-civilized races," that she sees as employing "exceedingly subtle rhythmic effects" (130). That year, the same year that Mamie Smith was recording her groundbreaking first blues recordings and Eugene O'Neill staged *The Emperor Jones*, so-called low art and high art—a decidedly indistinct and undistinguished binary "distinction" we will have to interrogate later—were finding themselves rooted in distinct African elements of the African American past that made its relevance obvious.

One caveat to this argument is that scholars do not know whether and how much African musicians had been exposed to European or African American music before African materials were first recorded on the page or on recording devices. The sometimes mystifying paths that folklore takes traveling from one village, country, even continent, are wondrous, and caution us against arguing absolutely for a total absence of connection, especially given the scantily documented arrival of Europeans on the continent of Africa with regard to such cultural elements. Given the extreme adaptability of African musicians, we can imagine an instrument, tune, or technique played by an early European visitor being incorporated into the local African musical tradition with ease. But that incorporated element could well have reflected a European appropriation of African American modalities. We must assert with caution.

A variety of elements of blues music seem to have taken particular influence from the cultures of West African tribes. We cannot always specify exactly which tribes contributed what people or characteristics to what region of America because of the shady and shameful way the slave trade was carried out, and the ways in which records such as ship manifests and other records have been mishandled. This tends to render arguments somewhat more impressionistic than we would like. We do know that the Senegambian region provided many of the captured slaves who were kidnapped and who brought blues-influenced music to America, and it was people from that region who brought the traditions that formed many of the first African American musics and helped transmit, through that, music elements that turned up later syncretized with Euro-American influences in the blues. West African music in general is frequently percussively performed, not only on the drums that are so connected in the popular mind with Africa, but also on the aerophones (wind instruments), chordophones (stringed instruments), and idiophones (instruments without strings or membranes) also found in the region. A 1964 recording of Fra Fra tribesmen by Paul Oliver, for example, features the percussive playing of a hollow gourd rattling with beads inside, with a sound similar to that of a washboard player in African American blues and jug bands, such as Amanda Sorter's playing with Jazz Gillum on "Riley Springs Blues" (1941); and ethnomusicologist Laura Boulton's recording of a "War Song" (1934) performed on a lute by a Tuareg tribesman has snapping and hammering of the type we hear on One String's "Rolling and Tumbling," recorded in Los Angeles in 1960. However, somehow the Fra Fra tribesmen might have heard a recording like "Riley Springs Blues," so we must beware the post hoc, ergo prompter hoc fallacy, while still understanding that a long cultural history renders the connections very *possible*.

Explanations from the nineteenth and early twentieth century frequently ascribe this percussive predilection to the "primitive" nature of Africans, and apply exoticized or horrified explanations of the characteristic through reference to the heart beat and racing of excitable human blood, as Elizabeth Kilham described a visit to a Sea Island church after the Civil War: "[there began] one of those scenes, which, when read of, seem the exaggerations of a disordered imagination; and when witnessed, leave an impression like the memory of some horrid nightmare—so wild is the torrent of excitement, that, sweeping away reason and sense, tosses men and women upon its waves, mingling the words of religion with the howlings of wild beasts, and the ravings of madmen" (White and White 103). It might be better said that the drumbeat can be elemental and essential—something, in fact, that connects us all—but human life is anything but uncomplicated and primitive. And so with the percussiveness of African music as well. The emphasis on percussiveness in blues music—Son House thrashing the strings on his guitar performing "Death Letter Blues" (1965), the accelerating, pounding rhythm of a Sonny Terry harmonica "Fox Chase" (1938), the thunderous drive of Meade Lux Lewis's "Honky Tonk Train Blues" (1927), the bleating of Red Prysock's saxophone on "Hand Clappin'" (1955)—indeed indicates an inheritance from a tradition with stronger percussive performance tendencies than that encountered by the first slaves arriving on American soil.

In West African music, percussion is employed in both polymetric (performing more than one meter simultaneously in a single performance) and polyrhythmic (combining more than one rhythmic pattern simultaneously in a single performance) ways that far surpassed the metrical and rhythmic developments of Western music in the nineteenth century. Polymeter is particularly disorienting, almost anarchic sounding, to Western ears, since monometer carries the day in Western music. And African polyrhythms and other techniques opened new vistas in European art. Such composers as Debussy, Dvořák, Hindemith, Milhaud (Composer Aaron Copland refers to "a fascinating blues section" in *La Creation du Monde* in 1929 [Kostelanetz 199], surely the call-and-response, syncopation, and prominent use of flatted thirds and sevenths in the second section), Krenek, Gershwin, and Stravinsky all employed elements that also had found their way into African American music. Copland, once a pop-jazz pianist who resigned his "jazz" position in 1924, wrote of jazz rhythms in 1927 as "different in quality and effect not only from those of the madrigals but from all others as well. The peculiar excitement they produce by clashing two definitely and regularly marked rhythms is unprecedented in occidental music. Its polyrhythm is the real contribution of jazz" (Kostelanetz 309, 87). Still, Copland's work, such as *Three Moods* (1920–21), is more Jazz Age pep than jazz, and his *Four Piano Blues* (1926–48) is wistful and reflective, but formally and sonically not African American blues.

Scholars such as Alan Lomax have speculated that the widespread use of polymeter and polyrhythm in West African societies may in fact reflect a community oriented toward finding ways to accommodate alternative ideas and counter-currents in the predominant flow of ideas in the community, as opposed to a rigid hierarchy that suppresses disagreement ("Song Structure and Social Structure" 448). This truly opposes a democratic spirit to a totalitarian one—a notion to be explored in later chapters. Indeed, Janheinz Jahn interprets the polytheism of West African communities to be related to the presence of these polymeters and polyrhythms in the music, and he accounts for the stark contrast in African and Western music as being attributable to a Western monotheism that encourages monometer, producing a thoroughgoing difference between the nature and aesthetics of the two (*Muntu* 219). This is an oversimplification of West African musical tradition, drawn from concepts found among the Alexis Kagame's study of the Bantu of Ruanda and not necessarily applicable to West Africa at large. Gerhard Kubik, for example, cautions scholars against adopting ideas "from just one delineated culture" to generalize about West Africa—a complaint applied to Henry Louis Gates in his use of Èṣù and Legba from Yoruba and Fõ culture. Further, Mandinka griot Foday Musa Suso, whose ancestral history as a griot goes back eight hundred years, asserts differences among the playing of West African griots: "The Gambia, Guines-Bissau, and Senegal are the home of the kora; here, it is common for kora players to also sing. The style in these countries is faster and louder than it is in Mali and Guinea, where musicians usually don't play and sing at the same time" (50). However, despite these cautionary notes, Jahn does raise an interesting point of general contrast between cultures through his comparison that opens up a space for the consideration of both major and subtle differences in emphasis.

Although polymeter did not carry over into the blues and jazz traditions in the United States, certainly polyrhythms are a major characteristic of the blues—as of ring shouts, minstrel songs, and ragtime before it. A listen to Blind Blake's breathless, bubbling guitar playing on "Righteous Blues" (1930); Louise Johnson's shifting clusters of rhythm on "On the Wall" (1930); the swinging and swirling brass and reed sections of Johnny Otis Orchestra's call-and-response riffs pumping up Ben Webster on "One O'Clock Jump" (1951); and Little Milton's blasts of brassy funk on "I Play Dirty" (1969) will testify to that. The polyrhythms of African American music may indeed reflect the temperament and aesthetic of a community that understands that counter-narratives exist to the master narrative of a society that ignores and suppresses them. Particularly in a supposed democratic society, people deprived of their liberty are aware of the irony of that narrative, and especially prepared to interrogate, dismantle, and reconstruct that ideal both in subject matter and style. Seeking to establish a "blues school" of literature (Jackson 296–97), author Ralph Ellison commented "the art . . . was what we had in place of freedom" (*Shadow and Act* 254–55). Thus, jazz and blues have frequently been seen as quintessentially liberated and liberating genres, emphasizing a generous polyvocality that affirms the variety of viewpoints within the commonality of a disparate and cooperative group. They are audible proof that one can find spiritual unity and euphony even in dissonant sounds. E pluribus unum.

This polyvocal and polyrhythmic predilection is related to another central feature of West African music that carries over into the blues: antiphony. Antiphony, of course, exists in a variety of musics, Gregorian chant among them. But it is far more likely that antiphony, or call-and-response, as it is also known, was passed on to enslaved African Americans from the West African tradition. "Ahanta Chant One," recorded in Ghana in 1979, exemplifies the use of overlapping call-and-response—where the call-and-response hand off to each other with a moment where each has a hand on the baton, so to speak, an Olympian interlocking of both parts even as they function as separable elements. The call portion of the performance may be passed around to more than one performer and may, in a sense, be improvised in relation to the individual, though the response is frequently standardized and stylized, providing an admirable unity and completion in the performance.

Similar types of call-and-response might be manifested a number of ways in the blues. Indeed, it entered, as Tony Bolden pointed out, into African American quilting style as well, setting up patterns that draw on similar visual interactions (59). For example, instrumentalists commonly respond to sung passages in spaces that frequently exist between the completed vocal performance of one line and the beginning of the next, as in Lonnie Johnson's "Blue Ghost Blues" (1927). A roughly inflected vocal line or lyric might evoke a similar rough sound from an instrument, or a contrasting tender one, as on Elmore James's "Something Inside Me" (1960). Blues stanza patterns themselves contain variations where the lines themselves are call-and-response patterns, from the most common AAB pattern (one line, repeated, with a final line that end rhymes and completes the thought in various ways, as in Henry Spaulding's "Cairo Blues" from 1929) to an AB refrain pattern (one line, followed by a different line that end rhymes, followed by a refrain carried across from stanza to stanza, as in Lucille Bogan's "They Ain't Walking No More" from 1930). Sometimes these refrains invite audience participation through a sing-along element, as in "Jim Jackson's Kansas City Blues" (1927), Allen Shaw's "I Couldn't Help It" (1934), or the quintessential "hokum" tune Tampa Red and Georgia Tom's "It's Tight Like That" (1928). Further, the solo within a song can be seen as a (frequently voice-like) response to the vocal, in an almost tension and release fashion. And there exist recordings on which there are voices that respond to what the singer is saying, as in duet recordings like "New Black Snake Blues" (1928) by Victoria Spivey and Lonnie Johnson or

Butterbeans and Susie's "Elevator Papa, Switchboard Mama" (1930), responsorial signifying on Big Maybelle's "Gabbin' Blues" (1952) and male or female choruses utilized on Little Esther's "Mainliner" (The Robins) (1952) or Ray Charles's "I Believe to My Soul" (The Raeletts) (1959), respectively. Robert Farris Thompson calls this "a means of putting innovation and tradition, invention and imitation, into amicable relationships" (87), and indeed the invited participation does produce a unified polyvocal performance. The point is, the blues (and jazz, gospel, and oral sermons) is imbued with this element of call-and-response, down to the performative element, which calls on the audience to respond to the performance personally and dramatically—to become part of the performance and to help ameliorate the frequent sadness of the subject matter through identification, unity, co-performance, and transcendence.

The polyrhythmic call-and-response characteristics of West African music and the blues, tapping as they do participatory elements that are more sparsely utilized in Anglo-American music, find further socio-cultural support in the technique Westerners term "syncopation." Derived from the word "syncope," meaning a skipped heartbeat, syncopation is an acknowledgment of the metronomic heart beat and the significant space surrounding it, displacing rhythmic accents from strong to weak beats. Richard Alan Waterman noted the importance of the metronome sense to African music—the need to have an absolute sense of where the beat is, so that polyrhythm, polymeter, and syncopation can be used by groups of musicians in a complex and effectively coordinated way (211). Recordings of the Donno drummers of Ghana from 1979 exemplify such a group of musicians whose performance might become anarchic without this metronome sense. Syncopated notes exist in the spaces just before or just after the metronome beat. They evince a tendency to topple or de-center Western listeners from a strongly imposed dominant beat into a realm less visited and understood by the Western musician and composer, though syncopation does occur in classical music, as in Handel's *Water Music*, for example. In a way, this space is claimed by and for the non-Western vernacular consciousness and voice, which must always know where the nodes of regularity are and dart trickster-fashion through the syncopated holes in the cabbage patch fence in order to survive. For an historically oppressed people, demonstrating the legitimacy of areas unexplored, unauthorized, indeed unrecognized by the dominant culture assists in transforming the dominant cultural narrative and social space, especially when, as African American music has done, the music teasing and circumventing the beats becomes the primary musical influence in the controlling culture. Of course, the recognition of this supercession can be gradual, even glacial, though it exists for a century, as witnessed by the great but underrecognized importance of African American music and culture for American white mainstream culture.

Style, of course, does speak to us, and this is particularly true with regard to manipulations of tone and timbre that produce specific communications in West African societies. Laura Boulton collected examples in the 1930s of the talking drums, as well as a remarkable recording of "Battle Signals" on a War Horn from the Kru tribe in Lagos, the sounds of which represent the tribal language and then English, commenting specifically on a battle scenario as it transpires. The messages of the talking drums function in a similar way, and the idea of the ability to communicate through drums in this fashion was the impetus for the suppression of drumming in the New World upon the arrival of African slaves, which itself may have created greater opportunity and privilege for those who performed on instruments other than membranophones. One of the greatest compliments one can pay to blues or jazz musicians is to say they made their instrument talk, or that they told a story through their solos. The remarkable "Mama Blues" (1927) by William McCoy features a harmonica performance that literally talks—literally forms the words "I want my mama" by inhaling the words into the harmonica holes while drawing in the breath and opening and closing the cupped hands to produce the word-sounds. McCoy produces the same type of simulation that Alvino Rey would later make on his "singing guitar," interestingly recording a "Mama's Blues" of his own and playing the words "Alvino Rey and his singing guitar" on *The Lawrence Welk Show* in the 1960s.

Further, the legacy of tone languages from Africa may in fact be operating in the African American improvisational tradition through the attachment of particular meanings to certain sounds or sequences of sound. For example, in Albert Collins's "Conversation with Collins" (1969), Collins clearly uses sometimes clipped, sometimes aggressive tone and phrasing to indicate a growing impatience with a wife who has stayed out past her promised time of return as the speaker struggles with the responsibility of taking care of the children. Collins rips off a razor-like phrase just as it becomes apparent that the wife has disregarded her promise. The musical conversation between husband and wife contains notes and sequencing that makes it clear that the two are cursing at each other—F*** YOU, MOTHERF***ER—climaxing in an explosive solo that indicates the emotional pitch at which their argument arrives. Through his narrative commentary, Collins makes explicit the meaning of his guitar solo. Still, in African American vernacular music, especially blues and jazz, all kinds of vocal sounds with verbal messages attached are pervasive.

We might even call attention to the convention in the early folk-blues to play something on guitar or harmonica in place of some or all the words of the line being sung, as in Furry Lewis's version of "John Henry" (1929), where "Cool drink of water 'fore I" is succeeded by a note played by the slide on the guitar, rather than providing the final word, "die." This close connection between what is sung and what is played emphasizes the identification between voice and instrument, and mirrors the notion that the instrumental music does deliver a specific message, especially if one is familiar with the tradition and language. It also emphasizes that there are sometimes "gaps" that must be filled in by listeners, making the song communally participatory. The Iserian reader or listener, then, is communally implied in the identification and interpretation of the meaning, with feet planted firmly in African American vernacular culture.

Further, since the blues is a music passed on over one hundred years or so from ancestors and represents a tradition, we may think of an individual blues song as speaking with a chorus of voices from the past as well. The form gains broadening and deepening meaning incrementally over the years and represents a historical, inherited wisdom as well as a current one. We might even see this as being manifested in the progression of a blues stanza which, with its response line, provides a statement and commentary that sometimes complicates the dilemma faced by the singer. For example, Bumble Bee Slim sings on "If I Make It Over" (1935),

> Well I'm blue and evil so many things to learn.
> Well I'm blue and evil so many things to learn.
> So many days to worry, so many ways to turn . . .
>
> Whistle keeps on blowin' and I got my debts to pay.
> Whistle keeps on blowin' and I got my debts to pay.
> I've got a mind to leave my baby, Lord I've got a mind to stay.

In this way, the music is communal and individual, and demonstrates the ways that the communal and individual feed each other in the context of passing on wisdom, knowledge, and culture.

Whooping, growling, buzzing, constricted shrieking, wavering, and quivering pitch spaces, and so-called blue notes, all elements identified with the blues, seem to stem from the West African tradition as well, as pointed out by Robert Palmer (25–39) and William Barlow (17–18). Western scholars have not always known how to deal with such elements, perceiving them as "primitive," "muddied," or "distorted" sounds, all of which have pejorative connotations in relation to the values of the so-called pure, clean sounds valued in Western music. Even to call them inflected, or literally "bent from a particular course," implies that there is a pre-existing standard from which these sounds depart, which establishes the Western as the a priori standard from which the African diverges. Graeme M. Boone points out that "blue notes are flexible melodic pitches (or pitch 'spaces'), opposable to the fixed pitches (or pitch 'points') that form the basis for most melody, and many musical instruments in the Western traditions. Blue notes are commonly situated around the third, fifth, and seventh degrees of the scale. The effect of these notes is striking: it includes moaning, crying, and other expressive vocal sounds that cannot be captured within a common fixed-pitch melody, but that have musical value in the blues" (63). This musical value, often seen as an emotional value in contrast to western pitch points, should be seen as having an intellectual message and value as well. That is, confronted with a social, economic, and cultural choice to capitulate to Western aesthetic values and sounds and leave the supposed "primitive," culturally vacuous past behind, the choice to retain distinctive elements of that past and fashion a new music is indeed an act of resistance, and of liberation, conscious or not. Rod Gruver articulates this notion in his discussion of the blues as a secular religion: "But organic man, man the irrepressible, wins a major victory in the blue note itself; for the blue note is a symbol of man's refusal to give up his unpredictable ornery-ness, his inalienable right to be himself and nobody else's. For there is in the blue note and the improvisations based on it a freeing of the spirit that gives full play to the creative imagination" (Tracy 223). David Evans reemphasizes the connections: "In this blues environment, where nearly everything is in a state of flux and few institutions or relationships have much permanence, except for the overwhelming institutional oppression that threatens from outside, blues functions very much like a religion and a mythology and the blues singer can be projected to a godlike status" ("Traditional Blues Lyrics" 40).

It is probably best to say that the African comprehensively embraces the spectrum of occurring sounds in the world, employing them for their intellectual, emotional, and musical value as they seem most appropriately to be used, even though the productions might, as termed by many whites, in the words of Peter Bailey, "sound out of place" (197) or inappropriate to "civilized" circumstances—such as the flatulent sounds of jug blowing on the recordings of various jug bands from Memphis, or the snorting of Albert Ayler. It seems to be a liberatory aesthetic actuated by a closeness to and acceptance of natural sounds. This, too, is reflected in the blues tradition. When Alfred Lewis whoops on "Friday Moan Blues" (1930), it resembles the whooping and echoic technique of the Fula flutist on "Bengsimbe" (1978). The growling of Tommy McClennan on "Brown Skin Girl" (1939), the nasal buzzing of Slim Harpo on "I'm a King Bee" (1957), the constricted shrieking of King

Solomon Hill on "Whoopee Blues" (1932), the wavering and quivering pitch spaces of Bessie Smith on "The St. Louis Blues" (1925), plus the multitude of blue notes "all around all of their beds," make the legacy clear and, in fact, contribute to the expansive variability of the blues.

Improvisation is a hallmark of jazz and blues, but it also exists in other types of non-African music, in different expressions, such as Bach's *Musikalisches Opfer* (1747) or Marcel DuPré's *Le Chemin de la Croix* (1932), and is what Ravi Shankar calls "the highlight of Indian music" in his recording "An Introduction to Indian Music." It also appears in art that can have nothing to do with jazz and blues, such as traditional Finnish epic poetry as characterized by Lauri Harvilahti, who derives her ideas from Albert Lord: "During the verbalization (composition) process the singer can elaborate some details according to his own preferences and purposes. But in order to produce an entire epic song, he has to activate a number of systems simultaneously. He therefore employs material formulaically organized. This means (using the terms of cognitive science) that the memory of the singer works on multilevel representations containing features of surface and meaning structure. Formulas, ideas, and images cohere; certain scenes and contents tend to include certain details, clusters of forms, and so on. Oral poetry is innovative and traditional at the same time" (97). The improvisational poetry that Angela Esterhammer describes in *Romanticism and Improvisation, 1750–1850* challenges the traditional notion of the isolated Romantic poetic genius through its public and collaborative nature (4–5). For purposes of this volume, the William Carlos Williams's *Kora in Hell: Improvisations* (1920) serves as a prime American poetic example.

Not surprisingly, improvisation is present in West African music and helps allow what seems (erroneously) to some as a limited musical genre to be much more varied. For example, there is a common 12-bar blues stanza pattern musically and lyrically that has dominated the genre—though it is by no means the only pattern. There are those who feel, then, that the blues is easy to play, and perhaps in a pedestrian sense, it is. However, to play it well, and in its spirit, one has to create an individual voice that connects to tradition and pulls it forward. Given how many recordings and performances of the blues there have been, this is quite difficult. Performers need to know how to improvise, making use of the wealth of percussive, call-and-response pattern, polyrhythmic, voice manipulative, and expanded sonic realm techniques, to produce their own styles, and then connect to significant phraseology, tropes, and subject matter to be an integral part of the blues music tradition. African American slaves, faced with the imposition of a hegemonic system that subordinated their African systems socially, politically, and culturally, could retain their inherited integrity by turning trickster and improvising with the varied palette bequeathed by the ancestors to create an art that not only resists but also advocates in a palatable way for both themselves and their oppressors, who have ultimately capitulated to the pervasive presence of African American music. As Ronald Radano asserts, "we can see black musical metaphyics emerging from America's own racial imagination in response to assimilationist intentions of erasure" and "challeng[ing] a vulnerable white supremacy that could no longer explain away the power and appeal of black musical achievement" (*Lying* 35). Such an amalgam of techniques and elements might well accurately exemplify the idea that a slave woman described to Jeanette Robinson Murphy: "Notes is good enough for you people, but us likes a mixtery" (White and White 51). The music exists not on the page or in fixed memory, but in broad-ranging performances that value spontaneity, ingenuity, and dynamic variation over stasis or fixed performance.

There is a philosophy associated with the blues that relates to both subject matter and style. A variety of blues lyrics express the idea of maintaining hope in the face of adversity. When critic Albert Murray contends that the music is of utmost importance—"Words as such, however well chosen, are secondary to the music" (*Stomping* 79)—he denies blues lyrics their proper importance in the blues performing and listening experience, and certainly undervalues these important building blocks of a blues ethos or philosophy. One thinks of the traditional lyric "The sun gonna shine in my back door someday" (William Harris, "I'm Leavin' Town" 1927) with its implication of even the sun having to sneak in to make its appearance, but the sense of assurance that it will do so. "Hard times here, there's better up the road" (Sterling Brown, "The Blues" 289) expresses the sense of agency associated with traveling to better times, a legacy, it seems, of the increased mobility that greeted slaves following the Civil War and during World Wars I and II. "You can mistreat me here, but you can't when I go home" (McClennan 1939) is a variant, with its implications of an eventual safe refuge. The traditional lyric sung by Ishmon Bracey, "I been down so long, down don't worry me" on "Trouble-Hearted Blues" (1928), suggests that times can get "better" through adopting an attitude that lays troubles aside. All, though, express that core hope for amelioration, for a home, a place to belong. And indeed the performance, distinctively African American as it is, with its adaptations of African modalities and European structures, provides that home—a place to mingle with the elders, the tradition, the community; draw on their strength; and affirm one's own ability to describe and transform individual and communal experiences into a transcendent art. The musicians call it "taking it back home," which is actually also "bringing it up *here*" through performance. That philosophy, sometimes articulated as "making my home where I hang my hat," combines this notion of seeking a home with the improvisational element so frequently associated with the music, as well as elements of tricksterism, demonstrating how closely these seemingly disparate characteristics sometimes cohere behaviorally, as well as musically.

Janheinz Jahn reads the central theme of the blues as "[a]n individual's right to an intact 'perfect' life." The life force which an individual possesses, or "magara," is a force that can be increased by the individual possessing it, but diminished by others (*A History of Neo-African Literature* 172–73). When that force is diminished, the individual can seek to increase it, and this relationship, Jahn theorizes, is represented in the response part of each verse of the blues stanza pattern, and especially at the "response part of the last verse." This reinforces the nommo, or life force which is exercised, and thus the blues stanza pattern "does not reflect but creates the mood" (Tracy, *Write Me*, 30). In other words, the blues provides agency for the performer to take the performer and the audience to a figurative place where they want to be, to a home-like place of comfort or relief or rejuvenation, even if only briefly. In Langston Hughes's *Not Without Laughter* (1930), the narrator comments about the blues singer/musician Jimboy, "When Jimboy was home, you couldn't get lonesome or blue" (46), because Jimboy's music produced a different mood. Whereas the spiritual produces God, the blues produces a mood, a mood that makes the muck, as in Hurston's *Their Eyes Were Watching God* (125), a merriment, even as it retains socio-economic disadvantages.

This notion highlights the connection between the realms of sacred and secular in African culture. As Samuel A. Floyd Jr. points out, African religion was the center of communal life: "The Africans' system of God, lesser gods, spirits, and the living-dead was a complex of imaginative beliefs, narrations, and symbols that served fundamentally and meaningfully as the basis for their culture. It was a symbolic field through which the nature of existence was observed and venerated, and it was kept alive through the artistry of ritual. African myth was the authority and support for African law, morality, and community. It explained the origin of the world and ratified, rationalized, and justified African community, social, and political systems" (22). Hence, the space normally recognized between the binary realms of the sacred and secular in Western music is less demarcated in African music, opening up the opportunities for nuances of meaning through the eradication of harsh and absolute distinctions. Not that sacred and secular distinctions are unrecognized in the African American community—certainly they are, as evidenced by the way that some in the Christian community have identified the blues as the Devil's music for its language, unsavory subject matter, and frequently promiscuous orientation of performance spaces. Any number of blues performers can attest to the fact that the stalwart among the "believers" can shake a pretty mean Bible at the blues backslider (even if a sister has been known to make a preacher lay his Bible down now and then).

But the possibilities of the way African religious music is used—to invoke and produce a "flash of the spirit" or the presence of a God or gods (Thompson xiii–xvii)—might well apply to invoking some power with what might be considered non-religious music. This is especially true given the intimate relationship between African music and society. As J. H. Kwabena Nketia asserts, "[s]uch is the unity of African music with African social life, that all sorts of subsidiary questions concerning the social setting of the music have to be considered before the music as a whole can be said to have been mastered" (29). This ever-present radiance of art in African society attests to the centrality of art to everyday life—a centrality that is substantiated in African American life not only through such evidence as the work songs and field hollers of slaves, but what Zora Neale Hurston described as the will to dramatize in "Characteristics of Negro Expression" and the prominence of front porch "lying" or storytelling in African American communities (50). To think of music as something central to life and the community, as something for "everyday use," as Alice Walker described it, is to think of art in a distinctive and crucial way that has implications for its nature. Indeed, Western Swing pioneer Milton Brown recorded a version of "St. Louis Blues" (1934, though with different lyrics) with Bob Dunn on the steel guitar quoting "When the Roll is Called Up Yonder" in his solo! What was it that suggested the connection to Dunn, a white musician, if not the strong implication of the continuum of sacred and secular in African American music?

Critics have offered a good deal of commentary on the traditional musicians known variously as griots (and, for women, griottes), jali, and gewel, especially as they may relate to those with the vocation of blues performer. As Thomas Hale notes, it can be very difficult to pin down the exact nature of griots, since their roles can be ambiguous, and community response can be ambivalent as well. Griots are most frequently found where Islam has had considerable sway in the community, and chiefs wield great authority. In savannah societies, griots are frequently professionals valued and employed by the heads of state. Especially in these circumstances, griots can be privileged, highly paid, and much admired for their skill, language, and knowledge, especially as it pertains to the history and culture of the society that it is their province to preserve. In Senegal, griots attached to a village frequently have a profession in addition to their role as griots. Still other griots may range broadly as griots-for-hire, and have no particular village to which they are attached. Thus, the functions they serve may be in part defined by their relationship to their society/societies (Hale 2–4).

The repertoire of a griot consists of praise songs, history and genealogy, songs performed for ritual ceremonies, and songs of gossip, wit, and insult. Their roles include genealogist, historian, advisor, spokesperson, diplomat, mediator, interpreter, musician, composer, teacher, exhorter, warrior, witness, praise singer, and ceremonial participant at namings, initiations, courtships, marriages, installations, and funerals. They are also frequently skilled musicians on instruments, a number of which are prototypes for folk instruments in the United States (see Evans "The Reinterpretation of African Musical Instruments"), such as the kora (21-string instrument), akonting and khalam (ancestors of the banjo), riti (fiddle), and balafon (or xylophone-type instrument). They can play singly, in small groups, or in larger ones depending on the circumstances, and more recent so-called world music recordings have found them performing with minimalist composer Philip Glass and avant-garde jazz reed player Pharoah Sanders on the CD *Jali Kunda* (1996), roots guitarist Taj Mahal (1992), and progressive world banjoist Bela Fleck (2008), as well as influencing such composers as Gyorgy Ligeti and Steve Reich. Thus, on the one hand they are traditional musicians who sing songs passed down through hundreds of years of performance through the hereditary line, while on the other they pass along information about contemporary events, and can innovate and manipulate old songs and language to use their considerable verbal powers to ridicule and cajole.

Whereas some griots are privileged for their verbal and instrumental prowess, elsewhere they are at the bottom of the social hierarchy—their dead bodies are even allowed to putrefy in the trunks of trees. Where sometimes they are admired for their skills, they are also feared sometimes as well, not only for their language but, in some locations, for an ability to produce spirits that are associated with evil (Nikiprowetzky). Hale notes that their training is comparable to a doctoral program's in extent, proceeding from respondent to accompanist to scholar to work as a journeyman griot to more study (172). Eventually the student becomes a full-fledged griot or griotte.

There are ways in which the roles of griot and blues singer overlap, and then there are ways they are different. There are also musicians who are not griots, whose music also reflects a blues connection. First we should say that not all griots are alike, and neither are all blues performers. Different birthplaces, parents, childhoods, musical influences and aesthetics, personalities, jobs—all contribute to the variety of performers and performance styles. It should not be necessary to point that out, and yet people sometimes do take stereotypes for reality, and limited knowledge for complete. Is blues singing a hereditary vocation or avocation? Not necessarily, though there are sons (Big Bill Morganfield, son of Muddy Waters; Shuggie Otis, son of Johnny Otis; Lurrie

Bell, son of Carey Bell; Jimmy Reed and Jimmy Reed Jr.), daughters (Shemekia Copeland, daughter of Johnny Copeland), stepsons (Robert Jr. Lockwood, stepson of Robert Johnson), brothers (the Carter Brothers; Richard and Willie Trice; Joel, John Henry, and Lightnin' Hopkins; Charlie and Joe McCoy; Lonnie, Bo, and Sam Chatmon; Big Smokey and Little Smokey Smothers), brother and sister (George and Ethel McCoy), nephews (R. S. Rankin, whose uncle was T-Bone Walker), nieces (Ruby Walker, niece by marriage of Bessie Smith), first cousins (B. B. King and Bukka White) that suggest that there can be family connections in the blues world. However, the arrangement seems to be less formal in the blues tradition, even if, as Art Tipaldi has exploreed in *Children of the Blues*, it does exist.

Blues singers, by the nature of their music, could, did, and do also play in various-sized aggregations, as griots do. Son House, for example, played almost exclusively solo on his classic 1930 recordings for Paramount. At his 1941–42 recordings for the Library of Congress, he performed duets, trios, and quartets in addition to solos, with a variety of instrumentalists and vocalists. Muddy Waters has recorded everything from solo to tunes with electric bands with brass sections (although the latter was a somewhat misguided commercial production). In some ways, the common musical and stanza patterns of the blues made it easier for musicians who didn't know each other to play together. This might very well happen at a makeshift recording session if someone showed up without an accompanist, or as in the case of the house bands that were formed for Bluebird Records in the 1930s and 1940s featuring Bill Broonzy, Blind John Davis, Black Bob, Josh Altheimer, Alfred Elkins, and others. These patterns also unified musicians with radically different styles, like Blind Lemon Jefferson and Charley Patton, and there are (unsubstantiated) stories of their playing together (Charters, *The Bluesmen* 27). The common themes, images, and formula-like ways of forming lyrics certainly made such arrangements easier as well. This highlights the nature of the blues performer who, like the griot, is a traditional performer, making use of inherited structures and content, while bringing individual stylistic innovation to the music as well. The ability to balance the two to the satisfaction of the audience accounts in large degree for the performer's success.

That success is something about which the blues performers must care, if they wish to continue making their living in the profession, from country supper to juke joint club to "chitlin circuit" to concert hall. Often it could be difficult to deal with the middle-class image of the blues performer as a loafer, a promiscuous person, a heavy drinker, and irresponsible lower-class riff-raff. Just as griots and griottes had various images with which to deal, so with blues singers, who were also admired for their facility with language and perhaps feared for their abilities to use that power to wound as well. Sometimes blues singers themselves encouraged the notion that they consorted with evil spirits—perhaps even to gain their power to perform, as the story goes in the case of Robert Johnson and many others. Others insisted that the blues was not the devil's music at all, but simply "the truth" of their existence (Evans 53–54, 58–59).

Comparing in terms of repertoire, certainly we hear songs of praise, especially of mates or spouses, in the blues, as in Blind Boy Fuller's "Meat Shakin' Woman" (1938), where "every time she shakes some man done left his home." But there is also praise for such qualities as sweetness and diligent work ethic as well—even if the term "hard workin' woman" is sometimes a sexual reference, too. Some blues songs praise other musicians—"Jazzbo Brown From Memphis Town" (1926) by Bessie Smith, "Ma Rainey" (1940) by Memphis Minnie, and "The Death of Leroy Carr" (1935) by Bumble Bee Slim. Others champion sports figures, such as "Champ Joe Louis" (1938) by Bill Gaither, "Did You See Jackie Robinson Hit That Ball?" by Buddy Johnson, and "That Last Home Run" (for Hank Aaron) by Willie Dixon with McKinley Mitchell. And even presidents garner attention, especially Franklin Delano Roosevelt and John F. Kennedy, as documented thoroughly by Guido van Rijn. There are also criticisms of more obscure figures such as Memphis Minnie's bad cop "Reachin' Pete" (1935) and presidents as well, including FDR, Truman, Eisenhower, and Kennedy, as demonstrated again in the works of Guido van Rijn. At least until the days of presidents Jimmy Carter and Bill Clinton, or Lee Atwater, no blues singer was a member of a president's "court" or entourage, though Josh White did make visits to the FDR White House. Big Bill Broonzy, in fact, sang in "Just A Dream" (1939):

> I dreamed I was in the White House, sittin' in the President's chair,
> I dreamed he shaked my hand and said "Bill, I'm glad you're here."
> But that was just a dream, a dream I had on my mind.
> Yeah, and when I woke up, baby, not a chair could I find.

Although the history presented in the blues is not formal or genealogical, there are copious references to historical events and common circumstances—instances of bad luck and burial—that amount to a social and cultural history of African Americans, from Brownie McGhee's "Born for Bad Luck" (1940) to Rosa Henderson's "Undertaker's Blues" (1924). A range of experience is represented in such recordings as Charley Patton's "Mississippi Boweavil [*sic*] Blues" (1929), Charlie McCoy's "The Northern Starvers Are Returning Home" (1930), Sonny Boy Williamson I's "Win the War Blues"

(1944), Casey Bill Weldon's "WPA Blues" (1936), "The Flood Blues" (1927) by Sippie Wallace, Cow Cow Davenport's "Jim Crow Blues" (1927), Richard Yates's "Sore Bunion Blues" (1927), "Bilbo is Dead" (1947) by Andrew Tibbs, and "Eisenhower Blues" (1954) by J. B. Lenoir. While these songs are first-person lyric presentations and not historical narratives, they do mirror some of the range of feelings felt by African Americans of the lower socioeconomic levels with an immediacy that is intensely personal as well as communally representative. Robert Wilkins sang in his "Jail House Blues" (1928):

Oh, look like I can see trouble in the air.
But it ain't only here, friend, it's trouble everywhere.

Blues performers, of course, have been the entertainment at countless events, though not likely at such ritual events as namings, baptisms, circumcisions, and courtships, which are not frequently celebrated so formally. Still, blues are sometimes heard at funerals, such as those celebrated instrumentally after the burial in New Orleans, and certainly wedding celebrations have included music from blues performers from time to time. Ultimately, the use of blues for ritual occasions of this sort is not extensive. Conversely, sometimes the blues performance is interpreted as a kind of ritualized scene in itself. Charles Keil, in particular, has called attention to the way that a performance, as the Bobby Bland spectacle he describes, may provide elements of cooperation, solidarity, and catharsis with the formality, depth, and sincerity of a church service, thus providing a "spiritual" response to everyday problems from the standpoint of someone experienced in those troubles (131–42). Once again, this reduces the space that separates "sacred" and "secular" in a conventional sense, and assigns to the blues an essential role in the amelioration of everyday problems. For those resistant to this notion, the role, for example, of early female "vaudeville" blues singers with regard to offering advice to women certainly reinforces the idea of blues performer as the voice of experience and a valid dispenser of advice. "I want all you women to listen to my tale of woe," Sara Martin sang in "Death Sting Me Blues" (1929—see 1 Corinthians 15: 55), and Ida Cox chimed in "Don't let your man know he can make you blue" on "How Can I Miss You When I Got Dead Aim?" (1925). "Lord, a woman is a fool to put all her trust in one man," Alberta Hunter added on "He's Got a Punch Like Joe Louis," and Ida Cox advised,

I'm gonna tell you something, I wouldn't tell no lie,
Wild women are the only kind that really get by,

on her quintessential independent woman's blues, "Wild Women Don't Have the Blues" (1924). Did the raising in blues songs of particular kinds of problems, such as domestic abuse, that were frequently taboo to talk about in public create a dramatic space for their acknowledgment and possible rectification? It certainly seems possible—and in these cases carried out in ritualistic fashion through the image and dramatization of a popular vaudeville blues woman who, by virtue of her talent, fame, and monetary standard, was an attractive figure of independent means, as Sherley Anne Williams advises (445–55).

Of course, the blues is rife with gossip, wit, and insult, and the figure of the itinerant blues performer fits admirably into this widespread African musical role. Frequently full of local details of the private lives of folks in the neighborhood, the blues often puts private business in the street and handles all kinds of private matters publicly—what Zora Neale Hurston calls in "Characteristics of Negro Expression" the "absence of the concept of privacy" (60). Joe Evans's "Down in Black Bottom" (1931) describes the shortcomings of women in the neighborhood known as Black Bottom, and especially one woman in particular who is "black and greasy." "Black Bottom," of course, also refers to skin color and anatomy, with some beauty measures of the times marking blackness as the least desirable color because of its distance from whiteness, and also a vigorous, at least semi-lewd, dance that was both shocking and, with the Charleston and such dances, the "rage" among dancers in the 1920s. Black could be awfully vigorous and stimulating, too. Sonny Boy Williamson II's "Don't Start Me to Talkin'" (1955) is all about gossip and signifying, touching on violence, promiscuity, and hairdressing issues in the course of its three minutes. One singer was even billed as Signifying Mary Johnson on her Decca recordings in 1936, another indicator of the prominence of signifying in the blues. In fact, sometimes there was so much gossip and revelation in public that there was even cautionary advice such as "Don't Advertise Your Man" by Clara Smith (1924) or Maggie Jones's "Don't Never Tell Nobody What Your Good Man Can Do" (1923). This employment of gossip, along with wit and insult, often intends, as folk materials sometimes do, to establish, subvert, or reestablish the order or power relationships within the community—and not only in relation to class, as Jim Jackson's "Dicty Blues" (1929) or Duke Ellington's "The Dicty Glide" indicate, but interracially as well. "Mister Tom was good, some said mean," Sleepy John Estes sang in "Tell Me How About It" (1940), adding "Haulin' these cotton bales, they ain't got no team." Here the hearsay ("some said mean") allows the singer to criticize the boss while seeming to praise him—a strategy employed in a variety of ways in African American culture to fool Mister Tom, Mister Charlie, or Mister Generic White Boss.

Insult is the particular province of the Dozens, a rhyming game that insults another person through derogatory—usually sexual—references to relatives, as in "your pappy is your cousin," or something about your mama "doin' the Lordy Lord." Commercially recorded versions are necessarily "cleaner" and more coyly double-entendre than the non-commercial recordings that may be closer to actual performances in the community—witness Lightnin' Hopkins's recorded version, or the "party record" "Dirty Dozens" recorded by Johnny Otis, both much freer and more profane with their language. This street corner game was recorded with music—sometimes called "The Dirty Dozens"—by Speckled Red (1929) and a host of others, including Charley Jordan under the title "Keep it Clean" (1930). Certainly the Dozens is not the only place where insult occurs in the blues, however. Roosevelt Sykes's "Dirty Mother For You" (or "Fuyer," 1936), Blind Boy Fuller's "What's That Smells Like Fish" (1938), Rosa Henderson's "Slow Up Papa" (1927), Bull City Red's "Black Woman and Poison Blues" (1935), and Edmonia Henderson's "Lazy Daddy Blues" (1924) are among many such songs, as is the lyric flung at many a mate in a blues stanza that turns up in Charley Patton's "Going to Move to Alabama" (1929), "you got a handful of gimme, and a mouthful of much obliged."

Although the language of the blues is sometimes known to be very coarse, direct, and blunt, many blues performers, like their gifted musical counterparts in Africa, including griots, have also been known to handle the language with witty nuance. Peetie Wheatstraw's clever play on scripture in "The First Shall Be Last and the Last Shall Be First" (1936),

> I was just sitting here thinking,
> Ooh well well which woman treats me the worst,

even found its way into Ralph Ellison's *Invisible Man* (172), Ellison claiming to have performed with Wheatstraw on occasion (Garon 64). Lonnie Johnson's "Hard Times Ain't Gone No Where" (1937), where Johnson says he is not worried about hard times because he "was broke when they first started out," plays with hyperbole—hard times don't worry him!—until he explains the dilemma of many African Americans at the time of the Depression. This is, of course, one of the ironies of African American life, that a disaster is not a disaster until it affects the white folks, approached very pragmatically and matter-of-factly by the witty Johnson, a performer known as a wellspring of the philosophical and urbane lyrics of the city blues—a legacy of his relationship with the vaudeville blues early in his career. That tradition produced a number of witty lyrics sung by Rosa Henderson, including "Poplar Bluff Blues" (1928):

I ain't no monkey, you don't see me tryin' to climb no tree.
The man ain't born who can make a fool out of me.

Hazel Meyers sings on "The Man Ain't Born Who Can Treat Me Like You Do" (1924),

I've got your pacifier, understand,
That there's lots of power left in my right hand,

continuing with,

Got a razor and a gatling gun,
Cut you if you standing, shoot you if you run.

Such amusing cleverness in expression—even with its deadly overtones—is common in the blues. In fact, many early female blues singers were labeled as "comediennes" on their record labels, and some of them were even featured as comedic entertainers in their live shows. On the other hand, the poignancy of such lyrics as Blind Willie McTell's "the blues came down like dark night showers of rain" ("Searching the Desert for the Blues" [1932]), or "In the wee wee hours just about the break of day / That's when the blues creep down on you and carry your mind away" ("Wee Midnight Hours" [1949]) indicate more of the range of the feelings expressed in the blues.

The blues, then, seem to have a number of possible connections with African music that establish it as a tangible connector to another continent, and a pre-slavery experience. Although these connections are not always as concrete and sure as we might like them to be, they are strongly suggestive of a quality of the blues to get "back home," to get outside of slavery and Jim Crow through the evocation of a spirit and a modality that inspired the performers of music before and alongside the blues, and the audiences, and subsequent audiences, including writers who needed to go to the well for inspiration and connection to a communal spirit, interpreted by an individual voice. African American composer William Grant Still, who had played in Handy's Orchestra, seemed to acknowledge this connection in his 1928 composition *Africa*. Consisting of three parts, "Land of Peace," "Land of Romance," and "Land of Superstition," each section utilizes elements of the blues to suggest that African identity, in peace, romance, and superstition, is imbued with what we have come to know as the blues. In the composition, Still makes some of his most experimental and provocative uses of the tradition, suggesting something previous to the American blues tradition, but still unmistakably bluesy in its tone and technique. Still's

Afro-American Symphony (1930) included a strain of "St. James Infirmary Blues" and a strong bluesy opening movement with call-and-response, syncopation, double time passages, and blue notes as well. The blues has another recurring sentiment: you never miss your water 'til your well runs dry. It ain't dry yet.

III

Obviously, the blues drew on Euro-American elements in its development as well. For example, most of the language used in the blues is English. This is not to say that there are not African-derived words that occur in the blues. Paul Oliver has pointed out that linguistic evidence from Dr. David Dalby's research has revealed that three-quarters of the words from blues sounds that are of black coinage "have a directly traceable Savannah origin," where Oliver locates the source of African American blues influences (Tracy, *Write Me* 73). Others suggest that, rather than words, African grammatical forms and usages are prominent (Evans). Further, Molefi Kete Asante argues that, in order to discern African elements in African American English, one must examine the "communication style" of a person or group—"the verbal or non-verbal behavior patterns that distinguish one person from another" and "observable relationships in the substantive social fabric of language behavior" (68). As has already been indicated, the communal and performative patterns of certain West African societies seem to be related to African American patterns. Such scholars as Samuel Charters, in *The Roots of the Blues*, have pointed out that the manner or modality of performance is similar in African and African American musics (117). Though the music frequently does not sound similar superficially, similarities in the manner of producing sounds and the nature of those sounds are clear if one learns to listen for them: "If a griot like Jali Nyama Suso had sung in English, the sound of his voice would have been difficult to distinguish from an Afro-American singer's" (Charters 119). The recording Laura Boulton made of "War Song" features a vocal that is similarly African American sounding, with the quavering pitch spaces, semi-growl, and descending vocal patterns one can hear in Mississippi Delta blues of the 1920s, with an insistent rhythm underpinning the vocal. As far as language in the blues goes, though there are recorded occasions of blues being sung in Pig Latin—Ollie Shepard's "Shepard Blues" from 1939 and the pseudo-"Pig Latin Blues" of LaVern Baker (1952), as well as blues from Louisiana sung in French (as sung by Clifton Chenier, for example)—and the contemporary international spread of the blues has produced a number of foreign blues bands singing in languages from around the world, still, overwhelmingly, the language employed in blues songs has been a dialect of English.

It is also clear that a period of acculturation made it possible for subtle exchanges of influence between African and European music. For example, Dena J. Epstein points out that the "process began immediately on board the slave ships, with exposure to the European instruments that happened to be aboard." Pere Labat reported in 1694 that, "Even at this early date some of the slaves played the violin very well . . . [t]he Africans had taken up European instruments successfully" (80). Slave Robert Anderson recalled a time when the absence of his master allowed time for a dance he described thusly: "We had a regular jubilee which lasted the greater part of the night. We danced the dances like the white folks danced them, and then danced our own kind of dances" (Epstein 44). And though it was clear that there was a differentiation between the two, "the style and degree of acculturation" (44) would be variously noticeable here. They had in effect become bicultural. The fact that the dramatic dance known as the cakewalk was itself a satirical take on a form of dance practiced by the whites demonstrates that, whether seriously or satirically, there were ways in which European models exerted some influence on African dance as well.

The major contribution of the Euro-American tradition to the blues—other than creating the appalling conditions that generated it—seems to have been the strophic patterns that identify the blues formally. In *The Roots of the Blues*, Samuel Charters differentiates between African and African American musics from his study conducted in Gambia: "Structurally, the two forms were hardly related at all. The blues is built on a strophic model and one popular form of the twelve bar blues has become so fixed a pattern that it has become a definition of the blues itself. The use of rhyme, the controlled line lengths—. . . these are all things that separate the blues from its African sources" (123). This use of strophes seems to have been adapted from materials generated on American soil, perhaps in contact with white mountain ballads with an ABAB or ABCB pattern. Paul Oliver has suggested that it was a marriage of the field holler vocal with the blues ballad structure—in such ballads as "John Henry," "Frankie and Albert," "Stagolee," and "Railroad Bill"—that helped to form the nascent blues stanza (*Story of the Blues* 22–25). Of course, African repetition is added to such a stanza to form an AAB pattern. Whatever the source of the pattern, and Oliver suggests that it followed "the simple harmonic progression of the British folk ballad and similar form" (23), it was distinctively applied, combined with African-derived pre-blues African American musical techniques and characteristics, such as instrumental breaks and repetition, to form a music so distinctive and powerful that it has lasted for over a century. Of course, European instruments, and perhaps, though not necessarily, iambic pentameter leanings also contributed to the transformation of the music as well. White mountain singer Clarence Ashley's "Dark Holler Blues" (1929) exhibits a heavy blues modality with a ballad stanza structure.

Because the stanza patterns of the blues are so important, a familiarity with their tendencies and varieties is necessary to understanding how they operate. First, here is a British ballad, "Child 63A, Child Waters":

> I WARN ye all, ye gay ladies,
> That wear scarlet an brown,
> That ye dinna leave your father's house,
> To follow young men frae town.

Juxtaposed to a "John Henry" blues ballad stanza, it is easy to see the similarities:

> When John Henry was a little baby,
> Sittin' on his daddy's knee,
> He pointed his finger at a little piece of steel,
> Said "That'll be the death of me.
> That'll be the death of me."

A repetition of the fourth line in "Child Waters" would render the two, with rhythmic freedom, roughly interchangeable, though there is a certain rushing syncopation to the third line in "John Henry" that renders it distinctively African American. As in Child 12 A ("Lord Rendal"), there are sometimes repeated lines, or, as in Child 21A ("The Maid and the Palmer"), repeated refrains that occur in Child Ballads that make the connection between the two more tangible. From here it is not hard to connect to to an eight-bar blues stanza with a rhymed AB pattern, such as in Willie McTell's "Searching the Desert for the Blues" (1932):

> You may search the ocean,
> You might go 'cross the deep blue sea,
> But honey you'll never find
> Another hot shot like me.

Eight-bar refers to the number of measures it takes musically to accommodate this lyric pattern. The blues most commonly uses what is called a I-IV-V chord pattern in its execution, meaning that the chords are built around the first (do), fourth (fa), and fifth (so) notes of the major scale. McTell's eight-bar pattern follows the following progression: I-V-IV-IV-I-V-I-V, the last representing a "turnaround," or announcement of the end of the stanza and preparation to start the progression again. Each Roman numeral in this notation stands for a single four-count bar. The indicators AB here refer to the end rhyme of the lines in the stanza. This is not the only eight-bar progression pattern, musically or lyrically. Tampa Red's "It Hurts Me Too" (1940) features a standard refrain in every stanza:

I can't be happy, mama,	I
For bein' so blue.	I
You keep me worried	IV
'Bout the way you do.	IV
Refrain: When things go wrong,	I
Go wrong with you,	V
It hurts me, too.	I-V

The numbers at the right margin refer to the chord progression, though because the chords sometimes change before or after the beginning of a new line, the change is only approximately indicated here. For example, the lyrics of the first two lines actually start on the last beat of the previous stanza, and are completed by beat one of the second stanza here, filled out by instrumental performance. There are, of course, many different ways that performers can embellish these patterns, from different styles of picking to chord substitutions to the use of a knife, bottle, or cylindrical slide, providing variations that prevent the form from becoming stale or a limitation. In fact, it is one of the challenges of the genre itself—to take a simple form and keep it both rooted and new and exciting.

The most common stanza pattern in the history of the blues is the twelve-bar AAB pattern, though other lyric patterns exist as well. Ma Rainey's version of "See See Rider Blues" (1924) features three different lyric patterns (ABB, AAB, and ABC), plus a chord pattern as listed in the right-hand margin of the first stanza that applies throughout:

See see rider, see what you done done, Lord, Lord, Lord,	I-I-I-I
Made me love you, now your man done come.	IV-IV-I-I
You done made me love you, now your man done come.	V-IV-I-V

I'm goin' away, baby, won't be back 'til Fall, Lord, Lord, Lord,
Goin' away, baby, won't be back 'til Fall.
If I find me a good man I won't be back at all.

I'm gonna buy me a pistol, long as I am tall.
Kill my man and catch the Cannonball.
If he won't have me he won't have no gal at all.

Here, the letters ABB indicate that one line is sung, then a different line that end rhymes is sung, and then the second sung line is repeated. In the second stanza, the first line is sung, then it is repeated, and then a third line different from the first two and end rhyming is sung. In the third stanza, three different lines that end rhyme are sung. The repeated words do not have to be exactly the same. They may be somewhat varied in terms of language or use of exclamatory words (as Ma Rainey adds to the end of the first lines in the first two stanzas), as long as the lines are recognizably similar. Indeed, singers are free to vary this pattern even more extensively if they wish in order to produce subtle effects.

The fact that Rainey uses three different patterns in this song suggests that she is trying for different effects in each stanza, since most commercially recorded blues of this time did not demonstrate this variety. In the first, rather than suspending completion to increase suspense, she repeats her second line, which effectively emphasizes her sad condition. In the second stanza, she emphasizes that she is leaving, as well as the length of time she will be gone, completing her stanza with a punch-line threat that leads to stanza three, a quick-moving stanza that contains the most words as she moves quickly to her conclusion. The lack of dwelling on a single line emphasizes her resolve to carry out her mission and conclude the scenario to her satisfaction: buy a gun, shoot, leave, and be satisfied.

It has been suggested that the repeat pattern in the AAB blues stems from the roots of the blues in field holler vocals and, before that, other types of African song. Langston Hughes speculated that the singer in the field might have sung a line and then found that time was needed to find a rhyming line. Repeating the first line provided the opportunity to come up with the rhyme. Hughes felt that "[s]omething like that must have happened the day the first blues was born" (*The Story of Jazz*). In this case, it might be suggested that the stanza sung by Henry Thomas in "Bull-Doze Blues" (1928) could be the result of a lack of invention:

> I'm goin' away, babe, and it won't be long.
> I'm goin' away, and it won't be long.
> I'm goin' away, and it won't be long.

This AAA pattern recalls to the listener that field hollers were sometimes called "over and overs," meaning that the lines or the melody were repeated often. This is not necessarily the case. Thomas does not always sing AAA stanzas (though he does mostly in this recording of the song), and he was certainly not in the field when he was recorded, so he had ample time to supply a different rhyming line. Perhaps there is a different motivation. For example, the singer insists he is going away, yet he delays his departure by singing that same threat over and over again. Could this indicate that the singer does not wish to leave, and is stalling in order to provoke some response that will allow him to stay? In that case, this stanza becomes a dramatic representation in which the repetition actually works in tension with the words—it won't be long, he says, and then he makes it longer. Though we can't possibly know, and the repetition of one line three times is used under other circumstances that do not indicate a desire to delay. In response to Hughes, it would be more accurate to say that something like that might have happened the day that the first AAB stanza pattern was sung. The variety of eight and twelve-bar stanza patterns collected by early folklorists in the field suggests that one pattern was not necessarily dominant. If this is the case, then something else may explain the different repetition patterns—other than simply the speed with which an individual singer could either invent or remember suitable rhyming lines. It seems more likely that the repeats were used in different places for their effects, and somewhere along the way the AAB pattern became more fixed and popular.

The other primary twelve-bar lyric pattern is an AB refrain pattern similar to the eight-bar pattern detailed above, but spread out over twelve bars. Walter Coleman's "I'm Going to Cincinnati" (1936) makes use of the pattern:

When you come to Cincinnati don't you get too full,	I-I
You're liable to meet the cop that they call Stargel Bull.	I-I
Refrain: Because I'm goin' to Cincinnati, the times is good,	IV-IV
I'm goin' to Cincinnati where they eat fried food,	I-I
And I'm goin' to Cincinnati, boys, where hittin' the bottle is good.	V-IV-I-V

This type of stanza very effectively sets up a sing-along refrain with which a listening audience can join in, offering the singer a chance to describe a particular location or person or activity and return to a central idea in every stanza—as with Cincinnati here, or Mister Tom in Sleepy John Estes's "Tell Me How About It" (1940), or the idea of there being "Nothing In Rambling" (1940) in the Memphis Minnie song.

Again, these types of stanzas can be and have been altered in various ways, as in Leadbelly's "Packin' Trunk Blues" (1935), which at first glance looks like an AAA stanza—one line sung three times:

Sittin' down here wonderin' would a matchbox hold my clothes.

Sittin' down here wonderin' would a matchbox hold my clothes.
Sittin' down here wonderin' would a matchbox hold my clothes.

I don't want to be bothered with no suitcase on my road.
I don't want to be bothered with no suitcase on my road.
I don't want to be bothered with no suitcase on my road.

Now, what would you do when your baby packin' up her trunk?
What would you do when your baby packin' up her trunk?
Now, what would you do when your baby packin' up her trunk?

Get you a half a gallon of good whiskey and get on you a big drunk.
Get you a half a gallon of good whiskey and get on you a big drunk.
Get you a half a gallon of good whiskey and get on you a big drunk.

And, actually, each stanza *is* an AAA pattern, but if you look at the "gap" between stanzas, you will find the end words of stanza one rhyming with the end words of stanza two, and the end words of stanza three rhyming with the end words of stanza four. This effectively makes the stanza both a twelve-bar and a twenty-four-bar blues, making a full twelve bars of weight to the question in the initial stanza and a full twelve bars of weight to the response to it. This technique is also reminiscent of a sixteen-bar blues stanza, which most frequently has an AAAB pattern, as in Sweet Papa Tadpole's "Have You Ever Been Worried in Mind?" (1930):

You never miss your water 'til your spring run dry.
You never miss your water 'til your spring run dry.
And you never miss your water, I said gambler, 'til your spring run dry.
You never miss your baby 'til you have blacked her eye.

Actually, Tadpole's song has a different harmonic progression than simply adding on another four bars to the traditional twelve-bar blues, which seems to be a nod toward the vaudeville blues tradition, the first blues tradition to emerge on the phonograph recordings that Thomas Edison helped to invent in 1877. It would be thirteen years before recordings were made by African Americans, though there were a variety of permutations of their music to be found before 1890.

Because many of the vaudeville blues were composed by tunesmiths who were attempting to "update" and commercialize the folk-blues tradition they knew, they frequently featured elements that were not part of the traditional folk-blues, such as 1) introductory narrative storylines not in the traditional array of music or lyric patterns; 2) chord patterns that varied from and extended longer than the eight-, twelve-, and sixteen-bar blues; 3) larger groups including jazz performers playing from charts; and 4) a stage production or presentation that seemed to critics like Sterling Brown to stretch the bounds of the blues to silly or smutty prurience, what he called "urbanized fake folk things" ("The Blues as Folk Poetry" 324). Margaret Carter's vaudeville blues "I Want Plenty Grease in My Frying Pan" (1926) has all four characteristics:

> (introduction)
> Beeper Street [sic] from New Orleans, he's the laziest man I ever seen.
> I was in my back yard, washing hard, and I happened to get me some lard.
> He made me so doggone mad and I screamed (?) it all day.
> He knew I could not fry my meat without lard,
> And this is what I said:
>
> I need a'plenty grease in my frying pan, 'cause I don't want my meat
> to burn.
> You know I asked him once to get me some lard
> But it seems that you cannot learn.
> You know I use plenty grease every day,
> But I ain't did no fryin' while you was away.
> I need plenty grease in my fryin' pan 'cause I don't want my meat
> to burn.

The introduction here lasts sixteen bars, leading to a main stanza that is also sixteen bars, but with a different chord progression, and including a stop-time section to emphasize and dramatize the lyrics. The obvious sexual double entendre are, of course, relatively common in the folk-blues, and are the kinds of elements that "respectable" middle-class African Americans would lament, especially in relation to the efforts of those on Striver's Row to move up in social class. As the type of blues that first reached a large mainstream American audience, however, vaudeville blues are of major importance in the history of American music, and the history of its influence on literature as well. It should be noted that Louis Armstrong's 1927 Hot Seven recording of "Melancholy Blues," which was launched into space on "Voyager's Greetings to the Universe" (1977), features one of these vaudeville blues structures, starting with a 32-bar form and then moving to an even longer one in the second section.

This rough discussion of the origins and nature of the genre of music known as the blues is obviously not adequate to present all of the nuances of the form, content, and performance. As the discussion continues, there will be more extensive treatment of all of these components as they relate directly to the times when the blues emerged and to the literature under discussion. It is important to emphasize that the music has been and continues to be a living, breathing force. It grew out of traditional African music, the experience of the Atlantic slave trade, the treatment of African American slaves, and the realities of Jim Crow conditions, focusing performers on particular incidents and experiences inherited from their past and operating in their daily lives that set the parameters of expression. West Africa, the American South, the northern ghetto; freedom of mobility, of spousal choice, of job opportunity; freedom from hunger, from racial violence, from educational discrimination. These and many other subjects are the heart of the landscape of the blues—the degrees of experience—about which Robert Johnson sang in "Preachin' Blues" (1936):

Well the blues is a achin' old heart disease.
Like consumption—killin' me by degrees.

IV

There are, of course, a broad variety of ways that elements of the blues may be manifested in literary works. One major problem is that there are elements that are characteristic of the blues that are also characteristic of other musical genres, and this lack of exclusivity can make determining whether the blues is at play very difficult. And because blues and jazz can shade into each other, can be difficult to differentiate at times (if they must be), the words are sometimes used interchangeably based upon the subjective understanding of what they are. Additionally, there are many jazz songs that employ blues musical form, and both jazz and blues regularly use improvisation and tonal variety. Bop players like Charlie Parker, after all, have a different manner of playing the blues from Frank Stokes in Memphis, or Cecil Taylor from Mississippi's Louise Johnson. Is it blues or jazz, we sometimes call out to ourselves, and we can only provide a subjective response based on our understanding of the percentage of characteristics that categorizes as one or the other.

For the purposes of this volume's discussion of literature from the 1920s, whenever possible we are limiting our focus to blues recorded before 1930, since music after that time would post-date the literature we are describing. This means that our primary resources for the blues tradition at this time will be commercial "race" records and materials collected by folklorists. Although neither can claim a balanced representation of types of blues from the time—being driven by the market on the one hand and field accessibility on the other—they do provide us with adequate examples from which to draw conclusions about various blues styles that coexisted during the era, from rural backwoods porches and juke joints to southern cities' street corners to the taverns and clubs up North. As white singer Marion Harris sang Walter Hirsch's lyrics over black composer-performer Spencer Williams's composition on "Paradise Blues" (1916), "There sits Ragtime Lew, / He can show you how to 'blue' / On that piano," the cross-cultural influence and implications became clear. The technique of "bluing," or giving the music a feeling related to the blues music tradition, was employed in a variety of different kinds of music. It was even the title of a song, "Bluin' the Blues," recorded by the Original Dixieland Jazz Band and Wilbur Sweatman in 1918, blackface singer Al Bernard in 1919, among others, and subsequently by Western Swing pioneer Bob Wills in 1936. And in the music of the 1920s, we can hear a "mixtery" of ragtime, coon song, spiritual, jazz, and blues in the repertoires—and sometimes individual songs—of black performers as well as white. Ironically, even the Ku Klux Klan created a Klan jingle, "Come Join the Ku Klux in the Old Town Tonight," to the tune of minstrel bandleader Theodore August Metz's ragtime-y "There'll Be a Hot Time in the Old Town Tonight" (with a grim, devilish play, one might think, on the word "hot"). Metz's musical composition of the well-known song ironically earned him designation of the "Father of Jazz" in some quarters at the time. As Richard Sudhalter explains, the terms were frequently fluidly perceived: "It's important to remember that in 1922–23 'jazz' was widely understood less as any sort of free-standing musical entity than as an atmosphere, a feeling. If Joe Oliver billed his octet as a 'Creole Jazz Band,' it was chiefly to give the public some thinly coded information. 'Creole,' like 'dixie' and 'dixieland,' implied that these were musicians from down south, and 'jazz' told potential customers they could expect a lively, good-time atmosphere for dancing—which in turn meant far more than just stomps and rags" (Sudhalter 92).

We can hear overlapping call-and-response, for example, in Angola prison work songs, or syncopation in Scott Joplin or James P. Johnson ragtime, or polyrhythms in jazz from Louis Armstrong to John Zorn—and we encounter all of these in West African music, a primary source music for the music of African Americans. Combining with European notions of art and life and community, what of the African has survived, and how is it manifested? Is the communal orientation of West African societies at work in the organized improvisation? Does this improvisation reflect a communal openness to various under- or counter-current voices that we see in blues? Do the polyrhythms so common in blues reflect these various communal voices as well? Is that where the polyvocality—harmonica player George "Bullet" Williams whooping and blowing simultaneously through his instrument on "Frisco Leaving

Birmingham" (1928), or guitarist Albert Collins carrying on a conversation with himself—comes from? Does the frequent sexual frankness of blues such as Memphis Minnie's "Bumble Bee Blues" (1930) reflect the fertility rites of the African ancestral homeland? And how about the notion of art as having an "everyday use," as Alice Walker's phrase would have it? Is that where the functionality of the blues comes from, and the valuing of vernacular art alongside its "high art" counterpart?

The answer to all of these questions is, in varying degrees, affirmative, probably, and yet how much they may be adapted to experiences in this country is certainly up for speculation. That speculation has been voiced by such major critics as Richard Alan Waterman, Paul Oliver, Janheinz Jahn, Samuel Charters, David Evans, William R. Ferris, and Gerhard Kubik, among many others, but is still mystified in the miasma that floats over the criticism like the haze over a Mississippi delta swamp. Spirituals deal with the trials and tribulations of this world as much as the blues do, and we find the spirit of hope and persistence in the face of adversity in gospel music as well. And so-called blue notes—we find them everywhere in African American music. Determining a particular *blues* influence in the absence of particular references to the blues can be very difficult, very subjective—but still a valuable exercise in mining the genre for wisdom and strength, and in establishing its relationship to other African American musical genres and thus exploring that flexible sacred-secular continuum in African American culture. We may not get the unequivocal answers we might be seeking, but we will get a valuable dialogue that explores a rarely mined terrain. As we think, then, about possibilities for influence, we need to keep these kinds of limitations—or should I say possibilities?—in mind.

Texts may present us with a discussion of the backgrounds of the blues—in Africa, slavery, Reconstruction, Jim Crow, work songs, field hollers, spirituals, coon songs, ragtime, etc. Are these backgrounds related to our understanding of how the blues has developed from these sources? Might they be setting up a philosophy, or a mode of understanding, or of playing or performance, or of meaning, that anticipates a nascent blues genre? Can we establish a development of ideas that are made manifest in the blues out of these elements? This is a circumstance when as readers we might feel the blues, or elements that will converge in the blues, coming, and can root our discussions in inklings of things to come.

But is it fair and reasonable to call something blues related if it was written before the genre of music emerged? Perhaps. Perhaps not. The blues song likely existed some time before popular or intellectual culture became aware of it, many elements of African American culture being below the radar of mainstream culture. We do not know exactly when the blues was first performed, though we think we can pinpoint it to within a decade or so of its genesis—somewhere around the 1890s. Before that, the elements that comprised the blues existed in various other kinds of music—work songs, field hollers, spirituals, game songs, ballads, and ragtime—but those elements had not come together to form the blues as we know it. It is important to note that it is not just the musical elements we are talking about here, but subject matter and spirit as well. There are blues songs, after all, that treat the concerns expressed in field hollers and work songs, particularly in such songs as Texas Alexander's "Levee Camp Moan Blues" (1927) (featuring an intractable mule) and Bessie Tucker's "Mean Old Master Blues" (1929) (featuring an intractable master). Hard work is on Big Bill Broonzy's mind in his "Plow Hand Blues" (1940), and the omnipresence of the unbearable sun (Old Hannah in some work songs) figures prominently in a brilliantly balanced stanza in Tom Dickson's "Labor Blues" (1928): "I don't mind workin', Cap'n, from sun to sun / But I want my money, Cap'n, when pay day come." All these and more show up in the blues. The need to persevere in resistance to harsh circumstances is a hallmark of the spirituals. The playfulness of game songs, particularly as they relate to the flirtatiousness of lovers, finds expression in such lyrics as "Sweet Home Chicago": "one and one is two, two and two is four / Come on, baby, don't you want to go?" and even Lucille Bogan's obscene take on the "Here's the church, here's the steeple / Open the doors and see all the people" in her unexpurgated "Shave 'Em Dry" (1935). Ballad heroes such as John Henry and Railroad Bill (outlaw Morris Slater) figure side by side in the repertoires of blues singers, as do rollicking rags and jump tunes that celebrate dance and instrumental music simultaneously, even giving us songs like "Raggin' the Blues" (1927) by Buddy Boy Hawkins. The point here is that it seems more appropriate to label, if we must, these elements not with a title of something that came after them, but something contemporaneous, and not that cherry-picks only one genre with the characteristics, but aims to be more comprehensive.

This seems to be at work in the arguments of Sterling Stuckey in his monograph *African Culture and Melville's Art*. In the book, Stuckey claims a particular distinction for Herman Melville: "In Melville's mind, the music of the blues is associated with various forms of suffering and not confined to blacks. Perhaps he was the first American to present the blues as the American national music" (9). The statement is surprising, and perhaps technically anachronistic, since the novel was published in 1851, three decades before most scholars agree that the genre known as the blues emerged. At that time, even the minstrel shows were still smaller affairs, just twenty years or so after Thomas Rice sang "Jump Jim Crow" and eight years after Dan Emmett's Virginia Minstrels began to perform. According to Allen G. Debus and Richard Martin, "[I] t was during the post-war period that the minstrel show began to change. By the mid-1870s, the shows had become larger . . . By the late 1890s, the cakewalk was already part of the show and ragtime songs were being introduced. For many, the 'new' minstrels seemed to be not far removed from vaudeville" (*Monarchs of Minstrelsy* 5). As Patrick O'Connor states, minstrel shows, tent shows, and medicine shows "prepared the rural and isolated audiences for other forms of music, blues and jazz, that later gave blacks an active, more genuine voice in the community" (57). While there was certainly overlap of so-called pre-blues and blues music in these shows—Ma Rainey being a prime example—it is clear that the images of minstrelsy that concretized white prejudices helped pave the way for the viability of blues-inflected tunes in both black and white stage and recording traditions later (see Abbott and Seroff *Ragged*).

Scholars such as David Evans speculate that the blues emerged as the first generation of African Americans born outside of slavery reached their majority (*Big Road Blues* 40). Without the wisdom of a generation of elders experienced in these new circumstances to help guide them in their choices and pursuits, this generation began to formulate a genre that drew upon previous musical genres in African American culture and envisioned new forms, subject matter, and possibilities. For example, the phrase "it was early in the morning, just at the break of day," which many people would associate with the blues genre, appeared in *The Narrative of Sojourner Truth* (1850; 1878, 116) in a hymn dealing with the resurrection of Christ. In blues songs, the words retain a more mundane meaning. These structural and textual continuities they combined with their new social experiences that foregrounded such major issues as geographical mobility and spousal autonomy, choice, and relations, which ultimately became the most common blues subject matter. As Michael Taft asserts in *The Blues Lyric Formula*, the twenty most common blues "formulas" are tied closely to these subjects (193), though David Evans feels that the formulas should be "studied as *lexical* rather than *semantic* phenomena" and takes a rather critical view of Taft's volume ("Formulaic Composition" 497).

The fact is, there are no references in print to blues music as a genre at the time of publication of Melville's *Moby Dick* in America in 1851. Of course, just because the blues was not mentioned in a press dominated by whites generally suspicious of or uninterested in the existence of African American culture does not mean that it didn't exist, at least in some nascent form. But publications like *Slave Songs of the United States* (1867) and the vogue for African American jubilee singers inaugurated by the Fisk Jubilee Singers (1871) indicated an interest in African American music that might have generated some discussion, or even just a mention. However, these sources emphasized the slaves' Christian music for its seemingly more palatably "sacred," less salaciously "profane," sentiments. On the other hand, the growing popularity of minstrelsy from the time of Thomas D. Rice's "Jump Jim Crow" (c. 1828) indicates an interest in African American music beyond its Christian incarnations. Still, none of the slave narratives published up until 1865, nor any other extant printed sources by African Americans or whites, mention the blues as a musical genre. Collector Gates Thomas and composer-musician W. C. Handy both recall first hearing something like the blues around 1890, Ma Rainey a decade or so later (Tracy, *Write Me*, 3).

Of course, just because the blues was not known by that name does not mean that it didn't exist, even if only in some embryonic form—as long as we understand that the embryo proceeded from a fully formed entity or entities. This seems to be the sense with which Stuckey uses the term. Whether we can still label it "the blues" retroactively is arguable, in this sense, but it is clearly a vernacular relative. Stuckey argues that the blues was born from slave spirituality (10), and that Frederick Douglass's *Narrative* and Melville's *Moby Dick* "give us reason to question the thesis that the spirituals preceded the blues" (82). He reasons that because Douglass describes a particular brand of sorrow akin to what he hears in the blues, manifested in Melville's novel as a "gloomy-jolly dialectic" (93), that we are brought to "that sacred moment when the spirituals and the blues appear to have been one, to that moment, however, when the blues is actually the foundational form" (82). With no formal stylistic relation to the blues evident, and not even a reference to some incarnation of the word "blues" in the text, even if there are parallel emotions, simply labeling it the blues rather than other later developments with similar emotions—such as field holler, jazz, or gospel, which all drew upon sacred and secular traditions, seems ill-advised. Blues singer Tom Dickson's recording "Happy Blues" (1928), is a twelve-bar blues, giving us something more to lean on in terms of the connection.

Stuckey's point of reference for these contrasting moods, for example, between the *Bachelor* and the *Pequod* in Melville's novel, "one representing the mournful march to the cemetery, the other the joyful return home" (97), is his understanding of the blues. However, Stuckey asserts that Melville attempted to hide these references deep below the vast surface of sea and language in the text: " . . . Melville made a particularly brilliant effort to hide the blues from us altogether. At times, as stated, he intimates the sounds of the blues while offering no recognizable clue that music is his subject" (19). This is, perhaps, tantamount to saying that the evidence is not there, but in the mind of the critic—which in some ways is always true, obviously, yet critics must have a peg on which to hang their hats and make their homes there.

This leads to a number of objections. What he is describing as blues music seems to have been only an ancestor, and would only develop into and be called the blues later. That is, part of the sound and sentiment would later be associated with what we would come to term the blues. At the time Melville was writing, this type of vocalizing would be more associated with work songs and field hollers—in fact, what Douglass is describing in his text, though Valerie Babb, mistakenly, I believe, refers to them as spirituals (371). Elizabeth Schultz suggests that "[i]n its development, all black autobiography might be compared to the development of the blues" (82), a statement that narrowly avoids suggesting that the blues informed the nineteenth-century slave narratives that preceded the emergence of the blues genre. Work songs and field hollers are both ancestors to the blues in the use of blue notes, and "pitch spaces" that allow variable points of attack and movement in performance. However, work songs and field hollers are generally more decorative and free ranging than the blues, the former group songs making extensive use of overlapping call-and-response, the latter the song of an individual without musical accompaniment, since the song was generated in the field. Neither adopted the variety of blues forms commonly associated with the blues, unless we think of the field holler, or "over and over" as it was sometimes called, as analogous to an AAA rhyme pattern. Was it the blues before it was called the blues? And is it the blues if it does not evidence the formal structures, common images and symbols, and such things as the blues do?

The problem seems to come down to whether the contrasting of opposite moods of joy and sorrow is unique to the blues. It is certainly ubiquitous, as in that common lyric "laughing to keep from crying," a phrase to which Langston Hughes concretely refers in his 1925 poem "The Jester" (*Collected Poems* 56), his 1926 poem "Homesick Blues" (*Collected Poems* 72), and his novel *Not Without Laughter* (1930). The question is, can this sentiment come from somewhere other than the blues music tradition, especially in Melville's time. Clearly it can. Certainly the instrument on which Pip "carried the burden of the blues" (93), the tambourine, is not an instrument commonly associated with the blues, but rather, with minstrelsy and, later, gospel music, though of course the blues can be performed on any instrument, or even without one. In an interview with Alan Lomax, blues singer-pianist Memphis Slim asserted "the blues came from slavery" (Lomax). Surely no one would suggest that the experiences of generations of African Americans had nothing to do with the creation of the blues as a genre. It can, thus, be useful to "read backward" from a knowledge of the blues to theorize about how the blues genre came into existence, and to chart an emotional course from slavery into the present day. However, technically, calling Melville's obscured musical references and contrasting emotions a usage of the blues seems to violate our historical knowledge of when the genre came into existence.

Now, Melville did refer specifically to "the blues" as an emotion in several places: in chapters 14 and 35 of *Mardi* (1849); in book 2 of *Pierre; or The Ambiguities* (1852); in "Sketch Seventh" of *The Encantadas; or, Enchanted Isles*; and in chapter 40 of *The Confidence Man* (1857). Melville also spoke of the blues in *Clarel* —"From out this same dull land so holy / Which breeds but blues and melancholy" (183)—but this was not a reference to blues music as a genre, and that volume was published in 1876, a quarter of a century after *Moby Dick*. We might also see Melville's rhyming of "holy" with "melancholy" as another instance of the yoking of emotions (as well as sacred and profane) together that in some way captures the "blues spirit" as we have come to know it. However, it still seems unseemly to suggest that Melville had blues music in mind as he wrote either the novel or the poem.

The question that arises, of course, is whether a detail is really a peg, and whether it will stand the weight of our cloaks. Stephen Crane's *Maggie: A Girl of the Streets* (1893) presents us with just such questions. Apparently written in 1891 before Crane moved to New York, though Crane may have revised it after he arrived there, the novel includes one passage that presents us with subject matter, language, and imagery consistent with what we have come to know as the blues music tradition. Title character Maggie's descent from innocence and "decency" into the profession of street walking echoes the sentiments of such blues recordings as Rosa Henderson's "I'm a Good Gal (But I'm a Thousan' Miles From Home)" (1924). The profession itself receives attention in any number of blues recordings, "Street Walker Blues" (1926) by Bertha "Chippie" Hill, "They Ain't Walking No More" (1930) by Lucille Bogan, and "I'll Keep Sittin' On It (If I Can't Sell It)" (1936) by Georgia White among them. Of course, the "fallen woman" story is not subject matter exclusive to the blues—it was frequently found in popular song as well. However, the passage in the novel in which Maggie makes her way toward her watery demise eerily "echoes"—or is that anticipates?—the language of the blues.

Wandering through the streets, Maggie confronts a number of characters in a nightmarish vision of her life as it stretches out before her. She wanders through "gloomy districts" filled with "blackness," "black shadows," and a "black hue," though none of the figures she confronts are described as African American. One voice stands out: "A drunken man, reeling in her pathway, began to roar at her. I ain' ga no money, dammit," he shouted in a dismal voice. He lurched on up the street, wailing to himself, "Dammit, I ain' ga no money. Damn ba' luck. Ain' ga no more money" (53). Again, though poverty is not exclusive to the blues tradition, such recordings as "Weary Money Blues"

(1927) by Chippie Hill, "No Job Blues" (1928) by Ramblin' Thomas, and "Repossession Blues" (1959) by Lightning Leon (white singer Billy Lee Riley) all employ the sentiment and phraseology. Further, the phrase "bad luck," sometimes read as a euphemism in the blues for racial discrimination, is ubiquitous in the blues, from the "Bad Luck Blues" of Kokomo Arnold (1938) and Ma Rainey (1923) to the "Bad Luck and Trouble" (1949/50) of Lightnin' Hopkins and the "Third Degree" (1953) of Eddie Boyd. The same is true of the common phrase "hard times," often meaning hard economic times, which occurs as "hard time here" in Skip James's 1931 recording "Hard Time Killing Floor Blues," and "It's Hard Time" by Joe Stone from 1933. Interestingly, and perhaps coincidentally, the phrase echoes a letter Harriet Beecher Stowe included in *A Key to Uncle Tom's Cabin* (1853) in which a slave named Tom Ducket, separated from his wife and children who had attempted escape aboard the schooner Pearl, writes to his master, "Hard times here" (172).

The soundtrack for Maggie's trek is the vigorous scraping of a fiddle (53), most likely some reel or Irish jig, perhaps some folk tune such as "Beaver Slide Rag" (1927), played on the streets by Peg Leg Howell's Gang, Henry Williams and Eddie Anthony, or "Alma Waltz" (1930) by the Mississippi Mud Steppers, or Booker Orchestra's "Salty Dog" (1927). In fact, the two traditions are not unrelated, as Oliver has pointed out (*Songsters and Saints* 24). Crane does not particularize here, so it is impossible to say. Were Crane African American, or if he were to make the speaker of these words African American, or if he mentioned some particular song from the African American tradition, the connection to the African American musical tradition would be more solid. Interestingly, critic Christopher Benfey, in describing Crane's employment of standard elements in this type of plot, points to Crane's variations on it as being similar to "a jazz musician toying with a 'standard'" (64). However, this seems to be more a trope utilized by Benfey than a technique of Crane. Historically speaking, an argument for a connection to the blues music tradition might be stronger if the story had been written and published a bit later than the 1891–1893 period.

Recent discussions of Gertrude Stein's short story "Melanctha," which was published as part of *Three Lives* (1909), partake of these reservations as well, though obviously the date of composition and publication places it *closer* to the era when the blues musical genre was emerging in the popular consciousness. Stein, of course, uses the word "blue" as a reference to the melancholy of Melanctha. Charles Bernstein points out that, in a conversation published in *The Review of Contemporary Fiction,* David Antin came across a sound recording of Gertrude Stein's *Three Lives* and "was blown away by the flattened blues music of 'Melanctha'" (March 22, 2001). What "flattened" blues music means is not quite clear, though listening to Stein, we do know where "flatness" comes from, and it is not from the third, fifth, and seventh notes of the musical scale, but rather from her own reading tone. A decade earlier, Kathy Ogren had suggested that a description of Melanctha's love relationships evokes the descriptions of the loves of classic or vaudeville blues singers (147). Stein would have done this, amazingly enough, with little verifiable contact with African American culture, and a few years before these African American blues singers became well known or recorded—though inklings of the blues were in the air, as discussed below.

Is Antin talking about the stream or flow of the consciousness that William James, one of Stein's influences, described as being able to encompass previous and future moments, his "specious present"? And does that account for our hearing the blues where it technically couldn't have been? Or does the linguistic repetition (or insistences, as Stein called them) practiced by Stein in some way suggest the repetitions and calls and responses in the blues? Her language is prose, after all, so more expansive, but the repeated phrases do build up an incremental meaning: "I don't see Melanctha why you should talk like you would kill yourself just because you're blue. I'd never kill myself Melanctha just 'cause I was blue. I'd maybe kill somebody else Melanctha 'cause I was blue, but I'd never kill myself. If I ever killed myself Melanctha it'd be by accident, and if I ever killed myself by accident Melanctha, I'd be awful sorry" (125). The modulated "kill yourself" and "never kill yourself" wrangle with each other for supremacy in the sentiments here, while the "because" and "cause" and "you" or "I" of being blue move back and forth between the identification of the two women with each other, especially when "myself Melanctha" occurs without appositive commas—the kind of identification, presumably, that helps the blues function so successfully in expressing for and alleviating the isolation and weariness of the audience. And Stein's reorganized linguistic representations, are they like the loose repetitions of the blues singer's lines, changing, adding, dropping words in the moment, as in Tommy Johnson's "Lonesome Home Blues":

> I woke this mornin' said my mornin' prayer
> I woke up this mornin' I said my mornin' prayer
> I woke up this mornin', babe, I said my mornin' prayer

In this one performed stanza, Johnson moves from his shortest line, which lacks the words "up" and the second "I," making it his earliest, lowest, and least first person "present" point, to a gradual opening up and presence in line two, to these two additions plus a direct address of the woman in line three. The statement becomes gradually more emphatic, full, and interpersonal with these small changes, without ever leaving his focus, the importance of his waking up (a gradual process in itself) and his morning prayer, which in this expression seems more automatic than fervent—habitual. Given that the song itself is about a man left by himself in his home, with no woman to speak for him, there is no need for verbal ingenuity or closure from the lines.

Of course, some critics assert that "Melanctha" "is not really a story about the ethnic realities of Negroes," with its stereotypical portrayals of the black characters, but a revision of *Q.E.D.* (Copeland 24, 67–68). If we were going to try to construct a connection between "Melanctha" and the blues tradition, the influence of a Cezanne portrait affecting Stein's writing at this time, of Cezanne's wife in a *blue* dress, might be the first linguistic block, even though it invokes a term not used in relation to music at the time. The iterations of the word "blue" in her text—a total of sixteen times, clustered together five times near the beginning of the story (125), and then closer to the end four times (232)—followed in five instances by references to suicide, may evoke the subject matter of blues lyrics as well. After all, songs that repeat the word "blues" emotively exist in titles—"Blue Blues" by Bessie Smith (1931), "Blues Blues" by Amos Easton (1934) and Streamline Mae (1941), and "Blue Room (Blues)" (1929) by Lonnie Johnson and Eddie Lang—and in song, such as Lucille Bogan's 1934 "Lonesome Midnight Blues":

> Blues and trouble have overtaken me
> And I've got those midnight blues, blue as I can be.

Songs entitled "Suicide Blues" were recorded by Leroy Carr, Thomas A. Dorsey, Margaret Johnson, Maggie Jones, Peanut the Kidnapper (James Sherrill), and Peetie Wheatstraw (William Bunch) in the pre-war era, and songs like the eventual blues standard "Trouble in Mind" called for letting "the 219 pacify my mind"—a reference to a train's estimated time of arrival. References to Melanctha's predilection to love "too hard" (127), to love "to do wild things" (128), and to have "bad luck" (222, 237) and "bad trouble" (227) could all come from blues songs with lyrics such as those in B. B. King's "Sweet Sixteen" from October 1959:

> Treat me mean, and I'll keep on loving you just the same,

or Ida Cox's "Wild Women Don't Have the Blues" (1924). Stein's references to razors (131), excessive alcohol consumption (129, 138, 141), and railroad yards (134) are also common to blues songs that have come down to us, such as Edith Wilson's "Rules and Regulations 'Signed Razor Jim'" (1922), Louisisana Johnny's "Razor Cuttin' Man" (1935), The Delta Boys' "Black Gal Swing"

(1941), Ma Rainey's "Dead Drunk Blues" (1927), Lucille Bogan's "Sloppy Drunk Blues" (1930), and any number of railroad blues songs so important to the migration that was prominent at the time of the emergence of the blues. The reference to James Herbert being "black and evil" (131) even evokes the title of blues songs recorded later by Alice Moore, Josh White, and Lil Johnson, which treated the notion that darker-skinned African Americans were rougher because of their "unmixed" blood. The reference to "hard forced laughter" (129) rings of the sometimes bitter laughter of the blues described as "laughing to keep from crying." Peetie Wheatstraw encapsulated the discontinuities and maddening ironies of African American life beautifully in a stanza from "No 'Count Woman" (1940):

> When I first met you, baby, you was beat just like a slave.
> You had one foot on a banana peelin', ooh, well, well, and another foot
> in the grave.

However, the point is that these are part of life itself, as well as the milieu in which the blues musical genre—among other things—came into existence, but the blues would have at most been in its early development at the time Stein was writing, and at this point in her life, it is not likely that Stein would have come into contact with that African American milieu. She did not meet Carl Van Vechten, later a Negrophile and supporter of the New Negro Renaissance along with the blues and jazz in its milieu, until 1917. As such, it seems that Stein's iterations, referencing of subject matter, and perhaps even her almost improvisatory-feeling sentences are either a sign that the blues was "in the air" at the time, or a remarkable coincidence that, while seeming to relate to a blues music tradition that she could become familiar with (and find sympathies with) later, do so primarily through our reading from our contemporary knowledge backward. After all, we can encounter improvisation and subject matter references in music and literature other than the blues.

There are ways in which texts that post-date the creation of the blues can reference an earlier period with the blues in mind. For example, texts may subtly reference the blues through references to the time period during which they seem to have emerged. Arguably, evidence from folklorists and sheet music and piano rolls suggests that some of what we identify as the blues *began* to emerge in the 1880s, and Emma Williams, mother of blues singer Mary Johnson, certainly remembered them "before nineteen-hundred" (Oliver, *Conversation* 23), though this was perhaps an earlier type of music bridging to what we know as the blues. This was a time at which the first generation of African Americans born outside of *de jure* slavery were coming to their majority.

Perhaps they grew up on plantations, perhaps not, but they did grow up with a different sense of their legal status, and thus the greater possibility of different attitudes regarding mobility, freedom of interpersonal relationships, and access to commodities and power. Not surprisingly, all of these elements are strongly characteristic of blues lyrics. Stephen Calt calls attention to a common phrase that occurred in black speech, as well as blues, from the 1920s until at least beyond the publication of Zora Neale Hurston and Dorothy Waring's *Polk County* (1944): "on the road somewhere," which means "leading a rootless existence" (175). The frequent restlessness encountered in blues lyrics is likely a legacy of slavery and Jim Crow social conditions.

Furthermore, they are frequently manifested in the evocation of one of the most common symbols in blues lyrics, the train. References to the train, of course, are recurrent in spirituals and gospel music. Frequently, at least superficially, the deliverance described in these songs is to an eminent afterlife rather than a deliverance in this life, though of course the strong masking tradition in African American vernacular music thinly veils, at times, reference to socio-political deliverance in this world as well. In the blues tradition, it is less God's or the Lord's train than it is a worldly vehicle that serves as a way of exercising one's own power to escape, pursue, arrive, or deliver in a variety of ways—or not. The lyric "train time here, track's all out of line" suggests the mobile imperative blocked by a confusion of avenues. The genre of boogie woogie, after all, was sometimes portrayed in a locomotive manner, as in Lemuel Fowler's "Express Train Blues" (1925) or Meade Lux Lewis's "Honky Tonk Train Blues" (1927), for the percussive and propulsive drive of the music, and well as for the meanings of the train in African American folklore. When Blind Lemon Jefferson sang in "Broke and Hungry" (1926), "I'm goin' away to build me a railroad of my own," which is echoed in the blues stanza Wright Holmes sang in "Alley Special" (1947), "One of these here days I'm gonna build me a heaven of my own," the idea of heaven is brought to Earth and made manifest in the power of the singers to seize control of the means of mobility, to take this power unto themselves, in a way that combines escape, pursuit, arrival, and deliverance in public and private, social and personal ways. The fact that Son House completes his lyric couplet with "[t]hen I'd give all my women a long long happy home" evidences this as a kind of sexual fulfillment as well, where "heaven" is a pleasure palace for his long and powerful phallus ("Preachin' the Blues Pt.1," 1930).

Of course, the sexual implications of trains and train tracks have always been obvious to blues singers, and the associations of sexual fulfillment with personal and social fulfillment have been clear, also, as were the limitations of that "freedom":

If I gits home to the land of de free
Pullman train'll be the place for me (Niles 54–56)

The singer of this song recognizes that even with nominal freedom, there is still a place designated for him amongst the servants—happy to have such a prestigious job—working on that selfsame symbol of freedom.

As we think about the ways the blues slowly became manifest in popular and "high" American and world culture, particularly literature, we must keep in mind the difficulties that questions of influence, definition, origins, syncretism, and adaptability to Euro-American literary uses pose. Historical, political, and social attitudes affect aesthetic choices in a plethora of ways that reflect the ongoing attempts of African Americans to achieve parity in a society resistant to offering it and only haltingly providing it, while embracing contributions made by African Americans as representative of American creativity, ingenuity, and labor. Many people overseas in the 1920s–1940s thought that American music *was* black music, and black music at that time was spirituals, ragtime, blues, and jazz. It is sardonic and hypocritical to accept credit for anything so violently and shamefully born.

The problem at the turn of the twentieth century was the issue of the color line, as Du Bois described it, and this line has continued to demarcate, blurred as it may be, as we progress through the twenty-first. "How does it feel to be a problem?" he characterized what was called "the negro question" in *The Souls of Black Folk* (11). What was to be done with the Negro? There are a number of ways, of course, that the question could be posed, depending on the source and viewpoint. A HUAC interrogation? A "where is you going, boy?" from the local police? A "why can't I swim in the public pool, mommy" from a five-year-old child?

A "why was I born?"

On a more general level, perhaps, and in a more involved mode, "how can we exploit/use/marginalize/eradicate the Negro?" Or was it "how can we express admiration for/produce a positive response to/live up to American ideals for the Negro?" Or even, "how might we tolerate the Negro while exploiting the resources/cultural productions of this fortunately-marginalized group?" Where was black agency? Why wasn't it being offered? And why did someone else have the right to offer it?

And how could you really tell what the question meant to each individual? The African American influence in the arts was a burgeoning field from at least the ragtime era on, even earlier with the emergence of minstrelsy and spirituals. Gershwin—was he a rhapsodic robber baron? Are we making a mountain out of an Antheil hearing boogie woogie in his music? Was Joseph

Lamb a ragtime wolf in sheep's clothing? Was Bix Beiderbecke really singing the blues? And do we really miss Sophie Tucker's blues singing some of these days? Were they an illegitimate part of the tradition of African American music? One-drop voluntary mulattoes suddenly recognized and affirmed after all those years? If they loved the music, did that make it legitimate? Or if they were good? Does art belong to a group or, once disseminated, is it up for grabs? Even if the history of treatment of that group is one of larceny on a grand scale, until the art is mostly what is left that belongs to them—and then it doesn't? When does something not from you become of you? How much imitation is too much? Who says?

It seems pretty clear that the answers to these questions are muddy at best. Some, like Furry Lewis, can peep through muddy water and spy dry land; others, when their left eye goes to jumping, don't know which way to go. In a much better world of equal opportunity and involvement, they might be easier to negotiate, but we do not have the benefit of those circumstances, nor the accrued benefits of an absence of institutional racism, to make our determination easier. Acknowledgement, of course, is not enough. It is a start, after all these years, one that has sometimes led to other types of remuneration for those alive to accrue the benefits, such as blues revivals, festivals, magazines, even Viagra ads and barbecue sauce, with a saucy wink toward old stereotypes. Answers to these questions are not something provided here. Answers to subjective questions like these are, like the blues, like consumption—they kill you by degrees. And in this case a degree doesn't help answer the question at all.

2
Paging Mr. Page

The Midnight Stage to Modernism

> . . . immigrants in the performing arts gravitated to gifted African-American colleagues and necessary African-American causes . . [jazz was] of limited interest to "serious" Americans in search of an indigenous high-cultural identity.
> (Horowitz 20, 44)

I

The emergence of the blues into American mainstream culture and subsequently into American literature was the result of a process born of the New World's ambivalent relationship with vernacular cultures, which jimmied the locked door of haute culture just enough to allow the white and black observers of the lower classes to get their vigorous-by-proxy, if sometimes condescending, hands on the driving wheel. It is useful to examine early examples of literature influenced by the blues in the context of literary history, folklore studies, popular and commercial culture, especially sheet music and recordings, Jazz Age aesthetics, and Leftist politics, in order to get a clear sense of the intercultural milieu out of which the earliest literary productions employing the blues sprang. This is especially true since early literary practitioners seemed ready to do battle from the beginning of the emergence of blues in literature with contentious middle- and upper-class forces, both black and white, that fought what they (sometimes mistakenly) saw as the commonness (not such a bad thing in America, and frequently very uncommon!) and "vulgarity" of the blues.

It is worth pointing out that, as the LP *The Unexpurgated Folk Songs of Men* and the historical CD *Actionable Offenses: Indecent Phonograph Recordings from the 1890s* show, there were a number of recorded whites who might be accused of vulgarity, too, not just blacks. These materials, interestingly labeled "blue," though not because they were necessarily *blues* recordings, found an ample audience, in the field, as demonstrated in the work of Gershon Legman and Vance Randolph, and in private and very occasionally commercial recordings. Whites were quite prolific at generating performances of frank and obscene material (see the LPs *The Unexpurgated Folk Songs of Men* and Ed McCurdy's *The Best of Dalliance* for examples from Elizabethan times to the present). Old-time or "hillbilly" performers took up the performance and commercial recording of double-entendre blues songs, in at least partially an African American style that suggested an association of "smutty" material with African Americans, quite readily—Cliff Carlisle's audacious "Mouse Ear Blues" (1933) and "That Nasty Swing" (1936), future governor of Georgia Jimmie Davis's (yes, the "You Are My Sunshine" composer) "Sewing Machine Blues" (1932) and "Tom Cat and Pussy Blues" (1932), and Smokey Wood's wild ride through "Everybody's Truckin'" (1937) among them. Those locating commonness and vulgarity primarily in the black community weren't looking in their own mirrors.

The blues, as they emerged into popular culture, were evolved from a variety of African and European modes and genres combined on American soil into a distinctive genre with fluid boundaries itself. What was called "hot" music included ragtime and minstrel music traced by David Wondrich as far back as 1843 (4), and Al Jolson was selling a contemporary mix of these elements and pop song in the so-called (but not) first talkie, *The Jazz Singer* (1927). In fact, Jolson had recorded a Vitaphone short of his regular act, entitled *A Plantation Act*, in which he appeared in blackface, a year earlier. However, labeling the tunes Jolson sang in *The Jazz Singer* as "jazz" shows how loosely and sweepingly the label was applied. In *A Plantation Act*, Jolson even commented (in blackface), "Mammy songs are the fundamental songs of our country" (*The Jazz Singer*); a writer of another of the fundamental genres of songs of our country, the patriotic George M. Cohan, "had written many coon songs in the 1890s" (*Monarchs of Minstrelsy* 20). "Hippodrome Minstrel Medley," recorded by Manuel Romain in 1916, shows the breadth of tunes included under the minstrel banner of the time—and indeed, some would be labeled jazz later. The medley includes war songs, coon songs, pop-ragtime, spirituals, and even the Bob Cole-James Weldon Johnson-J. Rosamond Johnson composition "Under the Bamboo Tree," among other works reaching back into the nineteenth century (*Monarchs of Minstrelsy*). And the minstrel shows remained popular, even nostalgic, to some segments of the population. There was a staging and filming in 1951 of *Yes Sir, Mr. Bones*, a minstrel show with minstrel entertainers such as Emmett Miller, Scatman Crothers, and Freeman "Brother Bones" Davis (yes, performer of the Harlem Globetrotters' theme "Sweet Georgia Brown"). An LP released by the Colpix label in the mid-sixties featuring Jack Benny, Milton Berle, George Burns, Phil Silvers, and Benny Fields performing a full-length minstrel show (*The Minstrel Men*), while Leroi Jones/Amiri Baraka was producing *Dutchman* and "Black Dada Nihilismus" (1964) and Gwendolyn Brooks was writing "Chicago Picasso" and "The Wall" (1967), gains force and irony through the juxtaposition.

This type of music was casually labeled "jazz" or "blues" because of the popularity of the labels and the similarities among the musics, especially the syncopation. Vaudeville blues singers, in fact, were frequently accompanied by jazz soloists or groups, further blurring the superficial distinctions between jazz and blues. The fluidity of transnational boundaries and the protean quality of American identity coalesce and contribute to the nature and uses of African American vernacular materials. It is good to be shifty in a new country, as Johnson Jones Hooper's Simon Suggs says, recognizing how the shifting of transnational boundaries helps determine the arc of culture and society that must be sight read or improvised for appropriate response. How the materials are used by the subjected to work against the paradigm of the dominant culture—initially and in relation to the co-opting and corrupting of those materials (as in minstrelsy) that then must be readjusted for appropriate social, artistic, and political uses—and how the use of those materials enters into and reflects integrative notions of American literature and democracy is a major focus of this study.

Of course, the use of African American blues elements in poetry in the twentieth century was anticipated and precipitated by important work in a variety of arenas, such as the productions of realist and local color writers like Mark Twain (a true lover of minstrelsy and African American spiritual and jubilee singing) and the southwestern humorists. Additionally, the collections of blues in American folklore studies, as well as the issuance of blues and material by black performers on sheet music, on phonograph recordings beginning in 1890, and on the first primitive juke boxes, assisted in satisfying the primary target audiences. It also helped create an interest in intellectual and popular culture circles that made it possible for writers to generate their own poetic experiments with blues and jazz that would be judged acceptable, at least to some audiences.

At the turn of the twentieth century, a number of other writers such as Paul Laurence Dunbar, Daniel Webster Davis, and James Edwin Campbell anticipated and/or contributed to an environment and range of artistic aesthetics and production in the area of vernacular music and poetry as well. Exciting literary activities in two major cities included attention to jazz and blues materials, appropriately enough since they were major recording centers as well. The Harlem Renaissance/New Negro criticism and poetry of James Weldon Johnson and Alain Locke certainly helped call attention to the possibilities of spirituals, blues, and jazz. The Chicago Renaissance drew on the "new" music as a reflection of the urban realism of the times. Vachel Lindsay's "higher vaudeville" explored the ways in which spirited, dramatic oral performances enriched the experience of poetry. The *American Songbag* and poetry of Carl Sandburg placed a variety of folk songs, including a number of African American songs, into the hands of readers who had encountered flashes of the material in Sandburg's poetry. Sandburg expressed his appreciation for the folklore collecting of Alan Lomax, connecting Lomax with the folk past and the modern temper: "[Alan] is intensely American and flagrantly and vagrantly modern . . ." (Hart 100). Though many of the activities of the Lomaxes (and all of Alan's) took place post-1929, they clearly approached folklore with an interest in traditions manifested before 1929. Maxwell Bodenheim and Kenneth Rexroth participated in poetry and jazz performance activities, as did Langston Hughes. In the southern folklore studies and "Black Ulysses" novels of Howard W. Odum, readers encountered attempts to contextualize African American folklore, while Sterling Brown's experiments with dialect and blues and jazz materials set the standard for honest and rooted folk expression. The journal *Blues: A Magazine of New Rhythms* (1929) used the blues as a metaphor for the type of modernist poetry emerging among those writers at the time. The leftist folk song movement of the 1920s and 1930s—spurred by Charles Seeger, Ruth Crawford Seeger, Carl Sandburg, Bob Miller, and others—helped usher African American folk music into the Popular Front scene, political appearances, supper clubs like the Café Society, the "From Spirituals to Swing" concerts, and mainstream American music, and moved the music even closer to the popular mind. And with poet Langston Hughes, there was the first foundational effusion of the African American folk-blues tradition into American literature.

It was the American local color impulse that first helped integrate American vernacular materials into American literature. From the earliest stock Yankee characters of "Yankee Doodle," Royall Tyler's *The Contrast*, and Washington Irving's and James Fenimore Cooper's prose; the Down East humor and frontier tall tales of Seba Smith, Thomas Chandler Halliburton, and James Russell Lowell; the humor of the Old Southwest reflected variously in the work of Thomas Bangs Thorpe, A. B. Longstreet, and George Washington Harris; the sensitive dialect renderings of James Whitcomb Riley, Daniel Webster Davis, James Edwin Campbell, and especially Paul Laurence Dunbar (the first and last of whom wrote in both Indiana Hoosier and African American dialects, among others); the versions of southern animal tales of Joel Chandler Harris; and the dialect and folk superstitions of Mark Twain's *Adventures of Huckleberry Finn*, one encounters reflections of the American vernacular in all its imagination, vigor, pride, condescension, and sometimes coarse and obscene glory. Blues poetry pioneer Langston Hughes was himself a Dunbar disciple, recounting in *The Big Sea* that some of his first poems he attempted to write were "Negro dialect poems like Paul Laurence Dunbar's" (28).

And in activities that nearly encompass his entire life, Hughes also described being enthralled when he first read *The Adventures of Huckleberry Finn* as a child, and praised Twain's portrayals of African American characters in Hughes's 1959 introduction to *The Tragedy of Pudd'nhead Wilson.* This is clear testimony to the fact of Hughes's familiarity with and admiration of an author whose gifts at employing vernacular language have been recognized as seminal in the development of American literature, at least as far back as Hemingway's famous, if somewhat blustery and arrogant, statement in *The Green Hills of Africa* (22) regarding the *The Adventures of Huckleberry Finn* as the source of all American literature. When Twain writes in Huck's voice that Emmeline Grangerford can "rattle off poetry like nothing" (173–74), he captures perfectly the vernacular phrase denoting "easily," but clearly, given the poor quality of her poetry, she also really does write poetry like nothing. Two jokes are embedded in Twain's skillful use of the vernacular—as is evident, for example, in the title of a blues song by Susie Edwards, "I Want a Good Man And I Want Him Bad" (1929) rather than "badly." This song was also recorded one year later by the white singer Annette Hanshaw.

Clearly, American culture was influencing and being influenced by the cultures of African Americans who were forcibly imported as property, chattel slaves. Manifestations of African language, stories, songs, proverbs, visual arts, religion, societal organization, and philosophy have been identified and discussed by such scholars as Melville Herskovits, Lorenzo Dow Turner, Janheinz Jahn, Paul Oliver, Robert Farris Thompson, Dena J. Epstein, Joseph Holloway, William R. Ferris, and others. The transnational mixing of African and European cultures on American soil was subjected to American racist stereotypes of ignorant, lazy, vain, and appetitive figures upon appropriation of these materials into mainstream American culture. The emergence of blackface minstrelsy in the 1830s gave impetus to the popularity of the African American song tradition as it had been stolen or borrowed and/or modified, adapted, and performed by white minstrel performers (and later black ones) in an often racist atmosphere. Such an atmosphere presented frequently stilted versions of African American materials that misrepresented the culture on one hand, and on the other fostered some embarrassment in the African American community, causing at least some in the community to reject the beautiful elements of African American culture victimized by minstrel distortions. In his *The Devil's Dictionary* (1911), Ambrose Bierce described the black face minstrel satirically as "[f]ormerly a poet, singer, or musician; now a nigger with a color less than skin deep and a humor more than flesh and blood can bear" (87), hinting at the ridiculous nature of the institution, as well as its tragic implications. Indeed, Mark Twain has come under attack for his use of the minstrel tradition in his own work, *Huckleberry Finn* included. In the meantime, accusations of outright larceny can sometimes be explained in an aesthetic sense. T. S. Eliot famously proclaimed, "The bad poet imitates; the good poet steals" (Richardson I, 421). This seems to support the artist in the defense of his felony, which on the one hand disregards the property rights of the plaintiff. Eliot says, "In my defense, I am a good poet." The good poet acknowledges tradition, works with past literary contributions and values, but must *possess* the material in order to make it reflect his own values and ideas. If you don't dominate it, it will become a time-bound, not timely or timeless, statement that develops organically depending upon the gardens in which the stolen object is planted. Is that a rationalization? Does it quiver with the arrogant arrow of the heartless (artless?) archer? Very possibly. Do the ends justify the means? Does the modification or transformation "make it new"? Well, as long as the appropriation maintains the crucial identification with the earlier work, it is necessarily a synapse that necessitates both. The new meaning represents a revolution of the object to a new perspective gapped from the past, and bridged to the next appropriation. It is personal and communal. Picasso's feeling about his own art is illuminating: "He did not want a painting to be an abstraction any more than he wanted it to be a facsimile. He wanted it to constitute a fact, a very specific fact" (Richardson II: 165).

In the meantime, while blackface minstrelsy was attracting the approbation, or at least the interest, of white mainstream American society, other cultural arbiters championed more "refined" examples of African American art. James McCune Smith, a prominent African American abolitionist and intellectual of the nineteenth century, invested his approval in the artistry of Elizabeth Taylor Greenfield, an African American operatic singer known as the "Black Swan." In an article published in *Frederick Douglass' Paper* in 1855, Smith praised her not only as an *artiste*, but as an embodiment of the argument for African American cultural achievement:

> In the world of art we have Dumas and Elizabeth Greenfield . . . Tropical nature vindicated in this child of the sun, in her department of Art, in like manner as Dumas in his department of Art . . . True Art is a leveler, and thoroughly isocratic: never was the Tabernacle so thoroughly speckled with mixed complexions . . . Miss Greenfield occupies a position of marked significance. Bending not one whit to the requirements of American prejudice, never shrinking for an instant under the cover of Indian or Moorish descent, she stands forth simple and pure as a black woman. This truthfulness is proof of the nobleness of her nature and fitness to become a Priestess in the Temple. Having selected as her aim the

> divinest of Arts that are requiring the richest endowments of nature and the most prolonged and arduous culture, it was but a light thing for her to meet prejudice face to face and crush it. (Stauffer 120–21)

Smith, comparing Greenfield favorably to Jenny Lind, finds her choice of European art of "culture" and "refinement" to exemplify the best that African Americans have to offer, with a clear undertone to her performance that cries out "'AM I NOT A WOMAN AND A SISTER?'" (121). Such middle-class attitudes that sought to prove African American worth through accomplishments in European genres, while certainly one side of the cultural achievement coin, tended to devalue African American genres that mixed African and European genres in a distinctive and original blend, such as the materials that were the sources for minstrelsy and that later developed into ragtime, blues, jazz, and gospel. Left to the performances of white blackface minstrels and the demands of white audiences, those materials degenerated into racist exaggeration and parody.

This mal(con)formation produced a need for proud and open-minded cultural arbiters to rescue authentic materials from the minstrel mess, among them Bert Williams and George Walker, Paul Laurence Dunbar, James Weldon Johnson, Sterling Brown, and Langston Hughes, all of whom attempted to balance on the precipitous tightrope of drawing on the roots of racist minstrelsy while communicating cultural pride and maintaining their constituencies in the African American community. A listen to the recordings by Bert Williams such as "You Can't Get Away From It" (1914), "Never Mo'" (1915), "I'm Gone Before I Go" (1916), and "Twenty Years" (1917) reveal an artist of great craft whose talent was not squandered on minstrelsy, but rather frequently signified upon its grotesqueries with sympathetic portraits. Dunbar and Johnson, too, sought to mitigate the insulting elements of minstrelsy in order to make the reclamation process possible. Dunbar's "When Malindy Sings" is among a number of his poems that champion the superiority of an African Amercan vernacular style, and his "A Negro Love Song" was recorded as a rhythm and blues song by Hadda Brooks in 1952, as well as later by rock and roller Gene Vincent. Johnson's "Under the Bamboo Tree" (1902) and "My Castle on the Nile" (1902), written with his brother J. Rosamond Johnson and Bob Cole (whose "A Trip to Coontown" was, in 1898, the first African American comedy to seriously alter the minstrel pattern) were composed around the time of "Lift Ev'ry Voice and Sing" (1900; sometimes called the Black National Anthem), demonstrating Johnson's desire to present a more acceptable image of African Americans. Hughes's poem "Minstrel Man" treats the subject directly, exposing the persona of the minstrel man that hides the man behind the mask. In all, there were a variety of commentators, critics, and artists at work on the accurate representation of the African American materials associated with minstrel tradition, which was a slow but steady process of sometimes subtle, sometimes major, alterations to a seriously flawed genre. Unfortunately, the white-controlled recording industry was still fostering racial stereotypes. Like white singers May Irwin and Clarice Vance, the white blues and jazz singer Sophie Tucker was billed with sixty-six different titles between 1906 and 1923, many of them before 1911 racially derogatory: Coon Shouter, Live Coon Shouter from the Sunny South, Refined Coon Singer, Manipulator of Coon Shouters, Coon Shouting Queen, Best Coon Shouter in Captivity (!), The Advanced Spring Fashion in Coon Songs, and A Revelation in Coonology among them (Ecker and Ecker 22–23). And not many black performers were even being recorded yet, though as Lynn Abbott and Doug Seroff point out, Ma Rainey, Bessie Smith, and others were all billed as "coon shouters" up until around 1916, when the popularity of the term "blues" in a song title transformed them into blues singers (4). Still, none of them would make it into the studios until 1923, which allowed additional time to mitigate the racist nomenclature.

American bard Walt Whitman, among others, provided an artistic aesthetic and poetic persona that was influential on the aesthetic and work of subsequent vernacular writers as well. This is reflected in Hughes poems like "I, Too" (1925) and "Old Walt" (1954), as well as in Hughes's editing of a children's book of Whitman's poems in 1946, including of Whitman poems in *The Poetry of the Negro, 1746–1949*, and mounting a notable defense of Whitman's work in the *Chicago Defender* in 1953. In these works, Hughes seeks to affirm Whitman's role as an American seeker of a democracy of the spirit, expressing in expansive and inclusive language that there is a space for African Americans in Whitman's poetic persona's America, even if Whitman, in his private and social life, frequently failed to live up to the spirit of his art in his attitude toward African Americans. By creating a poetic atmosphere hospitable to the breadth of American people and language, Whitman helped create a space for poets previously left to concoct in the kitchen. Into this atmosphere, prepared by a long and varied series of impulses and writers struggling with what it meant to be American (which cannot and must not be defined without reference to the African American meat and spices in the American stew) emerged the genre known as the blues, with its ragtime background, field holler melisma, reel-like abandon, and signifying playfulness with language, to become the music of what Hart Crane in *The Bridge* called the lament of the locomotive "Twentieth Century Limited" (*The Complete Poems and Selected Letters* 62).

Snatches of African American folk materials had begun appearing in mainstream print in popular magazines and such widely distributed works as Stowe's *Uncle Tom's Cabin* (1852) even before Allen, McKim, and Ware's *Slave Songs of the United States* (1867) helped spread knowledge of African American spirituals more broadly. Certainly the tours of the Fisk Jubilee Singers, beginning with George L. White in 1871, and touring black minstrel troupes of the same time helped spread the gospel of African American music as well. Among the African American forebears in the use of vernacular materials were authors such as Martin Delany in *Blake, or, the Huts of America* (1859–62); Frances Ellen Watkins in her "Aunt Chloe" poems and her novel *Iola Leroy* (1892); and dialect poets such as Paul Laurence Dunbar, James Edwin Campbell, and Daniel Webster Davis, all of whose poetry anticipated such work by Hughes as his October 1922 publication "Song For a Banjo Dance." Charles Chesnutt contributed most importantly in his conjure tales, whose "wise fool" trickster character Uncle Julius precedes Sterling Brown's "Slim Greer" and Hughes's "Jesse B. Semple." In folklore studies in general, the pioneering work of collectors like Mary Alicia Owen, who conducted research on African American folklore and voodoo in particular, presenting her results in 1891 to the International Folklore Conference, also helped foster a popular interest. Clearly these materials were necessary precursors, footing the path to be paved by later writers of vernacular literature.

Certainly these materials could use scholarly champions to lend their dignity to what were perceived as humble proto-forms, rather than acceptable specimens of art. In W. E. B. Du Bois's *The Souls of Black Folk* (1902), a seminal book read and cherished in many an African American home since its publication, we encounter an early serious treatment of what Du Bois terms "the sorrow songs," presenting a formative view of the importance of the words and music to African American life—and American life in general. Du Bois's pairing of snippets from the spirituals with epigraphs from European sources claimed a certain parity for this African American genre. James Weldon Johnson, whose pop-"coon" songs such as "Louisiana Lize" and "Under the Bamboo Tree" were written beginning in 1899 with his brother J. Rosamond Johnson and later Bob Cole, helped push on the boundaries that limited the accuracy and range of such songs. This, in turn, helped crack open the door for a number of writers and musicians to produce works for the stage, including Broadway. Shows such as *Shuffle Along* (1921) and *Runnin' Wild* (1923) benefited from the alterations to the minstrel show tradition that allowed black written, owned, and operated revues their space on the stage. Ragtime references and oral sermons in Johnson's *The Autobiography of an Ex-Colored Man* (1912; 1927) helped to demonstrate the effective uses to which such material could be put: more than window dressing, but as plot advancers and metaphors for the creativity of African Americans and the possibilities and limitations inherent in American society, in addition to commentary on the nature of time and the gap between low and high art. Johnson, too, was a champion of African American oral sermons and religious music, as his two collections and volume of oral sermons in the manner of the folk preacher demonstrate—in the 1990s, actual preachers recorded Johnson's oral sermons, including Reverend Calvin Butts of the Abyssinian Baptist Church (*God's Trombones*, 1993). Hughes's poems "Negro" (1922) and "Prelude to Our Age" (1951) both honor ragtime as a signal musical achievement of African Americans as well.

It was crucial for the emergence of the blues as a literary force that the materials of American vernacular culture work their way closer to mainstream American literature, even as the vernacular materials, subjected in life and in print to American racist adaptations and distortions, continued to evolve loosely out of field hollers, work songs, game songs, spirituals, minstrel songs, and ragtime into the blues. While at times these resources were mocked by the white and black authors that employed them, there were those who found philosophical lessons, survival strategies, aesthetic and social resistance, and just plain beauty in the vernacular culture of African Americans. Sometimes this was due to the acceptance of certain religious precepts such as piety and humility, as indicated in the spirituals. Others may well have identified in terms of experience or class or temperament with their African American counterparts. After all, haven't we all had the blues? It depends on which definition you are talking about.

II

As we have already said, references to the word "blues" denoting an unsettled state or a sad mood in the written tradition preceded our knowledge of the word as it was appropriated to refer to the African American musical tradition that began to emerge in snatches in the 1880s. According to the *Oxford English Dictionary*, we can trace in print the term "blue" meaning "discomfited, depressed" back to 1550; the phrase "the blue devils," meaning " baleful demons" to 1616; and "blue devilism" referring to the apparitions seen in delirium tremens to 1787 in the writings of Scottish dialect poet and ploughman Robert Burns. It is worth noting here that Burns's poetry sometimes approached a virtual poetic ethnography, full of folk materials and especially Scottish song influences that seem a template for the kind of work Hughes would do later for African American vernacular culture. Of course, as James Weldon Johnson pointed out in his introduction to *The Book of American Negro Poetry* (1922; 1931), the writers of the Irish Revival of the late nineteenth and early twentieth century provided an example for budding writers of the Harlem Renaissance of the 1920s (41), as later explored more fully in Tracy Mishkin. Variations of these "blue" terms occurred in the writings of Thomas Jefferson in 1820 and in 1825 in Byron's *Don Juan* (*OED* 236–37). Local colorist William Tappan Thompson's *Major Jones's Sketches of Travel* (1848) calls out the blues as well, as does Mark Twain in chapters 40 and 61 of *Roughing It* (1872), chapters 28 and 33 of *The Gilded Age* (1873), and in chapter 8 of *Pudd'nhead Wilson* (1894), where Roxy plans to fawn over the faux heir upon her return to Dawson's Landing. In chapter 16 of Harriet Beecher Stowe's *Uncle Tom's Cabin* (1852), St. Clare ironically tells chronic and demanding complainant Marie "you've got the blues, this morning" (244) while Marie criticizes "the race" for being selfish at the expense, and Robert Louis Stevenson refers to the emotion of the blues in chapter 19 of *Treasure Island* (1883).

Because of his importance in opening up literature to broader subject matter and freer versification—including for African American writers—Walt Whitman's employment of the term in *Notes Left Over* (1892) deserves special attention:

> I add that—while England is among the greatest of lands in political freedom, or the idea of it, and in stalwart personal character, &c.—the spirit of English literature is not great, at least is not greatest—and its products are no models for us. With the exception of Shakspere, there is no first-class genius in that literature—which, with a truly vast amount of value, and of artificial beauty, (largely from the classics,) is almost always material, sensual, not spiritual—almost always congests, makes plethoric, not frees, expands, dilates—is cold, anti-democratic, loves to be sluggish and stately, and shows much of that characteristic of vulgar persons, the dread of saying or doing something not at all improper in itself, but unconventional, and that may be laugh'd at. In its best, the sombre pervades it; it is moody, melancholy, and, to give it its due, expresses, in characters and plots, those qualities, in an unrival'd manner. Yet not as the black thunderstorms, and in great normal, crashing passions, of the Greek clearing the air, refreshing afterward, bracing with power; but as in Hamlet, moping, sick, uncertain, and leaving ever after a secret taste for the blues, the morbid fascination, the luxury of wo. . . . (1083)

This phrase of Whitman's, "a secret taste for the blues," indicates his sense of "the blues" that he is discussing. It is not what many commentators understand of it today (Albert Murray's *Stomping the Blues* notwithstanding), which is precisely a "clearing the air, refreshing afterward, bracing with power" that indicates this feeling quite apart from any blues musical tradition that might have been emerging in Whitman's time. For Whitman, this blues is merely temporal, robbing of power rather than providing it, a private and debilitating melancholy rather than a public and empowering pronouncement, and thus only the most superficial of ancestors of the musical genre that functions to express and alleviate such feelings of emotional distress.

Debra DeSalvo emphasizes seventeenth-century origins of the word "blues," particularly as they relate to "the intense visual hallucinations of 'delirium tremens,' the trembling and psychosis associated with alcohol withdrawal," making explicit the connections between blues, alcohol, and the type of dancing frequently fueled by alcohol in juke joints in the twentieth century (16–17). The term "blue Monday," often associated with blues and jazz parties, seems to stem from the German *der blaue Montag*, referring to "a Monday spent in dissipation by workmen" (*OED* 236). American poet James Whitcomb Riley, well known for his popular poems in Indiana Hoosier dialect—under Riley's influence, Paul Laurence Dunbar even wrote some in Indiana Hoosier dialect himself—used the phrase in this respect in his poem "Blue-Monday at the Shoe Shop"; Carl Sandburg refers to it as a term used in the 1890s in his 1952 autobiography *Always the Young Strangers* (81).

Charlotte Forten confessed in her journals to having the blues in 1860, ten years after the term first appeared in print in relation to music in a piece entitled "I've Got the Blues Today," and Washington Irving referred to "a fit of the blues" in *Salmagundi* (1807) (Levet 87). And certainly it is no surprise, given how lonesome Huckleberry Finn frequently feels, that he confesses to "feeling ruther blue" in *The Adventures of Huckleberry Finn* (231). Sandburg, again in his autobiography, described a character from before the turn of the twentieth century named "Nigger" Duke whose line of greeting included "my job is to chase away the blues" (284). Quite interestingly, the term "bloman" or "blueman," now obsolete, referred to a Negro in the fourteenth and fifteenth centuries as the result of the identification between the words, blo, blae, and blue, perhaps dialect variants (*OED* 237). It is interesting to note that obscene or vulgar material has been labeled with the term "blue," the etymology of which is unclear, but this sense of the blues as being associated in many locations with bawdy houses and sexual promiscuity may have strengthened the name "blues" because of these associations. Certainly there have been "obscene" recordings of blues, such as Lucille Bogan's "Shave 'Em

Dry" (1935), Jelly Roll Morton's "Winin' Boy" (1938), and Western Swing musician Smokey Wood's "Everybody's Truckin'" (1937), among many others. Of course, printed references do not tell us when the word "blues" referring to despondency emerged in the oral tradition, or from where, but they do give us a sense of when the term began to gain more mainstream currency: centuries before the African American music we know as the blues began to receive the notice of folklorists, journalists, and other interested parties.

Among the earliest references to blues music in print that we know of come from the observations of literate and performing blues musicians and folklorists, whose work was given impetus by the formation of the American Folklore Society at Harvard in 1888 and the Chicago Folklore Society in 1891, both of which established their own journals, as did Hampton Institute. Instances of blues or pre-blues performance began turning up all over the South as early as 1890. That year, folklorist Gates Thomas collected a blues-like song entitled "Nobody There" in south Texas, and W. C. Handy, blues composer and popularizer and a particular hero of Hughes's, heard a quartet singing the blues in Florence, Alabama. Two years later, Handy heard "East St. Louis Blues" in East St. Louis, and in the 1890s Ernest Borneman collected material related to boogie woogie. By 1901–1902, Jelly Roll Morton reported hearing the blues in New Orleans (though sometimes his dates are suspect), and Charles Peabody heard them in Stovall, Mississippi. Other important soundings include Ma Rainey in Missouri in 1902; Handy in Tutwiler, Mississippi, in 1903; John A. Lomax's cylinder recording of "Dink's Song" in 1904; the important collections of Howard W. Odum in Mississippi and Georgia from 1905–1908; John Jacob Niles in Pikeville, Kentucky, in 1908 (Ophelia Simpson's "Black Alfalfa's Jail-House Shouting Blues"); E. C. Perrow in Mississippi in 1909; Will Thomas in Texas in 1912; Anna Kranz Odum in Sumner County, Tennessee, in 1914 ("Leave Your House Rent Here"); W. Prescott Webb in Beeville, Texas, in 1915; John A. Lomax in Texas in 1917; Dorothy Scarborough (president of the Texas Folklore Society) in 1915; and Mary Wheeler along the Ohio and Mississippi (published in 1944). All of these instances of the observance or collection of folk-blues were occurring before or alongside performances by such bands as W. C. Handy's and Wilbur Sweatman's and occasional uses of the blues in sheet music and piano rolls, leading to the commercial African American vocal blues boom in 1920. Langston Hughes described in *The Big Sea* first hearing the blues around 1908 (at approximately six years of age) on Independence Avenue in Kansas City ("Jazz as Communication" 493), later adding that it was on a street corner near his uncle's barbershop on Charlotte Street ("I Remember the Blues" 152). There Hughes heard and saw the blind guitar players and folk musicians whose early work he clearly viewed as liberating, and whose performances would later form a basis for his own championing of the "low-down folks" and both the spirituals and blues that expressed their life experiences. Hughes's unashamed discussions of the blues influences of his childhood, alongside the sometimes condescending but frequently admiring commentary on blues from these other sources, increased the visibility of the blues in important ways for intellectual audiences.

However, the emergence of blues music into white mainstream American culture first came about through the publication of sheet music, followed by a trickle of recordings leading to the commercial blues boom set off by Mamie Smith's first recordings in 1920, with piano rolls by black ragtime and jazz players like James P. Johnson ("Mama's Blues" twice in 1917), Luckyeth Roberts ("Railroad Blues," "Irresistible Blues," and "Blue Fever," all in 1919), Jelly Roll Morton, Clarence M. Jones, Richard M. Jones, and Jimmy Blythe (and some white ones such as Zez Confrey, Pauline Alpert, and May Aufderheide) interspersed in the teens and early 1920s. Special mention should be made of Pauline Alpert, a multimedia star of concert halls, radio, piano rolls, recordings, films, and later television—she took the music to high-, middle-, and lowbrow stops on the countenance of American society. An attendee of Eastman School in Rochester, New York, Alpert's affinity for a ragtime-jazz-pop-classical blend allowed her to produce some remarkable, if underrecognized performances. Her piano roll "Blue Baby" for Duo-Art (1920) crackles with hot music syncopation. Her recording of "Hallelujah" for Victor (1927) so anticipates Art Tatum's style as it emerged on his recordings in 1932, with stride bass, slow and abrupt tempo changes, modulated chords, elaborate arpeggios, interpolations from other songs in unexpected places, and virtuosic speed and rhythmic rupture, that she must be considered a prime part of the air Tatum breathed on his way to piano immortality. Her composition "Ivory Tips" as performed by Sara Davis Buechner, reminds even more of the remarkable Tatum style, bringing the tips of her ivory fingers to keys both black and white that helped unlock the locked gate of multiracial expression that imbued the American identity.

Although 1912 has frequently been cited as the year the blues first appeared in sheet music, more recent scholarship has turned up earlier instances. Ben Harney, publisher of the first notated ragtime song, published the bluesy "Mr. Johnson Turn Me Loose" in 1896. Conductor Maurice Peress hears elements of blues in Will Marion Cook's "Swing Along," first performed in London in the 1903 production of *In Dahomey*, and later at the 1912 Clef Club Concert, organized by the first crowned "King of Jazz," James Reese "Jim" Europe (112). David Evans identifies Antonio Maggio's "I Got the Blues"

(1908) and Robert Hoffman's "I'm Alabama Bound" (subtitled "The Alabama Blues") (1909) as two other blues compositions preceding the watershed year of 1912 (*Cambridge Companion to Blues* 25). That year, Hart A. Wand's "Dallas Blues," H. Franklin "Baby" Seals's "Baby Seals Blues," Leroy "Lasses" White's "Nigger Blues," and W. C. Handy's influential "Memphis Blues" were all released, followed in 1913 by Handy's "The Jogo Blues" and in 1914 by Handy's "Yellow Dog Blues" and "St. Louis Blues" (see Abbott and Seroff, "They Cert'ly Sound Good to Me," 49–104). Indeed, Abbe Niles reports in his introduction to Handy's *Blues: An Anthology* that such figures as Dave Peyton, the *Chicago Defender*'s musical editor, Paramount employee Lovie Austin, and the white Leighton Brothers all helped contribute to the popularity of blues through transcriptions, publications, or arrangements (22–23). Peter Muir reports in his exhaustive study of the subject that there were "over 450 popular blues works [that] appeared, giving rise to roughly eight hundred known recordings on disc and piano rolls" (1); the proto-blues that immediately preceded the folk-blues are "almost all based on ragtime" (215). These compositions, drawing on the oral tradition and ultimately feeding back into it, made certain kinds of more sophisticated bluesy material available to a literate audience already familiar with coon and ragtime songs through the minstrelsy, medicine show, and New York stage traditions and ready for the next development in African American entertainment ripe for appropriation, music and vocal technique, stage persona, dance patterns, and all.

Undoubtedly, performance instances of the blues in the black community preceded its inroads into mainstream culture. Lynn Abbott and Doug Seroff assert in *Ragged But Right* that "[t]here are reports of blues singing in southern vaudeville theaters as early as 1910" (211), suggesting that the rumblings in the sheet music industry and the vaudeville theaters, both drawing as they did on the folk-blues tradition, were roughly contemporary in their employment of such material. G. W. Warford, for example, was featuring "The Blues and the Dream" with J. C. O'Brien's Famous Georgia Minstrels in 1912 (Abbott and Seroff 212). Clearly this type of blues was being disseminated to the masses of African Americans, who recognized the material as their own dressed up for stage performance, and thus the long, slow trek of blues into broader popular appeal was a slow one, built up from the ground in the journeys of African American entertainers from theater to theater and tent to tent. The earliest reports of blues in the minstrel shows, interestingly enough, came four years later, as evidenced in the references in the *Indianapolis Freeman* to blues performances by Wee Willie Nelson and Jolly E. Davis (Abbott and Seroff 211), at which point the flood gates opened to blues singers in the minstrelsy tent shows. Here were Ma Rainey singing "Morning, Noon and Night," with its reference to "The Weary Blues," in Tolliver's Smart Set Company, Bessie Smith featuring with the Florida Blossom Minstrels, and the aforementioned "Baby Seals Blues" featured in J. C. O'Brien's Famous Georgia Minstrels (Abbott and Seroff 145, 211, 212). Both Ma Rainey and Smith were known as blues specialists, but neither would make it into the recording studio until 1923, some seven years later.

On phonograph records, due to easier access to the recording studios, several important (and a fair number of not-so-important) white singers preceded blacks in recording blues-oriented material. This material, however, was not often of the traditional twelve-bar blues variety that seems to have been the most common pattern among folk-blues performers, and would be solidified as the dominant pattern as the era of commercial blues recordings progressed. Sophie Tucker's 1911 recording of Canadian Bert Williams imitator and songwriter Shelton Brooks's "Some of These Days" is an early blues-influenced recording, while vocalist Morton Harvey's recording of Handy's "Memphis Blues" in 1914 is generally considered to be the first blues song recorded by a vocalist (the song was recorded instrumentally by the Victor Military Band in the same year). The guitar duet instrumental "Southern Blues," recorded c. 1915, included one twelve-bar blues stanza among other stanzaic structures in the song. Recorded in 1916, Gus Haendschen's rollicking instrumental "Country Club Medley" (a twelve-bar blues in its first few stanzas), Nora Bayes's "Homesick Blues," and Marion Harris's "I Ain't Got Nobody Much" and "Paradise Blues" (both co-written by black entrepreneur Spencer Williams) were all in the blues tradition, as was the 1917 recording of the Memphis Pickaninny Band's raucous, full orchestra "Some Jazz Blues." George Gershwin stated in 1926 that one could get "excellent training in jazz rhythms" listening to Marion Harris's records (Wyatt 97)—interesting because Gershwin was known to have heard black performers and vocalists by that time, and he even acknowledged in a note to Handy on a copy of *Rhapsody in Blue* on August 30, 1926, that Handy's "early 'blue' songs are the forefathers to this work" (http://www.pinterest.com/pin/440508407273136483/). Special mention should be made of another song, not a blues, recorded in London in 1904. African American Pete Hampton, a singer and harmonica player, performed "Dat Mouth Organ Coon" featuring singing with a band, followed by virtuosic harmonica playing, including snatches of train and fox chase imitations—he even whistles and pays the harmonica simultaneously—that intimate things to come from later players such as Sonny Terry and DeFord Bailey (Lotz, *Black People* 89–124).

Abbe Niles reports that that same year Blossom Seeley sang "Hesitating Blues" (Niles 23), Ciro's Club Coon Orchestra, an African American band, recorded a spirited version of "St. Louis Blues" in London in 1917, while subsequently white shimmy dancer Gilda Gray performed that song on Broadway in 1918. Blackface performer and vocalist for the Original Dixieland Jazz Band Al Bernard recorded his first "blues" for OKeh in 1919, and was later credited by W. C. Handy as someone who helped Handy's "St. Louis Blues" become popular, as well as telegraphing the Western Swing genre with his easy blues touch. Sometimes (erroneously) referred to as the first recorded jazz song, though it did help to create a jazz sensation, "Livery Stable Blues" is a blues-inflected, and formal blues, recording by the white Original Dixieland Jazz Band from 1917, the same year the pioneering black jazz band leader Wilbur Sweatman recorded "Joe Turner Blues," with "Indianola" and "Dallas Blues" following a year later. The great African American artist Bert Williams recorded "I'm Sorry You Ain't Got It You Could Have It If I Had It Blues" in 1919, on the eve of Mamie Smith's groundbreaking, sophisticated and "stage-oriented" blues performances, which opened the floodgates for black vaudeville blues singers like Lucille Hegamin, Lillyn Brown, Lavinia Turner, Bessie Smith, and Ma Rainey (as well as for concert artist Mme. Anita Patti Brown, who recorded in September 1920). The blues, and this particular kind of blues singer, the saucy and independent female blues singer so promoted because of Mamie Smith's early success, were heading further toward the mainstream American consciousness.

Once the recordings ignited the vaudeville and cabaret blues craze, the film industry slowly became involved, producing movies with African American blues performers such as *Jazz Hounds* (1922) with Edna Morton; "St. Louis Blues" in *Darktown Follies* (1930) and Bessie Smith's version in *St. Louis Blues*; Mamie Smith's "The Jail House Blues" and "You Can't Do It" in *The Jail House Blues*; Maude Mills singing "I'm Gonna Lose Myself Down in Louisville" and Sara Martin singing "Cabaration Blues" in *Darktown Scandals Review*; Theresa Harris and the Dixieland Jug Blowers performing "Daddy Won't You Please Come Home" in *Thunderbolt*; Laura Smith in *Lazy Lize*; and some strong jazz performing by Nina Mae McKinney and Curtis Mosby in King Vidor's *Hallelujah* and Buck and Bubbles in *High Toned*—all from 1929. If you look closely at the Cotton Club–like cabaret scene in Dudley Murphy's film of Eugene O'Neill's *The Emperor Jones* (1933) featuring Paul Robeson, you'll see blues singer Alberta Hunter among the three women singing the blues. Although the peak years—1923–1926—of the vaudeville blues singer were in the past (Dixon and Godrich, *Recording* 20–21), the recordings of blues singers, including male singers around the country, would hit their pre-war peak in 1927–1930. In 1927, record companies issued five hundred blues and gospel records, an increase of 50 percent over 1926, with similar increases in the following years (Dixon and Godrich, *Recording* 41). The blues was clearly positioned to have its own impact and influence other genres as well.

One question to ask about this emergence is, why the blues (and ragtime and jazz), and why then? Clearly the subject matter and style of the music struck a soulful chord with various groups at the time. Motives, of course, were mixed, and not uniform among groups, but there were general trends and explanations. For the white working poor, the similar economic conditions and social prejudices would help them identify with lyrics and rhythms that dealt with these issues. The proximity of the residences of poor whites and blacks in the South fostered shared common stock musical repertoires. Close though frequently contentious relations in the North after the migrations following Reconstruction and around the time of World War I all contributed to a recognition and popularity of the music and lyrics among poor whites, prejudices and antipathies notwithstanding. There were many white versions of the blues among the old time and country performers of the 1920s that reflect this interest. For example, among the stellar country music performers who recorded either titular or formal blues at their first or second sessions (some in imitation of Jimmie Rodgers and his success with blue yodels) were Henry Whitter (1923), Emmett Miller (1924), Uncle Dave Macon (1924), Gid Tanner (1924), Charlie Poole (1925), Frank Hutchison (1926), the McGee Brothers (1926), the Allen Brothers (1927), Gene Autry (1929), Bob Wills (1929), Aunt Molly Jackson (1931), the Delmore Brothers (1931), the Prairie Ramblers (1933), Hank Snow (1936), Bill Monroe (1940)—even Roy Rogers, who offered the titular blues "When the Black Sheep Gets the Blues" (1937).

For the white middle class, with their own race and class prejudices, the novelty of the syncopation and rhythm appealed to their sense of newness and search for a distinct soundtrack for their jittery, rebellious generation. For the white intelligentsia and upper class, the music represented an instrument to fracture with the last nineteenth century generation. It suggested new sonic and formal possibilities in a newly cacophonous, cataclysmic world of violence, hypocrisy, and prattling verbal rationalization, as well as an escape from the banal, wearisome tedium of their lives. While there are obviously many exceptions to these appreciations of black music, and some just saw the music as an opportunity to go wild, crazy, silly, vulgar, or ludicrous, the way they perceived blacks to be, the music did have its various appeals.

Meanwhile, lower-class black audiences welcomed the chance to capitalize on and demonstrate the viability of their music, while upper-class African Americans like W. E. B. Du Bois trumpeted the influence of the music in the *beaux arts*, frequently privately classing off from the vulgar and embarrassing "black and blue sheep" of the family (Tracy 19–21). Du Bois, however, was not a highly popular figure in the black community in the 1920s (Lewis 21), including being personal disliked by Louis Armstrong (Harker 166), who felt the sting of class discrimination from the haughty among African Americans all his life, wives included (Harker 169). Samuel Coleridge-Taylor, a respected black composer from England, complained that ragtime "was the worst kind of rot" (Peress 54). He was offered the honor of becoming a member of the American Negro Academy of black intellectuals, who had formed to discuss, and frequently champion, their notion of worthy, "Talented Tenth," black art. Coleridge-Taylor criticized coon songs as being without melody or African American character, but the songs were defended by critic Sylvester Russell, who pointed out that Coleridge-Taylor had not heard "this low life phase of music which has electrified the world" in its best form: "[it] is better performed by degraded southern Negroes than by the best stage artists in existence" (Abbott and Seroff 14). Bar, tavern, and night club owners, as well as Tin Pan Alley, Broadway, and recording and film executives, would be anxious to exploit the latest fad. Black pianists Blind Tom and Blind Boone, the former favorite of Twain, are cases in point.

In fact, Carl Van Vechten thought that he had heard the first real American music in an Irving Berlin song. George Gershwin—who some commentators feel "personified the scandalous mixing of high and low" (Savran, "The Search" 463) agreed, considering Berlin the greatest of American songwriters—both men with reference to a tune of Berlin's entitled "Alexander's Ragtime Band" (Wyatt and Johnson 77, 116), with its minstrel language referencing "the bestest band what am." Bessie Smith recorded the song in 1927, though it may not have been her choice (Angela Davis 88), since it is obviously more cognizant of the white mainstream market than her usual repertoire. Gershwin even penned a composition entitled "The Real American Folk Song is a Rag" (1918), indicating how attuned he was to the trend of drawing on folk materials to provide a deeper feeling for commercial songs. Young people delighted in the opportunity to shock the old fogies, whether by eating goldfish or listening to negro music, it didn't matter. Ida Cox even recorded a song entitled "Fogyism" (1928) to distance her listeners from another generation's superstitions. It was fresh—meaning both new and extroverted—and vibrant. As the progressive Niagara Movement, NAACP, and Pan-African Conferences arose among people of color and their white allies, and the heyday of the Ku Klux Klan and *Birth of a Nation* flamed up, not just in the white alleys, but among all social levels just next door, the music had common, though conflicting, interests. Chicagoan Emmett Scott responded to Griffith film with his own three years later entitled *Birth of a Race* (1918), but the Griffith epic was seen by far more people.

The blues tradition made its mark on what was called old-timey music, now the precursor to country music. The repertoire of the tradition performed by white musicians included Anglo-American ballads, hymns and spirituals, pop songs, minstrel songs, ragtime, banjo and fiddle tunes, and the ballads and blues of the African American tradition as well. Certain tunes seem to have been shared as what were termed common stock tunes performed by both black and white musicians, but white musicians also made it clear that, like their black male counterparts, they had listened to the early female vaudeville blues singers. Dock Boggs described listening to vaudeville blues singer Sara Martin's "Down South Blues" (she didn't record the tune, so he may have heard it live or was mistaken in his identification) as a forerunner to his own version of the song (Russell 51). Additionally, black and white performers found themselves in situations where the exchanging of musical ideas was inevitable, resulting in the performance and recording of blues by influential white old-timey musicians such as Henry Whitter ("Lonesome Road Blues" 1923), Fiddlin' John Carson ("John Henry Blues" 1924), Samantha Bumgarner ("The Worried Blues" and "Georgia Blues" 1924), Charlie Poole ("If the River Was Whiskey" 1930), Frank Hutchison ("Cannon Ball Blues" 1929), Clarence Green ("Johnson City Blues" 1928), Dick Justice ("Brown Skin Blues" 1929), Larry Hensely ("Match Box Blues" 1934), Cliff Carlisle ("Ash Can Blues" 1932), and Darby and Tarleton ("Sweet Sarah Blues" 1929) (hear the CD anthologies *Mountain Blues, 1927–1938* and *White Country Blues, 1926–1938* for nearly four dozen examples from the 1920s). Jimmie Rodgers, the king of the white blues singers of the 1920s, listened to black musicians while he was hoboing, working, and traveling on the railroad lines in Mississippi and elsewhere, developing his personal style of playing blues—jaunty in the Memphis medicine show style, with a twinkle and a bounce and a distinctive yodel at the end of his stanzas.

The yodel may have stemmed from the vaudeville craze for Swiss music at the turn of the century, or from a modification of the West African falsetto leap or whoop carried over into the African American tradition, or indeed from Emmett Miller. Miller was a blackface minstrel performer who fused minstrel songs, ragtime, jazz, blues, and pop, some songs previously sung by the African American influenced white singers Sophie Tucker and Marion Harris, with a twist of yodel, into a highly distinctive and influential mix. From his first recording session in 1924, his style was one of the many tributaries that fed into the white blues and jazz. This was in part through the presence of white jazz performers such as Eddie Lang—who later recorded with black performers Lonnie Johnson, Texas Alexander, Bessie Smith, Gladys Bentley, about whom Langston Hughes wrote, and others—on his recordings. It also branched off into Jimmie Rodgers and Hank Williams streams down the line to help produce—with a deluge of influence from black music—contemporary American pop and roots music as we know it. Miller, it should be pointed out, was sometimes billed as performing with his "Georgia Crackers," another offensive label applied by someone in the record industry, this time to whites. Black performers Tampa Red and Frankie Jaxon were even billed as "The Black Hill Billies" on one corny-humored recording, "Kunjine Baby."

Wherever it came from, as Willie McTell told Alan Lomax, it was the idea of the white folks ("Monologue"), and it was widely popular and influential—years later, Howlin' Wolf would claim to have gotten his own howl from the Jimmie Rodgers style (*Screamin' and Hollerin' the Blues* CD set). Other black performers recorded Rodgers songs or songs in Rodgers's style, King Oliver, the Memphis Sheiks, the Mississippi Sheiks, and John Jackson among them. Rodgers also recorded accompanied by black blues and jazz performers as well—Lil Hardin Armstrong and Louis Armstrong, Clifford Gibson, and the Louisville Jug Band all appeared on different Rodgers recordings. Rodgers is now known as the "Father of Country Music" for his mix of blues and sentimental songs and his easygoing persona. The fact that of his 110 recorded songs, 108 have been covered by other performers—and they are still being covered today—is an unmatched ratio of recordings to cover songs in the history of country music (Ginell et al.). It is difficult to overestimate how important his own contribution was to disseminating this African American musical genre among whites whose country (Gene Autry), Western Swing (Bob Wills), bluegrass (Bill Monroe), country boogie (Merle Travis), and rock and roll (Jerry Lee Lewis) would be so influenced by the blues (*The Influence of Jimmie Rodgers* CD). He clearly embodied what Barry Mazor called "the humor and joy in the blues mingled with the loss, grief, and occasional anger, the 'we' of implied community balancing the 'I' of signifying, boasting, and self-expression" (46). He even had his recordings released in South Africa, and versions of songs by "Chemirocha" (native pronunciation of Jimmie Rodgers) were recorded on field trips among the Kipsigis of Kenya in 1950 (Mazor 102)!

Of course, notice of African American music in the world of classical music certainly made a difference to black intellectuals of the time who were searching for ways to champion African American social advancement. As tonality teetered on the precipice of relevancy in avant-garde classical music, composers seeking to express a national identity began to cast around for new perspectives on art music. Therefore, when Antonin Dvořák, in the United States to head the National Conservatory of Music, wrote in *Harper's New Monthly Magazine* in 1895 that "the future of music of this country must be founded upon what are called negro melodies" (Tibbetts 355), a wave of pride and excitement ran through the African American middle class. Under the influence of African American composer, arranger, and baritone Henry "Harry" T. Burleigh, who exposed Dvořák to "negro melodies," Dvořák had already produced his "New World Symphony" (1893) drawing on African American spirituals and Native American music.

After Dvořák's pronouncement, other composers followed in his wake, producing classical works rooted in black music. This is exemplified in relation to ragtime in works such as Erik Satie's "Prelude" in "Jack-in-the-Box" (1899), with its music hall anticipation of "Old Man River," French composer Claude Debussy's *Golliwog's Cakewalk* (1908), Scott Joplin's *Treemonisha* (1911), American Henry Gilbert's *Comedy Overture on Negro Themes* (1911)—and a variety of other works by Gilbert—Russian Igor Stravinsky's *Ragtime for Eleven Instruments* (1918) and *Piano-Rag-Music* (1919), and German composer Paul Hindemith's *Ragtime* (1921). There was even a recording "Ragtime Improvisation on Rubenstein's Melody in F" recorded by Melville Gideon in 1912 (Rust I: 615), and Pete Wendling's piano solo "Page Paderewski" with reference to Polish pianist-composer Ignacy Paderewski in 1923 (Rust II: 1813). This, of course, was nothing new: the text of Thomas Dartmouth Rice's "Jim Crow" (c. 1830) makes reference to a "roarer on the fiddle" who plays "Like Massa Paganini" (Alexander 128) near the dawn of blackface minstrelsy in America.

A listen to Stravinsky's *Piano-Rag-Music* demonstrates how a great composer avoids imitation while clearly drawing on a musical tradition. What we hear in this piece is similar to the way that blues, for example, draws on African music. It is clear that the modes of performance are derived from the source music—rhythm, syncopation, call-and-response, percussive attack, and so on. However, the musics do not replicate melodically, so that the musics do not so much sound the same as "feel" the same. The same is true of Erwin Schulhoff's haunting, decidedly non-Black Bottom number "Blues (pour Paul Whiteman)" from 1926 which was, as Jack Sullivan points out, "spookier than anything Whiteman could have conceived" (215).

Jazz examples include Frenchman Darius Milhaud's *La Création du Monde* (1923), "bad boy" George Antheil's *A Jazz Symphony* (1925), Czech composer Bohuslav Martinu's *Jazz-Suite for Small Orchestra* (1928), with its fine polyrhythmic prelude and pumping, driving force, and Austrian Ernst Krenek's *Jonny Spielt Auf* (1927)—the latter of which was a huge hit before it was banned by the Nazis, labeled "*entartete musik*" or "degenerate music" for its employment of African American sources. In fact, the Nazis denounced the piece as "Jewish nigger filth" in 1927 for its combination of "Black, Jews, [and] modernism" (Sullivan 216). This degenerate music concept was represented by a logo that featured a gussied up half-black man, half-ape playing the saxophone and sporting a Star of David pin on his lapel. The white, Catholic Krenek was even labeled a "nigger" and a "Jew" by the Nazis (Horowitz 110). Clearly, not everyone was enamored of the music or its sources, the Nazis aligning what they thought of as the primitive and savage negroes with Jewish intellectuals who they believed were hell-bent on dominating a mongrelized world. Later, when the Nazis used white German versions of African American jazz to deliver messages of racial superiority, it was one of the supremely devilish contortionist acts of the interwar/World War II period (*Swing Tanzen Verboten: Swing Music & Nazi Propaganda Swing During World War II*).

Such blues-influenced compositions as Gershwin's *Blue Monday* opera (in *George White's Scandals of 1922*), *Rhapsody in Blue* (1924) and *Three Preludes for Piano* (1926); Maurice Ravel's 1927 *Violin Sonata in C: Blues* (with its lugubrious violin sliding, "crushed" notes, and allusions to I-IV-V structures); William Grant Still's *The Afro-American Symphony* (1930) and "Lenox Avenue" (1937)—Still had earlier been an arranger for W. C. Handy and had performed with Eubie Blake—and George Frederick McKay's "Machine Age Blues" (1935) all demonstrated this direct connection as well. What made the George White revue a "scandal"? Why, sexual innuendo, bawdy or "vulgar" behavior, shocking familiarity with what was considered at the time these elements of African American culture, and—oh!—those hip-shaking dirty black dances. It was part of the times of avant-garde artists such as Sergei Diaghilev, who ushered in the "'post-armistice' school of composition in Paris, which set more store by an audacious frivolity and a desire to shock than by any deeper and more permanent qualities" ("Ballet" 384). But have not these elements become "deeper and more permanent" as a result of their introduction at this time?

Gershwin's *Rhapsody in Blue* was commissioned by the historically underrated Paul Whiteman, and orchestrated for Whiteman's orchestra by pianist-arranger Ferde Grofé. Whiteman himself had benefitted from the pioneering efforts of a bandleader from San Francisco named Art Hickman, who performed "rhythmic presentation of pop songs" with an instrumentation in the late teens that anticipated that of "hot" jazz bands, with the benefit of arrangements by Grofé (Sudhalter 88). The Whiteman concert was presented under the banner of "An Experiment in Modern Music" at New York's Aeolian (Aeolus again!) Hall in 1924. The concert also featured one of Gershwin's major ragtime influences and friends, white ragtime pianist Zez Confrey (Hyland 73), just three years past the publication of his wildly popular tune "Kitten on the Keys." With the composer at the piano, *Rhapsody in Blue* created a sensation for Gershwin, Whiteman, and the so-called jazz symphony, and became highly influential in the era, as did Confrey, who was later named as an influence by jazz pianists Earl Hines and Errol Garner. Handy even included an excerpt from Gershwin's *Rhapsody* and his masterful follow-up, *Concerto in F* (1925) in *Blues: An Anthology* (1926) as examples of contemporary blues usage. Though the compositions were deserving, their mention was an indicator of Handy's quest for "respectable" recognition for the blues, even as what Wallace Thurman described in his 1926 review of *Blues: An Anthology* as "the present epidemic of Negrophilia"garnered for the blues much popular support as well (185).

Interestingly, at the 1924 concert, a number of "judges" were gathered together to answer the question "What is American Music? " among them Russian pianist and composer Sergei Rachmaninov, Lithuanian violinist Jascha Heifetz, Russian violinist-composer-conductor Efrem Zimbalist, and famed Romanian soprano Alma Gluck, to whom Zimbalist was married (Wyatt 44). Ma Rainey's music would not be their answer, and *Adagietto con moto* would replace "slow drag" as tempo designation. White singer Marion Harris sang in "My Syncopated Melody Man" (1916), "Big music masters, they hate him, / They just can't appreciate him, / My syncopated melody man," but clearly all the music masters did not dislike African American music.

Ravel's composition grew out of a post–World War I jazz craze in Paris produced by the presence of African American troops and musicians (as well as Langston Hughes) in the city. Of course, there were nineteenth-century precedents: all of these came some fifty years after the nascent experiments of Louis Moreau Gottschalk with African American music of New Orleans and the Caribbean in the classical realm with "Bamboula," "Pasquinade," and "Le bananier," and the Afro-Classical blends of New Orleans Creoles Edmond and Eugène Dédé and Sydney and Lucièn Lambert. As David Baker points out, Brahms had his flirtations with ragtime (2), and Darius Milhaud (later a teacher of William Bolcom, Dave Brubeck, and Bert Bacharach) labeled jazz "as completely moving as any recognized musical masterpiece" (2). He made the first movement of his soundtrack for the creation of the world frenetic, like a windup jazz car running down and out, a bold and fitting precursor to Gershwinian rhapsodies to come. In fact, Milhaud had visited Harlem in 1922 and found jazz a "revelation," recalling that when he "went back to France, [he] never wearied of playing over and over, on a little portable phonograph shaped like a camera, Black Swan records [he] had purchased in a little shop in Harlem" (Alexander 358)—the Black Swan record label named for Elizabeth Taylor Greenfield. Black businessman and civil rights advocate Harry Pace's record label included Ethel Waters, Trixie Smith, and Josie Miles among its blues singers at the time. The label's slogan, "The Only Genuine Colored Record. Others Are Only Passing for Colored" (Robert A. Hill 416), was a sly twist on the racial passing phenomenon, as well as a discerning commentary on cultural passing in the form of begging, borrowing, or stealing elements of African American culture in some way foreign or resistant to the vagaries of copyright law protection. The slogan was also arguably false.

Although the music does not need to be legitimized by any connection to classical music, it was seen as a legitimization in some people's eyes, and certainly encouraged artists in various genres to take the material more seriously. When Ernest Ansermet, conductor of the Orchestre de la Suisse Romande and Stravinsky's Ballets Russes, and a conductor who premiered works by Stravinsky, Satie, de Falla, and Prokofiev, praised Will Marion Cook's orchestra, especially the playing of African American soprano saxophonist Sidney Bechet, who could not read music and was therefore even further from the Eurocentric classical music ideal, a new crowd began to listen and respect the music. Further, when Ansermet added, "I am inclined to think that the strongest manifestation of the racial genius lies in the blues," for many Eurocentric listeners stock in the blues went up as well (Ansermet 11). In 1926, Langston Hughes would look for "the genius of the great individual American composer who is to come" to utilize African American folk music to its fullest ("The Negro Artist" 308). Certainly he must have been motivated by this, in part, as well.

There is great value in listening to folk-blues, pop-blues, and ragtime-, blues-, and jazz-influenced recordings (and even marches) of the era side by side in order to see the continuities among the musics. There is a continuum of sounds among the musics that is striking, even as the instruments, structures, and audiences change. For example, one can hear the jaunty brass band bass on certain pop-oriented songs and early jazz band recordings such as the New Orleans Rhythm Kings' "The Weary Blues" (1923), and then hear the sound reproduced on the tympani in Milhaud's *La Création du Monde* (1923), now making the similarity to African drumbeats more obvious. The drum cadences of Sousa marches turn up on Wilbur Sweatman's "Bluin' the Blues" (1924). The clacking percussion on Ciro's Club Coon Orchestra's string band recording of "St. Louis Blues" (1917) turns up on the New Orleans Rhythm Kings' version of "Weary Blues" (1923). Bert Williams's "All In, Out, and Down" (1906), Sophie Tucker's "Some of These Days" (1911), and Marion Harris's "A Good Man is Hard to Find" (1919) all ply an interesting mix of connected talking (direct natural advice) and singing (artistic embellishment) in their presentations, and feature dramatic ritardando in their performance. And, interestingly, the neighing and whinnying of the Original Dixieland Jazz Band's

"Livery Stable Blues" (1917) relates to the laughing clarinet on Wilbur Sweatman recordings, the yodeling hilarity of Emmett Miller's "I Ain't Got Nobody" (1928), and even the clarinet glissandi of the beginning of George Gershwin's *Rhapsody in Blue* (1924), especially the version recorded by Gershwin with Paul Whiteman in 1927. Of course, the abandon, the syncopation, the foregrounded contrapuntal elements all create a continuity of sound as well, even if there are nuances of difference, too.

In the realm of dance, African American dance styles had influenced American dancing for decades. Sometimes parodies of white folks' dance demeanors, as in the cakewalks that Bert Williams helped popularize on the stage—he recorded an unreleased "The Cake Walk" in London in 1903 (Dixon, Godrich, and Rye 1031), at other times they were distinctive and energetic workouts that captured the notice of such observers as Charles Dickens and Lafcadio Hearn. Still, a book such as *Dance Music the Whole World Plays*, published in 1917, presented within 256 pages no songs related to the emerging "hot" music of the time, though songs collected in the nineteenth-century African American folk tradition, such as "Arkansas Traveler," "Fisher's Hornpipe," "Devil's Dream," and "Old Zip Coon" were included in the final pages of the book (Wier 252–56). Perhaps the "hot" music was a bit too scandalous for inclusion at this time. Still, the Charleston and the Black Bottom were in the air, and the white dance couple Vernon and Irene Castle, who insisted on dancing to the music of black bandleader James Reese Europe (Watson, *Harlem* 107), had already popularized the tango and taken such ragtime dances as the Turkey Trot and the Grizzly Bear to Paris, helping to bring new vigor to contemporary ballroom dancing. There was even a ragtime composition, "The Castles in Europe (The Innovation Trot)" published in 1914 (Sutton 39), that punned cleverly on the word "castle." The title referred to the structures themselves (castles), the impact of ragtime (the ancient and sturdy castles and cultures of Europe are affected by ragtime), Vernon and Irene (Castle), appearing in Europe, and the association of Vernon and Irene with James Reese Europe as well (Vernon and Irene Castle musically cross-pollinating with Jim Europe). The association of ragtime with the cut-a-rug cutting-edge movements that they all helped take to Europe are duly noted in the subtitle.

The "hot" music of the era emerged from earlier African American musical genres such as minstrelsy and ragtime, and began to incorporate elements of jazz improvisation and blues inflection, as well as brass band and string band and other pop song elements. As Alfred Appel points out, the twelve-bar blues is the most common harmonic progression in jazz, so differentiating among genres can be extremely difficult (48). "St. Louis Blues" was advertised on sheet music as "[t]he Most Widely Known Ragtime Composition" (Sutton 270). A ragtime composition entitled "Some Jazz Blues" (1917) indicated the undifferentiated fusion of terms, and "An Operatic Rag" (1910), "Operatic Rag" (1914), and "Ragged William (A Darkey's Idea of the William Tell Overture in Rag-Time)" (1899) represent interesting (and racist) offshoots. It was sometimes mixed in an interesting blend by orchestras like James Reese Europe's, whose "Castle House Rag" (note the punning title again—there were many ragtime compositions with cunning and punning wordplay in their titles) included a strong military cadence in the drum section driving the rhythm with minstrel spirit and ragtime syncopation. It created its own room to spread in American culture, and should be seen as part of what David Chinitz calls a "continuum" of music that drew from a variety of sources and fed into a variety of genres in world cultures, in conception and subject matter (10–11). For example, a listen to classical composer Charles Ives's *Study No. 9: The Anti-Abolitionist Riots of the 1830s and 1840s* and *Rough and Ready, or The Jumping Frog* reveals his use of ragtime-influenced chords among the chord clusters he explores in those compositions, though frequently in passing and as stepping-stones to exploring chords outside the nature of the ragtime idiom. Further, *Study No. 20* makes use of ragtime feel, chords, and a pastiche method of quoting a variety of sources in an almost improvisational-feeling style, transformed to fit the style and structure of the composer's work—and includes a reference to "Alexander's Ragtime Band."

There is, of course, a difference: as Russian composer Nikolai Kapustin observes of his own jazz composition experiments, "I'm not interested in improvisation—and what is a jazz musician without improvisation? All my improvisation is written, of course, and they became much better; it improved them" (96). And when African American artist Romare Bearden owned how he "played with the possibilities within the framework of his conception" (O'Meally 43) in his use of jazz in his work, he was expressing a similar aesthetic both to the jazz musicians and to classical composers like Ives and Kapustin, who both composed their music to "feel" improvisatory, to have the illusion of improvisation, even if that improvisation was frozen in the improvisational time of conception. Like classic blues and jazz solos or styles by Louis Armstrong, Clarence "Pinetop" Smith, Jimmie Rodgers, and Artie Shaw that have come down to us whole, admired and reproduced by generations of musicians, or the charts of Fletcher Henderson, Duke Ellington, or Ferde Grofé, there is room for copying or arranging elements that seem to be the perfect moment, even if jazz and blues always go back to the improvisational moment.

Hot music was helped along by white and black entrepreneurs anxious to employ, promote, and exploit the genre; composers seeking the newest "thing" in pop and classical music to contribute to the progress of their fields; and white folk musicians whose casual contact with black folk musicians helped produce an exchange of musical cultures that disseminated the blues, in various forms and feels, throughout white cultures as well. The wheels of many social breakthroughs for African Americans in this country have been greased by the music and its ability to draw people together. After all, it helped draw folks to Harlem and fuel a Renaissance there (and other major cities such as Chicago, Philadelphia, and in the District of Columbia). It helped capture the energy, passion, and aesthetic of the era, all the while retaining for many whites an air of the primitive, dirty, inferior, and inartistic while in black hands—a central paradox of the era we have come to know as the "Jazz Age." Irving Mills, white jazz music publisher, manager of Duke Ellington and many other jazz performers, and occasional vocalist and emcee at the Cotton Club, was one of the early pioneers of recording black and white musicians together. In 1928 he released a recording of W. C. Handy's sheet music composition "St. Louis Blues" combining the all-black Duke Ellington Orchestra and a white orchestra directed by violinist-composer Matty Malneck, who also recorded with Beiderbecke and Trumbauer, of the Paul Whiteman Band. Small world.

III

The notion of "Jazz Age aesthetics" is a bit tricky to describe. Inevitably, any single definition would be inadequate to the broad spectrum of meanings that jazz and blues had for the era of Prohibition, flappers, and lives of opulent abandon that some felt needed to be "wiped out as other bad and dangerous epidemics have been exterminated" (Radano *Lying* 236). And yet it is necessary to get a sense of what jazz meant to an age that had faced rapid urbanization and industrialization, faced off in race riots across cities nationally, faced down the Kaiser, and come through the burned-out ends of the modern landscape faceless and faithless with regard to the inherited middle-class values of the small town past. Hemingway's Harold Krebs of "Soldier's Home" (1925) represents this hopelessness, uselessness, and acedia, impotent in the face of meaningless social rituals. Ideas regarding race and gender in the Jim Crow era influenced the ways that African Americans and their cultural productions were perceived. Inherited notions of inherited "racial" characteristics resulted in essentialist assumptions that became part of the spirit of the age, the national consciousness and culture, as well. However, as Ronald Radano has pointed out, "[t]he legacies of oppression and segregation that undoubtedly contributed to black music's distinctiveness are not enough to sustain arguments of an unyielding black essence any more than parallel claims of totalities of European heritage or frontier independence defend white ones" (*Lying* 5). That doesn't stop people from trying to make those arguments.

The world in which various writers began their literary flirtations with hot music—ragtime, jazz, and blues—in the 1910s was fraught with change and upheaval. This upheaval was reflected in the constructions of race that prevailed at the time. Vestiges of minstrelsy were still prominent in the recordings of the time and on the stage, though, as has already been pointed out, such images were being challenged by a number of forward-thinking African American artists. A decade after the publication of W. E. B. Du Bois's *The Souls of Black Folk* (1903), as the First Pan-African Congress was beginning to take up Pan-African issues of the diaspora, the interracial Niagara Movement (1905) was moving further toward racial cooperation in opposing the conciliatory policies of Booker T. Washington as it grew into the NAACP (1909). However, the organization was seen by some as too conciliatory itself, with whites holding many of the prominent posts in the organization and directing an agenda that was confrontational but still perhaps a bit timid. This is especially true in light of the radicalism espoused by A. Philip Randolph and Chandler Owen in journals like the *Messenger*, as well as in another prominent social movement of the time. Marcus Garvey's arrival in New York in 1916 first put in place the major figure whose Universal Negro Improvement Association provided a revolutionary alternative popular with the African American masses and exposed a rift between middle- and lower-class ideas regarding the appropriate ways to confront racial inequities. There were at least ten recordings of "West Indies Blues" and "Black Star Line" that referenced the popular leader of lower-class blacks (Dixon, Godrich, and Rye 1089, 1301), and even two sides recorded by Garvey himself..

The black middle-class's notion of putting one's best foot forward—which frequently meant adopting certain Eurocentric social, political, economic, and cultural ideas in order to placate nervous and uncomfortable but supposedly "sympathetic" whites—trod uneasily on the people Langston Hughes called "the low-down folks" in 1926 in "The Negro Artist and the Racial Mountain" (306). Those lower-class African Americans, Hughes felt, placed an unselfconscious premium on individuality and self-expression, and were thus less enslaved to ideas of African diasporic inferiority and more likely to point the way toward independence and psychic health. This bifurcation of African American image and the strategies to approach and ameliorate the problems associated with it brought many arguments about how "the Negro" "ought" to act—as if there were one Negro and one standard of behavior. These arguments found expression in a variety of African American newspapers that spoke to and for African American audiences about contemporary issues—from the NAACP's *The Crisis* to the National Urban League's *Opportunity* (1910) to the more radical *Messenger* and the powerful *Chicago Defender*.

Of course, these arguments were problematized by continuing institutional racism reflected in the proliferation of Jim Crow laws; the chartering of the Ku Klux Klan in Fulton County, Georgia, court in 1915 and its weed-like proliferation in the American lawn; and the reporting on fifty-six African Americans being lynched that same year. There were responses to these affronts to the African American community, from the efforts of the NAACP, the National Urban League, and club women's organizations, in addition to the exposés of people like the pioneering Ida B. Wells in *Southern Horrors: Lynch Law in All Its Phases* (1892) and *The Red Record* (1892–1894) and Walter White in *Rope and Faggot* (1929). Carter G. Woodson's establishment of the Association for the Study of Negro Life and History and the *Journal of Negro History*, also in 1915, sought to establish scholarly attention on African Americans and correct egregious and subtle historical inaccuracies, and survives to this day as an important African American historical institution.

On the world stage, the outbreak of World War I in 1914 exposed human beings to carnage on an unprecedented scale and mounted a serious challenge to notions of Western cultural superiority when that "superiority" was placed in the service of mass destruction. When the United States entered the war—with the support of a Du Bois who urged African Americans to participate in the war effort even in the face of troop segregation ("Close Ranks") and the opposition of Randolph—a generation of African American males responded with the hope that making the world safe for democracy might make it safer at home as well. Those hopes were lynched, along with hundreds of black bodies, in the carnage of the "Red Summer" of 1919, which provoked political and artistic responses that contributed to the outbreak of the New Negro Renaissance. However, when Ambrose Bierce wrote that the definition of a riot was "[a] popular entertainment given to the military by innocent bystanders" (115), he was not far from describing that summer's events. Du Bois responded himself with vigor:

> We *return.*
> We *return from fighting.*
> We *return fighting.*
>
> Make way for Democracy! We saved it in France, and by the Great Jehovah, we will save it in the United States of America, or know the reason why ("Returning Soldiers").

Interestingly, Caspey, an African American character in William Faulkner's *Sartoris* (1929) expresses a similar sentiment in vernacular language, claiming "War unloosed de black man's mouf": "'I don't take nothin' fum no white folks no mo', he was saying. 'War done changed all dat. If us cullud folks is good enough ter save France fum de Germans, den us is good enough ter have de same rights as Germans is. French folks think so, anyhow, and ef America don't, dey's ways of learnin' 'um. Yes, suh, it wuz de cullud soldier saved France and America bofe'" (65). Of course, Faulkner has taken care to introduce Caspey as "a total loss, sociologically speaking," and a soldier whose only wounds stemmed from "a razor-hedged crap game" (64). Still, it was a sentiment recognized by both black and white writers, to whatever use it was put.

New Negroes had, of course, been around for some time, as had the emerging literature of the movement on stage and in print. The *AME Church Review* had been calling for a New Negro Renaissance as early as 1904. That literary explosion was fueled by the burgeoning literary modernism that responded to rapid industrialization, increasing urbanization as a result of mass migration of many Americans, African Americans among them, dizzying scientific advances that redefined the way human beings functioned and thought of themselves, and the desire to produce a new literature that replaced the worn out modes of the 1890s and reflected the contemporary restlessness, spiritual challenges, and disillusionment as the country transitioned into a new age. The Armory Show in New York in 1913, with its exposure of cubism and postimpressionism; Stravinsky's revolutionary *The Rite of Spring* that same year; "African Savage Art," America's first major exhibition of "primitive" art in 1914; and Duchamp's first Dadaist works in 1915 (the same year D. W. Griffith released the racist *Birth of a Nation*) all reflect the radical artistic experimentation—though not necessarily radical or progressive social beliefs and actions—that informed the arts of the time. Middle-class innocents on this side of the Atlantic got their bellyful of bayonets and bombs that blasted their beliefs and aspirations with regard to the underside of Western and American machinations. Oswald Spengler predicted the twilight of Western civilization in his well-known and influential *Decline of the West*, the first volume of which was finished in 1914 but not published until 1918.

The symbolism of African American music, especially those musics that were developing into and being called blues and jazz at the time, is rooted in contemporary class, race, and gender issues in this world of dizzying change, including popular contemporary stereotypes about the nature of African Americans. At a time when middle-class values seemed increasingly vapid and vacuous in relation to the habits and rituals of their lives, and repression of desires as explored by Freud especially in the period 1895–1919 seemed to define the order of Western culture, the notion of embracing values outside the mainstream—or at least thinking that you were, even if for only an evening's lark—appealed to the culturally weary or bored. As such, who might be considered more "outside" than African Americans, the descendants of imported chattel slaves who, in many minds, grew up far from the (perverted) values of the Western mainstream? And if contemporary rationality and sophistication seemed oppressive and empty, how might one get closer to the "primitive" in this country than the descendants of Africans—in the popular mind frequently and still cannibals in the jungle—who were still being portrayed as simple and/or animalistic in contemporary accounts in the media? And if life seemed passionless because of middle-class restrictiveness, who might better represent vice and sexual liberation, for men *and* women, than the African Americans who had been stereotyped as alcohol and drug abusers and sexualized as beasts and Jezebels in the popular mind? A contemporary schizophrenic ambivalence toward the concept of the primitive, which could easily be perceived more positively as "primordial," just as as "primitive mind" could be perceived as "collective unconscious," swung illogically and inconsistently between positive and negative (free) associations, and many contemporaries wondered whether God the watchmaker was still in charge.

Ambrose Bierce defined "prehistoric" as "[a]ntedating the art and practice of perpetuating falsehood" (103), clearly indicating how the "primitive" was considered honest and open in the context of contemporary duplicity. Of course, Upton Sinclair had already written his muckraking naturalistic novel *The Jungle* (1906), using the major naturalistic metaphor of the modern city as a lawless jungle. His intention to write the "*Uncle Tom's Cabin* of the labor movement" (Arthur 43), though he meant more exposé than racial revelation, was also a plea for the working class and their dire conditions in their work and life—in this case, the physical and moral decay of Lithuanian immigrant Jurgis Rudkus and his family is the focus. As such, the jungle was already criticized as a place where the philosophy of the survival of the fittest prevailed. There was no doubt, however, that these inherited attitudes about the primitivity of blacks had strong racist overtones.

Exposure to the African art exhibited in the 1910s, Gauguin's escape from the disease of civilization in the 1890s, the African-derived visual art of Matisse and the Cubism of Picasso, plus Stravinsky's *The Rite of Spring*, among other works, all helped produce a vogue for primitivism in art that, fed by racial stereotypes and intense contemporary interest in Freudian ideas of the centrality of sexuality to the lives of human beings, reinforced a popular attitude toward blues and jazz as a kind of dirty little guilty pleasure on one hand, and a welcome antidote on the other. In fact, Thomas Griselle published a ragtime composition in 1918 entitled "Cubist," recorded by him for Rythmik [*sic*] piano rolls in 1918, as well as in 1921 for the Gennett label by

Frank Banta (Sutton 73), that demonstrates how connections were already being made between black music and European art, in this case on mechanical, "futurist" equipment. Antheil, Stravinsky, Paul Hindemith, Marcel Duchamp, Ernest Toch, Gerhart Munch, and Percy Grainger all attempted to compose works that included player pianos, including Antheil's stunning *Ballet Mecanique* (*Piano Music Without Limits*). A year after Banta's recording, Erik Satie premiered his "Ragtime Dada," with the wonderfully ragged panache of a pun on daddy/dada, which in black hot music parlance often meant a female's sexual partner.

Between 1917 and 1942, there were thirteen jazz titles, one of them recorded six times, featuring "jungle" first in the title, including "Jungle Nights in Harlem," recorded (probably with tongue in cheek) by Duke Ellington in 1930 (Rust, *Index* 67). Even earlier, Eubie Blake had subtitled his "The Charleston Rag" (1915) with the words "Sounds of Africa" (Sutton 41). And, in fact, this exposure of African and black folk art even "caused some dramatic style changes for some [black] artists," such as Palmer Hayden, whose 1926 painting *Fetiche et Fleurs* endowed a conventional still life with two pieces of African art as a way of establishing the African American connection to the African continent (Patton 120–21). That same year, Hayden left the country to study in Paris.

The word "jazz" itself had sexual connotations, related etymologically, possibly, to jism, and reflected in such titles as "Jazz Me Blues" (Lucille Hegamin 1920), "I Want a Jazzy Kiss" (Mamie Smith 1921) and "Jazzin' Babies Blues" (Eva Taylor 1923). The word "boogie," too, had sexual connotations, meaning to have sex or to behave wildly or uninhibitedly, as in "I'm gonna pitch a boogie woogie," or as an adjective to refer to a prostitute or an STD, in addition to its musical meanings. The rhythmical thrust of lower-class African American dance emphasizes and celebrates, in some cases, sexuality and turns the dance floor into a field of action for fertility rites and a locus of sexual expression and release. The meaning of jazz in the 1920s related to thrills, excitement, and energy—William Faulkner has a white character, Pete, "jazzing his idling engine" at a policeman in *Mosquitoes* (1927)—reflects a thrilling and sexually energetic anti-authoritarian response as well (249). For some writers like Anne Faulkner Shaw, jazz, and its "black sheep" relative the blues, "put the sin in syncopation" (Walser 32), though a 1932 recording by Chick Bullock advised listeners to "Syncopate Your Sins Away" (Rust I: 213). And Kathy Ogren reports that the Cincinnati Salvation Army sought to prevent a movie theater from being erected (!) next to the Catherine Booth Home for Girls to protect the babies from "jazz emotions" that might seep in through cracks in the wall (3). (The home was closed in 1976, when the danger must have abated.) Opposed to the serious consideration of jazz, as well as the notion of jazz as aphrodisiac, H. L. Mencken, lamenting the ideas of "Christian workers and other intellectual cripples," found its rhythms "monotonous" and its tunes "puerile," "a sedative rather than a stimulant." To paraphrase Mencken and Bill Clinton, "it's the alcohol, stupid," not the music, which is exceeded by hymns at Methodist camp meetings, if the scandals that arise from them are any indication (Mencken II: 353).

Coupled with the dominant demeanor of female vaudeville blues singers of the early 1920s, the image represented for many observers a liberated figure free to dish out raucous criticism and bawdy advice with a whiskey in one hand and a feathered boa in the other as she picked up men and threw them down with aplomb. Of course this image could feed an opposite stereotype of black women: the sexualized portrait of the African American Jezebel was already ingrained in white American consciousness, and this image only added to the sexualized objectification of black women. But, as Tera W. Hunter points out in her discussion of the desire for autonomy in the lives of African Americans, "[a] central issue at stake was control over black women's and black men's bodies" (168), demarcating the occupation of physical space while creating and preserving the stereotypical erogenous zone of black female wantonness. Either way, the notion of the unboundaried, unrepentant, hard-living, experience-wisened female, whether positive or negative, was reinforced in the popular mind, as in Ida Cox's liberatory "Wild Women Don't Have the Blues" and Clara Smith's "Don't Advertise Your Man" (both 1924). In the decades that saw Jane Addams's reform era give way to the emergence of the feminist movement with issues of equal rights, individual freedom, and economic self-determination, strong and independent figures, as some commentators such as Hazel Carby, Daphne Duval Harrison, and Angela Y. Davis viewed these female blues singers, represented some possibilities with regard to women's social progress that may have been encouraging to the sisters in the crowds and among the record-buying public. It was truly seen as a rebellious music that represented contemporary youthful restlessness.

Not only that, but as an art form, the music called jazz and blues was seen by some as matching the contemporary discontinuity and need for reformulation of so-called high art and culture—to make it new and make it whole, as Pound advised, by piecing together from a different perspective to try to escape emotional paralysis and intellectual sterility. Composer and folk song enthusiast Charles Ives flatly stated that "[b]eauty in music is too often confused with something that lets the ears lie back in an easy chair" (McCleery 78), advocating for a music with intellectual and emotional energy to express the complex spirit of stimulation and exploration of an era. Similarly, black ragtime and jazz pianist and composer James P. Johnson recorded "You've Got to Be Modernistic" in 1929, with an aging 44-year-old King Oliver on board on trumpet and the younger Fats Waller doubling on the keyboards, reinforcing the modernism of jazz in a continuum of blues, jazz, and ragtime performers, and pointing toward some future pianistic developments of Art Tatum.

Of course, though the music was obviously a combination of African and European elements, those African elements made a huge difference in the thrust of the music. Music was now conceived compositionally, rhythmically, sonically, and functionally from a different perspective, inspiring African American jazz and blues musicians, and all manner of pop and old-timey music performers, as well as classical composers, to take up the charge to slur, slide, syncopate, and scintillate with contemporary art. The importance of improvisation in the music, and the emphasis on invention, imagination, and spontaneity, matched the contemporary fervor to live in the moment rather than wander through the endless rationalizations of human action, and to make each moment more immediate, in the context of the development of the weapons of World War I (also World War II and later), weapons of mass destruction that made instant mass obsolescence a frightening possibility. Jazz and blues emerged to fill an emotional and intellectual need in both the increasingly urbanized African American community, Jim Crowed and ghettoized but seeing the music as a possibility of expressing dissatisfaction in a concrete and more general and abstract way; and in white communities that faced their own disillusionment.

This is not to say that there were not positive, enlightened responses in the white communities to the blues. It was not all stereotype and fantasy that attracted whites, nor was it all desire to appropriate African American culture for personal gain. To suggest that would be a disservice to the artistry of the performers, as well as the temperaments and intentions of the audiences. There were strong, honest, valuable exchanges that took place in the era that demonstrated that the music was not always understood in primitivistic terms. Not all clubs in Harlem, for example, were segregated in the 1920s like the Cotton Club (with its slavery motif name), Connie's Inn—established by George and Connie Immerman in 1923 and famous for the *Connie's Hot Chocolates Revue*, a stage show that rivaled Cotton Club productions and strongly influenced the career of Louis Armstrong (Driggs 137)—or Small's Paradise. For example, whites and blacks mixed freely at the Savoy, as they did at the drag balls at the Rockland Palace, though mere mixing does not necessarily equal parity. Sometimes, as Rudoiph Fisher pointed out in "The Caucasian Storms Harlem," such visitation fed fantasy: "a group of 'fays' would huddle and grin and think they were having a wild time. Slumming" (Walser 63).

Some whites were in on the joke, as portrayed in the fictionalized Van Vechten character in Nella Larsen's *Passing*. How this stew of musical cultures eventually mixed into the poetry, fiction, drama, and nonfiction of the era is another complex and circuitous story that emerged from the bubbling stew of transitional Gilded Age to Progressive Era and Jazz Age policies and aesthetics. Modernist poet Louis Zukovsky, for example, localized the settings of his volume to *Connie's Hot Chocolates*, *Tanskin Revels*, *Hot Chocolate Drops*, and *Bon Bon Buddies* revues in his first decade of work in *A* (37–38), making explicit the journey—at least metaphorical—through African American culture and history that made up some of the fragments and "rags" of contemporary life. With American identity in the balance, what Michael North calls "rebellion through racial ventriloquism" (Eliot, *The Waste Land: A Facsimile*: 9)—the ventriloquist tradition extending at least back to Benjamin Franklin, president of an abolitionist society whose last public letter argued an antislavery position—"did the police in different voices" as a way of acknowledging, appreciating, and, yes, even limiting and controlling the African American part of American identity (4).

James Lincoln Collier even asserts that, for opportunistic political reasons, left-wing jazz critics created the myth that black jazz was primarily patronized by black audiences, even though the evidence proves otherwise in terms of presence in night clubs and radio programs oriented toward white audiences (89–91). Of course, it is more complicated than this. After all, black audiences were sometimes banned from certain white establishments, and even in mixed clubs might find racist treatment simply too much to endure. And the "orientation" of radio stations toward white audiences did not prevent blacks, who had gotten used to the orientation of many things toward white audiences, from listening, the same as, later, the black-oriented WDIA attracted white listeners. Furthermore, support of the music is indicated by more than monetary support. Emotional support, group identity and dynamics, pride in creation and accomplishment—in all of these elements certain portions of the black community supported black musicians, too. Still, as Collier asserts, the varieties of hot music, including black manifestations of jazz, were much closer to the mainstream of white American society than many critics were willing to admit.

3
Chicago, Chicago

Toddling on the Brink

I

With regard to poetry, the word "blues" as it relates to sadness had been appearing since at least Richard Brathwaite's use of the term in "Elspeth's Daughter In Law" in 1658. Somewhat ironically from a contemporary standpoint, John Wilkes Booth was rumored to have used the phrase "anything to drive away the blues" when he was asked to go get a drink at the termination of the Civil War (Burns). It subsequently appeared in works by such writers as William Gilmore Simms, James Russell Lowell, Samuel Woodworth, Fitz-Greene Halleck, Thomas Ongoldsby, Herman Melville, Frances Ridley Havergal, Albert Broderick, Jessie MacKay, James McIntire, John Godfrey Saxe, and James Whitcomb Riley in the nineteenth century, and by Will Carleton and Eugene Field at the turn of the twentieth century. Field, a Chicago columnist and poet whose father represented Dred Scott, in fact, continued to use the term "blues," twice in 1922 in the poems "Carlsbad" and "My Sabine Farm" ("My muse down with the blues"). However, once again it appeared as a generic term, not one with specific reference to African American culture. Field also composed the poem "Little Boy Blue," which is perennially popular and was a lyric source for Robert Lockwood Jr.'s Chicago blues recording "Little Boy Blue" (1941). Still, the phrase "down with the blues" or some variant thereof ("feeling low-down," "down and out," "down in the dumps," "down hearted," "down to the bricks"), is common in the blues music tradition—it was the first line of the song released on Chicago's Paramount label as "Ma Rainey's Mystery Record" in 1924—and the company contest to name the record was won by a person who suggested the title "Lawd, I'm Down Wid de Blues" (Lieb 25). Significantly, Bert Williams recorded "All In, Out and Down" in 1906, an earlier cousin of "Nobody Knows You When You're Down and Out" and a song that describes a number of troubles common to the blues music tradition.

However, the use of the term "blues" in relation to African American music really emerged in the writings of two revolutionary poets published, among other places, in the mid-1910s in Chicago native Harriet Monroe's *Poetry* magazine (established in 1911), Vachel Lindsay and Carl Sandburg. Both poets had evinced an interest in vernacular materials of American culture. Lindsay was an acquaintance of pioneering folklorist and author Dorothy Scarborough, who published collections of black folk songs in *From a Southern Porch* (1919) and *On the Trail of Negro Folksongs* (1925); Sandburg was a folk-song aficionado, collector, and editor. As a result, they offered their interpretations of elements of African American culture as it related to their own lives and their perceptions of the general public. Ezra Pound wrote in 1919 that "[t]he *first* artist ever to take up a neglected folk element has, historically, nearly always scored a success" (*Antheil* 103), and Sandburg and Lindsay were successes in their own ways, as Langston Hughes would be even more lastingly successful a bit later. Their cultural connections to Chicago proved valuable for the both of them, especially given Chicago's special relationship to blues and jazz history, in addition to a publishing scene that helped attract a variety of urban, forward-looking writers in the early twentieth century.

There was, after all, a Chicago Renaissance of great vigor burgeoning in the streets, pubs, union meetings, salons, and small magazines of Chicago at the time, one that began in the 1890s and would help give birth to a Black Chicago Renaissance that lasted into the 1950s. The urban vision of such writers as Hamlin Garland, Theodore Dreiser, Frank Norris, Upton Sinclair, Harriet Monroe, Sherwood Anderson, Vachel Lindsay, Edgar Lee Masters, Carl Sandburg, Eunice Tietjens, Alice Corbin, and others drew on the directness of newspaper journalism as it eschewed gentility for the grime under the cracked fingernails of Windy City workers. There were a number of writers in Chicago, such as Masters and Anderson, whose work was representative of what was termed the "revolt from the village," which portrayed the oppressive nature of small town life and a desire to migrate to the city. In some ways we could see the blues as part of this revolt as well—a quest for escape to the "Promised Land" of the North from the harsh environment of the South, though the blues also portrayed the shortcomings of the North with great clarity and specificity. Rosa Henderson's "Back Woods Blues" (1924) and Cow Cow Davenport's "Jim Crow Blues" (1927) typify the former, while Rosa Henderson's "Down South Blues" (1923) and John Lee "Sonny Boy" Williamson's "Down South" (1938) portrays a desire to leave the cold, hard North for southern climes again: "Well, now I'm goin' back down South, where the weather fits my clothes."

Chicago Renaissance writers' treatment of social and political problems frequently streamed from idealized American principles of democracy espoused by Walt Whitman. Whitman appreciated the music of the group called "Harmoneons," about whom he commented, "Indeed, their negro singing altogether proves how shiningly golden talent can be spread over a subject generally considered 'low'" (Tosches 15). Of course, given Whitman's openness to embracing words and subject matter from a broad spectrum of American lives, his love of the group's music reinforced his own aesthetic principles as expressed in his art. The aesthetics of Chicago Renaissance writers also drew from a variety of sources, including not only the American vernaculars of the streets and sympathetic material from the American literary tradition, but the European modernist experimentation of Pound, Joyce, and Stein. Indeed, Harriet Monroe's *Poetry* magazine and Margaret Anderson's *Little Review* provided both Chicago poets like Sandburg and Lindsay and "international" poets such as Pound and Eliot the space to mingle between the covers of an American volume. Newspapers such as the *Chicago Daily News* published the poems of Eugene Field, and Finley Peter Dunne's "Mr. Dooley" sketches appeared in the *Chicago Times*. The newspapers also kept journalists like George Ade, Carl Sandburg, and Chandler Owen in business. Owen moved from being "Lenin" to A. Philip Randolph's "Trotsky" when they co-founded the socialist *Messenger* in Harlem, to a somewhat more conservative position with the *Chicago Bee* in 1923. Harry Haywood moved to Chicago after the war, becoming one of the most important black figures in the Communist Party after he joined in 1925. White Chicago classical composer John Alden Carpenter (1876–1951) began experimenting with ragtime, blues, and jazz influences as early as his setting for Paul Laurence Dunbar's "A Plea" (1912–13) and *Concertino for Piano and Orchestra* (1915). His ballet *Krazy Kat* (1921), with its bluesy ragtime sound and instrumental smears at 10:20 of the piece, caused Diaghilev to commission *Skyscrapers* (1922–1923). *Skyscrapers* was influenced by African American folk songs and perhaps W. C. Handy's "St. Louis Blues" (Pollack, *Skyscraper* 136) along with Gerald Murphy's collection of jazz recordings that "represented the hurry and din of American life, and its association with jazz" (Pollack *Skyscraper* 212–13). The influence of "modern machinery and industrial sounds" in Italian Futurism, along with Chicago's burgeoning affair with skyscrapers, undoubtedly exerted their influence on Carpenter as well, and biographer Howard Pollack sees that work as combining "something of the alarm of [Henry Blake] Fuller and [Robert] Herrick, the awe of Dreiser and Norris, the exhilaration of [Harriet] Monroe and [Carl] Sandburg, and perhaps, above all, the whimsy of [George] Ade" (*Skyscraper* 217). He was the first classical composer to set (four) poems by Langston Hughes to music in 1926 (including "The Cryin' Blues"), as well as creating settings for works by Yeats and Li Po, and he carried on correspondence with Vachel Lindsay in addition to setting a Lindsay poem to music (Pollack 83). Indeed, Howard Pollack noted similarities between Carpenter's *Piano Concertino* (1915) and Scott Joplin's and W. C. Handy's work (134–35). Carpenter also sought to book engagements for J. Rosamond Johnson, Paul Robeson, the Hall Johnson Choir, and the Negro Quartet of Fisk University at the Chicago Arts Club in the 1920s, though he was not successful at arranging their appearances, nor one by George Gershwin (Pollack 387). Carpenter was indeed constructing a modernist house of urban richness.

Chicago's urban sprawl and toughness emerged from a history of violence. The battles with Native American Indians at the Dearborn Massacre (1812) and the Blackhawk War (1832), calamitous fires of 1839 and 1871, and the intense sociopolitical upheaval among employers, police, and anarchist internationalists of the Haymarket Affair of May 1886 mirrored the city's struggle for identity in the midst of the conflicting perils of American industry, ideology, and identity. The anarchist International Working People's Association was founded ten years after Albert Parsons, who was involved in the Haymarket Affair, moved to Chicago in 1873 with his African American wife, Lucy. This welter of political activity prepared the way for labor conflicts such as the Pullman Strike led in 1894 by Eugene V. Debs, the establishment of the *International Socialist Review* in July 1900, and the founding of the radical International Workers of the World (IWW or Wobblies) in Chicago in 1905. There were, of course, reformers who tried to ameliorate the situations of Chicago residents, particularly the increasing number of immigrants attempting to negotiate life in the city. Foremost among them was Jane Addams, a reformer and sociologist who established Hull House on Chicago's West Side in 1889 to deal with urban social injustice, penning such titles as *Democracy and Social Ethics* (1902) and *A New Conscience and an Ancient Evil* (1912) in the midst of her reform work, advised and aided politically by Florence Kelley. Additionally, organizations like the Illinois Woman's Alliance (188–1894) fought for women's labor and education, as well as against police harassment of prostitutes.

Chicago, too, had to deal with the mass "Great Migration" of African Americans around the time of World War I. With the visions of a land of milk and honey and the encouragement of *The Chicago Defender* newspaper, crowds of African Americans filled Highways 51 and 61 and the Illinois Central (I.C.) railroad line to make the often chilly trip from the South to Chicago, where foundries, stockyards, and steel mill jobs awaited, though not a number sufficient to accommodate the migration. Oscar DePriest was elected the first African American alderman in Chicago in 1915 (and later to the US House of Representatives in 1928), but race riots in the "Red Summer" of 1919 and the establishment of a "Black Belt" for African American habitation quickly drew the lines of social separation. These elements certainly contributed to the multiethnic complications that Chicago had suffered for its entire existence, and helped locate Chicago's extensive underworld and gang activities in the neighborhoods of the poor. There was mingling between labor leaders and African Americans, as well as among white and black writers who shared political ideals. The IWW, Socialist Party convention in Chicago in 1919, and John Reed Clubs all assured that there would be some intermingling, and the vernacular aesthetic of a number of Chicago Renaissance writers drew them to the lives and language of African Americans in Chicago for some of the gritty realism they desired for their portrayals of contemporary urban life.

African American musicians migrating from the South in the early 1900s found work primarily in carnivals and on street corners, in theaters, saloons, and house rent parties, helping to generate a vigorous African American street music scene. Frederick Ramsey estimated that over forty important New Orleans jazz figures had migrated to Chicago by 1914 and taken a place in the burgeoning night club scene. This scene was especially fertile in the "Black Belt" or "Bronzeville" during Prohibition, when Lincoln Gardens was a hot spot, suggesting that Chicago, and its gangsters, were welcoming African American music into certain parts of the city (Morris 25). Johnny Dodds, Al Wynn, Earl Hines, and, eventually, King Oliver and Louis Armstrong were all part of the early jazz scene. White jazz performers such as the New Orleans Rhythm Kings and Bix Beiderbecke hung out with black musicians and played in some joints together, and Nick La Rocca formed his Original Dixieland Jass Band there before recording in New York in 1917. Journalist and poet Frank Marshall Davis reveled in the work of Ethel Waters, Sidney Bechet, Noble Sissle, Louis "Satchmo" Armstrong, Butterbeans and Susie, and "the only cornet [he] had heard that [he] considered near Satchmo's class . . . Bix Beiderbecke" (Tidewll 179).

In fact, Beiderbecke and Frankie Trumbauer are prime examples of how folk traditions and marginalized social groups can feed into mainstream culture and, in turn, have an impact on direct manifestations of the folk tradition. The facts are that Beiderbecke and Trumbauer learned from the African American musical tradition to play jazz. Then they developed, in the spirit of the African American musical tradition, personal styles that, with somewhat easier access to the modes of advertising and distribution by virtue of their whiteness, found their style delivered via phonograph to both black and white hands. The great tenor saxophonist Lester Young heard, among other things, their recording of "Singin' the Blues" (1927), finding in their distinctive styles valuable ideas that he could adopt and develop into a personal style influenced by them. On the other hand, brilliant jazz performer Louis Armstrong offered that he "love[d] Guy Lombardo" (Wald 129–45), and adapted to his audiences between 1925 and 1928 by exhibiting what Brian Harker called a "split musical personality": "in the theaters and cabarets he played operatic melodies, show music, and society jazz, while in the recording studio he played polyphonic New Orleans jazz," later even merging the two in highly successful form (137). We find similar interchanges in the minstrel songs presented in exaggerated form in the minstrel tradition entering the repertoires of the same musicians who generated or carried on the black tradition in the first place. Still, might not something other than a mental illness or weakness account for such an uncommon breadth of appreciation of seemingly disparate music? Are not the variables greater?

For popularity and fame, Isham Jones's band was "[a]rguably the most influential Chicago dance orchestra of the early '20s" (Sudhalter 91), and the Mound City Blue Blowers gave Chicago jazz "a national—and soon international—profile in the early 1920s . . ." initiated by their 1924 recordings of Spencer Williams's "Arkansaw [*sic*] Blues" and "Blue Blues" (Sudhalter 95–961). The Blue Blowers' recordings from the 1920s include appearances not only by white jazz artists such as Eddie Lang, Gene Krupa, Glenn Miller, and Eddie Condon, but also black performers Pops Foster and Coleman Hawkins. Red McKenzie went to record with Paul Whiteman's Orchestra and with the black jazz string band the Spirits of Rhythm, which included guitar master Teddy Bunn and the very modernistic, even visionary scat/vocalese artist Leo Watson. Watson, in turn, went on to make some recordings with white bandleaders Artie Shaw and Gene Krupa, among others, in the 1930s.

Big Bill Broonzy, Ma Rainey, Papa Charlie Jackson, and Georgia Tom Dorsey represented a burgeoning blues scene that rippled with creativity. Blues artists sometimes worked in the same steel mills and stockyards as their audience, and remembered the same cruel and overt racism, boll weevils, floods, and conscriptions in the South as well. Big Bill, for example, recorded "Bull Cow Blues" (1932) and "Mississippi River Blues" (1934) alongside "House Rent Stomp" (1927) and "State Street Woman" (1930), bridging rural and urban memories and experiences. Broonzy's long career spanned stylistically from solo acoustic guitar to full amplified, pounding bands with horns—and back, in the 1950s, to the earliest folk style he could remember at a time when European audiences evinced an interest in early blues styles. Sometimes performers from a variety of genres appeared together in the clubs: Carroll Dickerson led a dance group with jazz performers Buster Bailey and Rudy Jackson, vaudeville blues singer Mary Stafford, and future hokum singer and dancer

Frankie "Half Pint" Jaxon (Sudhalter 86) all sharing the stage and blending the music. In fact, at age 17 Dan Burley combined blues learned from Chicago legend Hersal Thomas with hustling as a copy boy at the *Chicago Defender*. When he left the *Defender in 1927 to work as a lumberjack and musician,* it was with a clear handle on the music as well as the language he would later describe and analyze in *Dan Burley's Original Handbook of Harlem Jive* (1944) and *Diggeth Thou?* (1959, two important volumes that, combined with his musical experiences with Lionel Hampton, Brownie McGhee, and Dizzy Gillespie, made him a doyen and representative of the Chicago speakeasies. The extensive and impressive jazz and blues club scene in Chicago, however, was firmly under mob control and supplied by mob patronage (Morris 136).

An important venue for writers in Jazz-Age Chicago was the Dil Pickle, a night club founded in 1914 by former Wobbly Jack Jones, Irish revolutionist Jim Larkin, and a loose band of bohemians on the lookout for a welcoming venue for their revolutionary art and ideas. Sandburg (his banjo sometimes in tow) and Lindsay were among the gathered Dil Picklers, along with, at various times, William Carlos Williams, Sherwood Anderson, Kenneth Rexroth, Lucy Parsons, Clarence Darrow, and such African American luminaries as boxer-turned-jazz bandleader Jack Johnson (*Times Ain't Like* DVD), choreographer Katherine Dunham, "Walk the Dog" dancer Garrison Williams, writers Fenton Johnson and Jean Toomer, and a variety of musicians. Though most of the jazz musicians who reportedly appeared there are unnamed—Rexroth simply refers to them as "the Chicago jazzmen of the early twenties" (Rosemont 35)—such names as "Big Babe and the Honeycombers" and "Big Babe and Her Congo Kids" are evocative of the era, and the T. Thomas Taylor mentioned by Rexroth may well be the Tommy Taylor who recorded in 1928 and 1929 with the Windy Rhythm Kings, KC Stompers, Melrose Dixieland Thumpers, and Thomas' Devils. There was clearly an interest in African American culture—William Moore's "Jazz, the Hope of the Nation" being among the lecture topics (Rosemont 29)—as well as an interest in Whitmanian roots, exemplified in part by the old-timer whose favorite line was "I *knew* Walt Whitman" in the face of any criticism of the bard (113), perhaps the source for the episode in Jean Toomer's "Box Seat."

The abilities of Lindsay and Sandburg to recognize early on the importance of both traditional and emerging African American musics in various incarnations and to identify them as appropriate to their poetic output and the American tradition made them influential pioneers for the generation of poets soon to make up the vernacular poetry "school" of the Harlem Renaissance, and ancestors for subsequent generations of poets writing in the African American music mode. Both also clearly influenced Langston Hughes,

Lindsay not only in his advocacy of Hughes's work after an encounter with the busboy poet at the Wardman Park Hotel, but also as a spoken word pioneer who saw the practical uses of poetry as well—though his comments on jazz, discussed below, did not always seem so appreciative and welcoming. Sandburg demonstrated his influence in his vigorous Whitmanian heft and direct language but also in poems that were direct precursors to such Hughes poems as "The Negro Speaks of Rivers" and "Negro." As such, their influence, through Hughes, on blues-influenced literature was immense, though not unproblematic.

II

Time and criticism have not been kind to Vachel Lindsay, whose work was out of favor. If he, a suicide, is discussed much today, it is usually as more of a facile and melodramatic performer of rhymes rather than the avatar of the new poetry he was known to be in the 1910s. However, at mid-century, poet and critic Louise Bogan summarized the contributions and achievements of Lindsay with a more balanced eye than some less familiar with the spirit of his age. For Bogan, Lindsay, "with revivalist blood in his veins," gathered in "folk rhythms . . . the hymn . . . the question and answer technique of the minstrel show . . . circus and vaudeville . . . railroad songs and ballads . . . back-country legends . . . the neglected secular songs of the negro" and the syncopation and energy of ragtime and, later, jazz (42–43). He brought into American poetry, Bogan asserted, "an unmatched richness of subject and variety of dynamics" and "broke through the shallowness and sterility of poetic subject matter as one of his beloved circus performers would break through a paper hoop" (44). The metaphor, though an apt one, must be read carefully, for it is not the work of Lindsay that is being compared to the circus performer, but the ease and aplomb with which he rejected the relative timidity of the traditionalist Georgian poets. Eliot and Pound also rejected those poets—though these two were clearly of a different ilk from Lindsay. Pound supported an article by Edgar Jepson describing what he saw as the weakness of Lindsay's work in 1918 (Stock 216), and Eliot's startling poem "The Love Song of J. Alfred Prufrock" took second place to Lindsay's "The Chinese Nightingale" for Harriet Monroe's *Poetry* prize of 1915. If Lindsay was an outlandish nonconformist, he was, he felt, like Whitman—in the thick of things, pulsing on the course of pop, folk, and backwoods culture on his way to some religio-beatific utopia for all Americans.

Lindsay's "The Congo" (subtitled "A Study of the Negro Race"), published in 1914 in *The Congo and Other Poems*, evinced Lindsay's interest in treating

African American culture through his own particular lens. The poem had its genesis in Lindsay's visits to the office of black lawyer Charles Gibbs in Springfield, where the two talked about the race riots there and the problems that produced and resulted from them (Camp 852). Edgar Lee Masters, in his 1935 biography of Lindsay, called the poem "Beethoven jazz of the greatest success" (324), citing Beethoven's use of what he heard as (pre-)jazz-like effects in the scherzo of the B-flat quartet no. 6—a clear attempt by Masters to undercut the unique contributions of jazz and place Lindsay's poetry in a "headier" European company (though Beethoven's scherzo is interestingly syncopated and makes use of some lively sliding techniques in the violins, about halfway through the section, that nearly verge on black folk fiddling technique). However, given the composition year of the poem, it would be more accurate to associate the poem with the pre-jazz rhythms of the cakewalk and ragtime—at the height of its vogue from 1896–1920—rather than the jazz to come. Amy Lowell recognizes this when she labels the poem "a genuine bit of rag-time," which she associates with "a plentiful sprinkling of discord" and necessary dissonance in modern verse (150, 152). At the time, Lindsay saw the works in the volume as an attempt to move the "vaudeville form back towards the old Greek precedent of the half-chanted line" (Camp 851), so even Lindsay was conceiving this as a pop version of ragtime, and attempting to associate his work with time-honored Western traditions rather than the "vulgarities" of contemporary pop culture. He would return to this with a vengeance later.

Kathy Ogren sees Lindsay's onomatopoeia as an attempt at syncopation—itself prominent in ragtime—but if it is, it is a syncopation stilted by alliteration into overblown regularity. This takes the poem into the realm of popular parody of the cakewalk, which was itself rooted in slave parodies of the awkwardly stylized dances of their white masters. It is unlikely that Lindsay was aware of this, so his use of the cakewalk to "parody black culture"—as Ogren correctly states (148)—is an unconscious self-parody of white society of the time. Lindsay did not believe in the marriage of poetry and music: "Setting poetry to music, even the best music, is the destruction of poetry and the production of an amorphous and confused result. All poetry that has been set to music has been blasted thereby" (Camp 984). Neither did Lindsay see himself as a jazz poet—indeed, Masters writes that when he thought he was being disrespected in his work by 1920, he "began to see himself as a jazz poet, a kind of clown" (333). In his *Collected Poems* (1925), declaring "I am no improviser" (xx), he asserted "I have never used the word 'jazz' except in irony" (6), and his catalog of negative characteristics is telling: "no strain, jazz, spasm, or vulgarity" (7). Lindsay's language was even harsher in 1932 when he spoke of his invitation—the first for an American poet—to recite his work at Oxford University: "I use the word jazz ironically, have always hated jazz, and always will and considered *The Daniel Jazz* a mere after dinner skit, and was utterly disgusted, really horrified beyond words, to find it used as the title-poem of the English-Book when I arrived in England" (235). It is likely that this title was used because of the great popularity of jazz by the time of the release of *The Daniel Jazz* in 1920, though five years later it was turned into an orchestral piece by composer Louis Gruenberg. In 1919, Will Marion Cook's Southern Syncopated Orchestra—twenty-seven Afro-American musicians and nineteen singers—had helped popularize their version of African American music in London, performing on the club circuit, and also for the Prince of Wales at Buckingham Palace, as well as at the Royal Albert Hall. The great pioneer Sidney Bechet, who could not read music and was the only improviser in the group, was featured with the band, apparently specializing in blues performances. The title was a good promotional tool for Lindsay—except, of course, it wasn't jazz. And clearly Lindsay did not want it to be.

Of course, there were those like Anne Faulkner Shaw who saw jazz as "put[ting] the sin in syncopation" (Walser 32), a fear of African American music's deleterious effect on the youngsters of the age who were attracted to what proponents of classical music found to be the music's vulgarity. Erik Satie's *Parade* (1917), for example, "lampooned the banality of modern culture—including jazz itself" (Sullivan 204), though he was referring to music hall jazz, for some a dilution and degradation of "real" jazz. Just as the "Great White Hope" Jim Jeffries was touted to humiliate Jack Johnson and put blacks in their place in 1910, composer Roy Harris, who avoided African American influence in his work, was the "white hope" of classical music (Horowitz 408). Harris spoke of how "the jazz boys, chained to an unimaginative commercial routine which serves only crystallized symmetrical dance rhythms, are continually breaking out into superimposed rhythmic variations which were not in the music. This asymmetrical balancing of rhythmic phrases is in our blood; it is not in the European blood" (Alexander 372). His infantilization of the jazz performers, even as he uses them to typify American rhythmic sensibilities, is telling. Quick, now, name one of his compositions.

Though that harsh criticism of vulgarity was clearly not Lindsay's intent, he also did not embrace jazz music as a healthy enterprise. In fact, other prominent intellectuals of the time attempted to dismiss interest in jazz, perhaps even suppress it, through ignoring it: American composer Charles Wakefield Cadman observed that he "felt too much importance had been placed on this question of Jazz; too much worry has been given it. It is as silly to stir oneself up over the matter of jazz as it is to get into a fever heat over modern

Christianity and Fundamentalism" (Walser 42). Further, John Alden Carpenter, an excerpt of whose "Krazy Kat: A Jazz Pantomime" was included by W. C. Handy in his groundbreaking 1926 collection *Blues: An Anthology* (171), hinted at another notion of what "jazz" was for the contemporary public: "I am convinced that our contemporary popular music (please note that I avoid labeling it jazz) is by far the most spontaneous, the most . . . important musical expression that America has achieved" (Walser 43–44). John Philip Sousa, in fact, thought that "pep" was a suitable synonym for jazz (Walser 50), while Paul Laurence Dunbar asserted that black marching bands exemplified "Sousa played in ragtime" in their performances (*Collected Poetry* 178), and Pete Hampton sang of "When Sousa Comes to Coon-Town." But mere black minstrel performer pep, energy, or momentary rush of hijinks or hormones does not place African American vernacular music traditions in distinguished intellectual company, or to say it better, does not make it worthy of serious consideration for its insights on life, its vigor of language, or its keen mother-wit. Clearly there was confusion as to what exactly jazz was because, as with most artistic boundaries, boundaries are frequently imposed externally by someone other than the artists, from a variety of perspectives, drawing on contemporary notions of what is appropriate, and at the service of the dominant culture, in this case a capitalistic culture that seeks to profit from it and employs its resources in behalf of such exploitation.

Masters points out that, when Lindsay began writing his poetry, minstrel songs were popular (273), and Lindsay was influenced by those tunes, sometimes performed in a ragtime-to-jazz "hot music" style that associated all three names with the music and lyrics of such songs. Wilbur Sweatman, a pioneering African American bandleader and instrumentalist, helped the music segue from composed ragtime into more of a jazz improvising mode in a series of important recordings beginning in 1916, though he may have recorded "Maple Leaf Rag" as early as 1903–1905. Since jazz was, at this time, emerging out of a mix of genres that included elements of ragtime and would be part of a minstrel image in the popular white mind, it is possible to overblow the influence of jazz as we understand it on Lindsay's work. It is this transitional hybrid form in a minstrelly charged atmosphere that Lindsay understood as being jazz, not what became America's most lauded indigenous art form. Thus, Lindsay associated jazz with minstrelsy's supposed "lightheartedness" and simplistic, tuneful stereotypes, rejecting the label of jazz poet for something he considered more serious. Of course, there were jazz performers who were "mere entertainers" during that era, so it was possible for Lindsay to make this mistake about jazz based on what he saw and heard, but certainly some jazz actually was "serious" music at this time, as bands like Wilbur

Sweatman's and James Reese Europe's made the imaginative leap from ragtime composition to futuristic jazz improvisation. Still, they might also be perceived as mere "jungle" entertainments.

Lindsay's "The Congo" is his best-known poem, one that features the herky-jerky onomatopoeia that sometimes veers toward an approximation of rhythmic syncopation ("Boomlay, boomlay, boomlay, BOOM"), and he was proud of what he had expressed in the poem (even if the image of the "baboon butler" had previously appeared in a James Weldon Johnson lyric, "In a Castle By the River Nile," recorded by Bert Williams in 1901). In 1914 Lindsay, at the height of his powers, was quite upset that W. E. B. Du Bois and Joel Spingarn did not see the poem as a "hopeful . . . prophecy of a colored utopia" (Massa 169) based on Lindsay's earlier expression of a desire to see African Americans have "an equal yet distinctive society" and "quiet," not Marcus Garveyesque, "pride in Negritude" (Massa 166). Unfortunately, Lindsay's own "gospel" mentality, based on the seemingly admirable elements of "religion, equality, and beauty" (Massa 25), influenced his decision to dedicate the poem to a missionary to the Congo, Ray Eldred. This indicates the likely condescending colonial attitudes toward Africans that made their conversion "necessary" and associates Lindsay with Western arrogance—whatever his supposed rejection of dogmatism in favor of egalitarian ecumenism. Sections titled "Their Basic Savagery" and "Their Irrepressible High Spirits" draw from the stereotypes of the black beast and the black child current in American society. Its references to Africa, ragtime, and minstrelsy—bucks, bloodlust, and cakewalking princes—(lip)smacks of a primitivism and atavism later also remarked in some Harlem Renaissance writing, such as Claude McKay's *Home to Harlem* (1928) or Carl Van Vechten's *Nigger Heaven* (1926), as well as in H. L. Mencken, who rejected Van Vechten's championing of Stravinsky's rhythmic approach by calling attention to a similar approach among "modern Zulus and New Yorkers [and] the African Savage" (269). The idea that the primitive mumbo jumbo just may not die in the jungle is the whispered fear of the final lines. Though Lindsay emphasized the redemption of the jungle and its inhabitants in his comments on the poem, it is clear that a missionary notion of the need to save the land and people from their own pasts drives the poem, and the inescapable minstrel references communicate negative images of African Americans.

In the poem, Lindsay refers to "Mumbo-Jumbo" as "God of the Congo" (174), repeating that "Mumbo-Jumbo will hoodoo you." The primitivist retrogression to an earlier, uncivilized state telegraphs, in some ways, Eugene O'Neill's 1920 production *The Emperor Jones*, a work considered by many (Paul

Robeson included) an important landmark on the American stage and an impetus to Harlem Renaissance activities by African Americans. The term "Mumbo-Jumbo" itself, possibly from the Mandingo "mamaajamboo" and employed in 1795 by Mungo Park, refers very likely to a corruption of words that described an idol worshipped by Africans, but the corruption and attempt to make the term sound repetitious and nonsensical led the words to become synonymous with the notion of speech that is puffed up but empty of meaning. The connection to language used by the minstrel dandy, who frequently failed in his attempt to convince his audience of his intelligence through (a seriously flawed and convoluted mis-) use of words is also clear. The poem drew an unapologetic poetic response from Sterling A. Brown in "The New Congo," though Lindsay is still counted among Brown's poetic precursors.

Lindsay's "The Booker Washington Trilogy" (1917) is linked by the location of each section in various places in relation to the church: a sermon, a call-and-response song, and a poem-game, each of which delivers a story and perspective on the lives of African Americans and their enemies. The poem is especially notable for a vigorous vernacular portrayal of Harriet Beecher Stowe's Simon Legree in its first section, which Lindsay advises is "to be read in your own variety of negro dialect" (318), as if everybody has their own version to be trotted out for such occasions, or may supply their own improvisational version based on their own understanding of the tradition. Perhaps Lindsay merely meant to invite participation, but in this context the possibilities for parody and mockery are clear. The assumption is that the audience of the poem is not African American, and that they have some kind of personal or popular sense of the speech of the African American "other," whose speech is unlike standard English. The linguistic hegemony of the piece is unmistakable. Nonetheless, Lindsay comes out charging with his surprisingly dazzling, energetic, hyperbolic bad man description ("brass buttoned shirt," "snake skin necktie," "beard like a goat," "cheeks fish belly white," and "eyes like dirt") that makes Legree suitably rough-hewn and powerful in the manner of the Old Southwest's tall talk tradition of Mason Locke Weems and James Kirke Paulding and bad man ballad traditions of "Stagolee," and "Railroad Bill"—indeed, Bo Diddley was still singing of wearing a "cobra snake for a necktie" in "Who Do You Love" (1956). Lindsay's Legree cuts a fearsome figure, and his end in hell is suitably sinister, though oddly lacking in punishment for the man who revels in hatred and violence: Legree and the Devil gnawing together on a hambone, "shooting craps . . . playing poker and taking naps," like the description of the Devil "fat and fine" (318–20). Perhaps the congregation is meant to see that Legree does not even know that he has reached an ignominious end, and thus suffers even in his pleasure for all eternity. But Legree's ignorance certainly seems to be his bliss as well, even if the rest of the poem envisions a more joyful end for others who opposed his principles.

On the other hand, perhaps, just perhaps, Lindsay means to individualize the rendering of African American dialect by acknowledging a diversity of delivery and pronunciation. In that case, he encourages the drama that he practiced and encouraged in his performances, and recognized stylized dialect as in need of individuation. Thus, the voice in this poem becomes part of the performance milieu in which it is performed. It is immediate, personal, and alive.

The celebratory "John Brown" section employs call-and-response elements clearly related to an antiphonal African American tradition present in the work songs and spirituals, praising Brown and locating Brown, his wife, and his children in a clearly deserved heaven. The final section dealing with King Solomon and the Queen of Sheba anticipates an eternity of bliss for the congregation of the poem, bringing the suffering congregants to a suitable conclusion. The trilogy is successful in avoiding a few of the egregious stereotypes of some other poems. Additional poems also draw on African American elements: "How Samson Bore Away the Gates of Gaza" was based on an African American sermon style. *The Golden Whales of California* (1920) contains such jazz-referencing poems as the previously mentioned "The Daniel Jazz" (in a section titled *The Daniel Jazz and Other Poems*) and "The Modest Jazz-Bird," a poem which employs "jazz" as a reference to the bird's ability to improvise a variety of songs—a kind of archetypal American bird, which then flies off to the call of the American eagle to defeat the Kaiser and affirm the democratic strength of America. "When Peter Jackson Preached in the Old Church" is sung to the tune of the spiritual "Every Time I Feel the Spirit," and "The Conscientious Deacon," playing on the stereotype of the superstitious Negro churchgoer, races along in a style that Lindsay describes as "a song to be syncopated as you please" (380). Both have clear reference to elements of rhythm and improvisation in African American music, but, as Lindsay understood, not just jazz and blues, but the felicitous blend of minstrel music, ragtime, and spirituals as well. However, when reviewers began calling Lindsay "the jazz poet," a title Hughes later welcomed for himself, Lindsay made clear his displeasure (Burt 359).

More important for this study is Lindsay's "The Apple Blossom Snow Blues" (1916), perhaps the earliest reference in American poetry to the blues related to a type of music. Lindsay appends a note to the poem which associates the mood of the blues with "Milton's *Il Penseroso*, or a paragraph from Burton's *Anatomy of Melancholy*" (376), an invocation, perhaps, to the goddess Melancholy to bring Peace, Quiet, Leisure, and Contemplation, though the contrasting serious and satiric tones of the two works mentioned suggest a problematic time interpreting the association of materials from widely varying traditions. Indeed, it seems almost as if Lindsay may be inserting this "explanation" of the blues into the poem either to justify its use or to highlight an ironic intention in the poem. Lindsay may have done well to append a reference to Milton's companion poem "L'Allegro" to "Il Penseroso," given that the invocation to the goddess of melancholy in the latter poem is supplemented in the living blues tradition by the "busy hum of men" in the cities invoked by "L'Allegro." Lindsay firmly plants the poem in the ragtime, jazz, and vaudeville traditions by which the blues was influenced at the time the poem was published in 1916, mentioning vaudeville specifically in his introductory note and referring to ragtime, jazz, and blues throughout. The poem clearly telegraphs some of the elements upon which Hughes would draw in his later, vaudeville blues-influenced poems, though Lindsay does not seem to have tried or wanted to capture much of the gritty spirit of developing elements of the blues that were being performed, though not yet recorded, satisfying himself with references to various types of music in his quest for a "higher vaudeville."

In fact, the poem presents a dramatic scenario in which a performing couple act out a courtship which seemingly succeeds, but turns out to be feigned in the end, despite the best efforts of the male performer to praise his love's natural beauty. Lindsay uses italics to emphasize the formulaic reference to the woman's ("*Your*") beauty, as well as to reinforce the notion that what the performer "*Thinks*" is not necessarily true. Two stanzas later, Lindsay betrays the efforts of the man to "smirk and banter" to convince the woman of his love, and then reveals that

> he is her lover
> *And*
> Her dancing partner,
> In the blues he made
> Called "The Apple Blossom Snow." (376–77)

The blues is described not as the blues he *has*, but the blues he *has made*. The illusion of reality is actually arranged, the outcome known, and thus the emotion only for the audience's (and readers') benefits. This, of course, is much like the staged versions of blues of the era—formal, feigned, and flirting with African American culture in a refined way. The woman is described as a "fairy, / Yet a jazz-jump dancer" (326), contrasting an idealized version of her with a more earthy one, seeing them not so much incongruous as representative of a breadth of human desire, something magical and rare, yet common. Lindsay does, after all, refer not only to apple and cherry blossoms, but dandelions as well—a weed among the blossoms. It is, in fact, part of what he likes about her.

Quite interesting is the title of the poem, one of only two places where there is a reference to snow. Snow is never literally present in the story, so the marriage of the apple blossom and the snow in the title of the poem suggest that his natural love and what can end it are both inevitably part of the scenario—and life, which is a kind of dance with death, to use the medieval terminology. Ragtime, jazz, and blues are all metaphors for stylized spirited love and abandon in the illusory game of love, and the realization that whatever romantic illusions are evoked about the woman, she is ultimately the "rag time lady," and he is, as the poem ends, "The / Rag / Time / Man," two players in the fickle and fleeting game of life. The time, of course, is "ragged" because of the inevitable impediments that interfere with their happy union. What Lindsay had begun to recognize is the currency and popularity of stage blues performances and their ability to reach a younger audience unfamiliar, perhaps, with earthier forms of the blues. Lindsay exploits the entertainment aspect of blues performance and integrates it with traditional expressions of romantic love to make the contrast between artificial performance and true feelings, though they are still difficult to discern because one does not always know where the performance ends and reality begins. Lindsay's prefatory note regarding "the secret soul of a vaudeville man" introduces the ambiguity here—the stage actor whose true soul is hidden behind a performance that Lindsay will try to unmask (376). In this the poem has something of a connection to the "masking tradition" common in African American culture, in particular to Paul Laurence Dunbar's "We Wear the Mask" (*Collected Poetry* 71).

A poem Lindsay inscribed to Carl Sandburg in April 1923 indicates the disdain with which Lindsay came to consider jazz. In a letter in 1918, Lindsay had written about the poem "The Modest Jazz-Bird" and its positive meaning for America: "I insist that Jazz does not discredit America. I think the Jazz element in America is a sure sign of health. I have the utmost respect for [the] Jazz in the young people, and I feel that without it there would be no American armies in Europe today . . It is the same thing as Yankee Doodle was in the days of Washington" (Camp 879). Indeed, the "Scrap Iron Jazz Band" recorded a song entitled "The Ragtime Volunteers Are Off to War" in Paris in 1918, expressing just such a sentiment (Rust II: 1992). Five years later, in "Babylon, Babylon, Babylon the Great," Lindsay associates jazz with Babylon, the pagan city-state full of sin and pride and lust that made war on Israel and exiled the major citizens of Jerusalem to the city as well. John called Babylon the "Great Whore" in Revelation 19:2, and indeed it also represented the pride of mankind, building a tower to reach into the heavens and, in its overreaching, produced the plurality of languages that helped confound world efforts toward understanding. Moreover, it is Lincoln's speech at Cooper Institute in New York, from February 27, 1860, Lincoln's first address as a presidential candidate and thus representative of the birth of an American "new possibility," that, in Lindsay's words, "overthrew jazz—Babylon" (Camp 500). In it, a conciliatory unionist Lincoln asserted "LET US HAVE FAITH THAT RIGHT MAKES MIGHT, AND IN THAT FAITH, LET US, TO THE END, DARE TO DO OUR DUTY AS WE UNDERSTAND IT" (Lincoln 1859–1865, 130). By trying to understand and appease the South while calling for attendance to right and duty, Lincoln attempts to sail a *via media* that theoretically will preserve both integrity and the Union, though of course it is fraught with problems. Still, in trying to unify the plurality of languages in relation to the issues of the Civil War, Lincoln is portrayed as a holy figure.

Startlingly, Lindsay writes in a coda to the poem that he has "exhorted Sandburg to improvise," but not in the manner of jazz improvisation, which Lindsay labels with hatred "our most Babylonian disease" (502). Perhaps Lindsay has in mind the smaller deviations of rhythm and attack one might encounter in classical improvisation, or its further limited but acceptable embellishments, or the supplying of further counterpoints in an appropriate manner; perhaps he believes further that "[t]he apparently unfettered improvisation of the church organist or the jazz player is rarely entirely original but rather built upon an assembly and juxtaposition of received formulas" (Cummings 306). What is the cause of Lindsay's "Jazzophobia Blues" (the title of a song recorded by Henryette Davis in 1926 but by no one else, and a malady similar to Anne Faulkner Shaw's?)? Lindsay seems to intimate the source for his change of attitude, though not necessarily the magnitude of the change, in a letter to Katharine Lee Bates from October 28, 1924: "You see I was caught between two millstones. I was born with a voice so they thought me a weaker Bryan. I was born with dancing feet so they thought me Jazz. I used the word once or twice when it meant spice. But just *after that* the world, the whole world, went jazz-mad—a thing none of us could have prophesied and I have been worn to my soul, welcomed to a thousand towns where I have had to explain to thousands I was *not* a Jazz artist—and the Saxophone, which I hate, was read into everything I ever did" (Camp 883). Lindsay wrote later that jazz had come to mean—and he means as it had been co-opted in the popular mind—something "flip, snippy, 'fresh and smart alecky'" (Camp 900), and he would have none of it. Unfortunately, by responding to the popular image of jazz rather than the reality, he reinforced that meaning himself, and thus distanced himself from something that had contributed positively to his work.

As his references to improvisation continued, Lindsay expressed a desire for improvisation to be formulaic, refined, controlled, and "appropriate." He considers jazz to be none of these although, as Robert O'Meally points out, jazz "is never a free-for-all" (43)—and neither is the improvisation in Indian ragas, which Shankar describes as a "scientific, precise, subtle, and aesthetic melodic form" ("Notes" 16). Apparently unaware of this, Lindsay rejects jazz as a model for democracy and principled living.

Lindsay expounded upon this improvisation, "but the opposite of jazz" (Camp 503), in his "Preface to 'Bob Taylor's Birthday,'" a Phi Beta Kappa poem at Harvard commencement in 1922. Taylor, himself a fiddler, the reelected governor of Tennessee, is lauded by Lindsay as a representative of the good old days "when red or white roses were worn by every soul of Tennessee" and "local allusions . . . and improvisations on his own fiddle"—some lively tunes, some solemn, by a "picnic fiddler"—represented a kind of controlled or managed improvisation. Significantly, the improvisation is informed by the "old-fashioned, barn-dance, log cabin jig fiddler" associated by Lindsay with a white, not a black tradition (Camp 503). Of course, the influence of black fiddlers in the nineteenth century is well known now, and they can be seen as significant precursors to jazz and blues improvisers. Indeed, recordings by artists such as Peg Leg Howell's Gang and Stovepipe No. 1 (Sam Jones) show nineteenth-century African American musicians adapting to twentieth-century black musical trends even as they kept old tunes like "Turkey in the Straw" and "Dan Tucker" in their repertoires. Lindsay's is an idealization of "the short and simple annals of the poor" (Camp 505), and the white working poor at that, sprouting from the soil of an idealized Lincoln and Whitman. His improvisation is, unfortunately, fantastical and exclusive.

"The Jazz of This Hotel," from winter 1924–1925, extends this rejection of jazz improvisation by contrasting it to "the slower tom-toms of the sea" (a precursor of Hughes's use of the comparison in "The Negro Artist and the Racial Mountain"?) and "thunder," preferring what he calls "outdoor love, . . . outdoor talk and wonder" (Camp 576). Of course, judging jazz improvisation to be unnatural is purely subjective. In fact, some of the tone and intonation of jazz and blues performance is sometimes seen as stemming from elements produced or existing in nature and the environment. A harmonica player might blow both through and around his harmonica in order to produce notes and a barrage of wind to dramatize a train imitation or a fox chase. A singer like Chester Burnett might howl in a high falsetto voice as he reproduces the sound of the animal from which he adopted his nom du disque—"Howlin' Wolf." In "Come On in My Kitchen," Robert Johnson evokes the sounds of the wind with the sliding of a metal bar on his guitar strings. Wild

Jimmy Spruill and Jimmy Nolen were both known for the chicken scratching sounds of their guitars. And listen to those honking and screaming sax men like Illinois Jacquet, Joe Houston, and Albert Ayler bleat like sheep, honk like geese, and whinny like a horse in heat—as the Original Dixieland Jazz Band did on "Livery Stable Blues" (1917).

Lindsay finds jazz in the hotel, not in nature, but primarily because he does not understand its origins, energy, and importance. Also from 1924, "A Curse for the Saxophone" frenziedly associates jazz with Cain, Jezebel, Judas, Nero, Henry the Eighth, and John Wilkes Booth, portraying some of these and "twenty thousand pigs on their hind legs playing / The Beale Street Blues" (Camp 578). The song, composed by W. C. Handy and recorded by Esther Bigeou, Alberta Hunter, and Al Bernard, among others, was a hit for Handy, but Lindsay preferred the sweet fluty voices of a royal Queen—not a blues queen such as Hunter singing "My Castle's Rockin'" (1940). As a poet influenced by African American culture, Lindsay ultimately came to revile that influence and rail against the prominence of jazz, particularly as it had been perverted in the popular mind, as a technique from which skilled poets could draw to create contemporary work of great force and intellect. Feeling imprisoned by the designation, as Bert Williams was by minstrelsy or other black composers lamented the restrictions inherent in being identified as a "negro composer" or "jazz composer," Lindsay rebelled.

Lindsay's aforementioned "A Curse for the Saxophone," appearing in *Going-to-the-Stars* (1926), featured Lindsay's use of physical gestures, elements of chanting, and syncopated rhythms aimed at dramatizing his version of the new poetry for the masses rather than maintaining poetry as the exclusive province of the leisure classes—another aim of Langston Hughes, whose poetry tours to black schools and locations across the country were in the same vein. Lindsay's own performances, however, could sometimes spill over into a kind of self-parody filled with bombastic gesticulating, as Frost biographer Lawrance Thompson notes: "[a]wkward in his long-armed, long-legged struttings about the stage, he never seemed to guess that anyone might find an element of clowning in his performance" (270). Frost himself, though loathe to follow Lindsay in performance, produced a gentle parody of Lindsay entitled "John L. Sullivan Enters Heaven" that captured some of Lindsay's foibles. In fact, we may see Lindsay's dramatic performances spilling over into a kind of analogue for black minstrelsy of their own, with the exaggerated features of the itinerant folk poet being reinforced in the minds of contemporary audiences—in Lindsay's case, trading rhymes for bread rather than procuring gainful employment, and rolling his eyes in a fine frenzy.

In a lecture in 1908, Lindsay expounded upon the strengths and weaknesses of African Americans: the strengths were "Native Genius:—Sorrow Songs; Folk Lore; Oratory; Sense of the Picturesque; Minstrelsy" (Camp 914). It is not that Lindsay did not have an admiration for elements of African American culture, though his essentialist notions of the inherent dualities of a "race" are objectionable. It is not even that he doesn't recognize the ways in which African Americans were limited in their achievements, as portrayed in his essay "American Calling: Professor of the Whisk Broom" (Camp 914). But by the time another decade had passed he felt repulsed and trapped by the co-optation of blues and jazz. His general pronouncements painted the great music he previously embraced being performed by Louis Armstrong, Bessie Smith, and James P. Johnson with a "flapper" brush of pop-jazz and blues, some distance from the spirit and strength of less commercially compromised, popularly deflected and inflected productions. Combined with Lindsay's shrill rejections of jazz and blues and retrospective idealizations, these shortcomings have contributed to the failing reputation of Lindsay in the ensuing years. Hughes was never quite so animated in his performances, perhaps self-conscious about a criticism of his singing, perhaps just somewhat more reserved in personality or more tasteful in presentation, but the artistry of his work could produce a ringing power of its own.

III

Carl Sandburg, vigorous Chicago Renaissance poet, folk song collector, performer, and Lincoln biographer (each facet rooted in the same aesthetic), was an heir to the Whitmanian tradition in poetry, a crucial step between Whitman and Hughes vis-à-vis the employment of urban folk materials—and African American folk materials—in his work. Sandburg evinced this interest in a variety of ways. As early as "Nigger" (1916), Sandburg began treating African Americans in his work. Langston Hughes used the poem as a model for his own "Negro," a more refined composition than the colloquial and somewhat vulgar Sandburg poem that reflected the vigorous, racist language and attitudes of the Sandburg city. Philip Yanella points out that Sandburg admired the "dignity and wisdom" of black women (16)—an oversimplification of the natures and temperaments of black women, to be sure, but an indicator of Sandburg's *intended* sympathy for them and the working class culture in which many of them lived. Sandburg also reports in his autobiography that his father, an accordion player, expressed the opinion that "the Negroes played better, 'more loud and clear and you get the tune better'" (85). Indeed, Sandburg wrote about African Americans in Chicago in a series of articles following the 1919 riots, where he expressed how "appalled" he was "at the savagery of events" (Niven 341), printing the so-called radical NAACP platform and speaking with Joel Spingarn regarding the drowning of Eugene Williams (Niven 338).

Looking at Sandburg's poetry from this time, one can see clearly telegraphed some of the concerns, scenes, language, and structure of Hughes's poems, especially in "Nigger," "Harrison Street Court," "Old Timers," "Caboose Thoughts," "Dancer," "My People," and "Upstream," the latter also employed by Sterling Brown in "Strong Men." Here Hughes's concerns with the African and African American heritage, pride in that heritage, the cabarets and the blighted lives of performers in them, the street prostitutes, and later even the taint of commercialism find expression as Sandburg explores the tough urban street scene with unflinching eyes. If this is not always necessarily the tough, jaded, cynical, but energetic and tenacious spirit of the African American blues music tradition, it hangs the same faded overalls over its bony frame. Listening to Sandburg recordings of his poetry for Caedmon and Spoken Arts, one can hear a whispered weariness in his delivery, an evocative quaver that tells us that one part of this unequivocally *American* poetry is the blues.

Between 1918 and 1927 Sandburg made references to jazz in "Singing Nigger," "Honky Tonk in Cleveland, Ohio," "Jazz Fantasia," "Vaudeville Dancer," "The Windy City," and "Snatch of Sliphorn Jazz," and "Jazz Fantasia" has itself been noted for its syncopation-like effects (Niven 355) that seem to stem from his use of alliteration and onomatopoeia, as well as a mixed prosaic and elevated diction and cadence. Sandburg includes references to blues specifically in "Band Concert" (1918), "Honky Tonk in Cleveland, Ohio" (1920), and "Vaudeville Dancer" (1920). Interestingly, all three seem to relate to the recordings of the Original Dixieland Jazz Band, the white jazz group that helped inaugurate the popular jazz craze with their 1917 recordings, particularly the first, "Livery Stable Blues," to which Sandburg refers both in "Band Concert" and "Vaudeville Dancer." With its manic pace and lunatic barnyard sounds, "Livery Stable Blues" at times seems almost a parody of jazz—indeed Paul Whiteman parodied it at the famous 1924 concert at the Aeolian Hall, though much to his chagrin the audience actually responded warmly to what Whiteman considered to be a crude and primitive work (Sudhalter 23–24). In "Band Concert" (reprinted by Louise Bogan in her anthology) Sandburg seems to employ the song for just that reason—a nod to the silliness and superficiality of a public entertainment. As does "Band Concert," "Honky Tonk" mocks the "pony neighs and the tuba jackass snorts" of a jazz band fronting a "hopeless quartet of white hopes" singing repetitively "I got the blues," as if that captured the depth of experience and spirit of the blues tradition. Of course, the Original Dixieland Band was preceded by the Six Brown Brothers, whose own usage of such animal sounds and sounds of human laughter were displayed in 1911 on "The Bullfrog and the Coon" (*Those Moaning Saxophones).* In that same era, the echoic "hollering" of Jaybird Coleman on "Boll Weevil" (1927) and George "Bullet" Williams on "Frisco Leaving Birmingham" (1928), as well as even the broad glissandi and tremolo on the slide guitar on Jim and Bob's "St. Louis Blues" (1933), could be considered to be in the realm of these melismatic "animal" sounds. Much later, the heavy vibratos of Ben Webster, Illinois Jacquet, and especially Albert Ayler could be compared to animal bleatings such as mule braying as well.

A group of cartoonists in the honky-tonk, whose job it is to find humor in or create humor from frequently serious or topical issues, can only "weep in their beer" at the ludicrousness of the scene, while ship riveters play footsie with prostitutes in a meaningless parody of love (164). In this, Sandburg mocks the contemporary notions of pop-jazz as a soundtrack for the ludicrous lives of people trapped in the illusions of pop culture. In "Vaudeville Dancer," Elsie Flimmerwon has diverged from the path set out for her by her working-class parents, defying her mother's orders to "keep off the streets." For that act of resistance Elsie is rewarded by becoming a star vaudeville performer, though her act, which climaxes with her "shimmying a fast shimmy to 'The Livery Stable Blues,'" seems somewhat lightweight and superficial. And it seems all the more ridiculous for the Flimmerwon-shimmy-shimmy repetition, which identifies her so strongly with the fad dance, and the silly sounds of barnyard hilarity in the song itself. Significantly, her father's movements are described with a kind of dance language as well, as he moves "with the locomotor ataxia shuffle" (251), presumably an ailment caused by his employment. The juxtaposition of the shimmy dance and the ataxia shuffle undercut the seriousness of her "work" even more, though perhaps she can be seen as following in her father's footsteps after all. The question remains whether Elsie Flimmerwon has "won" at all, or is she only, like the S-shaped line outside the theatre, a snaking transient phenomenon of the street.

The reference to "locomotor," perhaps a reference to craziness ("loco" motor) as well as the railroad machine, establishes the connection between blues and jazz, the city, and the machine that seemed important to a variety of artists in the early twentieth century. At the end of *The Education of Henry Adams*, Adams confronts this new city in 1905, what he calls the "Nunc Age" as reflected in the energy it generates:

> The outline of the city became frantic in its effort to explain something that defied meaning. Power seemed to have outgrown its servitude and

> to have asserted its freedom. The cylinder had exploded, and thrown great masses of stone and stem against the sky. The city had the air and movement of hysteria, and the citizens were crying, in every accent of anger and alarm that the new forces at any cost must be brought under control. Prosperity never before imagined, power never yet wielded by man, speed never reached by anything but a meteor, had made the world irritable, nervous, querulous, unreasonable and afraid. All New York was demanding new men, and all the new forces, condensed into corporations, were demanding a new type of man—a man with ten times the endurance, energy, will and mind of the old type—for whom they were ready to pay millions at sight . . . A traveler in the highways of history looked out of the club window on the turmoil of Fifth Avenue, and felt himself in Rome, under Diocletian, witnessing the anarchy, conscious of the compulsion, eager for the solution, but unable to conceive whence the next impulse was to come or how it was to act. The two-thousand-years failure of Christianity roared upward from Broadway, and no Constantine the Great was in sight. (499–500)

And in short, he was afraid approaching it from his perspective, and seeing that "[t]he new man could only be a child born of contact between the new and the old energies" (500), though some, like Joyce and Antheil, pushed way out ahead.

In 1913, composer Claude Debussy declared that "[a] century of aeroplanes deserves its own music" (McCleery 14), and, indeed, it would have it. André Villeneuve noted that white jazz musicians in Paris in the twenties, for example, had transformed the (primitive black) music into an analogue for American culture—"mechanical and industrial" (Jackson 76). The freneticism they heard in jazz, the shifting cacophonous sounds, the unrelenting drive, the percussiveness, they associated with the relentless rush of city life. Fritz Lang's masterpiece *Metropolis* (1927) was an early screen treatment of the encroaching futurist machine age, also reflected in the music of Prokofiev, Antheil, and Honegger. Charlie Chaplin, who had published in Robert Coady's journal *The Soil* (1916–1917) alongside modernists Gertrude Stein and Pablo Picasso (Richardson II: 296), was placed by Hart Crane "with the poets (of today)" in honor of his artistry (Crane, *Library of America* 255). He would capture this futurist freneticism in his 1936 masterpiece *Modern Times*, which was vaguely anticipated by a film prepared by the Women's Bureau of the Department of Education in 1931. *Behind the Scenes in the Machine Age* depicts optimistically ways to avoid human waste on the assembly line established by Ford for his Model T in 1913—making the environment look more relaxed and harmonious than it actually was. The blues singer was not above embracing the power of the machine as a metaphor for her sexuality, either: Blind Blake recorded "Panther Squall Blues" in 1928, coupling the natural image in the title with "She got Elgin movements and a twenty-year guarantee," a spectacularly vivid description of his woman's acrobatically sexual charms. Not to be outdone, Cleo Gibson recorded "I've Got Ford Movement in My Hips" (1929), and Memphis Minnie, in "New Dirty Dozens (1930), chimed in:

> Now the funniest thing I ever seen
> Tom cat jumping on a sewing machine.
> Sewing machine run so fast
> Sewed ninety-nine stitches in his yas yas yas.

Embracing symbols of nature or the machine age, blues singers found reflections of their power and spirit everywhere in the world. American composer George Frederick McKay heard this in Sandburg's work, constructing a ballet entitled *Epoch: An American Dance Symphony* (1935) that tracked American literature from the romanticism of Edgar Allan Poe to the pastoralism of Sidney Lanier to the exploration of Walt Whitman to Sandburg's twentieth-century "Machine Age Blues." McKay modifies the fanfares, rumbling drum rolls, breezy movements, and light blues rhythms of the Whitman section into a noisy, clanging, percussive, syncopated, call-and-response, whistling, rivet-pulsed, sweeping, escalating locomotive rhythm in "Machine Age Blues." The saxophones blow discordant whistle sounds, and ostinato piano bass notes, sometimes almost boogie woogie–like, suggest a herky-jerky train-car clatter, leading to a pleasant pop-jazz melody that erupts once again into a polyrhythmic swirl of discordance that fades into hypnotic rhythm at the end of the movement. Each of the two sections has its slow rhythms, but Whitman's is the footsteps of a heavy but necessary trek, while Sandburg's is a blues-like dirge, gesturing toward the I-IV-V pattern while diverging, and using blue notes in the solo. As a poet of the city, of Chicago, Sandburg becomes, for McKay, a poet of the machine age that he associates with the blues—not only the tone of the songs and the sadness of the feelings, but the African-based modalities that helped express the frantic nature of modern life in the big city for a country changing through migration from a rural pastoralism to an urban crucible. Though McKay calls the drama "at present . . a tragedy" (McKay 4), the story is unfinished, leaving the future of America, and blues and jazz as an expression of it, shrouded. In McKay's mind, as in a number of others, the Sandburg, the city, and the blues were intimately connected.

When Sandburg said "Good Morning, America" in 1928 in his book of the same title, he walked and welcomed with the spirit of Whitman. Here was a twentieth-century Midwestern American bard who addressed and embraced—at least in poetry—all those, especially the poor working folks, who gave America the spirit it had. The title was a salutation, a recognition of the underappreciated diverse elements of American culture, an affirmation to counter the overwhelming "no in thunder" frequently directed at America's lower classes and countercultural picaros. The blues was there among those folks, in the body and in the mind, in the wind and in the fog, and in the subject matter and rhythms of the language, and all these were in Sandburg's heart.

"Baby Song of the Four Winds" (1927) was a poem that partook of African American vernacular music in soul and language. Indeed, nine out of sixteen of the lines of the poem have a demonstrable association with the blues and spiritual music traditions. The poem begins with the plea "Let me be your baby" (*Complete Poems* 342), the language and sentiment of a great number of blues songs from the 1920s on, including Alice Carter's "I Want My Daddy Now" (1921), utilizing the daddy/baby scenario common in many blues songs. Ma Rainey's "Southern Blues" (1923), with its line "let me be your rag doll," is one of the earliest employments of this formulaic phrase. White blues singer Jimmie Rodgers's recasting of traditional blues lyrics in "Let Me Be Your Sidetrack," recorded in 1931 with black guitarist Clifford Gibson (recorded earlier by Papa Charlie Jackson in 1925 and New Orleans Willie Jackson in 1926), and other titular phrases such as "Let Me Be Your Bo Weavil" (1939), "Let Me Be Your Boss" (1941), "Let Me Be Your Butcher" (1936), "Let Me Be Your Playmate" (1938), and "Let Me Be Your Winder" (1937) all testify to the commonality of such phrases in blues lyrics (Godrich et al. 1199). The sidetrack lyric, it should be noted, is also a part of the tradition of sexual railroad imagery in the blues, which, as we have said, has its sexual dimensions. These other title phrases have sexual connotations as well.

This blends associatively with another common phrase in African American vernacular music: "rock me," connecting the "baby" of line one with the rocking motion related to calming babies. "Rock me" was likely first employed in the African American vernacular music tradition in spiritual and jubilee songs before appearing in the blues, in the way that the biblical phrase "how long" appeared in spirituals before becoming the title of a hugely popular blues standard, "How Long—How Long Blues," recorded by Leroy Carr in 1928, as well as in 1921 by Albert Hunter under the title "How Long, Sweet Daddy, How Long." In fact, there are some nineteen titles, some recorded multiple times, recorded by blues singers before 1943. It is relatively common to "borrow" something from the "sacred" tradition and make it function in a "secular" manner (indeed, as we have said, the African tradition does not differentiate so sharply), and this is especially useful because it provides an even more complex concatenation of meanings by being both sacred and secular. It also demonstrates that there is not as much of a boundary between those traditions as there might be in conventional Western societies. Sacred and secular exist on a continuum, both being an essential part of daily thought and life that merge philosophically in a liminal area of culture. Songs such as "Rock My Soul in the Bosom of Abraham," "Rock Me, Shake Me," "Rock, Church, Rock," and "Rock of Ages" sit alongside "Rock, Aunt Dinah, Rock" (1925) by Leola B. and Kid Wesley Wilson, "Rock That Thing" (1929) by Lil Johnson, "Rock It in Rhythm" (1938) by Tampa Red, and "Rock Me in the Groove" (1941) by Sweet Georgia Brown. "The Rocks" was even an early name for boogie woogie piano style, recorded under that name by Clay Custer (George Thomas) in 1923, and the rocking, repetitive left-hand performance motion provides a vigorous sexual motion to imitate. More contemporary blues fans know the phrase "Rock Me, Baby" from recordings by B. B. King (1961/2) and Muddy Waters (1971).

It is even possible to locate both "rock" and "warm," which Sandburg also uses in line three, in the same blues song: Blind Willie McTell's "Warm It Up To Me" (1933), where he "shows these little women how to eagle-rock," following immediately with "you got to warm it up to me." Eagle-rock, in its reference to a dance, also becomes a euphemism for sexual intercourse, and "warm it up to me" is a clear invitation to the sexual dance. As such, the reference to "baby" in line one has not only connotations of infancy, but broadens to include implications of spiritual need, bodily movement, and sexual desire. Since blatant reference to sexuality in "polite" society was at that time considered gauche, the references to "rock" and "rock me warm" suggest a status that the blues was said to possess at the time—it was low-down and earthy. Thus, "rock me low" solicits the kind of "comfort" said to be characteristic of the blues community, belly-rubbing lyrically with spiritual stimulation.

References to a personified wind are also relatively common in the blues tradition. The wind is granted a kind of agency in the traditional lyric featured in Willie Baker's "No No Blues" (1929): "I'm a stranger, just blowed in your town." The wind is a harbinger of incongruous hard times in Walter Davis's "Howling Wind Blues" (1930): "The North wind is begin to howling, but the skies are pretty and blue." In 1953, Muddy Waters recorded "blow wind, blow wind, blow my baby back to me," contrasting an active and beneficial agency with the person who is being passively blown from town to town in Baker's lyric. In a more mystical vein, Peetie Wheatstraw projected his fantastical persona into the clouds and faraway lands in his "Pete Wheatstraw" (1930):

> Now this is Peetie Wheatstraw this morning, people want to know
> why do I frown (twice)
> Some say I frown in distant lands, some say I frown over the rising
> clouds.

In this case, the blues singer, who has had the racial mask of inferiority, docility, laziness, and so on forced upon him, gives himself a rollicking, funny name to retain the humor, but transforms the mask into a persona of mystical power, taking back his name, his identity, and his power—one way that the blues performer can undo the chains of Jim Crow musically. The power of this mask might be very apparent to literary artists working with personae (Pound, Eliot, Sandburg, Hughes, and Brown); visual artists working with tribal fetishes and masks (Picasso's "Les Demoiselles D'Avignon" from his African-influenced period of 1907-1909); white musicians working in blackface (Jolson, Sophie Tucker); composers constructing an American identity (Paul Whiteman, Georges Antheil, or Dana Suesse). He is more than William Bunch (his mundane daily "slave" name); he is Peetie Wheatstraw, High Sheriff from Hell and the Devil's Son-In-Law. Fats Domino even had a rhythm and blues hit with "Let the Four Winds Blow" (1961), a love song making clear use of folk materials to make his play. Now, of course, the wind plays a role in many folk traditions around the world, so the suggestion again is not that Sandburg necessarily took this from the blues, but that it certainly is not a violation of the tradition to which he seems to be making allusions so regularly in "Baby Song."

In stanza three, Sandburg requests of the North wind, "Change my ways," and such "changing" lyrics also occur in the blues lyric tradition, frequently relating to changing one's mind. However, "change my ways," "change your ways," and "change his/her ways" occur commonly as well. Blind Lemon Jefferson uses the phrase in "Christmas Eve Blues" (1928), Clifford Gibson in "Whiskey Moan Blues" (1929), Peetie Wheatstraw in "Cut Out Blues" (1936), and Sonny Boy Williamson in "Blue Bird Blues (1937). This changing is sometimes a result of a partner not "behaving," and Sandburg employs "make me behave" in stanza three as well. The use of the word "behave" in this context occurs in Blind Blake's "Too Tight" (1926), Bessie Tucker's "Penitentiary" (1928), Jake Jones's "Southern Sea Blues" (1929), Alice Moore's "Lonesome Dream Blues" (1930), Leroy Carr's "Blues Before Sunrise" (1934), and Minnie Wallace's "The Cockeyed World" (1935). Even Sandburg's phrase "shake me loose" has blues parallels, in the lyrics of Big Bill Broonzy's "Eagle Riding Papa" (1930): "We'll make you loose, we'll make you tight, / Make you shake it 'til broad daylight"; and white blues-influenced singer Sophie Tucker, who sings "I shook the shimmy now I don't pay the rent" (1919), making obvious the connotations of "shaking" and dancing. Of course, this sentiment has occurred elsewhere besides the blues tradition; and it is not suggested that Sandburg knew these specific recordings. Rather, with all the other connections to blues in the poem, and Sandburg's interest in folk materials, including the blues, as a collector, performer, and poet, it seems very possible that Sandburg was attempting to imbue this poem with the language, rhythms, and spirit of the blues music tradition.

This is a quite regular association of the poem with the content of blues lyrics, and they contribute feelings of desire and vigor, as well as double and triple entendre, to Sandburg's poem, giving it the energy, spirit, and toughness of the lower-class African American. In the context of this poem, the request for the four winds to take care of the speaker expresses the desperate need of the individual to be nurtured, combined with the implied absence of human nurturing. Blues songs and spirituals, of course, are full of lyrics about the motherless child, such as Ben Norsingle's "Motherless Blues" (1928) and Elvie Thomas's "Motherless Child Blues" (1930). Blind Lemon Jefferson even sings "I am motherless, fatherless, sister and brotherless, too" in "Broke and Hungry" (1926). This sentiment likely emerged from the conditions of slavery, where family ties were frequently suppressed or broken by the selling of family members, continuing as migrations from South to North or restless wandering, looking for better times, followed emancipation. The appeal to natural forces here represents the need to find comfort and support universally, in the four corners of the world, calling upon spirits other than God for support, from childhood's comfort rocking to adulthood's sexual sustenance, from beginning of day to the end, inside the home and out. This need, and its apparent lack in the poem, makes it ideally adapted to the spirit and subject matter of the blues.

Langston Hughes had made use of some of this language in his poem "Song For a Banjo Dance," a Paul Laurence Dunbar-influenced poem (*Collected Poetry* 29). Hughes first published the poem in *The Crisis* in September 1922, and later published it in his collection *The Weary Blues* (1926)—both before Sandburg's publication of his poem in *Good Morning, America*. In Hughes's poem, the speaker implores the woman to "Do that rockin' step" (*Collected Poems* 29), with clear dancing and sexual implications. Sandburg's "Shake me loose" parallels Hughes's repetition of "Shake your brown feet" and Sandburg's "Shake 'em low" relates to Hughes's "banjo's sobbing low," relating both described events to energetic movement and unhappy or base feelings and behavior. Hughes creatively personifies the banjo as the vehicle for expressing sadness in his poem, relating to the blues tradition of "making the instrument talk"—rooting the poem even more fully in the African American musical tradition. Hughes's poem also includes the regular repetitions of the words "shake" and rock," as well as reference to the sun, whereas Sandburg treats the wind. Furthermore, Hughes's poem "Ma Man" (*Collected Poems* 66–67), first published in 1926, makes reference to "eagle-rocking," with implications for both dancing and sexuality as well. All of these elements suggest that there is precedent in poetry, as well as in blues lyrics, for the kinds of words and techniques Sandburg employed in "Baby Song of the Four Winds." Sandburg had made earlier references than Hughes to "blues" in his poems, but Hughes's masterful usage of the tradition frequently both differed from and surpassed Sandburg's in terms of imbuing poems with the blues spirit.

Sandburg was known as a collector of folk songs and a folk performer as well. He was particularly interested in presenting folk materials to a non-academic audience—clearly also an interest of Hughes—and his *American Songbag*, a collection of 260 folk songs (including over a dozen blues songs) was published by Harcourt, Brace in 1927. It was one of the earliest collections prepared for such a mainstream audience (one might see W. C. Handy's collection *Blues*, published in 1926 in the form of composed songs rooted in folk materials and arranged for piano and voice, as a kind of predecessor, and an important one, and Sandburg indeed references it in his book). Among the arrangers for the tunes in the songbag was a young Ruth Crawford, future American composer, who, with her husband Charles Seeger, helped focus American attentions on the nation's folk song heritage from the 1930s on, through publishing, compositions, and transcriptions of songs in the Archive of Folk Song. Charles had earlier been an IWW sympathizer, and in the 1930s influenced the leftist Composers' Collective to aim at generating a simpler and popularly oriented music that would appeal to the masses—which soon became the Popular Front artistic aesthetic that influenced Hughes's artistic aesthetic in that decade as well.

Sandburg also evinced an early interest in recording with music, as Hughes embraced later in recordings of his work by Josh White, Paul Robeson, the cast of *Street Scene*, and others, and in his own recordings in the 1950s. Sandburg made his first recording the year before the *Songbag* was released, on March 4, 1926, for Victor Records, performing the ballad "The Boll Weevil." He released recordings subsequently on Musicraft, Decca, Lyrichord, Tiara, Society (coupled with some recordings by blues and folk singer Josh White), and other labels, and while the recordings never quite seem comfortable or stylistically "authentic," they do have an important place in the mainstream popularizing of folk music. Not many were blues recordings—"Careless Love," "Frankie and Johnnie," "C. C. Rider," "The Blues Ain't Nothin'" are among the songs he recorded—but the songs included in the book and among his recordings, and the quote he included in *Songbag* from Dorothy Scarborough, made his sentiments about Negro folk songs clear: "I urge that as a song hunter I should rather hear a Negro in the cornfield or on the levee or in a tobacco factory, than to hear [operatic coloratura soprano] Galli-Curci grand-operize" (*Songbag* 224). Zora Neale Hurston echoed such a sentiment, arguing in 1934 that she preferred the singing of a "cathead man in Florida" to that of Roland Hayes and Paul Robeson (Hemenway 54).

Early and acknowledged influences on the work of Langston Hughes, Lindsay and Sandburg provided some interesting and useful cues for Hughes's work with regard to embracing vernacular materials in his poetry, particularly urban ones that reflected the hard pavement of city streets. This was due in part to the influence of their political leanings on their poetic aesthetics. Heirs to the spirit and tradition of American radical poetry, both Sandburg and Lindsay were part of the Chicago "school" who looked back to Whitman and his champion, Socialist Horace Traubel, as well as to the Wobbly poets of the hobo jungles and open roads, for their precursors. From late 1907, Sandburg was involved in Wisconsin Social-Democratic politics, writing in the state for various newspapers, serving as a secretary to the socialist mayor of Milwaukee in 1910–1912, and then joining the *Chicago Evening World* in 1912. Though Sandburg allowed his Socialist Party membership to expire around 1914, he continued to sympathize with Socialist causes at other stages in his career. Lindsay, never as committed to the party as Sandburg, nonetheless wrote "Why I Vote the Socialist Ticket" expressing his dissatisfaction with contemporary social and political currents, a dissatisfaction that also found its way into the subject matter and style of his poetry-performances (subtitle of an early draft read "who am not a Socialist") (Camp 840). Though neither writer employed allusions to blues with anything near the regularity of Hughes, each offered early instances of some of the literary possibilities of blues, though with more reference to mainstream American culture than to African American resonances. As the 1920s approached, the blues was increasingly a new and exciting genre about to make history in a very commercialized form the comparison of which to its origins raises issues of ethics and authenticity. But both in music and poetry undoubtedly broke aesthetic ground for the fertile fields of Langston Hughes's blues poems.

IV

Less well known at the beginning of the twenty-first century but far more prominent at the beginning of the twentieth was Maxwell Bodenheim (1892–

1954), a poet and novelist who spent from around 1900–1915 in Chicago, publishing both in *Poetry* and *The Little Review*. He was well acquainted with a number of Chicago Renaissance writers, such as Sandburg, Lindsay, Masters, Sherwood Anderson, Floyd Dell, Theodore Dreiser, and Ben Hecht, and was known amongst prominent writers in New York where he moved in 1915. He even found his way onto a six-person "literary team" chosen by Ezra Pound in 1915 that "would beat anything that England could show among the new generation" (Stock 184), though by 1920 T. S. Eliot was calling him "an odd American Jew" and "rather pathetic, although foolish" (*Letters* 391). William Carlos Williams, in *Kora in Hell* (1920), calls him "a heroic figure" and "an Isaiah of the butterflies" (29)—presumably meaning a saint or a prophet of the beautiful—and Bodenheim met with the *Others* group at Williams's house, along with Marcel Duchamp, Alfred Kreymborg, and Man Ray (Watson, *Strange* 299). Interestingly, surrealist-dadaist-modernist artists had a special interest in African music and jazz, and dadaists were were known to frequently play that music at their meetings, though with a primitivist turn. Bodenheim also appeared in African American poet and critic William Stanley Braithwaite's *Anthology of Magazine Verse and Year Book of American Poetry*, a popular yearly anthology published from 1913–1929, where he was praised by Marianne Moore in 1926 (Moore 33). Today, he is at best a sparsely indexed entry in a few critical works on major modernist writers, his life past 1934 a ruin and his death an ignominious scandal.

But in a number of his works from the 1920s—after he had moved from Chicago, though he is generally grouped, if mentioned at all, with Chicago Renaissance writers, likely because of marked similarities to writing of the Chicago Renaissance writers, especially Lindsay—Bodenheim made prominent use of elements of the blues. References to black culture pop up in early poems such as "Chorus-Girl" (1918), which is one of a series of poems from around the time by such folks as Raymond G. Dandridge ("Zalka Peetruza"), Claude McKay, and Langston Hughes ("Midnight Dancer," "Nude Young Dancer") that deal with the bittersweet lives and experiences of objectified female dancers in clubs. "Negroes," too tells of blighted lives reflected in the voices and songs of people who had borrowed songs "from their elders," a man whose "life had found refuge in his voice" (*Selected Poems* 37), and a woman whose voice sounded "Like a quavering, feverish laugh / Softened in a long-forgotten cradle" (*Selected Poems* 38). Bodenheim is clearly attuned to the valuable artistic and survival gifts of black ancestry, as well as the hard, bitter laugh of the blues's "laughing to keep from crying" passed from generation to generation, even if he does not reference either nominally or formally elements of the blues.

In *Introducing Irony: A Book of Poetic Short Stories and Poems* (1922), Bodenheim published a poem, "Pronounced Fantasy," that made use of two snatches of blues lyrics to help portray the importance of the African American vernacular tradition, the conflicted mental state of an African American character, as well as the conflicted emotions of the speaker of the poem toward the woman, the vernacular tradition, his sexual attraction, and his feelings about African Americans more generally. The first section, which takes place in a location where the woman is playing a poorly tuned piano, foreshadows Langston Hughes's poem "The Weary Blues," in location and tone (*Collected Poems* 50); the second section, with its quotation from a now-well-known railroad folk-blues song employed by W. C. Handy in *Blues: An Anthology* (1926) and quoted by Hughes in his 1941 essay "Songs Called the Blues" (144), focuses on one of the major elements of the subject matter of the blues—geographic mobility—as well as one of the major symbols of African American folklore, the railroad. Bodenheim's use of specific African American blues lyrics in his poem just a couple of years after Mamie Smith helped spark a blues "craze" (with the song "Crazy Blues") demonstrates how quickly pop culture of the time was finding its way into literary expression, as authors attempted to express the times. The Newsreel, Biography, and Camera Eye techniques employed by Dos Passos three years later in *Manhattan Transfer* (1925) make use of just such snippets to capture the dizzying panorama of contemporary urban existence as it affected the lives of people being emptied into the city like wretched refuse through a garbage chute. Bodenheim's interpolations of lyrics provide important social and psychological markers for understanding the generator, object, and nature of the fantasy.

The poem introduces ambiguity of perspective and meaning from the first encounter with the title. Is "pronounced" an adjective, denoting that this is emphatically a fantasy? Or is it a verb, encouraging the reader to consider this a fantasy by directing the reader to the pronunciation of the following noun, "fantasy"? Whose fantasy is this? And why are we dealing with fantasy rather than reality? Or is it a reality that the speaker is trying to mask as a fantasy? And why would he do that? Even at the title level, the poem begins to question preconceived images and inadequate binaries (black/white; imprisonment/freedom; sacred/profane) that form and inform the fantasy in the boxcar of his experience.

The first line of section one presents us with an image that seems to assert existentialist humanity—"A Negro girl with skin"—yet the second line, "As black as a psychic threat," retreats frightfully into the fear of the African American as other, a haunting vision whose presence, though human, functions at a phantom level. She clearly represents more than she is in the mind of the speaker. She is socially codified as subhuman while clearly fitting the definition of human; a physical presence while clearly a psychological and social problem and challenge; and she is black and racially taboo, though oh-so-sensuous with her "swells of blonde hair" that bespeak whiteness and intensifying excitement. The ambiguity of feeling, the fear and excitement, arise from the forbidden blackness marked by the blonde hair as a violated boundary of desire in miscegenation. Positive designations such as "plentiful," "exultation," "quivering," and "strong" struggle with "threat," "vanquished," "shrouded," "violence," "prisoner," and "cell," while the notion of "buffoonery" often associated with minstrelsy and coon songs seems to mark the fulcrum upon which his conflicting feelings balance precariously. The speaker seems to be wrestling, then, with the spectrum of feelings run through the sociocultural and psychological alembic of his creative imagination. In Bodenheim's psychological portrait, this tragic mulatta is also clearly empowered, and triumphant in her art, even as she is imprisoned in society.

This is a faculty that the woman clearly possesses as well. She is a performer, a singer-pianist in the blues tradition that in the early 1920s was dominated in the commercial realm by women, and included other singer-pianists such as Victoria Spivey, Addie Spivey, Berniece Edwards, and Gladys Bentley. However, hers is not the glitzy opulence of the stage blues performer. She is, as in Langston Hughes's "The Weary Blues," the anonymous blues singer who nonetheless represents the bedrock strength and power of the tradition. Though she makes use of the "violence of minor chords" (often associated with the blues, which she is about to sing), nonetheless this violence and the strength of her hands are transformative—what was described earlier as audible proof that one can find spiritual unity and euphony even in dissonant sounds. Though her fingers are described as "vanquished" by the performance, it is this "vanquished performance" that provides her "midnight exultation"—a light in the darkness of her world—and encapsulates in her performance the tragedy of her life and triumph of her art. Her voice is described as a prisoner, expressing an anguish captive to the social definitions that pigeonhole her, but it is also a powerful, masculine entity unto itself. With his own hands, the embodied voice is "turn[ing] the bars of his cell / Into musical strings," from which, presumably, he can escape. Significantly, the skin and hair on which he had initially focused gives way to the "heart" that she expresses on the piano, not merely the visual cues freighted with social meaning but an aural and artistic cue that goes beyond the surface of his racial and gender preconceptions. Of course, he is not speaking of a literal jail cell, but a more powerful figurative one, one which traps the voice in the speaker's conflicting preconceptions even as the music empowers the voice to transform the bars and pluck the strings of his imprisonment. The male gaze of the speaker attempts to control the objectified adolescent (termed a "girl," not a woman, she may be either), who nonetheless reveals strength and passion enough to "lecture" about her feelings in musical terms.

The subject matter of her song is familiar in the blues tradition, even at this early date: lyrics about packing one's trunk to leave are recurrent in such songs as "Leavin' Gal Blues" by Bertha Henderson (1928), "Milk Cow Blues" (1930) by Sleepy John Estes, Tommie Bradley's "Pack Up Her Trunk Blues" (1930), or "Packin' Trunk Blues" (1935) by Leadbelly. So too is the sentiment of disappointment, as typified by the lyrics of Barbecue Bob's "Barbecue Blues" (1927): "Did you ever dream lucky, wake up cold in hand?"; and the notion that disappointment can lead to the blues and drug consumption, as in Sara Martin's "Death Sting Me Blues" (1929):

> Blues you made me roll and tumble, you made me weep and sigh.
> Made me use cocaine and whiskey, but you wouldn't let me die.

In this lyric, however, the girl bumps her head against the lowered ceiling of her possibilities, faces those limitations, "affirms" them, then sarcastically dismisses them through her acknowledgment of external forces that prevail in her life. Her language itself is set apart from the language of the speaker. It is italicized, phonetic, dramatically rendered, rhyming, primarily monosyllabic, and related in the first person. It is lyric, personal, heartfelt—extremely realistic, yet expressive of the illusion of satisfaction in a limiting world. To express the ambiguity and ambivalence, to make it sound real and create a space for its discussion, or at least acknowledgment, is in some ways to overcome it. The threat, the buffoonery, the shroud or mask, the strength and endurance and resolve are all parts of the image of African Americans in the white mind. The parrot symbolizes the clueless white response to African Americans, the squawking repetition of meaningless sounds coming from the vulgar space, white well of filth, the white spittoon. The girl responds to this unwelcome interruption with keen surgical skill, her "cursing / With religious incision" combining elements of the sacred (her self-defense of her art) with the profane (her use of socially unacceptable language). In this, she reflects the combination of elements of the sacred and profane in the blues tradition, its elements of artistic, psychological, social, and spiritual comfort on the one hand combined with its spittoon-weary worldliness on the other. Four years later, Langston Hughes would publish "Brass Spittoons" (*Collected Poems* 86) treating the spittoon as a symbol of the labor available to African Americans in the Jim Crow world, and seeing cleaning spittoons ironically as a spiritual endeavor.

The parrot, typically, does not stop its noise but continues the litany of squawking while the girl plays another song—presumably the song included in part two of the poem. However, the parrot does stop "in the midst of his squawk" at the sight of "her long blonde hair." One might question whether he is perplexed, shocked, horrified, or excited, but of course as a parrot he is none of those things. However, as a spokesperson (spokesbird?) for empty inane white attitudes toward African Americans in its ignorant commentary, his cessation of sound presents interesting possibilities. The long blonde hair, as a marker of miscegenation—and a very public one—raises social and psychological issues deeply imbedded in the white American mind. As the frequently unacknowledged taboo of race relations in America, it represents not only the lie of natural racial separation and superiority, but the acknowledgment of the attraction to what is in the public voice repulsive and shameful. It is as if white folks are able to see part of themselves in the girl, and their derisive comments are interrupted by this concrete manifestation of the false images and lies of racial hegemony.

Whereas we had been set down into the scene of her performance in part one, which suggests an "accidental" occasion, in part two the speaker tells us he has "found" the girl, so there is a deliberateness of encounter here. That suggests that he remains intrigued, presumably by the ambiguity and ambivalence she continues to represent for him, the "humour of sunlight" in the natural world disputing "the gloom of her skin," her racial experience in the world. Where in part one she was described as having "sensual swells" of blonde hair, in part two her feet and arms are "bare," for the speaker "sensual disappointments." Now she is in the process of balancing a burden, but a rather strange, seemingly light one that paradoxically dominates her demeanor and composure. It is not the trunk she was unable to find in her earlier blues lyric, but an egg, white like the spittoon, with a fragile, delicate shell that protects (barely) and hides what is beneath its surface. Beneath that surface may be the food she lacks—anticipating a Langston Hughes poem again, she is dining "upon the air," as Hughes later wrote in "Evenin' Air Blues" (*Collected Poems* 225)—or the life that it represents. That life is despairing to the point of suicide in the traditional blues lyric she uses, and yet enduring in its last-minute snatching of her head from the steely death on the tracks:

> Gonna lay mah head right down upon dat—
> Down upon dat railroad track!
> Gonna rest mah head right down upon dat railroad track.

An wen the train goes by—'m boy—
Ahm gonna snatch it back. (60)

This lyric was included in Mamie Smith's groundbreaking "Crazy Blues" (1920), and a version of this lyric was also recorded by Buddy Boy Hawkins in 1927 ("Snatch It Back Blues") and another by Will Wright for the Library of Congress in 1936. Countless other blues songs dealt with the subject matter and imagery of the railroad, including Papa Charlie Jackson's recording of "The Faking Blues" (1925), in which the singer boasts "I can get more women than a passenger train can haul," which was also used by white singer Jimmie Rodgers in a filmed version of his "Blue Yodel." Since the railroad and train is such a powerful symbol in African American culture, encompassing power, geographical mobility—movement, escape, and return—sexuality, and physical and spiritual transcendence among other things, it is fitting that it is the projected scene of death and resignation to/affirmation of life. She sings first that she is going to "lay" her head on the track, indicating that it is a deliberate placement, a conscious act. However, in the repeat line, which features some of the lyric improvisation perfectly appropriate to the blues, "lay" becomes "rest," indicating that the symbolism of this place in the African American vernacular tradition is, like a way station on the Underground Railroad, an avenue of liberation. And since the blues is such a powerful art form in the culture, it is fitting that it is the instrument of agency in her life. Freighted with so much meaning, the railroad is a fitting locale for the nexus of issues in her life and art.

Stylistically, Bodenheim does an interesting job of putting the lyric on the page. He renders the words ethnopoetically on the page, trying a capture the sense of performance rather than formal balance, as many lyric transcribers might have done. That is, rather than a six-line stanza, he tries to represent the rhythm of performance by rendering what would be formally lines three and four as a one-line rush of sentiment, indicating rhythmical and lyrical improvisation that is mirrored also in the sentiment of the lyrics—she intends to do one thing, but changes her mind and does something different. Thus, the spirit of performance and philosophy is presented in the poem. Additionally, Bodenheim does not overdo his presentation of African American vernacular speech. His one false move comes with the presentation of "when" as "wen": since there is no pronunciational difference, it seems unnecessary and condescending to leave out the "h" here as an indicator of difference, perhaps inferiority.

Here the speaker and girl finally actually speak to each other (something that doesn't happen in "The Weary Blues"), but only after she takes his white male gaze and breaks it on her "poignant" face. Only after this break, like the breaking of the shell of an egg, can he communicate with her about the issues she is balancing in her life, which seem to stem from that controlling gaze. We don't know whether she actually speaks to the speaker, since her lips are described as "motionless," but communication on a deeper level does seem to take place. Paradoxically, her hatred for the egg—white, fragile, and dangerous—causes her to maintain it, even though if she broke it she might open up herself, reveal her true self as opposed to the images created by the gaze. Indeed, the notion of female as "egg carrier" may well be another of the burdens she carries, limiting the scope and function of her activities in the world to procreation, which makes the suggestion of the breaking of the egg and undressing in the penultimate line carry both positive and negative implications. She is balancing "[t]he upturned remonstrance of her head," a pride and endurance she is unwilling to sacrifice, with her desire to be considered human and accepted as she is. Interestingly, since we do not know whether she actually speaks, the sentiment attributed to her at the end may be only ideas filtered through the gaze, and not hers at all. Still, the speaker at least imagines her in a different way, which is, after all, a crack in the facade that reveals the yoke of oppression.

Bodenheim's poem, then, asks us to question the perspective of the controlling gaze of racial hegemony. Behind the facade of the preconceived fantasy is a real person, a "girl" (perhaps an infantilized woman) wrestling with the ways that race and gender present her with burdens she must balance and false binaries she must negotiate. She must do this in order to free herself from her anomalous position in a black and white world that denies the transcendent nature of African American vernacular culture. However, the speaker's pursuit of the negro girl with blonde hair, with its intimations of miscegenation and sexual violence, is balanced by a desire to know her mind and life as well. If the traditional blues lyric "You don't know, you don't know my mind / When you see me laughin, I'm laughin to keep from cryin" ("You Don't Know My Mind Blues,"Clara Smith [1924]) is an accurate indicator of racial divide, then Bodenheim's poem may well be an attempt to bridge it.

Four years later, in the same year respected dilettante Carl Van Vechten published his sensational and controversial novel *Nigger Heaven* (1926), Bodenheim published *Ninth Avenue*, a mostly bleak urban chronicle in the tradition of Theodore Dreiser's *Sister Carrie* (1900), but spiced with a prominent interracial relationship and insights regarding the Harlem Renaissance, including Van Vechten's own role in its arrangement and promotion. Blanche Gelfant characterizes one incarnation of the American city novel, typified by *Sister Carrie*, as a "portrait study" that, through various events experienced by the protagonist, fleshes out the nature of the city, its dwellers, and its influence on the character, who experiences a "coming of age" (11). Bodenheim's white protagonist, rather obviously named Blanche, wanders through the stifling, claustrophobic urban wasteland that is Ninth Avenue, from one crude affair to another, until she finally breaks with her flawed, dysfunctional family's small-minded bickering and bigotry. Her excursion to Greenwich Village brings her into contact with Max Oppendorf and Ben Helgin (Bodenheim and Hecht), but more interestingly into the interracial circle that opens Blanche's mind to the social possibilities beyond the narrow-mindedness of Ninth Avenue. At the party of that interracial circle, Bodenheim introduces Blanche and his readers to the poet-publicist Eric Starling, sexual and racial politics of the Harlem Renaissance, and the blues.

Shortly before this party, on the outskirts of Greenwich Village, Blanche first encounters Margaret Wheeler, whose knowledge of the neighborhood, and unhesitating directness—she protests she is neither a criminal nor a lesbian, just a friendly person!—draws Blanche into the milieu. They meet while window shopping for clothes at a batik-shop that displays what Blanche finds to be a "soft, intricately veined gaudiness" that she terms "crazy," though "they suited her mood" (165). Margaret prefers the green and purple smocks, but Blanche prefers the blue. As Blanche transitions into this new environment, it is significant that she begins to embrace something more outrageous—though very lively, taking its "veins" into account—something crazy, and something blue. She begins to see herself in the garb of the Greenwich Village inhabitant or slummer, though she protests that she isn't one of the latter, and embraces their "outside" status as she moves from the margins to the center. The blue color of the smock, in light of what is to come, is significant.

Six years earlier, in 1920, Mamie Smith had helped precipitate an African American female blues recording craze with a song that had been known as "Harlem Blues," but whose name was changed by its composer Perry Bradford to "Crazy Blues." The song features lyrics that, after a brief introduction, proclaim "[t]here's a change in the ocean, change in the deep blue sea," but protesting that there "ain't no change in me." At this point in the text, Blanche is changing her own milieu, but a more precipitous change in her character is still some time distant. Mamie Smith protests that what has not changed in her is her love for a particular man—in fact, because that love remains, she is transformed into a sad and "crazy" person who proposes to "get myself a gun and shoot myself a cop." Blanche, on the outskirts of Greenwich Village is, like Smith, in an anomalous state, still sadly tied to her past but transitioning to a place of outrageous freedom—at least in her imagination. Both find that freedom in the blues—song or smock—and initiate their journeys,

Blanche through the agency of Margaret, whose relationships with men, like that in Smith's blues, have been unsuccessful. Margaret is herself in a socially anomalous state in her time. Significantly, as Blanche admires Margaret's figure, with "plumpness crowded in the buttocks and upper thighs," her attention turns to the "large blue eyes" set in the brown skin of Margaret's face (166). What she has not mentioned is now made clear: Margaret is mixed race, and the mix of black and white characteristics marks her to Blanche as "different" (166). However, she is an appropriate figure for Blanche to encounter in the border area of her journey from Ninth Avenue into this bohemian realm. She is someone who has already blended, telegraphing Blanche's future journey, and though the blue eyes are a sign of whiteness here, they are also unmistakably a marker of incarnations of the black blues tradition as well.

This association of African American jazz and blues with madness or craziness was not unique to Bodenheim, of course. The notions of white folks releasing their rational, conscious minds to the "barbaric" rhythms and feelings of black folks was to them like going crazy, going primitive. Songs from the 1920s connecting the two included Charles and Effie Tyus's "Jazz Crazy" (1925); Trixie Smith's "The World's Jazz Crazy, and So Am I" (1925); Mamie Smith's "Goin' Crazy with the Blues" (1926); and the Richmond Jazz Quartette's "Gone Jazz Crazy" (1928). Duke Ellington even had "Jazz Convulsions" in 1929. (This sounds suspiciously similar to the involuntary, nervous twitching critics proclaimed were produced by boogie woogie, then rock and roll.) In *The Beautiful and the Damned* (1922), F. Scott Fitzgerald quotes a song called "Jazz-mad," which may be his own composition:

> "Out in—the shimmee sanitarium
> The jazz-mad nuts reside.
> Out in—the shimmee sanitarium
> I left my blushing bride.
> She went and shook herself insane,
> So let her shiver back again——" (435)

Fitzgerald's narrator, too, likes his "Johnston's Gardens where they danced, where a tragic negro made yearning, aching music on a saxophone until the garish hall became an enchanted jungle of barbaric rhythms and smoky laughter . . " (338), unleashing a number of racist condescensions in one rush of thought. Additionally, there was a movie called "Jazz Mad" (1928) featuring Jean Hersholt, as well as a "Jazz Mad" Terrytoon cartoon in 1931. Attracted or appalled, the white world seemed to fear and recognize that its mental health would never be the same.

Blanche joins Margaret at Clara's tearoom, a joint with lazy literary pretensions, including "cubistic plagiarisms, slovenly sketches, and illustrations meant for the average magazine's check book but not quite reaching it," with a phonograph that plays "the latest fox-trot insinuations" (169)—what passes for "hot" music by employing just a tinge of the deeper jazz and blues tradition. The title of the song, however, expresses a hope or belief counter to Smith's "Crazy Blues" and Margaret's experience: "He Never Gets Tired of Me, No, Boy, Just Never Gets Tired of Me-ee." In a genre where Julia Moody's "He'll Do You Wrong" (1925), Rosa Henderson's "He May Be Your Dog, But He's Wearing My Collar" (1923), Florence Parham's "He May Be Your Good Man On Friday" (1923), and Lucille Hegamin's "He May Be Your Man But He Comes to See Me Sometimes" (1922) are far more typical, this bit of optimism seems naive, not hardy or enduring. It suggests that the people in Clara's tearoom are, like the surroundings, pretenders at art, culture, and life, another station on the way to her encounter with Eric Starling. Blanche negotiates her way through the blond-haired, blue-eyed cynicism and manipulations of Oppendorf, the effeminacy of Bob Trussel, and the bemused, adolescent malevolence of Ben Helgin to reach the party at which she passes from Helgin's curious clutches to the arms of Starling.

The party is a satirical portrayal of one of Carl Van Vechten's New York interracial soirées. Paul Vanderin's "opulent home and managed spectacles"—Helgin calls him a "ring-leader" who is "patronizing and eulogizing the negro" (201)—feature Christopher Culbert (clearly Countee Cullen) reading poetry "filled with adored colors and sentimentality that flirted with morbidity for moments" (205); an athlete singing the spiritual "The Blood Done Signed My Name" (Paul Robeson "with a crazy, half-sobbing, swaying quaver in his voice" 206); Miss Bee Rollins of the "Down South" night club (perhaps Edith May Barnes and the Cotton Club) dancing the Charleston (206); and other folks just generally, as the name of the Miller and Lyles and James P. Johnson Broadway stage show of 1923 put it, "runnin' wild" (209). In fact, Blanche continues to associate black culture with being "wild" and "crazy." She even sees the distinctive feature of African Americans, early in her first real encounter with the culture, as perhaps "a kind of insanity" (206), though Bodenheim clearly intends for the reader to play these feelings against Blanche's own family and cultural background to catch the irony. When she began to dance with "them" and catch their "rhythmical, subtle, audacious fervor," she found herself "swung into a happy harmony with their movements in spite of herself" (207).

At this point, her eavesdropping on other conversations brings her back to the blues and craziness. One man protests that a negro woman has "put a song in [his] blood," continuing "I'm crazy about you." Another flirting "negress" sings a song to her white man: "Mamma has her teeth all filled with golden bridges 'n' diamonds small, but po-oor papa, po-o-or papa, got no teefies a-all" (208). He responds by offering to prove he does have teeth (by biting her, a kind of sexual foreplay), that she must be singing about someone else. It is, of course, a "taboo" interracial game they are playing with each other, using the blues as the agent of attraction. Significantly, the blues here speaks of the riches, "gaudy" though they may seem to the white man's culture, that nonetheless attract him to the "exoticism" of the black female—like the "crazy" prints of which Blanche thought earlier. There were, of course, blues songs that mentioned gold teeth at the time—Madlyn Davis's "Gold Tooth Papa Blues" (1928), Tommy McClennan's "Brown Skin Girl" (1939), and Bertha Lee's "Mind Reader Blues" (1934)—and Diamond Teeth Mary McClain worked on minstrel and medicine shows, and was a contemporary of Bessie Smith. Sippie Wallace also recorded a "Lazy Man Blues" (1927) in which she protests, "He ain't got no teeth." The blues is here again an important marker of difference, as well as of interracial attraction, that was helping to bring about a cultural mixture, a cultural hybridity, fed in part by fantasy but effecting in some cases a cultural intermixture nonetheless.

Once again, Bodenheim pays attention to characteristics of black performance in his presentation of lyrics. Two common characteristics of West African music and African American vernacular music, including the blues, are melisma and glissando. Melisma is the singing of two or more notes to one syllable. Bodenheim represents melisma here in his rendering of "poor" as "po-oor" and "po-o-or," indicating that she is performing a one-syllable word in two and three syllables respectively. This is also a representation once again of rhythmical improvisation and emphasis: she changes the way she sings the same word in order to make it stand out, to "worry" it into heightened meaning—"papa" seems even more pitiful, or is being teased to a greater degree, through this emphasis. Glissando is singing or playing that glides between notes, emphasizing pitch spaces rather than pitch points. Since Bodenheim uses dashes here—"po-oor" instead of "po oor" or "po o or"—his intention may well be to indicate a gliding between sung notes. The techniques here seem to represent the "differences" in culture between "white papa" and "black mama." The song is used to play upon these differences as a point of attraction between the people of different races, and thus becomes an important stylistic rendering of subject matter.

Nonetheless, the newly initiated Blanche still experiences some resistance to the possibility of having a close interpersonal relationship with an African American: "Still, loving any one of them would probably be impossible—she still shrank a little from the nearness of their bodies, when the sorcery of the dances was removed" (210). At this point, however, a man with a number of white features—thin lips, narrow nose, brushed back light brown hair, pale white skin—but with "the least tinge of brown in it" (210), sits down next to her, with the bemused air of someone who has experienced the scene before and knows somehow what to make of it, though it still seems unreal to him. This is her introduction to Eric Starling. They compare their "pedigrees"—hers Hell's Kitchen, his Peoria Street—and she confesses that Greenwich Village has begun to make a budding literary artist of her, though she is still only being patronized by the artists Oppendorf and Helgin, who wish "to see how the slum-girlie would get along in the mi-ighty studio." These elements help the poor white woman and the man connect with each other, and in some ways help them feel superior to the lords of leisure and pretense. To Eric, the slummers are like addicts: "Do you know, people who patronize and bend down all the time, do it as a hop-fiend sniffs his cocaine. They might have to take a close peek at themselves otherwise" (215).

Significantly, Blanche responds with a reference to the blues, and a close look at her changing self: "When I think of all the dopes people use to kid themselves along, I get the Jailhouse Blues. I was just as bad myself, two or three years ago, before I commenced to get wise to myself" (215). Her use of the vernacular here has some connection, perhaps, to the experienced blues-singing persona—Lillie Mae sings "Wise Like That" (1930) and Monkey Joe Coleman "Wise to the Jive" (1939)—including the female vaudeville blues persona such as Clara Smith singing "Women be wise, keep your mouth shut" on "Don't Advertise Your Man" (1924). Bessie Smith (1923), Virginia Liston (1924), and Ida Brown (1924) all recorded versions of a song titled "Jail-House Blues," and although the songs may be only generically related to Blanche's comment, still, her way of describing her response to people's various addictions as an imprisoning blues certainly serves as an unconscious cultural connection to Eric, though it does not seem to be a patronizing one.

At this point, she does not know that Eric has any "black blood," and when she speculates on interracial associations in a way that lets Eric know she is unaware of this connection, it spurs much self-consciousness and soul-searching in Eric, who wants to tell her but is afraid to lose her. When he finally does tell her, she is shocked, but gradually becomes used to the idea of going away to have a life with Eric. She rather unselfconsciously calls him "boy" or "boysie" a number of times (259, 263, 266), though in a familiar and endearing rather than condescending way—their relationship seems to be above this terminology as an insult. Eventually she rebels, telling her mother, "I'm a grown-up person, ma, and not a slave" (240), which she presumably also understands is true of Eric, and professes her hatred of "this blind, mean world of ours" (245) to Margaret. Blues aficionados, of course, know the title "Mean Old World" as a song recorded by Big Bill Broonzy (1936), T-Bone Walker (1942), and Little Walter (1952), all after the publication of the novel, but likely in the blues tradition earlier and certainly present in spirituals. The epithet "mean" preceding some noun turns up in over four dozen titles of blues songs up until 1943, as well as in a variety of songs such as Bessie Smith's "Cemetery Blues" (1923), where she references "mean old graveyard eyes."

After she hatches a plot to fool her family into thinking she is no longer going out with Eric, they meet by chance at a club called "The Battery," where Eric is "walking along and trying to forget [his] blues" (263). Their blues bring them together again with a jolt, where they admit they can't live without each other and determine to run away to Chicago and get married, racist world be damned. The final look, a panoramic shot worthy of optimistic Hollywood schmaltz, is a bit much, but it cannot be said that Bodenheim has ignored important issues dealing with race relations. His characters are rounded, developing, thinking characters, and he avoids some of the overly philosophical or sensationalistic touches in other books on the subject at the time. When Eric criticizes Vanderin's *Black Paradise* for being merely curious, sensational, and insincere (266), he is countering the hopeful words of Helgin earlier, who says to Blanche, "What begins as a fad can end as an avalanche. I really hope it happens" (201). Despite the ending, Bodenheim really does explore real issues and feelings, employing the blues in some key places to help bring elements of African American culture to the fore.

In each of his next two books, *Returning to Emotion* (1927) and *The King of Spain* (1928), Bodenheim offers a similarly titled poem that may well be seen as different improvisations on the same theme: "Jazz Music" and "Jazz-Music," respectively. Both contain brief references to the blues, including Bodenheim's versions of blues lyrics, though they are clearly different, and arrive in different places. In "Jazz Music," Bodenheim writes a description of the nature and purpose of life and art through a description of jazz musical performance related to parts of a dancer's physical and spiritual being. Of course, the closeness of music and dance in West African and African American traditions has been noted (Stuckey, *Slave Culture* 16). Bodenheim's poem presents the combined performance as a call to artistic exuberance and imagination to synchronize a powerful, performative response to the repressing, bourgeois chains of the world.

In the poem's first section, the blues is associated with sensuality—her body twists and her breasts speak in blues rhythm to the music. Her "heart-beats" and the squeal of the flutes are tangled, and the saxophone expresses what she cannot verbally with a "clearness" that transmutes her sadness into transcendent sound. Bodenheim clearly connects this power with blackness, primitivity, and "madness" and craziness, though the pain the flutes express as "the lonesome, crying blu-ues" is "cra-zi-ly truthful," performed with "finesse." The music is clearly uniting opposing feelings here. She says of her man, "He's got a black, mean, orchid glow," setting each of the three adjectives off separately. "Black" is first, before "mean," as a way of separating the meaning of blackness from meanness itself—not mean black, but black *and* mean. The orchid itself is associated with virility and exoticism, which Bodenheim emphasizes in the stanza with the expressive strength, "heart-beats," and drawn out soul expression ("mo-o-oan" and "gro-o-oan") of the music. The glow, too, is also somewhat spiritual, like Christ's halo or illumination in the sky. Hurt, pain, suffering, frustration, glow, truth, soul, finesse—the blues express them all, almost paradoxically combined in one interpersonal relationship, except that the expression contains them both (16).

The comprehensiveness of expression in the music continues in stanza two. In section two, her body responds more and more to the music of the violin, cornet, and banjo, transforming her hips into "circular agonies of breath," which captures a sense of painful panting and physical effort expressed in movement. Meanwhile, her lips, her verbal means of expression, become "Musical challenges to death," and her eyes, windows to the soul, form into "bugles of light"—evocation of a military instrument that both awakes with reveille and announces death with taps. Her hands "measur[e] delight," and her boredom disappears (16). She becomes infused with the power of an "amazon"—the drum becoming the counterpart of the "military" bugle, and she the exotic counterpart to her mate, dancing producing words and "harmonizing all her heart and brain" through the expressiveness of music and performance (17). In stanza three her movements become the power that challenges the conventions of religions and gods; put up with the inanities of popular songs' imitations of jazz ("No, We Have Some Grapes" clearly suggesting the popular "Yes, We Have No Bananas" (1922), without the sexual appeal of the yellow fruit); and evoke a "dark lady" to counsel folks to "loosen up" in their response to the aesthetics of the performance of jazz—"a screech is as good as silence"—and throw off the "handcuffs and leg-irons" of conventionality (18) in the face of life's ambiguous meaning. Indeed, Bodenheim may even have been familiar with the "I've Got the 'Yes, We Have No Bananas' Blues," recorded in 1923 by several artists, since the title itself seems a mockery, as Bodenheim's title is. In this poem, the blues reconciles opposing or paradoxical forces by integrating art into life, private with public, music and dance and words, making the "lonesome, crying blu-ues" some of the sweetest sounds you've ever heard.

"Jazz-Music" from the following year contrasts the "cra-azy . . madness" (27) of the moon-dominated night with the "trapped and lo-one" (29) static nature of the daytime. Once again, music is associated with exoticism—"hot," hazy," "creaming," "weird romancing"—in the mysterious night, as well as with liberation: "The night's untied me" (27) and becomes a place "where a tune fights / The fears of life" (28). The night is a creative and fulfilling space where, through excellently managed enjambment, Bodenheim's female speaker proclaims both "the great night made me" and "made me / His leaping wife," thrilled into a dance movement where "nothing stayed" her (28). Not that the moon is uncomplicated or absent of pain: like the earlier poem "Jazz Music," it combines "tragic" with "lightness" (28), "grief and whiteness" into a satisfying, because complete, reconciliation of opposites. Where night has had a traditional western symbolism of the unknown, the dreamy, the unreal, or the hauntedly mysterious, here the speaker challenges the reality "that day was real" (28), and finds the daylight a place where she is "trapped and lo-one," as she sings in the blues that completes the poem (29). And if the night was a place where she suffered a bruise "where . . the moonlight—-sho-one" (29), she still fingers that bruise with a longing that is, as with the earlier poem, associated with "black," with the virility and exoticism of an orchid, and with the sensuous and expressive blues (29) that makes the moonlight shine.

Although the titles of these two poems refer to jazz music, Bodenheim acknowledges blues as the "heart-beat" of jazz—indeed, the word occurs in both poems (as it was referenced a variety of times by Langston Hughes, as in *Black Magic* 5). Surely Bodenheim participates in the primitivism and exoticism of his time—practiced by both black and white writers—that considered the music of African Americans in the context of an idealized and liberating jungle where caution gives space way to unbridled passions and sexuality. Still, he also acknowledges a range of meaning and function in the music, and a connection between performance of music, dance, and language, that presents a deeper dimension in contrast to the sometimes superficial treatments lamented by Langston Hughes, for example, in "Cabaret" (*Collected Poems* 35).

Bodenheim's novel *Georgie May* (1928) is another of his tales of urban wretchedness, this time the story of a prostitute, both created and chewed up and spit out by an oppressive Memphis. Roiling and moiling like a pressure cooker without a relief valve, "Rounder's Corner" proves too much for the titular character, whose headlong descent into suicide is told with no sordid detail of its pitiful squalor left unspoken. Georgie May herself marks her transformation from innocence to repugnance unsentimentally: "Must be two Gawgies . . One's lak ah was when ah stahted out, and t'othahs a fighting, boozing son of a bitch" (58). Significantly, she portrays herself as changed into a male (*son* of a bitch) in this harsh patriarchal, phallocentric environment, though Bodenheim does mount a challenge to the smarmy societal view of human sexuality in a parenthetical aside:

> (Civilization spits on sexual impulses and emotional promiscuity, and calls them unclean, perniciously abnormal, ruinous to the sturdy, healthily compromising, serenely healing structure of homes and knit-together families, but if these structures are indeed so strong and inevitable, how could they be destroyed, or even subverted, by that pagan individualism which society denounces as a sickly weakness, a wild futility? . . The truth is that civilization fears two extremes—paganism on one hand, and all the skepticisms of the intellect on the other—but civilization is an involved, shakily hypocritical braggart, who trembles at the slightest sound and jumps at the smallest opposition. Millions of homes and families remain uninvaded, snugly growing, immune to curiosity, but one man need only write a frank union of realism and intellect, or to display those nude, imposing, neurasthenic indifferences called unconventional, and a veritable little bedlam breaks loose in the scene surrounding him . . . .) (59)

This was particularly an issue related to jazz and blues in the 1920s (though not exclusive to that decade) as the protectors of middle-class morality saw jazz putting the "sin in syncopation," youth running wild to what F. Scott Fitzgerald described as the smutty soundtrack for a shell-shocked era: "The word jazz in its progress toward respectability has meant first sex, then dancing, then music. It is associated with a state of nervous stimulation, not unlike that of big cities behind the lines of a war . . For a while bootleg Negro records made everything suggestive, and simultaneously came a wave of erotic plays" (Kolocotroni 441–42). Sterling Brown, in fact, agreed that the phonograph records of the era were prurient products, but of the commercial record companies, not the African American folk tradition ("The Blues" 292). As we have seen, though, Bodenheim saw this sexual frankness as a challenge, a relief—an intellectual, social, and aesthetic stimulant—and in the novel this is even reflected in the architecture of New York City: "To the east and west, huddled apartment-buildings and hotels jutted into the sky, and their uneven, flat-topped, pointed roof-lines epitomized the ambitions of a city, where the buildings of height end in hard desistings; where the gradations between individuality are infinitely irregular and yet compressed into a small range; and where the practical compromise of angles reigns everywhere, with more imaginative and dauntless curves and circles limited to flesh and its diversions in theaters and jazz-palaces" (247–48). Where the city's architecture is all limitation, concession, and obstruction, sex and jazz and theater (Fitzgerald's triple threat) are more courageously creative, voluptuous, and flowing. In this, Bodenheim's view may be seen as a counterpart to Darius Milhaud's *La Création du Monde* (1922), which in its second section is a jazz fugue with a lurching, convulsive rhythm, a jagged and moody mechanistic rhythm, that places jazz at the rather difficult, very physical, birth of the world—surely a seminal creative act that required imagination, energy, and potency. Bodenheim's nihilistic view of life in the novel—life is like Georgie May's prison cell—thus offers some relief through these outlets, which are associated with each other in his mind, though, as Georgie May's life and death prove, they by no means provide a solution to the dilemmas of contemporary urban life.

Jail and the search for some kind of temporal freedom and relief proves to be a major novelistic metaphor in Bodenheim's next novel. In *Sixty Seconds* (1929), the decayed urban landscape is the scene for Bodenheim's compressed, Bergsonian time-dramatized passage through the life of criminal/sacrificial Christ figure John Musselman, whose memories of four different women are sparked by scenes from the landscape outside his cell window as he awaits execution. Another of Bodenheim's victims of family and environment, John unconsciously (at first) rebels against his family through a relationship with Elizabeth, who later in their relationship reveals to him that she is "[o]ne -eighth colored" (160). Bodenheim does a particularly good job of describing John and Elizabeth's conflicts at this point of discovery, as they filter personal and societal attitudes through their thoughts of "stuttering dismay and dazed reproach" on his side, "still and earth-quitting smotherings of emotion" on hers (161). Her tragic sense is associated at one point in the novel with the blues and its sense of despair modified by a hopeful bravado. On the afternoon following her assault at the hands of Di Alberti, Elizabeth finds herself walking down the railroad tracks, an important symbolic scene, especially as she recalls a traditional blues lyric, perhaps from a vaudeville blues source, that matches her situation: "As Elizabeth walked down the Burnside railroad-tracks on the following afternoon, she felt a century of effort and uselessness in each step, motion seeming to her just going nowhere, nowhere, with a mean attack here and a stone wall there, to make her detour and drag her feet in some other unprofitable direction . . . Got a travelin' mind but ah got no railroad, said ah got no ra-ailro-oad fare—got fa-are—but if mah shoes hold out, swe-eet bo-oy, ah'm gointa meet you the-ere, yes the-ere . . . Meet what? A bang on the head when they couldn't get you no other way; or the whole pack barking at you 'cause you loved a white boy; or nine hours of snipping at ribbons and pushing with needles in a shop; or staying at home too tired to stir your legs" (145). Her sense of her own tragic situation is here related to the post-Reconstruction, Jim Crow–era situation of African Americans, particularly African American women at the frequent mercy of sexual predators and sometimes guardians of the color line when it became convenient to do so. The lyric about a "travelin' mind" shows up in Mattie Delaney's "Down the Big Road Blues" (1930), as well as in the repertoires of other Mississippi blues singers, and lyricist Kay Swift told Sheila Davis that she heard the following lyric in 1916 in the Adirondacks:

> I got THE RAILROAD BLUES,
> I got THE RAILROAD BLUES
> But I ain't got the railroad fare
> I got THE RAILROAD BLUES
> But I ain't got the railroad fare
> If my shoes hold out, I surely will get there. (78)

Of course, the necessity of walking due to lack of money for transportation is endemic to blues culture, to lower-class culture in general: from 1923 to 1943, there were twenty songs with titles of "Walking Blues" alone that were recorded by African American artists, and two more entitled "Walkin' Blues" from 1923 to 1942 by country performers, along with numerous other blues, country, and jazz titles and songs that reference walking. What Elizabeth, only "one-eighth colored," resorts to here is the strength and wisdom of African American folklore, which tells her to synchronize her mental ("travelin' mind") and physical conditions (worn-out shoes)—to keep on walking until she finds what she really wants.

Interestingly, the next song that comes to her mind is a spiritual, with reference to Jesus washing the feet of his Apostles, and to Luke 7:45, where Mary, a woman described as one who had lived a sinful life, anoints and kisses the feet of Jesus:

> "Ho-ow d'you kno-ow that Je-esu-us lo-oves yo-ou? 'Cause he ki-issed
> mah fe-eet on the go-oldu-un stre-eet. Ho-ow d'you kno-ow that Je-esu-us
> lo-oves you? 'Cause he ki-issed mah fe-eet o-one da-a-ay." (145)

Elizabeth, who has been loathesomely mistreated by Di Alberti, recalls acts of humility, subjection, and forgiveness on the part of Jesus. However, in this case, she seeks for someone—Jesus—to kiss her feet, to anoint her, and then to take revenge on the man who had, in the words of the blues, "done her wrong last night" (146). The juxtaposition of blues strategies and spiritual strategies here demonstrates Bodenheim's grasp of the way these two types of songs function in style and purpose. Transcribed, like the blues song, with vernacular language and melisma and glissando in mind, the song expresses hope in the form of kind treatment that may not come in this life (the golden street is in heaven) and suggests a response (that Jesus will take revenge) that she herself rejects because "gawd, wasn't no punishment fit for him" (146). In the blues song, the agency is located in the singer, who must accomplish her goal by herself. In the performance of the spiritual, she takes on a more passive persona, looking to someone else to save her, but believing that Di Alberti would not be punished. She is, Bodenheim writes, a backslider: "Religion . . is a receptibility and seraphically mantled fear inherent in some people and completely lacking in others, no matter how temporarily it may be buried in the former, or earnestly professing in the latter . . " (146). Because "her religious side was kin to a lie but had never investigated itself sufficiently to produce any inner cataclysm" (146), the consideration of religious elements or consequences is not primary in her mind. She is more of the blues philosophy than the spiritual, the blues song expressing what *she* can hope to do, the spiritual what she would like to happen.

There is one more important instance of the use of African American vernacular music in the novel. John finds himself picking cotton among the blacks in the area—"shared their bondage in the field" (197)—and begins to reflect on who they are and what they mean to him. It is important that he be placed in their menial position at this point, though, as Bodenheim shows, John cannot get out of his white man's mind-set. Stealing other people's cotton when their backs are turned in order to supplement his own picking, John feels the hardness of a cotton-picking life, which finds relief in African American song: "He liked to hear the Negroes sing as their hands darted over the cotton bushes" (195). What follows is a representation of the frequently loose and seemingly disconnected progression of a work song, combining game song, work song, aphoristic philosophy, blues, and jubilee song, with shifting focus and mood. However, the progression, from courting to sex to hard work to the unfairness of the cotton system to blasted expectations and then on to heaven, is clearly associative, much like work songs, and the blues, could frequently be, especially in the folk tradition. Romance is usurped by the sexual urge, the sexual urge suggested (in the African American vernacular tradition, "work can be a euphemism for sex") and overtaken by the unfulfilling hard physical labor in the fields, which is supplanted by complaint, then nominal resignation ("We-el ah'm sa-ati-isfi-ied, ca-au-use ah go-otta a be-ee," they sing, echoing a sentiment Bodenheim had used in an earlier poem), climaxing in a day of jubilee and liberation, when they will "bl-o-ow i-it lo-ou-ud" (196), predicting a kind of ecstatic fulfillment that is not satisfied by sex or work, but by the expression of these sentiments in art. John sees this as "seem[ing] to be happy but they weren't" (196), expressing a "passion for making the best of things and extracting some cheer from their scorching work," though he "couldn't hate the negroes, or like them strongly" (196). There was a social wedge between John and these men, and that impediment made John think "of Elizabeth in connection with the negroes around him" (197). John is puzzled by this juxtaposition of different moods, but the rough, unpredictable nature of the lives of these men is reproduced in the structure of the song, and the simultaneous feelings of tenderness and lust, pride and resentment, resignation and hopefulness—happiness and sadness—are not a sign of simplicity, but a recognition of the complexity of moments experienced in life. John has been taught not to understand that, and his liaison with these men, and Elizabeth, is thus impossible.

Bodenheim's flirtation with blues in the 1920s was a fruitful one, helping him to produce some novels and poems that attempted to present a more complex picture of the relationships between whites and blacks. At times, it seems as if Bodenheim is veering close to some of the popular stereotypes of his time, as reflected in the following song from *George White's Scandals* (1931) and recorded separately that year by Kate Smith and Paul Robeson (!)—though one has to think that Robeson's take on the lyrics was decidedly ironic:

That's Why Darkies Were Born
(Music by Ray Henderson, lyrics by Lew Brown)
Someone had to pick the cotton,
Someone had to pick the corn,
Someone had to slave and be able to sing,
That's why darkies were born;
Someone had to laugh at trouble,
Though he was tired and worn,
Had to be contented with any old thing,
That's why darkies were born;
Sing, sing, sing when you're weary and
Sing when you're blue,
Sing, sing, that's what you taught
All the white folks to do;
Someone had to fight the Devil,
Shout about Gabriel's Horn,
Someone had to stoke the train

That would bring God's children to green pastures,
That's why darkies were born.

Bodenheim seems to have an ironic attitude toward these kinds of stereotypes as well. While he does frequently make African Americans "musical," and reference musical biblical figures such as Gabriel prominently, he does not suggest they were born for that, but rather that it is a way of dealing with the vicissitudes of African American experiences in this country. Bodenheim recognizes whites "cheating them out of most of their pay, or cornering one of their women and lining up on her" (196)—the difficulties of being black and female.

Blues and jazz were certainly a dominant force in the Chicago music scene in the years leading up to 1930, charting the "Chicago Bound Blues (Famous Migration Blues)" of Ida Cox (1923) and the transformation of southern men and women into the depictions described in "Chicago Man Blues" (1928) of Tillie Johnson and "Chicago Women Blues" (1928) of Nolan Welsh, working the jobs of Peetie Wheatstraw's "Chicago Mill Blues" (1940) and scuffling with the "Chicago Policeman Blues" (1926) as sung by Rosa Henderson. Arnold and Irene Wiley sang "You'd Better Not Go To 35th and State No More" (1927), where the State Street Swingers insisted there was a "Chicago Rhythm" (1936). The writers who wrote of Chicago's rhythms, its teeming street life, heard and saw how integral the music was to the life of the city, and the life of the country, and when they wanted to offer the "Chicago Buzz" (recorded by Junie Cobb in 1926) or the "Chicago Breakdown" (recorded in Los Angeles in 1926 by Sonny Clay, paired with "Plantation Blues"), they could take frequent recourse to the music that made "Chicago Flip" (Whistler and His Jug Band in 1924) and drove contemporary America to burgeoning heights and tumultuous depths of feeling in the investigations of what it meant to be human in the 1920s. Writers such as Lindsay, Sandburg, and Bodenheim, anxious to portray the contemporary scene in a vigorous and diverse manner, drew on elements of African American hot music's style and subject matter, filtered through folk, popular, and classical music lenses, to portray the contemporary scene as they heard and felt it, each with his own focus and aesthetic. Aided by other Chicago Renaissance activists such as editors Harriet Monroe and Margaret Anderson, they were able to disseminate their spirits and rhythms, inspired in part by hot music, including the blues, to fox-trotting audiences and globe-trotting poets such as Langston Hughes.

4
The Tale Ragging the Dog
Fragmentation and Ragmentation in the Modernist "Quarters"

I

With the inroads that African and African American materials were making on a variety of popular and highbrow genres of the time, it would indeed be a surprise if we did not find a blues influence or blues references among the work of the white modernists that began appearing in the 1910s. There were African masks of Picasso and the race recordings of Ma Rainey; the jazz- and blues-influenced work of Milhaud, Antheil, Still, and Gershwin to cartoons of "Felix the Cat" (Ann Pennington taught him to do the Black Bottom dance in a 1927 photo essay!) and "Betty Boop" ("St. James Infirmary Blues" in "Mysterious Mose" from 1930); from the folklore collections of Odum, Bradford, Sandburg, and Dorothy Scarborough to the folk-influenced art of Meta Vaux Warrick Fuller and the nightlife portraits of Archibald Motley; from the blues-inflected "old timey" recordings of Dock Boggs and Dick Justice to all of the "running wild" musicals on Broadway and the music of society bands like Paul Whiteman's; from Jolson's *The Jazz Singer* to Bessie Smith's *St. Louis Blues*. African and African American art and music was everywhere in American life.

In fact, the productions of African American communities around the United States can be seen as centrally important to the modernist endeavor, sometimes as a result of admiration for a different perspective on technique and expression, at others due to the association of Pan-African cultures with the "uncultured" impulsive, primitive response or a vital savagery. T. S. Eliot wrote in his final chapter of *The Use of Poetry* (1931) that "[p]oetry begins, I dare say, with the savage beating a drum in a jungle" (148). In *The Autoiography of Alice B. Toklas* (1933), Gertrude Stein writes about Matisse introducing Picasso to the sculpture produced by "negroes" and the effects it had on both artists, chiming in (in the third person) that "[a]s an american [*sic*] she likes primitive things to be more savage" (*Writings 1903–1932*, 723). Edgar Rice

Burroughs published his jungle fantasy *Tarzan* in 1914, and four years later Elmo Lincoln would swing onto the screen with the first of many filmed portrayals of the white ape man in Africa who becomes the master of the jungle.

Part of this primitivism was rooted in the audiences that were courted by the writers. For example, a white novelist such as F. Scott Fitzgerald might have criticized negrophobes such as Tom Buchanan, with his fear of the "rise of the colored empires" (13), but the jazz with which he sprinkles his novel is jazz for the "polite" class, used to satirize that class with only peripheral (if any) references to the blacks who created it and the conditions under which it was created. One might argue that that is not Fitzgerald's focus, but then again, one might ask why not. James Mellow tells us that Fitzgerald struggled to make the section dealing with the "*Jazz History of the World*" succeed, but that section, dealing with another (white) culture's appropriation of black music, he deemed a failure (221), likely because he wasn't quite sure about how he felt about the music or the interpretation of it he was describing. Fitzgerald often referred to blacks as "niggers" in his private correspondence (Mellow 420), and he felt that the Jazz Age had no interest in politics at all, obviously ignoring not only those outside of his social circle, but the political implications of the actions of those within his group as well (Mellow 95).

Jazz was sometimes more co-opted than understood in its socioeconomic complexity. Witness the speculative intellectualizing of Herbert Croly who, in Edmund Wilson's *The Twenties*, discussed the appearance of jazz in the ancient world, in the "soft Lydian measures" of Horace and the measures of Catullus's Attis (69). Now, we might see Catullus's poem about Attis as an attempt to reconcile paired opposites, and then compare it to the blues, which deals with the confusions of life, expressing pain and achieving transcendence, but overall the comparison to Catullus's poetry does not hold up well. Some of Williams's contemporaries, then, were attempting to use African American music seriously in their work, but it was, once again, divorced at least partially from its African American roots and pressed into foreign intellectual service. Picasso himself found the sculptures "by the anonymous artists of Africa" that he came upon in 1897 to possess "passionate and rigorous logic" that revealed them to be among "the most powerful and beautiful products of the human imagination" (Richardson I: 488).

The association of the primitive and the savage is also made by a number of composers, Antheil in his *The Profane Waltzes* (1919) and *Sonata Sauvage* (1923), Stravinsky in *The Rite of Spring* (1913) (this last work eliciting primitive and savage responses from his audience as well!), and Varèse's *Ameriques* (1920/21; 1926) among them. Stravinsky's revolutionary composition has been compared to jazz for its sonic and rhythmic experimentation, and prominent use of ostinato, and a big band jazz version of the entire composition with improvisation was performed in 2010 ("Stravinsky for Jazz Ensemble"). With jazz's constant syncopation and overwhelming rhythmic elements, some critics, such as Marcel Espieu, feared that the "obsessive rhythm of jazz" could, in Jeffrey H. Jackson's words, "easily be the music of the mob" (76)—and the mob had been a concern at least since the time of found[er]ing father Thomas Jefferson. Dancer Isadora Duncan objected, "It seems to me monstrous that anyone should believe that jazz rhythm expresses America. Jazz rhythm expresses the primitive savage" (Needham 198). George Gershwin demurred in 1925, stating, "We are living in an age of staccato, not legato" (Wyatt 90), adding the following year that "Jazz is the Voice of the American Soul," and that its "dominant note is vibrant syncopation" (Wyatt 91, 93). Black bandleader James Reese Europe chimed in that "[r]hythm is something that is born in the negro, and the modern dance requires rhythm above all else" (Tick 376), hinting at an essentialism about which many critics have disagreed. It was a raging debate at the time, full of sound and fury, signifying . . . some variety of things about various elements of American society in fiery flux and flower.

Admittedly, there were black writers who evoked these kinds of ideas in their poetry as well: Countee Cullen in his poem "Heritage" (1923), included "savage," "primal," and "heathen" among the words he used to describe his ambivalent feelings in relation to Africa, with "savage measures" related to "Jungle boys and girls in love," sexualizing, primitivising, and associating with violence both Africans and African Americans (James Weldon Johnson, *Book of American Negro Poetry* 221–25). Of course, notions of the primitive and savage were not unknown in jazz of the period. Witness Ellington's "Jungle Band" at the "Cotton Club," and such recordings as "Savage Rhythm" by Mills Blue Rhythm Band (1931) and by Cab Calloway (1937), "Savage Serenade" by Benny Goodman (1933) and Adrian Rollini (1933), and "Primitive" by Luis Russell's orchestra (1934). While such concepts appeared in the works of somewhat more sophisticated jazz bands, African American country blues artists, frequently from or primarily appealing to the so-called lower classes, tended not to find themselves either primitive or savage, unless it was through a nom du disque that established a larger-than-life, powerful identity—"the High Sheriff from Hell" or "the Devil's Son-In-Law," for instance—or unless researchers were looking for it. Primitivism was not only a race issue, but also a class and gender issue as well, and it stuck to (especially white) conceptions of the blues for years: Django Reinhardt recorded his "Blues Primitif" in 1947, and, especially in the 1950s and 1960s, blues researchers often sought out "authenticity" and "authority" by concentrating on the earliest blues performers—"finding" and recording 1920s recording artist Peg Leg Howell when he was embarrassingly far past his prime, though still interesting in knowledge and repertoire—and sometimes seeking out and recording far less talented performers at the expense of contemporary performers who weren't old and decrepit enough to be certified as legitimate.

Although modernist approaches were, inevitably, varied, there are some core principles and influences that help delineate the unsettled boundaries of the artists grouped under this banner, though we should note writers' vacillations on any number of these points. Ezra Pound, the major American modernist theorist and galvanizing force, delineated the goals of the group: to "make it new," eradicating clichéd, tired language through restless, unrelenting experimentalism, leading to original thought; and to "make it whole," providing a continuity that would help piece together historical and contemporary discontinuities, leading to an informed revitalization of culture. James Baldwin, in "Sonny's Blues" (1957) referred to jazz musicians as "keeping it new, at the risk of ruin, destruction, madness, and death . . ." (Tracy, *Write Me* 414) in their improvisatory solos and interactions, a modifying improvisation on the idea of these modernist writers. Influences included those prose writers Pound felt were more technically and artistically advanced than the poets: the disciplined realist Flaubert, whom Pound felt had cleaned up the language; and the psychological realist Henry James, with his building up of significant detail and his experiments with point of view. From Victorian literature they drew from the dramatic monologues of Robert Browning, which indicated an awareness of the character's perception of events in the monologue, in such works as Pound's "Sestina: Altaforte" (1909) and "Hugh Selwyn Mauberley" (1920) and Eliot's "The Love Song of J. Alfred Prufrock" (1915). Pound had quoted words from Browning in his epigraph to his 1908 tribute to the poet as being "*il miglior Fabbro*" (Eliot's phrase for Pound), "Mesmerism" (*Poems and Translations* 31). A year later, Pound put Browning on an unsolicited and condescending "reading list" he sent to William Carlos Williams (Simpson 236), though Tytell reports that in 1911 Pound "belittled Browning" (72)—and that same year he dedicated *Ripostes* to Williams (*Poems and Translations* 230). They also drew upon Walter Pater's emphasis on *le mot juste* and a unified sensibility of form and subject matter, though it was expressed in highly wrought, Epicurean prose inimical to imagism.

Other ideas sprang from the mind of Edgar Allan Poe and the work of Sigmund Freud. Poe, of course, was famously analyzed *in absentia* by Freud disciple Marie Bonaparte. The Symbolists Baudelaire, Rimbaud, Laforgue, and Corbiere, drawing from Poe, defined a symbol as an object or act with nuance—an idea Pound rejected because of the fuzziness of connotation, but which Eliot embraced as an objective correlative, as in Prufrock's "like a patient etherised upon a table," and Wallace Stevens's "The Emperor of Ice Cream." From Sigmund Freud came a focus on the irrational elements of human consciousness and the nature of the unconscious mind—both of which had been anticipated by Poe and the Symbolists—which prompted experimentation with point of view and a stream-of-consciousness style. The notion of the relativity of time, that chronology was not necessarily dramatic and that plot was not the only organizational concept, came from Henri Bergson, related in some ways to the technique of progression by association and the need to connect objects in this world with spiritual matters championed by the Symbolists. James Joyce and Virginia Woolf, along with Americans Pound, Eliot, and William Faulkner, found this idea very congenial to their experimentations. In order to contextualize what they saw as a degraded contemporary society, or to parallel contemporary degradation with the past, many modernists explored the role of myth and ritual in our lives—Eliot praised Joyce's mythical method, as well as the wealth of material collected and explained in Sir James Frazer's *The Golden Bough* (3rd ed., 1906–15).

Among the issues prominently addressed by the modernists were metamorphosis and the transforming moment; the search for regeneration and the significant gesture; a search for the diction and voice that will best confront these issues; the relation of artists to their countries, the "common people," and to the primitive or savage, including black modernists' wrestling with the African background, negro dialect, and folk culture. There was an ambivalence about the primitive: on one hand it was seen as liberation from the hypocrisy and rationalizations of society; on the other there was a recoiling from the thought of having the reins in their uncivilized hands. In "Redondillas, or Something of That Sort," which was a poem left out of *Canzoni* (1911), in a parody of Whitman's style, Pound offers up his view of the "common man" with unbecoming but all-too-common hauteur:

> I would sing the American people,
> God send them some civilization . . .
> I have met with the "Common Man,"
> I admit that he usually bores me,
> He is usually stupid or smug . . .
> I am that terrible thing,
> the product of American culture
> Or rather that product improved
> by considerable care and attention.
> (*Poems and Translations* 176, 177, 180)

H. L. Mencken was right: in "The New Poetry Movement" he said that Pound was among the "ardent enemies of democracy" (*I* 54).

Other modernist American writers were also attempting to come to terms with the meaning of jazz and its relationship to the avant-garde writing tradition. Daniel Joseph Singal asserts that "Modernism should properly be seen as a culture—a constellation of related ideas, beliefs, values, and modes of perception" (7), but the jazz that was part of this constellation was based not on an intimate and personal intellectual and emotional knowledge of the tradition as it related to blacks and their socioeconomic position. Rather, it was an intellectual and impressionistic knowledge of the commercial as it related to whites, or, for people like John Howard Lawson in *Processional* (1925), a conception of the needs and desires of the workers expressed in "the jazz today for the glory of the working class" (7). Many writers seemed to be interested in using jazz in a more abstract rather than concrete sense. Separated from the Afro-American tradition that created it, jazz became important as analogy, for how it could be used cut loose from an African American culture-specific message. Wassily Kandinsky and fellow theosophist Piet Mondrian both sought, for example, "to further through abstract (and hence unmaterial) art what (Kandinsky) in 1914 regarded chiliastically as 'The Epoch of the Great Spiritual'" (Alan Robinson 134); and Mondrian identified in 1943 a correlation between his work and one segment of jazz: "True Booogie-Woogie (sic) I conceive as homogeneous in intention with mine in painting" (Bradbury 30). But the browns of Mondrian's Parisian grids in 1910 were "colors presaging war and the sadness that follows" (Tytell 67), not the colors of Afro-Americans who created the music he conceived as homogeneous in intention with his work.

Those characteristics that made jazz, for some modernists and theorists, part of the modernist constellation—improvisation and spontaneity, rejection of middle-class values, emotional and sexual freedom, seeming primitivism, the concept of the artist as "outsider," disjunction and cacophony, and the seemingly spontaneous "orchestration" of group improvisation—all of these characteristics can be found outside jazz. For example, there is an improvisational tradition in classical music (one thinks of Roderick Usher's wild fantasias), and certainly a confidence man like Sut Lovingood is a master improviser as well. Williams's own *Kora In Hell: Improvisations* (1920) associates his improvisations in that volume with sexuality and life giving, as is evident from the cover design of an ovum in the process of becoming impregnated. Indeed, improvisation is a major characteristic of the objectivist school of poetry influenced by Williams. However, it should be pointed out that later, in a 1948 letter to David Ignatow, Williams called his improvisations "wild flights of the imagination" about which he felt "embarrassed" (Williams, *Letters* 267). At any rate, jazz seems to bring together this compendium of characteristics uniquely. Afro-American jazz musicians are seen, as human beings, to be paradoxically slaves in a "free" land, the dark side, the outsiders who transcend their social situation through exploitation of otherness; perceived as not so much human beings as things, a force to be used rather than a being to be accepted. They represented a way for white intellectuals to free themselves rather than an argument for intellectuals to commit to freeing Afro-Americans. Therefore, the music was perceived as a potent analogue for the revolution in contemporary literature, but not as a catalyst for revolution in contemporary race relations. Malcolm Cowley wrote "always, everywhere, there was jazz" (279), but it only accompanies "the atmosphere of a long debauch that had to end" (238). It is the primitivist illusion associated with jazz that suggests that "discipline and technical mastery are unnecessary, clarity and sophistication to be avoided" (Gioia 48), an avoidance of honest race relations rather than an attempt to deal with them, and a misrepresentation of jazz. Indeed, Ralph Ellison believed that white writers during the twenties ignored discussing the difficulties of the racial situation in this country more than at any other time in the history of American literature (*Shadow and Act* 17).

Obviously, these particular concerns have broad stylistic applications, but it seems clear that African American vernacular music had its stylistic and contextual relation to modernism. Hot music artists—ragtime, blues, and jazz artists, for example—were interested in relating to tradition, but also in generating an individual voice and style that was new, making sense out of lives that were blighted by oppression and limited by primitivist notions of African Americans in general. For some sociocultural arbiters, listening to the message and sounds of the blues could help correct discontinuities in American intercultural relations and revitalize American democracy and life through the exposition of issues in African American lives and the creative power of the genre. Because of the interesting relationship of the speaker in the blues and the group to which he is singing, and the role of the blues singer as the bearer of folk culture and folk ethos, some critics think of the blues as a kind of dramatic monologue that expresses, not the blues singer's experience and feelings, but common or possible experiences of members of the community (Gruver 222–30). Further, critics such as Albert Murray see even personal expression as "an artful contrivance, designed for entertainment and aesthetic gratification" (*Stomping* 87), which can be true, and half-true as well. The organization of blues lyrics, particularly in the folk environment in the 1920s, was frequently not chronological, with sharp discontinuities in lyrics and lack of transitions that suggest associative progression, as in Blind Lemon Jefferson's recordings of "Match Box Blues" where the subject matter is as idiosyncratic as his brilliant and startling guitar style (Evans, *Big Road Blues* 139–54). Improvisation, a hallmark of jazz and blues, certainly addresses the human concern for survival and mortality in a world where people felt they had to live in the moment and flout conventions as a way of rejecting the extreme violence represented by World War I, and of rejecting the radical innocence and hypocrisy that had not prepared the white middle class for the destruction of nationalistic and cultural ideals. The blues itself is a search for a significant gesture, the claiming of a voice, which will help transform African American realities. In their propensity for experimentation, blues and jazz also mirror modernism. That experimentation, made manifest in the styles that so provoked and interested the world in the 1920s, was also parallel to modernism in that, like much art, it teaches us *how* to respond to its newness or uniqueness *as* it expresses, in each case necessitating a new definition of what art can be as a radical departure from dominant practices.

The primitivism among modernist writers at the time sometimes carried with it the stereotype that sexually objectified African Americans. Since, under Freud's influence, the 1920s was an era of challenging sexual barriers and identifying the centrality of sexuality to identity, so-called primitives or pagans were frequently seen as sexually liberated compared to people considered to be part of society on one hand, and carried the yoke of sexual wantonness and degradation on the other. Pound, for example, in a letter to T. S. Eliot in 1922 concerning *The Waste Land*, recommends an alteration in Eliot's text: "Aristophanes probably depressing, and the native negro melodies of Dixee more calculated to lift the ball-encumbered phallus of man to the proper 8:30, 9:30, or even 10:30 level now counted as the crowning and alarse too often katachrestical summit of human achievement" (*Letters of T. S. Eliot I* 505). He ends the letter in minstrel dialect, which, as John Peale Bishop indicated, was one of his particularly bothersome practices: "He is delighted with his nigger, yiddish, and western accents, which he employs to wearing excess" (James Miller 390). Pound used and abused sexual and linguistic stereotypes, sometimes in tandem, sometimes insufferably, sometimes unselfconsciously.

Further, though writers like Pound rejected improvisation in art because he saw improvisation as antithetical to craft and precision, there are a number of musical and literary works that have a spontaneous, improvisatory air—we think of the stream-of-consciousness style. Indeed, these artists have striven hard to craft this feeling in their works, meticulously notating seemingly random, disorganized sounds, as in Pound's frequent changes in time signatures in his *Le Testament de Villon* (1923), which created a kind of improvisatory feel, though there is clearly no overt sonic influence of black music to be heard. Erwin Shulhoff, who later died in a Bavarian internment camp for the crime of composing so-called Entartete or degenerate music that drew upon African American sources, composed a piano concerto in 1925 that had little to suggest a relationship to jazz other than a brief suggestion of syncopation in an ostinato pattern in part one, more ostinato patterns and a brief, bluesy piano run at 3:30 in part two, and an interesting high hat punctuation at 00:20 of part Three (Schulhoff). Yet other piano recordings he had composed as early as 1926, but recorded himself in 1928, sound much more obviously jazzy, raggy, and bluesy—there were both obvious ways to employ the sounds ("Shimmy Jazz") and subtle ways to explore the modalities (*Piano Concerto*) represented in his early work. His "Blues (Pour Paul Whiteman)," honoring Whiteman and his contributions to mainstreaming jazz, uses a cacophonous experimentalism in bass ostinato that is both highly traditional *and* original, an underappreciated masterpiece.

There is some criticism among jazz musicians concerning the inferiority of "mechanical" performances. Sidney Bechet, whom composer Ernest Ansermet praised for his clarinet prowess, commented disdainfully, "Music like that, you could almost make a machine play it for you" (Bechet 65). Clearly there is an emotional and improvisatory element in jazz that emphasizes its *human* connection. However, few can listen to the well-oiled machine-like precision of Duke Ellington's Blanton-Webster band recording of "Cotton Tail" without thrilling to its technical force and brilliance. Perhaps Harry Heilbreich's discussion of the music of contemporary composer Iannis Xenakis suggests a parallel here. In Xenakis's comment about the law of probability that "[t]he complete mastery of chance does not exist by chance" (29) Heilbrech suggests is a clue to the composition and arrangement of what seems to be random loose and chaotic sounds. Heilbreich feels this leads to "music which contains a striking paradox: though 'calculated' cooly and rationally by mathematics and computer, it is music of a burning violence, of a force and expressive energy which apparently emanates not from the creative process, but from the finished product itself" (28). This seems in some ways to describe what Ellington and jazz orchestrators accomplish by cooly calculating the interplay of various sections of the orchestra, arriving, as in "Cottontail," at a "hot" performance partially made hot by by the prefabricated machinations of the composer, who has composed with the knowledge of a particular soloist in mind. In fact, Ellington can imagine what is possible from Webster based on what he has heard from Webster and where the composition might take him, and thus not only supports Webster, but helps him produce a performance textured by the creativity of Ellington himself. In jazz, however, there is still room for improvisation and chance in the work of the soloist, backed by what becomes a well-oiled machine in its precision and structural ingenuity in the context of Western conventions. The call-and-response, syncopation, pitch wavers, and such elements orchestrated into the charts make the playing seem vibrant and new, and set up those same elements pitched ingeniously into the solo, creating a gyrating mix that demands movement, *is* movement, even as it sits serenely on the music stand. When Pound and Antheil suggested that the industrial setting is more like an orchestra than a soulless machine, it is spoken first like people who have likely never worked in such a setting, and second with a respect for fundamental technical artistry that exists and has its place in African American "hot" music as well—as Ralph Ellison frequently argued (*Shadow and Act* 154–55). After all, though Bert Williams was praised as a great "natural" minstrel performer, in fact he was a formally educated, learned man who actually had to learn stereotypical minstrel speech and behavior before he could perform it (Debus, *Bert Williams: The Early Years* 7). The "natural" can sometimes be the result of a very long, technical, onerous learning curve.

Antheil's *Ballet Mécanique* (1924), which was generated as a soundtrack for cubist Fernand Leger and Dudley Murphy's surrealist film of the same name, is an outrageous and pertinent specimen of hot music–influenced classical composition. If one listens to the premiere performance with the original instrumentation intended by Antheil of *Ballet Mécanique*, one can hear what Randall Thompson calls the "acme of demented modernism" (*Bad Boy Made Good*) of the work. Yet there are blues and jazz elements there. At 14:10 of the performance there is a decided eight-to-the-bar boogie woogie feel introduced which, at 15:16, changes to another boogie woogie feel, primarily in the repeated bass ostinato figure. This eventually layers into a passage with a marked boogie woogie big band sound, the treble piano figures, with repeated riffs among the xylophone players, and the percussive attack of all the instruments reaching a tremendous drive (hear the performance on *Bad Boy Made Good*). These are all carefully orchestrated, of course, as were big band jazz charts.

Would Antheil have known these kinds of boogie woogie and blues elements in 1924, when the piece was first performed? Very possibly. Fletcher Henderson had made a recording of "Chime Blues," a boogie woogie piece, in early 1923, around the same time that George Thomas, as "Clay Custer," recorded the boogie woogie–themed song "The Rocks." This means that these kinds of performances using boogie woogie ostinato were being performed before 1923, as a number of African American pianists asserted. Eubie Blake referred to a man named William Turk playing music like boogie woogie around 1896 (Silvester 7), and Jelly Roll Morton chimed in his opinion that boogie woogie originated in Chicago around 1908 (hear *Jelly Roll Morton: The Complete Recordings by Alan Lomax*). The term "boogie woogie" itself was not popularized until "Pinetop's Boogie Woogie," recorded in 1928. Furthermore, when Antheil premiered *Ballet Mécanique* in New York in 1927, also appearing on the bill with his thirty-piece band was W. C. Handy (later called the "Father of the Blues"), whose blues compositions drew on folk-blues he had heard in the South. Antheil even played piano with Handy's band on a Handy jazz composition at the concert (*Bad Boy Makes Good* DVD 40:25).

Sheet music, however, may provide the answer. Pianist-composer-publisher-arranger and recording artist George Thomas published a composition in 1923 entitled "New Orleans Hop Scop Blues," a chorus of which contains playing "strongly suggestive of boogie woogie" (Muir 161–63). The song was popular as sheet music, piano roll, and disc recording, recorded by Sara Martin with Clarence Williams (1923) and Bessie Smith (1930), along with a host of jazz bands. It seems more likely that Antheil encountered boogie woogie by the time of his composition of *Ballet Mécanique* through this popular sheet music rather than in person, but it is impossible to say.

Jazz and blues artists who improvise have also prepared a long foreground for their "spontaneous improvisation." That is, jazz artists' improvisations are determined by the possibilities of the instruments they play, the physical strength they possess, the amount of practicing ("woodshedding") they do, the structure of the song they are playing, the size of their group, their imaginative proclivities, the feelings they have at any given moment, the responses of a crowd, and a collection of runs that are characteristic of their styles that are deliberately pushed and twisted—grabbed and turned every way but loose. In other words, it frequently requires much time, hard work, and craft to sound spontaneous. The upshot of all this is that the blues, in its search for public space for its vernacular voices, can be seen as an attempt to find a significant gesture to ameliorate the situation of African Americans, an ambitious attempt to revitalize a post–Civil War society in desperate need of reform, in which attempt it became a significant cultural contributor to the African American quest for civil rights through its ability to garner appreciation and admiration in both black and white communities.

Of course, the modernist scene was very much an international movement, with many avant-garde artists such as Gertrude Stein, Ezra Pound, George Antheil, and Ernest Hemingway resident for periods of time in Europe and enjoying the company of European modernists such as W. B. Yeats, James Joyce, Virginia Woolf, Wyndham Lewis, Henri Gaudier-Brzeska, and others. This seems at least in part to have to do with the continuing desire of American writers to establish their importance in a literary world that was for them still dominated by European writers and an avant-garde scene that provided some inspiration. Antheil, commenting on music, advised, "We have to look for the corners in our own music" (Pound, *Antheil* 90). Additionally, locales like Paris did not have the American middle-class puritanical restrictiveness that had confronted the great poet of democracy, Walt Whitman, in place and time. Although Pound had been able to get sections from *Ulysses*, for example, published in *The Little Review*, the novel, which came out in 1922 from Sylvia Beach's left bank *Shakespeare and Company* bookstore, had to wait eleven years before being published in the States because of its alleged obscenity. Five hundred copies were burned by British customs as well.

Indeed, as Tyler Stovall points out, Paris was "the creative center of the planet" (25) and a hotbed of American and African American creativity in the years after World War I (25–81). Interestingly, a number of blues and rag songs mention France. Composer, singer, and ballad collector John Jacob Niles recalled in *Singing Soldiers* (1927) hearing a number of songs personalized to the French war experience by black soldiers in France in 1917—"Goin' to get me a French gal wid nice smooth flanks / An' tell her de blacks is de best o' de Yanks" (26)—and 1918—"All dese colored soldiers comin' over to France / . . Goin' to help de whites make de Kaiser dance" (99–102). George Moran of the comedy duo "Moran and Mack," who did a blackface comedy act on the vaudeville stage and recorded some huge best-selling seventy-eights, wrote a book called *Two Black Crows in the A.E.F.* (1928), that referred to the presence of piano and guitar that had played some jazz and blues in their times (152), while a regimental band plays a version of the war song "Over There" "with a touch of jazz" (1928). Papa Harvey Hull sang, in "France Blues" (1927), "gonna stop by France / Gonna stop by there just to give these girls a chance." James Wiggins is even more international in "Gotta Shave 'Em Dry" (1930), where he sings, "Now the rooster crows in Italy, I heard him way down in France / The way she getting down these days you know I ain't going to have a possible chance." Blind Willie McTell chimed in in "Georgia Rag" (1931) that a woman "Came all the way from Paris, France / Come into Atlanta to get a chance / To do that rag . . . ." Each of these songs associate France with social or sexual freedom, with the black singers evoking images of interactions between blacks and whites—though, of course, the blues performers named would not have had contact with the intelligentsia of the artistic community. Some African Americans, including blues performers, had been overseas fighting with the French in World War I—the subject of Niles's book, as well as Howard W. Odum's *Wings on My Feet* (1929)—and would have been familiar with a racially freer environment there. It was well known enough to appear in recorded blues lyrics in the twenties and thirties.

In Paris, Gertrude Stein, Ernest Hemingway, F. Scott Fitzgerald, and Man Ray coexisted with Langston Hughes, Claude McKay, Jessie Fauset, Jean Toomer, Gwendolyn Bennett, Palmer Hayden, Augusta Savage, and Aaron Douglas, *La Revue Nègre*, Josephine Baker, Bricktop Smith, James Reese Europe, Florence Mills, Will Marion Cook, and Palmer Jones. James Joyce, Igor Stravinsky, Edgar Varése (whom black composer William Grant Still listed among his influences, along with African American vernacular music), and Picasso were working in the city as well. And a young Ravi Shankar was making some initial tentative pluckings on the folk instruments his brother collected in India, before the family moved to Paris in 1930, and meeting violinist George Enescu and Andrés Segovia there (Notes 4–6). It was likely the location of the highest concentration of great artists assembled at one time. Perhaps it was even where Shankar, who later experimented with combinations of music from around the world, was first exposed to the idea of cross-pollinating and transnationalizing Indian music. Certainly the *Exposition Internationale des Arts Décoratifs et Industriels Modernes* (International Exposition of Modern Industrial and Decorative Art) of 1925 was a major impetus for and expression of the Art Deco style, and Paul Colin's illustration "Bal Nègre" made explicit the influence of African-derived black Caribbean and Latin American music, along with futurism, on the style of the movement. And, as John Richardson points out, "symbolist Paris had been in the throes of a blueish obsession ever since the early 1890s" (Richardson I: 216). The monochromatic works, lower-class and depressing subjects—prostitutes, beggars, et al—and suicide of a friend all brand the Parisian "blue period" of Picasso (1901–04) with elements of emotional and aesthetic depression that, though not musical, are analogous to what the musical genre of the blues was treating. Aaron Copland suggested that the jazz craze had reached its peak in 1925 and petered out by 1927 for American composers (Kostelanetz 45, 87), retreating from what he saw as the limitations of jazz's two stops: "the blues and the snappy number" (Kostelanetz xxv). However, Copland underplays the range of possible emotions in jazz the way James Weldon Johnson did in his discussion of dialect poetry in *The Book of American Negro Poetry* (1922), before he was enlightened by Sterling Brown's work. Neither were American, nor European, composers done with blues and jazz. Even Copland's own "Symphonic Ode" (1928–1929) evinced elements of hot music.

Significantly, the scene included and drew inspiration from a good number of African American artists as well. As Charles Amirkhanian asserts, "The comparative sumptuousness and even erotic expression of Wagner, Brahms, and Debussy, salon music and the post-Romantics, found its antidote in Pound's adopted Paris in the pared down music of Satie and Les Six, Stravinsky, Antheil, and the influence of American jazz" (10). American hot music, including ragtime, blues, and jazz artists, found its setting among the avant-garde composers of the world, though it should be noted that there were two distinct jazz scenes in Paris in the 1920s. In the nightclubs of Montmartre and Montparnasse, the frequently black performers of the entertainment district appealed more to the bohemian artistic community, among others. Langston Hughes himself devotes several pages of his first autobiography *The Big Sea* (1940) to the music, performances, and fortunes of Palmer Jones, Cricket Smith, Buddy Gilmore, and others at Le Grand Duc (160–63, 176–78). Louis Mitchell even recorded a tune called "The Montmartre Rag." However, with the rise of the music halls all over Paris, a broader audience was exposed to jazz of a different nature. This jazz was "more symphonic," and "primarily performed by white musicians" (Jackson 69).

In Europe were the great artistic movements that made the avant-garde at the time, which influenced the formation of American aesthetic movements to establish the importance of the American avant-garde as well. The Pre-Raphaelite Brotherhood, Cubism, Expressionism, Italian and Russian Futurism—Pound called it "diarrhoea [*sic*] in writing" (Kostelanetz 151)—Surrealism, and Dadaism represented a variety of modes of experimentalism in literature in the Victorian era and beyond. At the time this experimentalism had its musical analogues in the works of the Russian Stravinsky, Germany's Krenek, Czech Martinu, Swiss Honegger, Milhaud in France, the Austrian Arnold Schoenberg, and Hungarian composer (and a founding ethnomusicologist) Bela Bartok, an admirer of jazz (Horowitz 117), among others. Bartok's interest in "pure" Magyar folk melodies in 1908—which he later felt had "technical and spiritual" affinities with jazz (Sullivan 220)—was contemporary with the nationalistic use of Russian folktales in Stravinsky's *Ballet Russes* with Diaghilev, and *L'Oiseau de Feu* (1910), which Langston Hughes heard in concert in 1925, shortly after visiting the jazz club Small's Paradise and the year before his own folk-influenced *The Weary Blues* was published (Rampersad, *Life* I: 114). American folklorist Howard W. Odum was also researching the lives and music of African American performers around Clark University in 1908 and published his work on African American religious songs in the following year. Odum also employed the folksongs and materials he collected in his own literary compositions. Composer-ethnomusicologist John Powell published his *Rhapsodie Nègre* in 1918, and Massachusetts composer-folk song–collector Henry F. Gilbert finally had his 1908 opera *The Dance in Place Congo*, rejected in Boston as "Niggah music" by Karl Muck (Darrell 9), performed in New York in 1918. Critics on the American Left found Bartok "an ideal antifascist solution to the dilemma of the alienation between mass audiences and concert music" (Laki 54). But Pound was not looking for that solution.

Although Americans were certainly influenced by such developments, writers like Ezra Pound and Amy Lowell—the latter, George Gershwin asserted, "loved jazz" (Wyatt 96)—sought to establish schools of their own, though sometimes in liaisons with British colleagues. The imagist movement anticipated by Ford Madox Ford (1898) and Remy de Gourmont (1908) and established by Pound, Lowell, T. E. Hulme, Richard Aldington, and F. S. Flint offered a manifesto from Pound by 1918 that called for 1) direct treatment of the thing, whatever it was; 2) the use of no unnecessary words; and 3) composition following the development of the musical phase rather than the metronome, all of which helped produce an economy of language and a liberation of the poetic line that represented a major reform of the literary tradition (see *The Literary Essays of Ezra Pound* 3–8). Pound's focus on economy of language was influenced by his acquaintance with the work of American professor Ernest Fenollosa, whose notes Pound edited as *The Chinese Written Character as a Medium for Poetry* (1918). It described, with what historians debate about as questionable accuracy (Mair 3), pictographic form and "grammatical elements that are minimal in the extreme"—"prepositions and conjunctions are rarely used, leaving relationships between lines, phrases, ideas, and images unclear; the distinction between singular and plurals only rarely and indirectly made; there are no verb tenses, so temporal location and sequence are vague; very often the subjects, verbs, and objects of verbal action are absent" (Hinton xx–xxi)—which fascinated Pound and inspired a concentration on an "ideogrammic" method in his work.

There were, inevitably, disagreements among the imagist poets, leading Lowell to branch off into what was called disparagingly by some "Amygism." This movement, as well as Pound's later delineation of the Vorticism that he (and several others such as Wyndham Lewis and Jacob Epstein) generated in *The ABC of Reading* (37) to account for the rush of energy that passed through images in his longer works through the uses of logopoeia (groups of words), phanopoeia (visual elements), and melopoeia (sonic elements), had a major influence on a variety of American writers at the time. Pound was looking for a stripped, spare, native American language to put up against the elevated language of Victorian and post-Victorian British writers as a way to showcase American autonomy and legitimacy—a search that led him, among other places, to African American dialect. A brief, abandoned essay entitled "For the Afro-American Language" features Pound arguing for the strength and legitimacy of African American dialect, but with an effrontery of terminology and tone that nearly erases his admiration: "God damn it I wish the yellow octoroons, quadroons, and spittoons wd. stop talking wd. stop talking like cheap whites . . Damn it, nigguh; when you got som'thin' better'n the white man;

why the hell can't you keep it" (Coyle 130). It may be Pound's idea of a joke to call African Americans "spittoons"—most jobs cleaning them were reserved for African Americans and other minorities—but his profanity and abusive language only make it a more disparaging, unfortunate passage. Pound seems to have known that it was better abandoned.

Of particular interest to this study is Pound's focus on the musical phrase as the guiding principle of the poetic line. Pound began work as a composer in 1919, with little formal musical training. What he lacked in training, however, he made up for with his poetic craft, a poet's ear, and a background in the musicality of the work of the troubadour poets of the Middle Ages. He also had the support and aid of his friend George Antheil to assist him in putting down his musical ideas, and because the two were attuned to each other's aesthetic, their association was very fruitful. Pound was a major devotee and supporter of Antheil's music, attested to by the fact that he actually wrote a volume devoted in part to Antheil's work: *Antheil and the Treatise on Harmony, with Supplementary Notes* (1927). Pound saw Antheil's music, in its foregrounding of divisions of time-space, as an analogue to the concentration on forms in the art of Picasso, Wyndham Lewis, and Gaudier-Brzeska that was outlined in the Vorticist manifestoes of 1913–1914. He also saw Antheil's use of machines "without bathos" as a mode of precision (51–52) that would benefit the poet. While Pound's championing of the musical phrase over the metronome did not lead him to make use of blues and jazz elements in his poetry, his advocacy of that idea may have encouraged others more congenial to black music to see the connection, and to employ it.

Pound reports Antheil's opposition to improvisation with relation to classical music (57), though Antheil was, of course, influenced by jazz and blues, and Antheil's sometimes patronizing remarks on African American music are sampled in the text: "I am beginning to get annoyed with Americans who tell me that jazz will be the music of the future. Young prodigy-composers from the US writing classic jazz in four-four beat throughout. My God, the African negroes have the American negroes stopped a mile for every kind of rhythmic and musical effect. American whites must have had a bad effect on their negroes, don't you think?" (87–88). Antheil asserts "Even jazz has lost its bites, the negroes are on Broadway and in the *Little Review*, and everything is becoming genteel" (88–89)—a sentiment expressed by Langston Hughes in "Note on Commercial Theater" in *The Crisis* in March 1940 (*Collected Poems* 215–16). The reference to the *Little Review* could not have been lost on Pound, who was the foreign editor for Margaret Anderson and Jane Heap's publication, which had published African American author Jean Toomer's avant-garde short story "Fern" in 1922.

Antheil, no fan of gentility anywhere, certainly lamented what he saw as the popularization of jazz as "art music" and theater fodder—though it is clear that great jazz and blues was still being performed on record, on the streets, and in clubs at the time, from Ma Rainey, Bessie Smith, and Ida Cox to Blind Lemon Jefferson, Blind Blake, and Charley Patton, as well as bedrock blues with finesse by Lonnie Johnson, Louis Armstrong, and Duke Ellington. In the section of Pound's book that contains notes by "William Atheling" (actually Pound himself, not the twelfth-century heir to the thrones of England and Normandy) plus comments by Antheil, jazz comes in for some sarcastic mockery by Pound, followed by an exasperated Antheil:

> The future of piano music lies in the Jazz, and we may soon expect a much louder and more varied contraption with xylophone, whistle and gong attachment in the treble octaves and solid steel bars in the bass. This new and forthcoming implement should, from present indications, present most of the advantages over the pye-ano that the original forte-piano did to its predecessors.
>
> *(Naturally. The one who screams the loudest is the greatest genius according to the new American standards—but don't get out of four-four time ever—my God. G.A.)*

Pound and Antheil's annoyance and impatience with what they saw as the gimmicky sound effects of jazz and the noisy, self-serving promotion bespeaks their chagrin over facile appropriations of the music. In truth, the white Original Dixieland Jazz Band was in part a gimmicky band burlesquing barnyard sounds on their first recording, "Livery Stable Blues" (1917—alternate title "Barnyard Blues") and there was enough exaggerated silliness to go around. On the other hand, to lump all jazz together under this umbrella libels the many fine, avant-garde, precise, serious jazz and blues musicians, black and white, who were performing in the 1920s: as George Gershwin noted in 1926, "[t]o condemn jazz . . . because there is much bad jazz in the world, is as absurd as to condemn all music because much bad music exists" (Wyatt 95). Indeed, in 1919 Swiss conductor Ernest Ansermet (who spent eight years as conductor for Diaghilev's Ballets Russes and premiered works by his friend Stravinsky) wrote a glowing review of the genius of a Sidney Bechet performance; and the character of "Pablo" in *Steppenwolf* (1927 in German; 1929 in English) by Herman Hesse (whom Eliot admired and corresponded with—see *Letters* 509–10, 543) was inspired by Bechet's playing as well. Pound's interest at this point just seemed to lie elsewhere. Amirkanian noted that jazz was a major influence in the 1920s, but listening to Pound's musical compositions and reading his poetry, it is clear that Pound did not indicate or acknowledge inspiration from jazz.

Then, too, Pound has been known for his racial prejudices—in the book on Antheil, Africa is "darkest Africa" (26) and the residents there are "savages" (137). Others are called "primitive" (141). We must admit first of all that America in the 1920s was a very racist and classist place. Though there were of course some exceptions, even many well-intentioned people could not escape centuries of prejudicial attitudes, though America was supposed to be the locus of great equalization, where the patrician did not rule (excepting Thomas Jefferson's notion of a "natural aristocracy"). These kinds of attitudes were held among the intelligentsia as well as the masses, the artists as well as the workers, the prostitutes as well as the presidents (Whitman's catalogs juxtaposed these last two, though his literary egalitarianism did not always extend to his personal feelings about race). The prevalence of racism in an era has been dubbed the "average racism" that prevailed as a way to soften charges of racism of a writer such as Edgar Allan Poe, and truthfully we must contextualize people's attitudes so that we do not judge historical figures unfairly by the standards of our own times (Kennedy 111). On the other hand, because people who rose above abhorrent attitudes did exist in those times, it was clearly possible to resist a prevalent norm. Unfortunately, many modernist writers in the 1920s had derogatory attitudes regarding race and class or, at least conflicted, harbored some of these elitist attitudes. Some critics even suggest that they were essential to their literary aesthetics.

As early as 1910, Pound had indicated the coming anti-Semitism that was more than just the garden variety, "normative" kind (Tytell 244): he asserted that "new Slavic and Jewish immigrants . . . were producing . . . a mongrel nation" (62). John Tytell asserts that by 1917, not only were Pound and his friend John Quinn "racially elitist," but Pound heard anti-Semitic remarks from Yeats and Wyndham Lewis as well, and the three, along with T. S. Eliot, believed that "democracy would gradually erode all cultural standards" without "the enlightened firm hand of a noble despot and a rigidly controlled economy" (139). In 1918, Pound told Quinn, "Of liberty, equality, fraternity, democracy . . . there ought to be as much . . . as possible. But art exists in spite of them—Any art that matters" (Moody 316). This is paternalism at its most condescending. African Americans were not Pound's primary social and economic scapegoats—"[t]he Jews were a favorite subject," Noel Stock offered about Pound's attitudes in 1942 (393), and Louis Simpson pronounced him "practically insane on the subject" (158). Pound even supported Hitler's favorable comments regarding eugenics related to humans (Stock 394)—though

Pound was certainly not alone in his support for a movement that garnered popular, scientific, and political advocacy in the early decades of the twentieth century. Donald Childs surveys the prevalence of eugenists among modernist writers in general, calling attention to the conflicting views of critics John Carey and William Greenslade as to what it meant:

> Carey regards the interest in eugenics on the part of many modernist poets and novelists as a particular expression of a more general fear of and contempt for the masses: "the principle around which modernist literature and culture fashioned themselves was the exclusion of the masses, the defeat of their power, the removal of their literacy, the denial of their humanity." The indictment he prefers [*sic*] against modernism is impressive. Yet so is the defense that Greenslade mounts. The latter argues that "the widespread attribution of deviancy and degeneracy to modern culture" effectively placed modernist writers themselves under the surveillance of eugenical discourse and so prompted in their work a complex defense of the rights of the individual as narrators and characters in their works explicitly or implicitly took on the role of "critical, combative humanist." (18)

Childs goes on to argue effectively "that the poet who called himself one of the last romantics [W. B. Yeats] was also, like [Virginia] Woolf and [T. S.] Eliot, one of the first eugenists" (230), indicating the prominent acceptance of eugenics among twentieth-century modernist writers.

Although Pound does not seem to have commented as much on African Americans as a group as he did Jews, this idea of mongrelization and the deterioration of cultural standards had been and would be used against African Americans. Pound's racial condescension can be inferred, and a number of critics—Michael North, Burton Hatlen, and Alec Marsh among them—acknowledge Pound's racism (Coyle 4–5). Pound did have contact with and admiration for at least one African American. From 1931 on he corresponded with Langston Hughes, and offered brief praise of Hughes in one of his infamous 1941 Italian radio broadcasts (Doob 16) and later in discussion with Nat Nentoff (27). However, in 1938 he was calling Hitler and Mussolini the "greatest statesmen alive" (Tytell 250), two years after Hitler had disrespected ethnic minority athletes, including four-time gold medal–winner Jesse Owens, at the Berlin Olympics by refusing to shake hands with any medal winners rather than have to shake the hands of people he deemed to be "inferior." Albert Speer, in his memoir *Inside the Third Reich*, reported on Hitler's private response: "Each of the German victories, and there were a surprising number of these, made him happy, but he was highly annoyed by the series of triumphs by the marvelous colored American runner, Jesse Owens. People whose antecedents came from the jungle were primitive, Hitler said with a shrug; their physiques were stronger than those of civilized whites and hence should be excluded from future games" (73). Pound, in fact, was working on an essay, never published, entitled "National Culture—A Manifesto" that same year, which included his criticism of "the total democracy bilge" and his belief that "[t]he disequality of human beings can be observed" (Tytell 250). Hughes remained supportive of Pound the old acquaintance and artist and, in fact, visited Pound when, pronounced insane to account for his "traitorous" broadcasts, Pound was incarcerated at St. Elizabeth's.

But Pound did exhibit the almost unimaginable effrontery in addressing Hughes in black dialect in their correspondence, as well as to correct Hughes's own use of dialect in one of the stories in *Simple Speaks His Mind* (Coyle 79). Wyndham Lewis referred to Pound's usage of his version of black dialect as "the Amos and Andy patter of his choice" (30). (Of course, before black actors Spencer Williams and Tim Moore began portraying Amos and Andy on television in 1951, the parts were played by white actors influenced by blackface minstrelsy.) Furthermore, Pound attempted to use Hughes to advocate for the importance of Leo Frobenius and the need for experts on Africa in black universities. He had a practical reason for courting Hughes's friendship, though he seems to have maintained a cordial attitude and genuine respect for Hughes's work. Hughes cultivated the friendship of Pound as well, which, depending on how much he knew of Pound's duplicity, must have been trying.

However, with regard to his pronouncements about African Americans as a whole, Pound shows a clear disdain for elements of the African American community. In his contribution to ex-lover Nancy Cunard's *Negro* (1934), Pound makes a pitch for Frobenius and laments the idea that others do not appreciate Frobenius's work as much as Pound does: "I should also have more respect for the Afro-American intelligentzia [*sic*] and for the Negro millionaires, etc., that are rumoured to flourish in Harlem if they had shown more alacrity in hearing of an author who has shown their race its true charter of nobility and who has dug out of Africa tradition overlaid on tradition to set against the traditions of Europe and Asia" (393). While praising African civilization—which Pound also did elsewhere, sometimes at the expense of African Americans—the piece indicates doubts about the existence of a black intelligentsia and extravagant wealth in Harlem. Is Pound merely indicating his ignorance of the Harlem scene, or doubting these achievements among African Americans? Several blues singers referred to being millionaires—Bessie Smith in "Nobody Knows You When You're Down and Out" (1929) and Blind Lemon Jefferson in "Right of Way Blues" (1927)—even if fictionally or hyperbolically. Of course, others, including African Americans (Nella Larsen in the Naxos—"Saxon" backwards—of *Quicksand*), expressed impatience and exasperation with the Anglophilia of African American institutions of higher learning at the time, but Pound seems to go a bit further in doubting their existence. This was not the only time that Pound suggested he knew better about African and African American issues than many blacks did.

There is another contribution dealing with Pound in Cunard's volume, this time "A Letter to Ezra Pound" (97), that may shed some light on Pound's attitudes. Cunard claims in *Negro* that she had not had time to secure permission to print the letter, so she left off the author's name. We now know that the letter was written by Langston Hughes. It reads as a response to Pound's contribution, which is printed much later in the text (393–94). This order almost seems to make this letter a preemptive strike, even though Pound's was written first. The letter explains to Pound that the two best institutions of higher learning for blacks, Howard and Fisk, "are trying desperately to become little Harvards," but suffer from being controlled by politicians and wealthy families, and headed by ministers. Hughes answers Pound's call for a chair in Africanology at a black university by asserting that the knowledge of the subject and its importance is not apparent at these institutions. He suggests that Pound contact Howard professor and Harlem Renaissance catalyst Alain Locke for a more informed view on the subject. Hughes is, in a sense, addressing Pound's doubts about Harlem intelligentsia and money by calling attention to them through Pound's well-known prejudices against what Pound terms the "ang-sax eddikater" in his contribution (393), and then follows with a note that there is a Harlem professor who is among the cognoscenti who could enlighten Pound. The letter is gentle and subtle enough to justify Cunard's claim at the end: "If any of my hundred per cent. white, Celtic or Asian, correspondents have done better during the past few months their epistles have got lost in the post" (97).

There are some brief references in Pound's letters that illuminate Pound's ingrained prejudice as well. In a letter to the *Boston Transcript* in 1915, Pound calls a reviewer of one of Robert Frost's works "a liar," due to his claim that Frost had done something other American poets of Pound's generation had done—had published a volume without external assistance. Pound laid earlier claim to the distinction, which he valued very much. He goes further in the next paragraph, speculating that the review was written by a "(? negro) reviewer" (62). It is not clear what prompted the presence of this musing on Pound's part, unless the implication of the speculation reveals a Pound trying to insult someone by associating him with African Americans. Pound in fact knew that the reviewer, William Stanley Braithwaite, did have African American ancestry, though he was very light skinned, but he was also a generally well-known and respected writer, poet, literary critic, and anthologist of the time. The fact that he was, by the prejudices of the time, considered to be a "negro" should make no difference to Pound's argument, unless it is a prejudice he holds. Pound does indicate in a letter to Harriet Monroe that he "did not write the letter to Braithwaite . . . Good heavens!!!" (67). Was Pound hypocritically afraid of revealing his own "true colors"? (In a letter from May 1920, T. S. Eliot complained to Pound of a negative review by Braithwaite of his *Poems*, wherein Eliot is called "An Exotic Poet" [1: 384].)

For example, an indelicate Pound does not hesitate to use the word "nigger" twice in *Guide to Kulchur* (1938): once speaking of his translation of the *Agamemnon* in which he "made the watchman talk nigger" and found that "by the time you had taken out the remplissage, there was no play left on one's page" (93); the other referencing the song "Nigger in the Woodpile" (recorded by four white country groups between 1924 and 1932) as Pound refers to a faulty paragraph of Aristotle (Arry) as "a woodpile in which you can hide an indefinite number of niggers" (324). In "Wyndham Lewis at the Groupil," he calls attention to a "pink shirted nigger" in a work of art. In a letter to W. B. Yeats (*Pound/Joyce* 95), Pound also refers to "niggers," and in the essay "Le Prix Nobel," Pound argues that Bengali poet Rabindranath Tagore was refused election to an academic committee "because they thought him a nigger" (*Pound/Joyce* 218). This rather casual use of the word suggests a level of comfort with its implications and exacerbates the imperiousness with which he dispensed his opinions. Psychiatrists appointed by the court to determine Pound's mental state in 1945 said Pound had "delusions of grandeur" (Blair 153).

This was a haughtiness he perhaps shared with Gertrude Stein, who wrote (sarcastically?) in *The Autobiography of Alice B. Toklas* (1933) that Carl Van Vechten "sent us quantities of negroes." Virgil Thomson, Stein's collaborator on the all-black production (with the Hall Johnson choir) of *Four Saints in Three Acts*, wrote to Stein, "Later we went to Harlem to a nigger drag and one of Carl's coon friends picked us up . . . ," indicative, perhaps, of a somewhat comfortable racist flippancy between the two (Holbrook and Dilworth 106). Among the Negroes Van Vechten introduced to them was the highly accomplished Paul Robeson, whom she said "became definitely a negro" when other people came into the room. She also dressed him down about singing spirituals: "They do not belong to you any more than anything else, so why claim them, she said. He did not answer" (*Writings, 1903–1932).* However, as Mrali Balaji points out, Robeson felt he could express the best qualities in his blackness through the Negro spirituals and the stage characters he embraced as complex" (25). One does not imagine Robeson being cowed very easily. By 1925, when he visited Paris, he was graduated Phi Beta Kappa and valedictorian of his class at Rutgers; a multi-sport athletic star; a Columbia University law school graduate; star of Eugene O'Neill's *All God's Chillun Got Wings* (1923) and *The Emperor Jones* (1920); featured in Oscar Micheaux's film *Body and Soul* (1924); and a short time away from appearing in an otherwise inconsequential amateur film shot by Ralph Barton entitled *Camille* (1926), in which he played Alexandre Dumas fils—in a film that also featured Sinclair Lewis, Anita Loos, Theodore Dreiser, Sherwood Anderson, Clarence Darrow, H. L. Mencken, Serge Koussevitsky, Alfred Knopf, Joseph Hergesheimer, W. Somerset Maugham, George Jean Nathan, Rex Ingram, Ethel Barrymore, and Charlie Chaplin (Chaplin, *A Woman of Paris / The King of New York*). Though he would understand her point of view, he must have been furious at her judgmentalism and gall. Robeson's firebrand preacher father had not cultivated a shrinking violet, though Robeson was aware of his position in contemporary society as a black man. As Balaji asserts, Robeson was "topically interested but defiantly unengaged" (35).

Stein's collaboration with composer Virgil Thomson, incidentally, led to Thomson's composition of "Piano Sonata No. 3, on white keys for Gertrude Stein" (1930). Stein's abilities to play the piano were apparently limited to the white keys, sometimes called the natural notes of the piano, while the sharp notes and flat notes of the black keys were left untouched. Since the black keys make up a pentatonic scale on the piano rather than heptatonic, they are connected with various kinds of music from around the world, including Celtic, Chinese, Japanese, and African music, and find particular applications in African American spirituals, blues, and jazz music. Whatever the reason for Stein's exclusivity with the white keys, it has an interesting counter-resonance with the attitudes of the African American narrator of James Weldon Johnson's *Autobiography of an Ex-Colored Man*, who professed a marked preference for the black keys of the piano, and found his inspiration and expressive outlet in African American music, including spirituals and ragtime.

Another letter offers ironic condescension on Pound's part: "Negroes in America love polysyllables and used to assemble most marvelous collections of unexpected syllables" (262). And in *The Spirit of Romance* (1910), Pound praises Villon with mockery of Whitman using a racial stereotype, claiming "Whitman is the voice of one who saith":

> Lo, behold, I am one who eats water-melons. When I eat water-melons the world eats water-melons through me.

When the world eats water-melons, I partake of the world's water-
melons.
The bugs,
The worms,
The negroes, etc.,
Eat watermelons; All nature eats water-melons.
Those eidolons and particles of the Cosmos
Which do not now partake of water-melons
Will at some future time partake of water-melons. (168–69)

These generalized views of African Americans amount to a stereotype—that of the minstrel dandy or comic negro whose attempts to indicate his intelligence are marred by hopeless mispronunciations and ridiculous neologisms; and the watermelon-eating darky who is equated with vermin (the Latin word *vermis* means "worm"). Pound habitually asserted prejudicial group judgments—about blacks, Jews (though he sometimes limited comments to Jews of the upper class who had power), and others—indicating an undifferentiated view of various groups. However, as Alec Marsh points out, Pound also linked dialect—and African American dialect—to authenticity, which he valued highly (Coyle 126). He seems to have vacillated between admiration, bemusement, and repulsion in relation to blacks.

The sum total of Pound's attitudes toward African Americans amounts to what Marsh calls "ambivalence": "[H]e simultaneously makes them the vessels of his own irrational fantasies and regards them as the most authentic Americans because they stand closest to the American heart of darkness, our tragic national legacy of slavery, racism and forbidden sexuality that could be construed as our true and secret history. Another reason, however, is that African Americans speak what Pound regarded as a truly American 'Afro-American language'—not English, but something original to our states" (Coyle 127). Of course, modernism itself was not without its ambivalences relative to social, political, and aesthetic issues. Gertrude Stein and Virgil Thomson's opera *Four Saints in Three Acts*, written in 1927–1928, was produced by the "Friends and Enemies of Modern Music" in 1934 (Thomson "Notes"). Pound's support for Hitler and Mussolini presents a huge stumbling block for those for whom the notions of a "master race," a "final solution," and fascism are entirely repugnant—and those things are not what contemporary critics admire about Pound. Norman Rosten's poem "Garland for Mr. Pound" sarcastically refers to Pound as being "apparently under no compulsion but poetry," adding "the circumstances of Mr. Pound's death continue to astonish his earlier poems" (Yoseloff 94–95).

Pound's racism is problematic for those whose appreciation for a literary work is affected by the writer's social and political views. We spend so much time on Pound here not because his poetry of the 1920s deals with hot music, or even that much with African Americans. William Carlos Williams commented in 1904 that "if he ever does get blue nobody knows it" (Moody 18), and though Williams was referring to sadness, he might just as well have been commenting on Pound's understanding of the musical tradition. An early draft of Canto Twenty from 1924 with Sambo and Dinah, minstrel language, and a razor-toting Negro who "cuts" President Washington is eventually excised in its published form. When the passage, arising phoenix-like from its ashes, resurfaces in Canto Twenty-One, references to Sambo and Dinah and getting cut disappear, and Jefferson only refers to "domestic servants" (*Cantos* 97). Pound seems to have been more cautious in his public speech on the matter. Racial issues and racist attitudes were in Pound's head, if less so in his published work. But the analogies between hot music and Pound's aesthetic theories discussed earlier, theories for which Pound clearly advocated among his friends, would surely have been apparent to other such disparate stylists as T. S. Eliot and William Carlos Williams, whose connections to African American vernacular music are more prominent, even if problematic racial attitudes sit uneasily with them side by side.

II

In a 1928 letter to Herbert Read, an English poet, literary critic, and art critic whom T. S. Eliot had known since 1917, Eliot described himself in his youth as "a small boy with a nigger drawl" and "a savage" (Chinitz 15). It was a sign of Eliot's difference, his feeling of "otherness," more a Frenchman, even more an Englishman, than an American (Read 15). The fact that he chose a characteristic of African Americans to represent his southern "difference"—he was born and grew up in St. Louis—from his New England schoolmates is telling, and even more significant is his use of the degrading term in relation to African Americans, and himself.

Of course, Eliot had used the term elsewhere, referring in "Ballade pour la Grosse Lulu" (1917) to an interview (made up by Eliot) in *The Outlook* journal with Booker T. as "Up from Possum Stew!"/ Or "How I set the Nigger Free!" The interview title, of course, parodied the title of Washington's inspirational autobiography, *Up From Slavery*, subtitled merely "*An Autobiography*"), one of Eliot's little minstrel "banjokes" (title of a 1927 Roy Smeck tune listed in Sutton 16) that he rather carelessly and insensitively found humorous. Eliot used as his refrain "Put on your rough red drawers / And come to the Whore House Ball!" (Eliot, *Inventions* 311), further associating African Americans with unbridled celebration of illicit sexuality. (An earlier reference in the poem to the use of bones as an instrument is glossed by the *OED* as an instrument used by "nigger minstrels.") Blues singer Kansas Joe McCoy recorded his "Dresser Drawer Blues" in 1932, and Carl Rafferty followed with "Dresser with the Drawers" in 1933. Chick Willis was still exposing women's drawers in his "Stoop Down Baby" in 1972. One might say that Eliot is again referring to the minstrel image, and is therefore using the word "nigger" for the blackface effect in relation to Washington. That, of course, would have to be fictional, since Washington himself would not, on principle or on behalf of his personal image-making, have used the term in such a way in addressing the white public. Washington's own recording of his "Atlanta Exposition Address" from 1908 (three years before the Eliot poem) shows him using the word "negro" exclusively (*Lost Sounds* CD). However, Eliot's reference would not have been the only parody of Washington's position and manner. Black jug band songster Gus Cannon recorded "Can You Blame the Colored Man" (1927) with mocking references to a man who "almost lost his color" when he met with President Theodore Roosevelt in 1901, making minstrel-like "goo-goo eyes" and getting drunk on wine—all unlikely, though exaggerated for critical effect.

Eliot's juxtaposition of this section of the poem with a reference to newspaper reports that "the learned horse/ Jim Key, was murdered in his stall" seem to associate Washington with a learned animal who was deliberately killed, presumably because he was more than he was supposed to be, outside his stall—as was Washington, the learned "nigger." This is again not necessarily Eliot's attitude, but his recognition of societal racism. Interestingly, there was a horse called Jim Key who was allegedly taught how to identify the ABCs, do math with numbers up to forty, tell time, know the days of the week, cite Bible passages, and differentiate among flags of the world. His owner and teacher was a black man, Dr. William Key, who trained the horse and exhibited him at the St. Louis World's Fair. The subtitle of a book about the horse asserted "he was taught by kindness" (http://www.beautifuljimkey.com/heroes.htm). The implications here for Washington, who was not taught by kindness but in the school of hard knocks, and even suggested that slavery was a "school" of valuable learning, are clear. African Americans were not taught by kindness, but, as with the horse's trainer, could provide an example of what kindness, not violence and murder, could produce.

Furthermore, the horse was not actually murdered, but experienced an easy and painless death, so Eliot has concocted the murder—as a newspaper report—for its juxtapositional effect rather than producing the truth. Another lie of the print media. The term "stall" perhaps triggers the reference to sexuality related to African Americans in the final lines. A common reference in blues to a sexually cheating partner is to say "you got another mule kicking in my stall" (hear Maggie Jones's "You May Go But You'll Be Back Some Day" from 1924). The word "ball" is a common slang term in the blues for sexual intercourse (hear Ethel Waters's "At the New Jump Steady Ball" from 1922)—"jump steady" is a barrelhouse term for both dancing and sexual intercourse, as stated in Calt 140). Since the two words end rhyme with each other in the poem, they are even more closely connected. The progression proceeds, then, from public embarrassment in the newspaper to murder to recourse to sexual abandon and celebration—perhaps the antidote for the first two, a little death ("*la petite mort*") from which one resurrects, "overcoming" the death that occurred in the stall. If, as Roland Barthes suggests, the aim of literature is to produce this effect in the reader, then perhaps Eliot's insights in the poem are intended to awaken the reader from racist lethargy to realization of the condition of African Americans. This would make the objectionable portrayals in the poem deliberately ironic, and present Eliot as an enlightened user of the terms.

However, it would not explain the objectionable scatological portrayals of blacks (presumably the reference is to an African village called Bolo in the Central African Republic) in Eliot's early "King Bolo and His Big Black Kween" and other King Bolo and Columbo poems—excised from a manuscript he sold to John Quinn—which were said to be favorites of Ezra Pound (Eliot, *Inventions* xv–xvi). The spelling of "kween" is in line with the dialect tradition of misspelling a word even though its pronunciation is accurately reflected in the normal spelling, which seems only to serve the purpose of intellectually degrading the dialect speaker. Interestingly, there was an instrumental ragtime composition by Albert Gumble published in 1908 entitled "Bolo Rag," but there is no information on whether Eliot might have heard it or not, and the rag itself has nothing scatological about it. Peter Ackroyd suggests that Eliot "seems to have derived a certain satisfaction from the description of sexual excess" (52), and that his sense of the "emptiness in all human affairs" produced "severe religious discipline or gross sexual indulgence [as] ways of alleviating those fears" (53). The fact that he blacked up—and sometimes jazzed up—to do so, however, is another thing altogether. Jonathan Gill further suggests that the Bolo poems "struggle with the very same tensions that dominate Eliot's published output—Old World versus New, high culture versus low, order versus chaos, tradition versus innovation, the dead versus the living—yet all within the formal conventions of the nineteenth-century African American minstrel song, and with a surprising racial, even racist, focus" (66).

It is not, perhaps, so surprising. Conrad Aiken describes his days with Eliot at Harvard, emphasizing Eliot's delight with American slang for its boundary-pushing, energetic neologisms: "How delighted we were with the word 'dinge' for negro!" (McIntire 37). Of course, their celebration of creative linguistic practices is not necessarily a celebration of racial epithets, especially since Eliot was clearly wrestling with his own feelings of otherness, but there is perhaps a disregard of racial sensitivity among him and his friends at Harvard that subordinates racist attitudes to the free rein of creative expression. Many would see that as a freedom appropriate to art; many others would suggest that art should not perpetuate ideas that take away others' abilities to enjoy their own freedom. That debate continues.

Listening to Eliot read his poetry, it is startling to hear how his Anglophilia has replaced his low "sass-iety" drawl with heavy English tones full of tea and crumpets and porcelain in late afternoon London "hah societay." In print that same year, in an introduction to Edgar Ansel Mowrer's *This American World* (1928), he referred to his loss of his "southern" accent (Miller Jr. 36). A public face versus a private face, preparing to meet the faces he met, a desire to appear less "vulgar," or a sign of ambivalence about his relation to African Americans? Or all three?

We know that he shared Pound's anti-Semitism, and shared it with Pound, though he denied the charge in his later years. He parallels rats with Jews in "Burbank with a Baedeker," and refers in "Gerontion" to a Jewish owner who was "spawned" in a low-class bistro in Northern Belgium, at that time (and still) the center of the diamond industry and the place where the first stock exchange was established. His social and economic associations of Jews with wealth, money-making, control, and vulgarity are clear. However, Louis Simpson distinguished between Pound and Eliot on this issue: "Pound was outspoken, Eliot more discreet" (134), his racism "intellectually fashionable rather than heartfelt" (158). Still, overt and covert racism are both insidious, the latter harder to ferret out. The point is that, if Simpson is right and Eliot was more discreet, figuring out his attitudes can be more difficult. And it also means figuring out the nature of his ambivalences—American and racial—can be that much harder as well.

Perhaps one key is found in Eliot's ancestry. Eric Sigg reports that one of Eliot's ancestors, grandfather Reverend William Greenleaf Eliot, moved from Boston to Missouri and "worked to end slavery" (26). Of course, even abolitionists had their racial prejudices, sometimes being opposed both to slavery and to race-mixing, a troubling ambivalence. The Reverend Eliot's last book, *The Story of Archer Alexander from Slavery to Freedom*, was highly descriptive and critical of slavery. Although the elder Eliot protested modestly in his preface that his book was "a plain story plainly told" (6), in fact it took up the central divisive issue in America in the nineteenth century with a frankness and a sometimes vacillating but clearly negative view of slavery. With paternalistic condescension he described blacks as a "docile and easily controlled race. Subordination does not come hard to them." However, with implicit allusion to the sword of Damocles, he is able to see clearly that "[o]ver the best and most pampered slave, the sword of uncertainty always hung, suspended by an invisible hair; from which it came to pass, that, under the best of circumstances, the best condition of slavery was better than the worst condition of freedom" (28–29)—all in the space of three sentences in one paragraph! He acknowledged that acts of "severity or cruelty" did occur, though they were "comparatively rare exceptions, and in no part of the South were they the rule" (28); yet he owns that "there is nothing in the scenes of 'Uncle Tom's Cabin' as given by Mrs. Stowe, to which I cannot find a parallel in what I have seen myself and known in St. Louis itself, previously to the war of secession" (91). He was an abolitionist, but criticized as irreligiously violent the activities of John Brown (43). And in an appendix on slave marriages as "concubinage" (117), he makes the unequivocal judgment that "truly the logic of slavery was the destruction of humanity" (118). Eliot is remarkably good at communicating Archer Alexander's feelings, and he rarely overdoes his transcription of the dialect that Alexander speaks. He is a remarkable combination of flawed advocacy, combining well-meaning prejudice and principled opposition to slavery.

In 1920, when T. S.Eliot's mother asked him which books he would like sent to him as she prepared to move from St. Louis to Cambridge, Eliot marked ten items on her list of books, including Shakespeare, Browning, Propertius, and . . . the Archer Alexander book (*Letters* I: 398–99). One wonders whether, in addition to the fact that his grandfather provided an "early model" for the poet, this particular book had any meaning to Eliot's racial attitudes. In an address in 1953 at Washington University (which William Eliot had helped found), he identified "standard of conduct . . . moral judgments, decisions between duty and self-indulgence" as streaming from his grandfather as if Moses himself were bringing down sacred laws from the mountain (Gordon 8). If there was a touch of *noblesse oblige* or paternalism about the attitude, it marked the notion of responsibility for community service deeply ingrained in Eliot. And the grandfather's sometimes unresolved attitudes about African American experience—infantilizing prejudice coupled with an urge to ameliorate their conditions—seem to anticipate the poet's own prejudices against and appreciations of black people.

Eliot was acquainted with "American society's cultural and racial compexity," showing in the 1920s a "highly delighted and critical immersion in records of 'The Two Black Crows'" and in the 1940s a propensity for singing "music hall songs . . . or Negro spirituals, such as 'Swing Low, Sweet Chariot'" (Sigg 25)." The Two Black Crows," George Moran and Charles Mack, were an immensely popular blackface comedy team in the 1920s and 1930s, presenting aurally, visually, and behaviorally stereotypical images of African Americans from the minstrel show tradition. They offered hokey jokes in a slow drawl, with images of laziness, violence with razors and bricks, dishonesty, gambling, and drinking, not without good comedic timing and some good material, on stage, radio, records, and films. Their recording of "In the Jailhouse" (1929) even features a rather pointed reference to being arrested "on suspicion of being hungry," a phrase that may well have resonated with poor black (and white) audiences. The phrase "Two Black Crows" itself had common conversational usage among whites referring to blacks, and Bessie Smith sang in Porter Grainger's "Homeless Blues" (1927) ""Wished I was an angel, but I'm a plain old black crow," as well as in the well-known blues song "Crow Jane." With their comedic talent and popular prejudice on which to hang their hats, their recording "The Two Black Crows" was "the runaway bestseller on Columbia in 1927, [selling] over 1.3 *million* copies" (Brooks 211). Their recordings even included on three sessions the great black ragtime pianist Charles Luckeyeth Roberts—whose own sides for Columbia done in 1916 were not issued (Rust II: 1186, 1425). There was no hesitation to degrade the culture that was being exploited—in some cases, there was a tacit admiration embedded in the mockery.

Eliot, of course, would have been familiar with ragtime, blackface routines, and spirituals from his boyhood in St. Louis, sometimes named as a birthplace and certainly a center of ragtime. He lived, after all, "only a short walk from the Chestnut Valley 'sporting district'" (Sigg 20). Between the early 1900s and 1914, there were four published ragtime compositions with St. Louis in the title, including Tom Turpin's "The St. Louis Rag," all of them recorded frequently (Sutton 271–75), and ragtime pioneer-king Scott Joplin chose St. Louis as his center of operations in the mid- to late 1880s (Berlin 8). One does wonder whether Eliot, a connoisseur of puns and allusions, connected these "Two Black Crows" to an epithet famously applied by Robert Greene to William Shakespeare, the actor: the "upstart crow." Greene, of course, was commenting on Shakespeare's plebeian birth, precipitous rise, and literary scavenging among other authors' works. Whether those works were well used or ill used by their authors, of the scraps that Shakespeare purloined from the carcass, critics have usually proclaimed of Shakespeare's transformation of the earlier materials, "Lord, what food these morsels be." So it is with Eliot's borrowings. Are these "two black crows," explicitly black, one a minstrel end man with societal pretensions, the other a lazy and stupid foil to his partner, both of humble birth, and burdened with the stereotypes of dishonesty and stealing—might these two be upstarts seeking to insert a black voice, even a stereotypical one, into the contemporary polyvocal discussion of race? Eliot may well be enjoying the masks of the "Two Black Crows" for these kinds of social implications as well. The comic "distance" of the "Two Black Crows" from Shakespeare lessens/lessons dramatically.

It is worth noting that Pound wrote in *Guide to Kulchur* (1938) that "[a] civilization definitely runs down when for its best you go *away* from serious books to the comics, from the comics to the theatre, from the theatre to the cult of the music-hall" (89). In this attitude he was contradicted by composer and folk song–collector Ralph Vaughan Williams, who declared in 1902 that "[w]hat we want in England is real music, even if it only be a music hall song. Provided it possesses real feeling and real life, it will be worth all the off-scourings of the classics in the world" (McCleery 47). Brazilian classical composer Heitor Villa-Lobos even went so far to embrace folk materials as to claim "I am folklore" (Brennan 3). Eliot was an intellectual rag-picker, scurrying through the seamy St. Louis streets for moods and music. Or perhaps, as he described in the poem "Cousin Nancy," he saw himself as "Riding to hounds / Over the cow pasture," outraging society in his own way, as Nancy "smoked / And danced all the modern dances" (*Complete Poems* 17). The title of George L. Lansing 1898 composition "Rag Pickings," recorded by white banjoist George Van Eps in 1911, puns in the same vernacular vicinity.

Mark Twain, too, was known to love black jubilee performers, and to sing their songs himself as well, as did many other whites of the time. Of course, the public debate over Twain's racism, particularly in *The Adventures of Huckleberry Finn*, still raises significant hackles today. Were both writers (and at least 1,299,998 other people) vacillating between appreciation and depreciation of African Americans, paternalistically responding either positively or negatively to their subjects? Eliot's "discretion" intervenes between question and answer.

Important developments related to African American music in classical music in the era when "Prufrock" was conceived and written have interesting parallels to Eliot's poem. What some commentators have considered the first radical classical music of the twentieth century first appeared in 1906. It was generated by the co-founder of an insurance company (similar to part-time poet Wallace Stevens's near lifelong connection with an insurance company) and composer whose interest in American folk songs as well as dedications to Whitman in *Symphony No. 4* and Robert Gould Shaw and his "Colored Regiment" in *Places in New England* are also telling. Charles Ives's *Central Park in the Dark* is a collage-like piece that interpolates sounds of Manhattan (not Harlem) night clubs, including pop and ragtime songs, into his composition. These are juxtaposed with the mysterious moods of the Central Park woods, providing an interesting, almost dangerous atmosphere, topped off by a massive musical pandemonium and staggering dissonant chord at the piece's *dénouement*. Comments that the middle section of Erwin Schulhoff's *Double Concerto for Flute and Piano* (1927) is "an intermezzo in blues tempo" (Bek 11) certainly misrepresents the variety of tempi in blues music. Tempo does not a blues make. Ives followed that same year with *The Unanswered Question*, another collage piece that approaches the cosmic question of existence with audacity—from its opening psalm-like serenity to its responsive asymmetrical and atonal layerings of brass and woodwinds implicitly interrogating the implied peacefulness of a receding tradition.

It is not difficult to think comparatively about the poem that Eliot would start five years after Ives's composition, though Ives's work was performed infrequently during most of his lifetime. "Prufrock's" collage techniques, shocking interpolations, dissonant allusions and voices, lack of logical transitions, enjambment, possible use of the rhythms and language of the blues, varied line lengths, and concern with questions of existence (Eliot's speaker implores, "Oh, do not ask, 'What is it?'") were in the air at the time. Might various forms of African American music, either directly or indirectly, either have generated these techniques, or reinforced them in such a way as to have made them an important aspect of his aesthetic universe and technique? "Prufrock" was intellectually part and parcel of what the age demanded. Along with all the sheet music, piano rolls, folklore collections, performances, and recordings of African American music, it was quite a heady air.

A number of critics have commented on Eliot's use of minstrelsy, ragtime, jazz, and the blues in his work. Perhaps the earliest, Clive Bell, in 1921 connected Stravinsky with what Bell called "nigger music," and then placed Eliot in the jazz poetry (hot music) school as well. Bell wrote, "Apparently it is only by adopting a demurely irreverent attitude, by being primly innocent, and by playing the devil with the instrument of Shakespeare and Milton, that Mr. Eliot is able occasionally to deliver himself of one of those complicated and remarkable imaginings of his: apparently it is only in language, of an exquisite purity so far as material goes, but twisted and ragged out of easy recognition that these nurslings can be swathed" (Chinitz 13). This attitude toward

Eliot as a "jazz" poet was repeated by Gilbert Seldes in a 1958 NBC television show entitled *The Subject is Jazz: Jazz and Other Arts*, where Seldes asserted Bell "hated jazz" but found it was "destined to become the essence of the modern spirit." Jazz poetry possesses an attitude, "irreverent" (only in relation to the dominant narrative of American society) in tone, that enables Eliot to generate a dramatic monologue in which the poet's personal feelings are masked by that tone and a language that is imbued with the syncopation and vernacular expression of ragtime. To be "twisted and ragged out of easy recognition" is at once to associate it with a mask of popular art or alternative culture, through which it is difficult to strike in order to discern the meaning beneath. When Eliot's grandfather notes Archer Alexander's articulation, "Now I'se a white man. Now I'se free" (88), he reports the practical truth of societal status for Alexander alongside a palpable falsehood of associating freedom with self-alienation. As the elder Eliot states, "[T]ruly the logic of slavery was the destruction of humanity" (118).

Paul Laurence Dunbar, of course, was one poet in a long African American tradition of masking, asserting "We wear the mask / That grins and lies" (*Collected Poetry* 71) as a way of unmasking the face of minstrelsy as false merriment—"laughing to keep from crying," as the blues tradition would express it. He also exposes the veneer of African American music, with its overlay of abandon and gaiety, to reveal what Langston Hughes would identify in *Shakespeare in Harlem* (1942) as "the tingle of a tear" (*Collected Poems* 412). It was this so-called counter-cultural temperament and transgressive linguistic flair that appealed to Eliot, who was himself challenging the distinctions between high and low art by revealing how the juxtapositions of various social, artistic, and linguistic contexts in his work can produce the kind of improvisatory-trickster feeling that had been necessary on Simon Suggs's American marginal frontier, and was still necessary to negotiate the demands of the modern world.

Part of the con, after all, is to frustrate attempts to get at the truth by being convincing in all of your guises, by making them all seem authentic and real. It is in that liminal area where the artificial boundaries and false dualities that Eliot was challenging might best be stretched like the suspenders of a bespectacled London banker, or a pot-bellied Missouri rube. So how should we presume to say whether Eliot's voice is one or the other; which is authentic; when the obvious polyvocality of his work resists—militates against—fracture, out of its fractured state made whole? The words of the dummy, after all, are not the dummy's, whether we see the lips, ventriloquist's or dummy's, move or not. Although Michael Borshuk is correct in stating that modernists who adopted black voices "too often sounded of stereotypical exaggeration" (256), it is also true that that stereotypical exaggeration was sometimes intentional, and ironic. In other words, sometimes white modernist writers were in on what I described years ago as the "great African American joke": "retaining African American cultural identity in the face of the standards of the 'high' culture of dominant whites . . ." that represented a history and authority that were never present on American soil ("Simple's Great African American Joke" 239).

Other critical commentary on Eliot and jazz correctly identifies "music hall jazz" (as in Satie's *Parade*) as a separate component of jazz that Eliot employs (Yeomans 269); the overlap of various genres such as blues, jazz, and ragtime and their influences on Eliot's work as he "blacks up" for showtime (Chinitz 7–8, 18); Eliot's use of "jazz staccato" effects in "Sweeney Agonistes" (Yeomans 268), which was also purported by Eliot to have a jazz tempo; and the scene in Eliot's "The Waste Land" where Eliot "took Lil's pain and set it to ragtime" (Groves 173). Craig Raine makes a provocative and sound (!) description of "Sweeney Agonistes" as "a dramatic fragment, half Greek choral, half Jazz riff—Aeschylus on sax . . ." (Raine 115). In some cases the support for such assertions is very concrete; for others, as is frequently the case with criticism, the feeling is very subjectively in the ear of the behearer. A closer look at Eliot's work of the 1920s specifically in relation to the blues should illuminate the extent of Eliot's employment of the African American vernacular music continuum.

W. E. Yeomans identifies the influence of jazz on Eliot's poetry to be found in "mood, tone, rhythm, and beat" (268), and specifically the mood and tone of the blues to be a particular influence (271). Since the words of the blues have frequently, though not always, been associated with sadness and hardship, the tone of such early works as "The Love Song of J. Alfred Prufrock" (1915) and "The Waste Land" (1922) seem prime candidates for comparison to the blues: Yeomans's assertion that "Eliot's poetry is sometimes said to be oppressive and depressive in the extreme" (273) unfortunately stems from an incomplete perception and understanding of the blues tradition. So, while he makes a number of good points in his essay, they are sometimes undercut by his mistakes.

The blues themselves are neither oppressive or depressive, but life-affirming and powerful, even as they frequently explore hardship and pain. However, because the transcendence is frequently achieved in performance, through the impressiveness and articulation of the sound, accompanied by frequently unique and bravura instrumentalism, this is harder to tell from the printed page—where Eliot is working. Yeomans claims that "[o]ne is lulled away from the anticipation from the future to dwell completely in the present mood" (273), but the blues are performed to link a particular mood to its expression and, through that, to a current and future transcendence that only the power of art can supply. His recognition of the importance of lyric and rhythmic repetitions in the blues is astute, particularly his point about the nature of jazz/blues performance producing a spate of spondees at emotional high tension, though he does not explore these very fully in his discussion of the poems. And he makes the common mistake of suggesting that blues are necessarily "'woeful ditties' sung or played extemporaneously" (273), since they need not be sad and are frequently thought or written out in advance (see Taft, *Blues Lyric Formula* 18–24), the improvisation bounded by a number of elements. And when Yeomans declares that the blues singer "is usually called upon to play the role of the self-confessed fool who knows he will never learn better" (275), he misses by a wide margin the number of roles that blues singers can play. From the traditional figure of the liberated blues woman Ida Cox who dispenses advice, to the dogged determinism of the hardworking farmer or stockyard worker such as Big Bill Broonzy, to the tough, urban, streetwise persona of Peetie Wheatstraw, and so on, the blues is polyvocal, polyrhythmic, and polyphonic. Still, Eliot's collage method, pulling together a community of commiserants through use of their language, and distinctive, *tour de force* organization and expression, may well provide a release and transcendence similar to the blues.

In other places, Yeomans reveals perhaps an unconscious received stereotype about the blues musical culture. Yeomans asserts that "[t]he addicts of the modern blues song want to be cast into a trance, to be caught up in a spell of emotional turbulence" (272). Others, such as Carl Van Vechten, had discussed much earlier than Yeomans's 1968 essay a phenomenon where they perceived a blues singer like Bessie Smith putting audience members into a trance-like state, perhaps not unlike the effect of African American spiritual or gospel music might have influenced a church congregation (Tracy 316). However, the way that Yeomans states his point produces negative connotations. The notion that blues fans are "addicts" and that they want to be put under a "spell" (a word Albert Murray uses in *Stomping the Blues* 10) that produces "emotional turbulence" implies a lack of personal control and agency, as well as a mystical or primitive "rite"—a word Van Vechten uses (Tracy 316)—rather than a conscious artistic communication that produces cathartic relief in the listeners.

Yeomans, in fact, declares that "[t]he words of the song seldom signify very much, but the way the singer plays around with the word-sounds signifies a great deal" (272). While the second half of this statement is certainly true, to deny the central importance of *both* words and music—as Albert Murray seemingly does in *Stomping the Blues* (79–83)—is certainly ill-considered and inaccurate. The prevalence of certain formulas, phrases, and historically and socially relevant subject matter in blues lyrics indicate that the content and formulaic expression of that content works with the musical performance to produce artistically the power of the blues. For Yeomans, the lack of necessity of words produces some of what some commentators have seen as drawbacks of blues lyrics in the 1920s and 1930s: there is "no special advantage of carefully elocuted words in the performance" (272). On this subject, Murray discusses what he considers to be the impossibility of understanding some blues singers and lyrics as proof that these singers' words are less important, though not *un*important (83), without, apparently, considering that a local audience may well understand the blues singer's words and subject matter more fully and easily because of familiarity with both. There are certainly blues singers who produced recordings for a local audience as a way to promote him or herself in the community and not more broadly for posterity. His or her audiences wanted to hear about events on Will Dockery's plantation, as they did in Charley Patton's "34 Blues" (1934), along with his copious local references in his other recordings. And if Blind Lemon Jefferson referenced the climate in China in "Got the Blues" (1926) with the words "so cold in China the birds can't hardly sing"—a brilliant and creative image reduced to naught by Yeomans's and Murray's dismissal of the frequently luminous linguistic invention of blues performers—his audience would have appreciated it much less if he had sung it *in* Chinese.

Eliot, like the speaker in "The Love Song of J. Alfred Prufrock," was metaphorically straddling two worlds, one brocaded slipper in the rarefied drawing room, the other hand-me-down clodhoppered foot in the grimy gutters. He was alienated from the one because of its vapidity, from the other because of his ingrained prejudices, and yoked to both. Therefore, a closer look at "Prufrock" presents some interesting possibilities of blues music connections, though they are speculative and perhaps not as concrete or exclusive as we might like. For example, like the primary subject matter of the blues, this is a song about difficulties in love relationships and the desire to connect or reconnect. Pruf*rock* is a person who has been "rocked" by his experiences, seeking both nurturing (rocking) and sexual connection (as in Sweet Georgia Brown's "Rock Me in the Groove," discussed earlier) to help him cope with the manner in which his world has been rocked by ennui and acedia. Of course, the phrase refers to getting into the proper spirit of things as well—certainly a Prufrockian passion, if pursued lethargically and wearily—his own "weary blues." The word is part of his name, his identity, his petrification. It locates him psychologically in the "stone" age of primitive fears and desires, while he resides physically in the age of artifice. It defines him.

The mood of loneliness and isolation of the speaker, paired with his restless wandering through the streets peering at "lonely men in shirt-sleeves, leaning out of windows . . ." (*Poems* 5) creates parallels to social and lyrical elements of the blues tradition. Loneliness and isolation is ubiquitous in the blues, though of course references to loneliness obviously occur outside the blues tradition. The issue here is whether, in combination with other elements, they reinforce a blues-like ambience in the poem. There are some 140 references to songs with the word "lonesome," and another nineteen to "lonely," just in Michael Taft's large but certainly not complete collection of blues lyrics from 1921–1942, *Talkin' to Myself*. These include early occurrences in Ma Rainey's "Last Minute Blues" (1923), Clara Smith's "Prescription for the Blues" (1924), and Ida Cox's "Lonesome Blues" (1925). And when the singers of blues lyrics get lonesome or restless, they travel geographically or psychologically, by foot, train, or boat, or by blues lyric. For example, in Ma Rainey's "Walking Blues" (1923), Rainey expresses her restlessness and despair which results, as it often does in the blues lyric, in walking:

> Walked and walked 'til I almost lost my mind.
> I'm afraid to stop walking because I might lose some time (1923).

The next year she recorded "Lost Wandering Blues," in which she sings, "I won't stop to wandering 'til I find my man," linking her wandering to wondering: "I'm sitting here wondering will a matchbox hold my clothes." The language of just these two blues songs shares the mood and language of Eliot's poem. Walking, mental instability, fear, concerns about time, being lost and wandering through an empty and love-starved world, and wondering about her condition and activities—all these relate to the speaker in "Prufrock." He walks though "half-deserted streets" similar to the lonely wandering of Ma Rainey (*Poems* 4); expresses fear ("And, in short, I was afraid") (*Poems* 6), including misgivings concerning his appearance ("They will say: How his hair is growing thin!'") (*Poems* 4); dread concerning rejection at the hands of potential partners ("I do not think that they will sing to me") (*Poems* 7); incessant fear about time (ten repetitions of the word "time" in the space of seventeen lines (*Poems* 4); the search for a stable and satisfactory relationship (And should I then presume? / And how should I begin?") (*Poems* 5); and exaggerated wondering from insecurity ("Do I dare / Disturb the universe?") (*Poems* 4–5).

As a result of these concerns, Prufrock's sense of isolation, haunted loneliness, and self-deprecation find masterful expression in Eliot's lines "I should have been a pair of ragged claws / Scuttling across the floors of silent seas" (*Poems* 5). This image finds a parallel in Blind Willie McTell's "Talking to Myself" (1930), where the lonely, love-crazed speaker, declares with audacious and voracious sexual appetite "I'll gnaw your backbone half in two."

This comes in response to the singer being talked about (backbiting), but in the context of a song where he discusses enormous sexual prowess. He continues humorously,

> I took a trip out on the ocean, walked the sand of the deep blue sea,
> I found a crab with a shrimp trying to do the shimmy-shee.

The element of fantasy here, as with the fantasies of the speaker in "Prufrock," provides an opportunity for the speaker to suggest a solution for or resolution to his problem, though McTell's humor, laughing to keep from crying, does not have the immediate sinister connotations of Eliot's soundless, dissociative scene. However, it does compare with the marginalized, almost voyeuristic longing of Prufrock, even if the singer conveys a tone of involvement in the "shimmying" not experienced by Prufrock in his song. And those "ragged" claws may well be more than just "rough" or "shredded." Writers, musicians, and composers of the time spoke of the technique of highlighting ragtime techniques in a composition as "ragging." Art is (one syllable) "ragged," passed through the alembic of ragtime genius, as in the 1911 sheet music composition that used a twelve-bar blues structure, "When Ragtime Rosie Ragged the Rosary" (Muir 203; Street Incredibles CD). In the parlance of the title of a Rufus and Ben Quillian recording, it is "Ragged But Right" (1929). What are the benefits of being ragged? The song benefits from a different perspective, an offbeat one that produces a different tone and thus a different response, one with more perseverance, more optimism, more abandon. This would transfer that sea from isolating and marginalized locus to a place of expanded possibilities. Both meanings inhere in the same phrase, producing complexity and tension, but also partial relief. All this results from the ambiguity of this one word making it possible to see Eliot as a crab in blackface, submerged in a fluid Atlantic Adam's ale.

Fantasizing about a solution to a problem, sometimes outlandishly or fancifully, is present in a number of blues songs. Just as Prufrock creates his fantasy concerning mermaids to dissipate his isolation and loneliness, his reverie is interrupted, and put to an end by the tedious patter—"In the room the women come and go / Talking of Michelangelo" (*Poems* 4)—from another room: "Till human voices wake us and we drown" (*Poems* 7). Though allusions to mermaids are not frequent in the pre-war blues (and Eliot, of course, obviously draws upon the story of the Sirens in Greek mythology), there is an indication that they did have a place in the folk-blues tradition. Blind Lemon Jefferson's startlingly idiosyncratic blues style belies the fact that Jefferson was also a traditional blues performer lyrically. Reflections of the folk-blues tradition in Jefferson's work receive their own re-crafting musically and lyrically in his work, but the traditional lyrical element does suggest that what Jefferson sang had occurred in lyrics before he recorded them. Jefferson's "Stocking Feet Blues" (1926) provides a provocative parallel:

> Somebody just keep on calling me.
> She got hair like a mermaid on the sea

as does his "Dynamite Blues" from 1929:

> I'm gonna get in a cannon, and let them blow me out to sea.
> Going down with the whales, and the mermaids make love to me.

In each case, Jefferson associates mermaids with something remote and alluring. In the first case, he connects someone that is close by with something that is remote; in the second, he connects something that is far away with an immediate need. In all cases, there is a psychological journey ("Let us go then . . .") to potential fulfillment, neither of which is achieved within the two blues songs, or in "The Love Song of J. Alfred Prufrock."

Finally, the speaker's indication of the banality of his life—"I have measured out my life in coffee spoons" (*Poems* 5)—reminds of the blues's use of coffee in a variety of instances related to deprivation and sterility. Blind Lemon Jefferson sang in "Dry Southern Blues" (1926), a song about a blighted life: "I can't drink coffee and my woman won't make no tea." This verse of the song amounts to the singer's measuring out his own life with coffee and teaspoons, lamenting, perhaps misogynistically, his own inability to satisfy himself, and his woman's refusal to do so. George Hannah's inability—one hesitates to say impotence, since the song is about a gay man—to have a successful heterosexual relationship finds this expression in "Freakish Man Blues" (1930):

> I sent her to the mill to have her coffee ground,
> Because my wheel was broke and my grinder could not be found.

In both songs references to coffee indicate a larger concern with some kind of emptiness or difference that defines the singers' lives in a larger way. That may be impotence, or sexually grinding braggadocio, but neither are spiritually satisfying. As in "Prufrock," it is not really about the Maxwell House (another sexual metaphor that occurs in the blues—good to the very last drop!).

The possible connections go even further. For example, Eliot uses (what he would call in *The Waste Land*) "demotic" language and energized rhythms in

"Prufrock," often seemingly in a rush of energy that provides a release from the suppressed thoughts and mannered and intellectualized language of the speaker. Ralph Ellison famously commented that Eliot's rhythms in *The Waste Land* were closer to jazz than those of many African American poets (*Collected Essays* 203). Listening to Eliot read "Prufrock," these changes in rhythm become even more apparent. For example, "Prufrock" gains emphasis and momentum from the frequent repetition of words and phrases that works in the way a 1920s jazz soloist might. State a written melody, restate the idea, modify it a bit, explore the implications of that sound or idea, until eventually it leads you to another associational phrase that lilts off into hundreds of other "decisions and revisions" before one lands back down in the middle of that less-inflected, more-conventional bourgeois, Tin Pan Alley melody. Louis Armstrong's Hot Five version of "Twelfth Street Rag" (1927) exemplifies this. Based on ragtime elements, it was a popular song that had become conventionalized as a fast, virtuosic showpiece with which many people were familiar. Given Armstong's status as a virtuoso, people were likely expecting swift and sublime fireworks. Signifying on their expectations, Armstrong gives the song an elephantine pace and an exaggerated, clunky brass bass intro, and proceeds to a different sort of virtuosity. Armstrong takes the melody to syncopated places that are impossible to anticipate, making the melody express a thrilling enthusiasm and shocking unexpected abandon that surpasses mere measured super-fleetness. Listeners are quite often left with the question of not only how Armstrong did what he did, but how he *ever* conceived it. Those spaces he explored are the result of his existing in places, as a lower-class African American, that provided him with a complex perception of and perspective on life and art. That rollicking rag now everybody actually *heard*—as if Armstrong is implicitly saying, "here is what you get if you really know it and listen to where it came from way back, way underneath." The song is a transformation of conventional expectations but, more importantly, it is a revelation of black creativity and art. We'll never navigate "Twelfth Street" in the same way.

It is the art, the song, with which the artists disturb the universe, is produced by the magic lantern of creativity that, plugged into the nervous system of the musician (and Prufrock) projects the art into the atmosphere for all to behold. The repetitions of words and phrases such as "time," "Do I dare?," "have known," "would it have been worth," "that is not," and "at all" all indicate a lively and restless imagination turning thoughts, emotions, and ideas "every way but loose," as Blind Willie McTell sings in "Southern Can is Mine" (1931).

In another sense, this kind of repetition occurs lyrically in the blues as well. The haunting Skip James lyric on "Devil Got My Woman" (1931) contains such repetitions that, combined with the eerie, minor-tinged guitar field he floats in the piece, seems to place the sentiment and ambience in a hazy psychological otherworld—deliberately, of course:

> I'd rather be the devil [than] to be that woman's man.
> I'd rather be the devil [than] to be that woman's man.
>
> Aw nothin but the devil changed my baby's mind.
> Aw nothin but the devil changed my baby's mind.
>
> I lay down last night, lay down last night I
> Lay down last night, tried to take my rest.
> My mind got to ramblin like a wild geese from the West
>
> The woman I love, woman that I love
> The woman I love, took her from my best friend.
> But he got lucky, stoled her back again.
> And he got lucky, stoled her back again.

What James has done here is used a loose and distinctive guitar arrangement, with unexpected and shifting polyrhythms, an unearthly falsetto, and an unsettling tone, to mirror his situation in terms of the relationship he is describing in the song. The arrangement, even more than some blues lyrics, produces shifting, suspended vocal silences that disorient the listener's sense of time—and at one point separates the singer from his act, a caesural sign of self-alienation. When the singer does emote, he does so with a hypnotic repetition that is almost incantatory. "I'd rather be" (twice), "Nothing but" (twice), "the devil" (four times), "mind" (three times), "lay down last night" (three times), "the woman I love" (three times), and the last two lines (twice): the lyrics are eerily repetitive.

But the lyrics do provide a psychological progression that is associational, revealing his fractured and contradictory feelings. James begins by singing that he would rather be anything, traveling to the fullest limit away from conventional ideas of goodness, the devil, than to initiate or continue a relationship with the woman he introduces in the song. This hyperbolic statement he wishes the listeners to believe is true. However, he continues using the image, but turns it slightly, now blaming the devil for their separation. If he were the devil, he would be capable of changing her mind. So, does he want to be the devil or not?

Suddenly the devil disappears and he finds himself restless and in the dark—a reflection of his ambiguity, feeling his mind flit between these ideas, in flight in between, and perhaps even away from, his dilemma. This is reinforced by the altered lyric pattern and rhythms in stanza three, which increases the repetition and heightens the emotional element, while replacing the main image of the devil in the first two stanzas with a natural image associated with migration and travel—his searching here a metaphor for looking for better times in general, an escape from hard luck and toward a heaven of his own creation, if we can have recourse to the Son House lyric mentioned earlier. And then, perhaps wishing to emerge from his uncertainties, not just about some immediate and temporal love, he describes how he acted decisively in taking the woman he loves from someone else, a comment, perhaps, on the unpredictable nature of relationships. Interestingly, James does not make it clear whether the woman of stanzas one and two is the same woman of stanza four. This is perhaps because the cynical blues singer does not believe in bourgeois notions of happily ever after, and reflects this as a way of expressing unambiguously that he desires stability and control to conquer the ambiguities of life and love. Eliot and James share a mood that is produced with similar technique.

Did Skip James get this from Eliot? I think not. He did not have access to the education that would have exposed him to emerging avant-garde poetry at the time. Did Eliot get it from the tradition that assisted James in expressing himself in such a startling fashion? Did he hear that in St. Louis, or among his friends at Harvard, or with the Parisian intelligentsia, or through its evocation in compositions such as Antheil's music, or in music halls, or on phonograph records? Perhaps they both awakened at 3 A.M. from the same insidious nightmare? Unfortunately, the more instances we must interrogate, the more possibilities send back their ambiguous reply.

The shifting, rushing rhythms are evident in a number of places in "Prufrock." One prominent occurrence comes in his stanza dealing with Prufrock's sexually charged attraction to the arms of the women—the purity of the whiteness, the sexuality of the nakedness, the eroticism of the juxtaposition of "bracelet" and hair—recalling Eliot's admiration, expressed in print in 1921, of Donne's line from "The Relic," "A bracelet of bright hair about the bone" (*Selected Prose* 60). The rushing lines are preceded by three longer lines of ten to twelve syllables:

> And I have known the arms already, known them all—
> Arms that are braceleted and white and bare
> [But in the lamplight downed with light brown hair!] (*Complete Poems* 5)

Two of them have medial caesurae, and two have caesurae at their ends; the words in the third are bracketed. The repetition of "and" in the second line contributes a monotonous tone and cadence to its expression. The third also scans smoothly in iambic pentameter. These elements tend to slow down and stretch out the time and space in which they occur.

Eliot follows with two startlingly quick lines that interrupt Prufrock's reverie, accentuate a sense of unwittingly revealing too much, and punctuate that sense with syncopation, galloping with anapestical rhythm but with modifying pauses—as if one is gunning an engine and jamming the brake at the same time. Metrically, the lines are iambic, with an anapest at the beginning of the first line. Rhythmically, they syncopate the regularity, producing anything but monotony. This modification comes in the first line with the addition of an extra unaccented syllable at midline, and in the second by reducing the metrical pattern in the first foot from anapest to iamb, and adding the extra unaccented syllable to the next foot of the line in the rhythm of the way the line is read. This makes the "modified" iambs rush even faster compared to the regular anapest, and to the shorter iamb.

> Is it perfume from my dress
> That makes me so digress?

The lack of medial or terminal pauses scuttles the line along as well, particularly when proceeding out of a smoothly scanned iambic line, reinforcing an interruption, a fracture—and an awakening. The rhyming of these two short, fast-paced lines contributes a musicality that, combined with the metrical and rhythmic "differences" that offer their rushing and syncopated feel, produces a boogie woogie–like pair of lines roughly comparable to something like lines in Tampa Red and Georgia Tom's "It's Tight Like That" (1928):

> Mama had a little dog
> And its name was Ball
> And if you give him a little taste
> He want it all

This type of blues, in the AB refrain pattern, is different from the AAB pattern. Rather than providing each two lines of lyrics with a four-bar musical space as the AAB pattern does, the AB refrain pattern provides the first four lines with four bars, followed by another four with eight bars. Because the four lines transcribed here occur within four bars of music, they are sung faster in the musical space, rushing some syllables, twisting and pulling accented and unaccented syllables, and creating the improvisatory feel of natural, unfettered speech.

The connections between the poem and these blues songs do not have to mean that this is where Eliot got the mood and language. Given his familiarity with the seedier districts of St. Louis, it certainly seems more possible, though Eliot makes no reference to black folks in the poem. Nor does he include obvious references to the word "blues" or some well-known title of a blues song, as a number of writers have done with "St. Louis Blues," which was coincidentally first performed in 1914, three years after Eliot had begun "Prufrock," but one year before the poem was published in Harriet Monroe's *Poetry* magazine. Still, Eliot shares mood and language similar to the blues here that is at least suggestive of a relationship, or a concern that is shared by modernists and the African American lower-classes in their art.

These kinds of connections were not limited to "Prufrock." *The Waste Land*, too, has been the focus of some critics' sightings of elements from African American music. This is in part due to Eliot's explicit reference to an actual rag published in 1912 and performed in the Ziegfield Follies of 1912, "That Shakespearian Rag" (McElderry 185–86). Both writers of this song were prolific composers, having connections with Edison's early Diamond discs—introduced in 1912—the Ziegfeld Follies, and ASCAP. One of the writers, Herman Ruby, co-wrote some bluesy material recorded by Marion Harris in the early 1920s; the other, Gene Buck, co-wrote (among many other tunes) "The Vampire" with Bert Williams and Earl Jones, a song Williams performed in the Ziegfeld Follies of 1914. Both, of course, were involved in the minstrel and hot music scenes as they translated them to popular media, and thus held an attraction and revulsion for Eliot, who appreciated the energy, rhythms, and dramatic monologues but gave the hook to its masses-pleasing, masked banality. Of course, Old Will was a bit of a lecherous linguist himself, keeping one eye on the cheap seats while he spoke for the patronages. Eliot, like Shakespeare, knew the "Sittin' on the Curbstone Blues" (the theme song of bandleader Armand Piron, and also an unissued Bessie Smith title from 1923), knew the seamy side was just the inside of the tuxedo, even if they both still have objectionable racial or ethnic attitudes, if we can interpret them correctly from their art. Their tentacles were spread, ready to grasp and suck on anything that floated near their crevices, so pliant that they can slip into remarkably impossible places.

The title of Eliot's work itself evokes a harsh, degraded, and empty landscape—Winston Churchill's "terrible century"—that needs reformation and rejuvenation, socially, politically, spiritually, aesthetically, and artistically. It is not hard to see this portrayal, in one sense, as the awakening of the white world to the cognizance of this state of the American world that would have been so obvious to African Americans, as well as lower-class whites—for whom Whitman's "Look for me under your bootsoles" would have had an entirely different meaning. The dark, seamy underside of the American image would have simply been "our side" for many lower-class blacks restricted to areas of racism and discrimination, with the reminders of slavery's relentless beating of the hot sun, laboring under the restraints of time, cries for water from the water boy, and fragmented families and identities, coupled with the squalor of African American lower-class urban neighborhoods, with their rats' alleys and stony rubbish. In response to these conditions, African Americans generated songs about these things that named them, complained about them, fixed them in formulated phrases that helped them manage and control those conditions by mocking them with irony and humor, and by expressing themselves with idiomatic creativity and ebullience. They have, to key into the end of *The Waste Land*, *given* their bodies and souls, *sympathized* with the hardships they shared with their brothers and sisters, and assumed a modicum of *control* of their lives that brought them a (musical) measure of a *peace that passeth all understanding* with a massive reclamation of the "human" in "human waste." As Bessie Smith sang, brilliantly bluing a pop song over a tinkling James P. Johnson piano accompaniment in "Wasted Life Blues" (1929):

> I've traveled and wandered almost everywhere
> To get a little joy from life.
> Still I've gained nothin' but wars [worries?] and despairs,
> Still strugglin' in this world of strife.
> Oh, me! Oh, me! Wonder what will become of poor me?

Even on the manuscript copy of the lyrics in the Library of Congress, her philandering, conniving, and violent husband Jack Gee has attempted to take the writer's credit, but his name is struck out (*American Treasures of the Library of Congress*), and the strong-willed Bessie's supplants it, like a tree that's standing by the water.

Eliot sets both literal and emotional scenes that relate, at least as analogues, to black life and music in his times. In the opening section, "The Burial of the Dead," Eliot juxtaposes elements of signs of life and liveliness with elements of depression and weariness, as in "breeding lilacs out of the dead land," "mixing memory and desire," and "stirring dull roots with spring rain." In each case, an active participle precedes something that grows, causes growth, or indicates active attraction, along with elements of death and dullness. Much like in a blues song, elements of hard luck and ennui are put in a setting that encourages movement—dancing and singing along. In fact, the blues is intended to lift the spirit, even as it expresses the depression of mind. Out of the juxtaposition of the two comes a way of dealing with the sadness and maintaining the hope that is endemic to the blues. It is the consolation of the artistic endeavor, which is strengthened by the ability to exult in the mastery and domination of the experience, even if only for three minutes. And it is an aim of Eliot's as well.

However, it is extremely helpful to have the concrete reference to ragtime, even if it is a white version of ragtime, in order to be able to survey the landscape of his wasteland with a compass that provides comprehensive directions to the diversity of sites. A look at the drafts leading up to the final version of *The Waste Land* reveals that Eliot had more than just Othello doing the "Grizzly Bear" dance on his mind. A crucial change to his original manuscript, one recommended *so* erroneously by Pound, was the elimination of the epigraph from Joseph Conrad's *Heart of Darkness* (1902). Its perfect relevance and synchronization with Eliot's tone makes its elimination difficult to fathom. Pound said the passage was not "weighty enough" (Brooker and Bentley 44), and Eliot deferred to Pound's judgment. The passage's connection to the jungle, primitivism, and relationships between blacks and whites—the blacks mysterious, frightening others—would have enriched and reinforced a number of textual points, and certainly fed into Eliot's serious rag-tomfoolery. That is not to suggest that what he replaced it with is inadequate. The starkness of the void echoes in the Sibyl's response to the question of what she wants: "I want to die" (*Complete Poems*). This is a sentiment frequently expressed, sometimes in a brilliantly vivacious way, in the blues. Ma Rainey articulated a tortured plea in "Slave to the Blues" (1926):

> Blues do tell me, do I have to die a slave?
> Do you hear me screamin'? You're goin' to take me to my grave.

Though the term can certainly be hyperbolic or metaphorical, Ma Rainey very clearly expands the context of her song to the African American slave past. This makes her lament something much more than one woman trapped in a bottle or jar—though that extreme circumscription is certainly enough—and an issue that must be understood in the broader slavery–Jim Crow continuum, just as it clearly refers—in a vulgar boast by a lower-class Roman in Petronius's *Satyricon* appropriated by Eliot—to more than ancient mythology. Barbecue Bob adds in "Hurry and Bring It Back Home" (1928),

> I got them blues, and I can't be satisfied.
> Got them so bad, I could just lay down and die.

His easy and matter-of-fact manner of welcoming death—just lay down and die—indicates the relief he would feel from the omnipresent dissatisfaction—he *can't* be satisfied—that he experiences while he is suspended in his limited life, waiting for his mate to return.

The Conrad allusion would have interacted with other elements that Eliot chose to exclude from the final version. In an early incarnation of "Burial of the Dead," at around line 35, comes the comment "Myrtle treated me white," (Eliot, *A Facsimile* 5), meaning "decently," as opposed to how a non-white person would expect to be treated. Blues performer (at the time) Robert Wilkins sang in "Falling Down Blues" (1929), "I'll certainly treat you just like you was white," though he followed with the threatening, "That don't satisfy you, girl, I'll take your life," which shows the implicit frustration with the idea. The comment is echoed by Eliot in another deleted passage later on, where the speaker is portrayed thusly:

> Then he wished he had been a young girl
> Caught in the woods by a drunken old man
> To have known at the last full moment, the full
> taste of her own whiteness. (*Facsimile* 93)

Just a few lines down, another passage refers to "his whiteness and his redness," from being penetrated by arrows of Christian sacrifice, satisfying him (*Facsimile* 93). Clearly Eliot has in mind racial identity, along with the symbolism of whiteness as purity, though at this point sullied by violence on one hand, sexual attraction to Christian self-sacrifice on the other—and made more explicit in Eliot's rewriting of the passage before he deleted it (*Facsimile* 97). Thus, Eliot emphasizes that whiteness is not quite the innocence it is knowingly and hypocritically portrayed to be. The "redness" may even be an oblique reference to Native American Indians, with savage and primitive undertones as well. This reference to race and class relations would certainly have broadened and deepened Eliot's social commentary, and fed directly off of the energy from Conrad's novel. Further, Eliot's allusion to Dickens using the language "he do the police in different in different voices" can certainly be connected to minstrel language, with the lack of proper agreement between subject and verb. The phrase even explains Eliot's concluding eleven lines in the poem, with their polyvocal, polylingual expression which is eerily like a possessed Linda Blair spewing voices out of a haunted well in *The Exorcist*. It also evokes the tradition of African American parody of white folks in such performances as the cakewalk, which parodied white folks imitating blacks, which was then re-adopted by whites! Criticizing the police as authority figures is also quite frequent in early blues, as in Rosa Henderson's "Chicago Policeman Blues " (1926), Dessa Foster's "Tell It to the Judge" (1931), in which the policeman is portrayed as following a brief knocking with a gruff "Open the door before I blow the knob off," and Coley Jones's "The Elder He's My Man" (1929):

> Ashes to ashes, dust to dust,
> The police don't get you, now the undertaker must.

Actually, we all do the police in different voices, prepare faces to meet the faces that we meet. For example, I speak to casual friends with a relaxed grammar and tone and what some people might call white midwestern intonation. For my academic friends I produce formal diction and careful pronunciation, with expanded, Latinate vocabulary. When I speak with other musicians, my voice drawls in a southern manner, more informal, and unfortunately more profane. And when I sing, I am a full-fledged southern growler and shouter, more assertive and bold than a shy little boy ever thought about being. Even my harmonica voice is different—huge, manic, staccato, relentless. The fragmented me seeking to integrate the pop, folk, vernacular, formal voices, the adult and child voices, the male and female (Tiresias) voices, the life and death voices. And each of these voices has an authority of its own, ruling and controlling one aspect of my life and personality. Which voice is mine? Which me? Do they embody a supernal oneness, or an infernal twoness? Emerson and Poe await the answers in the wings.

An integral figure and voice of the poem, Tiresias, he of the "wrinkled female breasts," combines not only man and woman in one body, but also embodies the eternal struggle between males and females regarding sexual supremacy. In the classical mythology in which Tiresias answers that women get more pleasure out of sex than men do, Tiresias is both blinded and given the status of a seer, making him blind but "sighted." The fact that he is described as "throbbing" in two consecutive lines (*Complete Poems* 43) signifies both the sexual attraction and sexual tension for Tiresias in the poem, as it highlights the signifying relationships between male and female blues singers on the stage and on records. These kinds of battles between duet-singing blues singers are legion, including Butterbeans and Susie ("Elevator Papa, Switchboard Mama" 1930), Lonnie Johnson and Victoria Spivey ("New Black Snake Blues" 1928), and Grant and Wilson ("Have Your Chill, I'll Be Here When Your Fever Rises" 1930). But we might even go one step further with Tiresias, comparing this blind prophet to the proverbial blind blues singer whose voice is the communal voice, male and female, lamenting, and transcendent.

There are stories, for example, about blues singers such as Blind Lemon Jefferson and Blind Willie McTell being able to navigate their ways through complex city streets, or tell the different denominations of money merely by feeling them. Is the contemporary Tiresias the voice of the blues singer, self and other, describing the state of contemporary society through the hybrid music, myths, and lives of the conglomeration of voices that was less part of the melting pot than lagniappe of central importance? Or is it the hermaphroditic blues singer "Peach Tree" Payne, who shares his own sexual ambivalences in "Peachtree Man Blues" (1923).

Bolstered by two other references to minstrelsy and ragtime, snatches from "By the Watermelon Vine" and "Cubanola Glide" (Eliot, *A Facsimile* 5), Eliot would have had a direct inroad into the heart of American darkness. The fact that these elements were eliminated does not make them irrelevant—they still form part of the context out of which the poem was conceived. And it must be clear that Eliot felt these references important enough to include at an early point in the poem, yet not important enough to make the final cut. Why not? Was "Shakespearian Rag" to be the sole vortex through which this energy passed? And was it sufficient?

"That Shakespearian Rag" was a white pop version of a ragtime song ultimately sprung from minds of "black and unknown bards" (James Weldon Johnson, *The Book of American Negro Poetry* 123). This immediately flashes upon us issues of fragmentation; appropriation; commodification; popular, vernacular, and high art dichotomies; African American identity and African American voice and expression; American identity; the necessity and strategies of masking (preparing a face, again) for both blacks and whites; racial relations; and ragmentation that could make even ragtime fingers dizzy. Shakespeare himself was known to pun on his name—how about associations with the primitive, so prominent among modernists at the time, manifested in the shaking of a spear? Shaking as a dance we have already discussed, as well as the relation of shaking to sexuality, which suggests the connection of the phallic spear/sphere, and perceptions of African Americans as possessing an exaggerated sexuality. That orifice-like repetition of expletives in the quote from *Hamlet* (not originally in the song), "O O O O," echoed in the following two lines with the repetition of the word "so" buttress this sexual meaning.

The song-stage "O," however, is not the "O" of the Shakespeare play, which Shakespeare may or may not have written, but does not occur in the original song itself. The "O" also has associations with the Hindu-Arabic numeral zero, meaning "nothing," which certainly connects ("only connect" say the symbolists) with Eliot's repetition of the word "nothing" in sections two (just before "Shakespehearian Rag") and three (lines 301–02), as well as with the sense of the desolate and empty scene of the end of *Hamlet* and this section of the Eliot poem. The stretched and exaggerated, vaudeville pronunciation of "Shakespehearian"—you can almost see the Jolsonian singer drop down on one knee, "jazz hands" quivering at the furthermost reaches of his outspreading arms, selling the song with cheesy emotion—brings a bit of low humor into Eliot's poem. The song is neither elegant nor intelligent—as ragtime can sometimes be—in this incarnation, but ludicrous on one hand, and tragic on the other (Wheatstraw's "One foot on a banana peeling, and the other foot in the grave"). We don't know whether to laugh or cry. Hamlet has finally acted, which is good, but he has paid a terrible price. Of course, African American music intends for us to act with it as well, with a communal expression that touches different segments of the community, expressing the individual, but satisfying the community as well. And the noble heart that cracks, is it not a designation we could apply to the role of the blues singers, who, though their motives were certainly not always innocent or noble, cracked their hearts for the community's sake. When McElderry claims that ragtime is written music, not improvisatory (85), he reduces ragtime to one incarnation of its different facets, since ragtime in the "joints" by non-reading musicians clearly contained a good bit of improvisation, although some memorization, possibly, as well. And when he says that the blues is the opposite of ragtime, he creates a false binary, since minstrel, field hollers, ragtime, blues, and jazz are only some of the musics that exist on a continuum of expression and meaning, and even black Christian religious music, though it expresses different takes on holiness than these other musics do, should be heard in that continuum as well. But I digress.

This commercialized ragtime did sell. It did pass to some for "high" culture. And it does parallel Eliot's fusion of "high" and "low" culture to the techniques of a classical composer like Stravinsky's use of the jazz idiom (Raine 88), or any of the other classical composers discussed in similar terms in this text. How does its use relate to the African American ragtime tradition, to that back story? Why can we not just unmask? The contemporary world cannot ignore these contexts, no matter how hard it tries, and this one brief reference reveals a world of phoniness, duplicity, pretension, and violence masked by open-armed loving gestures and praise of created and imposed stereotypes. A handful of dust thus becomes fear.

As discussed in relation to Prufrock, the repetition and rephrasing of words or verbal constructions sometimes suggests a musical improvisation perhaps akin to African American music. Eliot's repetition of the word "time" in a variety of places and cadences certainly can suggest not only improvisational phrasing but elements of call-and-response as well. Certain phrases are repeated: "There will be time" (*Collected* 4) and "Hurry up please its time" (*Collected* 41–42), for example, present a sense of urgency in seemingly casual social situations. "He'll want a good time" (*Collected* 41) and "the time is now propitious" (*Collected* 44) both refer to sexual liaisons. The allusion to Andrew Marvell's "at my back I always hear," in Eliot "at my back from time to time" and related to the time of the dead ("a rattle of dead bones") (*Collected* 43), yokes themes of *carpe diem* and *memento mori*. Other references to time include seasons (winter and spring), day and night, the empty niceties of "tea-time" (*Collected* 4) and the sinister "violet hour" (*Collected* 43), which later straddles both time and atmosphere with a reference to the "violet air" (Collected 48). In African American music, of course, it is elements of time that create ambience—syncopation, polyrhythm, melisma, glissando, rubato, fragmentation—in ways that mix laughter with tears, a laughing to keep from crying, a grim irony not lost on Eliot, whose comic elements in the poem are underrecognized. Another sinister reference to a famous poem, Whitman's "Out of the Cradle Endlessly Rocking" as "out of the window perilously spread" (*Collected* 44), ironically juxtaposes youth and eternity with precariously placed drying unmentionables in preparation for a mechanical assignation that does not partake of the idealized endlessly rocking cradle. There is a call-and-response in the relation of mechanical duration to Bergsonian dramatic time invested with emotions—fear, anxiety, excitement, boredom—that produces an active interplay in these elements in syncopated phrasing, contrapuntal agitation, and antiphonal recurrence that produce an activity and a spirit not unlike that in African American improvisatory musics, what Langston Hughes calls the sob of a jazz band with the rollicking laughter of the performance. It makes the poem shake with anticipation, rattle the bones of the past, and roll with ennui through a ragtime landscape, gambling that the dance with death and decay will result in a piece that passes all understanding.

To these rhythmic elements might be added Eliot's frequent enjambment in *The Waste Land*, as in the opening lines of the poem. By spilling over the meaning of his words to another line into another line, he emphasizes particular parallel words with the slight hesitation or fracture of his cadence. Words like "breeding," "mixing," "stirring," "covering," and "feeding" (*Complete Poems* 37), placed as they are, all produce the initial word of the following clause with the words of the previous one, providing a lurching or anticipatory effect not unlike a brief interlude of syncopation. This effect also occurs at line 43 (38), in conjunction with a change to less formal diction and the slang phrase describing the pack of cards as "wicked." The cards, of course, are not inherently evil. In fact, "wicked" does not imply evil here at all, but Madame Sosostris's ability to manipulate them in virtuosic or impressive fashion. "Wicked" as a term that is ironic in the context of its original meaning appears in F. Scott Fitzgerald's work in 1920. It is, in a sense, a trickster-like taunting of notions of wickedness, similar in motivation to the appropriation by African Americans of "nigger" in a positive sense, or "bad" turned around to mean "good." In this case, Eliot offers one enjambed line, and splits his main clause, suspending meaning across two lines, producing something like a syncopation effect that accompanies the nonstandard word usage, giving the lines as they are read a shifting, halting, then motoring feel like a snow globe being observed from various perspectives, or a jazz clarinet solo.

In "The Music of Poetry" (1942), Eliot wrote of Edward Lear's mid- to late nineteenth-century poems employing nonsense language as being a "parody of sense." Those poems of "unrequited passion" are, in a sense, similar to the blues, in which we "enjoy the feeling of irresponsibility towards the sense" (*Selected Prose* 110). Eliot's extensive use of sound repetition in *The Waste Land* (twit twit, jug jug, ta ta, Weialala, leia, la la, drop drip drop, co co rico, Da, Datta, Dayadhvam, Damyata, swallow swallow, Shantih shantih shantih) come close to suggesting Lear-ing nonsense sounds (jug jug especially, since it was by this time a slang term for female breasts), as well as scat singing evident in ragtime performances by performers such as Joe Sims, Ben Harney, and Tony Jackson (Morton CD set), along with recordings by Gene Greene in 1909, and an Al Jolson recording of "That Haunting Melody" from 1911. Ethel Waters's premier recording of "That Da Da Strain" (1922—also recorded by Annie Meyers, Mamie Smith, and Eva Taylor around the same time) is extremely suggestive in its nonsense syllable references to Dada (as baby talk for "father" but also unintended allusion to the artistic group with its ridicule of modern art and culture and prominent collage techniques), and thematic employment of shaking, dancing, insanity and craziness, wildness, and reeling brains—all of which have connections with the times and literary works under discussion in this study. Hindemith himself can be seen as wedding dada and jazz in his work of the time (Horowitz 120). Two other important recordings, one by Louis Armstrong in "Heebie Jeebies" (1926) and the other celebrated use of "beedle um bum" in Tampa Red's hokum blues trailblazer "It's Tight Like That" (1928) are also notable. Of course, Eliot's "O O O O" from his allusion to "Shakespearian Rag," helps solidify the connection.

Once again, *The Waste Land* employs repetition of words in a variety of places. Lines 111–26 feature the repeated words in various places in the line, with various emphases. This placement also conveys a frantic darting and shifting that indicates the movement of a distraught and desperate mind or, for an artist, an attempt to portray these feelings with artistic vision and verve:

> "My nerves are bad tonight. Yes, bad. Stay with me.
> "Speak to me. Why do you never speak? Speak.
> "What are you thinking of? What thinking? What?
> "I never know what you are thinking. Think." (*Complete Poems* 40)

This is an extended portrayal of various usages and meanings of central words much akin to a solo that moves from a whimper to a scream with various stops upon the way. For example, the word "speak" opens and closes the second line, first in a three-word dactyllic sentence that through the imperative commands direct communication with the speaker; then in a one-word imperative sentence that seems to reduce to "just say something!" with the back-to-back stressed syllables in the latter producing even more emphasis. In between, there is a five-word, six-syllable sentence that interrogates the person being asked to speak. This middle sentence presents a somewhat uneven fulcrum for what surrounds it, abrupting into the notion that meaningful speech, serious speech, even any speech is seriously lacking in the marginalizing existences of the contemporary world.

If only there were some real "speak-easy" that would break through the masks, repeal the prohibitions, unfetter the inhibitions. Speakeasies, of course, were widespread during Prohibition especially. They were bars and clubs that sold illegal alcohol, and frequently featured blues or jazz entertainment, and were mentioned in King Oliver's "Speakeasy Blues" (1928), Georgia Tom (soon to be Thomas A.) Dorsey's "Been Mistreated Blues" (1930), and Ethel Waters's "Loud Speakin' Papa (You'd Better Speak Easy to Me)" (1925). For Eliot, and a number of others, it seems, putting on a black mask, which is not the same as unmasking, sometimes got the "other" juices flowing. However, like the unmasking of Lon Chaney's character in *The Phantom of the Opera* (1925), what it reveals is the misfit beneath.

From this external and verifiable act, the next line proceeds to three questions about what supposedly precedes speaking, thinking. Here the interrogative "speak" is repeated more than anything else in the line (three times), followed by "thinking" (twice). The sentences themselves gradually shorten until the end of the line, while the final "what" actually expands the question—not what specifically, but what at all? This suggests a deeper burrowing into the mind of the person to whom the questions are posed, and a tension between reduction and expansion that increases the pressure of the expression. The following two-sentence line repeats "thinking" and "think," the first a question in a sentence of seven words, the second a command in a sentence of one word. This seems to magnify the intra-line relationships of the other three lines, and juxtapose the most extremely divergent two sentences in terms of length. These various sentences with repeated similar words, sometimes starkly different from what becomes before and after, suggest a deliberate playing with rhythms on the same ideas, with percussive staccato effects, rolled into a little crystal ball that reveals the inner mind of the respondent, with its grim and sinister alley, dead men, and bones. It is a dirge-like, arranged improvisation, full of energy and not the least bit obtuse, artfully portraying skillfully and passionately the state of the contemporary mind. The expression of these elements as the speaker portrays his own excessive troubles captures both the difficulties and will to express and prevail. The spirit of the blues.

The entire section has an immediate, improvisational, syncopated feel, Eliot playing with phrasing to tease out the emotional and intellectual content of the words, what the blues singer might call grabbing it and turning it every way but loose. A phrasing of emotion through sound, with a changing (de)cadence of words to guide the sound. This reminds of what John Coltrane did in a section of *A Love Supreme* (1964), actually playing notes that conformed to the cadence of a prayer he wrote and included in the liner notes to the album, and milking the sounds for all their emotional content. Perhaps Eliot and Coltrane drank from the same well, no empty cistern or dry well, since despite the blues lyric "You never miss your water 'til your well run dry," the blues well never runs dry.

Other popular British slang references take us to the land of blues as well. When *The Waste Land* mentions "hot gammon" in section two (*Complete Poems* 42), the contexts of lower-class slang, "hot music," and sexual and anatomical euphemisms in the blues come gushing from the pork. Relating African American "hot" music to African Americans regarding sexuality was common at the time. To evoke ham or bacon is to open up the field of appetitive metaphors in the blues. Such sexual references to ham and bacon occur in Bessie Brown's "Pork Chop Blues" (1924), Ed Bell's "Ham Bone Blues" (1927), and Charlie Nickerson's "Everybody's Talking About Sadie Green" (1930), the latter of which praises Ms. Green with "Legs look as nice as a Georgia ham," as well as numerous songs discussing the attractions of "pig meat," such as Mae Glover's "Pig Meat Mama" (1929) and Georgia Tom Dorsey's "Pig Meat Papa" (1929) and "Pig Meat Blues" (1929), along with The Hokum Boys's "Pig Meat Strut" (1930). The reference to a shapely and attractive leg of a woman as a "gam," dating to 1775–1785 (1110), makes the double entendre meaning obvious, and thus this episode crackles to the sizzling of the blues.

The scenario of Mrs. Porter and her daughter provides another vernacular moment, not necessarily African American, but certainly in the recognizable spirit of unexpurgated African American toasts. First, "O the moon shone bright on Mrs. Porter" (*Complete Poems* 43) reminds of the white southerner Stephen Foster's "Oh the sun shines bright on my old Kentucky home," a white romanticized version of the southern slave environment, and a palpable falsehood that renders ironic the reference to the theoretically illuminating light of day. Folk anecdotes about a "randy" woman and her nubile daughter abound in world folklore. But Eliot's song takes an unexpected detour from the pornographic in having the two women wash their feet—unless a foot fetish is implied. In unexpurgated songs, the women baptize their genitalia. "The sounds of horns and motors" evoked by Eliot recalls the futurist preoccupation with contemporary industrialization as urban thermometer and soundtrack, as in *Ballet Mécanique*, which they themselves also associate with the contemporary rage for "hot" music stemming from African American culture. Indeed, Le Corbusier would call skyscrapers "hot jazz in stone or steel," and John A. Kouwenhoven felt that jazz and skyscrapers were "the climactic achievements of the vernacular tradition in America" (Pollack 218). All of these interpenetrating elements and the evocation of rhythms of "naughty" toasts and "bawdy" music-hall songs lead to an overwhelming question about the application of blues modalities to this passage.

The employment of signifying—a common verbal strategy in African American culture that relies on indirection, though not exclusive to African Americans—is certainly a central trope in African American culture. Thus, the employment of that strategy in the section treating Lil and her demobbed husband, especially considering the setting in a bar; the lower-class language; the illicit sexuality frequently associated at the time with African Americans; and repeated references to the pressure and value of time (relating both to life and musical time) mobilize the blues forces for interpretive action. When one female speaker slyly suggests that Lil's husband may be appreciated more by other women, Lil responds archly, "Then I'll know who to thank," punctuating her thought with a "straight look" (*Complete Poems* 41). This is clearly signifying of the type reflected in Romeo Nelson's "Gettin' Dirty Just Shakin' That Thing" (1929): "The broad catch you signifying, you breaking her down." It is also possible to wonder whether the situation of demobilization, slanged to "demobbed" here, might possibly gloss to the violence perpetrated upon African American soldiers upon their return to society in the "Red Summer" of 1919, and further to the dangerous lynch mobs that pursued African Americans like so many hellhounds. Perhaps this might not even have occurred to Eliot, though the East St. Louis, Illinois, riots of 1917 were very prominent precursors to the 1919 riots, some of which occurred in St. Louis. The tingle of African American tears tinkles remotely on a battered upright—not a *grand*—in the dog whistle range of this passage.

The vicissitudes of the deactivated soldier are not foreign to African American music of the time. Examples of "military blues" include "Soldier Man Blues" by John Jacob Niles before the publication of *Singing Soldiers* (1927). Even earlier, Howard W. Odum reported soldier blues by African Americans as treated in *Wings on My Feet* (1929). John "Big Nig" Bray's recording of "Trench Blues" for the Library of Congress in 1934 is an extended treatment of black experiences in World War I, while laments about Uncle Sam separating black couples are fairly common in the era. None of this necessarily plants Eliot's episode in the poem in African American experience, but it is suggestive of issues in the era that relate Eliot's experiences to those of African Americans.

Further situations and language shared by the blues (and, of course, many other genres as well) and *The Waste Land* include "lidless eyes" (41) preventing sleep, as in Mamie Smith's "Crazy Blues" (1920), which begins "I can't sleep at night." Waiting for a knock on the door, or hearing one, is also fairly regular, as in Papa Charlie Jackson's "Coffee Pot Blues" (1925):

> It was early one morning, just at the close of four,
> When Dolly Smith knocked on Evelyn's door.
>
> She jumped up, sweet babe, tipped on across the floor,
> Hollerin' "Long tall daddy, don't you knock no more."

Coming between the song that derives from a song about Mrs. Porter and her daughter washing their pudenda in soda water and the suggestion that Lil's husband might be given a "good time" by someone else, this tale of sexual longing and frustration might clearly be associated with the meaning of this passage.

Women and men being done wrong (41–42) is ubiquitous in the blues, as in the recording of the blues ballad "Frankie" by Edith Wilson (1921) and "Frankie and Johnny" by Nick Nichols (1929)—and, as pointed out earlier, both collected and recorded by Carl Sandburg in 1927. River banks (42, 47, 50); humble backgrounds (46) such as coming from the bottoms—also sexual—as in "Low-down Mississippi Bottom Man" (1928) by Freddie Spruell; "once was, now am" scenarios (46–47) such as Bessie Smith's "Nobody Knows You When You're Down and Out" (1929)—it *is* a mean old world to try to live in. And when you face death? "The rattle of the bones, and a chuckle spread from ear to ear" (43) mixes unsettlingly with "laughing to keep from crying." Whose chuckle is it? And is that a minstrel rattling the bones, blackface with a huge, ludicrous smile painted on? It certainly complicates the image Eliot presents, suggesting death's chuckle at our coming, the minstrel's mockery of our sense of reality, and the hopeless gullibility of the crowd's belief in those illusions that rule our lives. The traditional song often called "See That My Grave is Kept Clean," "Two White Horses in a Line," or "One Kind Favor" deals ominously with toning bells, coffins sounding, interment, and the unchanging desolation of death that seems related to images and tone in section five. As Blind Lemon Jefferson sings (1927), "the poor boy's in the ground"; and the "Dry Bones" (*Collected Poems* 49) perhaps a reference to the biblical story or even the African American spiritual, offer no threat, because, as Jefferson proclaims, "the poor boy's dead and gone," and "it's a bad way [wind?] that don't never change." This kind of entrapment, of course, leads Eliot to contemplate life as a prison, something common both in black chain gang songs and the blues, where songster and older-generation blues singer Henry Thomas sings in "Don't Leave Me Here" (1929), "She bring me coffee and she bring me tea. / She bring me everything but the jailhouse key," thinking of the key that confirms not only his immediate physical imprisonment, but a fear of abandonment and loneliness that may be cosmic. When Bessie Tucker moans her melismatic, field holler blues "Key to the Bushes Blues" (1929), she refers to having the way to escape the penitentiary, through the bushes and into freedom, though it is a boast that seems not to be true, only confirming her imprisonment as well. Of course, one needs hope, perseverance in the face on incalculable odds, some fragments to shore against the ruins of one's life to keep on fishing (see Henry Thomas's "Fishing Blues" 1928), trucking (see Big Bill Broonzy's "Trucking Little Woman," 1938), and singing.

So if, as I expressed earlier, *The Waste Land* is one long lament, personal and communal; rooted in tradition; polyvocal, with vernacular language, metaphors, and situations; using touches of repetitions and syncopations that combine lamentation and hilarity; with a philosophy of endurance in the face of death and destruction, leading to artistic and human transcendence, is it the blues? Well, not in a conventional African American musical sense. But of course we have seen that there is so much more than the conventional African American musical sense to the blues. The poem is a complex mix of elements related to emotional, social, and aesthetic aspects of the black blues as they have fanned out into popular manifestations in cabaret, music-hall, and pub performances, sheet music, player piano rolls, classical experiments. They have siphoned through racial prejudice, class inequities and antipathies, and discriminatory aesthetic binaries of "high" and "low" art. If it suggests, as does the blues, the validity of treating African American art as a local manifestation of internationally applicable situations and feelings, even if some prejudices are still on display, is it sister-song to those of Mamie Smith, Sophie Tucker, and Dana Suesse's *Jazz Nocturne* (1931)—itself a Gershwinesque classical composition that led to Suesse's pop-jazz songs such as "My Silent Love," performed by the monumentally popular white singer with a jazz feel Bing Crosby? Connect the dots to Al Jolson, Emmett Miller, George Gershwin, William Grant Still, and George Antheil? And Palmer Hayden and Katherine Dunham and Piet Mondrian?

There are, of course, other poems by Eliot from this time that can be related to the African American blues music tradition, including the blues. The decision to focus on "Prufrock" and *The Waste Land* in a comprehensive manner springs from the idea that, since these are Eliot's major works pre-1930, an extensive treatment of these two works can provide a template for further studies. Because of Eliot's elusive and evasive techniques and polyvocality, obvious, direct, and concrete references are not frequent. This forces us into perspectives from the marginal, "othered" areas of American society and culture. Obvious and suggestive meanings emerge from below the Mason-Dixon line, outside the *salons* of Paris, and up above on that "high old lonesome hill" from which Bessie Smith took the measure of her disaster-laden existence in "Back Water Blues" (1927). (Hetero)glossing Dante, Eliot quivers, "I had not thought death had undone so many" (*Complete Poems* 39). For Bessie Smith, it was "I had not thought African American life had undone so many," though, as Sterling Brown asserted in his poem "Ma Rainey," which quotes Bessie's "Back Water Blues," "undone" does not preclude re-done, death does not preclude resurrection (Brown, *Collected Poems* 62–3). Because Eliot's life, ideas, and attitudes paralleled the complexities of his poems and times, wandering the half-deserted but crowded streets of his psyche, shrinking from but fascinated by the baby-faced bats haunting the soundless seconds of interminable time, the clues are often vague and murky. As the rags of time emerge into the rags of art, it is perhaps best to attend to the syncopated, the skipped and skipping heartbeats, that make the rags what they are.

III

The decade of emerging literary modernists termed "The Jazz Age," with "hot" music deep-hued and in tune with the "out of tune" feelings of Pound's own Hugh Selwyn Mauberley, was striving to come to terms with blacks and blues and jazz, sometimes only half seriously, as a trendy or avant-gardist pose (Bone, "Preface" ii), in part as a way of effecting a literary renaissance. It is not surprising that William Carlos Williams, searching for a new measure and a new form to challenge the artificial forms of the past, seeking to be colloquial, and revolutionary, "ragging" on Eliot for his Anglophilic elevation, might be attracted to the music and what it might represent. In "For a New Magazine" (1929), Williams wrote a manifesto for Charles Henri Ford's journal *Blues* that suggests what blues and jazz represented for him at that time in the context of his poetic work, implying that the posture and achievements of blues and jazz were another analogue to his modernist aims.

The year 1929—the first year of publication of the journal *Blues: A Magazine of New Rhythms*—marked the end of the first decade of systematic commercial blues recording by black artists. As we have said, the early years of commercial blues recordings were dominated by women singers, from the earliest recordings of Mamie Smith, Lillyn Brown, Lavinia Turner, Daisy Martin, and Lucille Hegamin to the milestone recordings of Bessie Smith and Ma Rainey—as well as their white counterparts Sophie Tucker, Marion Harris, Annette Hanshaw, and others. Godrich and Dixon report that the years 1923–1926 were the years of the ascendancy of the vaudeville blues singers, "professional singers who sang mostly for city audiences, using fairly standard song material" (33), written often by professional songsmiths interested in altering traditional folk-blues forms and language to lend it a popular appeal. It was these blues singers, sometimes ostentatiously dressed as exotic "hot mamas" for the stage (as opposed to singing their blues alone in fields, at picnics, or on front or back porches where they had originally been heard), who established the broad popular city audience often first identified with blues music and its various commodifications in recordings, sheet music, and piano rolls (even if a strong connections with southern blackface minstrelsy frequently informed its image). Indeed, these women dominated the numerous resident and traveling stage shows and revues of the twenties, indelibly fixing them as the central figures of the first blues craze, though they had already, to varying degrees, left behind aspects of their folk-blues roots for a broader urban expression and appeal.

Blues: A Magazine of New Rhythms in some ways left those blues roots behind as well. With industrialization, modernization, and militarization promoting migration from South to North, the branches of American tradition stretched far beyond its roots, though the thematic and stylistic connections were still organically related to the American rural past. The changes in American folklife, from traditional speech, clothes, food, worship, song, dance, and other elements to the city ways that seemed colder, more dizzying, more avant-garde, more convenient, and more financially remunerative affected the orature and literature in significant ways. It rendered the orature, through the local color and realist movements, more available as a resource to the literature, particularly as a way of marking the contrast between the two, and what was lost and gained by each approach. This revolution in interest and perspective touched many of the black and white literati of the time, who saw contemporary developments of especially African American regional folklife to be the future direction of the development of American identity. As we have already discussed, the emergent African American "hot" music captured the interest of artists of many different genres and schools as a way of modernizing. Williams was one of those modernizers.

Among the various groups important for Williams were the surrealists, with their avid interest in jazz and blues. Drawn to jazz in part because of the primitivism that such critics as Mary Ann Caws and Anna Balakian identify as centrally important to the group, surrealist André Breton perceived jazz to be revolutionary in nature, though mysterious in method: Breton wrote in *Introduction to the Discourse on the Paucity of Reality* (1924), "In the flow of a phrase as well as the mysterious wind of jazz, reveal to me your plans for the coming revolutions" (Garon 25). In 1976 Franklin Rosemont reiterated the connection between blues and surrealism: "Surrealism is the exaltation of freedom, revolt, imagination and love. The surrealists could hardly have failed to recognize aspects of their combat in blues (and in jazz), for freedom, revolt, imagination, and love are the very hallmark of all that is greatest in the great tradition of black music . . . We find the blues to be, rather, a magnificent dream implying the total transformation of reality—an ardent appeal for a new life of all travestied hopes" ("Surrealism and Blues Introduction" 19). And, Rosemont continues, blues singers were singing such things when "the 'official' poetry in English was saturated with servility, puritanism, guilt, remorse, and decay, its stale rhythms marked by the clicking heels of fascist law and order" ("A Revolutionary Poetic Tradition" 20), references, it is likely, to Pound, Eliot, and Wyndham Lewis, whose "making it new" was in fact, in terms of attitudes and prosody, sometimes very traditional. This attack on central modernist writers, who saw themselves resurrecting and revitalizing English poetry, is an attack on one solution to the modernist dilemma, seen by some as the culturally chauvinistic authoritarian approach, though the issue is more complicated than that. While jazz would not be very much a part of Pound's method, it might be part of the democratic approach of Langston Hughes, or John Howard Lawson, or e.e. cummings, or William Carlos Williams. Indeed, Hughes was an important influence on Negritude and surrealist writers such as Louis Aragon, Etienne Léno, Léon Damas, Aimé Césaire, Léopold Senghor, and Ted Joans (Rosemont and Kelley 15, 23, 117, 130, 220).

Williams, we know, had contacts with surrealists before and during the time he contributed to the journal *Blues*. He contributed to a "surrealist" pamphlet *Aesthete* (1925) (Nadeau 30- 31), served as American correspondent for Ribemont-Dessaignes's *Bifur* in 1930 (Nadeau 32), and as American spokesman for surrealism in "Midas: A Proposal for a New Magazine," published in 1940. Ribemont-Dessaignes was an ex-Dadaist, described as being "most inventive in annoying their public," railing against the bourgeois and sometimes forming choirs in "imitations of the aboriginal negro chants" for shock value (Moholy-Nagy 98). Paul Christensen maintains that Williams saw that surrealism and jazz both "seemed fraught with protest and complaint" and that both "bore against restraint, calculation, and limits of any kind" (155). Of course there *is* calculation and restraint in jazz, and the question of how much social protest and complaint is implicit or explicit in blues and jazz has been argued unendingly. Suffice it to say that Williams had the perception of this aesthetic connection between surrealism and jazz, and that both would have been attractive to him for their championing of this freedom principle.

In addition, Williams received a letter from fifteen-year-old Charles Henri Ford, a blue-eyed Brookhaven, Mississippi, teenager touched by the surrealist's search for a new language and a juxtaposition of images possessing the logic of dreams, as well as by Walt Whitman and the rhythms of jazz. Ford (who dropped out of high school to carry out the project) and his associate editor Kathleen Tankersley Young sought editorial assistance with a new journal, and Williams seemed to fit the "bill." Gertrude Stein would later, in *The Autobiography of Alice B. Toklas*, call the journal "the youngest and freshest" of the little magazines attempting to liberate verse (Rood 193). A list of the writers who contributed to the short-lived journal contains some of the most significant writers of the time. Paul Bowles, Kay Boyle, Erskine Caldwell, James T. Farrell, H. D., Eugene Jolas, Alfred Kreymborg, Ezra Pound, Kenneth Rexroth, Laura Riding, Gertrude Stein, Williams, and Louis Zukovsky all lent their talents to the budding journal. So did New York poet and communist Herman Spector, who contributed, among other works, "These Are Those Back-Again, Once-Before, Home-Again Blues," where the speaker contrasts rural and urban environments while on a street corner, "dangling like a fly" (*Blues* 83).

Williams at this point would not have been influenced by Ford in any major way. Indeed, Williams's own experiment with surrealism, "The Agonized Spires," appeared in *Spring and All* (1923) some five years before he heard from Ford (Perkins 252). However, this young man struck Williams as a resourceful poet who had a talent for "using the banal to escape the banal" (*The Garden of Disorder* II). Karen Rood cites "Dicty Glide in Central Park Menagery" as an example of a poem that "draws together the clichés of modern culture to satirize that very culture" (199), and the title itself uses the common African American vernacular language to refer to a "snobbish, upper class or stylishly sophisticated" person or thing (Townley 94). It appears on record as early as Edna Hicks's "The Dicty Blues" (1923), as well as later in a 1929 Duke Ellington recording "The Dicty Glide." The term itself is an attempt to deflate the puffed up, as is Ford's poem, and Ford injects a bit of jazzy bravado into the address of the speaker to the anachronistic cowboy whose end is foretold in the poem. Such style and subject matter would have certainly appealed to the poet who wrote "Shoot It Jimmie" and "We wash too much and finally it kills us" (*Collected Poems* 216, 310).

Williams did see the influence of jazz on Ford's poetry, asserting in his introduction to *The Garden of Disorder and Other Poems* that Ford's poems create the state of mind necessary to understand them, and that state of mind is associated by Williams with "the radio jazz and other various, half preaching, half sacrilegious sounds of a Saturday night in June with the windows open and the mind stretched out attempting to regain some sort of quiet and be cool on a stuffed couch" (9). The effect "is to revive the senses and force them to re-see, re-hear, re-taste, re-smell, and generally re-value all that it was believed had been seen, heard, smelled, and generally valued" (9)—what Williams had written in 1923 in *Spring and All* his "Improvisations" had done for him (*Collected Poems* 203). The connotations of "radio jazz" are various. For one thing, it takes the music out of the immediate performance context and places it more firmly in the impersonal commercial and mechanized realm of which Ford and Williams were both critical, though the futurists would have embraced it. For another, the jazz that would have been heard on the radio around that time would have far more likely been jazz by white bands, like Paul Whiteman's, Ted Lewis's, Sam Lanin's, or the Casa Loma Orchestra's pop-jazz interpretations. Since Ford's poems contain his own (white) versions of jazz, neither the jazz of the music's creators nor for black jazz's original target audience, the reference is entirely appropriate in terms of pigeonholing Ford as an interpreter in some ways distant from the source of the music but in touch with its implications for the popular (white) mind. Radio jazz is the aesthetic coeval of Ford's poetry, but Ford's "jazz," for Williams, retains the ability to revise established traditional aesthetic concepts, partially through the surrealist connection, which did not seem to Williams an incongruous connection.

The questions concerning what Williams knew about blacks, jazz, and blues at this time in his life are important for establishing their relationship to his own aesthetic and setting a backdrop for the "manifesto" written for *Blues* and Ford. Mariani describes a Williams whose heroes, like his father's, were not "great egoists . . . but rather nameless figures;" and a poet who sought to be "part of a larger quasi-anonymous community of poets rather than emphasize his individual contribution" (10). Such admiration might easily dispose him to appreciate the contributions of anonymous blues and jazz performers playing in the trenches, so to speak, and expressing often communal concerns and values of a particular segment of the black community, all the while expressing their individuality in colloquial language as well. But there is not much evidence that Williams viewed the people or the music in this way at that time. Williams seems to have been somewhat insulated from the blacks and immigrants on the fringes of Rutherford by the "comfortable old Yankee money and showy opulence around" (Mariani 23), as well as in New York City, where Williams worked around 1909. There, surrounded by various immigrants in the high crime area of New York, Williams concerned himself with chamber music, opera, Isadora Duncan, and Gilbert and Sullivan, referring at that time to one of his black patients as a "coon" (Mariani 55). In *The Cultural Front*, Michael Denning reports that radical Mike Gold felt in 1935 that "[w]hen somebody writes the future history of the pioneer beginnings of proletarian literature in America, I am sure W. C. Williams will be somewhere large in the table of contents" for Williams's portrayal of "the unorganized American worker, and the horrors of the slum life he leads" (213). Nonetheless, despite his portrayals of ethnic figures, it was not entirely clear how well Williams understood them, or their cultural productions. Certainly he didn't explore the environment and issues as closely as, in an earlier generation, Paul Laurence Dunbar did in *The Sport of the Gods* (1902), nor as fully as his contemporary James T. Farrell did in his Studs Lonigan trilogy (1932–1935).

Williams's attitudes toward blues and jazz at this time are not as clear as they could be, but we do know that he cultivated an interest in classical music openly and made far more references to it than the vaguest references to jazz in his poetry, as in "Postlude" (1913), "Mezzo Forte" (1913), "The Death of Franco of Cologne" (1913), "Danse Russe" (1917), "Ballet" (1917), and "Divertimiento" (1917), as well as in his prose. Williams's black characters rarely achieve a three-dimensional status—he uses the word "nigger," which Alain Locke labels a "formula," frequently, as in the stories "Four Bottles of Beer," "The Right Thing," and "Above the River." Frequently blacks are associated with sex, as in "Sick African" (1914), "Canthara" (1917), and "Impromptu: the Suckers" (1927), or merely the physical, as in "Apology" (1917) or "Overture to a Dance of Locomotives" (1921). Paul Mariani avers that black women were "half-mythic, Amazonian presences to Williams" (15), as portrayed in the story "The Colored Girls of Passenack—Old and New"—sexually vivacious and irresistable, even if they are horrible housekeepers and cooks (*Collected Stories* 51–55). But Williams, like other modernists, found the so-called primitive to be immediate and valuable, as he wrote in 1923: "The primitives are not back in some remote age—they are not BEHIND experience. Work which bridges the gap between the rigidities of vulgar experience and the imagination is rare. It is new, immediate—It is so because it is actual, always real. It is experience dynamized into reality" (*Collected Poems* 220). In order to make things new and whole, as Pound and the imagists suggested, one needed to subject the primitive to the transforming imagination to make a bridge between the experiences inherited from the past and current realities, the mundane realities of the past and the procreating potential of the imagination.

Of course, while growing up, Williams's imagination was stoked by many things, including materials related to black folks. Williams's father read to him the dialect poems of Paul Laurence Dunbar, connected by many folks with the minstrel tradition, though in fact he was often reclaiming black vernacular English from minstrelsy, as William Dean Howells observed (Dunbar xiii–xx), though he was unable to recognize the high quality of some of Dunbar's non-dialect poems as well. But Williams was perhaps insightful enough to see Dunbar as he did black poet Melvin Tolson later on: Williams praised Tolson as a "cultured intelligence turning back to praise native intelligence, negro to negro—no white" (Mariani 610). It even may have represented how Williams viewed his own vernacular work. Unfortunately, Williams identified with the "tension of opposites he saw both in himself and in his father": "a silent northern figure who found himself growing up in the buzzing tropics of the Caribbean and who tried to distance himself from that world by the ordered harmonies of piano and flute until he managed to exile himself even from that earthly paradise to follow the insistent cicada's cry of duty" (Mariani 13). How does the white intellectual cope with the conventions and values he has learned at the Ivy League university, when his own native intelligence leads him in a different direction? Is part of him always striving to gain entry to the Valhalla of culture, all the while feeling the instinctive pull back to the side pockets of the pool halls? The question is strikingly similar to the one Countee Cullen asks in "Heritage," though there are important racial parameters that must be considered.

Living in the so-called Jazz Age and cultivating a position in the avant-garde community, Williams would have heard jazz of some kind, but just what kind is not clear. He had heard, we know, the "radio jazz" he mentioned in his introduction to *The Garden of Disorder*, and had talked with George Antheil—Pound's close associate and collaborator—about Antheil's jazz opera *Transatlantic* (1930), but he was not especially forthcoming about particular jazz and blues performers (*Autobiography* 93–94). Mariani reports that Williams was impressed with Nancy Cunard's black assistant/lover Henry Crowder's knowledge of jazz in 1931. Crowder was a jazz composer, pianist, bandleader, and booking agent who had spent some time playing with famed jazz violinist Eddie South—and had even been booked to back white singer Marion Harris in Paris in the 1920s, which eventually led to his meeting Cunard at a gig in Venice, Italy. His international and insider knowledge of the jazz milieu would have interested the cosmopolitan-localist Williams greatly as he participated in the international scene without loss of local connections and values. But Williams's more serious consideration of jazz emerged over a decade later, during the New Orleans jazz revival.

The co-opting of black jazz by whites Williams saw as analagous to Eliot's supplanting of indigenous forms in American poetry (Mariani 515), so Williams felt some brotherhood with black jazz people thrust into a similar situation. However, and somewhat strangely, it might seem, the music in which Williams had become interested was a music that he realized was "nostalgic" (Mariani 824), somewhat anachronistic. It was not the cutting edge of jazz in the 1940s, but the reemergence of the 1920s New Orleans jazz that was championed by the so-called mouldy fig jazz critics so horrified by the frantic and frenetic bop revolution. In a letter to me, Allen Ginsberg surmised that Williams "must have heard regular Benny-Bix 20's, 30's swing" (Goodman and Beiderbecke), and he seems not have gotten much beyond that in his appreciation of jazz. And, in fact, by 1961 Williams would tell Walter Sutton that not only did music not mean much to him—he preferred "old fashioned music" to "this modern atonality" (53), a swipe at Schoenberg and his followers—but that he didn't like jazz: "I don't like jazz. The artists in Paris rave about jazz, but it's too tiresome, it's too much the same thing . . . It merely exists; there's no subtlety at all" (55). The central problem, Williams felt, was that it was not "advanced enough from the primitive" (55). The comment reveals not only Williams's feelings concerning black primitivity—an element, as we have said, of the response to African Americans in the 1920s milieu—but also his short-sightedness concerning the elemental emotional and intellectual power of jazz and his limited view of the advancements that had been brought to jazz from the very beginning by artists from Armstrong to Ellington to Parker to Ornette Coleman, if indeed he knew of them.

But in 1929, Williams's attitude toward a jazz-related music, a music contained within the broad designation of jazz and, certainly in 1929, a music married to jazz in the work of the popular vaudeville blues singers and in the work of white pop bands, was quite different. In *Blues* vol. 1 no. 2, Williams wrote a manifesto, "For a New Magazine," that associated blues, in an abstract way, with the kind of revolution he felt was necessary for American poetry. Williams is abstract in the sense that he makes no specific references to particular blues singers, blues songs, or aspects of blues performances. Rather, he concentrates on popular and intellectual perceptions of the blues from the vantage point of outside the culture of the people that had created the blues. Attention is drawn, therefore, to the poetry revolution, and a perception of how the spirit of the blues functions in the intellectual constellation of Williams's poetic revolution is implicit but not explored.

This is emphasized in the opening sentence of Williams's manifesto. "Blues is," he writes, in a manner that causes the reader to anticipate definition; however, he completes the clause with "a good name for it" (30), immediately deflecting the focus from the blues, and to "it." "Blues" becomes a "name," a label, an association. In fact, Williams mentions the word "blues" only once more in the essay, again in the opening paragraph and again in reference to the sexually implicit "pushing new venture" (30), before his attack on the state of contemporary poetry and his insistence on the need for *Blues: A Magazine of New Rhythms*. Williams never uses the complete title of the journal, however, nor is the word "blues" italicized or punctuated in any way to differentiate the magazine from the music. The intent seems to be, like Emerson's use of *Nature* and Whitman's of *Leaves of Grass* as titles, to effect a complete identification between the writing/journal and the "other medium" (30), which Williams finds so valuable for the creation of poetry. It is perhaps even a reference to *Palms* (which is also neither italicized or punctuated), an avant-garde magazine with a major commitment to African American poetry, including an October 1926 issue devoted to African American poetry and the engagement of Countee Cullen for a short time as assistant editor. However, Williams accompanies his reference to the use of other media with the example of studying Ingrés or Manet rather than Louis Armstrong or Bessie Smith, so the importance of the jazz medium is underplayed in his example. This suggests that Williams is indeed playing a type of free association game with the blues, buttressed by serious references to "high" art.

Williams seems to think that *Blues* is a good name because of the association with personal sadness of the type to which he refers as "getting blue" in a 1906 letter to his mother (*Letters* 6). In this case he is invoking a lament for "all the extant magazines in America" which are "totally, completely dead as far as anything new in literature among us is concerned" (30). His lament is for the state of contemporary poetry as well: not only for the academic poetry of T. S. Eliot, but for the young writers who needed to be able to recognize what is trite and banal and either avoid it or, as Ford was doing, use it to advantage. Blues are, of course, often but not always laments, but rarely laments about the inadequacy of the art of the blues itself. A famous lyric goes "I got the blues so bad it hurts my tongue to talk," but that doesn't stop the singer from expressing that feeling in his blues. Blues may be either first person autobiographical laments or the laments of a blues persona created by the singer, most often discussing interpersonal difficulties between men and women. Such lyrics, however, may at times mask laments of a broader social and racial significance through the technique of indirection that characterized the common practice of signifying among African Americans. Thus, when Williams applies the term "blues" to what he perceives as the contemporary state of decay in the arts, he is only doing more obviously and directly what may be occurring covertly in its own way in the blues tradition itself in reference to the decadence of contemporary American society. Importantly, the laments of *Blues*, like the laments of blues, often celebrate attempts at creating individual voices and expression that become celebrations in the act of lamentation.

On the other hand, Williams suggests that *Blues* is such a good name for the magazine because it is associated with a number of qualities that would be valuable to the new poetry revolution. First, since Williams thinks that all the other magazines are "dead," blues is associated with life or liveliness, a common enough association since blues is dance music, syncopated music, requiring movement and "life"; since it deals with real life situations or fictional possibilities or fantasies that reflect psychologically cogent representations of fears and desires; and since the performance enlivens experience as art and often evokes cries of recognition, acknowledgment, and sympathy from an audience. That audience recognizes a common experience and/or identifies with the validity lent to African American creativity by the artist who chooses African American expression over some other, white, middle-class–oriented form. Williams may have, in fact, associated what he perceived as the agitated excitement of jazz, which certainly drew from such elements, with his own "nervous nature" and "excited pace" ("I Wanted to Write a Poem" 15). That nature and pace, Williams felt, prevented him from writing the long lines of Whitman and assisted him in establishing his own voice, one that was free to be natural and colloquial and seem spontaneous, though, of course, there was a long background to the improvisation that burst from either the horn or pen and into art.

Blues has also been perceived as music of lower-class blacks, of juke joints, and gin mills, often sexually explicit or euphemistic, and thus associated with procreative acts, whether performed for that end or not. When Williams wrote of "banjo jazz" in *Spring and All* (1923), saying "Our orchestra/is the cat's 'nuts'," he was, of course, partially invoking the sexual nature and power he and others saw in jazz. After all, the phrase "cat's nuts" was far more commonly the "cat's pajamas," "cat's whiskers," or "cat's meow," all far more "refined" than the reference to the cat's gonads. A slow blues, for example, might be called grinding music; boogie woogie, as music or dance, derives from references to a prostitute as a boogie or syphilis as boogie woogie; the "scrontch" or "scrontching" refers to both a dance and sexual intercourse. Such dances that s(t)imulate sexual intercourse seem to stem, as Melville Herskovits points out, from "the simulation of motions of sexual intercourse also found in certain quasi-ritual African dances" (271), indicating yet another kind of life, that of cultural inheritance that helps establish group identity and, in this case, individual expression.

The association of blues music with such ritualistic dances that simulate sexual intercourse, as well as with the lives of what were perceived as lower-class bestial primitives, apparently accounts partly for what Williams sees as the connection of the blues with the taboo: the middle-class fear not only of frank representation and discussion of sexuality but also of the demarcated racial lines across which whites were brought up not to cross for fear of being infected with a jungle primitivism that would, as Tom Buchanan says, cause the white race to "be utterly submerged" (13). Clearly vulgarity is part of the blues for Williams. He refers three times to vulgarity, twice in a positive sense, finding the hesitation to be "a little vulgar and so accurate" (30) to be a tragedy for contemporary poetry and suggesting that "frank vulgarity even would be relief enough" (31). Williams's vulgarity in the negative sense is the condition to which we sink when experimentation and invention fail us and mire us in "vulgarity and dullness" (31). In this sense, Williams's positive vulgarity is the "vulgarity" of Dante (one thinks of his *De Vulgari Eloquentia*), Chaucer, and Whitman, their expansion of the acceptable materials of poetry. The status quo, the norm, then, becomes negatively vulgar, while the frank, the challenging, the revolting (in various senses), becomes heroic.

And certainly the blues is associated by Williams with revolt: "Blues comes as near to stating the implied revolt from this (regimentation) as one could get to entitle a pushing, new venture" (30). The black middle-class view of the blues, of course, would have held that the blues was not a revolt or progress, but a retrogression; the blues was the devil's music, and Langston Hughes, for example, was "the poet low rate of Harlem" in part because of his use of the blues in *Fine Clothes to the Jew* (*Chicago Whip* February 26, 1927). Hughes, on the other hand, saw the jazz and blues he used as "the tom-tom of revolt against weariness in a white world" in "The Negro Artist and the Racial Mountain" (308), and indeed the surrealists saw such a revolt in blues and jazz as well, relating it across class, racial, and national boundaries to the artist's search for freedom. In fact, for Williams, the blues was something "new," a word he emphasizes three times at the outset, in the title and first paragraph of his essay, something "bizzare" [*sic*] to the "common mind" (30) but a "pushing new venture" (30) to his, valuable for its newness, its currency. Though the black blues was some fifty years old by the time Williams was writing his essay, it was only ten years on the phonograph record watershed started by Mamie Smith and a bit longer on the stage; therefore, its relatively popular explosion was, in fact, indicative of something different and unusual to popular ears, and Williams was calling for "unusual and more radical work" in his essay (32).

Part of the radical revolt Williams championed was against the forms of the past, and indeed the blues was different from the "perfect sonnets, perfect drawings, dainty bits of blah" (30) that sickened Williams. Here were new forms, twelve-bar, eight-bar, sixteen-bar, thirty-two-bar, or fourteen-and-one-half-bar or stanzaic mixtures if the singer felt like it, imbued with life by the oral tradition and pushed rhythmically by speech patterns from real life. True, more popular and jazz-oriented blues performances were more highly arranged and polished but, since it was likely that Williams and the American public at large had few of the folk-blues to compare them to, even these more arranged blues seemed remarkable for their twisting, lunging abandon and their strange syncopated energy barely contained in flexible forms and structures. In addition, Williams called here for poets to "speak plainly" (31), and for magazines to publish "unedited observations" (32); and plain-speaking and relatively greater freedom, particularly with sexual material, is characteristic of blues both in the oral tradition and in commercial recordings, though of course unexpurgated recordings like Lucille Bogan's "Shave 'Em Dry" (1935) and Jelly Roll Morton's "Winin' Boy" (1938) were not commercially released at the time of their recording. Such amazingly explicit blues are far outnumbered on recordings by the blues that use plain metaphors, like "hot dog," and outrageous ones, like being a "deep sea diver" or "whipping it to a jelly," still material that, like the poetry that Williams seeks, is not "salable in the usual market" (31) because it offends in some way middle-class values or expectations. Blues singers were not interested in speaking over the heads of their audience: they wished to speak to their audience, and as their audience would, because communication is the essence of the blues performance. That does not mean that the language cannot be poetic, or that the form is chaotic. It does require the reorientation of basic aesthetic values for someone outside that tradition, and it is that type of reorientation that Williams felt necessary for contemporary poetry.

Looking at the poem known as "Shoot it, Jimmie," we can see these associations. The poem, suggested to be an interaction with e.e. cummings's "jimmy's got a goil," has been read by Paul Christensen as his version of "scat singing" (155), though there is nothing like scat singing in the poem. Scat singing is a kind of vocal improvisation using sounds, often not recognizable words from the dictionary, to communicate, and Williams and cummings merely repeat recognizable words in these poems. Rather, the poem is a rendering of the sexual and aesthetic boasts of a (likely white) musician about the power and energy of his orchestra's jazz music, in a world where many people considered white bands pale imitations of the black, though there were also many who preferred the music Whiteman-style to what they considered to be the "lower" and "raunchier"—funkier—black bands. Of course, the situation was much more complicated than that.

As Ann Douglas suggests, the poem is both "slanging and ragging" twentieth-century culture (261) to rebel against its stiffness, but also against facile adoptions of African American vernacular speech. The reference to "savage beast" in relation to rhythm in the middle of the poem clearly differentiates the speaker of this poem from black culture—unless the words are spoken ironically, as Duke Ellington might do. But the speaker pulls back from the vulgar "the cat's nuts" to the milder (pasteurized) expression "a lot of cheese" rather than something more forceful (bullshit, crap, shit), undercutting his own vernacular freedom and "authenticity." A search through various jazz, blues, and ragtime discographies, as well as blues lyric collections, collections of black vernacular English and blues words, and my own memory produces nothing in the way of "a lot of cheese" in African American hot music (though "blue goose cheese"—a reference to the black part of town—and limburger cheese turn up in 1930 in titles and raunchy lyrics by Teddy Bunn and Roosevelt Sykes), nor of "the cat's nuts," at the time, though there are three jazz recordings titled either "The Cat's Pajamas" or "The Cat's Whiskers" from 1923 (Rust, *Index* 16)—the year of the publication of the poem. In her horrifyingly marvelous 1935 recording of "Shave 'Em Dry"—twelve years after *Spring and All* was published—Lucille Bogan makes a brilliant comparison of testicles ("nuts") to the clapper in a church bell tower, playing off the old "here's the church, here's the steeple" hand manipulation game, but there is no "cat" in the steeple but the man she is describing. African American toasts, of course, have specific reference to "nuts" as testicles (the Signifyin' Monkey pleads, "Please Mr. Lion, let my nuts out the sand," and Merline Johnson sang the song "Hot Nuts"), and blues have plenty of double-entendre references to nuts meaning testicles, "crazy," and a visit from or to the peanut vendor. In the poem, Williams uses the phrase "the cat's nuts" to mock the innocence of "the cat's whiskers," while "a lot of cheese" moves in the opposite direction, cleaning up "a lot of shit." Thus, the two usages indicate the tensions between the two approaches, which are also apparent for the contemporary poet like Williams who doesn't want to sling snot in the salon or nibble *petits-fours* pinky finger up in the honky tonk.

The speaker's inconsistency in usage exposes even more his ventriloquist disguise which, though it liberates him in some ways, makes him an inauthentic or inaccurate *imitator*. In this case, in Williams's hands, the usage indicates an "essential rebelliousness" that is characteristic of jazz itself, but it challenges culture from the vernacular to the *beaux-arts*, admiring the speaker's process of rebellion, if rejecting his product. The poem champions improvisation rather than sheet music—the oral rather than the written tradition—for its fertility (of mind and body), using a fresh language that combines Shakespeare and contemporary and vulgar slang to promote the "harmonies" of the music—even while the people go "crazy." This, it seems, is "the key" (*Collected Poems* 216)—to freedom, individuality, and the American idiom. Find the sexual charge (cat's nuts, shoot it). Add some flash (nickelplated—a fine coated finish, preventing rust, and not as expensive as gold). Turn up the volume—as Antheil complained, "*The one who screams the loudest is the greatest genius—according to the new American standards*"—(amplifier). Crank up the rhythm, the wildness (savage), and the altered perspective (crazy), and you have both the key to American individuality and the communal thrust (in the orchestra) to set the imagination off on its own path. The fact that a sexual suggestion is also violent only complicates and exposes more the combative nature that produces sexual power.

Williams uses all of these elements of the spectrum of jazz approaches, then, to champion once again his own modernist aesthetic. The fact that he uses a persona in the poem only reinforces Williams's feeling that a variety of voices, even this "adopted" and artificial-feeling voice, can express and expose the American character through language. The poem, as easy as it might seem to mean, expresses a complicated view of Williams's attraction to and rejection of jazz based on the conflicting ideas and values that engaged each other as he tried to mediate between the individual and the communal, the white and the black, vernacular and high culture. Certainly, though, Williams's recordings of his poems give no trace of a jazzy presentation (he did not record "Shoot it, Jimmy"), his light, slightly high-pitched nasal grandfather voice (much later, of course, than the poem was written) bringing no lilting, fragmented, angular, or suggestive feel to what he reads.

Finally, in "For a New Magazine," Williams professes his interest in inventing new mechanisms—he repeats the word "mechanism" four times—adequate to expressing contemporary ideas, wishing to create dynamic new constructs that lead not to further regimentation, but to revolt, anticipating his famous statement "A poem is a small (or large) machine made of words"

(*The Collected Later Poems* 4) from his introduction to *The Wedge*. Williams is following not only T. E. Hulme's prediction that art would be "associated in our minds with the idea of machinery" (13), but Apollinaire's call "to mechanize poetry as the world has been mechanized" (15) and, perhaps, the machine drawings of Picabia. One of the heroes named in "For a New Magazine," Henry Adams, expressed a passionate ambivalence about the dynamo, a moral force symbolizing infinity on the one hand, an anarchical force symbolizing chaos and multiplicity on the other. Whereas for Adams the power of the machine "seemed to have outgrown its servitude and to have asserted its freedom" (*Education* 499), Williams was the creator of his own mechanism and thereby asserted his own freedom. This "simultaneity" that Williams attempts to achieve, which he admired in Picabia, Picasso, and Juan Gris (Perloff 181), seems much like that field of action encountered in New Orleans jazz, including the performances of jazz musicians accompanying the blues singers. There we find a "spontaneous" orchestration of strands of improvisation, a working mechanism that is functional unto itself, though it may violate the rules of various other systems. New Orleans jazz finds roles for various and individual colloquial voices that alternate and interweave strong, direct improvisations rooted in chords and melodies that are altered, transformed, by those voices into a constantly moving, constantly changing message and construct. Williams's new poetic settings, his modernist machine, had to be inclusive of the range of American life: new, experimental, frank, unusual—challenging. And these things, Williams implies, are characteristic of that segment of jazz music known as the blues. And though Williams's knowledge of blues music is only vaguely outlined by him, and though his interest came to be more in what he could take away from it rather than its value as a genre unto itself, it is clearly part of the constellation that interested him and the mechanism he wished to set in motion.

IV

The poetic work of e.e. cummings should also be seen through the prism of African American hot music, again as it came to him in various venues and guises. cummings's playful humor and then-startling sexuality; radical break from tradition in his use of vernacular language with nonstandard poetic voices; challenge to the fundamental order of society through his rejection of conventional punctuation and capitalization, which produced fragmented lines and poems, offbeat accents, and unexpected silences that always kept readers a little off beat; and restless, improvisational feeling (but clearly not) are certainly characteristics his work shares with the hot music tradition, even when his subject matter does not ostensibly deal with related subjects. In his foreword to *is 5* (1926), cummings recognizes how serious the novelty of the world is, and moves center stage, cracking silly jokes that call attention to the fact that people often do not say what they mean. His response is not to say what they know, but, cubist-style, to make them pay attention to the substance of precisely what they mean without allowing formal elements to obscure the day. It is humorous and extremely serious simultaneously, though it takes some time to see through the quirk to the quintessence of his style: "At least the theory of my technique, if I have one, is very far from original; nor is it complicated. I can express it in fifteen words, by quoting The Eternal Question and Immortal Answer of burlesk, viz. 'Would you hit a woman with a child?—No, I'd hit her with a brick.' Like the burlesk comedian, I am abnormally fond of that precision which creates movement" (*Complete Poems* 221). Comparing himself to a burlesk [*sic*] comedian brings along with it associations of exaggeration and parody, social and political satire in the music halls of England in the nineteenth century and, progressively in twentieth-century America, a succession of variety acts such as contortionists leading up to the striptease that was only a small part of the show at Moulin Rouge and across Europe. It was the poor and embarrassing cousin to more "legitimate" theater but, like listening to hot music, it takes discerning senses to see how important it *really* is and can be to "serious artistes" as well. Cummings himself can sometimes seem like a contortionist stripteaser in his early poems, twisting the poem, his speakers, and his readers into all manner of poses as he explores the sexual fears and fantasies of those involved, the works exciting in their possibilities, but somewhat sad and pitiful in the lack of human sexual contact and fulfillment in the observation. cummings had found the perfect metaphor for his technique, in some of this early work combining contortionist, jazz music, and a revealing display of sexuality.

Work by cummings that references jazz or the performance milieu turned up very early in his career. The earliest poems were in the 1922 manuscript of *Tulips and Chimneys*, put together in 1919, and then delayed because of the experimental and sexually frank nature of some of the works. Tulips and chimneys are, of course, yonic and phallic respectively, so cummings tips off pretty early that the book itself will be sexual, even if the manuscript found itself a bit castrated on first book publication by Thomas Seltzer. Cummings also manages to juxtapose in one statement in stanza two the oral and phallic functions of the (two)lips: "whose arched occasional steep youth swallows / curvingly the keenness of my hips." As Williams wrote in his introduction for Allen Ginsberg's *Howl* (1956), "Hold back the edges of your gowns, Ladies" (8), and if they weren't quite going through hell, it was an "unsavoury" earth as a stop on the way.

The 1919 manuscript was generated in the same year of a recording of a tune entitled "I Want a Doll" by a black string band called the Versatile Three. This is a song that cummings references in *Sonnets—Realities* XI of the *Chimnies* section of his first book, "god pity me whom (god distinctly has)." The poem is an audacious one, managing to reference god (no caps), female pubic hair, ejaculate, and jazz all in the first stanza. His elliptical style produces reasonable ambiguity over god's relation to sex: in line, he calls on god to pity him, and then in a parenthetical phrase suggests that god has pitied him for his Adamic inability to resist the sexual impulse, a sin in the Christian churches of his time. Or does the parenthetical phrase interrupt the main clause and imply that god "has" her body, that *god* is tempting him? The poem leaves us wondering whether god's response to human "capitulation" to sex is to pity or to tempt—in the Christian mythology, god was a tempter in the garden of Eden, creating the garden and then placing it off limits. However, in the poem it pretty quickly seems that the speaker doesn't quite care which is god's plan, given the "svelte," "arched," "curving," "twitching," "breathless," "wise-breasted," "lisping," "wispish," "sliding" body at hand, and all sensuously available.

Interestingly, what cummings does is use words that are clearly sexual, though sometimes he combines them with non-sexual terms—arched (not "back" but) "youth," slid (not "in and out" but) steps—as a way of suggesting sexuality and then withdrawing, or perhaps seeing youth as one long arched interval to which sex is central, undeniable, seminal. At other times, he combines terms related to oral sex, such as "swallows," with not the phallus but the hips and vaginal region, substituting one part of the body for another in a way that produces both, doubling the pleasures. Still other times he uses somewhat crude, though inventive, terms for sex—"thread the fattish drone," the stinging creature so frequently the vehicle of sexual activity in many traditions, including blues like Alberta Hunter's "Stingaree Blues" (1923) or Memphis Minnie's "Bumble Bee Blues" (1930). The physical attraction of the sexual relationship is clear.

And then he retracts from the sexual image to relate it to an African American recording that is a coy mixture of fantasy and reality. "I Want a Doll" is about a young boy who loved to play with dolls when he was younger. His mother said "his daddy was that way," at which point the young man admits he is still that way, taking after his father. All this leads to a refrain "I want a doll, I want a baby doll / To play with me, to play with me," which soon makes clear that he wants one "just like the dollies they have in the follies." This turn in the situation overturns the innocence of his childhood play, and suggests an inherited patriarchal attitude toward women as objects of innocence and sexual objects of temptation—the same issues of pity and temptation of line one—and both of which manage to be sexual within those patriarchal attitudes. He the beastly rogue pursued by the twentieth-century Diana, huntress who is a "cracksman," who really needs only a laughing body and "wise breasts" to "thread him." This metaphor also occurs in blues songs, such as Victoria Spivey's 1928 recording of "My Handy Man"—"He threads my needle"—and Memphis Minnie's "New Dirty Dozens" (1930), in which she sings,

> Now, the funniest thing that I ever seen
> Tomcat jumping on a sewing machine.
> Sewing machine run so fast
> Sewed ninety-nine stitches in his yas yas yas.

As Memphis Minnie takes a bemused attitude toward what happened to the tomcat, and as the figure in "I Want a Doll" sees two opposite views of the woman's role, so the woman in cummings's poem, having experienced his "dribbling moan," tousles and parts his hair at departure, like someone who has used him as a man and then infantilized him at the end, smoothing out his saxophone—the phallic instrument of the black man in the Nazi Entartete Music poster—and his dialect accent that labels him as metonymic, a type of the Irish lover for her. In fact, he wants to "play" with her, as she wishes to "play" with him, though the connotations of "playing" are, as in the song, doubled. And, since the poem is clearly a performance of a scene as well, it becomes a "play" as well, describing his feelings and perhaps even "making a play" for the woman.

What we see here is cummings using images or words related to African American hot music to turn up the heat in his clearly sexual poem. Cummings does make the contemporary connection between black music and sex, but he does it for a philosophical reason that makes the music more the consideration of the bounty of sexuality rather than some merely "licentious" end (Thomas Wyatt's "Whoso List to Hunt" keeps running through my head!). Although he makes the connection clearly physical—moan, bee sting, needle—it is at the service of a poem that champions the ambiguities of what god provides, expects, or forbids in the context of this very enjoyable, boundary breaking, cross-vernacular experience. So what should we think—about sex, about societal boundaries, about god? Well, "god" drops out after line one, and we are left to watch the sex, and unless we are simply voyeurs, we want to get involved. Though there does seem to be a bit of sexual stereotyping going on here, cummings, to be fair, uses sexual symbols and allusions in other poems where he doesn't reference African American hot music.

Cummings makes a reference to a jazz band in number five of *Sonnets—Actualities* (*Complete Poems* 158) that does not seem particularly sexual. In the poem, the speaker, who is contemplating drawing a female figure, is held back excessively from engaging his subject by his intellectualizations of his fears. When he finally voices two five- and six-syllable words—"perspicuity" and "susceptibility"—either the posed body or the speaker's own consciousness, or both, direct him in two single-syllable, direct words, to

shut

up.

At this point the poem pivots to treat his desire to be seen by her, to be passive in the connection with her, though he suggests in the following line that being seen by her has "nothing on something," the something presumably a direct physical move. However, with the reference in the final three lines to the jazz band—"did you ever hear a jazz / Band?"—and to passive men who drink without preparing their food, cummings contrasts *hearing* the active—and interactive—jazz band with *shutting up* the passive male. Not only that, but the line placement in those two lines gives us at least double meaning or the two lines: a *jazz band* (article, adjective, and noun) or a jazz *band* (article, noun, verb—the group banding together for a common purpose). The jazz band is clearly an exemplar of the active role the speaker wishes to take, juxtaposed with his fear of being shut down by a female intolerant of his seeming social paralysis. So, while there may be sexual undertones in the poem, its main message is that the mere evocation of a jazz band denotes energy, activity, decisiveness, in contrast to a Prufrockian ennui and indecision—even though his mind is actively exploring his situation.

Also in *Tulips and Chimneys*, there is a brief cubistic portrait of a ragtime performer in "ta" (*Complete Poems* 78) that breaks down the performer into component parts, and then pulls it all together quickly in the final speeding line. Cummings stretches out the description of the performer by dividing "tapping" in stanza one, "hippopotamus" in stanza two, and "genteely" and "lugubrious" in stanza three each into three separate sections, followed in stanza four by three words run together into one ("LOOPTHELOOP") and in the final lines four words run together.

The pace of the lines is like that of a performance. It starts emphasizing the rhythmic and percussive toe tapping in three syllables, moving quickly and setting out the speed and rhythm of the piece. At double the syllables it simulates chording, perhaps, in stanza two's six syllables with the massive back, suggesting underlying strength and power of the performer and the music. In the seven-syllable, two-hyphen line, the grace under pressure indicated by the gentility reflected in his eyes seems to shore him up in the face of the dismal state of his life. This seemingly slows down the time by imposing a motive and melody that supersedes the rhythm. In the enjambment bridge between stanzas three and four we have the yoking of the exaggeratedly tragic with the humorous eyes that also perform the minstrel-like comedy of exaggeratedly rolling to create and maintain his image as entertainer of white folks, in a CAPITALIZEDANDFOOLISHLOOKINGREMINDEROF-HISSTATUSTOHISAUDIENCE. Perhaps, as David Perkins has suggested, the doubled Os are like eyes (43), visual representations of the scene, followed by the pausing space at the end of his introduction—the "as" set off in its own line, climaxing in a rush of music, as indicated by the four words being run together rather than stretched out like most of the other words and phrases.

The meanings of "loop the loop" may well provide a complex background meaning for the poem. Significantly, there was a ragtime composition that cummings may have known by Jean Schwartz entitled "Loop the Loop (Cake Walk)" recorded by (Fred) Hager's Orchestra in 1902 (Sutton 163)—the same Fred Hager who agreed to record Mamie Smith in 1920, helping to set off the commercial blues boom in the recording industry. Remembering that cakewalks were sometimes black folks' parodies of white folks' parodies of black folks introduces a bit of minstrelsy backdrop into the poem that brings significant meaning. The Wright Brothers' flight at Kitty Hawk in 1903 also helped advance manned flight and with it the development of the flashy flight trick known as the "loop the loop." A high school friend of Orville's was black writer Paul Laurence Dunbar, for whom the brothers carried out printing jobs. Their knowledge of Dunbar and his literary output may well have sensitized them to the masking issues that Dunbar lived and explored in "We Wear the Mask" (1896). Linking in the reference to loop the loop a desire to fly (flee) with a desire to fly (escape the bonds of earth and transcend), this acrobatic element relates to the machinations through which black folks had to go to be able to live their lives and play their music—turning their lives upside down in the process. The looping slip knot, which binds in a tight fashion, may well have relevance here in terms of the binding done in lynching, which was at the time actually experiencing an upturn in incidence with a revival of the KKK. And in American slang, "loop de loop" has reference to the sexual position often known as the "69." The connection to ragtime in the composition, the desire to escape limitations, the worries about lynchings and bindings, and the perhaps repressed sexual feelings that come out in banging the rag may all be reinforced in cummings's poem by these historical connections.

What the poem emphasizes is the importance of the back story, the prelude to performance in understanding the music and the performer. The poem emphasizes strength and sadness restrained, the attempt to achieve dignity under the imposition of foolish masquerade, the eyes as windows to the soul as well as primary deceivers. And then, the music. Preceded by an opening stanza of one- and two-syllable words, and then two stanzas with five- and four-syllable words, the poem reduces to all monosyllablic words in two of the last three lines, though more than the simple single syllable words since they are all united in one great explosive (bang), perhaps even sexual (bang) rush, becoming three- and four-syllable words in their poetic performance. And these are vernacular words as well—banging ragged pattern with fat hands (these are workingman's hands, not soft, slender classical fingers) on a piano is music? Yes, it is. Thus, cummings portrays a complex social and aesthetic scenario, a performance with its complicated racial context in shifting language and patterns that represents a ragmentation—a piecing together vernacular style—of the conditions that represent the performance.

A poem mentioned earlier in connection with William Carlos Williams's "Shoot it Jimmie," cummings's "Jimmie's got a goil," published in *is 5*, does seem to be related to Williams's poem (*Complete Poems* 233). Although there may be an improvisatory air to the poem, buttressed by the vernacular language, it is actually carefully ordered in a variety of ways. For example, the words "goil," "shake," "gurl," "sal," and "Jimmie" or "Jimmie's" are each repeated four times in the poem. "Got," "shimmie," and "talk" are each repeated twice. There are two periods, one halfway through and one at the end. There are four commas, each one in the same line (the third) of each six-line stanza. And there are four apostrophes. There is a progression in the poem from calling the young woman "goil," to "gurl," to "gal," one who progresses from shimmies to shakes to twist-and-twirls, and then becomes associated with a full-blown seductress and cold-blooded agent of death (as the biblical story of Salome and John the Baptist goes, and to which Eliot also alluded in "Prufrock"). It is rather like the poet's formal orchestration of a hot music song based on vernacular hot music, much like those recordings by white society bands of the time. This allusion to Salome seems to work both ways in the poem: the objectified girl is clearly attractive to the speaker, but she is also "dangerous" because she is named as "Jimmie's"—we don't even get her real name. The fact that she is "dangerous," coupled with the allusion to Salome, seems to suggest that Jimmie's goil is at fault, rather than the speaker who finds her attractive, a typical male response to the "seductiveness" of women. In terms of the position of the lips and mouth in vocalization, there is a progressive opening up in the application of the noun to her. The New Jersey vernacular "goil" simulates a pucker, while for the more midwestern "gurl" the lips open a bit wider, the tongue retracts, and the roof of the mouth arches. For the perhaps more southern "gal," the lips are at their widest, the tongue moves down, and the mouth cavity is at its largest, as if his expression of his attraction grows with each stanza, or as if he is preparing to devour her in lingual celebration. While the expression of attraction changes with the poem's need to rhyme, the vernacular variety seems to suggest an attraction beyond the local, and a situation that is common rather than rare, as if her being "Jimmie's" is part of the attraction in a patriarchal world of possessions and power.

With its repetition of words and structure and references to dancing, the poem is like a song itself, but not the kind that one would sing in front of Jimmie. Therefore, like the girl, the song is seductive—he wants to express it—and dangerous, too, and it is hard to imagine the occasion for it to be sung. Perhaps it is not meant to be sung by the speaker, but relayed with arrangement by the poet. The poem becomes the highly arranged objectification of the speaker's inner thoughts about the girl, a ritualistic, nearly incantatory sexual praise song in a white culture that at least nominally does not praise such things in public, but has permission to do so as a horny adolescent in blackface. The song is associated with a black dance that involves both shaking the shoulders (thus the shirt or chemise) and leaning in to welcome—also co-opted by white dancers such as Gilda Gray—and turns up in hot songs of the time, such as The American Republic Band's 1916 "military band" recording of Spencer Williams's "Shim-Me-Sha-Wobble" (Rust I: 28), Sophie Tucker's "Everybody Shimmies Now" (1919), Sara Martin's "Blind Man Blues" (1923), and Papa Charlie Jackson's "Shave 'Em Dry" (1925). These popular occurences reinforce the possibility of the poem's connections with black culture.

The reference in this poem to the shimmy dance is reinforced by another poem in the volume, "death is more than," which climaxes with the line "hate laugh shimmy" (*Complete Poems* 236). The poem is a confrontation with death and what it means, juxtaposing "ourselves against the worms" with "hate laugh shimmy" as a way of suggesting valid active responses shoring up his fragments against the ruins of his life by moving from unexpressed hatred to outright laughing to the engagement of the entire body in a celebratory dance. A few pages later in the volume, "(and i imagine" (*Complete Poems* 239) climaxes with reference to the famous black ragtime-cum–jazz bandleader: "stood sharp angels with faces like Jim Europe," a response to what cummings describes in the poem as a "fat, stupid" animal world where people "slobber . . . in the darkness" as "the messiah tumbled successfully into the world." The identification of the angels with Jim Europe implies that it is he who is vigilant and, this line being set off by itself at the end of the poem, both outside of the darkness and stupidity in the poem *and* the climax of its meaning. We are reminded again of Williams's intro to Ginsberg's *Howl*, which came much later but still seems relevant: "Poets are damned but they are not blind, they see with the eyes of angels" (*Howl* 8). It was his poetic ability as a black man to ingratiate the worldly Europe itself with his music, work with popular white dancers Vernon and Irene Castle to popularize black dances worldwide, and to organize the hugely important Clef Club and its orchestra, which played music by black composers, and thus exposed the world to black musical talent that gives him significance in a tawdry world.

The "mulatto" or hybrid nature of culture and the importance of the visionary artist is implied in the poem, as it is in a later poem in *is 5*, "Will i ever forget that precarious moment." In this poem, the Prufrockian speaker, who is waiting on the railroad tracks for some train to come along and kill him—a passive suicide—reflects on his difficulties with controlling his desires and the need to do so, his dissatisfaction with various elements of societal order, and the inscrutable nature of existence. In both the first and third person he rehearses his confusion and dissatisfaction, indicating both his self- and societal alienation. As he reflects on endless tea parties with well-known authors and the bits of events that occur there, he muses, "a watermelon causes indigestion to William Cullen Longfellow's small negro son, Henry Wadsworth Bryant" (260–61). In this "confusion" of names, cummings suggests that the lions of the New England romantic, and thus American literary, tradition are intimately related to each other and a powerful dominating tradition of patricians, even though both were antislavery poets. This undifferentiated mix of men father a child whose inability to eat a watermelon without indigestion suggests that theirs is an inbreeding tradition that marginalizes African Americans who, according to that tradition's stereotype, are watermelon eaters, even though the evidence shows that the child is given indigestion by the ingestion of such stereotypical materials. The implication is that such an exclusive tradition must be broken, freeing African Americans from such forced stereotypes, producing a healthier tradition of poetry rather than the dyspeptic regurgitation of a "genteel" racist antislavery tradition that still supports marginalization.

In all, cummings seems to use jazz in terms of formal concerns, language, and subject matter in a way that is embedded in his manner. He is humorous and satirical, but not as condescending or stereotypical as many other poets in his employment of hot music elements. His extreme typographical, punctuational, and linguistic experimentation, like the opening of the mouth in the "Jimmie," opens up his poetry to the world's social and sexual possibilities in these poems, and his use of jazz in this way seems related to Whitman's wide embrace, and his directive to "Unscrew the locks from the doors, Unscrew the doors themselves from their jambs!" cummings screws and unscrews simultaneously, in some ambiguous mid-kingdom with the paradoxical nature of the modern world.

V

Another bridge to that mid-kingdom was built by Ohio-born mystic-romantic-machine age–poet Hart Crane. It was a bridge from Whitman to modernist poetics through American history and culture, including a significant view of African American culture. Encompassing hot music from shaking tambourine to blues ballads to ragtime fiddle and dances to the rhythm of the rods on down to old Broadway, Crane's spirit and imagination hopped a freight through geographical, chronological, cultural, and aesthetic space in a span of less than twenty working years to arrive at his new myth for America. Along with Christopher Columbus, Pocahontas, Whitman, Poe, and an optimistic view of the modern and futuristic elements of contemporary American culture, Crane arranged elements of improvisational African American hot music in his vision, synthesizing them all in a structure that demonstrated how they were all connected and represented America. His references to black musical culture in various forms and use of its rhythms mark him as an important employer of hot music.

Crane's "logic of metaphor," in which the "motivation of the poem must be derived from the implicit emotional dynamics of the materials used, and the terms of expression employed are often selected less for their logical (literal) significance than for their associational meanings" ("General Aims and Theories" 221), has a marked similarity to the associational methods sometimes characteristic of the procession of lyrics of some folk-blues performers, whose associational method eschewed chronology. This essay, which deals with the inception of "For the Marriage of Faustus and Helen," treated below, discussed "the very real and absolute conception of beauty," which seemed to "consist in a reconstruction in these modern terms of the basic emotional attitude toward beauty that the Greeks had" (217). For Crane, this approach "was really building a bridge between so-called classic experience and many divergent realities of our seething, confused cosmos of today, which has no formulated mythology for classic poetic reference or for religious exploitation" (217). In other words, his imaginative, poly-intuitive, polyvisual, and polyvocal approach and output find him seeking an appropriate language: "the voice of the present, if it is to be known, must be caught at the risk of speaking in idioms and circumlocutions shocking to the scholar and historians of logic" (223). Crane means to exploit the "fluid" nature of language to express the traversing that America has done and must do historically, culturally, aesthetically, and viscerally in order to generate an imaginative poetic act that encompasses no less than a theory of beauty large enough to define a polychromatic America. In Crane's work, we may not so much be impressed by the volume of references to hot music, but their philosophical and stylistic congruence.

Biographically speaking, Crane was predisposed to identify and exist as a marginalized outsider, even to embrace the condition. He came from a volatile family, his parents separating when he was nine years old and, after reconciliation, divorcing when he was eighteen. Sexually abused by an older man when he was young, he found his homosexual identity under siege by his mother's Christian Science beliefs that made him a pariah in the world. Crane turned his extreme alienation into a strength, crediting it with giving him the mystical power to be the visionary necessary for his poetic calling. He was awakened to the power and energy of New York City upon his first visit in 1917 and, according to Waldo Frank, he was ready to apply and alter Whitman's vision based on his perception of the contemporary city: "For Whitman, the founding of Zion in America meant the experience of the Scriptures applied to the crowds on his Broadway, to the prairie and the Open Road. To Crane, it meant these also, but in the jungle of the Machine, in the airs of jazz, in the matrix of skyscraper and subway" (*Complete Poems* 270). The jungles of Upton Sinclair and Frank J. Webb, the jazz of Ellington and Whiteman, and the urban scenes of John Alden Carpenter and Claude McKay, all these and more were fodder for Crane's poetic sensibilities.

Crane was, not coincidentally, a music lover who "fancied himself . . . a music critic" (Unterecker 135), though a significant focus was on classical music, such as his "Wagner records" (Unterecker 140), including the "Processional" from Wagner's opera *Parsifal* (Unterecker 173). This was perhaps an odd choice for Crane, given Wagner's opposition to miscegenation and his racialist and anti-Semitic views, which verged on suggesting a final solution for Jews in Germany. However, it was likely Wagner's grand and synthesizing musical vision and wide and encompassing influence that attracted Crane. Unterecker mentions Crane "going to cabarets" in 1919 (133), but as far as his specific familiarity with hot music, Unterecker is silent. One of Crane's patrons, Otto Kahn, was a supporter of the arts to whom composer Henry F. Gilbert dedicated his composition *The Dance in Place Congo* (rev. 1916), a "symphonic poem" based on work by George Washington Cable dealing with the important locus of African American music in New Orleans in the eighteenth century and beyond. Still, if Crane was getting the cityscape whole, his "camera eye" vision of it as "a series of exposures intense and rather savage," that "presents . . . more entrancing vistas than any other location I know of" (Unterecker 138) must have been informed by a variety of incarnations of hot music—from the basement storeroom where he wrote "Black Tambourine" to "the Metropolitan roof garden with a jazz orchestra" where section one of "To the Marriage of Faustus and Helen" was set ("General Aims and Theories" 217).

"Black Tambourine" takes the black porter where Crane worked in the basement of his father's restaurant in Cleveland in 1921 as the point of inception of a poem actually written in that basement storeroom (Unterecker 188). There he had easy and genial relationships with black cooks and dishwashers whose demeanors and language were part of his exposure to the vernacular character of America. Crane sympathizes and identifies with the African American/black artist who, in contrast to the fable(d) composer Aesop, the slave possibly of Ethiopian origin, finds himself in a degraded situation created for him by contemporary society. Since the poem is titled "Black Tambourine," Crane's focus is primarily on the instrument of his (in)expression and how it has become virtually paralyzed and silent, described in language that seems familiar with Eliot's Prufrock's fear of "The eyes that fix you in a formulated phrase" (Eliot, *Collected Poems* 5), though pinned without the wriggling. The tambourine may not be black in color, but rather represents African American spirit and vision, artistry and performance, the imagination neutralized by that "formula," as Alain Locke labeled it, for people of African descent in America. Thus, it is actually not just about this particular black man; it is about Pan-African expression subordinated to white American hegemony and image. We can identify a variety of reflections of hegemony in American culture of the 1920s, of course, that reinforced the subordination of African Americans. In the movies, we think of Elmo Lincoln, whose last name was actually Linkenhelt, not Lincoln, in *Tarzan of the Apes* (1918)—his co-star was Thomas Jefferson, creating an almost Ishmael Reed-ish irony (?) and satire (!) likely lost on the film's producers; the white-controlled book, music, and art publishing industry that required a Van Vechten–type intermediary to recommend publication; and the mammy and sex-crazed stereotypes of the general white public as expressed either concretely or as insinuation virtually everywhere and at any time among them. Trapped in between depictions of beastliness and childishness, violence and docility that distort African American reality, the grotesque image of the black man imprisons a spirit in a maze of illusion.

Crane characterizes the poem as "a description and bundle of insinuations" that finds "the negro (in the popular mind) sentimentally or brutally 'placed' in this midkingdom" (Unterecker 190–91). The percussive tambourine that normally shakes in performance, sometimes assisted in African gourd performances by the rattling of beads, evokes the common reference to "shaking" in blues combining dancing, sex, and gambling as in the phrase "shake, rattle, and roll," sung in Memphis Minnie's "Shake Mattie" (1931). The tambourine's presence also evokes religious ceremony, both in Africa and in African America, where Wright Holmes sings in "Alley Special" "The woman I'm come to lovin', she's a holy woman and she beat that tambourine." In the poem, however, the tambourine is silent, stuck on a wall, both placed, as an artifact, and fixed and immoveable, as a remnant of musical, spiritual, and physical days long gone. The soul of the beat is silent. The continuum of sacred and secular performance—a distinction less recognized in West African culture—is interrupted and degraded. Symbolizing the attrition of African traditions in the American landscape and the immobilization of African Americans and their communal artists, the lone figure in the cellar neither hears the incantations atop Aesop's grave nor sees the dead and decaying carcass symbolic of Africa's demise—a demise brought about by the desolation of African spirit and art in the American tradition. In the poem there is no vigor—no dancing, no sexual energy, no risk-taking activity that sometimes comes to fruition. Just the silent artifact, lynched on a wall where its former vitality and present immobility can be displayed, an ironic (and modernist) depiction of a significant past juxtaposed with a powerless present.

Crane, of course, did not mean that these things did not exist among African Americans in America. He had heard the music and seen the culture, albeit at times in artificial or degrading contemporary commercial presentations. He was commenting, rather, on the interference of a racist society with the complete development of African American possibilities in society and in art as they took distinction and strength from a significant African past. So while Booker T. Washington, W. E. B. Du Bois, James Weldon Johnson, Countee Cullen, Louis Armstrong, and Augusta Savage may not have been drunk and alone in a cellar, it is not for lack of society's trying to put them there with the "closed doors" (*Complete Poems* 4) that confronted them. And whatever achievements they might attain, in the created images of many white folks that subterranean space is always where they could be located. There is, in fact, a minstrel song sung by Gus Cannon, "Can You Blame the Colored Man" (1927), that portrays Booker T. Washington, a temperate man, as being "drunk on wine" and "feelin' fine" despite his distinguished image and nature. Jamaican poet Claude McKay expressed his ideas concerning brutal, exclusionary racial prejudice in the poem "The White House" with "Your door is shut against my tightened face" (*Passion* 123)—a poem that he insisted was not about *the* White House, but any white house, though the symbolism of both meanings run through the poem. Zora Neale Hurston demonstrated that the idea was well known among the poor black masses, offering in *Mules and Men* the folktale in which a recently freed slave is admonished by his ex-master, "But 'member, John, youse a nigger" (90) as John, who has just won his freedom, leaves for a life of "freedom" that will be severely undercut by his status as a black man, even if he is no longer a slave. And, if John does, the image will become self-fulfilling for others without the vision to see past it.

Actually, the flies on the lion's carcass here may be a reference to white American culture feeding on black culture as well. The reflections of a co-opted African American culture are everywhere in American society, so feeding upon a dead or dying carcass supplies an apt metaphor for the sustenance and rejuvenation of a culture of diseased gadflies seeking for something new and modern to provide vital expression. Crane surely saw and heard the disparities between commercialized "pop-jazz" frequently played by polite, tuxedoed, white orchestras and the playing of black performers who grew up closer to the genesis of hot music. Those black musicians have been frequently seen as playing a "purer" version of the music than, say, Lawrence Welk and his Orchestra, which recorded the jazz tune "Doin' the New Low-down" in 1928, or Guy Lombardo's Royal Canadians, who nonetheless could play "hot" when they wanted to (Rust II: 1052), though, as Ralph Ellison has taught us in *Invisible Man* (196–230), these notions of purity can get awfully clouded. The superiority of black jazz was a sentiment being expressed during Crane's time, as Paul Giles points out, by Paul Rosenfield and Waldo Frank, among others (Giles 98), but Crane's avowed aim was bridging the commercial and high artistic aims of jazz in a way that preserved its dignity in the face of pop culture assault.

The primary movement in the poem is the "carcass quick with flies" (*Complete Poems* 4), the feeding frenzy not of large scavengers but the potentially pestiferous insect that moves quickly to take what it can. Crane phrases this ironically as a carcass that is quick—since it is dead—and then introduces the flies to produce the movement. Suggesting the biblical phrase from I Peter 4: 3–5, the association implies that the lion and the flies shall be judged for their acts, as American society shall be. The technique is similar to what Crane has done in the title of the poem. Since African American hot music was frequently used in mainstream and artistic culture to describe the rapid pace of contemporary society, the notion that society is driven and sustained by a subjected African American segment of the population, by slave or virtual slave labor, is another social and cultural point in the poem. If one has seen the activity of flies on a carcass, it is frequently frenzied, overwhelming, multi-vocalized hysteria—there was a "Hysterics Rag" published in 1914 (Sutton 137)—characteristics that were frequently applied in the popular conception to African American hot music. These associations make Crane's image not only visual but aural, perhaps even gustatorial in its associations.

The scene in the cellar places the entire poem in an underground region, which obviously has associations with death and burial—though once again, Ellison warns that not all basement rooms are coffins (*Invisible Man* 6). Though Crane was relatively happy in the position he had at the time, remember that he was literally writing underground as well, suggesting a certain concrete identification with the person in the poem and the environment in which he lived. Since the black man has already been associated with the lion's carcass, Crane has made this connection with death explicit. However, the frequent reversal of the meanings of high and low in African American culture suggests that the situation may possibly be redemptive, though the poem remains firmly negative on the surface. Being from way down in the bottoms or "down home" was often seen in blues culture as a measure of one's authenticity and authority. Being this "lowdown" conversely connotes being exalted, privileged in the world of blues appreciation. Songs such as Ethel Waters's "Down Home Blues" (1921), Clara Smith's "Down Home Bound Blues" (1925), and Ada Brown's "Down Home Dance" (1929) all suggest a certain vigor and honesty associated with the rural southern setting to which Africans were brought following their kidnapping, a place where *real* was as *real* as it could get. George Jackson's composition "Down Home Blues," recorded by Z. Z. Hill in 1982, reflects the post–black power movement embracing of "down home" as a place where African American culture was born. Thus, although there were negative connotations to *being* down home, especially among upwardly mobile middle-class "strivers," the *choice* of *going* down home was often really taking it to a sweet spot. Going to the cellar or basement can also suggest an earthy and fecund relationship, a kind of returning to the roots, so to speak, as Ma Rainey sang in "Down in the Basement" (1926):

> [Spoken]: Oh, this is one of my low-down days, boys,
> Take me to the basement.
> I've got a man, piano hound,
> Plays anything that's going around.
> When he plays that highbrow stuff
> I shout, "Brother, that's enough."

Take me to the basement, that's as low as I can go.
I want something low-down, daddy, want it nice and slow.
I would shimmy from A to Z, if you'll play that thing for me.

The singer's rejection of the supercilious *high-brow* for the sensual (*low- pubic*) is indicative here of the need to escape from pretension, puritanical sexual denial, to the real, low-down, exalted expression of the blues, a full-bodied embrace of African American identity that recognizes society's heathenish attempt to bury and the heroic attempt to survive that characterizes the strength of African American culture.

Were Hart Crane a black poet, it might be easier for some to see this reading as operating in the text—a work of art that uses death as a call to life among the "people" of the poet. Frequently jungle references in relation to African Americans among whites were intended to be derogatory, though black composers like Duke Ellington and William Grant Still and some whites shook off the negative connotations and embraced the spirit of the culture. As Daniel Mark Epstein has pointed out, Crane was "listening to jazz in pursuit of the systematic derangement Rimbaud required of poets," and he "[built] sonorous lines from golden phrases while measuring his progress against jazz riffs" (12). Crane's identification with the victim in the poem, however, also makes it easier to read it this way for Crane the poet as well, since for him the poem may be any cast-off and degraded artist who is kept from practicing his artistry. However, the separation and isolation from home continent and community, the juxtaposition of an active and communal life and art and a death only active in its decay, and juxtaposition of folk culture and popular misconceptions and stereotypes, serve to add even more telling Pan-African context to the portrait for Crane. This allows Crane's portrait to be both culture specific to African Americans and universal simultaneously. This was certainly an issue of concern to African American writers in the 1920s like Countee Cullen, whose longing to be considered a poet, not a black poet, sparked some substantial disagreements. Black *as* universal was actually a revolutionary idea at a time when, in the West, universal meant white.

As Crane was preparing to write "For the Marriage of Faustus and Helen" in 1922, he was writing to Allen Tate of his desire to "invent an idiom for the proper transposition of jazz into words! Something clean, sparkling, elusive" (Weber, *Letters* 89), as a way to bridge and reconcile the spectrum of space between so-called high and low culture. The idea that he felt that the proper (presumably principled, not anesthetized) conveyance of jazz would be typified by these three adjectives—clean, sparkling, and elusive—conveys the gist of his attitude toward jazz as it related to his artistic vision. Especially since we frequently hear the blues described as "low-down and dirty," as in Leroy Carr's "Low-down Dirty Blues" (1928) and jazz as springing from questionable environs—not always true—Crane's use of "clean" may puzzle some. However, clean may here be a synonym for fresh, immaculate, pure, or sparkling, reminding us that Crane frequently sought out in his poetry the spirit of innocence in notions of ultimate beauty, insisting that innocence and beauty are not always found where we expect them to be. In fact, he turns upside down notions of high and low, much the way African Americans did with that terminology at the time of the Harlem Renaissance, in order to suggest that the experienced can be made innocent again, the soiled pure—wash me and I shall be whiter than snow—through artistic vision.

This type of vision is something like what his friend Jean Toomer was writing about in his short sketch "Fern." There, the men in the community, who don't understand Fern's mysterious nature, begin to see her, who has taken many men, as a virgin whom they need both to satisfy and to possess (*Cane* 16). Their motivations are not pure, not even the narrator's, though he protests that they are. To them, she *is* what they *see*, not what she *is*, just as Karintha and other female characters in the collection find themselves defined by others' visions, primarily male. Crane, looking for a new and optimistic vision to counter that Eliotic ennui of *The Waste Land*, seeks to bridge ancient notions of art, beauty, and hierarchy in order to achieve the harmony that his mythic ideal requires. That inner purity will be reflected in a sparkling surface, an allure that will attract both spiritually and bodily, though this ideal beauty and spirit will be elusive until a unified being and sensibility, and a unified country, responds to her.

Part Two of "For the Marriage of Faustus and Helen" takes us to a rooftop and a place where oversight—both positive and negative—is possible. Here, where the lay of the industrial landscape is on display for all to see, a jazz band provides relief from a world sometimes too much with us, though somehow somewhat closer than it seems. The setting is a rooftop garden which, in the days before air conditioning, were better places for dancing than the insides of buildings. Jazz recording titles such as Graham W. Jackson's Seminole Syncopators' "Roof Garden Get Off" (1930) and Ted Weems's "Rooftop Serenade" (1930) evoke the era's high society slumming, and some orchestras were sometimes even billed on recordings, such as Don Parker's "Strand Roof Orchestra" (Rust II: 1318). Helen, having just left a streetcar named Desire, where she was bombarded by the omnipresent barrage of facts and figures until her metaphorical seduction supersedes those temporal imperatives, finds herself in a garden. It is an artificial one, to be sure, shooting down its roots not too deeply into the concrete scalp of the top of a building, though deeply enough to make the connection between classic and contemporary beauty and explore notions of "love, beauty, death, renascence" ("General Aims and Theories" 217).

Of course, it is no Eden, being man-made and as such fallible. The concept of Eden and its inhabitants at conception had been jostled a good deal in hot music of the time. In blues songs, Genesis itself was sometimes called "Genessee," as in Blind Willie McTell's "Southern Can is Mine" (1931—likely too early for the can to reference a beer can!). The pun places the origins of humanity and God's special place for humans in Rochester, New York, and probably at the first brewery established in Rochester, which changed its name to the Genessee Brewery in 1878. Hociel Thomas asserted outright "Adam and Eve Had the Blues" (1925), Butterbeans and Susie recorded another song about "Adam and Eve" (1925), and a well-known lyric of the time offered by Blind Bogus Ben Covington went "Adam and Eve in the garden of Eden surely musta shook that thing" (1928). The notion of Adam and Eve's fall seemed to recognize that the blues, and sexual "transgression," has been with us from the beginning, and the genre embraced both in artistic aesthetic and subject matter in a celebratory way that must have displeased preachers of the time. The roof garden is no Eden, though perhaps it is subjectively a seriously qualified one. And then God, the orchestra, and Crane create the music, and God says, as James Weldon Johnson has it, "That's good!" (*Book of American Negro Poetry*, 117).

There are regular references to music in this section—"tremolo," "opera bouffe," "melody," "harmonic laws," "song"—that make it clear there is a rooftop orchestra at work. The introduction of "nigger cupids" in line eight suggests that its members are black, and other musical descriptions suggest the music is exciting jazz, what jazz symbolized in its challenging relation to traditional Western artistic aesthetics. This music is "brazen," "hypnotic," "magnetic." This is *not* your grandfather's tea party. It *is*, as the title of one jazz song punningly suggests, "Doin' the Uptown Lowdown" (Venuti 1933). It is much more active, shocking, even "primitive" in its trance-inducing allure: the African American exotic and demotic in the stars.

Here the traditional figure of the Roman god of passionate love becomes "nigger cupids" who "scour the stars" (30), bridging from a hierarchical single figure to a group of figures that represents how the band is full of searchers for subjects—subject matter and human beings—in the heavenly stylistic spaces. The communal nature and function of African music transplanted to America here challenges traditional Western paradigms of hierarchy, replacing an idealized white boy with the very uncommon "common man." The reference to "nigger" here is not meant by Crane to be pejorative. Crane does not seem to have used the word with any frequency in his poetry, prose, or letters, though he did on occasion—a 1927 letter to Samuel Loveman contains the couplet,

> There once was a cannibal nigger
> Who ate up his enemy's frigger . . . (Crane, *Library of America* 520).

In the published poem, the word's distinctness and uniqueness come from the juxtaposition of the traditional handsome young white male with the vulgar stereotypes that accompany the word "nigger." Yet the "lowest down" in a (supposedly democratic) American society here succeeds the traditional Roman cupid, traversing heavenly spaces to find the *musica universalis*—the music of the spheres—reflected in a new vision of the structure and order of the universe. The entire band works in concert—communally and in performance—reversing the hierarchy of "lowest down" to highest up as they explore new ways of seeing and producing art, cupids still as fecund as ever. What we get here is the African American lower-class view of low-down, meaning both "earthy" and "honest"—elements too often neglected in the artificial praise of the sonnet tradition, for example, reflecting contemporary distaste for the artificiality and vapidity of a postwar world. This music is "crashing." It will "ricochet," "snarling" with "rhythmic ellipses" that lead to the barnyard—remember the early animal imitations in jazz recordings by bands such as the Original Dixieland Jazz Band—back down to animal earth. It creates a startling skyway from the mute moon to the movement and music of the animal farm, where boundary-crashing revolution in and of itself is not bad and the elliptical syncopation can be understood as the unspoken, resentful passion about the conditions that led to the birth of the music.

Crane's reference to opera bouffe suggests that there is something comic going on at this location, farcical, parodic, or satirical. Kenneth Lohf has also suggested a comic opera intention in the manuscript of Crane's "The Dance," which includes references to ragtime, "Gichigume Blues," and "Sitting Bull Blues" in its lists (Lohf 41–43). The French opera bouffe tradition includes such works as *La Vie Parisienne* (1866), Jacques Offenbach's initial attempt to portray Parisian life through the lives of the wealthy and the gay dandies of the time interacting with the socially *gauche*, sexually promiscuous demi-mondaine. The opera rouses itself into a party in act three that treats the earthy and sensual debauchery of Parisian high life, a high life that lasted into post–World War I Paris, where avant-garde artists from around the world translated the hot music they heard there to their own contemporary artistic visions. While on the one hand the reference to opera bouffe indicates the minstrel-mask smiles that black performers frequently had to wear, on the other it indicates a satire on contemporary society, parodying their responses to black music. They have "a thousand light shrugs" as they dance "splayed like cards from a loose hand" and "fall downstairs . . . / With perfect grace and equanimity," "[w]hile titters hailed the groans of death" (*Complete Poems* 30). Their self-perceived fall *with* grace rather than *from* grace indicates their assurance of the old verities of class and culture while ungracefully unbalanced by new perspectives that challenge their vision of the world. They "titter" in response to the music made of the death groans of the lower-class African Americans performing in front of them, superficial in their perceptions of and responses to black music. As Langston Hughes commented in "Lady's Boogie," if she listened beyond the surface of the music, she would hear "the tingle of a tear" (*Collected Poems* 412). Truly it is a "divine grotesque" (*Complete Poems* 31), divine in the performance, grotesque in the response.

Such responses recur in the "metallic paradises" (*Complete Poems* 31) that he and Eliot's "Prufrock," "have known" in such frequent social gatherings. There the musicians skillfully produce in their stylistic autobiographies themes of catastrophe and death—presumably social and racial—amidst the noise of birds and awnings, prattling and laughing that does violence to the dignity of the music and musicians, making it seem mere cacophony rather than the exalted music it is. For the speaker of the poem, the "music has a reassuring way" (*Complete Poems* 31) of bridging the divine and grotesque. In the end, Crane juxtaposes recording and performance, guilty song and innocent siren, waxed recording and waxed floors, as a way of indicating how jazz in this setting, where it is cultivated by "cultivated" people in a cultivated garden, still holds a special, sexual (dipping as they dance), timeless beauty, even if the others are only skating across its surface while the speaker is skating among the stars.

The reference to wax here is interesting for its double, perhaps triple (Edelman 113), meaning. We think of it in terms of the dance floor at this gathering, providing a surface-protective and light-reflective layer that gives the gathering some of its artificial sheen. It is the base from which all activities depart—either in mundane, tipsy chatter or in the trip to the stars. But wax may also refer either to the wax cylinder recording process (Edelman 113) or its employment in creating the original wax master disc of a recording before it is pressed into a mixture of shellac and other elements as part of mass production and distribution. This is the process that preserves, in its rather brittle, 78 RPM way, a classic (or not-so-classic) jazz performance for the ages.

However, it also fixes forever this improvisational music in one arranged performance, which other musicians might copy by reproducing this one performance endlessly in reverence, rather than plugging into the improvisatory spirit of the piece. Likewise audiences may come to expect the ossified, shellac-hardened musicianship rather than the active interplay of a live performance. It is not a long leap to seeing the recording as potentially expressing a rehearsal of the past—musically, sexually—rather than the desire to have, as one of his major influences, Emerson, wrote, "an original relation to the universe" ("Nature" 7). The dabblers in Negroes stay on the level of the record, on the polished floor, frittering away their jazz and human heritage in mimicry rather than soaring *themselves*, as the artist must do. The classic recording can bring back an exalted memory, but it can also dead end into that memory unless the performative nature of the idiom is given full play, to create new insights, new styles, new memories.

The interplay between these two meanings, as well as the ambiguities of meaning elsewhere in the text, reproduce elements of call-and-response in the poem that again imbues the poem with a jazz spirit through an improvisatory feel. Crane has obviously carefully crafted his words, arranged them, but in such a way as to suggest immediate dialogue, from Greek to contemporary times, from person to person, intellectual to "high society," from race to race. "Taking" the young, innocent siren of the springs of guilty songs—sexual guilt, racial guilt, class guilt, and the artistic guilt of the poet who fails to envision contemporary beauty—means assuming it all, possessing it all in fecund ecstasy, and reconciling it in an art that expresses the contemporary and futuristic as it serves the divine-grotesque human. This is what literature, malleable as the wax moulded into disc, protective and gleaming as the gloss on the floor, must do: recognize its malleability, protect its exaltedness even as it searches on the floor (the bottoms, the low-down) for the holy vernacular materials of poetry, polish it to its appropriate finish, and ascend to the firmament.

All of which brings us to what others have described as either Crane's monumental failure or his climactic masterpiece-in-transit, *The Bridge* (1930). Most scholars who have written about Crane's use of hot music in *The Bridge* have rightly focused on the section called "The River," about which Crane claimed "the rhythm is jazz" (*Complete Poems* 250). However, Crane does make what might be a reference to hot music in the preceding "Rip Van Winkle" section. Rip, the perennial slacker rescued by Whitman's defense of loafing in "Song of Myself," here finds himself time-traveling from the land's earliest European days/daze down to Crane's time, still rejecting, like the hoboes elsewhere in the poem, the rigid Dutch sense of industry and responsibility to wander over the vital, life-giving land, though now Rip is relegated to sweeping "a tenement / way down on Avenue A . . ." (*Complete Poems* 58). Crane once again places his subject at the nadir, at the place of (way) low-down, though here it may have contradictory connotations as well. Avenue A, after all, ran the length of Manhattan, bordering a variety of neighborhoods such as Spanish Harlem, the Gashouse District, and Ira Gershwin's neighborhood, about which he wrote in his 1925 composition "I'm Something on Avenue A":

> There's a part of Manhattan
> that's Jewish and Latin:
> my neighborhood, Avenue A.
> Though gunmen may roam there
> I'm proud of my home there,
> No matter what people may say.

The section deals with the dutiful diligent "progress" of history that loses sight and memory of the mythic value of Rip, of random switches and fleeting, suppressed benignity of the Lord's day doffed to the "beard and certainty" of the dashing conqueror Smith. Rip now realizes that he is no longer potent in contemporary times, his organ ground and he "*not here / nor there*" (60), unsure whether his memory torments him or brings him the slightest pleasure from a past and a present that a mere nickel's worth of "change" can abandon. The desire to alter Rip, in his own time and presently, brings him a sense of "responsibility" from which he needs to escape, be it into the freedom of the mythic Catskills or on the long Natty Bumppo pathfinder route from Far Rockaway to Queens.

The italicized stanzas of this section both have a rhythmic lilt, as if an incantatory nursery rhyme, somewhat akin to a jazz feel that found itself expressed in a number of jazz recordings of nursery rhymes or solos that incorporated snippets of nursery rhyme melody or phrasing. The songs combined the innocence of childhood and a well-traveled experience (like Rip), as also found in a New Orleans tradition of incorporating folk rhymes into second-line rhythms that leaped exuberantly along the long road to the cemetery, the celebrants later departing as more solemn, lessoned people. Is the loafer "low-down," a chastised member of the community, or really high up, still able to visualize Catskill daisy chains in May long before and after the white bright lights of Broadway have lost their lustre?

These stanzas serve as improvisatory interpolations that signify on the solemnity of the prosaic and reflective blank verse of tradition, which badger Rip to move along with the "Times," which can be a negative geographical move, but a positive visionary journey that allows the river, the train, the human spirit to *flow*. Like Oscar Hammerstein's 1927 lyric "Ol' Man River" for *Show Boat*, Crane places his "Joes" in the human stream to provide Greek choral comment on the ebb and flow of human life, from endless tie to tie, river to sea, local to universal. As sung by black actors Jules Bledsoe and later Paul Robeson—who recorded it with white bandleader Paul Whiteman in 1928—and directed by the openly gay James Whale, who brought the story of another misunderstood futuristic primitive to the screen in 1931's *Frankenstein*, it commented, too, on the endless flow of human spirit and human misunderstanding that connects it to Cranc's "Thc River." Crane's flow, though, is clearly more optimistic than Eliot's "A crowd flowed over London Bridge" in *The Waste Land* (39), especially given that it is "falling down" at the end (50). Crane's bridge clearly partakes of what it spans, since a river can be a bridge as well.

It is meet that "The River" section is driven by the jazz rhythms of the train, an icon of American and African American folklore. Acknowledging the desire to escape from something to something, be it from de facto slavery to nominal freedom, from a world of trouble to a heaven of rest, from social and sexual powerlessness to the road to fecundity, from formal ossified structure to vernacular fluidity—it is *so* good to be shifty in a new country. In jazz parlance of the time, to "ride" meant "to keep perfect time" (Burley 223), to let the jazz performance flow with energy; a "rider" was a sexual partner, the rocking motion simulating sexual intercourse. In the hoboes riding trains, Crane unites musical style and performance with potency, a way of producing or augmenting one's power through art—certainly a feature discussed by Jahn in his work as a characteristic of West African and blues traditions. This, in turn, makes the hoboes examples of the kind of artist Crane wants to be, just as Ma Rainey provided an artistic aesthetic for Sterling Brown in the poem "Ma Rainey" (1932). Keeping close to the earth, charging into new territories, revising the landscape as they re-encounter it, clothes at the end of a craggy stick, stuffed in a ragged bundle, they have the spirit.

Trains are, of course, ubiquitous in the blues and gospel tradition, from the fifteen titles of blues beginning with the word "train" recorded between 1917 and 1943 (Godrich, Dixon, and Rye 1290–1291) there have been multiple recordings of the train motif, in gospel: "The Funeral Train" and "Death's Black Train is Coming" (1926) by Rev. J. M. Gates; in blues: "Freight Train Blues" of Josie Miles (1924), the "Honky Tonk Train Blues" (1927) of Meade Lux Lewis, and white-recorded train blues such as Grayson and Whitter's "Train 45" (1927) and Frank Hutchison's "Train That Carried The Girl From Town" (1926); and in jazz: Lem Fowler's "Express Train Blues" (1925) and Duke Ellington's first session recording of "Choo Choo" (1924), among hundreds of other recordings. Classical music has its entries, too, notably Arthur Honegger's churning 1924 "Pacific 231," perhaps a forerunner to Belgian jazzman Django Reinhardt's "Mystery Pacific" (1937). In nineteenth- and early twentieth-century America, if you wanted a symbol of power, one that might over-match the water power and majesty of the mythic Mississippi, barreling into the future with a visionary gleam in its eye, savage howl in its smokestack, and mystery and adventure across every trestle, you wanted a train.

Crane roots/routes the forward progress of the twentieth century in a journey through elements of the African American past. It starts out its journey "rushing" to the beat of a different drum, taking Horace Greeley's "go[ing] west—young man" (62) out of the wagon train and into the iron horse, ticking the barrage of advertisements and minstrel playbills as they pass. The reference to minstrel icon Bert Williams emphasizes that, even in 1930, minstrelsy was alive, that the past was in the present. Williams actually died in 1922, but Moran and Mack were still with us, and Crane effects his temporal shift in the poem's time through metaphorical meaning—ragging the time into frenetic, kalcidoscopic images of the remembrance of things past rendered at present Bergsonian mobility and fluidity of time. In fact, the poem shares Proust's novel's multiple perspectives and recollection of past events that impinge upon the present: "Time's rendings, time's bendings" (64). Here, however, the lines are like fleet, leaping hot music improvisations that can be heard and seen correctly through the logic of metaphor, syncopating over enjambed bridges in synaptical splendor. Then, setting us down in the middle of hobo wanderings—on the wane by the time of the Great Migration of 1914–1919 but on the increase since the stock market crash of 1929 (Garon and Tomko 17–18)—Crane takes advantage of the times to see America, the land and what has grown from it, in the slower pace of the old train, and the hobo who hops it.

What we get are several different types of songs. There are plantation school idealized memories of days before the war ("My Old Kentucky Home"), which was only recorded once by a jazz band pre-1942, and that by Gene Krupa's band in 1939, compared with seven versions by country artists. We also get folk songs about maverick heroes pushing beyond the limits ("Casey Jones," recorded separately by the jazz group Straun's Pullman Porters in 1925, white singer Gid Tanner and His Skillet Lickers and Furry Lewis in 1927, and DeFord Bailey and Mississippi John Hurt in 1928, as well as reported by numerous folklorists collecting music in the South). And then there is religious music in the projection of a warm and welcoming day off in the future, presumably when the travails of life shall all be over (Charley Patton recorded "Some Happy Day" in 1929, and the blues "Some Summer Day Pt. 1" in 1930). It is the romanticism, vigor, and hopeful vision of the past, sandwiched in the poem between the present-day Bert Williams, an educated and dignified man who had to *learn* to speak "Negro dialect" for his act, and "road gangs" (64), pressed by frequently trumped up charges into perpetual and backbreaking service. It is a vision like that in Peetie Wheatstraw's brilliant recording, "No 'Count Woman" (1940):

> When I first met you baby you was beat just like a slave.
> You had one foot on a banana peeling and the other foot in the grave.

Yet, as in the Sterling Brown poem "Strong Men" (1932) drawing on Carl Sandburg's "Upstream," they "keep comin' on" (Brown): one of Crane's hoboes exclaims, "But I kept on the tracks" (64). As Paul Garon and Gene Tomko explain in their book *Black Hoboes and Their Songs*, quite a few of those hoboes were African American—including Furry Lewis, who lost a leg to a freight train, and Peetie Wheatstraw, who recorded several songs having to do with the "hobo jungle" and died after being hit by a train, both mentioned above. "When I first started hoboin' hoboin' hoboin'," sang John Lee Hooker, "I took a freight train to be my friend" (Garon and Tomko 3). It is that friend that helps provide an optimistic, ever hopeful vision, for one life, for all the hoboing lives, for the whole country, through its unsettled geographical, historical, and personal journeying, each tie different, but linked by rails in restless harmony.

We also hear these hoboes talk about real people and experiences unshackled by minstrelsy and chain gang victimization. Here are people cherishing Aunt Sally Simpson's smile and watermelon days sans rolling eyes and white folks acting up, just black folks *of* theyselves, *by* theyselves, and *for* theyselves, understandin' Bert bustin' rock out on the county road and the chain gang cake-walkin' across the stage, intercha[i]ngable. And movin' on.

These men feel the spirit of America—the trains, the natives, the songs, the river, the skyline, the history, and the alluvium of time, and they remember it and pass it on. They are like the musical hoboes who journey through Americana, recording "Casey Jones" and "Steamboat Bill," as the white California Ramblers did at the same session in 1927, and "Missouri Joe" as country singer Bob Miller recorded in 1929. They are in touch with the spirit, and with the vision and art that drives it, reshaped into new deposits headed for the Bank of America in the Cannonball, humming down the tracks. Crane knows that the flow of America, in train, river, or imagination, is clearly and cleanly seen by its black hoboes, whistled and sung and scratched out of black soil by its black searchers in a black Passion that led up to an uncivil release, and a spoiled Resurrection limping along the road to Emmaus, itself a warm spring contributing to the heated waters of the big sea of twentieth-century race relations.

In this section, Crane imbues modern times with perceived frantic nervousness of contemporary jazz, but takes time to touch that which produced that twentieth-century feeling. He moseys through the nineteenth century and mines its riches, though with the omnipresent "Sheriff, Brakeman, and Authority" (68) dealt with in blues songs like Charley Patton's "High Sheriff Blues" (1934), Jimmie Rodgers's "Brakeman Blues" (1927), and Blind Blake's "Third Degree Blues" (1929), the latter describing unlawful arrest and violent interrogation, always shadowing the figure. These authorities were there to drive the chain gangs, capture the runaways, massacre the natives, take the blessed rest of the spiritual "Deep River" (a well-known spiritual that also appeared in Toomer's "Rhobert," [*Cane* 43]), and turn it into the melody for the pop song "Dear Old Southland." This popular song, recorded in twenty-one jazz versions between 1921 and 1942, including Louis Armstrong's version from 1930, is a sentimental evocation of a desire to return someplace where the horrors have been smoothed and overlain with a veneer, or perhaps a distillation, of burnished glory. Crane doesn't want to throw the baby out with the bathwater, but the baby just isn't coming clean. Crane's vision here makes clear that wholesale rejection of the past by the artist—break for brake's sake—will simply run the train into a ditch.

Crane employs materials associated with hot music in several other places in *The Bridge*. The bluesy-sounding language in "The Tunnel," where a fandaddle daddy is admonished "if / you don't like my gate why did you / swing on it . . " (109) is most interesting as a companion to "The River." This time the speaker is traveling through a subterranean world, on the subway, as opposed to the land-touching super-way of the train. Once again, bits of conversations and events flit past, but this time insignificant or vulgar conversations, though not without their creativity. "Fandaddle" is apparently a word of Crane's coinage, a neologism perhaps created out of "fiddle faddle" and "skee daddle," combined with its alliteration with "daddy," perhaps with a brand spanking new fanny (used commonly enough in blues and jazz) along for the ride. The word may well be related to "fandango" as well, referring to both Spanish music and dance that also occasionally turns up in the repertoires of Afro- and Anglo-American songsters. Apparently, it refers to a man who is exasperated and going about the nonsense of asking his paramour for change from what he paid her to do, presumably something sexual. "If you don't like my peaches, please don't shake my tree" is a common enough lyric in the blues (see William Harris's "Hot Time Blues" [1928]), almost formulaic, which would lend itself to the common strategy of plugging in different words to formulas to create new lyrics and songs. Swinging on a gate occurs in Fiddlin' John Carson's recording "Gonna Swing on the Golden Gate" (1927), also recorded by the Utica Institute Jubilee Singers in 1928 as "Swingin' On the Golden Gate," though neither seem to be reaching for the bridge pun, and the gate in the songs is in heaven. Given that heaven can sometimes be a sexual metaphor in blues songs, Crane may well be complicating the conversation here by suggesting that the man has attempted to suggest that the affair was good rather than bad, indicating how difficult to negotiate sexual politics can be in a society that places restrictive limits on sexual expression, a metaphor itself for artistic freedom and vision in the poem. The point here is that the tasteless behavior comes alive through the metaphor the woman uses to vivify it, an occurrence of creative vision amongst those in vernacular culture that suggests that valuable ways of doing and seeing things exist even on those subterranean rides we take through hell.

Interestingly, in the conversation she stylizes her communication, performs her words as a blues song rather than simply speaking plainly. Crane compounds the puns here by mixing golf references (links and holes) to stops on the train route (Fourteenth) and golf technique (swinging), which relates back to the man's infidelity and segues to the emergent jazz that would dominate the 1930s, swing music (109), dropping the readers off at "phonographs of hades in the brain" (110). The instance is a performance by a woman fit into a particular circumscribed role of lover, and Crane's suggestion that the gate or portal to somewhere else is part of what *she* would like to swing, to make happen. The word "swing" has been complicated to encompass sexual, social, and artistic meanings that unfold with every snatch of conversation. The seemingly random concatenation of these references actually pulls these bits together under the banner of the games, dizzying speed, tawdriness, and desperate desire for love and mobility necessary in the contemporary world, along with the quest for artistic vision to make it whole. It is a jazzy, improvisational-sounding arrangement that, heard correctly, has the "logic of metaphor." In its way the poem "feels" like Arnold Schoenberg's *Suite, op. 29* (1926), particularly the "Ouverture," which has the same feeling of randomness, and a violation of conventional melodic, harmonic, and rhythmic elements that makes it seem individually "in the moment," rather than written down. It is thus like the idea of hot improvisation, where interpolations of melodies or rhythms from a popular song can have a metaphorical logic. (In rock music, for example, the highly blues-influenced performer Eric Clapton features four bars of "Blue Moon" [Rodgers and Hart 1934] as the first four bars of his solo for Cream's rock-blues "Sunshine of Your Love," playing off the contrast of sultry ballad and hard blues, moon and sunshine, wistful ballad and hard rock twelve-bar blues approach, idealization and sexualization of the lover.) It is no wonder that Schoenberg so impressed a number of jazz players later in the century,

Yusef Lateef, Bill Evans, and especially Anthony Braxton among them. Even though he himself was not impressed with jazz, there were, especially "out," avant-garde jazz players who responded to his advances.

It is important that we understand Crane's complexity regarding hot music in the works under discussion. The *hearing* of the hot music, at whatever velocity or extent of presentation, becomes a synesthetic aural metaphor for the vision of the artist as he sees it working and dramatizes it in his work. Crane's style forces us into to swim in his fluidity and follow the flow wherever it can go, something like the building momentum of Illinois Jacquet flying home, or better yet the Lonnie Johnson–Eddie Lang guitar duet "Hot Fingers" (1929), which mixes the elegant Johnson's monumental improvisational blues soloing over Lang's unmatched jazz harmonic invention. Though Crane is not as idiomatic as either, he does bring together black and white, formal and improvisational traditions in an individualistic style, writing out of his own experience, which encompasses hot music as well.

Yes, yes, yes, critics since the 1930s have been working that punning bridge metaphor in relation to Crane's work. I've done it here. We could call a moratorium on bridge metaphors except that, doggone it, they work. So, if we can suspend the moratorium for a span of a few lines, let us say that Crane has bridged in his work lower and upper classes, black and white, vernacular culture and the beaux arts, sound and sight, past and future, individual and group, real and ideal, local and universal in a stunning and passionate way that reminds of no less than the blues recording made by country singer Jimmie Rodgers with Louis Armstrong and Lil Hardin Armstrong accompanying, "Blue Yodel No. 9 (Standin' on the Corner)" from 1930, the same year *The Bridge* was published. Here black and white, male and female, the father of country music and the king of jazz, both harassed by the system for just hangin' on the corner or hoppin' a freight, come together in a sublime stylistic and visceral meeting that brings us for a few minutes a visionary ideal, country and blues traditions flowing toward the wave of the future. Crane, perhaps, did not use hot music references frequently enough in his work to call it a major influence. But that spirit comes shining through, the logopoeia and phanopoeia flowing through melopoeia into his work.

VI

It has been in the last dozen years or so that scholarship on Mina Loy has shifted to a higher caliber, even though she has counted big guns Gertrude Stein, Ezra Pound, T. S. Eliot, and William Carlos Williams among her admirers and showed up in many biographies of important figures of the era (Conover xii). She was even touted by the *New York Evening Sun* as an exemplar of the "modern woman" in 1917, just shortly after she arrived in the States (Burke 224). She has gone from a crescendo to a grace note to a melody in the modernist symphony of the times, but a futurist-feminist melody, not some lullaby-like luller of the human spirit, her "one last tentacle of intuition" seeking "to quiver among the stars" (*Lost Lunar* 41). She was there to mine alloy—both the pockets everybody thought were rich, along with the so-called cheaper, inferior metal of African American culture that itself had been making an alloy of American culture and redefined the word "alloy" not as something that degrades that to which it is added, but something that enriches.

We would not say that Loy made heavy use of African American hot music in her work. As poetry scholar and critic Marjorie Perloff points out, Loy did not come to America's bohemian community in New York to live until 1916 (and then left in 1918). After returning to England and the Italy, she moved to a Paris filled with African American hot music in 1923 and returned to New York in 1936, when she was in her mid-thirties (Perloff, "English"). However, her poems, which were seen as too radical by Harriet Monroe's *Poetry* standards, were central to the establishment of the new journal *Others* in 1915 (Hanscombe and Smyers), and Ezra Pound wrote of Loy's "distinctly national product" in 1918 as if she had been born in America. Virginia Kouidis enumerates characteristics that make Loy "American"—realizing the inadequacy of traditional poetic structures and subject matter for contemporary poetry; compressed diction and employment of spoken language; and uses of the techniques of futurism and Cubism, combined with Perloff's addition of her "polyglot language," the arguments are convincing in relating Loy to Stein, Stevens, Marianne, Moore, and Williams (Perloff "English"). The most important of her poems of the twenties that did use hot music, "The Widow's Jazz" and "Lady Laura in Bohemia" (both completed in 1927, though published a bit later), show an original and distinctive use of the materials of hot music as analogues to the characteristics of Loy's poetry listed above.

In her essay "Modern Poetry" (1925), Loy emphasized the musical modality of poetry: "Poetry is prose bewitched, a music made of visual thoughts, the sound of an idea" (*Lost Lunar* 157). Poetry casts a spell. It takes us over body and mind, perhaps in the way that Carl Van Vechten described the performances of vaudeville blues singers like Bessie Smith or entertainers like Josephine Baker as enchantment or transport to another region (Tracy, *Write Me* 316–17). The blues is, after all, poetry, visual thoughts, sounds of ideas, and this fact allows us to deal with the blues in ways that we would deal with what arbiters of "high art" call poetry. Hot music allowed delusional white people to act differently from "normal," to imagine themselves as someone else part of something somewhere else—maybe in Harlem, or even in the jungle. Loy, in fact, knew the widely connected Van Vechten socially at least as early as 1914 (Januzzi 549), and she even said she trusted the publication and layout of *Songs to Joannes* (1917) to him (Schreiber and Tuma 104). The name-dropping Van Vechten (Mellow 178) himself had been familiar with black entertainers since around 1903, and had been championing African American writers since 1917. He frequently conducted excursions to Harlem for the white and curious (Woodson 1201), and his close friendship with Loy found her explaining her feminist politics to him. Loy was a staunch advocate of reading poetry, not just for the sound but the *serious sound effects*, for the meaning that the sound brings in the concatenation of poetry and music: "More than to read poetry we must listen to poetry" (*Lost Lunar* 157). In helping us to hear the poem produced, performed, and contextualized, Loy made it come to life.

Loy's poem "The Widow's Jazz," according to Natalie Clifford Barney read by Loy in her salon on May 6, 1927 (Barney 213–16), is one of the poems most frequently mentioned by Loy scholars in relation to jazz. Among titles in African American hot music, it is much more common to find an adjective preceding the words "rag" or "blues" rather than "jazz": "The Junk Man Rag" from 1913 by Luckey Roberts (Jones and Jasen 142), the pianist on some of the Two Black Crows sides, or "Some Class Rag" (Sutton 147, 264), or Clara Smith's "Every Woman's Blues" (1923) or Edna Hicks's "Cemetery Blues" (1923). Still, "The Widow's Jazz" seems to be within that tradition as a title, describing to us what is distinctive about the widow's jazz, in the languages of the widow's jazz. Loy may have wished to avoid this being a popular rag, with its frequently uptempo, happy feel (though of course, Scott Joplin felt that rags should be taken at medium tempo), or a blues, with its sad associations in the popular mind. It is, in fact, dual—an overlapping appreciation and lament, exploring inside and outside, private and public, black and white.

Essentially, the poem explores the hissing snakepit of turbulent conflicting feelings experienced by the speaker upon the death of her lover—the fear in line one, the sadness in line three, the sinister and sexual in line four, the ancient and mysterious "new" territory of loneliness in lines five and six, the invitation to new perspective in lines seven and eight (*Lost Lunar* 98). The poem is presumably located by the repetition "Chicago! Chicago!" in that city, though it might take place in any such location. Chicago, of course, was known as a tough, wide-open town with numerous gangster ties, especially during Prohibition (ratified January 16, 1919). In the well-known song recorded in jazz versions by "The Georgians," "The Caroling Serenaders," and "Bailey's Lucky Seven" in 1922 and employed in the film *The Story of Vernon and Irene Castle* (1939), it is hailed by its name twice in exuberant recognition that it is a "toddlin' town" that couldn't even be broken down by legendary fire and brimstone Christian evangelist Billy Sunday (whose vehement and colloquial sermons made him popular with segments of the population at the time—Jimmy Swaggart without the scandal and "Killer" cousin). The poem presents us with a scenario in a Chicago club, a place where one might go to break loose or unwind, where the arrogant white man can yield to the vision of "colored folk . . . [with] de moon in dere eyes" (*Lost Lunar* 95). The word is, obviously, related to the "lunar" in the title, with its connotations of pining and dreaming, being either visionary or crazy, and perhaps even baring the buttocks—all are addressed in the poem.

The speaker confronts social and sexual "sobbing taboos," the desire to challenge boundaries between love and hate, life and death, happiness and sadness, black and white (and maybe even legal and illegal—clubs were a place to procure bootleg liquor). Black jazz would have been considered an obvious choice for the soundtrack, given its associations in the popular mind with "[a]n uninterpretable wail," "ecstasy," the primitivism of the "primeval," "dissonance," the "electric," and the pain of loss and separation—simultaneously the thrill of the improvised moment and the imposition of isolation and loneliness on the left behind (pun intended). But the jazz club is also the place of casual and meaningless sexuality, where "shampooed gigolos" are the prize and the musicians sport metal-hard, swelling instruments beckoning both to her spiritual and lusty feelings—metal is, after all, a good conductor of heat. The subject is not unknown in jazz songs. The Original Capitol City Orchestra, "the only Mississippi riverboat band to play and record in England pre–World War II" (Rust II: 1276–77), recorded a song entitled "Gigolette" in 1924 that refers to the distaff side of that phenomenon, indicative that indeed these types of issues were treated in hot music of the time. At one point, though, the music seems to break down the spiritual aspects of the feelings, the communal loaf being eaten by the doves of peace, leaving her with her warring feelings facing the "colossal absentee / the substitute dark" (*Lost Lunar* 96), her lover, the former colossal presence and light of her life.

In this setting of illicit sexuality and flaunting of taboos, she indicates her resentment at his abandonment, accusing "you cuckold me with death" (*Lost Lunar* 96). The middle English word "cuckold" is an interesting one to use here. It accuses the husband of infidelity or sexual betrayal, but immediately takes it to a symbolic level by having death be a physical betrayal. "Cuckold" creates a linguistic distance from the phrase—an outdated, almost "literary" term—while the meaning makes it personal and palpable. Simultaneously, the "flames of sound" and idealized and idyllic native "tropic breath" of jazz raise both her ire and her passion for the absent lover. The jazz both "bellow[s]" and "cajoles" in "a synthesis / of racial caress" (*Lost Lunar* 96). There, in that club, with that jazz, where black and white mix in a torrid zone of "mime" (*Lost Lunar* 95), "murdered laughter" (96), and "everlit delight" (97) she finds the language to communicate across the boundaries, though only temporarily—the electric does get turned off.

The use of esperanto here—a language that is artificial yet intended to be "universal" (though based on European root words)—indicates the desire to find a language and an expression equal to her meaning: a common modernist concern. Since the word literally translates as "a person who hopes," it also indicates her optimism at maintaining contact with her lover, even from beyond the grave, though ultimately the poem descends to impenetrable mystery and isolation. And then, amid the teeming crowd, the blaring jazz, the artificial but electric sexuality (Loy's futurism shining through), and the triumphant expression that jazz makes of her feelings, these recede from her and, as in Toomer's "Esther" (*Cane* 27), she emerges into the void "of unpeopled space" (97).

Ultimately, jazz is used as an expression of and foil for her conflicting feelings. This jazz has elements of ragtime and the blues, moiling and roiling in the process of their expression, traveling wherever the feelings go, improvising in the voices we all have, communicating, if we listen, to all. The esperanto of hot music's languages—vernacular as in Geeshie Wiley, sophisticated as in Duke Ellington, in the French of "Le Blues de Petit Chien" (1934) by the Breaux Freres, the pig latin of Ollie Shepard's "Shepard Blues" (1939), and even the wordless moans and shouts of countless blues singers—is clearly a multivocal expression, just as the poem voices various aspects of attitudes the source of which is frequently ambiguous, and it is projected loud and clear from Chicago dives to bohemia.

Of course, bohemia was a favorite haunt of American avant-garde artists, and frequently those artists had an interest in African American hot music. Afro-Canadian George Bohee recorded a banjo solo entitled "Bohemian Galop" "[b]efore 1898 in England" (Godrich, Dixon, and Rye 91)—though this was possibly a composition from Irish composer Michael William Balfe's *The Bohemian Girl*, which had international success in the 1840s, and several songs of which had been adopted in burlesque on the minstrel stage (Mahar 3, 19, 101, 151). White ragtime composer Joseph Lamb's "Bohemia Rag" (1919) also contains sufficient characteristics of a Czech polka to make the European region at least in part a source of the name (Schaefer and Riedel 87), but it is definitely a rag as well. Still, there were other jazz-oriented bands that were given pseudonyms such as Bohemian Dance Band or Orchestra (Rust I: 162) to suggest that there was a pun on the name connecting Czech culture to the avant-garde communities—a characteristic that was frequently part of the naming of ragtime compositions. As a final note, Czech composer Bohuslav Martinu composed jazz-influenced pieces such as *Jazz-Suite for Small Orchestra* and *La Revue de Cuisine* in the late 1920s, demonstrating how fluid the process of exchange could be.

"Lady Laura in Bohemia" demonstrates how awkward and out of place this upper class "lady" meeting "vulgar" Americans can be in bohemian Paris. The name "Laura," obviously connects to Petrarch and the inception of the sonnet tradition of a poet writing to an unattainable love. Petrarch's Laura is idealized by him as a most beautiful, pure, and unattainable figure that caused him intense desire and unspeakable pain in her inaccessibility. In a real sense, his trouble is his own fault, since his inability to see her clearly results in his pain. She is "above" him, this broken, fragile glass of a man, and even his ability to create beauty out of his love in his sonnets is to no avail in "winning" her. In fact, sonneteers have struggled with the perception of their fervor as artificiality, mere broken wind in the heat of passion. Since notions of unattainability, boundaries, class, and sexuality are prominent in Loy's poem, it seems reasonable to assume the connection to Petrarch—who himself helped to establish a ruling tradition in poetry in English. Thus, his position must be contested as well.

Perloff points out that "trained" is the first word of the poem, which reminds us of Hart Crane's use of the train as symbol in *The Bridge*. Where Crane's poem uses the train as a symbol of freedom, power, and vision, Loy's usage of the similar word places the emphasis on "social and cultural control" (61), which is what the lady thinks she has, and is used to having, as a "lady." Compared with Crane's punning railroad reference to the "Twentieth Century Limited," this lady is circumscribed by her vision of herself in society, but near enough to a power that can overcome it, if she has the vision, desire, and will to take it on. Reading the two poems in tandem, and with music in mind, like Charles Ives drawing some of his musical ideas from being in a park and hearing several bands playing simultaneously, helps produce a blues- and jazz-informed reading that draws meaning from the juxtaposition.

But "Lady" is also used in the expression "lady of the evening," which means something quite different in the shadows than it does the light of day, or candlelight of the drawing room. The phrase was a common one, one that also also served as a title to a recording by the California Ramblers in 1923 (Rust I: 261), and the Original Capitol Orchestra (that recorded "Chicago" in 1923) in 1923 as well (Rust II: 1276). Training, however, is also associated with taming animals—surely her feeling about the bohemians before her—and has associations with taking aim, as with a gun—she keeps this impulse under control—as well as the long end of a dress that trails behind the aristocrat who wears it, which one might expect her haughtiness to be wearing. As Januzzi asserts, there is a "serious *regression* from the norms of civility" (Schreiber and Tuma 433) in the poem, and this regression is potentially positive (the norms, after all, are artificial and need challenging) and negative (the danger is always that the challenge to norms merely creates another artifice to buy into, or comes to sit alongside the other artifice in blissful ignorance).

However, it becomes clear that Lady Laura does not have social and cultural control in this setting. She is immediately divided as she "proceeds recedingly" (98). Unable to overcome her "reticence" (98), which is hidden by her hauteur ("lifted chin" 98), she possesses a sense of a descent into the hell of a perceived horizontal social arrangement, a democratic political and social idea never quite fulfilled for most poor immigrants, including America's forced immigrants, African American slaves. Presiding over what the speaker sees as a divinely decadent religious celebration, complete with communal gin fizz, is a combination abbess-prostitute—a description that could be applied to Lady Laura or one of the bohemians. A bohemian would be chaste abbess as director of the bohemian culture, prostitute in the more egalitarian social world. Lady Laura would be the symbol of purity in her bearing but a whore selling her soul for an illusory superiority. One attendee's casual fling with the young boy Detruille shocks Lady Laura with the knowledge that this woman has met her "*people*" (100), wedding and contrasting her obviously sexual affair with the attendee to Lady Laura's sense of her purity and exclusivity. She even calls the bohemian woman a "bounder" (100), an ill-bred and obnoxious person, with clear associations of crossing a boundary of Lady Laura's creation. What Lady Laura does is assign the bohemians to a rung on her social ladder, one above the jazzers but below herself, who would never stoop to join, even to conquer or exploit, such a group. Loy makes it clear that the bohemian world is artificial as well, and the poem is a parody of two parodies: white folks playing "jazz" and white folks playing "anti-jazz," with the black jazz playing some artificial and illusory role in their salvation on the one hand (the boy has the eyes of a Buddha, and is described as divine) and Lady Laura's exclusivity on the other. It comes close to functioning like a cakewalk—a parody of a parody, a burlesque of an unconscious burlesque, a cross-racial fantasy and nightmare riding on its own meld.

On the other hand, Lady Laura is not what she thinks she is either—not a "natural" aristocrat in a well-manicured world. She is assigned by the speaker to a circus, more of a place where one might expect to find clowns and minstrel performers in blackface singing their folk-influenced, raggy sounds for the masses. The same Versatile Four that we mentioned earlier in relation to "I Want a Doll" recorded a song entitled "Circus Day in Dixie" that demonstrates that connection between the circus and the budding hot music. Thus, Lady Laura's milieu becomes the circus masquerade, while the jazz mass becomes a liberated if degraded good time. When one of the partygoers insists that she wants "to stay here and behave like a grue-u" (99), her tone is clear—she recognizes the hypocrisy and pettiness of the setting and its inhabitants. What a "grue" is is open to speculation, though it seems to be a French word for a "crane," as well as denoting "gore" and the feeling of shuddering—a response to gore. Cranes are known as noisy birds that nonetheless are quite outgoing and sociable, flying with their necks extended as if loathe to miss something. Something like the behavior at this gathering. Shuddering, in a sense, would be a shrinking from the gathering rather than a joining in, which might express more accurately the feelings of Lady Laura.

There may also be an embedded meaning related to Joyce's *Finnegan's Wake* (1939), which Joyce had begun in 1922—the same year Loy sketched Joyce for *Vanity Fair*. In *Finnegan's Wake* Joyce uses the word "gruebleen," a mixture of green and blue in which the initial two letters are transposed. Because there are some cultures that do not have words that distinguish between blue and green, these words for the colors might be blended as symbolic of their linguistic unanimity. This combination would bring to the poem another reference to boundaries, this time ambiguous ones, as a reflection of Lady Laura's clear sense of violated taboos from the perspective of her artificial world. This modification of the word "blue" also refers to the changes wrought upon African American hot music by whites. Blue is, of course, a primary color, so mixed with other colors, like green, it still maintains its own character, modified to blue-green. In fact, since green is made up of blue and yellow mixed, blue-green is actually two parts blue, and one part green. The blue predominates, even when cut by another color, and the blues just overwhelm.

The final line, in which the speaker labels her as being "like a diamond on a heap of broken glass" (100), is again ambiguous. Of course we associate diamonds with great value and multiple facets. Lady Laura may have worldly wealth, but her superior feelings demonstrate the poverty of her morality—even as she looks down her nose at the (im)morality of the bohemians. She hardly seems multifaceted in her ability to understand and accept those different from herself. She *is* hard in her judgments, created out of centuries of enormous pressure to sit upon her subjects and mold them in her social and hierarchical image. However, the domain the speaker sees her ruling is not only glass—sometimes used as a cheap imitation of a diamond by unscrupulous vendors—but *broken* glass, perhaps broken by weight of her opinions.

And what do we see in glass but images, and broken ones in broken glass? This is a modernist contemporary world of surreality, a mockery of surface, a refraction of the blues; yet its common materials, the broken glass of a shattered, forced-immigrant world and consciousness, reflects a deeper reality that stunned a world unprepared for sound wisdom from the slave quarters.

There were, of course, other American poets who made references to African American hot music in their work at the time. In fact, a major chronicler of the period, Malcolm Cowley, recognizing African American music as an important social and intellectual force of the 1920s art scene, wrote a number of poems published by 1929, which included references to genre, song, and performers in the jazz and blues milieux. He had arrived in New York from the war in 1919, "where he starved as a poet and free-lance book reviewer" (*Blue Juniata* i), joining the staff of *The New Republic* in 1929. In the literary collection *The American Caravan* (1927), section five of "Biography" is entitled "The Farewell Blues," and includes references to traditional blues lyrics and subjects in a Chicago setting (57–58). "Commemorative Bronze" referred to jazz (*Blue Juniata* 84), while "Kelly's Barroom" employed the traditional blues line "take me back" (*Blue Juniata* 33); "Variations on a Cosmical Air" references "Frankie and Johnny" and the "ashes to ashes, dust to dust" biblical parody sometimes employed in blues songs (*Blue Juniata* 34–35); "Three Songs for Leonora" includes a section entitled "Tennessee Blues" (*Blue Juniata* 72–3); and Harlem and Duke Ellington turn up in "The Eater of Darkness" (*Blue Juniata* 75), along with performer Florence Mills in "The Lady from Harlem" (*Blue Juniata* 82).

Also published in *The American Caravan* in 1927 was a poem by John Dos Passos entitled "Lines to a Lady" that references a jazz band in section seven (Brooks 458), then follows up with references to that "ashes to ashes" blues parody and interpolations from Handy's "The Hesitating Blues" (1924), delivering the poem to a jagged wasteland (Brooks 460). Dos Passos uses hot music in his prose as well, in *Manhattan Transfer* (1925) referencing Eubie Blake's ragtime song "I'm Just Wild About Harry" (303), as well as a "sacrilegious" combination of the bawdy "Foggy Dew" and the spiritual "One More River to Cross" (250), possibly compounded with Irving Berlin's 1924 pop song "What'll I Do" (304). Among the interstitial welter of pop lyrics and slangy language in the skyscraping "City of Destruction" (366) that for some typified the sound and energy of the Jazz Age—John Alden's Carpenter's *Skyscrapers* debuted at the Metropolitan Opera in the following year—lie the jazz in which Dos Passos indicated an interest in *The Garbage Man* (1925), though especially related to "melodrama and burlesque" interests and associations (Wagner 73). The music was still getting a serious workout in contemporary literature—after all, this was also the year of Langston Hughes's virtuoso blues volume *Fine Clothes to the Jew* (1927).

Columbia University graduate and poet Florence Becker demurred in *The American Caravan*'s "Ante Bellum's Belly Ache," using a mixed formal and vernacular voice to recognize twenties literature as "advertis[ing] the rupture of your eggs / To the whole damn stockyard" by advertising "with huge letters, electric lights, and jazz bands" (Brooks 757). On the one hand, the speaker advocates for proletarian literature in a vernacular voice, while on the other extolling the virtues of John Keats (much like Countee Cullen) to her antagonists, the modernist poets who seem all flash and no heat. It was a time both when the nascent idea of the Popular Front (officially born in 1935) was groping for a stronger relation to the songs of the masses and many writers were migrating ever more leftward, slouching toward the Great Depression. Poets were reevaluating their relation to African American hot music—Langston Hughes writing fewer blues poems, for example—and other social and political relationships began to develop that would employ the music in new ways. In this liminal area, in this liminal volume, Paul Green, Malcolm Cowley, John Dos Passos, and Florence Becker co-existed, along with the Mike Gold of *Hoboken Blues* (1927), to be discussed below in the drama section. The volume also published Gertrude Stein, Ernest Hemingway, William Carlos Williams, Edmund Wilson, Eric Walrond, Margery Latimer, Babette Deutsch, Louise Bogan, Allen Tate, Robert Penn Warren, Hart Crane, and Eugene O'Neill. "Hot music" was hot music, and running in a variety of very good circles.

Ultimately, the work of Euro-American modernists reflects an interest in and concern with finding ways to employ the lessons of blues and jazz as they are related to social, psychological, emotional, and aesthetic concerns as they emerged in the modern world. While these artists were not always cognizant or respectful of the performative lessons of African American music, they were just as assuredly as their Chicago counterparts knee deep in their own interpretations of the blues. These interpretations were variously formed out of variety of materials and attitudes that were informed by the class, race, and gender prejudices of the time. And they were run through the modernist mechanical alembic to distill just what seemed to matter in particular ways to make the tradition match their ideas. The supposed gulf they dug between "high" art and "low" was sometimes only skin deep. The racial ugliness was to the bone.

5
Folks in New York City Ain't Like Folks Down South

The Folkloristic Writers

I

The late nineteenth century upswing of interest in folklore in general and African American folklore in particular emerged naturally enough out of the contact between different cultures precipitated in part by the Civil War. The result was the coming of age of local color and realist literature in response to fears that the "old ways" would pass in the light of rampant urban industrialism replacing rural agrarianism, the domination of northern interests, the passing of *de jure* slavery, the waves of migration North, and the pull and pace of modernity. The formation of the American Folklore Society at Harvard in 1888, the Chicago Folklore Society in 1891, and the Hampton Institute Folklore Society in 1893 were all extremely important to the appreciation of varied pockets of American folklore all over the country—pockets that were full of folklore of all manner of coinage, with more being minted every day. Both organizations published their own journals, which helped assure an outlet for the burgeoning interest in American materials, from cowboy to Native American to even the Dutch lore used by Washington Irving. African American minstrelsy and choir and quartet versions of spirituals and jubilee songs were already exerting their hybrid influences on an American popular culture thirsting for something old (folk past), something new (an updated version of the previously little-heard), something borrowed (from African American culture), and something blue (blues). As the nation attempted to reestablish its bearings after the Civil War and take its place by the time of World War I on the international stage, American writers built on the nationalist sentiments seeking to establish a political and artistic identity indigenous to American culture, not always with a full sense of the irony of borrowing/stealing it from a subjected segment of the population kidnapped from another continent. With Henry James's discussion in his book on Hawthorne of the elements of culture present in Europe but lacking in America blowing in the wind (*Haw-*

thorne 43), folklorists sought to collect and explain the continuities and discontinuities of American folklore in relation to the rest of the world. While some would focus on the survival of Child Ballads and other European connections, however, others examined the very distinctive elements represented by the blending of African and European traditions that gave America one of its most distinct and characteristic creations—African American folklore.

Because many collectors of folklore were university trained, white, and male (though there were also notable women), the modes of collecting folklore from African Americans represented a significant obstacle to the interpretation of materials collected at the time. The approach of late nineteenth and early twentieth-century white southern folklorists, for example, to a frequently terrorized southern black community prompted guarded responses, professions of ignorance of certain black traditions, and the placing of the minstrel mask between performer and collector, as Bryan Wagner explores relative to the Lomaxes and Howard Odum in *Disturbing the Peace* (213–38). The lack of insider knowledge about the community and its traditions, and the frequent racist socialization process under which whites had grown up, precipitated styles of dealing with, collecting from, and condescending to informants that closed down valuable avenues of exchange. The technological shortcomings due to the absence of recording devices many times meant that a folklorist relied on notes or memory for the oral "texts," and, because not all were trained in musical notation—and European notation was inadequate to appreciate and transcribe African-based instruments and sounds—the accuracy with which folk materials were represented was sometimes questionable. Still, folklorists persevered, and some prevailed, in representing the materials in an honest and dignified manner when warranted, reining in their prejudices as they spurred themselves on in their quest to document and define the American character in as scientifically controlled a manner as possible.

Previously termed "popular antiquities," the word "folklore" was coined by William Thoms in 1846 (Thomas A. Green 331). Besides being an unwieldy term, "popular antiquities" could, by the twentieth century, complicate the process of identifying folk materials—already a difficult process—by confusing folk and popular elements, which was to become particularly difficult in a century where an expanding media and burgeoning recording industry meant the translation of folk elements to popular culture (and vice versa) with inordinate speed and insipid disregard. Additionally, since oral folk elements were sometimes altered by copywriters and transcribers for consumption outside the community/ies of origin, sometimes the materials were quite different from the original variants collected in various locations. And once those recordings began to turn up in the communities of origin, they began to feed back into the oral tradition, altering it through its emphasis on new or favored formal patterns, stylistic individuality, virtuosity, favored subject matter and lyrical expressions, beauty, opulent visual presentation, and, finally, hucksterism. For those bent on haggling over boundaries, it could be quite difficult to differentiate folklore from what Richard Dorson termed "fakelore" (Thomas A. Green 275), someone's original creation passed off as folklore, and "poplore," which attempts to neutralize the negativity of the word "fake," though the musicians—who as always knew what felt real and when it was wanted—took the various manifestations in stride and gave their audiences what they wanted. For example, Robert Johnson used to perform the pop song "My Blue Heaven"—popularized by white crooner Gene Austin in 1928—and, horror of horrors for the blues "purist," between meeting with the devil at the crossroads and being relentlessly pursued by hellhounds, might even have enjoyed it!

After random but significant encounters with the blues by people like Gates Thomas, W. C. Handy, and Ma Rainey just before or after the turn of the twentieth century, the combination of tent show performances, sheet music, piano rolls, stage shows, and the rise of the age of the American folklorist produced an increasing number of references to African American folklore, including blues music, and further scholarly interest. Important books by John Wesley Work II, Thomas Talley, Dorothy Scarborough, John Jacob Niles, Newbell Niles Puckett, and even Carl Sandburg symbolized the flow of African American folklore toward mainstream white channels (and sometimes toward black commercial channels, Handy's publishing company and Black Swan Records among them), where they were directed by money or inherited values and attitudes toward their "appropriate" docks. Therefore, what we encounter in folklore—and folk-blues—is "hot" music, certainly, but not "hot music," the more commercialized manifestation of the folk materials that were generated in the backwoods, on the back porch, and back in the alley where the blues came from. Of course, one hesitates to attempt to segregate one from the other too fully, since they did exist side by side, sheet music or piano rolls, for example, springing originally from and sometimes feeding back into the folk tradition. But there were elements that were introduced into or standardized by commercial products that can betray the mass market nature of the materials. Folklorists frequently attempted to avoid, even weed out, commercial songs as in some ways choking off the folk tradition.

Folklorists, of course, were collecting important African American folk materials in the 1920s, though not always with a fictional frame or a narrative to present, or as much of a focus on materials that might be termed hot or "pre-hot" music, though at times some music related to blues music, for example, might be included. John Wesley Work II's *Folk Songs of the American Negro* (1915) deliberately emphasized, as many scholars had before him, elements of religious music that did not take into account how sacred and secular distinctions were more blended in West African cultures. Thomas Talley, a Fisk chemistry professor with an interest in African American folklore, responded to Work's volume with *Negro Folk Rhymes* (1922), which demonstrated the existence of "secular" folklore of a type that had been little collected and studied. Dorothy Scarborough's *On the Trail of Negro Folk Songs* (1923) collects some fascinating material and provides interesting commentary on the works, though sometimes reflecting racist attitudes concerning "the colored mind [being] not essentially logical" (272). Roark Bradford, Sterling Brown, Zora Neale Hurston, H. E. Krehbiel, Charles Peabody, Newbell Niles Puckett, Gates Thomas, Will Thomas, W. Prescott Webb, and others contributed to the slowly increasing knowledge of African American folklore, of course a primary source of African American hot music of the 1920s. Pride of place goes to Edward C. L. Adams, a South Carolina physician who, though a white man well positioned in the white community, nonetheless found himself a confidante of black laborers who trusted his empathetic posture and willingness to help. His *Congaree Sketches* (1927) and *Nigger to Nigger* (1928) present a bold directness and honesty from his informants that anticipates the work of Lawrence Gellert, whose own collected material was challenged as inauthentic (some of it *was* written by him) because of its brutal frankness and predominance of protest materials. Adams, like Van Vechten, made use of the "nigger" epithet in one of his book titles, two years after Van Vechten's book had sorely offended some readers, but as Robert O'Meally points out, Adams was an insightful and sympathetic observer whose purpose was not to shock, but to share (Adams lxiv).

Naturally, there were those toiling in the fields of folklore that evinced a socio-political and literary interest in the materials they encountered. After all, the Civil War had not finally decided what to "do" with still-objectified African Americans given their *de jure* freedom, but those on opposing sides still intended to make their arguments in a variety of ways. Thomas W. Dixon, D. W. Griffith, and a variety of others following Mencken's "Sahara of the Bozart" (Beaux arts) certainly made their pitches, and those whites who opposed them, even if their own notions of race and class were not necessarily radically different from their enemies', found public ways to manifest their views. Among these people, folklorists were frequently nearest the people "furthest down," since because of their connections of folklore with the past they had a tendency to collect from isolated pockets of older members of the population. If this supposedly put them in touch with the "real spirit" of African Americans, folklorists' attitudes toward the lives and art of the folk as expressed not only to other "scientists" in their journals, but perhaps in magazines and novels excerpted from their experiences, could provide special insight into "the "Negro problem." This is especially true if "enlightened" attitudes allowed them to view and hear events with something like an enlightened democratic outlook.

One of the first to emerge among these literary folklorists was Howard W. Odum (1884–1954), a sociologist and folklorist from Bethlehem, Georgia, with degrees in English (BA), Classics (MA), Psychology (PhD), and Sociology (PhD). His early days were passed in Georgia and Mississippi, where he was easily familiar with white and black southern culture and attitudes and their relations to each other, viewed especially from a white perspective. After earning his PhDs at Clark and Columbia Universities, he proceeded to work in a variety of jobs, including teaching, where he eventually settled as a distinguished professor at the University of North Carolina in 1920. Between 1905 and 1908, he studied and collected materials from local black populations in Lafayette County, Mississippi, and Newton County, Georgia, forming the basis for his important early seminal articles on sacred and secular music among blacks. The first installment, "Religious Folk-Songs of the Southern Negro," was published in 1909, followed in 1911 by "Folk-Song and Folk-Poetry as Found in the Secular Songs of Southern Negroes." Odum was exploring the roots of what was soon to infiltrate pop culture in hybrid forms. In fact, Guy B. Johnson ("Double Meaning" 12–20) and Sterling A. Brown ("The Blues as Folk Poetry" 324–39) both commented in the 1920s on the issue.

Odum's early collecting expeditions in the South produced the most significant African American blues and blues-related materials collected before those of Alan Lomax, Lawrence Gellert, John W. Work III, and Lewis Jones, and extensive work done by Paul Oliver, William R. Ferris, David Evans, Bruce Bastin, and others later. In his publications, he reported from his field collections the lyrics that would be showing up especially post-1920 on the recordings of African Americans during the blues boom, though he took the time to place them thematically, aesthetically, and stylistically in a (sometimes faulty) context. Inexplicably, Odum destroyed the cylinder recordings he had made of the performances, a significant loss to the study of folklore, but at least the word "transcriptions" remain to demonstrate how the music existed in a primarily non-commercial setting, though even folk musicians were familiar with the songs from piano rolls and sheet music and would work them into their repertoires, as Odum himself pointed out (Tracy, *Write Me* 136–37). Odum also took the extraordinary leap of employing the materials he collected in a "Black Ulysses trilogy" of novels which would test his sociopolitical beliefs and tax his artistic abilities to their fullest.

Despite being born in Bethlehem, Odum was not wrapped in swaddling clothes and laid in a manger of racial understanding. Odum's early work reveals racist underpinnings that he had absorbed from his surroundings, asserting at various times that the Negro was most characteristic in "his wanton and reckless moods" (Tracy, *Write Me* 93) and suggesting that blacks could not possess "conceptions of higher love, married life, and the relation of the sexes" (*The Negro and His Songs* 166). Odum required a tag-team of experts to assist him in examining his racist attitudes, and he got them through his work with colleague Franz Boas, student, protégé, and colleague Guy B. Johnson, and informant John Wesley Gordon. Boas, the esteemed "Father of American Anthropology," lecturer, and head of the new department of Anthropology at Columbia University beginning in 1896, brought his insights into non-Western cultural groups to bear on Odum's prejudices, as he would later guide Hurston to her collections of folklore among African Americans. Guy B. Johnson's collaborations with Odum revealed that the more involvement the younger and more progressive man had in the production of the text, the less racist it was, as can be seen by a comparison of *Social and Mental Traits of the Negro* (1910) and *Negro Workaday Songs* (1926). Both were extremely important for Odum's social transformation.

Perhaps the most important of the three "experts" who brought his experience to bear on Odum, was not the wise old German anthropologist or the younger, highly esteemed sociologist, but the itinerant black man and folklore source/informant who, as Lynn Moss Sanders points out, became a cultural collaborator with the white southerner Odum (165–66). To call this a cultural collaboration is to acknowledge the important contributions of Gordon to the text. For Gordon, he was giving his life, his speech, his spirit, his art, to the project. It would not have been possible without him. Odum is, in a sense, a go-between, a transcriber: without him, there is not access for an audience that needs to understand Gordon's life and has the ability to change the conditions that torture him. If Gordon stands on one side of the gulf, and white society on the other, then Odum is the bridge in between, a bridge, perhaps, like that which Hart Crane envisioned in his masterly poem. Not that Odum was merely a passive conduit. He had to choose what to include and exclude, what to compress, how to order properly to offer narrative integrity, how to make the language and experiences accurate and accessible to the audience. And, in the first and third novels of the trilogy, he provides commentary that contextualizes what is offered in a more academic and/or Western literary style. Presumably—though this is not verified— the monetary proceeds of the book went to Odum, who prepared it in the accepted manner for dissemination in his culture, and thus reaped those benefits. In that case, the sower, as had been unfortunately too true in the past, may not have gained monetarily for his toil, though we do not know for sure what their arrangement was. The benefits could be more gradual—as was frequently counseled as advisable by "sympathetic" whites—a type of breaking ground of attitudes and planting seeds that would sprout in a generation or two. It was a start definitely needed by the society in power, which notoriously disregarded the lives of the present—a weird blues: hardship now, hope later, on OUR terms, in OUR style, in OUR time. The weight of the wait weighs heavily on the waiter. This cultural collaboration was inherently unequal, yet this does not make Odum an exploiter. He clearly did put a great deal of work into projects of his choosing that provided then and now a greater understanding and appreciation of African American culture that, over time, created an environment in which certain adjustments and improvements could be made to ameliorate the situation of African Americans. He clearly admired Gordon, foregrounded him in the books, and acknowledged it publicly. Revolutions are lit by sparks, before flame throwers.

John Wesley Gordon was Odum's bridge to understanding and appreciating an African American worldview and strategies for survival. Gordon's nickname was "Left Wing" because he'd lost his right arm in an accident after the war and was left with only his left "wing." This type of nicknaming was a common practice in African American culture. For example, white Chicago jazz trumpeter Joe Manone lost his arm in a street car accident and became "Wingy Manone;" Lovell Alexander, who recorded a tune called "Howling Man Blues" (1934), was called "One Arm Slim," perhaps as a result of having his arm cut off!; and Joshua Barnes Howell's damage from being shot in a fight resulted in his peg leg, and the monicker Peg Leg Howell, on record. The surprising thing about Gordon's injury, however, is that Odum barely ever mentions it, as if it doesn't have any significant effect on Gordon's life, personality, or survival skills. Gordon, in language Faulkner employed for Dilsey, endured, but in a more vigorous, independent way than Faulkner's servant. What we note in the three novels is that Odum genuinely admires Gordon's ability to survive and thrive amidst tragedies of epic proportions, using his shit, grit, and mother-wit to face down all the hardships life has to throw at him.

It is also quite possible that Odum employed the nickname for another, more political reason. The term "left wing," meaning liberal or radical, emerges from the nature of seating arrangements at the French National Assembly in the late eighteenth century. There, the more radical members sat on the left side or wing, while the conservatives took their places on the right. Since the term was thus current in this meaning at the time Odum wrote this novel, it may well be that Odum intended to term Gordon a liberal or radical in his social ideas, or indeed to label himself as a radical in his admiration for Gordon's life and language. Especially given Odum's later concentration on Gordon's extensive wartime experiences in France, this Franco-historical approach seems possible, but not verifiable.

By the time of his novelistic trilogy of the late 1920s–early 1930s, Odum had begun to transform into a "progressive" southerner, in contrast to the traditionalism of the Fugitives Allen Tate, John Crowe Ransom, and Robert Penn Warren, advocating for a greater understanding and cooperation between the races. Sterling Brown looked back from 1931 on Odum's career from the vantage point of a review of *Cold Blue Moon* (1931): "The list of books by Prof. Howard Odum on the social conditions of the South is a long and honorable one. If report be credited, he has repudiated an early book of his which dealt with racial characteristics in rather sweeping fashion. Since then his works have been characterized by candor, scholarship, and interpretive power. In addition, he writes in a manner unlike that of many of his fellows in the social sciences; it is obvious that he is a poetic craftsman as well as a social observer" (Brown, "An American Epoch" 187).

Positive reviews from a number of Harlem Renaissance reviewers for his novelistic trilogy, including Walter White, Thomas Talley, Countee Cullen, Langston Hughes, and Eric Walrond, demonstrated an admiration and acceptance of Odum's talent, materials, and motivations for creating the work, though a couple of dissenters with regard to Odum's works, Gloria Goddard and a jealous Zora Neale Hurston, discussed below, made sure that it was not an unqualified or unanimous approval. As Emory Bogardus wrote, Odum the sociologist sought "the integration of all regions into a national whole and then into a societal whole" (448). One of the imperatives of this plan is that there be interracial understanding in the South, which Odum undertook to achieve in a variety of ways in a variety of venues, teaching, publication, and committee and organizational work among them. In his Black Ulysses trilogy, he sought to "explain" the life and value of a previously unfathomed black man to his white "neighbors" around the country, revealing the unwarranted fragmentation of the black and white worlds and advocating for a constructive harmonization of the contemporary world. This would help demarcate the line between the old southern order and a new, better southern order that he was helping envision (299). If this seems a bit arrogant—one comment frequently floated concerning white southerners was that they "know their negroes," sometimes better than they know themselves—it is still Odum's heartfelt attempt to contribute a sympathetic mind and pen to the cause.

With the optimism, expansiveness, and sometimes the ecstatic language of both Walt Whitman and Carl Sandburg, Odum set out on his own odyssey to describe the odyssey of Left Wing Gordon. Odum's three novels, *Rainbow Round My Shoulder* (1928), *Wings On My Feet* (1929), and *Cold Blue Moon* (1931), make copious use of African American folklore, including the blues, in ways that indicate its value to African American and American culture, and in ways that show its adaptability and usefulness thematically and stylistically to unite America through understanding and bring its united culture to the world stage, while remaining remarkably personal and thematically and stylistically rich. Odum, who in the first novel of the trilogy uses italicized print to differentiate his words from Gordon's in order to help direct the picaresque narrative and make his sociological and myth-making comments stand out, runs the risk of implying that of necessity Gordon needs an interpreter with lofty formal language in order to be considered an important figure. This is neither thematically nor stylistically Odum's intent. His respect for the communicative power of the blues and the integrity of Gordon's artistry would not allow that, even if he feels he needs to employ that kind of language for his expression and voice—formally educated, trained in classics, sociology, and psychology, a teacher and scholar, with W. E. B. Du Bois (53), Langston Hughes (252), Professor Howard Mumford Jones (270), Carl Sandburg (272), and white folklore collector E. C. L. Adams (300), and the entire classical tradition in the wings for support. The italicized portions of the text are what express *him*—race, class, and gender—more effectively than anything else. Just like Gordon and his blues.

The trilogy lays out Gordon's life, from family to childhood experiences to work, play, chain gangs, war experiences, the ghosts of southern gothic past and present, and the sweet consolations of folk materials and sweet women to help him roll his time on out. His personality was likely expanded a bit by Odum to include bits of songs and stories, and people that he had met as well. It is no coincidence that a rainbow is the major symbol of the title of the first novel. Its archetypal symbolism as a connection between disparate or distant things in this and other worlds gives context to Gordon's skill as a repository of folklore supreme, an elemental conjure man, and a loud, fast, and big talking American hero. What exactly was Gordon bridging—for himself, for Odum, for art, and for America? Black and white; northern and southern culture; upper and lower-class; vernacular art and the beaux arts; Odum's folklore, classical studies, and sociology; the great gulf of American democracy? The distance it takes to get *home* in a heart[h]less world? The distance between one human heart and another? It took a genuine respect for the strength, dignity, skill, and talent of Gordon for this collaboration to work, and Odum seemed to have that for Gordon. If there are times in the book that Odum idealizes Gordon as a symbolic embodiment of African American spirit, which is too much weight for anybody to carry, he also includes a fair number of faults and drawbacks that suggest he realizes he is dealing with a human being. Odum tries in a number of ways to "explain" black people through the rehearsal of all too common African American life stories of difficult struggles with poverty, broken homes, violence, and low ceilings of expectations. If Odum was going to demonstrate how powerful African American folklore was, he was going to need an awfully powerful figure, an epic hero, to represent it, and sometimes with all of those glorious epithets, they can be just a bit hard to bring down to earth.

The construction of Gordon's character is a little difficult to speak of here, because Odum allows that he has attempted to portray Gordon accurately in terms of personality, actions, and language. The figure first turned up in Odum's *Negro Workaday Songs* (1926), with Gordon's character pretty much as we find it in the novels. However, Odum also told Leon Whipple that "the very sentences are transcriptions of Negro talk, not always of one man but nothing else but Negro" ("War Blues" 163). So when was Odum telling the truth? And what is "Negro talk"? Is Odum suggesting that all black folks speak the same way, or that black speech is most accurately portrayed by lower-class, itinerant, southern blacks? This is a real problem in a time when a black individual in many white minds symbolized an entire "race," and black minds thought about that, too, because they wanted every member of the "race" to keep up the entire race's image. In separate reviews of Odum's works, Langston Hughes and Sterling Brown both emphasized Odum's portrayal of "proletarian life" (Hughes, "Review of *Rainbow*" 149) and "a certain type of Southern Negro" (Brown, "Black Ulysses at War" 383), but as Hughes continued to emphasize, "[N]ot all Negro life, of course" (149). Hughes, in fact, used the occasion to slam black critics for expecting that only "the 'best' things" about African Americans would be portrayed, lecturing "[t]he deplorable conditions shown in these chapters really exist, like it or not" ("Review" 149). And Brown added in 1933, [m]any of the stereotypes are overthrown in *Rainbow Round My Shoulder*, although comic, and brutal, and submissive Negroes may be seen there. These are viewed, however, "in the round," not as walking generalizations about *the* Negro, and Odum is intent on making us understand how they got to be where they are (*Negro Cavalcade* 638). However, there were a number of white reviewers who wrote that Odum was portraying "the

Negro" in their reviews, including Percy Hutchison, who saw Odum's character as "the eternal home-grown coon" (12). Despite Odum's protestations that Gordon was an individual, which he clearly was, writing about him as a symbol of something larger and more general makes him seem like more than himself, which he is. However, he is not "Every-Negro."

In *Rainbow* Odum calls what Gordon represents "folk backgrounds," "folk-urge," "folk-soul in the making" (316), and says of Gordon, "one could scarcely imagine a better summary of the lonesome road, if made to order" (207). Seeking these things is not how one buys a townhouse on Striver's Row on West 138th and West 139th in Harlem. Unfortunately, some reviewers did not differentiate between classes, and so Odum was sometimes hung with the label of portraying the "race." On the other hand, Odum was suggesting that, deep down, the race did all come from the same place, and therefore did share something deeper, more primitive. Back in time and space to the "jungle throats" that Odum connects to "red lips like watermelons" (271), minstrelsy, blues, and jazz. Odum does not seem to be using these images in a pejorative way. In fact, he goes to some length to offer a positive view of Africa and African American life before the war. Rather, Odum seems to be trying to portray the communal artist, the one who speaks and acts both as an individual and the community, first person singular and plural, as in Langston Hughes's "The Negro Speaks of Rivers" (*Collected Poems* 23) and, ultimately, with its source in West African communal art transplanted to American soil. A connection to a proud heritage, to the ancestors. Race relations and keeping up or building an image were so complicated, however, at that point in time, that it is somewhat difficult, especially for both black and white authors, to carry this off, especially if they want to evoke jungles, watermelons, and minstrelsy for a middle-class scrambling for Palmer's Skin Success, pomade, and quail on toast.

The subtitle has already told us that this man is a black Ulysses in a time when such designations would have been considered "ludicrous," as Odum himself acknowledges (317). Ulysses was, after all, a hero whose Homeric story of "arms and a man" (with apologies to Virgil) cannot be played out—Gordon only has one arm! With this additional handicap, Gordon undertakes his relentless journeying, his "black epic in a white world" (53), in a world that is not his, with no significant connections to any gods that might save him. Like Ulysses, he does not have the boundless strength of Hercules; like Ulysses, he must depend on his prudence, sagacity, wisdom, and his ability to lie fluently. The first three of these qualities were not associated in the popular mind with the African American. The end men in the minstrel shows were lazy fools or unduly vain pseudo-dandies. Odum's audiences might have wondered whether Odum was serious in this lofty characterization, or merely making a mockery of the African American by the seeming disparities of the comparison. At the beginning of *Rainbow*, Odum makes it Gordon who "might have been thinking of himself as some noble Ulysses" (1), setting us up for a suspected ridiculing of the vain minstrel stereotype we have come to expect. But then the negative stereotype of the black person as compulsive liar begins to operate in the portrait, particularly as Gordon is revealed as a wanderer and a musician. Odum contextualizes the lofty language to come in chapter 5: "*Black Ulysses starting as no more than an 'average' nomad, reflects a rare cumulative Odyssey*" (68).

However, Odum seems to be using Ulysses to make a point about Gordon and the type of black folks he represents. Ulysses lies to protect himself, for example, from Polyphemus. Should Ulysses fail in his deceit, he and his people will be killed. It is not an unfathomable leap from Ulysses's need to lie to Polyphemus and the vicissitudes of a black man's life that necessitates deceit. We think of the extensive and multifaceted masking tradition in African American culture, as in Paul Laurence Dunbar's poem "We Wear the Mask" (*Collected Poetry* 71) as one reflection of this. Figuring out how to get out of tight racial spots such as those explored in the folktale "Caught the Old Coon at Last," by Richard Wright in "The Ethics of Living Jim Crow," or Ralph Ellison in *Invisible Man* (59), do involve quick thinking, social discernment, and multi-perspectival strategizing. A one-eyed Polyphemus/southern cracker has no depth perception, but with two eyes and a ton of training in extricating himself from close calls, Gordon will do just fine at negotiating the tyrannical dangers of the Jim Crow South. In fact, one of Odum's main points in the texts is that African Americans have developed skills and strategies from their African tribal past, experiences during slavery, and the Jim Crow present that make their lives, through Gordon's, comparably epic to the wanderer Ulysses's. Furthermore, the notion of "lying" conveys different implications in a black community where people call tall tales and stretchers "lies" and celebrate the ability to tell them. The lie is a creative act, an entertaining act, a way of explaining inexplicable elements in the world. Explanations of the presence of white folks and black, how stars were made, and such things foster creative thought that begins to explore social aspects of the lives of African Americans through tongue in cheek, ironic, even outrageous transparent falsehood that attempts to match the insanity of life itself. To be a sayer, to speak things into existence, is empowering, part of the game of life itself, as all speech, as Chaucer says, is but broken wind, though all smells are not created equal.

What does Gordon have to help him survive the comparison to Ulysses and the Jim Crow South? The knowledge of the fatherland, the love and perseverance of his parents, especially his mother, the wisdom of the elders, and the ancestral gift that has been passed down to him through African American folklore, especially the blues. The fact that he has "never yet found the bottom of his bag of songs" (272)—perhaps a sidewise glance at Carl Sandburg's *American Songbag*—has a particular significance. Throughout the entire series, Gordon draws upon the wisdom, strength, and beauty of African American folklore to sustain, strengthen, and revivify him. This goes all the way back to the African continent, described by Odum as a clear explanatory source of the backgrounds of African American philosophy and aesthetics, as well as the source of human life. In one of the rapturous italicized sections preceding each chapter, Odum calls on the ancient power of African song, advising Gordon, "*REPRESENT YOUR RACE*" (270), with generations of African Americans supplying not only more finished products like work songs, coon songs, jazz songs, and blues, but the essential rhythms that form the basis for the art. When Odum admonishes African spirits to sing "*THAT WE MAY REMEMBER, ALWAYS REMEMBER*" (271), he means remember not only the slave trade and the horrendous inhumanity and sin of the system, but also past that, "*INTO THE PRIMITIVE EARTH, THE BROWN, BLACK EARTH . . . WHERE WE CAME FROM*" (272). The acknowledgment of the essential connection of all human beings in the most distant past in Africa is one of inter-continental and intra-continental community, evoked to point out that the primitivism that overlays African American identity stems in part from the originality of Africans and their evocations of the spirit of primal passions and art. After all, Odum feels we must confront these realities, these passions, these songs "*THAT WE MAY REMEMBER, ALWAYS REMEMBER*" (272) that history and kinship. How does Odum say we are reminded of it, how do we remember it? Through the lore, the song, communication. And that communication must come in an appropriate style and language and rhythm—the rhythm of the earth that is the rhythm of the song that "conjures" us. Although this sounds to some ears like primitivist jungle voodoo, as in Lindsay's "The Congo," and Odum does refer to Gordon as "primitive" (251) and "childish" and "self-pitying" (2, 251), Odum actually is directing us toward accepting the unified subject matter and style of African song that will bring the spirit of America into unity with the rhythm of Africa so that America may learn, not to capture that rhythm, but to liberate the rhythm from American captivity. Whereas Odum sees Gordon and what he represents as "[a] part of the nation, and apart from it" (315), in another use of the rainbow in the title, Odum asks us to follow it to the pot of gold.

Odum sought to liberate the music by collecting it, appreciating it, and exposing it to an audience that knew very little about it, save through the distortions of popular culture. The "folk-urge" that he discusses in relation to Gordon includes the messages, modes of communication, and purposes for which folk materials were put to use. One of the major symbols of Gordon's artistry is his guitar, "Twelve String Laura in the Rough" (1), the name of which titles the first chapter of the book. Gordon is very clearly identified body and soul with music. This is not a surprising depiction, given that the racism of the time frequently portrayed African Americans as naturally musical, even "set to music" (Stowe). These kinds of sentiments were even mouthed by people of African descent of the time, such as British composer Samuel Coleridge-Taylor, who offered "the Negro is really and truly a most musical personality. What culture may do for the race in this respect has yet to be determined, but the underlying musical nature cannot for a moment be questioned" (7). Coleridge-Taylor's own *Twenty-Four Negro Melodies* impressed Booker T. Washington, who felt that Coleridge-Taylor's work revived interest in plantation melodies with what Jack Sullivan has called his "Anglo-Negro hybrid" (35), though Coleridge-Taylor hated ragtime (37). In fact, black folklorist Arthur Huff Fauset, in a review of Odum and Johnson's *The Negro and His Songs* (1925), commented, "I believe we can say this with safety: the negro is never more himself than in his songs" (228).

But Odum clearly shows Gordon to be a special case, not a stereotype. Not many sentences go by in the text without some snatch of a folk melody, frequently a blues, jubilee song, or spiritual, sung in Gordon's own rough-hewn way. If Gordon's roughness here is unvarnished, it nonetheless has the authority of knowing whereof it speaks, having accompanied him to and in thirty-eight states (2), some multiple times, in his quest for peace. He becomes the quintessential type of the wandering, guitar-toting, hard-living, womanizing blues singer of American legend—a proto-Leadbelly without the prison time, before Leadbelly gained his fame. He has the wanderlust—he sings a snatch of a blues lyric that also turns up in white Jimmie Rodgers's recording of "Blue Yodel No. 9" from 1930 (98), and speaks of the train symbol in literal and metaphorical contexts: "gonna ride them cushions to the promised land" (322). Gordon stands up for himself in a variety of circumstances in the text—confronting the brakeman (226), insisting he will not die for the white man (303), or "be no black leaf blowed about by some white man's breath in some dam' fence corner" (304). His pride in himself, his desire to stand up for himself, is very much part of the folk heritage he represents.

Significantly, his guitar is named after a woman, with the obvious associations with handling the female shape, inspiration by a muse, and the attempt to bring masculine and feminine into sexual and spiritual harmony. The fact that she is a rough one matches his own origins and aesthetic. One needs a rough guitar for a rough music expressing a rough life, though for all that a homemade "box" still has all the notes that a Martin does, and sometimes a few nobody ever thought of without it. Gordon is not from "blue vein" or "dicty" society—not light enough to see the blue veins in his arms or highborn enough to feel the starch in his collars. He is down home, low-down as they come, and his straightforward and unabashed unpretentiousness finds its most vigorous expression in his description of one of his drunks: "Jes' let me git alcohol behind my eyes, good-God-a-mighty I'm right wid the world, rockin' in the slime" (129). This distinctive phrase, "rockin' in the slime," is as peculiar and appropriate an expression of vulgar, unrestrained, unrepentant *testosterone*-saturation, as pure and ebullient an expression of disgusting male celebratory excess as one is likely to find in four words that are still pronounceable in your mother's presence.

As one would expect from a sociologist, Odum portrays where Gordon comes from with a general bit of sociological language in chapter 2, "Remembering First Things" (17), but it is clearly the memories that Gordon has that are of primary importance, not the statistics. His mother was a hardworking, responsible, education-oriented woman who had aspirations for her children (22, 40, 44). She was also a harsh disciplinarian in the mode of the mother in Wright's "The Ethics of Living Jim Crow," beating him for playing with a white girl (26). His light-skinned father, lighter than either the mother or the boy, is frequently cruel and violent, but he likely thinks he is "toughening up" his children for a cruel world when he beats them. However, he does not lower the ceilings of their expectations: "what anybody else do an' you can see it you can do" (28). Gordon has done many things, like Sterling Brown's protagonist in "Odyssey of Big Boy," he's "done done" them, and he'll do until he don't no more. It was a hard lesson to learn, but the father thought it was better to learn it early. Unfortunately, the violence that the father perpetrates on the mother necessitates that she kill him to protect her family, whereupon a long tribute to black womanhood and the sufferings of their lives explains what Odum sees as a particular devotion of children to their mothers.

Yet Gordon is not a sociopath. He is just a human being with his superego on a "time out" for good behavior. Gordon's life does seem to have its associations in the novel with stereotypical "black" behavior that some people might find to be offensive. The defense here is that this is Gordon's life, and Odum simply reports the events, though of course the way they are reported has a good bit to do with how we perceive them. Alcohol, knives, guns, domestic violence, profanity, lack of formal education (though Gordon can read and write, 22)—they are all here, as they are, obviously, in many blues songs of the time as well. Blind Willie McTell sang, "I drink so much whiskey I stagger when I'm sleep" in "Dark Night Blues" (1928); Josie Miles's version of "A to Z

Blues" (1924) deals with carving the alphabet in a mate's body; Robert Johnson's "32–20 Blues" (1936), based on Skip James's "22–20 Blues" (1931), describes how he'll take his gun to his woman and "cut her half in two"; Lucille Bogan out-Herod's Herod with her profanity in "Shave 'Em Dry" (1935 unissued); Gabriel Brown had the "Education Blues" (1935); and Big Joe Williams sang about a cruel parent in "Mean Stepfather Blues" (1935). Odum, however, recognizes these things not as innately racial problems but, thinking as a sociologist, knows they are bred of society's seemingly unintended but sometimes deliberate functional malevolence.

This malevolence creates the dilemma of what Odum calls the "Negro and his four selves" (211): who he is, who the white man thinks he is, who he might be, and who he desires to become. Rob Lawson calls his ambiguous living space a "Jim Crow Counterculture" where call-and-response evoke accommodation and resistance (1). Given that he is also separate from the nation, part of an old, restrictive order, a black man in a white world, his identity problems—a quadruple consciousness, to paraphrase Du Bois's terms—receive an explanation that blames environment for the epic problems faced by blacks, and sympathizes with the women who try to hold things together. The scene interestingly anticipates the trial scene in Zora Neale Hurston's *Their Eyes Were Watching God* after Janie has killed Tea Cake, near the end of the novel, where white women understand and empathize with Janie, since Hurston has revealed to us Janie's position as a woman and partner in the social world. Here the intersection of race and gender make Gordon's mother's violence justifiable, as Janie's is (176–79).

One of the most positive influences in Gordon's life is his grandparents. They are portrayed as strong, supportive folks whose pride in heritage and knowledge of the lore of African Americans not only allows them to sustain themselves but to provide Gordon with the equipment to support himself as well. Significantly, the grandfather tells the story of his enslavement, sale, and escape that contextualizes the cruelty that the father has visited on Gordon. When the grandfather returns to his mother—and Odum has devoted a section to the worship of mothers and their special burdens (39–40)—she rejects him with the retort "go back an' work fer whut [you] gits in life" (57). The ten pages worth of discussion of the grandparents Uncle Simon and Aunt Mandy makes it clear, however, that life was not all rot gut, piss, and blood. There is plenty of evidence that African Americans strove to live clean, sober, and humanistic lives in the face of adversity and squalor—a point Olaudah Equiano made in comparison of Africans to Europeans in *The Interesting Narrative of the Life of Olaudah* Equiano—even if Equiano did falsify the record in his reportage. Their house is whitewashed clean (54), and they work hard to furnish it with food and furniture that make the children comfortable when they are there. Some of the things they have they made themselves, casting them as functional artists in materials of the earth as well as folklore.

Uncle Simon was a Baptist, so when he scolded the children for their transgressions, he made sure he personified the devil for them, and the children "delighted to hear him tell stories" (56), even if they were about his enslavement. Odum makes it clear how important emancipation was to blacks by portraying Aunt Mandy as frequently telling stories about that day, those times. That among the rejoicing there were "some folks all puzzled an' didn't know what to do" (57) portrays the fatally flawed plans for Reconstruction and the ways in which Gordon's family was doomed to difficulties by the societal malevolence that blocked Thaddeus Stevens and others from carrying out more felicitous plans for African Americans post-war. Of course, spirituals and jubilee songs are another gift of the grandparents, who have learned and retained this part of the African American heritage that is not so strong among the altered lives of their children. The importance of the extended family and the wisdom and pride and joy that the elders have to offer is a blessing for the children that manifests itself in Gordon's love for the stories and songs of the African American oral tradition.

There are few pages that pass in *Rainbow Round My Shoulder* that do not contain some reference to a lyric from the blues and spiritual tradition. While the blues have sometimes been portrayed as antithetical to the Christian music tradition, it is quite clear, as Odum understands, that the two may rest side by side quite easily, protestations of the "devout" notwithstanding. Though many believers suggest that all of one's works and thoughts ought to be directed at the Christian life and worship, there are blues singers who own that their abilities come from God, but that the music they play increases the enjoyment of more people if it deals with broader subject matter from their secular lives and travails. After all, we live in this world, so if we render unto God the things that are God's, there is no problem if we render unto Caesar. Albert Washington, a well-known blues singer, started as a gospel singer, and brought a great deal of the gospel feeling to his blues songs. Like Sam Cooke or Ray Charles, he sometimes received criticism for mixing gospel and blues sounds, and for playing in clubs on Saturday night and then being in church on Sunday. According to Albert, he was using his God-given talents to support his family and please crowds who were out seeking entertainment and relief from their daily worries, into which he was tapping with connections to the African American oral tradition. He was trying to ease their worried minds, so the intertwining of what are sometimes divided by Christians into sacred and secular traditions is carried out without irony or sense of wrong.

In his mind, he needed neither to quit night clubs nor the church, since he thought of himself as serving wherever he was.

Similarly, Gordon has no conflicts here either. His grandparents were devout Christians, and his mother was, too, though a bit less so than her parents. As such, Gordon performs songs such as "Steal Away to Jesus" (53), "Glory Glory Hallelujah When I Lay My Burden Down" (59), "Soon One Morning" (207), and "Down By the Riverside" (244) alongside his blues as reflections of not only his whole person, but also of the whole community tradition. That is, he sings in the first person, and expresses in the third person, the concerns of the community, in the songs and style of the community, when they serve both individual and communal concerns. Gordon is not accurately termed a blues singer, then, but rather what Odum identified from community terminology as a "music physicianer," a person who traveled from place to place and was expert in making songs and playing an instrument (Odum, "Folk-Song" 257–58). Besides blues and "sacred" songs, his repertoire included ballads such as "John Henry" (92; see Furry Lewis) and "Railroad Bill" (190; see Will Bennett); folk songs such as "Bully of This Town" (182; see Joe Harris and Kid West); game songs such as "The Skin Game" (131–34; see Lucille Bogan and Peg Leg Howell); and coon songs such as "Travelin' Man" (230, 235–36, 277; see Luke Jordan). Though the phrase "music physicianer" is left unexplained, it may in fact be related to the practice in the African American music tradition of calling of an expert piano player a "professor"—New Orleans blues pianist Roy Byrd, for example, sang, "They call me Doctor Professor Longhair." The notion of being a "healer" certainly jibes well with West African and blues music traditions of the consolatory healing power of the blues, and, in fact, brings those divided notions of sacred and secular together quite nicely.

Thus, Odum's regular use of the blues in the novel is offered within the contextualized portrait of a variety of African American folk performance, as well as in the context of Gordon's relationship to the various communities in which he performs the music. Although Gordon is generalized by Odum to something like the spirit of African Americans, Odum gives us enough of the individual personality of Gordon to make him himself, as well as a reflection of the community. And Gordon is not merely an object here, but a speaking subject of his own, even if the words are filtered through the mind and pen of a white sociologist-folklorist, however accurately he transcribes Gordon's words. Odum is not just using Gordon for his own purposes—though it is expressing his take on Gordon, and he is writing and monetarily benefitting from the publication of the novel—but offering Gordon a platform for his own benefit as well. Odum's use of Gordon's life and words, then, is somewhat different from the usages of Sandburg, Lindsay, Eliot, Loy, and others, in that the focus here is clearly of Gordon's life and African American art as it is related to the American experience.

But the blues seems to be most important to Gordon's life and expression. As the novel nears its close, Odum asserts, "Black Ulysses singing his Blues indescribably characteristic of his wanderer's soul. Black Ulysses IS the blues. No other form of expression can portray him fully as he is. His sorrow song the expression of self-pity, childish yearning, struggle for survival, folk feeling and all that is crowded into his singing moment. Black mirror reflecting song technique of obtaining food, shelter, money and sweet mama. Blending of folk romance of work and imagination, primitive, physical and spiritual expression. Appetite turned to song, song attuned to appetites" (251). The passage demonstrates Odum's feelings about the blues, its essential relationship to Gordon's life, and its expressive power as an art form that is uniquely capable of delineating Gordon's life. The blues is an expressive spirit that is inhabited by the individuals who feel it and perform it. It is a spirit and an individual. Gordon becomes the blues, and the blues is very becoming to him, and to the community. The blues style and form is seen as an artistic form that is physically, spiritually, artistically necessary, perfectly reflective of the life and lives of Africans on American soil. Although some critics may argue with Odum's references to self-pity, childish yearning, and primitivity, surely performers may have felt these things in addition to feelings of transcendence and assertiveness when performing, and perhaps "primitivity" is a poor word choice for the idea that the spirit and feelings of ancestors are evoked in performance that empower and direct one's playing. For Odum, the blues is clearly both incidental and visceral, and it is both a cause and a solution.

Thus, the frequent occurrence of blues lyrics in the text. Even before Gordon's narrative, Odum quotes a quintessential old blues, as old in theme as the African shackles and as recent as the hoot owl at sunset: "Poor Boy Long Way From Home," recorded as early as 1926 by Bo Weavil Jackson. Set immediately alongside some other old and archetypal lyrics in the associational style of some of the oldest blues ("Trouble I had it all my days" and "Got the blues, too damn mean to cry"), it becomes like digging down to that deepest root, exposing that rawest nerve, touching the most visceral art and saying this is where it comes from, and this is where we are going.

Blues lyrics are not only sung by Gordon here, but they are spoken, part of his everyday language. This is a reflection of Odum's feeling that the person *is* the blues, and that the language of the blues is that which is spoken, not some rarefied concoction for special performance occasions. Any occasion is a performance occasion, and any act of speech is the occasion for creativity. On a variety of occasions, Gordon spews forth a long spiel of lyrics that are familiar from blues songs that might seem a bit artificial, Odum over-the-top. However, in fact these kinds of improvisationally formulaic instances do occur. Ralph Ellison was clearly aware of this when he has Peter Wheatstraw name himself in a long string of terms (*Invisible Man* 176), and singers like Pigmeat Jarrett have been known to speak their identities this way as well: "My name is Big Time Black, Muck the Muck Man, Chief of Black Diamond, some call him lucky but he gone again, better known as E.D., Walso, Steno, jive for short. This is old Pigmeat, y'all. Thank y'all" (Tracy, *Going to Cincinnati* 93). The performance entertains, mythologizes, challenges boundaries of identity, and embodies the traditional lyric "you don't know my mind." It is shape shifting at its best, much like the medicine show performer who tells a number of unbelievable stories or "stretchers" in order to lower the bar for the claims of the "medicine" pitch man (as performed in *The Last Medicine Show).* For Odum, the technique is both functional and symbolic.

Other lyrics occur throughout. East Coast performer Blind Blake sings the lyrics "walkin', walkin' talkin' to myself" in his 1928 "Walkin' Across the Country" (3). Atlantan Barbecue Bob's "Barbecue Blues" (1927) includes "I ain't so good looking, teeth don't shine like pearls" (10), and we may recognize the lyrics "mama may have" included much later in Arthur Herzog and Billie Holiday's "God Bless the Child" from 1941 (58). Mississipians Son House and Willie Brown recorded "Camp Hollers" for Alan Lomax, John Wesley Work III, and Lewis Jones in 1941 echoing "ham string poppin', collar cryin'" from *Rainbow* (121), and the "cool drink of water 'fore I die" can be heard in Memphis's Furry Lewis's 1929 version of "John Henry Blues" (92), as the "peep through muddy water and spy dry land" (129) also occurs in Lewis's "Dry Land Blues" (1928). Another blues ballad, "Railroad Bill," was recorded in 1929 by Will Bennett (190). The "toad low shaker" references in the book (128, 162, 237), suggesting how earthy one can get sexually, occurs in Cincinnati's Bob Coleman's "Tear It Down" (1928), and Texan Blind Lemon Jefferson's recording of "Bed Springs Blues" features the sexual boast "I got somethin' to tell you make the hair rise on your head " (218). Sticking with Jefferson, "Long Lonesome Blues" (1926) starts with the memorable line "The blues came to Texas lopin' like a mule" (265), and his 1927 version of "Match Box Blues" includes "If you want your lover, better pin him to your side" (157). Alabaman Lucille Bogan (1935) and Atlanta's Peg Leg Howell (1927) both sing "Skin Game Blues," and Robert and Charlie Hicks (Barbecue Bob and his brother) even re-created one in their 1930 recording "Darktown Gamblin'—Part 2 (The Skin Game)" (131–34). Howell's "Turtle Dove Blues" (1928) features the "If I had wings" lyric (273), an interesting mix of the Bible and the blues. And of course there is the ubiquitous "Laughin' to keep from cryin'"

(311), as recorded by among many, urban blues singer Clara Smith as "You Don't Know My Mind" in 1924. This is not all the occurrences, but the omnipresence of the blues is clear.

Odum, in fact, collected all of these lyrics *before* they were commercially recorded, in Mississippi and Georgia between 1905 and 1908, from unknown sources, so it seems clear that the lyrics that were recorded existed before the era of recording, and likely had a much more widespread occurrence than the two locations mined by Odum. Of course, that was likely because the singers were like Gordon—ramblers from state to state, sometimes performing for a living, and thus carrying what might have been local songs at some remote point it time to a regional or national audience—certainly national by the time of recordings. Since Odum uses these songs in his writing, in Gordon's performance, and in Gordon's speech, it is fair to say that the novel is imbued with blues lyricism, and expressive of its spirit through the voices of Gordon, the tradition, and Odum. Formally speaking, the blues has particular characteristics that are reflected in Odum's novel as well. Call-and-response is extremely important to African American hot music, including the blues, and Odum uses it here in the give and take between the white folklorist's and the black informant's "conversations" with each other. These conversations are not direct, but rather take the form of juxtaposed expressions of ideas that form a communication between the two of them, as well as between them and the audience. In this case, Odum's reformation and subsequent adaptation of his training to his heightened sensitivity to African American culture allowed him to be a medium through which Gordon, and African American culture, might gain a public voice and a novel audience.

Whipple called Odum an "audacious artist" (163), and indeed there does seem to be a certain daring to Odum's techniques in the novel. Within the "picaresque tension" (316) of a wandering life, Odum has managed to pack the sometimes loose, associational, and hybrid nature of African American musical genres into the movement of the novel, following the blue trail blazed by Gordon through the ups and downs and all arounds of a blighted life made epic by his physical, spiritual, and artistic perseverance. Odum calls Gordon's expression "this tougher fabric" from which must come "the more sensitive and creative fiction true to and worthy of the innermost life and character of Black Ulysses and other physical and spiritual adventurers like him" (316). Odum's sentiments echo some of the language of Harlem Renaissance writers projecting in the future the fulfillment of the beauty and promise of African American folk culture. If they fail to see the orature as equal in its way to literature, they were at least at a step on the way.

All of which returns us to the rainbow of the title, a symbol more complex than previously explained. On a surface level, the phrase was quite common in 1928–1929 in jazz recordings—no fewer than ten jazz versions of the song "Rainbow Round My Shoulder" were recorded during those years, including a version by McKinney's Cotton Pickers. James Weldon Johnson's re-creation of black folk sermons by that title had come out a year earlier, in 1927. In Johnson's *God's Trombones*, it is God who wears that rainbow around his shoulders, preparing to create all the creatures of the world, and finally a man in His own image. Thus, as Gordon wears it, it identifies him with a power and spirit larger than mere humanity. It places him in the heavens with Christian and classical gods, beautifying the world with his wonderful garment, a sign of his gift of folk artistry. And as the rainbow comes with the sun, shining through a period of storm and stress, indeed it represents the spirit of the blues, the sun gonna shine in my back door—maybe even the front door—someday. This is the spirit of Gordon, the spirit of African Americans. And it is also the spirit of Odum, who envisions the country coming through the Civil War and Reconstruction to a place where the sun is going to shine on a unified national America not fragmented by a sectionalism that had already nearly torn it apart. It is a political bridge from slavery to freedom. A social bridge from class inequities and misunderstandings to behavioral contextualization. A racial bridge between whites and blacks who have only to learn about and understand each other as individuals. An educational bridge from the ignorance of a variety of cultures to the understanding fostered by learning and challenging the inherited standards of education. An artistic bridge from Cyclopean shallow vision to the vision of one who can "peep through muddy water and spy dry land" (129). Gordon is undeniably "part of all that he has met" (316), not just proletarian or African American, but American, and ready to take his place among the Pleiades, his use of the vernacular intact.

Something beautiful there for all to appreciate.

Wings On My Feet differs from *Rainbow* in a variety of ways, even while it shares the reverence for African American folklore, and for Left Wing Gordon, obvious in the first book. Where are the italicized passages of yesteryear, readers might ask, and why have they gone? In the second volume of the trilogy, Odum has done away with his italicized contextualization and commentary and given over the book to Gordon's voice. Whereas the commentary in *Rainbow* did help set up Gordon's voice and life and establish a voice that contrasted to and supplemented Gordon's ideas, some contemporary critics felt that those sections were a bit bombastic (Walrond 3). They might also be construed as operating the way that introductions in American local color humor did: supplying a standard of language and discussion that served implicitly to criticize the education and diction of the lower classes. This was clearly not Odum's intent and, having provided the commentary in the first volume and set up a number of themes he wished his audience to consider, Odum felt he could essentially let Gordon speak for himself here. This new strategy allowed Gordon and Odum to develop those earlier themes from *Rainbow*: exploring his philosophy of life, the strength of the African American folk tradition, mutability and the need to seize the day, the necessity of self-sufficiency and perseverance—stoicism—in the face of adversity, the ravages of American racism, and rewriting the American story in both style and subject matter. While Odum intended to give shape to the episodic narrative with his comments in *Rainbow*, the uninterrupted flow of Gordon's narrative in *Wings* more nearly captures the spirit of Gordon's liberated voice and narrative. Of course, a slave once told white collector John Henry Faulk that the whites who "set them free" had no right to enslave or liberate anyone, having only wrongly assumed the power to do so. Odum's assumption of control over the narrative might be seen as arrogance, and the tactic of *Wings* presumptuous as well. Perhaps Gordon should have been the author, making authorial decisions.

Wings On My Feet also broadens the context for Gordon's ramblings, taking him out of the American post-slavery Jim Crow crucible and into the European theater, a move that de-familiarizes Gordon for many who did not think of African Americans as being involved in the war, and that provides Gordon with the opportunity to see American racism in a different light. Gordon's presence at the European battleground allows him to perceive certain continuities between this segment of his life and the lives of his ancestors, and highlight the way he responds to the world. Though he is a long way from home, as the blues lyric says, he has been a long way from home before. Therefore, he draws upon what he knows to help him adapt to situations that, truth be told, are really only superficially different from the life he knew in America.

Of course, Odum still exerts his influence on the book, selecting what Gordon says and the sequence in which he says it. There was likely a great deal of other material, some perhaps trivial, some other perhaps more important to Gordon than to Odum. We assume that this selection process was Odum's, and therefore that he had the ultimate control over the text. Given his sympathetic stance toward Gordon and African Americans, we expect that he was reasonably accurate, though any inaccuracies would reflect on Gordon, not Odum. Gordon's, in a sense, was all the risk with, it might seem, few immediate benefits—a deck stacked a long time before Odum and Gordon came along, and the last card has not yet been flipped.

In this volume, Odum maintains the classical comparisons, still calling Gordon "Black Ulysses" and introducing another classical element to span time and space the same way the rainbow/bridge metaphor did in the first work. This time it is the allusion to "wings on my feet" that connects Gordon to the *talaria* or winged sandals of Hermes/Mercury, as well as the *petasus* or cap that Mercury wore. The association with Hermes as "messenger of the gods" is an apt one with regard to the function Odum has Gordon serve. Gordon is, after all, delivering his own message (and Odum's as well) of the power and viability of African Americans and their traditions, bridging various segments of society. As this type of messenger, he also serves as the patron of travelers and shepherds by, in a real sense, speaking up for them: Hermes is the patron of people like Gordon, who both travel and tend to African American artistic traditions by keeping them up and passing them on to others. Hermes also conducted souls into the infernal regions, making him unique among the gods in terms of frequenting both upper and nether regions. This is certainly also true of Gordon, whose carrying and performing of music associated with heaven (spirituals) and hell (the Devil's music, the blues) mark him as a figure with personal experiences that partake of both, and generate music out of both as well. Along these lines, Hermes is also noted as the inventor of a seven-stringed lyre, which he not coincidentally gave to Apollo in exchange for the caduceus that started out this whole discussion. Of course, Gordon's greatest gift is his gift of speech, which also characterizes Hermes, the god of eloquent speech. In all, Gordon continues as a traveler, a seeker, and a bridge, embodiment of African American folk spirit, who exercises his powers, as Odum shows, by adapting his abilities to his environment—another characteristic of the depth and breadth of African American folklore.

This is particularly true of the way Odum uses his blues in this book. By revealing the experiences of Left Wing Gordon throughout the process of the draft, basic training, shipping out to Europe, exploring the new land though working, fighting, and gambling, carrying out the postwar cleanup, returning (belatedly) stateside, and attempting to reintegrate into American society, Odum reveals the experiences of black soldiers in World War I, positive and negative, and the remarkable resilience and adaptibility of the black soldiers under difficult conditions. Part of that adaptibility is in the folklore itself, which continues to serve its functions of expressing, explaining, and ameliorating or transcending conditions. Thomas Wentworth Higginson's *Army Life in a Black Regiment* (1870) had earlier showed some of this adaptation of black song to a wartime experience, this time as the blacks served as soldiers in the Army of the Lord and Union volunteers: "Dere's room enough in heaven for the sojer: / Can't stay behind" (17). Most obviously, the World War I soldiers who were blues singers would begin to generate songs about war experiences, and we encounter these in the recorded blues tradition in songs such as Edna

Hicks's "Uncle Sam Blues" (1923), Kid Coley's "War Dream Blues" (1931), and John "Big Nig" Bray's "Trench Blues" (1934). What frequently happens in these kinds of circumstances is that traditional blues lyric formulas serve as frames for particulars related to the local experiences of the war. For example, the traditional song "T' Ain't Nobody's Business," recorded in one version by Frank Stokes in 1928 (*Wings* was published in 1929), undergoes this substitution in Europe:

> Joinin' army to git free clothes,
> What we fightin' 'bout nobody knows,
> Nobody's business but my own. (103; see also 267)

That same lyric about having a derby on quoted in relation to Solomon Northup, Bo Carter, Howlin' Wolf, and others is also used here, this time worn by a "big black soldier" (209). And another lyric about eating pork and beans turns up in a Willie Dixon song, "Back Door Man," recorded by Howlin' Wolf, this time with the singer "on the ocean / Dodgin' submarines" (180). When Tommy Johnson sang, "Lord I wonder will I ever get back home" in "Cool Drink of Water Blues" (1928), he may have been thinking of a number of circumstances stretching all the way back to Africa, but Gordon uses it to face his mortality in the war (20). The loneliness for sexual companionship takes on a particular urgency in war times, so the lyrics Peg Leg Howell sang in "Rock and Gravel Blues" (1928), "It takes rocks it takes gravel to make a solid road / It takes a lovin' fair brown to satisfy my soul," serves Gordon particularly well (107). Gordon uses that same "it takes" formula again, this time "it takes a rubber ball to bounce," with a variant of a lyric recorded by Jim Jackson in "Jim Jackson's Kansas City Blues" (1928) and Bob Coleman on "Cincinnati Underworld Woman" (1929). And whereas Gordon is on the sea when he sings that his mates should throw his body in the sea when he dies (198), it worked just as well for a landlocked Little Walter years later in "Blue and Lonesome" (1959). The immediately previous lyric, linked associatively with the "whales" lyric, though not necessarily always performed together, about having wings to fly and light on one's lover, is familiar through Peg Leg Howell's "Turtle Dove Blues" (1928). These and many more lyrics—"I been down so long" (87, 91), "ain't got no drivin' wheel" (100), also sung by Lonnie Clark in "Broke Down Engine" (1929), even Gordon's use of the insult rhyming game "The Dozens" (94), recorded as "The Dirty Dozen" by Speckled Red in 1929, reemphasize the importance of the blues tradition to Gordon, wherever he is.

Gordon makes shrewd and effective use of religious music as well, including materials that likely existed in the tradition and printed collections. He takes the traditional lyrics "The Blood Done Signed My Name" (recorded by the Novelty Four Quartet in 1928) and "Death Is in This Land," for example, and unites them with stark wartime experiences:

> Gonna take my shirt an' swab out my gun
> Gonna shoot big hole in dam' old Hun
> Lord, the blood done sign my name. (253)

His use of "Down by the Riverside," recorded by the Elkins-Payne Jubilee Singers in 1923, is even more startlingly and perfectly adapted to the horrors of war:

> I'm gonna lay my old gas-mask down,
> Down by the riverside.
> Lord, I ain't gonna study war no mo'.
> Down by the riverside. (263–64)

Recalling other, spiritual battles that have been fought, Gordon brings a pacifist message to his current experiences in this physical war where, of course, he cannot literally lay down that mask at any real riverside, only dream of it in the midst of apocalyptic experiences (41). Perhaps even more startling is Gordon's version of "I'm Gonna Walk All over God's Heaven," typically about looking forward to getting there. However, Gordon replaces the traditional "I got a-shoes" and walking all over God's heaven with something that suggests that man gets the heaven that he creates for himself:

> You got a gun, I got a gun,
> All God's chilluns got a gun,
> When I git to heaven,
> Lawd, gonna shoot off my gun,
> Gonna shoot all over God's heaven. (97)

Clearly the war experience has given Gordon the opportunity to challenge traditional notions of heaven with the further revelation of man's warlike nature in this international conflict. It was enough to evoke memories of a blues song to Gordon: "Oh, my Lord, wished I was in Georgia singin' jail-house blues" (44). Gordon makes it clear that he has been in this kind of conflict before, dealing with the Georgia "officials" and their incarceration system in the Jim Crow South. Though Gordon judges the war to be worse, it is not really so "foreign" to his experience.

And the stunning reminder of what awaits him at home, something comparable to what he experiences in the middle of violent battles, begins to explain the subtitle and pull the book together. This is "Black Ulysses at the Wars," not just "at war," so there are other wars, other enemies, other horrors implied by the title. Gordon repeats a number of phrases formulaically in this book to set up particularly important ideas, one of them being "been mighty change since I been born" (57), which usually highlights not only a change that has taken place during his lifetime, but certain continuities that have remained:

> Been mighty change since I been born. Change where I been but ain't change me. I remembers hearin' my mama's papa, fine, ole, gray-haired colored man, tellin' 'bout bloody fightin' tribes of Africa. Fightin' one 'nother, fightin' white folks tryin' to run 'em off or comin' to take slaves. Now here I is, side by side with black soldiers from Africa, fightin' with white man 'gainst 'nuther white man. Neither is I in Africa where my mama's papa come from, neither in America where I was born. Neither is I fightin' white man, neither white man fightin' me. Maybe I'm fightin' white folks. They tell me Germans is white. Well, I don't know, Lord, I don't know. An' white folks been fightin' my people ever since I been born. War an' me the same thing. I'm jes' natchel magic black boy, rainbow round my shoulder, wings on my feet. (57)

Here, Gordon is sifting through things his grandfather has told him about the African past that help throw current circumstances into relief. With another reference to his grandfather's storytelling abilities, he describes himself as a fighter: "I been fightin' as a boy, I been fightin' ever since. I'm African chief, I'm travelin' man, I'm in American Expeditionary Force, naming name of a soldier. I'm last week an' next Sunday. Yet I ain't bother yet, I ain't bother yet. War never got me, never will" (58). There have always been battles and wars, always racial and national and international conflict, just as he finds himself in the midst of it now. In fact, there are in this passage particular connections made through violent behavior that link Africa, particularly the fierceness of its people in war (58–62), the slave trade, the Civil War, Reconstruction, and World War I to each other in one long painful episodic narrative that defines humanity as violent, and leads to an end to the passage that describes Gordon's survival strategy: he embraces it.

The repeated phrases "War an' me is buddies" (13, 18, 41, 67, etc.), "War an' me the same thing" (57, 88, 95, 98, etc.), and "War never got me" (13, 35, 40, 52, 58, etc.) all indicate that he has acknowledged and accepted the propensity of human beings to commit violence upon each other, and he does what he needs to do to survive. In this sense, it is the quintessential statement of the "bad" man in African American culture. In order to survive in white society, with all its racism and violence, the figure must become "badder" than the "bad" in society in order to overcome it. He is essentially taking the club of relativism to societal values and producing a perspective where the worse (badder) society thinks you are, the better (badder) you are. As Langston Hughes does in a story like "Jazz, Jive and Jam," he is reversing traditional designations such as good-bad, black-white to force readers to see a different perspective on the value judgments. This is a type of Sartrean "noughting nought," where the vapidity of societal values receives an infusion of African American meaning, whereby that original emptiness is replaced by black identity and structure.

Not that violence is all. The formulaic way he states his identification with war, which provides both continuity and touchstones in the work, also shows his folk tendencies to use stories to teach lessons, acknowledging that propensity even more fully when he calls himself "magic," and connects himself to the heavenly and the gods as well, through his rainbow and his wings. He is both war and peace, hate and love, secular and sacred. He is proud of his African past, his African American past, his parents, and himself, because, like the spirit of the blues tradition, he survives and has hope in the face of all of that endless adversity. Not just in formal wars, but in undeclared wars of whips, chains, starvation, and illiteracy.

Such huge paradoxes will of course produce tensions, and these tensions are expressed through his secular and sacred songs and stories, the performing of which blends them into a kind of syncretistic ragmentation, a joyful performance that shakes the devil's hand in friendship as it hurls him back to hell. Two other phrases he repeats are "Feel my hell a-risin'" (116, 141, 143, 146, 183, . . 301, etc.) and "I ain't bother yet" (91, 100, 104, . . 306, etc.), phrases that produce a straining tug of war with each other. It is not just that his temper that is rising here, but his hell, which, one imagines, rages more furiously than just a temper. And to have a hell inside him is to suggest that he lives with it, controls it by some means which can sometimes, under extraordinary circumstances, get away from him. If his hell is rising, he is certainly getting "bothered," or is about to be—the use of litotes here unmistakably signifies an imminent blast of passion.

This circumstance may hint at another function of these formulated folk-phrases, related in a way to the blues. The blues can be sung to *express* something that is felt, but it can also be used to *produce* a feeling as well. He can make himself rev up or calm down by using the languge in a way that indicates what might be coming if things don't change. This use of formulaic phrases and blues lyrics reconnect him to something larger than himself, the fighting spirit of ancestors and Algerians, the persevering spirit of enslaved forebears, and the creative resistance of the folk.

When Gordon expresses these tensions, he does so with a clear sense of where he stands as a black man in the war and in contemporary society. There are times when he feels "Neither wus we black, neither white, jes' soldiers of the world" (221). However, at other times he calls ironic attention to the "principles" of white soldiers: "Some white officers principled up like this, every colored soldier wus no more than dog, jes' sumpin' out there to work" (119). In this statement he voices a common complaint regarding the menial tasks assigned to African Americans in the military, revealing the so-called principles of the officers to be nothing more than traditional systematic racism dressed in the appropriately named "fatigues." There are over thirty-six blues songs recorded pre-1942 the titles of which begin either with "Tired" or "I'm Tired," and a number of jazz songs as well. Admittedly, these songs frequently deal with being fed up with the actions of a mate, but certainly they may also stand symbolically for a broader societal mistreatment that would have been much more dangerous to express in those sociopolitical times. The French, on the other hand, in a situation that mocked the values of American democracy, were more welcoming to blacks than their own countrymen: "French treated us fine, better than we had been treated befo'" (199). Still, Gordon knows the precariousness of his sitution as a black man. He tells of seeing white soldiers making a young black boy jump off a bridge (87)—a malicious use of what has been a positive symbol in the text, and an acknowledgment of how dangerous the bridging process can be, given the trolls that lurk beneath. And later, when soldiers string up a black soldier and riddle him with bullets, Gordon has no trouble deciphering the enigma: "Army don't have to fight Jerries, got plenty colored folks to fight" (90). The realization that he has more than one battle front makes him keenly aware of who and what his allies are, and how to draw upon them.

Ultimately, Gordon understands the nature of war in the following terms: "War don't make things no better. Maybe neither worse" (304). It is just a large-scale expression of the nature of mankind: local conflicts, petty jealousies, prejudices, and hatreds, (un)settled by bayonets and gas. For Gordon, it is more of the same old thing: violence, lynching, hypocrisy, illusion. In need of something to manage it, something to make the lonesome road less lonesome, something to "rock trouble to sleep" (309), he contextualizes—

> Lord, I been down so long,
> Down don't worry me. (87).

This snatch from a blues lyric, recorded in "Trouble-Hearted Blues" (1928) by Ishmon Bracey and in two different variants by Furry Lewis in "I Will Turn Your Money Green" (1928)—"I been troubled so long trouble don't worry my mind" and "I been down so long, seem like up to me"—is part of the blues's genes. The lyric, though clearly partially ironic in its attempt to downplay the magnitude of trouble in the hopes of convincing oneself not to worry, seems also to suggest that one learns something from being "down" that assists in dealing with bad luck and trouble, hard times, and the wind howling at your door. Thus, the lyric references not only the trouble, but the mechanism for dealing with it, and employs it in performance—an exemplary exemplification.

The other image, of trouble as a baby being consoled, is a complex one. Rather than suggest a single strategy for response to trouble, the statement presents us with a phrase in which there occurs a word that has special meanings within the African American vernacular, and the ambiguity of the phrase suggests a variety of possibility. Part of the ambiguity comes through the meaning of the word "rock," which, as we have said, suggests several different actions. The one most obvious projects "trouble" as a baby to be rocked to sleep. Sometimes, the way to deal with trouble and tension, as we have said in the discussion of "my temper is rising," is to relax or deny its power. As such, infantilizing the trouble makes it more manageable, and brings out what seems to be the nurturing and soothing side of the "rocker." That may not be the case. Any parent knows that when the baby is crying, it can be very difficult to be soothing. So, you suck it up and act that way. It requires knowing what soothing is and pretending to be so, and it can be extremely difficult unless you are adept at the masquerade, not just in your face or your arms, but in your bones, and babies can tell when you are tense. One of the strategies the phrase "rock trouble to sleep" suggests, then, is dissembling. Sometimes it is the only way to protect yourself, with particular applications to the lives of African Americans in the Jim Crow South, who would need the ability to get out of all manner of irrational and unexpected difficulties, instilling confidence in a hostile audience.

On the other hand, rocking trouble to sleep can simply suggest calming *oneself*, since trouble, frequently expressed as "troubled in mind" in the blues, is in the mind of the be-thinker. One must, then, learn to *handle* trouble in mind—and one way to do that is to evoke the community and the spirit that makes you know you are not alone, and expressing it in creative and appropriate language that defines and controls it, to some degree, through artistic expression. Formulaic phrases and lyrics of folklore songs would both come under this category.

Conversely, the other two meanings eschew the soothing approach for actions more physical. With its sexual connotations, to rock someone to sleep means to use one's sexual power to overcome someone. Since sexuality is a vital urge, it can sometimes be a greater desire than the one that brings opponents to battle. In a broader sense, the phrase would simply mean to consider all the alternatives and choose what can be sacrified. This is still positive force, because it offers powers of fecundity as counters to trouble, something (pro)creative and life giving, an infusion of life force, in response to trouble. The third, a show of raw force, to rock or topple the enemy, is the most direct, but the sense of the term can apply to either of the other approaches as well, since in any case, the world is overturned, changed. These types of double entendre and triple entendre can be found easily in the examples of blues recordings we have from the 1920s, suggesting that this is in fact an important element of the blues tradition. This makes sense, because it is a kind of masking tradition in itself. They allow people to say taboo, dangerous, or subversive things with impunity because they are hidden beneath the cover of a superficial meaning that makes sense. In Martin Delany's *Blake, or The Huts of America*, for example, the biblical phrase "Stand still and see the salvation" is made to mean different things at different times in the text, based upon the actions Blake wants to evoke. And is that really a chariot coming to take someone to heaven, or a wagon North?

Finally, the volume presents one of the few and first published depictions of the experiences of African American soldiers in World War I, joining the pioneering and exhaustive work of Emmett Scott and *Singing Soldiers* by John Jacob Niles, discussed below. The book helps extend the understanding of African American lives and folklore through the prominent use of the subject matter, style, and strategies of the blues and other African American folklore. The collaboration between two remarkable artists and men provides a great deal of insight into the lives of African Americans and the lies of America through the lore of the folk. And, indeed, it also demonstrates how folklore adapts to its circumstances by retaining its spirit while adjusting its particulars in a manner that draws on, describes, and produces hope and life in a word of violence and desolation. From turnrow to bunker, the blues "can make a billy-goat butt a lion" (67).

The third novel of the trilogy, *Cold Blue Moon*, actually lies a bit out of the parameters of this study, though a few words are appropriate here. In it, Odum returns to providing the textual commentary that was present in *Rainbow*, but excluded from *Wings*. Perhaps Odum sought to return to more overt polemicism in this volume, emphasizing the ways in which the history of African American slavery interacted with the African American folk tradition—to ghost story lore—that has particular historical and sociopolitical implications for slavery and the problems of the American "democratic" system. Odum did, of course, accomplish this in both of the other volumes. But perhaps felt he needed to set up audiences for something alien to their experiences—an insider portrayal of African American lives told not in minstrel language but a more respectful vernacular— in *Rainbow* and *Cold Blue Moon*. These books both took place on American soil, so the perceptions of African American lives were all tainted by racist attitudes in the popular mind. On the other hand, since the popular audience was more familiar with more accurate war stories and novels, especially from the unprecedented number of war novels produced about World War I, including Henri Barbusse's *Le Feu* (1916), John Dos Passos's *Three Soldiers* (1920), Virginia Woolf's important sub-plot in *Mrs. Dalloway* (1925), and Erich Maria Remarque's massive international best seller *All Quiet on the Western Front* (1929). Possessing that context, *Wings* could proceed without Odum's commentary, instead offering another voice that provides another perspective on a foreign war that is both further from (geographically) and closer to (in terms of historical familiarity) the general public.

Whatever the reason, Odum continues using folk materials—more stories than songs here, though there are still a fair number of lyrics that are recognizeable from the recorded blues tradition. For example, Odum refers to "crazy blues" nine separate times in the novel. Though this is not necessarily a reference to the Mamie Smith recording from 1920 (or the re-recordings by Mary Stafford in 1921, or white country performer Cliff Carlisle's 1930 song by that title [though it is a different song], or the jazz versions by the Noble Sissle and Eubie Blake in 1920, the Original Dixieland Jazz Band in 1921, Joseph Samuels in 1921), "Crazy Blues" was certainly famous enough to have been familiar at least titularly to Odum. If it was textually familiar, that would have provided him with an example of anti-authoritarian blues lyrics in its final stanza, in which the singer proposes to get a gun and shoot a cop. In a text that deals with the manner in which the nation is haunted by the insane workings of authorities, such a song would have clear resonances. It is possible that Odum simply wished to reproduce the notion of craziness in a text that dealt with ghost stories, while still rooting them in historical reality in order to emphasize their reality and *surreality*. There are certainly *many* black blues songs that reference the word "crazy," including thirteen black blues song titles alone that begin with the word "crazy" recorded between 1920 and 1938 (Dixon, Godrich, and Rye 1107). Blending history, pathology, ghost stories, southern gothiciam, and verbal artistry, the use of references to insanity in the novel makes for an eerie and stunning consideration of race relations during and after the Civil War.

Of course, "crazy" does not always mean "insane." In fact, crazy was a word sometimes applied to African Americans who wouldn't stay in their places, who stood up for themselves, as Big Bill Broonzy and Memphis Slim told Alan Lomax (*Blues in the Mississippi Night*). Gordon talks plenty about his attitudes toward white folks, and Odum's decision to include this material may have been somewhat uncomfortable for Gordon, but is likely an eye-opener for those familiar only with the happy darky mask. This is particularly true in *Rainbow*, where Gordon confronts a white brakeman (226), avows he won't die for (303) or be blown around like a leaf for the white man (303), and says white folks look like monkeys when they get old (304), though he claims he knows the strategies for dealing with white folks (308). "I thinks my duty to please white folks," Gordon says, adding "white folks ignorant 'bout colored folks" (309). The bottom line for Gordon Gordon's dissatisfaction comes in *Wings*: "'cause I ain't free" (94). And, stated more directly, "I want to be free" (170, 216).

Other references appropriate to the era mix blues, coon songs, spirituals, ballads, and folk songs. It is important that, even though the volume focuses on ghost stories, it does not drop references to the songs that existed side by side with other forms of oral lore. Thus, we find references to lyrics that also occur in the recordings of Blind Lemon Jefferson's 1929 "Bed Springs Blues" (18, 183, 216); Bo Carter's 1928 "Good Old Turnip Greens" (126); Charley Patton's 1929 "Pony Blues" (98); Booker T. Sapps's 1935 "Mule on the Mountain" (95); Moses "Clear Rock" Platt's 1933 "Run, Nigger, Run" (134); Furry Lewis's 1929 "John Henry" (273); Leadbelly's 1940 "Stewball"; John Byrd's "Old Timbrook Blues" (1930); the Jubilee Gospel Team's 1928 "These Bones Goin' Rise Again" (145); and Jim Jackson's 1928 "Old Dog Blue" (171), along with further references to "I been down so long" (38) and "St. Louis Blues" (265). What becomes clear is that Odum, in piecing together from Gordon's words an account of the black man's life, attempts to offer a holistic presentation, pulling together numerous types of lore and examining their artistry and function in delineating, explaining, and dealing with important sociopolitical issues in Gordon's life. Rather than some one-off quote of a lyric or passing reference to a blues singer, the book focuses on the life of an African American as lived and represented through folklore, including very prominently the blues, but not the blues to the exclusion of other pieces of the contextual puzzle. As such, Odum's book is an extremely valuable attempt to understand and portray African American life on and in its own terms.

II

John Jacob Niles wore many hats in his lifetime, and made comfortable homes where he hung them, be it as ballad collector, performer, dulcimer and lute maker, composer, writer, or farmer. Born in Louisville, Kentucky, on April 28, 1892, the young Niles sang the Child Ballad "Barbara Allen," taught to him by his father, in a Louisville singing contest when he was nine years old. The performance started him on his way to becoming one of the earliest folklore collectors and popular folk-composers in America, beginning his collecting in 1907 (while he was still in high school), almost ten years before established British folklorist Cecil Sharp arrived from England to collect folk songs with assistant Maud Karpeles in 1916–1918. In Louisville, Niles heard the music of unidentified local jug bands such as those of Clifford Hayes, while nearby his house "Bony Miser Rockfish and Professor Pankhurst" set up their medicine show (Pen 20), which, like many medicine shows, likely employed a songster who included the blues in his repertoire. During the time Sharp was collecting, Niles enlisted in the US Air Force just after the start of World War I, supplementing his military duties by collecting folk songs from his fellow soldiers and, after being discharged due to injuries from a plane crash, he went to school in France, where he also met Gertrude Stein.

Back in the States, he continued his schooling and worked on organizing the songs he had collected. Increasingly he became known as a performer, singing with the Chicago Lyric Opera Company and on the radio for Westinghouse in the early 1920s. He published his first song collection, *Impressions of a Negro Camp Meeting*, in 1925, evincing a clear interest early in his career in African American folklore. The volume was a collection of eight impressionist-influenced spiritual arrangements by Niles, part of an interest demonstrated during those years by the publication of volumes of Negro spirituals by J. Rosamond and James Weldon Johnson, Clarence Cameron White, and Harry T. Burleigh (Pen 79)—the same Burleigh who also exposed Dvořák to the spirituals. Niles drew from his four trips in 1928–1933 to the Appalachians with photographer Doris Ullmann (Axelrod 358) for some of his subsequent folk song publications, memoirs, and eventually, recordings both of folk songs and his own compositions for RCA, Asch, Tradition, Vanguard, Folkways, and other record companies. He became a high-profile singer and composer, writing such popular songs as "I Wonder As I Wander" (employed by Langston Hughes for the title of the second volume of his autobiography), "Go 'Way From My Window," and "Black is the Color of My True Love's Hair" heard in recorded versions by such artists as Marlena Dietrich, Placido Domingo,

Linda Ronstadt, Kathleen Battle, Joan Baez, Burl Ives, Jo Stafford, the London Symphony Orchestra, Barbara Streisand, and the Fendermen.

Called the "Dean of American Balladeers" by Barry Alfonso, Niles was known for his high-pitched, hearty delivery and deep passion, making him one of the forerunners and founders of the folk music boom of the late 1950s and early 1960s in America. With a desire to "preserve and popularize American musical folklore" (Alfonso), he lent all of his spirited talent to doing just that, resulting in his induction to the Kentucky Music Hall of Fame in 2006, a quarter of a century after his death in 1980. His was truly a life spent in contact and creation with all types of American folk songs, and, in *Singing Soldiers* (1927), with African American folk songs and blues that he had collected a decade earlier, just before the African American recorded blues boom.

Niles dedicated *Singing Soldiers*

> To the
> Amercan Negro Soldiers
> Who Made
> This Writing Possible (v)

An interesting dedication. Normally, one thought of African Americans at that time in terms of illiteracy, yet this aviator, Lieutenant Niles, a white man, was crediting blacks with some element of the book's production. Since it was most likely that they were not the owners of a press at that time, we can only surmise that there was some element of inspiration in their speech, actions, or both, that was the impetus for the book. Given that Niles's avowed aim was to collect and preserve oral culture, it comes as no surprise that he would acknowledge the great contributions that the oral tradition had made to the written word and, given his deep love of not just the lore, but the people and their spirit, that he would provide an acknowledgment for the voiceless, to whom he is now giving a public stage for them upon which to speak and act.

Singing Soldiers is not a novel but a contextualized folk song collection-memoir. Niles is more of a character in this book than Odum is in his, and he states his avowed aim directly: "to make as nearly as possible an unexpurgated record of of the words and to write off the tunes" for songs sung by his fellow soldiers, as Theidore Botrel had done for the French. While he had initially determined to do this for all American soldiers, he found that "the imagination of the white boys did not, as a rule, express itself in song" (vii). Deriding the professional stage writers and their moon-June rhymes, he eschewed their safe and silly songwriting for the oral compositions of the African American soldiers whose spontaneity, vigor, tone, and directness fascinated him, even if they did resort to "music-hall" (viii) material from time to time: "The negro soldier had not only the mellow, resonant vocal qualities so necessary in singing, but he had abandon and an emotional nature which, with his ability to dramatize trivial situations, many times produced the most affecting performances" (viii–ix).

Niles had been set up to like the music of African Americans by hearing and appreciating it since he was a child in Kentucky. Of course, he was not immune to the occasional stereotypical comment, as when he speaks above about an "emotional nature" that dramatizes what Niles feels are "trivial situations," and calls them "natural-born singers" (viii), denying them credit for the artistry of their work, implies that the black soldier was not up to snuff (ix), and occasionally makes them seem a bit simple. Even if Thomas Wentworth Higginson had earlier labeled them as "childlike" (190, 203) in *Army Life in a Black Regiment*, he never cast aspersions on their soldierly abilities, commenting, "It was their demeanor under arms that shamed the nation into recognizing them as men" (206). Despite the negative implications of Niles's attitudes, with some extra guidance from W. C. Handy (called "W. H. Handy " in the text) (ix), Niles intended to capture the music as much as he could, admiring mostly their musical abilities, and admitting that the "tunes and harmonies [were] ofttimes too subtle for my clumsy fingers and my improvised score paper" (viii). Indeed, Niles claims that their "music had some part in the success gained by our arms in the past war" (ix), but primarily does not delve into their other qualities. In this, his book is more limited in focus than Odum's, the portrait less complete.

Biographer Ron Pen has some harsh words for the volume, referring to Niles's "condescending paternalism," "commodif[ication] of black culture," depictions of the "exotic other," and "insensitivity." However, he also commends Niles for his startling focus on the soldiers who were largely ignored or taken for granted (89), and feels that Niles manages the dual nature of the book as narrative and song book extremely well and succeeds as both storyteller and musician (90). Contemporary book reviews were full of praise for Niles's work (Pen 91–93). The optimistic Niles even contacted the NAACP in 1927 to secure their interest. In the end, Niles produced a fascinating work, a bundle of remarkable strengths and notable weaknesses that render it a significant book of its time.

Although Niles does not deal with the blues to the same extent as Odum, there are some important references here to blues and folk music that demonstrate some ideas similar to those in Odum's books. Niles prepares his readers for the coming of the blues by creating a milieu that characterizes both the blues and the men who sing them. The first instance turns up immediately after a crap game is presented, linking the blues with such environments and illegal activities. Niles presents a black man mispronouncing the French word "dix" (dees) as "dicks" (23), simultaneously mocking his intelligence and associating blacks with the sexual (followed by a "hard" joke, 25). What follows next is a dramatized scenario in which a black soldier is portrayed as too cowardly (smart?) to ride in a plane with an officer because he was afraid he would have to get out and crank while they were up in the air. This is clearly a joke that could cut two ways at once: either the black soldier is comically afraid of flying—we can almost picture him mugging and cringing in the movies—or simply knows that if something goes wrong, the black man will be the one to have to deal with the danger—in this case, ridiculously step out of an airplane and fall to his death. Some joke.

The first blues song Niles allows us to see is "Hoochey, Coochey Hilda," the adaptation of some variation of a blues song to German (and French) soil, having more of a pop-blues structure and rhyme scheme than the folk-blues. Jazz pianist Lem Fowler had recorded a "Hoochy Coochy Blues" in New York in January 1925, suggesting that the term, which had been conceived in 1876 at the Philadelphia Centennial Fair to describe a faux-Turkish belly dance, had currency in the black community, indeed as it did nationwide. The song is, as Niles writes, a kind of generic blues where a man who has left home returns and hopes to be taken back by his mate, repeating stock phrases like "take me back" and "I'se done you wrong" in his archetypal blues. However, the song is now personalized to the war experience that opens up several possibilities. The reference to making the Kaiser "ball de Jack" is an interesting adapted way to say that they want to push the Kaiser to risk everything on one big gamble—the gambling meaning of the term, which relates to the crap game in process. However, because the "hoochey coochey" was a popular dance in the 1910s, something akin to the old gunslinger meaning of the term—the bad man attitude—may apply: they want to make the Kaiser "dance" by shooting at his feet. "Balling" obviously has a sexual meaning, including in the blues, as in Jim Jackson's version of "St. Louis Blues" (1930), which also portrays train tracks as a sexual symbol:

> A red-headed woman make a freight train jump the track
> And a black-headed girl will make a preacher ball the jack.

The attempt is to get the Kaiser to do something sexually humiliating in order not just to beat but to embarrass him.

These kinds of sentiments were not unknown in African American toasts, though they were rarely recorded. Lewis Jones and Alan Lomax recorded a startling one dealing with Adolf Hitler on August 2, 1942:

> . . . in his last hitch
> We was after his ass, the son of a bitch
> We's gonna cut off his dick and split his bag
> Gonna wipe our ass with his own flag
> We gonna banghole his wife and cuss his luck
> For not havin' enough women for us to fuck
> We gonna eat his bread and drink his gin
> Gonna fuck every woman in old Berlin
> We gonna skin his dick like a rotten banana
> Til his asshole whistle "Star-Spangled Banner"
> We gonna walk in his palace and shit on his floor
> Hang Old Glory up over his door
> So here his is [?] with his last hitch
> May his asshole rot off with the seven year's itch
> When the war is over we'll sail back in mass [en masse]
> And tell all the boys how he had to kiss our ass ("Hitler Toast")

This would surely be the "unexpurgated" material that Niles suggested he would report but didn't!

Beyond the desire to humiliate Hitler, there is prominent misogyny and sexism here as well, but also, given the history of African Americans in this country, another whole dimension to this story. The graphic violence with which Hitler is attacked seems to be *overkill* and, prefaced by the pronoun "we," implies a group attack. It is not far from there to the kind of mob scenario that faced blacks in the form of lynching. This is especially true as we look at the extreme sexual nature of his torture, frequently a gleeful component of black lynchings and the taking of "souvenirs," as Richard Wright describes in "Big Boy Leaves Home" (49). The suggestion of doing these things to a white man's genitalia would have been allowable under these circumstances—the criticism of Hitler—and thus a safer than usual outlet for even this extreme expression of violence—though this is the only collected toast of its type recorded during the era. After all, by wiping their asses with the German flag, they are wrapping themselves in Old Glory, which is clearly foregrounded in the toast as a reminder of patriotism. It even reminds of the flag tattoo that Ellison would later describe as tattooed over the pubic region of his fake-blond kewpie doll dancer—exploitative sex and stereotypes are as American as apple pie (*Invisible Man* 19). Even further, the expressed desire by a black man to "fuck" Hitler's wife and "every woman in old Berlin" exhibits a kind of warped misogyny that implies that Hitler can't protect "his" women; meanwhile, he is actually stating a desire to attack sexually a large group of white women. It is clear that Niles couldn't touch this, if indeed he encountered anything like it. It does suggest that some of his material, like much literature of the time, was homogenized. What we have, then, is the equivalent of the commercially recorded blues, which had to substitute double entendre such as balling the jack for explicit language.

The singers follow with a quasi-quartette version of what he describes as "the famous old tune of 'Ashes to Ashes, Dust to Dust,'" a biblically named tune which, if I have identified it correctly, can become a violent and obscene song as well. Blind Willie McTell sang in "Southern Can is Mine" (1931) "Ashes to ashes, mama, dust to dust / Show me a woman that a man can trust" and "Ashes to ashes, mama, sand to sand / Every time I hit you you think I got a dozen hands." On the other hand, "Pigmeat" Jarrett used to sing a song that went, "Ashes to ashes, dust to dust / If it wasn't for all these young men you know what mm mm mm would rust," leaving out the "dirty" parts. The song for which something like these lyrics serve as a refrain is an associational blues, verses not crucially connected to each other but moving from like subject to like subject. It may be that part of the purpose is to sneak in a stanza like the last one Niles transcribes:

> Goin' get myself a French gal wid nice smooth flanks,
> An tell her de blacks is de best o' the Yanks." (260)

This type of sexual boast is common in the African American folk tradition, although the racial comparison, which feeds on a sexual stereotype, might be a little touchier to sing with whites around, who we have already said frequently manifested their anger in the genital region of African Americans. Further, it is only implied that the singers are saying that the blacks are *sexually* the best of the Yanks—you have to combine the second line with the first in order to get that meaning. It could mean that they are boasting that they are the best all-round—though, conveniently, that textual reading could be reasonably denied as ambiguity or wording for safety's sake. This was a common strategy for delivering comments or criticisms around whites that may be denied because of their double meanings.

All of this material is delivered within the context of the crap game, ending with a song about "Crap-Shootin' Charley," celebrating his nominal abilities, though there is a stanza about a woman shaking her "stuff" mixed in, probably a parallel to the shaking of dice and "supple" movements as they sang. Ultimately the craps, the sex, the movement, the song all become one holistic force, and Niles has the piano playing become less like music and more like drumming—that primitive and elemental force frequently associated with blacks at the time, and a revelation of Niles's attitude toward this type of communal aesthetic. The entire episode serves to make him homesick for the good old days of his youth when the levee was full with "piles of merchandise" to be moved and removed by blacks and "Robert, the colored boy" cleaned out the spittoons and practiced superstitions like spitting into his hand and tapping it to see in which direction a bug went (28). And even if slavery in Kentucky was represented as being more "humane" than deeper in the South, one doubts that it was this idyllic, if at all, for very long. Once again, Niles reveals his own mind, different from Odum's, on the issue of black mistreatment and resentment. It is difficult to tell whether he understands the subversive nature of their songs, especially since he is trying to portray himself here, too.

The "Ashes to Ashes" tune returns for the next blues song, this one sung by a man described in derogatory terms by Niles. He was a "sawed off sooty black boy from Natchez," a "blubber-lipped lad" who sang grotesquely, "rolling his eyes in wide circles" as he attempted to bilk money out of a group in the guise of a preacher, though he was actually a beggar. The song he sings is about a vamp—a common misogynist term drawn from Bram Stoker's *Dracula* (1897), F. W. Murnau's *Nosferatu* (1923), and the stage play before Tod Browning's *Dracula* (1931)—for a "[w]oman who sought to exploit men by using feminine wiles" (Calt 259), as recorded in songs like Edith Wilson's "Vampin' Liza Jane" (1921) and Alberta Hunter's "Vamping Brown" (1923). It turns into a warning to "all o' you gals with fire in your blood" to repent and "drop your change right in de plate." Niles makes it clear that the singer is a confidence man who (mis)uses the song for personal gain, emphasizing that these types of tunes may be exploited for whatever personal benefit they might bring. The tune, sung seriously, would be a warning about good behavior, but as Niles presents it, it is only a scam—another point where Niles admires the music, but paints a bleaker portrait of the characters. He does not comment at all at the end of the song, preferring to end on the black preacher's selfish plea for money "in de plate" (35). Interestingly, in calling for the crowd to change their ways, and to put "change" in the plate, he is associating the positive behavioral alterations with giving *him* money. That is, itself, an adaptation of the tune to circumstances, demonstrating how, for better or worse, folklore is adaptable in time, space, and circumstance.

There have been a variety of blues songs dealing with war, more so for World War II than World War I, but still a fair number during the 1920s and early 1930s. These include "War Horse Mama" (1924) by both Clara Smith and Hazel Meyers, "Soldier Boy Blues" (1930) by Phillips' Louisville Jug Band, and "War Dream Blues" (1931) by Kid Coley. "The Soldier Man Blues" in this text is in that tradition, though it is again a rather rambling text, dealing in the first two stanzas with the war and then moving mundane but necessary activities such as maximizing your potential (a woman without style who has a great smile), trying to get by without being qualified (sneaking into heaven), the necessity sometimes of going backward rather than forward (an impeded train), and finding the things that certain animals—or men—are good for (possum in pot liquor juice) (92–94). Again, Niles makes no comment after the song, so the readers wonder about the point. Since the first two stanzas deal with the soldier's sadness and the his desire to determine his own actions, the different scenarios in other stanzas may represent symbolic strategies he can adopt to deal with that problem: getting ahead through making yourself look good; sneaking in; moving backward to go forward; and simply finding a way to lazy through. Behind this may be the lesson that the black soldier, being prevented from achieving much praise, status, or reward, is simply playing a game of strategy: how to deal with the unfairness thrown at him—in and out of war—by the man.

There are other blues songs in *Singing Soldiers* as well: "The Deep-Sea Blues," blues about President Wilson, about the war effort (98–99). "The Jail-House Blues" (103–05) is not the one recorded by Bessie Smith (1923), Sam Collins (1927), and others—obviously one can have many experiences in a jail house. A low-down "grave-diggin' feelin' in my heart"—Sam Collins recorded a "Graveyard Digger's Blues" in 1931 (131–35) that evokes the sinister and visceral beautifully. "Papa's In the Jail-House Now" (perhaps a relative to the "He's in the Jail House Now" of Blind Blake or Jim Jackson's 1928 recordings, or Leroy Carr's "Papa's On the House Top" from 1930) is sung by a quartette such as those blues recorded by quartettes like The Excelsior Quartette on "Jelly Roll Blues" (1922) and The Norfolk Jazz (and Jubilee) Quartet on "Monday Morning Blues" (1921). All of these songs are presented in similar style to the earlier songs in the text, reinforcing their notions of the blues and the men who sing them.

Niles does finally make a point about sadness in black song, one that deserves consideration: "The Negro has no so-called love songs . . . Some folks have said that the Negro finds happiness through self-commiseration. This is not altogether true. The constant recurring note of sadness in the music of the black man is like the ripple of a stream of water running around a rock—the water being his thought-stream—the rock, suppression" (154). Niles is, first of all, technically wrong that "the Negro" doesn't possess any of his own love songs. In fact, saying "the Negro" is his first problem. Acting as if one can generalize about all African Americans is absurd, and further suggesting that they don't sing love songs (experience love as whites do?) is ridiculous, and can be contradicted from several perspectives. First, there is the actual evidence of loving lyrics, such as the common "I love my baby better than I do myself" or "I love you baby, tell the world I do." Poet Paul Laurence Dunbar even includes "A Negro Love Song" among his dialect poems (*Collected Poetry* 49). While it was suggested at the time that blacks did not have the higher feelings of love that whites did, that idea can be contradicted by numerous examples on both sides of the color aisle. A second objection, that perhaps whites are not aware of all of the marginalized black peoples' songs, don't have access to them, has certainly been an assertion that blacks such as Zora Neale Hurston (*Mules and Men* 2–3) and whites such as Howard W. Odum have made. It is part of the strategy behind the "you don't know my mind" lyric in the blues, which acknowledges that holding back or masking in front of whites serves just such a purpose. A third objection is that perhaps Niles is suggesting that the nature of the love songs is different, that there is less idealization of spouses or situations, more cynicism about the realities of love in the world. Such negative-sounding titles as Butterbeans and Susie's 1926 "Love Me and the World is Mine (Hit Me and the Jail is Yours)," Leroy Carr's 1929 "Love is Dead," Lonnie Johnson's 1932 "Love is Just a Song," Ruby Lee Woods's 1933 "Love'll Make You Drink," Roosevelt Sykes's 1939 "Love Will Wear You Down," and Walter Davis's 1938 "Love Will Kill You" certainly all testify to that element in the blues. This is a track that semanticist, English professor, and US Senator S. I. Hayakawa followed in his essay "Popular Songs vs. the Facts of Life." While such an assertion is not entirely true, since there are blues lyrics that are unrealistic and sentimental, exposure only to certain types of black songs could leave that impression—and of course being unsentimental and realistic about love can be an excellent antidote to the oversimplifications of pop song discourse. Such terms as "forever" or "all night long" come to mind.

The metaphor of water running around a rock does not quite work here either. While Niles does not deny the possible partial truth of finding happiness through commiseration, his suggesting that the water is his thought-stream and the rock his suppression suggests that the song produces only a personal benefit, that of empowering his own thought-stream. This denies notions of group identification and empathy produced in the listener, who may well have had similar experiences and thus enjoy hearing them named and overcome. Undoubtedly the liberating ability to produce art has a positive effect on the performer, but an inability to "commiserate" with the performer would likely cause such a song to become extinct. Niles's use of *suppression*, which frequently refers to restraint of emotions, rather than *oppression*, which is more a physical and political concept, is instructive. What Niles limits response to is the individual, a person restraining his or her own emotions, which disregards the cause for such restraint—in this case, the oppression of blacks by whites that forces a network of secret meanings and unknown events or circumstances, sometimes represented in symbolic terms. Making the rock *suppression* avoids naming its source, and minimizes the significance and culpability of the oppression. Bringing *oppression* to the slavery–Jim Crow race equation acknowledges both group responsibility (primarily white) and group victimization (primarily black), and allows the art work to operate in a "commiscrating"—perhaps better commisero-combative—mode.

Singing Soldiers is an interesting genre mix of folklore collection, war chronicle, and memoir. It is primarily interested in the music seemingly cut loose from much sociopolitical commentary. The songs contain that commentary from time to time, but it seems either underrecognized or underused by Niles, who seems willing to go along with some of the old stereotypes in the name of celebrating the music's beauty. Niles sees the music as a real, lasting contribution, but unfortunately doesn't root it enough in sociopolitical realities to highlight what it reflects or how society should respond to the people who generate and sing it. Perhaps Niles warned his readers of this in the title. It would better have been an understatement.

By the 1930s, the field of interest in folklore was expanding. John A. Lomax took over for Robert W. Gordon as Honorary Consultant and Curator of the Library of Congress in 1934, and Alan embarked on a series of recordings with other folklorists and collectors such as Lewis Jones, John Work III, Mary Elizabeth Barnicle, Zora Neale Hurston, Willis Laurence James, and Roscoe Lewis that grew the archive into a most impressive collection of African American folklore. Hurston's own collecting, begun in 1927, continued, growing eventually into her prized publication *Mules and Men* (1935). By the 1940s, the Popular Front had picked up on the performing of country blues singers and songsters such as Leadbelly, Sonny Terry and Brownie McGhee, and Josh White, following high-profile appearances in New York clubs like Café Society and the "From Spirituals to Swing" concerts at the end of the thirties. From the humble but significant efforts to collect and represent African American folklore in the 1920s had grown a formidable movement in the 1930s that would bring black folk materials much closer to mainstream American culture than ever before, though hot music was becoming an ever more burgeoning popular music growing ever farther from its folk roots with the emergence of big band swing in the 1930s.

6
Angels in Harlem

The Harlem Renaissance

I

What scholars call the Harlem Renaissance, or the New Negro Renaissance, was a major impetus behind the emergence of literature employing elements of hot music. Like the folklorists of the time, many artists, black and white, were interested in the folk roots of African Americans. However, these artists explored those roots as they could contribute to the establishment of a regional, national, or racial identity, or indeed as they could establish an African American contribution to American identity. Drawing perspectives from local color writing, dialect poetry, the Irish Literary Renaissance, and modernism, they sought to make expressive culture an arboreal expression of African America. Rooted in the soil and soul of experience in the South, branching out into urban migratory expressions of contemporary identity, and bearing artistic, social, and political fruit to feed the future, the culture ran deep and stretched high and far. The movement was called by some scholars the New Negro Renaissance because they (rightly) observed that the renaissance was a national phenomenon with cultural centers in Washington, DC; Virginia; Chicago; and Pennsylvania. Additionally, excursions to the South by folks like Langston Hughes and Zora Neale Hurston, international outposts where people like Hughes and Claude McKay wandered, and the cultural and political business of Alain Locke and W. E. B. Du Bois overseas demonstrated that this movement was, indeed, international, Pan-African, and polyvocal, not merely the lark of a lone urban detachment.

Because New Negro Renaissance writers attempted to harness and thereby liberate this spirit from its minstrel associations and express its ever-expanding urban manifestations as well, they became the major and central source of literature that dealt seriously with the music with its racial connections and connotations. That is not to say that there were not commercial depictions of contemporary hot music in African American literature, but rather that, writing with generally a better knowledge of the music's past in African American environments, they were more likely to tease out racial nuance and magnify some of the ironies of commercial or white liberal representational excess. Certainly different writers emphasized various approaches to and appreciations of the music. For some, it provided a local color, sometimes even an exotic, backdrop for their ideas; others sought to make contemporary events clank harshly among the euphonious sounds of the ancestors; still others emphasized the emotional and intellectual strategies of city-dwellers laughing LOUD to keep from crying in the noisy industrial wasteland. Women expressed their strengths and sorrows, men their frustrations and conquests, children wondered as they wandered, and the writers found the music big enough to express it all. There were, of course, class differences that sometimes made these missives from the lower class unwelcome in certain organs of the movement that emphasized uplift, though there were elders such as Locke and James Weldon Johnson who made their appreciation known. And with the patronage of wealthy whites and artistic sympathies of some among the literary avant-garde and well connected, there was now a stream of money and a few publishing outlets that would deliver certain kinds of material to a variety of audiences.

Harlem was, of course, one of the places where stereotyped commercial representations of hot music were concocted for crowds of slumming white patrons, as well as for white artists exposed to the music by white cultural arbiter and ambassador Carl Van Vechten and others. With the delusional supposed intent to rebel against society and/or middle-class values by virtual-hitching their imported Bugatti Royales to the outsider status of African Americans, the faux primitivity of an invented African and slave past, and the stereotype of roaring passion and sexual abandon among blacks, whites exercised their feelings of discontinuity in a fragmented world. They did this, in their minds, by exalting improvisation, invention, imagination, and spontaneity through their mini-masquerades to jazz performance, which they thought impulsively allowed them to abandon rationality, sexual taboos, emotional paralysis, and intellectual sterility for a cracking good primitive time. In New York, in order to see Negroes in their "natural habitat," one went to Harlem, where at places like the Ubangi Club or the Cotton Club one could hear "jungle music" in a theatrical atmosphere of tuxedoes, evening gowns, and painted palms.

Of course, there were many venues for the burgeoning market. There was the Roseland Ballroom, where Louis Armstrong first played in New York with Fletcher Henderson; the Savoy Ballroom, where Henderson, Jimmie Lunceford, King Oliver, and others held court; the Lafayette Theater, featuring

Wilbur Sweatman and Duke Ellington; Connie's Inn, formerly the Shuffle Inn, which put on the "Keep Shufflin'" and "Hot Chocolates" revues, plus Luis Russell and Fats Waller; Small's Paradise, where the waiters did the Charleston and spun their trays on their fingertips to the music of Charlie Johnson; and of course Owney Madden and Frenchy De Mange's Cotton Club, with Jack Johnson greeting at the door and Ethel Waters and Earl "Snake Hips" Tucker among the performers to the music of Andy Preer's Missourians, Duke Ellington and his Orchestra, and then Cab Calloway. Slightly more off the beaten path were the Rockland Palace, with its Drag Balls, various "buffet flats," with a broad palette of musical and sexual performances, and the black underworld joint recommended by Ethel Waters called Edmond's Cellar. A performer at various venues including the Cotton Club and Harry Hansberry's Clam House on 133rd Street, in the 1930s, the openly lesbian singer Gladys Bentley headlined at Harlem's Ubangi Club with a chorus of drag queens. Was it a social and artistic form of the blackface minstrel show, projecting hidden fears, anxieties, and desires onto a swarthy "other" for whose actions one does not have to take responsibility? A relief from the commitments and beliefs that rule the habits and rituals of their lives? A brief tryst with a bait and switch twist? Or something more serious?

Many felt that white crowds flocked to places like the Cotton Club or clubs like those mentioned by Rudolph Fisher in "The Caucasian Storms Harlem" merely to feed their fantasies about the primitivity of blacks. For example, in "Gotham," published in *Blues: A Magazine of New* Rhythms in 1929, Harvard-educated poet Witter Bynner describes his escape from the world of "polite society":

And there were professors
Around the whiteness of the sepulchral table
Plucking at the weight under which they were buried
And never knowing
That the motion of their fingers
Was caused by earth-worms.

So I hurried away from them to Harlem
And danced at a cabaret till dawn
And saw dark bodies
Waving for poise
Like wings on a dark twig
And hugged to my heart cymbals and drums
And rose up to the long yowl of saxophones. (*Blues 45*)

And it was in part just such an interest on the part of wealthy white patrons that helped sustain the New Negro Renaissance even as it fought hard to free blacks from such facile, racist, and delimiting stereotypes. Ironically, at the same time they were being accused of fostering those stereotypes as well, since without them the palates of many of the audiences could not be satisfied. But as easy as it is to be cynical about white intent, there were black people connected with the Harlem Renaissance who seriously welcomed some white involvement and believed in its sincerity (James Weldon Johnson, Claude McKay, and Langston Hughes among them), even as they propagated myths of exoticism and atavism and constructed jungle scenarios in their own lives and works.

Blues and jazz found an important place in the work of many New Negro Renaissance authors who saw them as "racial" expression, though not all middle-class blacks or religious blacks could or would accept as their own what they deemed such ignorant and sinful creations of vulgar commoners. Frequently, they preferred either sacred music or versions of white Western art products influenced by the African American tradition to help mainstream themselves into white American society, as in the work of Dvořák, Gershwin, Stravinsky, William Grant Still, and others. But jazz was a burgeoning industry in the 1920s, a cultural phenomenon, and thoughts about its symbolism were not to be ignored by contemporary African American writers. Langston Hughes called jazz this "tom-tom of revolt against weariness in a white world," associating it not with whining resignation, defeat, or ignorance, but with African roots and racial struggle ("Negro Artist" 308). Its beat and cadence, as we have discussed, was also an aesthetic marker and catalyst for modernist writers of widely different stripes, such as T. S. Eliot and William Carlos Williams, though sometimes through popular versions that had traveled some distance from the African American community. In its variety of incarnations, it refracted the heat, light, and spirit of African American creativity and resistance into uses and meanings not approved of by all, but part of the music's diffusion into American consciousness.

For example, many black artists such as Sterling Brown and Zora Neale Hurston were less than wholly pleased with the commercialization of their people's music. This commercial representation of the blues in the "vaudeville blues" of the time was criticized by Brown, who found the "crudities" and the "sophisticated smut" present there to be a reduction of the blues to the level of "cabaret appetizers" (Brown 339). However, negative representations were not, after all, unknown in the folk-blues tradition. Fed by stereotypes, they became part of American society's feeble and somewhat misguided efforts to come to terms with what an American identity would include from African

American culture, and how it would express itself. Coming at the time of Freud's emergent popularity, a sexual revolution, a mass migration of African Americans to urban centers, and a rise in Klan membership, the sexuality of the blues became a convenient and vigorous expression of the younger generation's feelings of being repressed, while at the same time serving to liberate artists to deal in more meaningful ways with their art and society. But delimiting stereotypical roles would also serve to control the progress of blacks in the twentieth century by reducing them to mere entertainments and sexual stereotypes, whatever expressions of appreciation whites might mix with their takes on African Americans associated with primitivism, atavism, sexual and emotional abandon, and simplicity and naiveté in their work. Of course, all of the vaudeville blues singers did not find themselves thus reduced, even if many were painted that way by unperceptive whites, and vaudeville blues singers contributed greatly to the poetry of Langston Hughes as opposed to the "high road" of Keatsianism and Victorianism employed by Countee Cullen, the allusive learned and allusive modernism of T. S. Eliot, and the poetic chickens and rainwater of William Carlos Williams's unpacked wheelbarrow artistry.

During the 1920s, writers of the New Negro Renaissance like Langston Hughes, Sterling Brown, Wallace Thurman, and Zora Neale Hurston were attempting to forge a new and revitalized literature. They drew on the poetic inspiration of the spirit and productions of African American folklore, especially, for Hughes, the blues, both in its folk forms and in the vaudeville blues get-up that had emerged leading up to the breakthrough recordings in 1920 and had dominated the blues recording industry for most of the first decade of recording. Others in this New Negro Renaissance such as Countee Cullen, Claude McKay, and Jessie Fauset drew upon the music for its symbolic importance as well. Slightly earlier, Vachel Lindsay of the Chicago Renaissance had attempted to achieve a "higher vaudeville" and the rhythms of black music, like jazz, to create his own new poetry. Sherwood Anderson in *Dark Laughter* (1925) wrote of songs of blacks that demonstrated an "unconscious love of inanimate things lost to whites" (106) that "had sometimes a way of getting at the ultimate truth of things" (248). But Lindsay felt himself slandered as a "jazzer" (xxxii), and he focused on the "picturesquely exotic" (Brown, *Negro Poetry and Drama* 94–95), thus capturing some of the heat, but not the light, of jazz; and Anderson's romanticized view presents blacks as primarily lovers of sex and gaudy things, cloaked in a rather laughable mysticism that looked upon "the folk" as noble savages.

Sterling Brown knew what was behind the depiction of blues on the vaudeville stage and in the popular mind, for he was, as the general public was not, familiar with the folk-blues tradition as it existed and was documented by pioneering collectors such as H. E. Krehbiel, Guy Johnson, Howard Odum, Gates Thomas, John Lomax, and others. Zora Neale Hurston herself was a valued collector of African American folklore, and she and Hughes traveled together in the South for a brief period and heard a number of folk performers (Hughes, *The Big Sea* 296), perhaps artists much like those Hughes and Hurston had both heard in their youths. They were familiar, in other words, with various styles of folk-blues that began to achieve commercial record release later than the popular or vaudeville brand, though the folk-blues predated the vaudeville style. The five years of blues recording following Mamie Smith's recording of "Crazy Blues" were dominated by female performers. At that point, male blues singers began to emerge in their own right, while female singers still held their own. During 1927–1930, the peak years for issuance of blues and gospel records (Godrich and Dixon 104–105), five hundred blues and gospel records were released per year, and field excursions by major record companies to Atlanta, Memphis, Dallas, New Orleans, and other locations greatly expanded the types of blues issued for the "Race" market, but not so much so for the popular market (read white market). Therefore, the use of the word "blues" signified a different and broader group of musics for many African American artists in the twenties (and later) than for their white modernist counterparts, so the use of that term by modernists like Williams must be read in the light of their familiarity with only a segment of the variety of blues music and their often racist responses, deliberate or not, to African Americans, while the variety of blues heard by certain New Negro writers was greater.

As blues emerged in small towns, on street corners, back porches, and juke joint floorboards across the country, traveled in carnival caravans and to tent shows, and leaked out on piano rolls and sheet music, artists began to listen. Artists both black and white listened with both aesthetic and capitalist ears to the sound of what Dunbar may have called "a jingle in a broken tongue" (*Collected Poetry* 191) and made their moves to market the music. As has already been pointed out, white literary artists such as Sandburg and Lindsay made prominent use of the music early on. And Langston Hughes, who had heard black America singing firsthand at the behest of Whitman and Du Bois, now read it in Sandburg and Lindsay. When he dropped his own poems alongside Lindsay's plate at the Wardman Park Hotel in Chicago, blues were among the poems on Hughes's menu, and Lindsay responded sympathetically to the beat.

Of course, Hughes was listening not only to white writers such as Sandburg and Lindsay who were familiar with hot music, but black ones as well. This is particularly true of Old Guard and transitional guard writers like W. E. B. Du Bois, James Weldon Johnson, Alain Locke, and Charles S. Johnson, important elders and mentors whose writings and editorial connections helped establish a sympathetic terrain for younger African American writers, even as they resisted some of the more avant-garde strains of Harlem Renaissance–era folk aesthetics. The notion that a great people showed their culture and worth by generating great works of art, and advanced through the demonstration, was an influential one at the time of the Harlem Renaissance, espoused by James Weldon Johnson and others as they jockeyed for African Americans' political progress.

For many African American intellectuals, spirituals were the most important African American folk songs extant. In 1923, John W. Work, for example, ranked Stephen Foster's melodies behind spirituals but ahead of "any of the secular Folk Songs of the Negro" (337) in terms of their value and beauty. Du Bois's *The Souls of Black Folk* (1903) and James Weldon Johnson's anonymously published *Autobiography of an Ex-Colored Man* (1912; 1927) spoke lovingly of spirituals (Du Bois) and ragtime music (Johnson actually championed both). Each man emphasized the importance of the folk culture, while Johnson recognized the value of both urbanized commercial developments of those materials and haute culture transmutations of base folk art into classic gold—ragging the classics and classicizing the rags—as ways of caressing and communicating the spirit of "the race" and contributing to the national culture and reputation of America. Johnson's introduction to the *Book of American Negro Poetry* (1922), published in the year after Hughes's first poems appeared in print, emphasized the importance of finding a "racial flavor" (Huggins 300), as Synge had done for the Irish, to help create an indigenous African American literature. Johnson's interest in African American folk religion was reflected in his co-authoring with his brother J. Rosamond Johnson of *The Book of American Negro Spirituals* (1925) and *The Second Book of American Negro Spirituals* (1926), as well as his acclaimed volume of oral sermons, *God's Trombones* (1927). In the preface to the former volume, Johnson emphasized the importance of religious song leaders such as "Ma" White and preachers such as Singing Johnson, and in *God's Trombones* he discussed the artistry and importance of the folk preacher called Singing Johnson in *Autobiography of an Ex-Colored Man*. Thus, in his editorial, fictional, and poetic work, Johnson emphasized the importance of folk materials for the advancement of African Americans through their creative work to political advancement.

Significantly, Du Bois wielded influence as editor of the major organ of the NAACP, *The Crisis* (along with literary editor Jessie Fauset), while James Weldon Johnson's important and influential work as contributing editor for *The New York Age* demonstrated his political and cultural commitments and gave him a platform from which to influence the next generation of writers.

Alain Locke and sociologist and editor of the Urban League's journal *Opportunity* Charles S. Johnson seemed better able to appreciate African American secular folk music than Du Bois and James Weldon Johnson, Locke as a net-casting theoretician who came musically under the influence of the younger Sterling Brown, and Charles Johnson with his belief, expressed in 1925, that the much ridiculed decadent and primitive jazz was the "key to the interpretation of the American spirit" (133).

In his introduction to *The New Negro* (1925), Locke emphasized that "in the very heart of the folk-spirit are the essential forces" (xv); that same year, Arthur Huff Fauset claimed for religious songs, work songs, social songs the "power" to express the "Soul of Black Folk" and "to get down to the real soul of the Negro" (228-29). And though Locke still leaned, as did Du Bois and James Weldon Johnson, toward the spirituals as the great contribution of African Americans to folk song, his pronouncements, along with those of Du Bois, J.W. Johnson, and Charles S. Johnson, did help aesthetically legitimize, in the eyes of younger artists, a variety of forms of African American folk materials. When Langston Hughes complained to his benefactor Charlotte Mason that he was not a rural southern poet, but instead "was Chicago and Kansas City and Broadway and Harlem" (*The Big Sea* 325), he did not mean that he did not know the South; after all, he had left it. He just meant that the northern road was long and dusty and a hard road to travel, and it led away from shacks and mules and plows and cotton crops to tenements and cars and steel mills and skimpy paychecks, from stream-of-consciousness guitar playing folk-blues to whirling tuxedoed orchestras with more than one kind of brass on the road to modernity.

II

From the year 1920, when Mamie Smith made the sides that launched a craze for African American blues recordings, starting with "That Thing Called Love," "You Can't Keep a Good Man Down," and "Crazy Blues," the blues was largely a woman's field in terms of popular recordings. Early recordings by artists such as Lillyn Brown, Lavinia Turner, Daisy Martin, and Lucille Hegamin helped create an atmosphere that led to the ascendancy of the so-called classic or vaudeville/stage blues featuring female artists during the years 1923–1926. It is not surprising that Langston Hughes, who considered himself an urban and not a rural poet, would be attracted to these kinds of blues featured on phonograph records and in larger urban venues. That is not to say that Hughes was not familiar with the street corner blues of itinerant singers. He reported that his poem "The Weary Blues" contained the "first blues verse [he'd] ever heard way back in Lawrence, Kansas when [he] was a kid," along with a number of blind singers and guitar players and piano players in Kansas City as well (Tracy, *Langston Hughes and the Blues* 105). In a variety of writings, though, he frequently mentioned female singers of this type as among his favorites or among the best singers in the tradition, especially Ma Rainey, who he heard in Chicago's Monogram and Grand Theaters in his teens, Bessie, Mamie, Clara, and Trixie Smith, Victoria Spivey, and Chippie Hill (Tracy, *Langston Hughes and the Blues* 108–09, 118–19). As Godrich and Dixon point out, though, in 1924 the trickle of black male blues-oriented performers, beginning with Barrelhouse Ed Andrews and Papa Charlie Jackson in 1924 and especially Blind Lemon Jefferson in 1925–1926, heralded an era of black male blues performers that would help nudge out the earlier vaudeville blues performers (*Recording the Blues* 33–34), Some of the women continued to record, however, and the work of Lonnie Johnson, from his first recordings in 1925, evidenced the influence of the vaudeville blues style, though now recorded by a man, as few had been previously been.

Though as we have already shown, Hughes's references to the blues were preceded in a variety of ways in the work of other poets, Hughes was the first creative writer to embrace so thoroughly and completely the style, ethos, and subject matter of the African American genre known as the blues. His influence on other poets using African American vernacular forms is incalculable, though the way was prepared for him by artists and scholars whose own expanded understandings of the breadth of American literature allowed Hughes to make revolutionary and groundbreaking choices in his work. For most of the period covered by this volume, Hughes's work was the benchmark for the use of blues in literature, and he remains the central figure related to literature touched by the blues.

Hughes's "blues poetry" first began to appear in print in *The Crisis*, starting in October 1922 with "Song for a Banjo Dance" (*Collected Poems* 29), which provides a template for Hughes's imaginative use of the blues genre. First, the title connects the song, and the poetry, with dance, an important cultural connection given the centrality of dance in West African musical performance. In this, Hughes establishes firm cultural roots, African associations of which African Americans had been taught to be ashamed. Hughes, however, is unashamed in his implicit associations here. It is also clear from line one that Hughes is looking to the language of the everyday African American, the vernacular, for the language appropriate for his poetry—another element that middle-class values would have taught him to shun. However, in this he establishes a connection to the great "dialect" poet Paul Laurence Dunbar, whose popularity among African Americans exceeded that of any other African American poet, until Hughes. Third, Hughes is speaking not *in propria persona*, but in the voice of a speaker, one of many individuals that Hughes was to invite to speak in his poetry over five decades. His use of the word "honey" in this poem reminds of Dunbar's "A Negro Love Song," itself a dance song that repeats a refrain including the words "jump back, honey" (49). Moreover, Hughes establishes from the beginning that this is not one of your light-skinned chorus girls on whom he is focusing. While light skin was a requirement for many chorus girls in Harlem, a reflection of color stratification that favored a complexion closer to white as superior, in Hughes's poem it is brown feet that shake the world of the speaker, who translates the rhythm of her spirit, and her dance, into a world-shaking poem.

The second stanza of the poem in particular evinces elements of the blues' ABC twelve-bar pattern, not the most common pattern in the blues, and an early indicator that Hughes knew and would draw on varied blues elements, not only the standard ones, in his work. Thus, Hughes emphasizes the variety and adaptability of the form to the emotional, intellectual, and formal exigencies of his poetry, emphasizing that the genre is not a limited or limiting form, but a flexible, suggestible foundation for his poetic fancy. Since this is Hughes's first published overt use of the blues stanza, it is useful to see that he is already transcribing the twelve-bar blues lyric pattern, which implies three lines, in six lines. In this he acknowledges the medial caesurae that frequently occur in performed blues vocals, highlighting Hughes's desire to convey performative oral elements in his written poetry. This performative element is reinforced by Hughes's employment of emphatic repetition in the final lines of the stanza, which sometimes occur improvisationally in performance as a rush of words whirling into a small unit of time:

> Shake your brown feet, honey,
> Might never dance no mo' . . .
>
> The sun's going down this very night—
> Might never rise no mo'. (*Collected Poems* 29)

In this case, it suggests a certain urgency in the dancing, a seizing of the moment before time is up, even as it suggests greater rhythmic speed in relation to meter. Complicated rhythm produces a tension related to the importance of this dancing to the dancer's life, and also captures a frantic polyrhythm that emphasizes the communal nature of performance. Combined with references to shaking and swiftness, Hughes provides a nuanced sense of polyrhythms in the poem.

References to the sun going down and sobbing may draw on the blues tradition, as in Pinetop Burks's "Sun Down Blues" (1937) and Sara Martin's "Sobbin' Hearted Blues" (1924). Interestingly, Hughes describes the banjo as producing a sob. One does not usually associate that sound with a banjo, which has a rather plinkety-plunk tone, and whose strings do not sustain a note as long as a guitar, which might better produce a sob or a whine. Since we are in a period of transition from guitar to banjo at this period of history in hot music, it is entirely consistent to present a banjo in a jazz band. And, in truth, Hughes will make this kind of application of "mismatched" instruments and sounds in "The Weary Blues" later, referring to the piano as moaning. This, of course, is an aural signal that the musician is working his transformative magic on an instrument, making it sound like we think it cannot. Perhaps, Hughes suggests, it is because we approach the instrument in a limited way, underestimate it, as we might underestimate a human being from whom we are taught to expect little. Perhaps we can transform everything around us through our imagination, and make it reflect our moods, our worldview. Perhaps we can speed up dance time in order to crowd so much more of this wonderful "dark time" into the minimal space left before dawn. Or, if dawn may never come again, into the minimal time left for this kind of pleasure. Given that philosophers such as Henri Bergson were exploring conflicting notions of durational time and dramatic time in human consciousness in the era, and that it became a major influence on literary modernist experiments, the implications in Hughes's poems seem clear. Transforming durational time into dramatic time, traditional sounds into individually distinctive ones, the transformative power of African American cultural performance is clearly an answer to the worn out accepted notions of the past, and the ennui and acedia that plagues contemporary culture.

Other poems that preceded publication of Hughes's first volume emphasize hot music on the landscape as well. Poems such as "Negro" (1922) reference the contributions of ragtime, and "Jazzonia" and "Cabaret" from the August 1923 issue, as well as the March 1925 "Negro Dancers," refer to jazz and the club milieu in which urban blues might be performed, though only the laughter with the sob beneath the surface of "Cabaret," with its possible connections to the well-known blues phrase "laughin' to keep from cryin'," connects explicitly with the blues tradition. Both "Young Singer" (1923) and "Negro Dancers" populate their lines with jazz people. Interestingly, Hughes's "Laughers" (1922) refers to "jazzers" among those adjectives that describe his persevering people.

In May 1925, Hughes seized the opportunity, in the journal *Opportunity*, to publish his first explicit "blues poem," "The Weary Blues" (*Collected Poems*

50), the title of which was common as the "weary" or "worried" blues in the oral tradition. By the mid-1910s, the lyrics from the oral tradition began turning up in print and on phonograph recordings. Black ragtime composer Artie Mathews published his version of this folk-blues in 1915. The title had been utilized in minstrel shows as far back as 1913, and instrumental songs recorded as "Weary Blues" appeared by the Louisiana Five in 1919, Windy City Trio in 1920, the Cardinal Jazz Band in 1921, the New Orleans Rhythm Kings in 1923, and Vic Meyers and Jelly Roll Morton in 1924, and by Clarence Williams as "The Weary Blues" in 1923, all before the publication of Hughes's poem. In fact, Clara Smith sang in "My John Blues" (1925) "You take a southbound regular, you ride my weary blues away," one of the earlier references to the weary blues of Hughes's title. Later, such recorded singers as Henry Thomas, Gladys Bentley, Frank Hutchison (all of whose sources likely predated Artie Mathews), and Hank Williams recorded some version of the worried or weary blues, which became a generic title for what the blues were all about, eliding easily through pronunciation the distinction between the two related meanings. Though the Hughes poem was not, at the time, the explosive time bomb that Richard Wright's *Native Son* was in 1940, "The Weary Blues" was a revolutionary aesthetic volley, the visceral beginning of the blues poetry era and, thus, a genre-altering moment the importance of which has only become clear gradually, and in hindsight, even though it was certainly welcomed in the twenties.

Taking the title and lyrics of "The Weary Blues" was certainly no accident. Weariness and worry were in the air, from the lingering Lost Generation effects of the war to the Great Migration to lynching and Jim Crow to rapid industrialization, so everybody, but especially African Americans, could identify with the title. It was not just "weary blues," but THE weary blues, something more than just temporal mundane concerns, but weary blues for the times, and for all times. In this it may be seen also as a volley in the battle over the "universality" of African American poetry at the time. While some seemed to feel that one had to erase references to African Americans to become "universal," Hughes challenged the notion that white poetry could be universal without erasing such markers. The singer is identified as a Negro, in a black neighborhood, singing a genre of music associated with African Americans. There is no question as to his race, nor does Hughes suggest that his great skills come from anything other than placing his black hands on the white keys of the piano, and expressing his black man's soul. And yet, these blues, placed within a narrative structure and dramatic scene, gazed upon by a nameless narrator, have a universal lesson to convey along with their local habitation.

Fittingly, for the poem Hughes returns from his current age of twenty-three to the time of his youth for the title and inspiration for his poem, to "the first blues verse [he'd] ever heard back in Lawrence, Kansas, when [he] was a kid" (*The Big Sea* 215). It was something that had been with him for much of his life, as it had been with his people, and thus represented a lifelong cultural keepsake that accompanied him in his travels. Now he would use it to express himself, expressing his people, expressing their troubles and their determination to persevere and reinvent American culture, as Hughes determined to reinvent himself as the poet his classmates thought he would "naturally" be. From adolescence in Kansas to maturity in the Harlem of the poem, the poet himself had taken his own great migration from his grandmother's lap to the bosom of the New Negroes in Harlem, where those old blues songs were shaking off some of the plantation soil and moaning in the flashing lights of New York.

Hughes was a city poet with a strong rural ancestry in the folk-creations of his people. As such, this poem must reflect both of those interests faithfully, while allowing the poet his own creative approach. This is where the blues fit in so beautifully. Since the blues took a variety of different forms and stanza patterns in their folk incarnations, and found a similar variety in the vaudeville blues incarnations that were electrifying the era, their sure structure, adaptable to a flexible democratic looseness, between and within stanzas, captured the ethos of group dynamic, individual expression, improvisational immediacy, resistance to arbitrary authority, and indomitable perseverance that Hughes felt were hallmarks of black culture that would be a gift to America.

What Hughes struck upon for the stanza pattern in his poem is a personal modification of the vaudeville blues tradition, itself a modification of the folk-blues tradition practiced by songwriters with varying levels of exposure to the folk-blues, among them Perry Bradford, Clarence Williams, and the blues women themselves. Since the folk-blues seemed to some commentators to be overly rough and vulgar, there was an attempt to clean up the folk lyrics, without losing a certain earthiness, in order to make them more pop oriented and appropriate for the stage. Even in their sanitized versions, however, some lyrics strained the limits of acceptability, even from the mouths of Negroes of whom it was to be "expected," and piled ludicrous *double entendre* on top of *entendre* to the pretended horror (but sometimes titillation) of the middle-class listener.

Rosa Henderson, one of the excellent undersung vaudeville blues singers of the 1920s, provides an example of a vaudeville blues song structure that was common at the time, and on which Hughes may have drawn for his poem "The Weary Blues." The Henderson song, "Slow Up Papa" (1927), begins with a narrative section that describes Henry, the reckless, speeding chauffeur, who gets moving violations daily, violations that extend to his trips with his "gal" as well. As the main sixteen-bar section of the song begins, a section that also serves as a refrain, she admonishes him in no uncertain terms:

> Slow up papa, slow up papa.
> Mama likes to take her time.
> Your gas is low, so take it slow
> 'Cause you've got a hill to climb.
> Now your spark is weak, your tire is flat,
> You can't go the distance if you speed like that.
> So slow up papa, slow up papa,
> Mama likes to take her time.

This type of sixteen-bar stanza, common in vaudeville blues, allows more space for the unraveling of a plot or making more elaborate claims, while often losing the pithiness and gritty force of the eight- or twelve-bar stanza. With its intro, it even lends itself to greater dramatization on the stage or in tent shows, where such songs were frequently performed. The introduction also sets up the obvious coy sexual double entendre that provides a source of laughter concerning Henry's mobile malfunctions. The more elaborate song structure, narrative introduction, and dramatic stylization—along with Henderson's clear diction and controlled singing—tend to mark this song as an urban vaudeville variation of the folk-blues. Ma Rainey's "Lucky Rock Blues" (1924) also contains an introductory section, but this time leading into twelve-bar stanzas for the rest of the song. There was a good bit of variability possible in this manifestation of the blues, variability which Hughes employed in his own creations.

Hughes uses some of these elements in "The Weary Blues" to mark his song as an urban work as well, though he also makes use of eight- and twelve-bar stanzas, as a number of vaudeville blues songs did. Mixing eight- and twelve-bar blues stanzas in the same song also occurred in the folk-blues tradition, as in King Solomon Hill's "The Gone Dead Train" (1932), but usually not with a stylized introduction. Thus, it mixes the folk-blues of the rural South with the urban blues of the North, along with narrative, dramatic, and lyric elements and commercial and literary elements, to offer a unique hybrid that embraces various manifestations of the blues tradition. It was an auspicious beginning to the strongest, most nuanced vein of blues literature.

In the first stanza, Hughes forms another connection to the vaudeville blues tradition by treating the subject of a musician who will be praised for his musical talent. Like such songs as Alberta Hunter's version of Richard M. Jones's "Jazzin' Baby Blues" (1922) or Bessie Smith's version of Fletcher

Henderson's "Jazzbo Brown from Memphis Town" (1926), Hughes describes a particularly affecting performance he heard on Lenox Avenue in Harlem; unlike them, Hughes's featured performer remains nameless. This is significant because Hughes, in addition to championing an individual performer, is writing in praise of a tradition. When he writes that he heard "a Negro play," the words "a Negro" are, like the title of his poem "The Negro Speaks of Rivers," both singular and plural. This negro, important in himself in the poem, remains unsung individually despite his importance, but is raised to the level of representative of a broad tradition as well. Thus, he mirrors the aesthetic of a community, West African and African American, which connects individual to community through and in performance. This establishes a relationship between singer and audience, or more appropriately caller and responder, which Hughes will explore more deeply and crucially as the poem begins.

The poem begins with the sound of a drone, a deep humming sound that can be produced either by the human voice or by an instrument, marking an immediate close identification between voice and instrument that is endemic to the African and African American musical traditions: the instrument is an extension of the voice, and to say that an instrumentalist can "make it talk" or "tell a story" is high praise. Furthermore, the drone sound is frequently a significant part of African music, especially as some type of resonating device such as a gourd can be attached to an instrument to extend the life of its tones. A drone is also created by lowering the pitch of a string by a semi-tone to make it vibrate against other pitches. In either case, it provides a departure from Western practice, as well as a solid sound base for extending notes or improvisation, at times eschewing chord changes for a type of modal playing that allows for easier improvisation and can be very hypnotic, as in the playing of Lightnin' Hopkins or John Lee Hooker. In this case, the source of the drone is ambiguous, because the syntax of the line is ambiguous. Who is droning and rocking in the poem? Although we expect it is the pianist, the syntax connects these activities to the "I" or speaker in the piece, who is an observer. What Hughes creates with the syntax here is an immediate and close connection between the speaker and the performer, as well as between both of them and the music. "Droning," "drowsy," "syncopated," "rocking," "mellow"—all of these elements of the music become potentially a part of the personalities of both of the figures in the poem, bringing them together into a community of performers exchanging, call-and-response fashion, the distinctive elements of the blues music tradition.

But there is a tension that serves as a catalyst in the poem, a meeting among the milieu, moment, and music that suggests a "disruptive" performance practice that nonetheless produces an uneasily casual, even dreamy, mood. Hughes's juxtaposition of the words "drowsy" and "syncopated," like his reference to the song played by the performer as a "sad raggy tune," implies a relaxed or depressed milieu that is belied by the momentary disruptions produced by syncopation. Stemming from the word "syncope," which means a skipped heartbeat, syncopation is, in Western terms, the alteration of a metronomic beat that throws the listener into less-familiar spaces in the temporal world of the song. In African music, it is business as usual. Thus, rather than letting the listeners relax into the conforming beat, it displaces the listeners, moving them a "super-regular" (rather than irregular) space that contrasts with the conventional time while calling attention to it. It is one of the features of African American music that makes it a dance-oriented, participatory music, even while it can produce a lazy, relaxing feel. It calls attention to difference while it emphasizes alteration of a norm, in this case conventional monorhythmic European time and rhythm. The "d" alliteration in "droning" and "drowsy" connects the two, and indeed the drone does frequently produce something akin to a trance-like state. "Syncopated," the word with the most syllables in the line, is itself as long as those two words, and produces a rushing, syncopation-like effect through the following of an accented initial syllable by three unaccented syllables—it is what it says, almost a form of onomatopoeia, and produces what it says in the line, starkly contrasting to the somnolent regularity of the first five syllables of the line. Because this type and frequency of syncopation appears in West African music, syncopation cannot be said to disrupt the nature of that musical tradition. It is European tradition, encountered in the context of African American performances, that is the beneficiary (or victim) of such disruptions, disruptions recognized by surrealists as "an ardent appeal for a new life from the other side of all travestied hopes" (Rosemont 19). As Lucy Lippard said of the surrealists, "The Surrealists hoped eventually to draw from the juxtaposition of these dislocated fragments a new, superreality, rather than a mere destruction of the old" (Rothenberg and Joris 466). The word "rocking," in and of itself, produces a similar effect. While on the one hand it suggests the soothing movement designed to put a baby to sleep, on the other it refers to raucous music and movement, as pointed out in the discussion of Sandburg's "Baby Song of the Four Winds." Now, for Hughes, the single work encapsulates and reinforces the tension of relaxation and stimulation produced by the performer in the poem.

Critic Donald Dickinson sees the opening stanza of the poem as being "an alliterative innovation in the style of Vachel Lindsay's 'The Congo'" (120), and indeed the popularity of the poem and Hughes's acknowledged familiarity with and esteem for Lindsay make that entirely possible—poet Sterling Brown responded to this Lindsay poem himself. However, one need not resort to Lindsay for a possible source for the stanza when the vaudeville blues tradition provides us with a concrete and likely source. Vaudeville blues and jazz songs, as well as pop manifestations, which reference characteristics of the music such as syncopation (as in Lucille Hegamin's 1923 recording "Syncopatin' Mama") and crooning (Jabbo Smith's 1929 "Croonin' the Blues"), or responses such as laziness or swaying (in Casey Bill Weldon's 1937 "Red Hot Blues," not a vaudeville blues) were certainly present in the vaudeville blues, and Hughes certainly showed an interest in that tradition. The stylized repetition of the "lazy sway" line connects it with a performative or dramatic tradition, as well as an African American tradition where "worrying" a line through repetition can help emphasize, deepen, or multiply meanings latent in the language and cultural milieu itself. Furthermore, the rendering of the word "of" as "o'" suggests at least orality, if not musical performance, and certain titles in the blues tradition were rendered in this fashion as well. Because the speaker here is offering the description, and nowhere else in the poem does he put forward a dialect rendering of his own words, it seems as if this is yet another entrée by the speaker into the spirit of the tradition, another, at least musical, identification with it.

Simultaneously, because of the difference from the language he uses elsewhere in the poem, the spelling he uses here also emphasizes some distance between him and the singer as well—one of the elements of the poem that the speaker seems to be attempting to work out. After all, the singer is only designated by race, never by name, and the speaker does not seem to make any effort to find out more about him. The singer-pianist is just an anonymous performer in a particular place at a certain time that causes the speaker to reflect on the nature of the blues tradition in relation to himself. It seems to be a rather odd tension between involvement and detachment, like the earlier tension between movement and relaxation, unless we see this as a reflection of the ability of the blues and its performers to both entertain and relax on one hand, and to agitate and propel on the other. The blues, after all, is important as musical performance—entertainment and artistry—but it packs a sociopolitical punch in its challenge to Western notions of art, outlet for suppressed black voices, and reaping of individual and group power through the exercise of facility, flair, wit, and will. The speaker states it, after all: "I heard a Negro play." This public voice, particularly for an anonymous lower-class African American, clears a space for him not only to be listened to, but to be *heard*, much as vaudeville women blues singers were able to garner space for explorations of women's issues in their songs and performances as well. Given that the 1920s was a decade during which African American voices were beginning to be heard with greater impact than ever before, including in poetry like that of Langston Hughes, the statement, while seemingly of little significance, actually resounds in a poem that is about performance, and employs alliterative sound effects and onomatopoeia as well.

This Lenox Avenue pianist performs in the area of Harlem called Jungle Alley, 133rd Street between Lenox and Seventh Avenues (including many clubs catering to fledgling white visitors, such as the Cotton Club), a district that held the largest number of fancier night clubs in its area of any in Harlem, with the seamier joints nearby enough to provide somewhere else to go for more private entertainment. Since the time of the poem is described as the "other" night, Hughes sets up the expectation that we will visit the "other" Harlem, the real one behind the glitter and glitterati, and thus explore an "other" experience. Therefore, the speaker takes us "down" to this location, a descent into something deeper and more real than the champagne and chorus girl blues of the high life, and he takes us there at night, when the harsh light of day gives way to the freedom to explore provided by the curtain of night. Not that the light does not intrude upon the scene: the "pale dull pallor" provides an almost mock lighting, in contrast to the lights of the large clubs, and the "old gas" source of the light makes this an experience associated with the past, the run down, not the up-to-date and high octane. The association of dullness with the paleness and pallor of the chiaroscuric illumination compares the harshness of whiteness with the freedom of night and the black blues tradition, the single gaslight and single performer and single observer all similarly isolated—no one else is mentioned—alone with each other, and with the weary blues.

The speaker emphasizes this black and white distinction specifically in the poem by remarking how the ebony of the pianist's hands touches and transforms "each ivory key." Ebony, of course, implies strength, durability, richness, a worthy synonym for the power of the blues tradition, while the pianist's touch on "each" key implies the total transformation of the instrument from its similarly valuable ivory representation of the Western music tradition to something new, expressive, and compelling, yet as aged and venerable as the roots of the tree or Western musical tradition. And the transformation that he effects, applying the skills and aesthetic of ancient West African traditions to the venerable piano of the West, brings about a music unlike that which the piano has seemed to be able to make in the Western tradition. Yet it is not a violent transformation: the line itself is full of alliteration—three "m" sounds and initial two "p" sounds—"He made that poor piano moan with melody"—that blends the mechanical sounds of the "poor" broken down piano with the performer-maker's soulful ability to make mountains out of mole hills.

In the Western tradition, as the piano is not usually thought of as having the ability to moan, neither is melody a moaning feature, therefore not only the instrument but the nature of the melodic tradition is remodeled, this time on an African American prototype that makes both possible. Since the piano is an instrument on which, when one strikes a note, a hammer hits a string inside the piano, with no possibility of bending or stretching, as would be possible on a guitar or harmonica, the Western listener is left to ask what sort of magic—as Equiano had queried earlier about European handiwork—produces the moan. The answer is to think of the keys and sequence of playing in a different fashion. Playing two or three consecutive notes simultaneously on a piano produces, in the Western tradition, a vulgar, inappropriate, dissonant sound that one would usually make, before the modernists, only accidentally. However, such "rough" sounds frequently occur in the West African tradition, along with the effects of resonators and other elements that recognize that what Westerners consider harsh sounds can represent intellectual or passionate ideas and elements that express the broad palette of emotions of human beings, and thus the aesthetic of the artist. Such a spellbinding renovation can spark in the speaker of the poem little less than veneration. He responds not with the merely surprised "oh," but with an exclamation of worshipful wonder, "O Blues!"—an expression touched by the traditions of biblical and mythological glorification, at which point we notice the first of three exclamation points in the poem, all venerating the blues. Of course, the pianist-singer also manifests that veneration, identifying speaker and subject with each other once again.

One would expect, then from this veneration a similarly respectful description of the pianist. However, the pianist is characterized as playing "like a musical fool," as he sways on his stool, perhaps a poor substitute for the throne one might expect from the previous line. And yet the stool itself is not incongruous. The performer is a creator and entertainer, responsible for generating his own music as well as communicating to an audience which he wants to respond and participate—in the communal tradition—as well. Thus, his "sad raggy tune," itself a seemingly incongruous mix of unhappiness and syncopating movement, needs selling. He isn't the *fool* fool, he is the wise fool, playing the "dirty" music of the blues tradition in all its exaltation, if only people can recognize it for what it is. He is making it heard, even if one person at a time, by syncopating the sadness. It is that syncopating sadness that helps make the blues "sweet," as the speaker calls it, in another exclamatory phrase. This designation again may seem incongruous—how can this sad music be sweet? The answer, of course, is that in expression and performance, the words produce a transcendence of sadness, a lifting of patting feet and an elevation of spirit. Without the connection to the mundane stool, the everyday problems of the masses that the singer describes might not be available to him, and his music might be less authentic, less soulful. The African American style of performance produces style, flair, and wonder that transforms the sadness; and its source, as the speaker recognizes, is the "black man's soul." Thus, this soul, this spiritual source for all of this creative and passionate power of reconciliation, deserves its third brief, two-word exclamatory paean of praise, "O Blues!" This eight-line section of the poem, describing the power, meaning, and importance of his performance, encompassing the sadness and sweetness of what he is and does, now brings his human voice and words to the poem, another connection between speaker and performer in the poem, and a reminder that they do the same thing, and that those connections, and their connections, are what makes the speaker's poetry matter.

Having heard the piano "voice" of the performer, the speaker now turns to the "song" voice, the words that interact with and express in human language what the music exalts. Very few of the blues singers recorded throughout time can be described as having deep voice, if by "deep" we mean "low." An early recording by Buddy Moss, "Gravy Server" (1935), stands out, but it was likely pressed at a slow speed, which accounts for the super-low register, at least baritone, voice, though Moss himself did have a low voice. The description of the voice as having a tone that is "melancholy" reminds the listener with alliteration (m) and assonance (long o sound) related to line ten about the piano moaning with melody. The speaker's interest in connecting the piano playing and the voice in this way is his way of emphasizing the symbiotic relationship of music and words, the way they adapt to each other, reaffirm each other, according to the rules of African American aesthetic practice. Both voice and music will moan, in a balance as sure and artful as the line:

> I heard that Negro sing, that old piano moan—

With its medial caesura providing a symmetry for the poet's line visually, as the performer might very well sing the line in halves divided by a brief pause in his singing, the poem proceeds into the first blending of voices of the two, technically a transcription of a performance, but aesthetically a twin vision that acknowledges the superiority of language and music in the blues tradition for expressing African American integrity.

The first recognizable folk-blues stanza that Hughes interpolates in his poem is the eight-bar AB musical variant. While the twelve-bar AAB stanza was more common, the eight-bar communicates a certain pithiness and directness, lacking the "repeat" line, that drives directly to the heart(break) of the situation:

Ain't got nobody in all this world
Ain't got nobody but ma self.
I'se gwine to quit ma frownin'
And put ma troubles on the shelf.

The sentiment and phrase "I ain't got nobody" is, of course, most common in the blues. Feelings of isolation and loneliness are a core feeling and expression, evoking the poor boy/gal long ways from home that itself may link to expressions going as far back as the Middle Passage. Of course, the famous Spencer Williams composition from c. 1915 "I Ain't Got Nobody" was well known at the time through its popular recording by white jazz singer Marion Harris in 1916, and subsequent recordings by Virginia Liston, Ida Cox, and Bessie Smith, all from 1925, the same year Hughes's poem was published. The poem, however, shares little lyrically with the Williams song other than the title. And, it should be pointed out, it doesn't even share all of the title: the song of the performer in the poem omits the "I." This is, of course, entirely consistent with the vernacular and popular blues traditions, which allow the singer to omit things like pronouns because in performance the singer would be understood as the complainant. Mary Stafford recorded "Ain't Got Nobody to Grind My Coffee in the Morning" in 1926. Indeed, Hughes uses other oral elements in the song, such as "ma," "I'se," and "gwine." Some commentators might argue, though, that omission of the pronoun permits listeners mentally or verbally to place their own "I" in the song, identifying with the experience and participating, call-and-response style, with the communal group and acknowledging the persona nature of the blues-singing voice. If such a scenario seems unlikely in the oral tradition, perhaps the notion that the literary artist Hughes seeks to use this aspect of the vernacular tradition to emphasize the singer's isolation seems more likely—he sings that he has nobody but himself, but even his self-reference is gone in his vocalization of the lyrics.

There is, however, a repetition in this blues stanza, even if it is not a twelve-bar form, or, perhaps better, a corrective extension of line one, in line two. Where the singer first states that he has nobody, he modifies that by stating that he has nobody *but himself*. This is an important distinction, because it points the way toward the resolve he expresses in the rest of the blues stanza. It is a turning point at which he acknowledges his own agency and determines a strategy for handling his troubles: he will refuse to allow them to be foremost in his mind, and persevere despite them by minimizing their importance so that he is not dominated by weariness. Thus, singing the weary blues is about driving the weary blues away—a kind of anti-weary blues. It is a strategy to express and create and transform in place of being weary and worried. The strategy is not necessarily merely an avoidance of the troubles, but rather an acknowledgment that one can attack problems in more ways than one. Rather than sinking beneath his burden, the singer will do what generations of African Americans had done to lighten their loads: create songs to ease their trouble in mind, to help pass the time. Or, better yet, not to have the work as the center of their purpose and the music to ameliorate the situation, but have the music at the center, and let the work be subordinated to it. This would effect a central redefinition of who they are—not beasts of burden, but begetters of beautiful blues. It puts the first stanza on a fairly optimistic plane, with a resolute singer, his voice finally exercised, using a song connected to his African American heritage to make an individual decision to employ his agency.

It would have been entirely understandable if Hughes had ended the poem on such an optimistic note, but then again perhaps not so realistic. The blues, after all, keep on dogging people around, as Sodarisa Miller sang in "Don't Dog Me 'Round Blues" (1924), so we might expect something to follow, as it does heralded by triple onomatopoeic thumps of the performers shoes on the floor. They do not interrupt the performance—many blues performers were known to use percussive effects like knocking on a guitar or foot stomping to enhance a performance. Rather, the stomping announces the return of the troubles, as if the singer is indicating that he is digging in for another round, gaining momentum in the music as he returns to the vicissitudes of life. Stephen Calt points out that in the barrelhouses, "stomp" or "stomp down" was "[a] Southern intensifier meaning downright" (232), and as a noun it referred to a rowdy, no-holds-barred dance party (233). In either case, the intensification is clear. In a bar which seems to be empty other than the performer and single listener (and likely a bartender, not mentioned), the singer kicks into high gear as if a whole crowd were there, as if he were singing for the world.

Whereas the first stanza he sang took an eight-bar musical form, this one is bigger, longer—twelve bars, in an AAB pattern, the most common stanza form of the blues, right back down to the bedrock form. It is not uncommon for a singer to mix eight- and twelve-bar stanzas in a single song—Tommy Johnson did so in "Canned Heat Blues" (1928), among many other examples. Hughes, however, is mixing vaudeville-style intro with eight- and twelve-bar stanzas, with a concluding return to narrative—again, an experiment in style and form. We wonder why Hughes decided to employ the twelve-bar AAB stanza, and it may well be that the troubles named here are so pervasive as to carry more weight, though not obliterate, the perseverance of the eight-bar stanza. By repeating "the weary blues," he emphasizes it as a looming presence that produces dissatisfaction. That repetition, though, is with a difference. Again this is entirely consistent with the oral blues tradition, but carries weight in the written tradition as well. In the first two lines, the singer employs the first person singular pronoun twice; in the repeating second pair of lines, the pronoun disappears; in the final two lines of the stanza, the pronoun returns three times. Technically, then, both the A and the B are there with the pronoun intact, while the A is also present without it, and in the center of the stanza. Interestingly, this technique emphasizes the singer as speaker, a person with an identity and lie in the frame of the stanza, while in the core that self disappears. The stanza, then, becomes a visual and verbal representation of the affirmation and nullification that do battle in the lives of African Americans, and in their blues, the expressive individual and his creation always just a bit stronger than the power to eradicate his life and art.

How can this be possible when the last two lines express the desire to have died? To express the desire to have died is to indicate that the death did not occur: to sing about death, or suicide, is not the same as death or suicide. It is the intensifier of the moment, not the act itself. If he now wishes he had died, he could do something about that, but he does not act in a destructive way—he acts in a creative way. The resonance of his downheartedness with the speaker is clear: the rest of the poem consists of the speaker's description of an approaching void, with the planets fading into darkness, and the singer becoming metaphorically either like an inanimate object—a rock—or a corpse. But being *like* something is not the same as *being* something, the same as wishing something is not the same as doing something. The man is not dead, either in his own lyrics or in the poem the speaker has generated. In the speaker's mind, the weary blues may echo "through his head," but his croon and his tune outlasted the night, just as they have outlasted the 1920s in the poem. While the speaker suggests visions of insensibility and death, the hard and cold end that comes at the termination of the poem, the song and spirit survives, not rose colored or candy coated. There is a deep connection to weariness and death in the man, but it is only sleep, rest, a time to put his troubles on the shelf before he awakens to create again. There is, perhaps, another connection to the blues tradition in the "slept like a rock" line. The famous W. C. Handy composition "St. Louis Blues" (1914) contains the line "my man's got a heart like a rock cast in the sea," the simile the same though the deadliness is different. The image of Handy is more vivid and active, using the symbolism of heart, sea, and the action of throwing to invigorate the scene, but Hughes's usage, while perhaps clichéd, is a solid reminder of how far the man must travel in order to rest from the blues compositions he creates and sings.

"The Weary Blues" offers us a nuanced and complicated musical mixture of hard times and transcendence, life and art. The two (or four) are not isolated, as, though the two never directly communicate, the speaker and performer are not isolated, but spiritually conjoined—as is Hughes, the poet whose "Weary Blues" encompasses all and echoes through our heads as well. While Wallace Thurman wrote in "Negro Poets and Their Poetry" (1928) that too many of Hughes's twelve-bar blues poems such as "Bad Man" and "Suicide" were "modish and ephemeral" (214), he felt that "The Weary Blues" "justifies his experiment" (215) with the blues. Indeed, as a transformation of eight- and twelve-bar rural blues forms into a vaudeville structure that retains the feel and elements of the structure of the more remote blues tradition, and thus demonstrates how the blues was being transformed not only commercially, but artistically, it is an evocative masterpiece.

In these works, Hughes demonstrates a nascent interest in drawing upon elements of his contemporary urban experiences with the transformed folk products of the Great Migration. Those products are not only the songs, which at times receive a cold urban makeover to express the street corner and night club ethos, but the people, many of whom seem to wither in the metamorphosed milieu. So while linguistic and structural elements are apparent in a few of the poems, the vernacular voice and persevering attitude of other poems published previous to his first volume, such as "Mother to Son," the folk ethos rooted in such poems as "Aunt Sue's Stories," and the admiration of black beauty in "When Sue wears Red" all seem, especially once they were interspersed among the linguistic and structural markers of the aforementioned poems in Hughes's first volume, poignant or wistful reminders of the spirit of the blues. Is this a product of preconceptions about the poetry because Hughes is black, and therefore associated with the genre? Perhaps. But once again, Hughes's ability to use skillfully vernacular language, to capture the idioms and symbols of the tradition, to present varied personae in blue moods, to reflect near resignation rescued by shit, grit, and mother-wit, these capabilities seem to validate the feeling that, in his poetry, the blues is so frequently ready to grab his characters around midnight, and not turn them loose 'til day, and *we* feel it.

Because I have spent an extensive amount of time elsewhere discussing Hughes and the blues, my intention is to focus on a couple of blues poems at the beginning, and then speak generally about Hughes's two volumes from the 1920s. In these volumes Hughes not only included individual poems, but also an ethos and connections that fit the blues, as well as spirituals and gospel music, and laughter, tears, anger, and contentment, into daily life. They are in conversation, in many different voices, because people and ideas do correspond with each other, and aggregate that variety into a kind of unity that expresses an ethos, a folk-ethos transplanted to overcrowded urban tenements. Hughes's first published volume, *The Weary Blues* (1926), the first section of which was titled "The Weary Blues," contained in total sixty-eight poems. Of those poems, fourteen out of fifteen poems in the first section referred to or utilized jazz-related materials. Only three, "The Weary Blues" (1:1), "To Midnight Nan at Leroy's" (1:7), and "Blues Fantasy" (1:14) referred specifically to the blues. The others in section one (except for "Prostitute") either mentioned jazz or reflected some aspect of what we might call "blues feeling"—isolation, loss, loneliness, ennui, or resoluteness in the face of adversity, including "Young Singer" (1:5), "Cabaret" (1:6), "To a Little Lover-lass, Dead" (1:8), "Song for a Banjo Dance" (1:13), and "Lenox Avenue: Midnight" (1:15). In other sections jazz is mentioned ("Harlem Night Song" 4:2) or features those blues feelings: "Troubled Woman" (6:2) and "Suicide's Note" (6:3). Only "The Weary Blues," "Song for a Banjo Dance," and "Blues Fantasy" make use of the structural stanzaic elements of the blues.

These poems are contained primarily in the first section of Hughes's first book, both entitled "The Weary Blues," giving primacy to African American blues voices. That is important because Hughes is acknowledging the presence of blues voices, even as he invokes a blues ethos. In this section are elevated voices ("Jazzonia"); vernacular voices ("Negro Dancers"); foreign language voices ("Young Singer"); singing voices ("To Midnight Nan at Leroy's"); "hot" cabaret voices ("Harlem Night Club"); wistful, ironic voices ("Young Prostitute"); bitter voices ("Lenox Avenue: Midnight"); authoritative voices ("Proem"); the shibboleths of respectability voices ("To Midnight Nan at Leroy's"); the male voices ("Song for a Banjo Dance"); and female ("Blues Fantasy"). All of the poems reflect blues and jazz milieux, voices, and feelings—with blues and jazz voices leading the varied way. These elements are woven into subjects in a black tapestry encompassing life (numbers list section and poem number within section):

* romantic love ("Harlem Night Song" [3:2]) and tawdry assignations ("To a Little Lover-lass, Dead" [1:7], "Young Prostitute" [1:11]);
* a variety of employments, all treated with dignity ("Mexican Market Woman" [6:7], "Young Singer" [1:5], "Young Sailor" [5:7]);
* beautiful art ("The Weary Blues" [1:1], "Aunt Sue's Stories" [3:6]) and shameful artifice ("Port Town" [5:4]);
* racial pride ("Nude Young Dancer" [1:10], "The Negro Speaks of Rivers" [3:1], "Proem" ["Negro"] [prologue]) and racial plague ("The South" [3:4], "Cross" [3:2]);
* night clubs ("Jazzonia" [1:2], "Cabaret" [1:6], "Negro Dancers" [1:3], "To Midnight Nan at Leroy's" [1:7]) and sanctuaries ("Dream Variations" [2:1], "Poem" [3:7]);

* dreams ("The Dream Keeper" [6:10], "Dream Variations" [2:1]) and nightmares ("Afraid" [7:3]);
* exploitation ("Lament for Dark Peoples" [7:2]) and redemption ("Joy" [2:6]);
* African heritage ("Jazzonia" [1:2], "Danse Africaine" [7:7], "Proem" ["Negro"] [prologue], "The Negro Speaks of Rivers" [3:1]);
* laughing ("Blues Fantasy" [1:14]), and laughing and crying ("The Jester" [3:3]);
* seascape ("Seascape" [5:8], "Sea Charm" [5:10], "Death of an Old Seaman" [5:11], "Young Sailor" [5:7]) and land ("Young Prostitute" [1:11], "Our Land" [7:1]);
* and identity ("I Too" [epilogue]) and oblivion ("Suicide's Note" [6:3], "Troubled Woman" [6:2]).

While much of the explicitly blues and jazz material is contained in the opening section, that section introduces themes that recur throughout the volume. This indicates a primacy for the blues and jazz spirit, and a suggestion that in fact the blues treats a range of subject matter. It is not merely there for titillation or sexual innuendo, as the pop songwriters sometimes had it, though that is of course part of life. This interaction among the sections demonstrates how the blues are wide ranging in subject matter and distinctive in style—certainly worthy of their status as poetry as Hughes expresses them. By making water, land, darkness, and sun prominent in section titles and poems, Hughes makes the material archetypal and elemental, though still with a local habitation and a name. As with Milhaud's *La Création du Monde* (1923), Hughes places blues and jazz at the beginning, leading us right down to the final "Mother to Son," "Poem" and "Epilogue," which, in their styles and language, exfoliate from the directness, ecstatic energy, overwhelming hardship, perseverance, and wistful reflections of the blues.

Hughes experiments with these elements as a way of demonstrating how adaptive and malleable the blues tradition is, how much it makes use of call-and-response elements inherited from African and previous African American music, how important the audience response is to the performance and ambience, and how the movement from hurt to hope, from static immobility to movement and transcendence in his works mirrors a blues aesthetic and tells a well-rounded and complete story. These experimental uses of the blues tradition in the poetry, revolutionary in their day, nonetheless draw on elements already in the blues tradition for their genesis, representing not so much a violation of traditional elements but an extension of them into the literary terrain. With Hughes especially we feel the sadness and hope, the dejectedness and pride, the poverty and richness of the blues tradition.

One other poem that falls under the banner of reflecting the "blues feeling" is "Suicide's Note." Looked at through the lens of the blues tradition, it can help provide a pathway into Hughes's more subtle employments of that tradition. A brief three-line, thirteen-syllable poem that does not fit any conventional blues stanza pattern, it is, nonetheless, expressive of a common theme in the blues.

> The calm,
> Cool face of the river
> Asked me for a kiss. (*Complete Poems* 55)

With its haiku-like brevity, it expresses a sentiment like that expressed in Peg Leg Howell's 1928 recording of "Rock and Gravel Blues":

> Honey, let's go to the
> River and sit down.
> Honey, let's go to the
> River and sit down.
> If the blues overtake us
> Jump overboard and drown.

Blind Lemon Jefferson's "Match Box Blues," recorded in 1927, deals with the issue as well:

> I'm goin down to the river
> I'm gonna walk down by the sea.
> I'm goin down to the river
> Walk down by the sea.
> I got those tadpoles and minnows
> Arguin over me.

Hughes seeks to distill that sentiment here, to squeeze it calmly and deliberately, and with a haiku-like pithiness, into thirteen syllables that evoke the emotional and physical attraction of the river for someone seeking to escape weariness. The archetypal symbol of the river, ancient, natural, mutable, and eternal, a source of life and avenue of escape that would have resonated with slaves escaping to the "Promised Land," to use biblical typology, are all present here in the blues lyric and Hughes poem. The sentiment of going to the edge of the riverbank for escape and comfort is one so strong in the blues tradition that we can still find it occurring in Percy Mayfield's 1952 recording of "The River's Invitation":

I spoke to the river
And the river spoke back to me.
It said, "You look so lonely,
You look full of misery.
And if you can't find your baby,
Come and make your home with me."

While Hughes's first book publication does not overwhelmingly feature formal elements of the blues tradition, it does evidence prominently in the title, a section heading, and in several poems the importance of African American vernacular music and the social and political tradition from which it came, along with other blues-influenced or blues-inflected poetry. This blues current in the volume would become a torrent in Hughes's next volume, signaling Hughes's complete immersion in the materials of rural folk culture wrenched into a tough and cynical urban setting.

However, in the late 1920s, while Sterling Brown was marshalling into print his first endeavors (Zora Neale Hurston had published a variety of pieces in such locations as *Stylus*, *Opportunity*, *Messenger*, and *Negro World* before Hughes's first book publication), Hughes was publishing a two-page collaboration in *Opportunity* magazine between himself and artist Aaron Douglas, both of whom spent time among white and black artists in Paris. Hughes contributed six blues poems, and Douglas five illustrations, each complementing the other and demonstrating how the two genres "can suggest the complicated experiences of African Americans" (Carroll 116). Like a blues performance, the works of both have a rhythm, vibrancy, and wonderfully interactive cross-genre dynamic—aural and visual. The collaboration is a charted, organized jam session, clearly arranged, but with the immediacy of two musicians swapping call-and-response licks in a virtuoso display of sight, sound, and style. That is, like improvisations, they have the energy and feel of spontaneity, while they are clearly based on the long foreground of mastery of form and subject matter, along with the joy of bandmates feeding off of flying high together. Douglas's bold, expressionistic work, with its sharp angles, spatial asymmetry and disproportion, extravisual aural elements, and powerful geometric presences reflect the audacious gutsiness of the blues, with its offbeat (but decidedly *on*beat and *up*beat) syncopation, palpable soul and energy, and colossal presence.

Next up was his second volume of poetry, the controversially titled *Fine Clothes to the Jew*, in 1927. Hughes's reference to the stereotypical store-owner "Jew" in the title of his second volume and the poem "Hard Luck," which had been published in Harriet Monroe's *Poetry* in 1926, provoked some disapproval and complaint, even with fashionable anti-Semitism making the rounds in American society of the time. Hughes *had* to have known that there would be some controversy, and perhaps even courted it with this usage, showing artistic independence by flaunting what some folks felt was a prominent dissonant note in his literary spotlight. Of course, there were many so-called dissonant—dissident—notes in the volume, but that was, after all, the low-down folks, that was the blues, and they were Hughes's emperor-has-no-clothes, the-men-don't-like-me-'cause-I-speaks-my-mind-but-the-women-all-love-me-'cause-I-takes-my-time avatars of honesty. Interestingly, Hurston wrote a letter to Hughes in 1928 telling him how his poem "Hard Luck" had entered into a skin game in a turpentine camp (Kaplan 121–22).

Reference to Jews are not exactly rampant in the recorded country or vaudeville blues of the time, a single stanza in which the singer states "I'm gonna tell you, baby like the [Chinaman/Dago/Gypsy] told the Jew" being the most prominent mention, sung with the Chinaman variation by Trixie Smith in "Sorrowful Blues" (1924). In "Tight Haired Mama Blues" (1931), referencing a vernacular name for short hair (Calt 247), Charley Jordan sang, "Baby, now, you got good hair, but you bought this from the Jew," referring to the desire to have what was called "good hair" in line with white standards of beauty, which required black women to buy wigs. But in neither instance is the reference overtly critical of Jews, as Hughes is with his stinginess stereotype in the individual poem. Portrayals of Jews may have been more common in the folk tradition, but Hughes seems to be interested in dealing with the issue of non-black shopkeepers as affecting the black community in a negative way. Importantly, the gender of the speaker is indeterminate, but the speaker is not Hughes, but rather one voice in a community of voices. None of the other voices express this sentiment, though they may respond to it personally in their community, so it represents one more person, idea, or feeling in an African American world that is artistically portrayed, warts and all, openly and honestly, dicty audience be damned, Jewish audience understand. Hughes is walking a social, political, "racial," artistic line here, pushing on the boundaries, trickster fashion, but stressing a blues angle of directness and honesty in the face of artistic disingenuousness. If "hard luck" is a blues euphemism for racism and discrimination, then the poem feeds from the practice and flows back into it, perhaps, which may well be Hughes's point.

Fine Clothes to the Jew was a landmark experimental volume in the history of American literature. Imbued with a jazz and blues form and spirit that cuts a broader and deeper swath through the aesthetic terrain than any African American vernacular music-influenced work that came before it, the volume marked out a visionary milieu and horizon for hot music-rooted poetry attained by no one previously, and by few who came after him. This is no mere *post hoc, ergo prompter hoc* occurrence. Out of a total of fifty-seven poems, at least over half either mention or make use of the blues in style and subject matter, including the selections and sections that open and close the volume. Coming out only a year after *The Weary Blues*, the poems were written contemporaneously with those of the earlier volume. The advance was in the sheer number of blues poems in form, subject matter, and spirit, an unflinching, unashamed, numerical, political, and aesthetic rebuke to stereotypes about lower-class African Americans, as well as hot music performers and lovers. Not that "lower-class" existence was devoid of vice, but that the people were not totally defined by that vice, nor was their openness to sexuality and pleasures of the body necessarily so bad. It was almost as if Hughes were saying, "all right, before we get mired any further in this racial mess, let's jam"—much as his speaker Jesse B. Semple would *still* have to do later in "Jazz, Jive, and Jam." Hughes himself commented later in *The Big Sea* (1940) that *Fine Clothes to the Jew* "was a better book than [his] first, because it was more impersonal, more about other people than myself, and because it made use of the Negro folk-song forms and included poems about work and the problems of finding work, that are always so pressing with the Negro people" (263). Here African modalities and African American experience and artistry transmute Anglo-American form into America's bubbling orature stew.

The poems are frank and explicit for the times, confronting contemporary middle-class sensibilities and social markers in a variety of ways. Hughes, of course, had written of the admirable openness and unrestrained temperaments of the "low-down folks" in his essay "The Negro Artist and the Racial Mountain" in *The Nation* in 1926. Here he seemed intent on exploring the nooks and crannies and crux and fannies of their loves and lives through the blues, unafraid to explore offensive material that might bother a number of his Jewish friends—though not Joel and Amy Spingarn (Rampersad, *Life* I: 140)—perhaps in the same mode as his friend Carl Van Vechten, to whom Hughes dedicated the volume, had done in his novel *Nigger Heaven* from the year before. Suicide, violence, superstition, gambling, prostitution, promiscuity, alcoholism, social stratification by skin color—all of these subjects are addressed in the volume, at a time when the best-foot-forward black middle-class strivers would rather have projected more positive images of African Americans as a means of achieving racial progress. While white critics frequently praised the volume, there was a blast of hot and angry air from some black critics calling Hughes a "sewer dweller" and the "poet low-rate of Harlem." But neither does Hughes focus on only one location in the poems. Though the landscape is predominantly the northern American city, there are poems placed in the

South, and even in Paris, that help provide a broader context for the portrait that Hughes paints of struggling lower-class African Americans who, he said, "are the people I know best" (Rampersad, *Life* I: 140).

Interestingly, Hughes makes use of a variety of blues structures in the volume, from the most common twelve-bar blues stanza (in twelve poems), to eight-bar stanzas (in seven poems), blues ballad stanzas (one poem), and more sophisticated vaudeville-type blues stanzas (in two poems). Furthermore, fifteen of these poems feature female speakers, six feature males, and nine are indeterminate. It is as if Hughes is trying to paint a picture of diversity both in terms of subject matter and form, even as he focuses on only one segment, and a frequently most stereotyped one at that, of the black community. The predominance of women's voices in the volume bespeak Hughes's lifelong interest in the lives of women, perhaps a legacy of the important women in his life, especially his grandmother Mary Langston, the "Aunt Sue" of "Aunt Sue's Stories." Certainly the "double whammy" of race and gender discrimination would interest Hughes, a sympathetic male whose admiration for women and their storytelling abilities, as evidenced by "Aunt Sue's Stories," "When Sue Wears Red," and "Mother to Son" from *The Weary Blues*, while not ignoring his male poetic forebears, was intellect driven and heartfelt. Additionally, a number of the poems of the volume were written as early as 1923, when the blues recording industry for African Americans included only women, and the vaudeville blues firmly held sway from 1923–1926 as male blue singers such as Ed Andrews, Papa Charlie Jackson, Lonnie Johnson, and Blind Lemon Jefferson began to record. As such, though Hughes had clearly seen male blues singers in his childhood, the bulk of the blues singers he encountered in Harlem and Chicago, and in Montmartre, were females as loquacious, bodacious, and hellacious at times as they are deceived, bereaved, and grieved at others. They, too, are America—diverse, and "somewhat" free.

"Hey!" The opening poem of the opening "Blues" section of *Fine Clothes to the Jew* is a vernacular volley. Hughes begins with two lines that he will repeat in an AAB blues stanza pattern:

> Sun's a settin',
> This is what I'm gonna sing. (*Complete Poems* 112)

Hughes's second collection is a revolutionary, attention-grabbing volume, with an annunciation as memorable and vigorous in its way as the opening notes of Beethoven's Fifth Symphony, though quite different. The single word is more immediate and direct that Beethoven's, Beethoven's more formal notes giving way to this informal gut forceful attention grabber, an exclamation that says listen, pay attention, I am here, I have a voice. It is not the voice or language that the poet uses in his daily life—Hughes was more meticulous about formal pronunciation—but it is another person speaking through Hughes, part of Hughes's vast storehouse of materials that make up his heritage, African American and otherwise. However, the *reason* for this reveille is not clear. "Hey" is a common enough word, used for a variety of purposes. For example, here the poet could be greeting in an informal manner, warning about an impending mishap, or objecting to being pushed. It serves, in fact, as a greeting—to the volume and to the audiences unfamiliar with the "neighborhood" or seeing that neighborhood depicted sympathetically—even with warts and all—in a book. Dixon, Godrich, and Rye list seventeen recordings beginning with the word "Hey" between 1924 and 1942, the first Rosa Henderson's "Hey Hey and He He, I'm Charleston Crazy" (1924), four of them followed by exclamation points (1151)! Of course it occurred frequently elsewhere in blues performance, as it did, admittedly, in the daily lives of many people. Carl Van Vechten himself even used it repeatedly in his 1926 novel *Nigger Heaven* (10, 13, 157, 242, 248).

"Hey!" may be a greeting, but it is a warning, too. The poet is also saying "here comes that unfamiliar world, in an unfamiliar setting, so pay attention and try to overcome a feeling of strangeness or disorientation—it belongs here, though it has not quite been here before in this way." It becomes not only an immediate but also a cultural warning. And of course, the word might well be objecting to racism, poverty, distrust, and aesthetic and artistic hegemony that forces the man "furthest down." The spirit says, "Hey! We're out of chattel slavery, up from the South, back from the war, and through keeping quiet. It's time!"

And what time is it? In the poem, the sun is setting at the end of day, a traditional symbol for the end of an important event or epoch or action. It might be a momentous time for great change, as were Hughes's times, with the tremendous violence and upheaval of war, rural to urban migration, industrialization, gender advancement, and aesthetic experimentation of the 1920s forcing the nineteenth-century capitulation to the arrival of the modernist twentieth. Many people would suggest that this is a strange place for a volume of poetry to begin, at an ending. It is neither the most common place for a blues song to begin, the phrase "woke up this morning" being endemic to the blues and its unpacking of subsequent experience. But, first of all, Hughes did not write "The sun is setting." He wrote "Sun's a settin,'" and there is a vernacular world of difference in that phrase. First and foremost, it is an alliterative line. Using only three words, two of them beginning with the consonant with another wedged between them, Hughes has brought sound to the support of circumstance. As with the exclamatory tag "Hey!" the alliteration stresses the significance of the elemental (solar) importance of this genesis, along with what the blues symbolizes or may come to symbolize in this new setting of so-called high-culture poetry. The alliterative voice here is a harbinger of change, a hissing out with the old and salute to the newness emerging from the dark.

This short line, which is repeated exactly in line three of Hughes's rendering of the twelve-bar AAB pattern, reinforces the seemingly paradoxical notion of creation at sunset, combining ending and beginning. This effect continues as the poem progresses to the second line, which expands the visual space of that line to twice as long as the first line, though within the blues performance it fills approximately the same aural space, reinforcing a sense of retraction for the sunset and expansion for the action of singing to be initiated by the speaker—what he is going to (gonna) do, a poetic equivalent to a great migration. The line is also clearly not one that initiates a standard European metrical pattern, especially when the second line is much longer and necessarily metrically different. Part of this metrical difference is produced by the vernacular language in line one: the first apostrophe in "Sun's a settin'" contracts out a syllable, which is then picked back up through the insertion of an unnecessary syllable grafted onto the beginning of the third word. By reworking the syllabic emphasis, Hughes uses the "a" to produce a rushed, offbeat, even syncopated feel to the end of that first line—U/U—an artistic correlative of the rapid setting of the sun on the worn out sociopolitical and aesthetic world of the twentieth century. However we read the line, "settin'" having two syllables or "a settin'" having three, certainly the sun is getting gone.

The second line of the poem, in response to the ending of the first line, rushes on through in a burst of ambition itself: /UUU/U/, an emphatic accent followed by three rushing unaccented syllables, abrupting into an iamb, and a period. The resulting end-stopped couplet implies that his song is going to be about sunset, an end. It is an action, but contained within the confines of the opening end-stopped couplet. He will create a song of setting sun, of ending. However, as is standard in this blues form that he is employing, he proceeds to repeat those two lines in *almost* exactly the same fashion. Almost. Here, rather than construct an end-stopped couplet in the manner of lines one and two, at the end of line four, Hughes places a colon. Rather than looking backward from a period, the line projects forward to a future, achieving a different movement and direction from the colon at the crossroads. In a sense, this is how the repeat in the blues stanza functions: the second line cleaves to the language of the first, and then moves forward to trigger some new sentiment or language that will move the song forward. Hughes is negotiating the aural space of the oral tradition and the visual space of the written, blending them almost imperceptibly through the clash between period and colon. Now, what is gonna be his song is about what the blues—the feeling, the style, the artistic aesthetic, the social revolution—is gonna bring:

> I feel de blues a comin',
> Wonder what de blues'll bring? (*Complete Poems* 112)

What he is going to sing about remains to be seen in the volume ahead, but clearly from our vantage point the overwhelming number of blues songs, style, and subject matter predict what has in fact occurred: the twentieth century, dubbed by cultural and political chauvinists the American century, might very well be baptized the blues century.

As Hughes knew, the blues expressed a great deal about pain, hardship, and suffering, before and beyond. At this juncture the poet is vowing not only to remember and continue to confront those feelings, but to harness the power of the blues to express, transform, and revolutionize through a liberating style that produces relief, empathy, and transcendence through connection to the ancestors and stylization in performance. It is why the speaker expresses himself in the blues genre: the message is not to be delivered without the proper mode. The blues, as the speaker feels it, is a tradition, a mode, a feeling, a means and an end. Whatever the blues bring, he, and the world, must respond to the call of the blues.

A seemingly simple six-line poem actually announces the beginning of a complex and nuanced poetic volume. The volume is revolutionary in its use of black vernacular English, its reversal of traditional Western symbolism, its metrical irregularity, even formal metrical indifference—syncopating effects, and its mixing of materials from the black oral and Western written traditions. It trumpets the power of African American art that finds its birth, like Milhaud's creation of the world, in a darkness that from rupture produced synergy out of acculturation, the action of which springs in part from Hughes's poem.

Fine Clothes to the Jew employs poems with relation to hot music in every section, even, arguably, the "Glory! Hallelujah!" section, the double titular exclamation points pointing toward the final poem of the volume. Poverty, suicide, meanness, social stratification by skin color, the North and the South, death, the working people, relations between lovers, mistreatment, superstition, disgrace, youthful difficulties, violence—these are the subjects of the blues, and of Hughes's blues poems. Hughes deals with some of these issues in a number of poems, such as social stratification by skin color, as in "Misery," "Gypsy Man," "Evil Woman," "Black Gal," and "Gal's Cry for a Dying Lover." The singer's reference to a "blue-gummed" mate in "Evil Woman," which means an African American who is extremely dark due to little admixture of white blood (Townley 37), has its counterpart in the "Blue Gum Blues" (1923) of Sara Martin. The notion of darker-skinned African Americans as being more earthy, more "low-down," less able to have their choice of lighter-skinned African American mates occurs here, as it does in the blues tradition. Ida Cox's "Southern Woman's Blues" (1925), in which she discusses color and origin ("no northern black or brown"); Bo Weavil Jackson's "Some Scream High Yellow" (1926), in which he discusses how out on the street the "black won't turn you down;" Barbecue Bob's "Brown Skin Gal" (1927); and Bull City Red's "Black Woman and Poison Blues" (1935), along with the songs of Alice Moore, who recorded four songs with "black" and "evil" in the titles out of a total of thirty-six released sides (eighteen 78 RPM records), are part of a fairly prominent number of blues that treat the issues.

Hughes seems to conceive of the volume as organic as opposed to a set of discrete units. In particular, a number of his blues poems pair up well, in subject matter, style, and layout (on facing pages) in the text: for example, "Hard Luck" and "Misery" couple hardships and the ability of songs to alleviate them. Note that "Hard Luck" contains a variant of the "mule kickin in my stall" lyric—here, the speaker doesn't even have a stall, which has both habitation and sexual implications!

> I'm so low-down I
> Ain't even got a stall. (*Complete Poems* 82)

"Suicide" features a woman wondering whether she should kill herself or her man, followed by "Bad Man," a poem where a man exults in beating "his" women. "Gypsy Man" is in the voice of a lonely female, followed by the lonely male voice of "Po' Boy Blues," which plays on the blues lyric that showed up in Blind Joe Reynolds's "Outside Woman Blues" (1930)—"When you lose your money, please God don't lose your mind." In "Po' Boy Blues" the North is cold, followed by the homesickness" for the South in "Homesick Blues." In "Cora," the woman laments being mistreated by men, followed by a "Workin' Man" who laments mistreatment at the hands of his woman. "Evil Woman" leads to "A Ruined Gal," "Minnie Sings Her Blues" and "Dressed Up" describe a couple and a single person on their way out for a night on the town, and in "Gal's Cry for a Dying Lover" a female voice lamenting her lover's death in language related to Ma Rainey's "Black Cat Hoot Owl Blues" (1928) passes on to a woman reflecting on the death of her girlfriend as it evokes thoughts of her own mortality. Hughes puts the poems in dialogue, sometimes playing up similarities, sometimes differences, creating a blues dialectic that champions voice, exchange, and unity between his opening and closing poems, while still accepting and containing the seemingly paradoxical blending of the meanings of the blues.

Bookending the volume is another poem that takes the AAB, twelve-bar blues form. If Hughes made hay with the opening poem, he made some new moan hey in the body, and he made it doubly effective at the end. "Hey! Hey!" recommences what Hughes had started over fifteen poems earlier by returning to his attention-grabbing exclamation, letting it ride one more time, and, having found out what the blues brought, asserts the primacy of the blues for both the opening question and closing assertion. This time, at the close of the volume, we get, as in the end of Jean Toomer's *Cane*, a rising sun, a harbinger of new beginnings (because we frequently ignore that it is the end of something as well). In Toomer's case, his first sketch also begins with a setting sun—"Her skin is like dusk on the eastern horizon," with Toomer refocusing our perspective, cubist fashion, from the fantastic and fiery display on the western horizon to the rich, deep, darkness at dusk. What Spengler described as the heroic but doomed Faustian Western civilization in decline informs Toomer's quest for unity and wholeness, as it does Hughes's attempt in this volume to take the tragic, isolated figure and reconnect to the community through polyvocal portrayals of the community at the Harlem Renaissance crossroads. "Hey!" is the call, "Hey! Hey!" the response—no need to change it, it has done the job of the volume. Redouble it. Problem and solution; trouble and deliverance. The "gonna sing" of "Hey!" becomes the "ma song" of "Hey! Hey!" The notion of putting the blues behind is where we arrive.

In *The Weary Blues*, the poem "Blues Fantasy" says it: "Hey! Hey! / That's what the / Blues singers say" (*Collected* 91). When that poem ends after hardships and music, the singer shouts again, "Hey! Hey!" and the sister rides off on the railroad to a new place. Here Hughes is joining the blues tradition by echoing one of his own blues in another poem of his, in the loose, associational style of folk-blues lyrics, but with a strong literary purpose. His speakers know the blues, from closet to clothesline, and they have shared with Hughes.

The rising sun figures in many blues lyrics from the era, such as Barefoot Bill's "Mean Conductor Blues" (1927):

> I stand here lookin up at the risin sun
> Some train don't run, why be some walkin done.

An expression of restlessness, mobility, and determination, the lyrics project a general feeling of ennui and desperate wanderlust that finds more particular origins in Sam Collins's unissued (at the time) "My Road is Rough and Rocky" (1931), clearly a lyric that could trace its lineage to slavery times:

> I got up this morning, looked at the risin sun
> Can't nobody run me like them bloodhounds done.

A remarkable recording that includes five stanzas about the pursuit by bloodhounds and human trackers, this initiatory stanza of the sequence connects his perception of the rising sun with his frantic flight from these agents of bondage and captivity. Hughes's poem takes the readers from the sunset of apprehension and anticipation to a sunrise of assertion and self-definition.

Of course, the phrase "all night long" is ubiquitous in the blues, as in the "stayed out all night long" of Barbecue Bob's "Crooked Woman Blues" (1927) and Lonnie Johnson's "the nightmare ride me all night long" in "Blue Ghost Blues" (1927), both preceded by Ma Rainey's recording of Guy Suddoth's "Those All Night Long Blues" (1923). It also occurred in country music from the era, from Frank Hutchison's "All Night Long" (1927) to Richard D. Burnett's 1927 "All Night Long Blues" to Hank Penny's "All Night and All Day Long" (1939) (Russell 1015). The phrase is sometimes a reference to sheer determination, relentless carousing, sometimes sexual stamina, sometimes to persistent worry or sadness—sometimes all of the above. When Hughes's speaker says he has "been blue all night long," especially forceful from the alliterative repetition of the "b" consonant in the previous line, the conversion from the conditional "could be" to "been" indicates a determination to leave the negative feeling of the blues behind, though he retains the blues in supportive spirit, form, language, and subject matter to help him do that. "All night long," of course, is usually a hyperbolic intensifier, and here it seems to be like a journey from the dark night of the soul to a union with God, here from the dark night of the soul of enslavement to community through the agency of song. "Long" also means to yearn, and adds additional weight to the emotional force of the phrase, as does a further meaning of "long," extended duration. Hughes leaves us to contemplate the meanings of the final couplet and the nuances of its words at the break of day he has created in his volume.

III

The response to Langston Hughes's work was divided in the 1920s. Though today he is seen by the predominance of critics as the major poet of the New Negro Renaissance and a revolutionary champion of African American culture, in the 1920s he often came in second (or lower) place, especially among Old Guard Renaissance figures and middle-class blacks—who had the money to buy his books—to another poet whose stylistic differences and sanctioned credentials made him the poster poet for uplift. Hughes used him as a model of the misguided wannabe-white poet in "The Negro Artist and the Racial Mountain" a couple of years after their earlier friendship had ended, perhaps the victim of the breaking of homosexual silence between the two—or three, if you count Alain Locke in the mix (Rampersad 1: 98). Countee Cullen had the social framework, impressive education, and aesthetic purview to surpass the sailor-turned-busboy poet, even if Hughes's education and experiences were ultimately impressive as well. Although Cullen's childhood past was mysteriously shrouded, his acting (though never adoptive) parents were Frederick Cullen, pastor of the well-attended Salem Methodist Episcopal Church and his wife Carolyn, highly respected in the Harlem community and important enough to garner Cullen a society-sized and publicized (but ultimately unsuccessful) wedding to W. E. B. Du Bois's daughter, Yolande, in 1928. By that time Cullen was quite a catch in may people's eyes: impressively educated at DeWitt Clinton High School, Phi Beta Kappa at NYU, and with a master's degree in English and French from Harvard (1925–1927), he had published in Mencken's *American Mercury* and Harriet Monroe's *Poetry*, among many other magazines, won a host of prizes, published three volumes of refined and finely crafted poetry, won a Guggenheim Fellowship, and engaged in may other social and literary activities.

During the time, some among the literati in Harlem felt that art would help establish the culture, intelligence, and worthiness of African Americans to take their places alongside their white counterparts. The fact that Cullen idolized John Keats and other British Romantic poets pleased a constituency that desired proof of black competency at traditional Western and European poetic forms and genres to help make inroads into white American society. Cullen certainly dealt explicitly in a variety of his poems with race, but most often his elegant and elevated style was remote from the lives of the masses, though he could write with an impressive monosyllabic and bisyllabic facility that was quite direct. In a 1942 interview with James Baldwin, Cullen indicated his preferred audience: his forthcoming book would be "one of [his] few attempts to get at the masses" (Early 605). However, Hughes's lack of multisyllabic elaboration and cultivated, polished sophistication and circumlocution was not the result of impaired education or insight on his part: he chose it. To speak to the masses, and through the masses, directly, was his goal. To Hurston, as she stated in a 1928 letter to Hughes, Cullen was "Nice, safe, middle-class" (Kaplan 116).

The appearance, then, among his poems of a poem entitled "Colored Blues Singer" (Cullen *My Soul's High Song* 144) has surprised some, particularly in light of his own comments about some of Hughes's vernacular blues poetry:

> If I have the least powers of prediction, the first section of the book, *The Weary Blues*, will be the most admired, even if less from intrinsic poetic worth than because of its dissociation from the traditionally poetic. Never having been one to think all subjects and forms proper for poetic consideration, I regard these jazz poems as interlopers in the company of the truly beautiful poems in other sections of the book. They move along with the frenzy and electric heat of a Methodist or Baptist revival meeting, and affect me much in the same manner. The revival meeting excites me, cooling and flushing me with alternate chills and fevers of emotion; so do these poems. But when the storm is over, I wonder if the quiet way of communing is not more spiritual for the God-seeking heart; and in the light of reflection I wonder if jazz poems really belong to that dignified company, that select and austere circle of high literary reflection that we call poetry. (*Opportunity* February 1926)

More than lamenting what he feels will be a trendy and paternalistic praising of jazz energy, Cullen questions the validity of the poems themselves within the confines of the traditional high-low art dichotomy, finding the poems primitive (frenzied) and artificial (electric light) rather than properly and meticulously maintained and cultivated. Whereas Whitman described Poe's work as "brilliant and dazzling, but with no heat" (*Specimen Days* 231), Cullen criticizes Hughes as being dazzling and *with* heat! Perhaps in his unadopted state, and with the stigma of homosexuality motivating him to go through with a sham marriage to Yolande, Cullen could not stand the heat from a man to whom he was attracted.

Published in *Copper Sun* (1927), later in the same year as *Fine Clothes to the Jew*, it is interesting to see this lone "blues" poem in Cullen's volume as the counterpart to the flood of them in Hughes's book, though it is likely Cullen's was at press already when Hughes's was released. Still, coming on the heels of *The Weary Blues* and Cullen's criticism of jazz poems, it might be considered a stylistic rejoinder on the subject matter, Cullen's "if you are going to write about the blues singer, do it with class, elevation, sophistication, and restraint—one is enough."

Cullen measures his phenotypical blues singer against famed beautiful operatic soprano prima donna Maria Jeritza, and the lively subject matter of the blues singer against the celebrated notated staffs of operatic über-composer

Giuseppe Verdi. Perhaps Cullen was thinking of Verdi's breakthrough *Va, pensiero* from *Nabucco*, also known as the *Chorus of the Hebrew Slaves* (1843), in which thought flies on golden wings and seers play harps of gold to inspire crude lamentations regarding the lost homeland, written following the recent death of Verdi's wife and children. Of course, the applicability of biblical typology of the Babylonian exile to the conditions of African Americans makes a strong connection as well. Certainly Jeritza was on the cultured radar of the New Negro intelligentsia: Hughes mentioned wanting to see her in a 1923 letter to Locke (Rampersad I: 67–68).

Labeling the blues singer here as "colored" has particular significance, since the racial signifier suggests that there are other than colored blues singers at the time, which, indeed, there were, pop-blues singers Sophie Tucker and Marion Harris among them. As in Hughes's "The Weary Blues," the singer is assigned no name, so the adjective bears an even greater importance as the primary descriptor and important characteristic of the singer. As with the dominant trend in the industry from 1920 to 1926 or so, the singer is likely female, especially since she is compared with other women in Africa, and contrasted with a female opera singer, Maria Jeritza, later. Otherwise, there is once again a nameless subject whose strength seems not to be in her individuality but in the tradition of the vocation or avocation to which she is related. A primary difference is that Cullen employs a traditional ballad stanza and ABAB pattern, as opposed to Hughes's formal employment of blues stanzas, vaudeville, twelve-bar, and eight-bar, to help carry the meaning of his poem and connect him formally and spiritually to that tradition. Hughes's use of the vernacular in parts of his poem contrasts with Cullen's use of standard English, though both use primarily one- and two-syllable words (except for "melody" and "Jeritza" in Cullen). Cullen's "keenings" and "kraal" (*My Souls's High Song* 144), however, might have sent his readers to the dictionary. Formally, Cullen seems more distanced from the blues singer than Hughes, providing international and mythical context that seems to suggest someone from another culture, or trained to another culture, appreciating the artistry.

Interestingly, the figure who ultimately becomes Jeritza is first portrayed as an undifferentiated performer, generalized in the way the blues singer is. This effect established a relationship between the two that is to be explored. The opening reference to "some" is contrasted with the more specific "you," even though later this "some" will become more specifically named Jeritza in the final stanza, while the blues singer never gets a name in the poem.

Some weep to find the Golden Pear . . . (line 1)
But you go singing like the sea . . . .(line 5)

Cullen suggests that this classical group has the ability to achieve individual fame and status as a result of its connections to the European art tradition, the written tradition of Verdi (line 17), while the blues singer's connections to an oral tradition of common and mundane origins proves a disadvantage in cultures that privilege written over oral traditions. Cullen accomplishes in his poem what was rarely produced in real life: the prima donna or "first woman" (this one a beautiful, world-renowned figure with a marquee name) finds herself in a place she rarely, if ever, visited—the confined space of a twenty-line poem alongside a nameless purveyor of mundane melodies of grief and mourning drawn not from myth or literature, but from non-Western life in Africa. However, the two share an artistry that is pertinent and instructive in their juxtaposition.

In fact, initially the opera singers are not even singers: they "weep," while the colored blues singer will "go singing," a designation that that implies a mobile and active artistry in the blues singer. The opera singer's song is a lament of disappointment and self-defeating rigidity—they "grow cold as ice" (line 3); the blues singer's song is a lament with agency—"You make your grief a melody" (line 7), emphasizing the creative response through alliteration as well. That this poem is about beauty and vain self-importance is emphasized through what the opera singers treat in their works: the Golden Pear of Prometheus, which distracted three goddesses who vied among themselves and in their own minds for the designation the most beautiful goddess of all. While the goddesses argued, Prometheus stole fire—light, heat, civilization, creative energy—for human beings, the lesson being that such vanity and abstract, subjective speculation can be self-destructive and pointless, bringing the power of gods and human beings to closer parity. While these opera performers weep in character over the illusory value of *things* that appear golden but find themselves degenerating like all else in life, their response to the degeneration may also take the form of a haughtiness that suggests that mutability and degeneration can be willed away by the proud-enough presence, an arrogant ignoring of the lesson the fruit teaches them, that it only looks golden. And appearances can be deceiving. A practical, clear-eyed look might get one closer to the truth, and to beauty. Somewhere people are weeping in reality over other humans, the tragedy of which is more palpable.

By contrast to this frosty illusion, the blues singer receives more felicitous comparisons: the symbol of the sea, the great mother, the source of life, the agent of journey, flux and eternity. Much later, in 1940, it was the title of the first part of Hughes's biography, *The Big Sea*, a metaphor for the vastness of experience and the Whitmanian yearning to experience it all. The object of attraction is not an object at all, but a departing lover. As with the Golden Pear episode, the lover causes grief by leaving, but the singer, rather than producing merely scripted weeping or pride, becomes a creator—fashions the grief into a song that accompanies and comforts the singer even as the lover's backside grows increasingly distant. This is the great comfort of the blues, that it fosters creativity and provides solace, ameliorates rather than merely dramatizes a situation. Further, the songs of the blues singer connect to hidden personal origins, not merely mythological stories from foreign cultures but real songs and occasions of loss. In the descriptions of the blues singer's inspiration, Cullen employs "lovers" twice (lines 6 and 11), not the self-enamored but those enamored of living companions who leave or die in the flux of life but whose pain, it seems, exists eternally. The losses of the singers are real—in specific huts, with "rotting flesh and bone" (line 12) replacing the fruited maggots of the pear. In Africa, in the hut villages rather than on Parisian stages, in the real human drama of the ages that connects Africans to African Americans to all, are the source tragedies of triumphant blues.

In the final stanza, as the blues have been established in their power, Cullen finally invokes the beautiful and famed Jeritza. Jeritza was no pampered pup: her beginnings in provincial opera, where she worked her way up to fame when she was plucked by Emperor Franz Joseph, were well known at the time. But Jeritza is described as breaking her own heart in a kind of self-induced tragedy that seems self-destructive and self-defeating. Not only that, but her heart is broken on "symbols Verdi wrote" (line 18), representations of something abstract rather than concrete, and second-hand visual symbols passed on by Verdi to posterity. The language is contrived to convey the performance as abstract, distant, and impersonal, as opposed to the concrete, personal directness on the blues. The blues singer's frequently personal keening comes from a real place. The blues singer, tearing the strings not just of her heart but her soul apart (line 19), not just the seat of her emotion but the repository of her essence, expresses so much more. If she plays her soul as one would an instrument, she plays percussively, even violently, on her soul, her art matching the pain and violence of experience.

This blues poem from Hughes's major aesthetic challenger of the time presents an interesting and admiring look at the blues singer. However, it is plagued by a distance and lack of aural description, including the onomatopoeia employed by Hughes, that would make it more immediate and real—exactly the way Cullen describes the genre and singer. While it is a major failing in the poem, Cullen still manages to instill the poem with an attraction for what the blues is able to accomplish in its earthiness ("rotting flesh and bone"), sensuality ("mellow-bosomed maids"), passion ("dark tears"), and vital starkness ("blood dripping note by note"). Still, Cullen lacks sufficient admiration for the style, language, and performative aspects of the blues to employ them in his poem. Perhaps he intends it for a portrayal of the way a Jeritza aficionado might appreciate the blues, or of the way a poet who would write an equivocal work like "Heritage" might vacillate between the African and European. Whatever the intent, it is not a compelling poem.

IV

While Cullen was not asking for any aesthetic guidance from Hughes at the time, another acquaintance was: novelist and gay bon vivant Carl Van Vechten, who knew both men, Cullen from a jazz band soiree at the Rockland Palace where Cullen's shy nature, along with Van Vechten's readings of Cullen's European-inflected poetry, convinced Van Vechten of Cullen's aloofness. Van Vechten, who had met Hughes in 1925, liked Hughes's blues-inflected poetry much better than Cullen's work, and sought out Hughes at Lincoln University on October 30, 1926 (Rampersad I: 137) when copyright infringement threatened to derail his commercial powerhouse novel of the Harlem Renaissance, the controversially titled *Nigger Heaven*—a novel spiced with hot music references. A comparison of the fourth and seventh printings of the novel helps reveal the substance of the changes. Bruce Kellner has a brief discussion of some, though not all, as Arnold Rampersad points out (I:137), of Van Vechten's misuse of other people's compositional work in the novel, including Papa Charlie Jackson's (registered a Jean Paul Henriques and Troy Rami composition) "Shake That Thing" (1925), taken from an Ethel Waters recording (1925); Gus Kahn and Walter Donaldson's "Yes, Sir, That's My Baby," recorded by The Goofus Five in 1925; Harry Harris's "I Had Someone Else Before I Had You (and I'll Have Someone After You're Gone)" (1924), recorded by the Goofus Five in 1925; Pearl Delaney and Tom Delaney's "Nobody Knows the Way I Feel This Morning," recorded in 1924 by the Red Onion Jazz Babies accompanying Alberta Hunter; and Bessie (not Clara, as Kellner says) Smith's "Nobody In Town Can Bake a Sweet Jelly Roll Like Mine" (1923), along with James Weldon Johnson's "Sence [sic] You Went Away" (Kellner 87–96). Van Vechten also replaced Jack Palmer and Spencer Williams's "Everybody Loves My Baby" (1924); Edgar Dowell's "While You're Sneakin' Out (Somebody Else is Eazin' [*sic*] In"), recorded by the black and blackface gaspipe clarinetist George McClennon in 1926; and Brown, Rose, and Henderson's "If You Hadn't Gone Away" recorded by the Kit-Kat Band in 1925. Interestingly, Van Vechten retains the snippet from "Everybody Loves My Baby" in his prologue (14) as well as "My Man Rocks Me" (or "My Daddy Rocks Me"), recorded by Trixie Smith in 1922 (and again in 1938 as a stamina-busting two-parter!), just as his prologue ends (16), perhaps through fair use. Another couplet about "teeth like a lighthouse on the sea" (8) quotes from Ida Cox's recording of Lovie Austin's "Any Woman's Blues" (1923) or the recording by Bessie Smith slightly later that same year. One is not surprised to find this many quotes from the blues and jazz tradition in a novel that takes place in one of the three top centers of performance and/or recording of such music (Chicago and New Orleans are the other two). The mixture of blues, pop-blues, and sheet music sources is also characteristic of the scene in New York.

Neither is one surprised to find it in Van Vechten's work. Music and drama critic–turned-popular-novelist of contemporary decadence, Van Vechten cast a dilettante's urbane and sophisticated monoc[g]le on Harlem, affecting some of the the innocence of the sympathetic advocate while projecting some of the debauchery of the decadent dilettante as well. The references to music that populate Van Vechten's text come both from the world of the Langstonian "Weary Blues" bar and cocktail cabaret, race record company and sheet music publishing potentates, tawdry back alley blackness and marquee luminosity, set down powdered cheek by dusky jowl in a sensational—in both senses of the term—manner and volume bound to make Van Vechten's novel a slice of life, place, and time disputed for its accuracy and intentions. And a great name dropping, erudite confabulating, drag ball docking, highball tippling, titillating and teasing time was had by . . . some.

But if the novel seems at times too breezy for academia's hallowed halls—a decidedly windier affair—another look demonstrates that it is not only local color posturing that guards the entrance of Van Vechten's novel, but a fine sense of how such a mix of high and low culture juxtaposed in resplendent energy and with admiration in a scandalously titled novel might be contrived to challenge the social and linguistic tyrannizing potency of such a title, shattering it into shards of illumination. After all, Van Vechten used as epigraph four critical lines from Cullen's "Heritage" in which parched pride and fevered passion yearn for sociopolitical, intellectual, and physical reconciliation of a long-standing perplexity of interrelations that interrogate the contextual definition of Africa. Simon Suggs's notion that it is good to be shifty in a new country can certainly depend upon the racial temperament of the trickster con man. Individual hierarchical shifts in race, class, and culture can be much more fraught with difficulty for African Americans than whites because of limited social mobility, increasing the desperation, and frustration, of exploratory challenges to the system. What results in *Nigger Heaven* is a kind of risky revelation of bifurcated social attitudes that bristle into print. Hence Du Bois's "a blow in the face;" hence Paul Robeson's "NIGGER HEAVEN AMAZING" (Pfeiffer xiii, xxx). "What is *Nigger Heaven* to me?" asks Byron Kasson, searching among the blues and art songs, librarians and divas, in dim and glaringly glittering places for his answer, knowing the Negro entrance is typically around the back. Van Vechten exploits his juxtapositions of songs to dredge up the unflattering detritus of the Negro attitudinal heritage both in and out of the text.

There were contemporary minstrel and hot music compositions that contained the epithet "nigger" in the title: George Schweinfest's 1900 recording of Frank S. Mazziotta's ragtime tune "Nigger Fever" (Rust II: 1485), a dozen or so songs listed in Tony Russell's *Country Music Records, 1921–1942* (1114), and two compositions in Allan Sutton's international ragtime discography covering 1894–1930. There was even a recording from 1932 by a combination of British dance band and symphony musicians under the direction of Fred Elizalde, *The Heart of a Nigger Suite* (later retitled with sensitivity and tact *The Heart of a Coon*), that featured a "Nigger Heaven" section recorded for Decca in London—the other sections were "Watermelon Memories," "Coloured Love," and "Dissipation" (Rust I: 518)! Interestingly, the suite was written in 1927 and produced in 1928 by ballet impresario Sergei Diaghilev, which is indicative of the current attitude toward racial epithets among at least some of the intelligentsia, in Europe and America. Unlike Van Vechten's novel, the suite was not a satire on racial attitudes. And there was the important early sheet music publication of "Nigger Blues" (1912) by Leroy "Lasses" White, which was among the first sheet music publications of the blues.

To some, the term was an indicator of race and class, though to others only undifferentiated members of the race. The use in popular media, of course, was not unprecedented. However, from the "discriminating" polite circles of society matrons to the middle-class movers of Striver's Row to the "patronized" black artists of the publishing houses, it struck some as at least distastefully gauche, others as a belligerent affront to mannered propriety, still others as an incendiary that blasted them back to the plantations, and a few as either a hilarious joke they were almost ashamed or afraid to acknowledge, or a secret attitude they preferred to titter away. Satire can be gentle and violent, microscopically focused or indiscriminate as an atom bottom—and all points between. Or a combination. Van Vechten dropped his bomb in the title, and then laughed as the fallout variously affected his characters and readers.

Though blues are most frequently referenced, in fact Van Vechten quotes from a variety of musical genres in the text, and places a good bit of action on hot music's varied territorial grounds—street corner, bar, pub, and cabaret, with Florence Mills of *Shuffle Along*, appearing in 1926 in *Lew Leslie's Blackbirds,* prominently mentioned as well (120, 162). Obviously different characters stand for different parts of and attitudes in the community, or those like Byron caught in between. The issues Van Vechten raises through the deployment of the music of Hughes's "low-down folks," both profane and pristine, hang the unwashed, raggedy, and hol[e]y unmentionables on a summer clothesline. Many questioned whether Van Vechten had the write/right to pin them there.

The blues songs not only help provide the text with local and chronological color, but demonstrate the pull that this manifestation of African American creativity, in various guises, has on the lower-, middle-, and upper-class communities of blacks, as well as upper-class whites. At times they provide a common denominator from which white and black numerators draw according to their fractions of understanding or prejudice, or provide foils among black characters negotiating race, class, and gender through the alembic of sexualized music and dance. For example, aside from the blues songs already mentioned, there is the multiple repetition of "Hey! Hey! Do that thing" (10, 13, 157, 242, 248) that likely stems from the 1924 version of the song recorded by Rosa Henderson. She was accompanied, significantly enough, by Fletcher Henderson's Club Alabam Orchestra, which was located at West 44th Street at the time. Van Vechten mentions Henderson twice in the text of the novel (77, 151), solidifying the probable source of the phrase. In the not-so-subtle world of hokum music of the times, the phrase "that thing" was deliberately left vague for the attainment of multiple entendre in the double entendre world of alcohol addled titillation, where one might do that thing, shake that thing, smack that thing, put that thing, play that thing, ride that thing, tap that thing, rag that thing, ease that thing, and even, mercifully, stop that thing. The first reference to this song in the novel is to a "lad of six" who is dancing on the corner of One Hundred and Thirty-Seventh Street (10). Using this *double entendre* song in this context connects the innocent boy on a recreational spree with the sexual lyric, and the frequently at least vaguely sexual nature of African American popular dance, suggesting that it might be both innocently or irresponsibly performed. Van Vechten may well be associating sexuality even with pre-adolescent black youngsters, suggesting that African Americans are inherently or behaviorally more sexual than whites. In his primitivistic romp, black grown-ups and children alike shake that thing, perhaps Van Vechten's way of emphasizing the sensuality of black "primitive" life. Bessie

Smith's niece by marriage, Ruby Walker Smith, herself exposed the "queer," "drag ball," "buffet flat" aspects of the Harlem community in a recorded interview with Chris Albertson, suggesting that these elements attracted both white and black visitors to Harlem as much as the admittedly outstanding music (*Besssie Smith: The Complete Recordings Volume 5).* Van Vechten, in fact, references sexuality connected with primitivism, the savage, and the jungle multiple times in the text (12, 14, 89–90, 145–46, 164, 277–82), frequently in relation to dance—especially the Charleston, which Van Vechten specifically names (on 10, 13, 30, 141, 160, 213, 242)—and jazz or blues music. The cultured Mary herself has an interior monologue relating the "savage" music to the "beat" and "rhythms" of jazz (89), lamenting that she has "forfeited her birthright" (89), as James Weldon Johnson's "passing" protagonist did in *Autobiography of an Ex-Colored Man*, and wishing that "she could only let herself go, revel in colour and noise and rhythm and physical emotion, throw herself into the ring with others, figuratively shouting and hurling their assegais" (90). Of course, the music did have these associations in the minds of many blacks and whites at the time, even though some blues singers did seek to project an image of respectability with elaborate costumes on the stage, or community gatherings around the back porch.

And yet, we should note that Van Vechten uses bits and pieces of spirituals to expose black and white attitudes about respectability as well (37, 50, 59–61, 73–76, 84, 103, 107, 120, 187), with references to Paul Robeson and Roland Hayes on display (50, 120, plus Robeson on 180). Such is also the case with art songs, the pathetic Webb hauling out Shakespeare's "Hark! hark the lark" from *Cymbeline*. A counterpart to "Hey! Hey! Do that Thing" in its purpose to "penetrate" Cymbelene in a way that previous crudities did not, Webb Leverett sings the song to demonstrate his stiff Eurocentric credentials, which are not, to Mary's taste, so sure. However, his faults disappear when he begins at Mary's suggestion to sing spirituals (74–75), when even the old white ladies begin to move to his rhythm. Though Webb does not seem to be very accomplished, the question becomes whom Van Vechten is satirizing. Is it the striver Webb chasing after European culture to prove his humanity? Is it the white audience that hears the spiritual more enthusiastically than the art music to prove their generosity toward African American talent and/or to validate their stereotypes about African American rhythm? Or is it Mary, whose "cleverness" in creating a scene places her in condescending relief to both?

Interestingly, the final scene brings together blues context and spiritual message to represent Byron's ultimate downfall. In a variation on interior monologue, in a chapter 9 loaded with blues songs in the air at the Black

Venus, Byron, feeling the racial vises tightening on his confused consciousness (which takes us back to Cullen's epigraph), mixes jazz, blues, and spirituals in his thoughts, hot music and cold weather in his soul:

> What was going around and around in his head? My way, my way's cloudy; go send them angels down! . . Gin, golden-browns, Blues, and snow. Where did they get the snow? He wanted some. He was about to call a waiter when he heard a voice announce, Shine butter an' egg man.

"My Way's Cloudy" had been recorded by the Dinwiddie Colored Quartette in 1902, and Marian Anderson in 1924; Charlie McCoy recorded the "send me an angel down" lyric in "Last Time Blues" (1929), though of course it occurs in "My Way is Cloudy" as well; Louis Armstrong was having success with Percy Venable's "Big Butter and Egg Man" in 1926; "Shine" was a song written in 1910 by Cecil Mack, Lew Brown, and Ford Dabney, also recorded by Armstrong. Though of course "Shine" refers literally to whether the butter and egg man (a term for big spender) wants his shoes buffed, it certainly adds to the dizzying stream-of-consciousness images of jumbled high and low, hot and cold, sacred and secular, stereotype and reality. When he notes that his enemy, Randolph Pettijohn (petty john), also called the King (in ironic contrast to the petty john surname), is coming toward him and feels shots whizzing by his head, Byron thinks of Robeson singing "Were You There (When They Crucified My Lord)?"—a song that was recorded by Robeson in 1925 and reprinted by James Weldon and J. Rosamond Johnson in *American Negro Spirituals* in 1926. This whole notion of being crucified in a bar called the Black Venus certainly contributes to Byron's sense of confusion and disorientation, leading to his final action of firing into Pettijohn's dead body, whereupon the "innocent" Byron is arrested, professing to his girlfriend (not mother) Mary that he is innocent. There is a sense here of "Father, forgive them for they know not what they do," since Byron is being falsely arrested. On the other hand, there is a sense that "they" have the man they want as well—the black man. And Byron? Kneeling over the King at the Black Venus with a discharged revolver, at the location where the words "Nigger Heaven" were first spoken about Harlem and the club in the novel (15), neither Harlem nor the Black Venus, nor for that matter where Byron is headed after the murder, seem to be a Nigger Heaven at all, but more of a nigger purgatory where a heavenly and hellish pendulum swings unsteadily back and forth between the two. Unlike Poe's narrator, who is liberated from the Inquisition at the end of his story, Byron has now realized that he has been caught in his own pit the whole time.

V

Anthropologist, folklorist, raconteur, and writer Zora Neale Hurston was, with Sterling A. Brown, most felicitously placed to make use of the folklore of the South to enliven her literary work, as well as help establish her credentials as a leading folklorist of her time. By now with her "rediscovery," a word used here as uneasily as it is applied to the "re-activated" 1920s blues singers beginning in the late 1950s, her background in the remarkable community of Eatonville, Florida, where she grew up with a preacher father and a mother who encouraged her to "jump at de sun," are legendary, in both senses of the term. Resident there from the time she was three until she went to Jacksonville after her mother's death in 1904, her early experiences in an all-black community nurtured her pride in African American creative activity, especially the extensive "lying" (storytelling) and singing she heard on the front porch of Joe Clarke's store when, as a youngster and a female, she would have been privy to stories considered somewhat "inappropriate" for her age and gender. Later, in her Library of Congress recordings, she seemed embarrassed not for herself but for other folklorists when she explained that some songs she had collected and was about to sing were considered to be songs of "jook women," a designation that perhaps the defiant and vigorous Hurston welcomed in the face of the prissy alternative—losing the songs that few others could collect.

She was recognized by her mother, teachers in Eatonville, and travelers visiting the community as a bright, creative, and spunky spirit beyond the pale, and after work as a domestic and assistant to her brother's wife caring for her children in Memphis in 1914–1915, she went to Maryland, where she graduated from high school, moving on to Washington, DC, in 1918. Working as a waitress and manicurist at a black barber shop—where she may have heard a few interesting stories as well—she began in 1920 a stint at Howard University, from which she received an associate's degree. Her presence there helped her concentrate on the study of linguistics with Lorenzo Dow Turner and her creative writing, and she produced her first short story, "John Redding Goes to Sea" (1921). Ultimately, she planted herself in the literary salon of Georgia Douglas Johnson, where she met some members of the burgeoning New Negro literary movement of the time. By January 1925, she was in New York, where friendships with Fannie Hurst and Annie Nathan Meyer and encouragement from Georgia Douglas Johnson brought her a scholarship at Barnard College, where she majored in English. The leading American anthropologist of his day, Franz Boas, then at Columbia University, recognized her talent, pressing her into service doing "field work" in Harlem.

It is a testament to Hurston's character, personality, and drive that she carried out—boldly or foolishly—her activity of measuring the heads of blacks on Harlem streets to prove "scientifically" that blacks were not mentally inferior to whites. Also at this time, on November 1, 1927, a Hurston "composition" entitled "Jelly Look What You Done Done," was recorded for OKeh Records by Victoria Spivey, a vaudeville blues singer with recordings accompanied by the great Lonnie Johnson and Porter Grainger to her credit, the classic "Black Snake Blues" (1926) preceding Blind Lemon Jefferson's "That Black Snake Moan" by six months. Clara Smith also recorded the Hurston composition on May 10, 1928.

The Boas connection helped determine the course of her next few years, when a 1927 research fellowship from the Association for Negro Life and History, secured with the help of Boas and Carter G. Woodson, allowed her, with her insider insights as one of the "folk" and a budding folklorist herself, to travel to Florida, Tennessee, Alabama, and Georgia, among other places, to ferret out the hidden and sumptuous caches of folklore that she knew firsthand existed. In addition to meeting with her family, she also met up with Langston Hughes in Alabama on his first trip South, filling him with her excitement and regaling him with stories, and taking him to meet Bessie Smith, a short time after visiting Booker T. Washington's grave with Jessie Fauset. Her meeting with wealthy widow Charlotte Mason at the time, through the connection of Alain Locke (who was receiving support from Mason, as was Langston Hughes), provided her with an important but exacting benefactor who would fund future trips collecting folklore from 1928 to 1931, though her contract with Mason gave "ownership," as if such things could be owned, to Mason. Hurston was deliriously happy and enchanted by the sumptuous folklore she could barely spare the time to transcribe, a feeling that shows in her later spirited portrayals of the lore she encountered on these trips.

By 1929 she was working on the manuscript that would become the groundbreaking literary-folkways collection *Mules and Men* (1935). Unfortunately 1931, the year Skip James recorded his sonorous, Depression-starved lament "Hard Time Killin' Floor Blues," found Hurston split both from Mason and from Hughes, who had his own bone of contention with Hurston over authorship and control over a co-authored play, *Mule Bone*. Hurston's extensive personal and professional connection with southern black folklore placed her in an important position as both creative writer and professional, and, though the bulk of her most important creative writing falls outside the chronological scope of this study, what she did produce, and the interest she helped generate at the time, was important for a number of New Negro Renaissance writers.

The first short story in which Hurston exercised her blues experience was

"Muttsy," published in the August 1926 issue of *Opportunity*. Winning second place in the *Opportunity* awards for short stories that year, the story seems at first as if it is not really well managed, almost an ill-paced, underdeveloped non-story. However, heard with the aid of a blues ear trumpet, the story has a rhythm that is both steady and syncopated, a tone that is cynical and tough-edged, and a "so-low" from the "hero" that stomps down to the bricks like a barrelhouse boogie. The character Muttsy, who does prove himself to be something of a dog whether he is a gambler or foreman on the dock, is a Harlem buffet flat blues pianist and gambler whose errant ways are on full display as the story opens. While Hurston does not go into the sexual details noted by Bessie Smith's niece Ruby Walker in her interview with Chris Albertson, the implications of the ambience of the "front" (41) parlor are clear. While some find his character rather unconvincing because of his hairpin willingness to throw over his old gambling life for the love of an innocent Eatonville newcomer to the big city, Hurston may well be trying to point out that his change of heart actually stemmed from the fact that he never intended to quit gambling in the first place, no matter what he had promised. His desire to be a "big man" was fulfilled on the docks, but he knew that eventually, in an urban patriarchal world unfamiliar to Pinkie, he could mould her once he reeled her in. Finding her unusually difficult to convince, even with a diamond ring and promise of marriage, he simply did what he needed to do to make her "his." Hurston, in order to establish the linguistic ascendancy of the omniscient narrator by contrasting his paternalistic vernacular language with the characterization of his whispered chauvinistic aside as being "sotto voce" (42), an opera term that refers to speaking in a lowered voice for emphasis. The term indicates a bit of condescension on behalf of the narrator toward the haughty blues-performer-on-the-make.

His avocation as a blues piano player as described in the opening paragraph makes this clear. While the piano is described as stuttering and wailing, sure signs of nervousness and unhappiness, Hurston's description of the pianist keeping "time with his heel" reveals him to be in perfect control. Not only that, but he dramatizes "an imaginary deserter" and, even though stuttering and wailing, still brags confidently that his "slow drag"—a hypersexually, grinding dance that suggests his love-making prowess, as portrayed in "Slow Drag" recorded by Cow Cow Davenport in 1929—will surely cause her to return. Although the song is a "mournful . . . plaint," the music's tom-tom rhythm gives it an earthy, elemental, hypnotic feel (41). The description reveals the power of the blues to turn sadness into control, into agency, through the creative concoction of an art and image that exudes strength and confidence, even in full wail. Hurston reveals to the readers that Muttsy is a poseur, feigning indifference to the newcomer's appearance, but his control of his outer image is sure, if we can judge by the subordinate responses of the other men to him. While he plays in Ma Turner's back parlor, he goes to meet Pinkie in the receiving room, the "front," where he attempts to lure Pinkie into his orbit, at first, and then into his life as his attempts fail to attract her. While he gloats prematurely in his excessive possessive desire to dominate and control "She's *mine*! . . . All mine!" (52), he fears later that "Ada an' all uh them laffin—they say ah done crapped" (51). For Muttsy, who worries twice about having "crapped" (51, 55), this will never do. He must restore his reputation not only for others, but himself.

Muttsy's first mask-to-face meeting with Pinkie comes significantly at an evening gathering at the flat, ushered in by the sound of a black pianist playing the blues and singing another lyric common to the blues tradition:

> Ahm gointer make me a graveyard of mah own. (46)

Furry Lewis sings this "I'm gonna buy me a graveyard of my own / I'm going to kill everybody that have done me wrong" in his "Furry's Blues" (1928), but this type of formulaic structure also used "railroad" and "heaven" in its body, as we saw earlier in Blind Lemon Jefferson's "Broke and Hungry" (1926). In either case, the desire for ownership and control in a world where such power is infrequently available to blacks is explicit. His desire to make Pinkie all his makes clear Muttsy's obsessive male desire with control, one that cannot be easily altered. A boasting Blind Willie McTell, for example, sings,

> Pull down your windows and lock up your blinds
> I'll tell you something that will change your mind

in "Come On Around to My House Mama" (1929), a song akin to Muttsy's boastful lyric at the outset of the story. Coupled with the other lyric, which describes a journey that culminates in death and transportation on the cooling board, which appears in Papa Harvey Hull's "Hey, Lawdy Mama—The France Blues" (1927), it describes clearly the intention to live out on the smoky road, "smoky" meaning "low or mean" (Calt 222), or even "black," and "on the road" a "rootless existence" (Calt 175), until he dies. Significantly, the black piano player in the house first sings this, and then it is repeated by Muttsy as he enters the house, indicating his own intention, as expressed in the communal blues tradition, even if temporarily sidetracked, to shake, rattle, and roll to his demise. But clearly Pinkie, this "kack girl," as Ada calls her, meaning respectable or refined girl (Calt 44), who threatens to put her "on de bricks," or in a hard situation, perhaps with connotations of street walking, has at least a temporal pull on the usually cock-sure Muttsy. This is barrelhouse language, the rough language of the type Hurston must have learned in her travels collecting folklore. As such, it is subject to a barrelhouse aesthetic, which is do what you need to do to get what you want to get, and let the jook roll on. Big Bill Broonzy and Memphis Slim described an altercation in a jook that resulted in the death of a man whose body was then pulled up to a pool table to use as a step stool (*Blues in the Mississippi Night*). That is what you call really crapping out. But Muttsy's gambling, and his image, are sacred to him, and they must be restored.

Thus, at the end, as Muttsy dives back into his gambling ways, he combines the language of the church and the blues. With his "take" accompanied by a "doxology"—the near-sacrilegious "praise God from whom all blessings flow!"—he takes his friend "Bluefront," whom he calls "Blue," for his entire roll and, firmly in charge, he plots a course to "keep" his wife and the dice. The dice are called here "bones" (56) in vernacular parlance, since they were originally made of the bones of an animal and had the tetrahedral shape of the knucklebones. The connection to the use of the word "bone" in the blues tradition, meaning, as in Barbecue Bob's "Chocolate to the Bone" (1927) or Blind Lemon Jefferson's "makes the flesh tremble on your bones" in "Bed Springs Blues" (1929)—or, indeed, in Emily Dickinson's "Zero at the Bone" in "A Narrow Fellow in the Grass" (460)—emphasizes that the activity is practically a part of his structural DNA. Further, there are sexual connotations here through the association of the word "bone" with the lyric "meat shaking on her bones" as in Tommy Johnson's "Big Fat Mama Blues" (1928) or "rocking" someone like their back ain't got no bone. In all, his return to gambling signifies his energetic return to "control" of his lifestyle and relationship, which he sees as proper, and thus the story ends abruptly with his whole-boned precipitate reentry into his old life.

The story reveals Hurston's keen understanding of the flow of human blues in human veins. From the pianist's foot-tapping command of time in the beginning of the story, which foreshadows the stuttering and wailing to come, to his gambling command at the end, from the opening blues to the closing Blue, the story directs a drama the interaction between downhome innocence and blues experience. Pinkie, like the little finger or toe, seems small and cute, and though she gains a temporary ascendancy over Muttsy, he eventually emerges in the patriarchal blues world as the victor. However, as the blues song that he picks up from the other pianist acknowledges, he is constructing himself a graveyard toward which he is most assuredly slouching once he has crapped out with his deceitful ways. Thus, the story, while it contains Muttsy's blues lyrics and focuses on his story, contains implicitly the blues of Pinkie as well.

Hurston's "Eatonville Anthology" (1926) is a cubistic collage of fourteen folk-pieces stylistically positioned between the poetry of Edgar Lee Masters's *Spoon River Anthology* (1915) and the prose of Sherwood Anderson's *Winesburg, Ohio* (1919) with, perhaps, Jean Toomer's *Cane* (1923) lending an example as well. There had been other short fiction cycles, such as Sara Orne Jewett's *The Country of the Pointed Firs* (1896) and Hemingway's *In Our Time* (1925), but all of these works were longer than "Eatonville," providing more continuity to the collections and usually more development to each section. Anthologies themselves became popular in the twentieth century as showcases for a variety of poets whose work might receive greater acclaim from the exposure in a collection. William Stanley Braithwaite's annual *Anthology of Magazine Verse* (1913–1929), for example, attempted to fulfill such a role, though as an African American Braithwaite had little sympathy for Afro-conscious poetry, being himself something of a conservative arbiter of taste. Of course, Hurston's anthology was not a Spoon River–like revolt from the village, nor was it a collection of works by different authors as in the case of Braithwaite. Although the "Anthology" does expose some of the grimy drawers of Eatonville, nonetheless, with its occasional wry humor spicing some of the more pitiful portraits, and elements of folklore enriching the fading rurality of a postwar community, it arrives, not like Joyce's *Dubliners*, at "The Dead," but at a folktale that reinforces the remote origins of contemporary behavior that explains human nature in a fanciful way that at the time was quaking in the wake of scientific, psychological explanations that were largely beyond the ken of the common person. Marking its territorial end with "stepped on a tin, mah story ends" (72), a traditional folk formulaic ending rendered as "stepped on a *pin*" in *Mules and Men*, the anthology clearly leads us through a narrative that defines linguistically, musically, and spiritually a community that bears, celebrates, and expresses its vicissitudes through continuity with folk past and folk culture while never avoiding the inevitable and time-proven tragedies of human existence.

Section XI, "Double-Shuffle," exemplifies this mixtery through the use of music and dance, contrasting through the voice of an elder the rich songs and dances of the days of yore with the developments since the war, when buck dancing gives way to the new-fangled, ragtiming foxtrot which, though popularized by Vernon and Irene Castle, had its origins in the black community. The first lyrics appeared in a similar form in Langston Hughes's "Negro Dancers" in *Crisis* in March 1925 (*Collected Poems* 625), though Hughes later changed the "buck" to the "Charleston," a contrast that Hurston herself seems interested in making in this work. In fact, the lyrics are traditional, and Hurston complained in a letter to Cullen that Hughes was passing off traditional material as his own (Kaplan 84). Perhaps a promised complaint to Van Vechten prompted Hughes's change to the "Charleston," which matched his urban milieu better anyway. Hurston also changes the word "ways" as it appears in Hughes—a brag about invention and creativity in dancing—to "days," which serves to set up the speaker's point here that, as the blues lyric says, "my time ain't long."

In those old times, folks mixed in the sacred and secular elements of the community, "Deacons clapping hard as the rest" (65), as the celebration encompassed folk beliefs, good-time self-criticism, and unbridled joy that ultimately gave way to the ordered customs of courtship that paid fealty to the past. It is the type of criticism that one began to find in works by Dunbar, Daniel Webster Davis, and James Edwin Campbell around the turn of the century, as in "De Linin' ub de Hymns" by Davis, lamenting the idea that the illiterate among the folk were being left behind by the use of hymnals they couldn't read. Indeed, it had more than sufficed, it had sustained, nourished, and overcome, only to be cast out by a new generation unsympathetic to tradition. In this section, the old comfortable, time-tested, traditional familiarities and formalities, "scattered about during the war" like the boys and girls of the story (66), receive only brief and untutored recognition, the picking up of feet during dancing ignoring the differentiation and distinction in old times between sacred and secular dance.

The meaning is in the shuffle. The double-shuffle, of course, refers to the knowledge of older traditions and, even more than knowledge, respect for them. To double-shuffle is to dance with both feet on the ground, without violating religious proscription, as well as containing connotations of being thoroughly grounded in one's life as well. For people who have fewer material goods to pass on, these elements of folk culture serve as a vital legacy in the face of materialistic impoverishment, therefore the seeming rejection of traditional modes of performance and entertainment indicate the encroachment of materialism, and *modernism*, on the traditional culture. However, the term "double-shuffle" has further connotations. It refers to a fast syncopated dance, one that is presumably difficult to execute. This definition can cut both ways in the story, since the older speaker and the younger objects of derision each have difficulty executing the other's dance, finding themselves near hopelessly flat footed and placing them at stalemated odds. The term was also reserved for a vulgar dance, one that is either considered informal or vulgar, and thus applicable to either dance as well. The title, then, in its ambiguity, opens the field for an exploration of a community in transition, part of it clinging to outmoded ways that carry elements of the wisdom and ways of the elders while another segment flees to an age that matches not the shuffling gait of the old, but the double-shuffling pace of the new. As Sam Townsend sang in "Lily Kimball Blues" (1930), "I'm bound to lose."

The elements in the other lyrics that Hurston quotes here can be commonly found among the recordings of black vernacular singers of the 1920s. For comparison of potential mates by skin color, see Texas Alexander's "Yellow Girl Blues" (1928) or Edmonia Henderson's "Black Man Blues" (1924), which contains the "blacker the berry, the sweeter the juice" line. Harmonica player, singer, and medicine show performer Peg Leg Sam was still performing the "electric car" lyric in 1972, and Bobby Leecan's Needmore Band recorded a version of James Whitcomb Riley's "Shortnin' Bread," with which the lyric has been sometimes associated, in 1927, in addition to a passel of recordings of the song for the Library of Congress (Dixon, Godrich, and Rye 1263). Peg Leg Sam's version, which Hurston's echoes (or vice versa), is actually a parody of a religious song called "Hand Me Down My Silver Trumpet, Gabriel," adding even more to the deacons' magnanimity in joining in in the continuum of sacred and secular music characteristic of West African, and sometimes African American, music. References to "cabbage" in a sexual context are also common in 1920s blues, as in Maggie Jones's "Anybody Here Want to Try My Cabbage" (1924). And criticism of the preacher, of course, is ubiquitous in black folk song, including the blues, as in Madlyn Davis's "Too Black Bad" (1928) or the Mississippi Sheiks' "He Calls That Religion" (1932).

"Eatonville Anthology," then, is a collage-story much like a traditional improvisational blues lyric, which can be associational, sometimes seemingly incoherent and non-thematic, while still forming a possible urtext for others to follow. That is, Hurston juxtaposes the polyvocality of the folk tradition in a way that manages to give voice and value to the tradition, while revealing parts that need adaptation to survive in a changing and modern world. By ending with the folk story formulaic ending, she indicates that the heat of the folk past has not yet died out. Neither is it to be forgotten, nor can it be wholly clung to. Hurston's conscious distortion of space and time here, as in experimental work being done by the Cubists, Dos Passos, and others to come, nevertheless does not subordinate the traditional community to contemporary motives. Rather, the snippets of folk narrative and portrait and performance retain their essence, while converging in an anthology that points to the future.

VI

Langston Hughes knew that his orientation as a writer was toward life in the urban landscape because that was the landscape of his life: "I was Chicago and Kansas City and Broadway and Harlem" he asserted in *The Big Sea* (325) in 1940, later adding "I am not a Southerner" ("Jazz as Communication" 492). There were other African Americans who were beginning to mine *that* territory very valuably. Premier among them was Sterling Brown, who, despite a middle-class upbringing that found him valedictorian of his high school class, Phi Beta Kappa at Williams College (1921), an MA in English from Harvard (1923), and a complexion that nearly made it possible to pass for white, identified closely with the rural southern lower-class characters like "Big Boy" Davis that he encountered in places such as Virginia Seminary and College at Lynchburg, Virginia, where he went to teach after graduating from Harvard in 1923. After teaching at Fisk University in 1928–29, he settled into a forty-year stint at Howard University in 1929. Although it would be three years before his first book of poems appeared—*Southern Road* (1932)—Brown had begun writing in the 1920s, honing his skills as an observer, informal folklorist, raconteur, scholar, and poet—and above all a folk-identified aficionado—as a run up to one of the most remarkable debuts of a poetic volume in American literature. His "Odyssey of Big Boy" in Countee Cullen's collection *Caroling Dusk* (1927), "When de Saints Go Ma'ching Home" in *Opportunity* in July 1927, "Long Gone" in V. F. Calverton's *Anthology of Negro American Literature* (1929), and "Riverbank Blues" in *Opportunity* in May 1929 demonstrated forcefully his deep knowledge of folklore and its place in the lives and aesthetics of the folk. "Odyssey" and "When de Saints" in particular, with their references to the restless, some might say—erroneously, for Brown—profligate, and heroic energy, and the form and spirit of the "John Henry" blues ballad in the former, the spiritual in the latter, showed Brown's crucial understanding of the relevance of secular songs to the lives of the folk, not only as historical marker, but as visceral expression and sustenance. His "Riverbank Blues" follows in a similar channel, reflecting the rich folk tradition, as well as Hughes's famed 1921 poem "The Negro Speaks of Rivers." While his work was mostly written a long way from Harlem, it was forged in the seat and soul of the Renaissance, and is among the most exceptional achievements of twentieth-century American poetry.

Brown's debt to singer-guitarist Calvin "Big Boy" Davis, which he acknowledged in a number of places, including in several poems, was clear. What has not been widely acknowledged is that there are recordings that were made by a "Big Boy" under the auspices of Roscoe Lewis in Hampton, Virginia, and sold to the Library of Congress in 1941 (van Rijn, *Too Late* 4), and that these recordings are possibly of the performer Brown knew, though "Big Boy" was a common nickname for an African American male. Brown, of course, had met Big Boy much earlier, when he taught at Virginia Seminary and College from 1923–1926. Brown assisted Professor Roscoe Lewis of Hampton Institute in the Virginia Writer's Project research on *The Negro in Virginia* (1940), which was published just before the recordings were made (Tidwell and Tracy, eds., 10), but there does not seem to be evidence at this time that Brown acknowledged the recordings. While it may seem presumptuous to suggest that this is Brown's Big Boy, a look at the songs he recorded for the Library of Congress makes a firmer connection. In addition to "Hobo Song," "Careless Love," "Shine on Me," "Everybody Living Gotta Die," and "Train Song," Big Boy recorded versions of "John Henry," "John Henry Hammer Song," "When the Saints Go Marching In," and a "Blues" (Dixon, Godrich and Rye (69, 1072). While these songs are common enough in the African American oral tradition, the fact that these are among the songs recorded by Big Boy, and among the songs prominent in Brown's early poems, when linked with his association with Virginia and Lewis, suggests that this is the Big Boy of Brown's inspiration.

Big Boy's recordings reveal, indeed, a masterful blues performer, with powerful vocals supported by coursing guitar in a Robert Wilkins vein, only more muscular, though Kip Lornell compares the playing to Furry Lewis (14). Teasing slide guitar emerges in spots on his masterful "Blues," which includes a narrative with snippets from "Nearer My God to Thee," "Ever Been Down You Know Just 'Bout How I Feel," "Trouble, Had It All My Days," which is mentioned also in Brown's poem "When de Saints Go Ma'chin' Home," a stanza from "Match Box Blues" (1927), popularized by Blind Lemon Jefferson, and a reference to "Alabama Bound." Tony Russell suggests that this song might well be the "Train Song" listed in discographies, though this is not clear (Liner Notes 2). The recording of "John Henry" is similarly rhythmically powerful, though featuring weak vocals by two singers, as well as a hacking cough that betrays the informal recording conditions of the session. Still, it is a nearly five-minute performance, rivaling the length of Furry Lewis's two-part recording, which makes it a kind of ur-performance as the longest single continuous recording of the song in the pre–World War II era. The recording, unfortunately, fades out as Big Boy begins a solo on slide guitar. The recording of "When the Saints Go Marching In" has not been released. Listening to what is available, however, affirms why Brown was so enthusiastically inspired by Big Boy, evoking snippets of this work in various poems.

"Odyssey of Big Boy" reveals Brown's earnest, fervid belief in the force of the folklore and mythology of African Americans to parallel in extent, heroism, allure, and importance the favored productions of Western classical mythology. This is an odyssey, after all, conjuring the wanderings of Odysseus after the fall of Troy, looking for a home and doing battle with the formidable forces of the irrational and petty juggernauts of democracy. Brown, the epic poet, actually allows his Odysseus to be his own Homer, offering a first person narrative that weds voice to exploits, demonstrating how, in times of self-examination when the heritage of a group is weighed and tested, an epic arises to reveal, sum up, and assert autonomy. Significantly, Brown's hero Big Boy is, like Odysseus, not the part-god, part-human supernatural hero but the "common" man, surviving, like Odum's Left Wing Gordon, by his shit, grit, and mother-wit to give witness to his spirit to persevere, a living embodiment of the spirit of the blues. Just as Odysseus puns on his own name to escape the wrath of Polyphemus by calling himself "no-man," so is Big Boy "no man" in the eyes of his "captors." He is a "big *boy*." This is at once a derogatory term used by whites to infantilize black males (boy), as well as a descriptive term employed to provoke images of fear and the threatening of blacks' physicality for whites (always "big" blacks). However, when the black object adopts the name for his own, he becomes a self-identified subject, a strategy on the part of the victimized black to accept and wear proudly and positively a term meant to insult and degrade. Richard Wright's own "Big Boy" from *Uncle Tom's Children* (1938) finds himself having to grow up very fast from youngster to adult, from innocent to initiated, from game player to murderer, with virtually no bridge or transition from one to the other. He is the common experience, but only one incarnation, of the laboring and labored life of the African American male. Importantly, like Odysseus, Big Boy is trying to find his way *home*, not in this case a geographical place but a spiritual pantheon of powerful folk figures who help define the strength and ethos of African Americans.

Not only does Brown provide space and time for Big Boy to speak for himself, but he also provides a special and timeless structure with which to unburden himself: the blues-ballad stanza. Combining the distinctive blues modality of African American culture with the ancient, traditional ballad stanza of yore, the form is both European and African, blending ancient and contemporary elements of both in experience and expression. Through word and style, it sums up and integrates a clash of cultures as it reinforces the values and vigor of an African American culture that sustained itself through horrors unmentioned, though not unfelt, in the poem. This blues-ballad stanza is the one used, appropriately enough, for the ballad hero John Henry, he of the thunderous nine-pound hammer, who out-muscled the steam drill on legendary tracks all over the South to prove his mettle and worth in the face of dehumanizing racial characterizations, and for the entire brotherhood of human beings as the machine threatened to prove them obsolete. John Henry's presence, never explicitly mentioned in the poem until the very end, envisioning the twilight of Big Boy's life, is the vehicle of expression, that distinctive space where his voice is heard and immediately recognized, welcomed, and nurtured.

This ten-bar stanzaic pattern had served as the rough agent of John Henry's continuing power for a generation by the time Brown employed it, an old friend that evoked the spirit of perseverance even without the words, which were sometimes completed at the ends of lines in performance by an instrument, such as Big Boy Davis's slide guitar, that "vocalized" the sentiment the listeners already understood. And make no mistake, the power is in the performance, the individual evocation of an indomitable communal spirit. Brown's ingenious decision to employ this stanza pattern transforms the poem from an outsider's observation to an insider's incarnation of the spirit and presence of African American history and power and the centrality of its importance. Given the attitudes toward African American "secular" folklore at the time, that Brown chose the form is testimony to his mastery of the sacred-secular continuum of African American art, and his extraordinary insight into the possibilities of African American orature for written expression.

The first two words of the first three lines of the poem reinforce Big Boy's desires: "lemme be" (*Collected Poems* 20). Big Boy wishes to be left alone to his independent wanderings, to his restless search for adventure and experience. When he is not left alone, he becomes a manipulated object in the hands of these irrational pseudo-gods. Instead, he articulates his desire to be his own man: let me *be*, he says, who I am, rather than who you think I am. The repetition of the third word, "wid," in each of those lines, stipulates that he wishes to choose his own company. He does not wish to be grouped by others as they see appropriate, neither with other blacks with whom he may have some arbitrary connection, nor with whites, in whom he seems to have no interest, nor with whom does he seem to envision any advantage. His three-word reiteration—a technique common in African American orature—is further articulated in appropriate vernacular language, signaling immediately that Big Boy, given his own platform and voice to speak by Brown, speaks like John Henry, like a "nach'al man," when his time finally comes.

Big Boy is reflecting at this point on his demise, looking back over his life with a blustery braggadocio revealing his celebrations, complaints, surprises, and wonder at his cumulative experiences. His sense of himself is forged in part from his individual experiences, part out of the communal revisioning of those vicissitudes to form an epic spirit and character that transforms the mundane into the momentous. Hence, Big Boy seeks to choose the companions whose lives have become stellar, substantial, who emphasize the significance of "the man furthest down," who despite, perhaps even because of that status, takes on greater stature by proving the worth and legitimacy of *all* human beings through his individual actions. It is a communal burden, responsibility, and gift that grants most special status to the bearer, and it is testimony to the strength and commitment of the man who faces not Cyclops, not fearsome dragons, not supernatural terrors, not the fanciful terrors of legend, but the bleak terrors of reality.

John Luther "Casey" Jones, he of Wallace Saunders's ballad, a brave engineer on the Illinois Central trying to stop his train and save lives; and Stagolee, the man who shot Billy Lyons over a Stetson hat: these two stood out as the intended faceless, voiceless wraiths who lent substance to their existence, their *be*ings, by becoming something other than the nondescript, inferior scarecrows they were intended to be. Both songs traveled around in the oral tradition, but also entered the popular realm as well. Published as sheet music in 1909, a version of "Casey Jones" was recorded commercially by Furry Lewis in 1927; Ma Rainey recorded her version of "Stack O' Lee Blues" in 1925, while Missssippi John Hurt recorded his version of the ballad three years later. While Stagolee's life may not seem to fit a "positive role model," in a sense, because he was considered to be a "bad" man, a formidable force, in a society considered by blacks to be "bad" or dysfunctionally functional in itself, he stands out as a Big Boy, a looming figure shouting no in thunder to the drab character he was expected to be.

Some suggest that his name, sometimes articulated "Stack O' Lee," partakes of the stature of the smoke*stack* on a steamboat, tree toptall and bellowing its strength at the top of its furious lungs. Certainly there is, again, the restless element of travel. As Big Boy travels through Kentucky, Virginia, Maryland, Georgia, South Carolina, Tennessee, Maryland again, Southeast Virginia again, Southeast Massachusetts, New York, Georgia again, Maryland again, Virginia again, Arkansas, Tennessee, Louisiana, and Washington, DC, climaxing in the nation's capitol, his restless and circuitous route, seemingly unplotted and without, as they say, rhyme or reason, does arrive at the episodic summit of Hughes's racial mountain. The rhyme of the stanza pattern is, of course, there, as is the reason for this wandering life. A look at an interview with Peg Leg Sam, a medicine show performer and itinerant wanderer, reveals a remarkable similarity to the folk spirit, and perhaps Whitmanian spirit, of Big Boy's catalogs: "I traveled all out through Ohio, all down in Missouri, up in Minnesota. I never did go no farther thisaway than Baltimore [with a show]. I went the other way around—all out West. Come on down to New Mexico, Colorado. All down Georgia, Alabama, Louisiana, Mississippi, Texas, and all that. Back up through Kansas, that way. I stayed around Rocky Mount, North Carolina a long time. I stayed there about four months of the year for 25 years" (Bastin 2). Peg Leg Sam's clear pride in his wanderings and self-sufficiency clearly relates to the pride that Big Boy expresses in the poem as well.

The work of stanzas two through six, the transition of stanza seven to the interpersonal relationships of stanzas eight through ten, and the philosophy that sprang from and guided the direction of his life in stanzas eleven and twelve, brilliantly culminate in a valedictory affirmation in lucky number thirteen. It is a full circle wandering journey, like Odysseus, like Walt Whitman, with a purpose but no set route save the direction of the river, wind, or highway bent to time, circumstance, and whim. While some would call this an aimless life, it is because they do not value the sanctity of the journey, nor recognize a destination without walls. That seems to be acceptable to Big Boy. He merely repeats, "Lemme be."

The sense of accomplishment and culmination in the poem stems in part from Big Boy's repeating of the word "done." Twenty times in the poem he repeats the word, a construction so ubiquitous in the blues that it begins the titles of nearly two dozen African American recordings between 1890 and 1943 (Dixon, Godrich and Rye 1118), without even counting all of the occurrences in the bodies of blues songs. Songs such as Clara Smith's "Done Sold My Soul to the Devil" (1924) and Margaret Johnson's "Done Made a Fool Out of Me" (1925) exemplify the root of this expression in the African American vernacular with which Big Boy speaks. Most of the time, it is a vernacular expression meaning "I have already accomplished this." Still, there is some sense of finality to the expression. "I have already done that," he says; "no use to do it again." Instead of a life of settling, of the quiet desperation of settling down, Big Boy chooses, like the train, like the river, like the spirit of freedom he seeks in a land of slavery and Jim Crow, to highball it, to roll on, to *be* what he wants. The ever-living, ever-loving embodiment of the spirit of African American survival, swinging that hammer against the odds, the ultimate "jazzbo" in two ways: embracing the negative stigma of the black man as a useless "jazzer" (lazy, frivolous, sexually promiscuous) and transforming it into the ultimate repository and expression of black strength and beauty. This black Odysseus who is his own Homer, seizing the time as he acknowledges in stanza eleven, becomes timeless.

Big Boy Davis is the acknowledged inspiration for another of Brown's poems from this era, "When de Saints Go Ma'chin' Home" (1927). Noting that Davis was "*Chased Out of Town for Vagrancy*," a subject touched upon in Ramblin' Thomas's "No Job Blues" (1928)—"and the policeman came along and he arrested me for vag"—Brown refers to Davis as a "*Friend*" who provided him with fond memories (*Collected Poems* 26)—a significant statement in a world where Harvard MAs did not frequently appreciate or listen to, much less converse with, folks of Big Boy's class unless under duress. Actually, the performer was never out of work, even though—and quite unfairly—what he did was usually called "playing." Big Boy provided the entertainment and expressed the mood for a harried community worried and troubled, and even stepped on occasion outside the "rôle," made more formal and serious by the *circonflexe* over the o, and somehow more artificial in terms of what is to come in his *in propria persona* performance of his mother's sanctioned and sanctified selection. More than creating and expressing a mood, now he invokes and embodies a spiritual world, invokes the incarnate flash, the troubled world of days, measured by minutes, toward the infinite, rooted in the unruly rhythm, rumbling low and scattering high, of a humble hymn of hope and faith.

This poem, in third person with flashes of first person dream revealed to the poet in the singer's deep sorrow and hypnotic vision, thanks to the vision of the poet, is about home again: the mother longing for her home in the skies, Big Boy's going home to mother memories, the speaker's marching unpretentiously to his memories as well, all couched in communal memories and meanings that imbue the songs with the performative, poly-rhythmic, holy-rhythmic sounds of comfort and peace, the closest thing to heaven on earth. The saints, of course, are the exceptionally holy, though as the speaker makes clear, they are not the economic elect, the masters of commerce, or the perfect exemplars of appearance. They are the common folks, for whom a reward has been prepared because, like the singer's mother, they have "defeated the grief / Life piled so closely about [them]" (*Collected Poems* 29).

Clearly, not everyone can be admitted to this heaven. This heaven is a personal and communal creation matched to the exigencies of experience. Henry Thomas sang, "I'm gonna build me a heaven of my own" in "Texas Worried Blues" (1928), one where things match his previously powerless conception of how things ought to be. Unlike the heaven imagined in Western texts, though, with its sure divisions, here beautiful women like Sophie, so lovingly described and remembered in the poem, might still stir up trouble, and so must stay elsewhere with the drinkers, carousers, and gamblers. As in this world, the saints still have their struggles, their memories of "trouble deep down in [their] soul." That is, in fact, what puzzled the performer, who must work out what to do with the good white folks who went beyond the pale, even while they still retained the identities that entitled them to a reward less grand in heaven. It is problematic, this creation of a heaven, even if you know what you hope for, and hard to envision a world where many white folks won't impose their whiteness on a more sainted world. Cullen wrote of this in his poem "For a Lady I Know" (*Collected Writings* 11), challenging the definition of "lady" by revealing her decidedly un-heavenly condescension. Big Boy's dream of heaven struggles with the ugly residue of racism, the flawed nature of human beings, and the complex road to glory.

So Big Boy transcends mere rôle, mere dramatization, mere mundane consideration. This is not the man who merely induces the slow drag mood, the buck-dancing abandon, the shuffling relief. This is the songster, a blues player par excellence, who nonetheless travels spiritually through his music to a place where, as the text said, they could not follow him, but surely not merely to his girlfriend Sophie, or to other Saturday night dances. He may carry Saturday night with him, but he carries Sunday morning, as well. Like, perhaps, the Wallace Stevens poem of that name (*Collected Poems* 66), Brown's poem is a (largely) blank verse reverie on the meaning of life as reflected in its perceived purpose and conclusion. Both poems relate religion to memories of female figures connected to mothers and companions, Sophie for Big Boy, Elsie for Stevens. While Big Boy is not on a fancy patio with the presumed monetary and formal educational requisites that accompany it, neither is he in church, as Stevens's modernistic woman is not. Her sacred and secular considerations of this world and the next compare to Brown's poem as well, though the financially impoverished figure Brown chooses, and the song that enlivens the lines, remove any sense of a "fashionable" consideration of religion for a figure who does not, after all, question his faith, but does look forward to "imperishable bliss" (Stevens *Collected Poems*, 68). Big Boy the wanderer never wanders any further away from heaven than his fingers and, like his instrument, he is an instrument of grace as well.

Two other Brown poems from the 1920s partake of this spirit of travel, "Long Gone" (1929) and "Riverbank Blues" (1929). "Long Gone," following "The Odyssey of Big Boy" in *Southern Road*, portrays in the first person vernacular that unexplained wanderlust that both puzzles and pleases the speaker, but only puzzles the woman to whom he delivers the lines. Exploring the impulse, the speaker is drawn by looks (st. 3), sounds (st. 4), possible mobility (st. 5), anticipation (st. 6), adventure (st. 8), and compulsion (st. 9): "I cain't stay here" (*Collected Poems* 23), a counterpart to blues singer Clara Smith's "You Can't Stay Here No More" (1929). Not only that, but the images suggest his feelings: the upward movement of the train in stanza three, hearing the emptiness in stanza four, the letting off of steam and the switching of direction in stanza five, the desire to "highball" it in stanza eight. All suggest dissatisfaction, frustration, or exciting possibility that even feelings of home cannot overcome. It is, he says, just not natural—perhaps another John Henry reference—for him to sit still: he says, "I'se jes dataway" (*Collected Poems* 22). As he speaks naturally and behaves naturally, he names himself naturally as well:

> Jes' my name and jes' my habit
> To be Long Gone. (*Collected Poems* 23)

Blues performer Alice Moore sang a lyric, "I'm black and I'm evil and I did not make myself," on "Black and Evil Blues" (1929) that may well be thematically related to the poem. The song and the poem both say, "I am who I am, and I do not apologize for who I am because I am just this way *naturally*." Though never specifically mentioned, the common African American folk songs "Long Gone," "Long Gone Lost John," and "Long Gone Blues," as well as the superb version on the recording "Kentucky Blues" (1930) by Little Hat Jones, resonate in the lines of the poem. W. C. Handy discussed the song in his notes to his 1926 anthology *Blues: An Anthology* (36–37), with which Brown would certainly have been familiar as well.

In "Riverbank Blues," Brown returns to the site of the river, so common in blues lyrics of the time (Mississippi River, Coal River, Tallahatchie River, Trinity River, the Blood Red River, and so many others), to explore how the speaker of the poem feels both the pull to stay and to leave in the current and voice of the river. Comparing the poem with Hughes's "The Negro Speaks of Rivers," we see in Brown a more equivocal attitude toward the river, which retains its immediate strength and importance but works its ambivalence on the mind of the sojourner, who is wondering which way to go. Although the poem does not use formal elements of the blues, its portrayal of tough, elemental, and ambivalent choices and portrayal of the tiny voices of doubt that creep into consciousness make it a blues nonetheless. Songster Peg Leg Howell sang on "Rock and Gravel Blues" (1928), "Honey let's go to the river and sit down, / If the blues overtakes us, jump overboard and drown." His attitude here is distinctly more carefree, apathetic, or indifferent than the speaker in "Riverbank Blues," though that may well be that he has a woman to sit on the bank with him. The location of the poem, on the riverbank where both hard ground and water present alternative pulls, juxtaposes opposite choices that loom largely in the future of the speaker, and the water is "muddy" (*Collected Poems* 100) and not easily read, though perhaps someday, as in Hughes's poem, that muddiness may turn to gold. Unlike the spiritual "Down By the Riverside," this is not a person laying down his sword and shield but about to embark, perhaps, on the quest that Big Boy was finishing. He is not quite at the stage where he can ignore ambivalence and just live and *be*, nor so much invested in the tradition that it buoys him with confidence. Thus, on the liminal riverbank, neither here nor there, he retains his burden, and the water rolls on.

Brown would go on to write many important poems and essays drawing on the African American musical tradition, including the blues ballad in the monumental "Strange Legacies," the blues in the masterful "Ma Rainey," the work song in "Southern Road," and jazz in "Cabaret." Though his contributions were not as numerous as Hughes's, they were as unique, masterful, and deep as any use of folklore in the American tradition. Coupled with early essays such as "The Blues as Folk Poetry" (1930), Brown's practice and influence, though not often hailed for the importance it has, is staggering. No writer better liberated the African American folk spirit into literature than Brown, nor combined it with the traditions of social realism and protest in such holistic, natural ways. That literal odyssey of Big Boy was the figurative odyssey of Sterling Brown, who takes his place with Big Boy, Casey Jones, Stagolee, and John Henry in the heroic pantheon.

Other writers of the New Negro Renaissance employed African American hot music in the 1920s, though not with the frequency and high profile of Hughes, nor as remarkably as Hughes, Hurston, and Brown would continue to do in the 1930s and, in some cases, beyond. Wallace Thurman's review of Handy's *Blues: An Anthology* (1926) made clear his cynical ambivalence to the blues and its employment in literature, though he clearly appreciated Handy's contributions. Later, Thurman would try his hand at using blues for mood and local color in his play *Harlem: A Melodrama of Negro Life* (1928), co-written with William Jourdan Rapp. There the phrase "shake that thing," associated with the Papa Charlie Jackson song that got Van Vechten in trouble, is employed, along with lewd references to a woman who "whips it to a Jelly," a common phrase that gave title to Clara Smith's "Whip it to a Jelly" (1926) and a "red hot mamma" (337), another typical phrase that also occurs in Trixie Smith's "Black Bottom Hop" (1925). When the play ends with the murder of Kid Vamp—a reference to jazz age people who, like vampires, hypnotically dominate and drain their victims dry, as in Mae Glover's "Vampire Woman" (1931), it is a jazz band that crescendos to closing. Thurman's 1929 novel *The Blacker the Berry*, which also appears lyrically in Leroy Carr's "Good Woman Blues" (1934), features Thurman's evocative descriptions of a piano performance, with such phrases as "sock it" and "dirty no gooder" reflecting words encountered in blues recordings such as Keghouse's "Sock it Blues" (1928) and Bessie Smith's "Dirty No-Gooder Blues" (1929), setting the sensual stage for barroom observations (457–60). Thurman was clearly familiar with the spirit of the music, and brought a voluptuous vitality to his descriptions of hot music and dance.

Nella Larsen is not frequently grouped with the African American authors mentioned here in terms of the content and style of her work, especially since many critics have considered the adjective in the phrase women writers to be synonymous with *genteel* in that era. The more we study, of course, the more we see the imitations of that view, as the work of Maureen Honey, Deborah McDowell, and Thadious Davis, among others, expose us to underexposed writers and reevaluate the work of those falsely accused of being the prudish and pretentious in polite society.

Daughter of a Danish mother and a black West Indian father, in a race-restricted, xenophobic, and sexist society, Nella Larsen was, depending on how you approach it, either extremely well or badly situated to understand the interactions of all of these elements. Davis tells us that Larsen attempted to "resist marginality and to create a coherent narrative of her life" (4), though she also "sought access to [the] middle-class African American world as an alternative to a dreary existence as a working-class female" (5). And McDowell sees Larsen's heroines in *Quicksand* (1928) and *Passing* (1929) as featuring "daring and unconventional heroines, in the end—sacrifice[d] to the most conventional fates of narrative history: marriage and death, respectively" (xi). However, positioned as she was, even if she were outwardly middle class in her demeanor, might Larsen not have understood more about the situations these women were in than to oversimplify her own message regarding their lives? That is, perhaps the author here is somewhat like the powerful blues singer on stage, singing, "I want all you women to listen to my tale of woe," as sung by Sara Martin in "Death Sting Me Blues" (1928). The warning, in fact, may well be not that women should be more conventional and careful, not more middle class and acquiescent, but how easy it is to lose what you had, and how many ways it is possible to lose it, not just to the cult of true womanhood (piety, purity, submissiveness, domesticity), but to all the race, class, and gender cults that have their prescriptions [proscriptions] for women's behavior, written in patriarchal hand and sure prescriptions for the blues—incidentally, in the singular the title of a song sung by Clara Smith (1924). In this sense, when the female blues singer describes the procession of vari-colored or vari-featured women who try to take "her" man, she acknowledges the extreme competition and frequently the unfairness of a situation that might call on her to play the traditional female roles, such as "lady," laborer, cook, or sex object, to win back her man. What's an author to do?

In *Quicksand*, Larsen may well be acknowledging this type of scenario and, while seeming to reject the culture of the blues and jazz clubs, may actually be providing a warning to middle-class African American women caught in the large gray area between middle-class prim conventionality and lower-class assembly line child production. We can think of the story as having the trappings of a John Henry–like blues ballad: told in the third person, describing the exploits of someone who is fighting a battle similar to ours, exemplary in some way, and whose life provides a lesson for the audience to hear and internalize.

In a novel where the protagonist wanders from place to place, always becoming overcome with an "indefinite discontent" (81) after a short period, what she really seems to want is an autonomy and assurance nobody either can or wishes to offer. Certainly in the antiphonal, call-and-response, give-and-take of the blues we can see such indecision built in structurally to the music. Uncertainty is not a stranger in blues lyrics either, though not many songs make it as prominent as in Bumble Bee Slim's "Uncertain Blues" (1937), recorded by Jazz Gillum in 1938:

> Well, I started to write a letter
> No, I believe I'll go back home,
> Yes, I start to write a letter, baby,
> No, I believe I'll go back home.
> After she reads my letter
> I believe she'll travel on.
>
> I started to cook me a chicken
> No, I believe I'll take my rest.
> I start to cook me a chicken, baby,
> No, I believe I'll take my rest.
> Maybe I'll go back and sleep
> Maybe I'll dream the things is best.
>
> I started to sell my jewelry,
> No, I believe I'll pawn my clothes.
> I start to sell my jewelry, baby,
> No, I believe I'll pawn my clothes.
> Yes, my watch ticks so lonesome
> Up and down this lonesome road.
>
> I started to break this twenty,

No, I believe I'll spend my change.
I started to break this twenty, baby,
No, I believe I'll spend my change.
I started to buy a wood stove,
No, I believe I'll fix my range.

I start to say that I'm worried,
No, I believe I'm satisfied.
I started to say that I'm worried, baby,
No, I believe I'm satisfied.
I start to walk around the corner,
But I believe I'll take a ride.

Recorded a few years after Larsen's book was published, the lyric is not offered as something Larsen specifically drew upon, as is the case with most examples in this work, but an occurrence of the subject matter or structure contained in the blues that reflects that the blues encompassed these ideas, even though they assuredly existed in black communities outside of the blues tradition as well. Gillum's almost pathological indecision, of course, comes off as much more humorous than Helga's.

As is clear from her early interview with Dr. Anderson, Helga is a very sexual woman, but also very repressed, "sublimating," as the rich patron Mrs. Ellsworth in Hughes's short story "The Blues I'm Playing" might say, her sexual desire into notions of middle-class feminine propriety. As the two speak of "service," an ideal of middle-class feminine behavior at the time, Helga Crane's feelings are described in one 6-sentence, 106-word paragraph using words such as "yearning," "throbbed," "urge for service," "insistent," "sprang," "stirred," and "desire," with the word "stirred" coupled with "shamed" as well (20). However, Helga's mixed shame, fear, and double conscious "frigidity" (7) causes her to beat back her acknowledgment of these feelings, the same way in which she felt guilt about even articulating the "one *nameless* way" (8; my emphasis) that she had power over James Vayle, which she describes as an "ancient appeal" (8). The mind-body duality or binary by which she has been taught to operate seems to allow for no gray in between, even though the text foregrounds the colors black, white, and gray as an almost ocular mockery of her dilemma. "She could neither conform, nor be happy in her unconformity," Larsen notes (7), and she detested "such non-sensical soul-searching" (82) to search for answers she did not wish to find, in this case why Anne Grey(!) wanted the person she couldn't consciously admit she herself wanted.

When she responds "Yes and no, to both questions" (101) to James Vayle's query about returning to Denmark, she is revealed in all her Prufrockian trepidation. She doesn't know what she wants to commit to, because they are all traps infected by a sexist societal view that has an ingredient label for every jar a woman climbs into.

Now, if she were like Hughes's "low-down folks" in "The Negro Artist and the Racial Mountain," those blues and gospel singers, drinkers and guffawers, she wouldn't care. If she were like Mrs. Hayes-Rore, the middle-class "race woman" who announces "I'm interested in girls" (39), she wouldn't care. But she couldn't allow herself to be bound to Anne Grey's racial chauvinism, where "the most wretched Negro prostitute that walks One Hundred and Thirty-Fifth Street is more than any president of these United States, not excepting Abraham Lincoln" (48); she also asked herself quite seriously, "Why . . . should she be yoked to these despised black folks" (55). Cleverly, Larsen deliberately uses ambiguous language to describe Helga's feelings when she got her inheritance from her Uncle Peter and prepared to leave for Denmark: "She was about to fly" (56). Was that to transcend, to soar, to find her autonomy and independence, or was she merely fleeing? Yes and no to both questions. Like the *Quicksand* of the title, she intends her struggling to free her, but it seems to pull her down, but the counter intuitive impulse to relax, which would presumably allow her to float, is simply not possible in a world that bedevils her with umpteen codes of behavior.

Thus, the section where Helga visits the jazz club in chapter 11 is important for the way it exposes her fear of something to which she will flee later on. The club itself is described as subterranean, with implications of her "ancient appeal" to Vayle. The night itself is "sulky, humid," described then by Larsen somewhat surrealistically as "furry," with "electric torches that shone like silver fuzz" (58). With these implications of the pubic regions and genitalia, Helga nonetheless insists that it is "an atrocious night for cabareting" (58), though in fact it is really only an atrocious night for Helga to confront her sexual and social fears. Inside Helga is described as some variant of "oblivious" four times (59), as she is carried away by the scene. However, she may not be oblivious as much as she is penetrated—Larsen uses the word repeatedly (2, 22, 35, 54, 79, 113, 128)—by fear of what she might have to admit about herself and feel shame about. Flying on the buoyancy of the music, nevertheless she flees when it is done. Here Larsen repeats the word "jungle," along with a "savage" and the "syncopated jangle" of the music to reinforce Helga's extreme fear and shame, not simply that she "had been in the jungle, but that she enjoyed it" (59). A 1912 recording by the Peerless Orchestra, "Bacchanal Rag" (Dixon, Godrich, and Rye 1324) seems to capture the sexual frenzy associated with the music, and points to language used later in the text in relation to activities of the Reverend Pleasant Green's ministerial life, which is neither pleasant nor green, but to Helga stifling and unnatural. Later, she watches admiringly the "primitive," "throbbing," "panting," languorous dancing of Audrey Denney with Dr. Anderson, which produces similar feelings in Helga, who leaves in a sweltering sweat of unconscious sexual thirst. There is a schizophrenic instructiveness about Helga's mind that causes her to push to some cataclysmic epiphany that she denies, yet returns to shortly later, though also with disastrous results. On the evening when Helga is preparing for a party and is interestingly described as being "impregnated still with the kindly warmth of the dead Indian summer" (98)—clearly foreshadowing some contradictions to come—she comes upon both Vayle and Anderson at a party. Rejecting Vayle's middle-class condescension, she is broadsided by a passionate kiss from Anderson, who later explains away his actions. Fleeing the hypocrisy of Anderson, whose cowardly advance and denial earns him the resounding smack he deserves, Helga now takes the step that many readers can't buy, and the one that cannot be explained without the context of her sexual power over Vayle, sexual interest in Anderson, sexual admiration of Denney, or her sexual ecstasy and repulsion at the club: she flees almost instinctively to the storefront church of Rev. Pleasant Green, and flies on the wings of angels to the Lord in physical—and yes, sexual—rapture.

The spiritual activity of the church service is described in the most physical and lustful terms. Ironically, she is recognized as a "scarlet 'oman" (112) from the first, a blessed relief from the hypocritical avoidances of Vayle and Anderson, even though she is not the kind of scarlet woman of which they are thinking. As the service begins, it generates slowly a "Bacchic vehemence" that, with its "mixture of breaths, its contact of bodies" is itself a mixtery of the spirit of the church and the physical, sexual being, for the first time providing Helga with the (illusion of) innocence that she needs to carry out her activities. At the climax, Larsen floods her paragraphs with words like "penetrated," "orgy," "possessed," "madness," "brutal desire," and "obsession" (113), with an orgasmic "Oh God, mercy mercy" preceding women described as being like "reptiles" (remembering the "ancient pull" of human feeling and the sexuality of the subterranean club) tearing off clothing and "dropping hot tears and beads of sweat upon her bare arms and neck" (114). Finally, sex for which Helga does not have to feel guilty—heaven.

However, Helga finds out rather quickly that it is not heaven. When bluesman Son House sings "I'm gonna build me a heaven of my own, / I'm gonna give all these women a long, long happy home" in "Preachin the Blues" (1930), it is clearly a euphemism. Helga finds that once again she has been drawn into something that is neither satisfying nor truthful. Pleasant Green is neither pleasant nor green; it was not a holy ceremony that he visited upon her; she could not be satisfied with this life; and she was not a "natural" mother (not like John Henry, who was a natural man) in love with the pain, filth, and stink of human existence until her body gave out. As had happened in every move that she had made—from the college at Naxos to Chicago to New York to Denmark to New York to Alabama—she felt that old dissatisfaction coming back. This time, however, we might expect that, having been shocked by this experience into a clearer notion of a balance of mind and body, she will soar. The last line of the story is one of the most breathtaking, shockingly nihilistic moments in literature, surpassing Hemingway's "our nada who art in nada" in "A Clean, Well-Lighted Place" (383) and the emptiness at the conclusion of Toomer's "Esther." This is particularly true since, having been schooled, however briefly, at the jazz clubs to her sexual nature and having finally seeming to have come to terms with it, Helga leaps into an illusory relationship with the veneer of piety (the church), purity (marriage), submissiveness (the preacher's helpmeet and wife), and domesticity (mother and housewife), realizing the illusion just before the biological trap is sprung again. She is foiled again by the curse of the multi-headed patriarchal juggernaut, who can sing, like Tampa Red, "I can't be happy, mama, for being so blue" ("It Hurts Me Too" 1940). The redeeming factor is this: that Larsen tells the story as a cautionary tale that, like the blues song, describes troubles but transcends in the performance of the story.

VII

Rudolph Fisher's prominent use of African American music in his work has been examined briefly by John McCluskey, who sees Fisher as associating the "Southern tradition" with spirituals and the "Northern urban tradition" with the blues (193). Indeed, Fisher has a fitting background to exploring such elements. He was son of a Baptist clergyman John Wesley Fisher, later "compil[ing] an unpublished collection of Negro spirituals" (Claudette Brown 223) and employing titles from the spiritual tradition prominently in his works. He is also said to have worked as a pianist and arranger and in other musical capacities for his friend Paul Robeson (McCluskey, ed., xiv). Converesely, Fisher was tagged by Langston Hughes as employing "the sharpest and saltiest humor" (Hughes, *The Big Sea* 240), and Sterling Brown identified him as evidencing his main interest "in the life and language of Harlem's poolrooms, cafes, and barber shops," which Fisher portrayed with skill and aplomb (*Negro Poetry and Drama* 136). Arthur P. Davis, attempting to kill two with one blow, even derisively called Fisher a "Van Vechtenite" for his willingness to expose this side of Harlem life through his work (286). A neglected work such as Fisher's "The Promised Land," however, demonstrates how skillfully Fisher could marshal the forces of both traditions to explore, in call-and-response fashion, seemingly antithetical elements of the sacred and secular in the urban ghetto. While identifying how those elements actually blend to present a complementary view of that life, Fisher presents a unified vision of the messages that both traditions deliver.

Published in the *Atlantic Monthly* in January 1927, the story presents yet another view of one of Fisher's favorite themes: the way that the transplanted southerner is worried, like a blue note, by his fledgeling northern experiences. The biblical typology that accompanies Mammy's singing of the spiritual "How Low Must I Bow" sets the context for a story that will examine the interaction of suffering and reward as it is reflected in the creative traditions of blues and spirituals. Both allow people to express and lament mistreatment in an ungodly world; both provide performative occasions for transcendence of that situation, at least temporarily, through a celebration of survival, steadfastness, and style. In terms of subject matter, not all blues are sad; neither are all spirituals songs of praise. As Fisher points out with his brilliant metaphorical setting at the initiation of his story, there is a place where these seemingly fundamentally opposed traditions come together, mix and mingle, even marry, in a soundscape that exists all throughout the neighborhood: an airshaft. And it is in that airshaft where the story amplifies both dilemma and resolution of the question of how one reaches "the promised land."

As Fisher makes clear, this airshaft is a communal and democratic place. An airshaft is "the central opening ventilator shaft in a . . . tenement block which, in warm weather when windows are open, acts as a sound amplifier" (Townley 145). Symbolizing the necessary venting of the atmosphere and emotions of inhabitants in need of fresh air and relief, the airshaft accomplishes this venting by the opening up of community windows and the amplification of the varied voices of community expression. While to some this intermingling of sounds might seem chaotic or anarchic, indeed it is polyrhythmic, even polymetric, in its reflection of the countercurrents of community attitudes and styles. The two "opposing" songs, significantly not named until the third paragraph, issue from locations described as existing "at a certain level" (53), a level not specifically mentioned but seemingly one that could be located easily within the community. At this point in the story, in the communal airshaft, Fisher prefers to emphasize the spatial and spiritual relationships of the songs to each other, rather than the physical locations of disparate dispositions. However, it is clear that both the songs are flung outward and upward, like prayers that "spent themselves like mist" (48) in their soaring and dissipating hopefulness for on the one hand, the love of God, and on the other, the love of man.

The blues song is, significantly, reproduced by a phonograph, an up-to-date mechanical device that vents its frustrated power from behind the closed boundary of a shut window that the music "labors against" (48). Here the music is confined, trapped, a common naturalistic trope for the urban ghetto that (poorly) housed recently arrived southerners, and thus mirrors the secular imprisonment against which the master's tools strain. Conversely, the spiritual does not strain against a closed barrier, but is sung full force into the shaft by Mammy. Unfortunately, for Mammy, full force must be filtered through the age and infirmity she feels. Here are two elements of the community often dealt with by Fisher in what Eleanor Tignor calls the "grandmother as guardian" group (94): the elder of the community with her abiding and time-tested faith in traditional religion, and the contemporary youthful figure hopping a different freight to his heaven. Mammy's vision of their pastoral childhood in the South is now undercut by changing streets and circumstances, seriously affecting any unity with her grandson that she, perhaps illusorily, felt existed. Thus, though Mammy's literal song does not strain against any barrier, there are the barriers of her memories, sense of the deterioration of morals and ethics, and her age and infirmity with which she struggles as she expresses herself.

Fisher introduces the lyrics of the first song in a visual, auditory, and tactile way that emphasizes the strength and presence of the sentiment in her life: "Like her eyes and fingers, her hymn sought comfort, sought while it most despaired" (48). Ingeniously, Fisher has located a song that sonically represents Mammy's pain, even as she hopefully pleads for guidance:

> Bow low!—How low must I bow?
> Bow low!—How low must I bow?
> Bow low!—How low must I bow
> To enter in de promis' land? (48)

Here the visual and aural elements resist each other, contrasting the look and pronunciation of the words. Fisher's employment of rhyme subtly raises questions about meaning itself. The –o sound in "bow" is pronounced differently than in the word immediately juxtaposed to it, "low." Then the following word return to the first pronunciation in "how." There is an indeterminacy, an almost frustration of the language, as it alternates pronunciation in our visual field. However, looked at (or rather heard) another way, there is no problem: however the words look, we can hear them pronounced properly. If we do not know the pronunciations of the words as we look at them, we will mispronounce 40–60 percent of the –o sounds in this line. The inconsistent rules applied to the visual lines, then, would cause us to misapprehend, while the experience of the oral/aural tradition would reproduce them accurately. Here, Fisher emphasizes the need to negotiate different perspectives on issues affecting us, especially those crucial ones that give us pain and pause. Further, the –o vowel sounds, when isolated, offer us a sense of Mammy's pain:

> ow-oh!-ow-oh-ow?
> ow-oh!-ow-oh-ow?
> ow-oh!-ow-oh-ow.

Surely this is incessant moaning, persisting for three long lines until the fourth line provides the relief of arrival to the promised land—and contains neither ow nor oh. However, the rules Mammy attempts to apply to her grandson, generated in and for another location and occasion, are hampered and hamstrung in this environment.

Furthermore, the internal rhyme of the lyrics redoubles the emphasis on what Mammy is asking, making the need to bow even more incessant, perhaps, at this level of overkill, even demeaning. Certainly this is an attitude that a younger member of the community further from the experience of slavery might well feel. These emphatic sounds even suggest to us that we can focus on them without the different rhyme, winding up with "how bow," which is a different though related and, perhaps, relevant question. The stuff of these first three lines could well be the content of a blues lyric, a questioning of social and secular-spiritual status with no mention of God at all. In fact, if this were to occur in a blues song, it might be considered a "protest" lyric, since there is no spiritual metaphor to remove it from the realm of mere social commentary. The frustration expressed in these lines, in fact, may be seen through the veil of creative strategy: the religious lyric can bring in God to mask the social meaning, and the blues song can avoid the reference to God and hide its deeper spiritual associations. But both can accomplish similar ends.

The other element that makes this lyric like a blues song is what is left out. In the continuing exchange of the first three lines, *directive*, bow low, is followed by *question*, how low must I bow. In perhaps a catechismic way, what we might expect at this point is an answer to the question. However, none is forthcoming. Instead, we merely get a continuation of the question, this one indicating the goal of action. Many might consider this something of a disappointment, and indeed without this resolution, we are stuck in the indeterminacy of the bowing stage, with a goal but no real assurance that we are using the proper technique to arrive. This is a common complaint about the spiritual life—that it demands obedience without concrete assurance. This just leaves some people with the blues.

Dialect spelling adds one more significant element to Fisher's meaning. While the song clearly refers to the traditional promised land of the Old Testament, in fact Fisher renders it, wholly in character with oral vernacular performance, "promis' land." At first glance, this seems inconsistent, since Fisher drops the –d from "promised," but leaves it on "land." However, for readers of standard English, the meaning of "promised" is changed by the dropping of the –d, whereas the meaning of "land" is not, so this may well be a vernacular-linguistic clue from Fisher. The promised land *is* a determinate place, one that demonstrates God's commitment to nurture and take care of his "chosen" people. However, the "promise land" adds further meaning by suggesting that you may get to a land that will promise, but not deliver, God's people as in the formal agreement. Once again, the look of the spelling may well contrast with the intended meaning of the sound, delivering to the reader a sense of ambiguity that emerges from careful use of vernacular language.

Other religious references in the text abound, reinforcing Mammy's religiosity, even while at times, in the lamentations "Lawd have Mercy" (49) and "Good Lawd" (51), reminding of similar ejaculations in the blues. One detail that more significantly correlates sacred and secular positions is the reference to the dancing at the party. A popular dance at the time, the "Camel Walk," which was represented by a flurry of jazz recordings in 1925, was a vaguely intimate dance of the ragtime/jazz era—the girls rested heads on the boys' shoulders in a display of intimacy, and simulated the shuffling of a camel. It is this dance that is performed at their party, and which evokes associations with the Magi of the Christian tradition, along with John the Baptist, who was clothed in camel hair. Clearly the boys are not searching for Jesus or God in their "camelling": the dancers are described as being "warmly fused, bending to the sensual waves of the 'camel,'" which causes Mammy to wonder, "Where was God in that?" (49). Indeed, later Sam is turned into a Christ figure when a jagged piece of glass gives the illusion of a "wound in his side" (56). The fact that Mammy's Bible has broken the glass emphasizes how an antagonism has risen between her world and that of Sam and Wesley, who has been overwhelmed by materialism, and how that antagonism is destructive to their relationship and to the community.

Fisher's blues lyric is introduced at the rent party, a significant social gathering of the time that served the purpose of gathering rent money for an apartment by providing entertainment and food and drinks for which people paid, hopefully in excess of what they cost. Ironically, this type of party seems to have derived from a church social, though evolving into something that Christians might describe as decidedly irreligious. The parties were well known for featuring individuals or smaller groups of performers who played ragtime, jazz, and blues, and figured in titles and subject matter of blues songs such as Virginia Liston's "House Rent Stomp" (1923). The song, which Mammy recognizes as having relevance but lacking reference to God and reverential occasion, bears a similar formulaic structure to the song she sang:

> Lawdy, Lawdy, I can't help but cry an' moan.
> Lawdy, Lawdy, I can't help but cry an' moan.
> My man done gone and lef' me—gone an' lef' me all alone. (49)

Though we might say that the Lord's name is evoked here, it is done in a much more casual, almost irreverent way: "Lawdy" is a familiar corruption of the title, almost like taking the Lord's name in vain, since she is lamenting an earthly loss rather than taking solace in spiritual comfort—she is singing the blues. While Jon Michael Spencer argues that these types of references are "an abbreviation of the religious and ethical orientation that blues singers made explicit in various ways" (38), certainly the tawdry reputation of the blues among many blacks in the Christian community, their notion that such an epithet is worldly and blasphemous, and their direction to get right with God rather than with man forces a more complicated interaction with the implications of the use of the word. In this case, the parallel repetition of "Lawdy" produces an expectation of a heavenly reference at the beginning of the third line. However, the reference to the Lord is replaced with "My man," which Mammy sees as the central problem of her irreligious grandsons: putting man in the place of God. Whereas the spiritual lyrics seek to gain an entry into the promised land, to find a haven, the blues lyrics describe being abandoned, left behind. Both still project a feeling of loneliness, since the spiritual provides no answer, and the blues precludes one. In fact, when Fisher describes the dancers as "abandon[ing] [themselves] to the dance" (49), he suggests that the dance is a substitute for true connection, and a performance of fleshly contemplation in place of the spiritual. Though Mammy continues to contemplate the spiritual, it is in fact a powerless and hopeless contemplation, almost as if she has abandoned herself to the past and formal ritual, her dance with "the Lord," not one who is fulfilling a promise, but one who merely presents a land of empty or broken ones.

Both the spiritual and the blues lyrics are repeated later in Fisher's story with significant alterations that contrasts with their earlier settings. At the end of section three, the blues lyric is repeated first, now no longer a "hoarsely phonographed blues" but a version voiced by Wesley, singing while he works. Wesley's adaptation of the song to a personal experience—"My gal done gone"

(55)—serves to personalize the lyrics to match his own situation, as the tradition is wont to do. Other alterations are entirely consistent with the vernacular blues tradition. As Wesley performs the song, he reduces it by roughly one-half: he eliminates the repeated first line, the exclamation "Lawdy," and the first person pronoun "I." Thus, stripped down, the song seems less formulaic, more like a stylized personal statement. Dropping the four "Lawdy" references is part of the process Mammy sees taking place in contemporary life—even the casual mention of religion disappears. Most significant is the elimination of the "I" from the first line. Ironically, this represents a diminution of Wesley's presence, his life force, even as Wesley alters the song to fit his own situation, presumably making it more applicable to him. This weakening of Wesley as he personalizes the lyrics foreshadows the altercation with Sam. Sam and Wesley's first altercation came right after the interpolation of this song the first time after the party. There, the reference to the man leaving has less to do with the situation than the lyrics personalized to Wesley's life do. Wesley's attempt to "stay the light of day" (55), the song nonetheless causes Wesley to reflect on his relationship with Ellie, whereupon he decides to leave Sam to Ellie, who will "swat him for sixty bucks a week" (56)—not a generous or thoughtful gift for him to offer. However, it is Sam's belligerence, not the blues song, which precipitates their final conflict. The blues song is a reflection of their lives and a reflection on their troubles, but neither the cause of nor the solution to them.

The lyric from Mammy's spiritual is presented in abbreviated form as well. It, too, is reduced by nearly one-half, offering only the final two lines. The emphatic repetition of moaning sounds from the earlier version of the lyric is significantly reduced here, producing more of a last gasp than a continuing, perseverant fervor. Coming at the climax of the story, and thus reduced, we get a sense that the experiences of the story are wearing down and away that same art, since half the original lyrics and the stanzaic form both disappear. Wesley, who sang the blues, is dead; Mammy, who sang the spiritual, is bowed and weakened; and Sam is impervious to his guilt and remorseless in his scarcely interrupted pursuit of Ellie. The concluding scene places Mammy once again at her window, but now the meaning of her song is altered by the events that have transpired. Mammy has lied about how Wesley died, bowing to Sam's menacing and the threat of the white man's retribution in order to "save" her grandson—only to see him return to his evil ways "in a week" (59). This is the same airshaft, same Harlem sky, same hymn, but a different Mammy, one who, like the blues-singing Wesley, has fallen from her innocence into the experience of the urban North that renders her strategies inadequate to the temptations and dangers with which she must deal.

In "The Promised Land," both the spiritual and the blues lyrics depict a weakness and deference that highlight the characters' dismay at the harshness of urban ghetto life for transplanted southern blacks. Though the setting for the blues here is not, as McCluskey suggests it usually is, in a "cabaret, speakeasy, or ballroom" (193) as it is in "High Yaller," "Common Meter," and "Blades of Steel," it is in perhaps a more significant venue: in the home, and especially in the airshaft where the melodies suggest a commingling of spirit, perseverance, and purpose created from their lives and structured by tradition, will provide greater strength and unity in a threatening environment. As demonstrated here, Fisher uses a sensitivity to the contrasting oral and written, traditional and modern language and lifestyles to confront linguistically the ability of the vernacular to adequately portray the contradictions and ambiguities of that life. Although the "sacred" song is clearly associated with a fondly remembered and romanticized past that may not have existed, and the blues song with the harshness of the urban ghetto, both are now on that turf, and neither achieves precedence of value in terms of coping with their difficulties. The spiritual, at the end, makes no mention of God; the blues lyric merely takes the name in vain. By the end, the religious message is usurped by social situation, God is replaced by the white man, and the old hymn is still dissipating in Harlem's black sky. In 1925, Fisher wrote to Van Vechten out of frustration that his medical career prevented him from fulfilling his literary program: "I am Moses on the mount, gazing hopelessly to the promised land" (Tignor 87). What kind of promise is it if you can't get there?

There are of course other writers and works we could discuss here, such as the work of Claude McKay in his story "Highball" (1927) or his novel *Home to Harlem* (1928). And there was a great deal of work to come in the 1930s and beyond from Hughes, Hurston, Brown, Fisher, and McKay, leading up to the emergence of Richard Wright. In the work of these New Negro writers, we see the most sustained and nuanced use of the materials of hot music—not just folk and race record manifestations, but more commercial and pop-influenced elements as well—that existed in the 1920s. Empowered by the strength of the tradition and convinced of a justification to use the tradition because of its origins, New Negro writers, especially Hughes, Hurston, and Brown, produced a body of work that was startlingly rooted *and* original, as well as instructive for future writers who might try their abilities at using the features of hot music in their works.

7
Enter Stage Left

Dramatists' Blues

I

At the beginning of the twentieth century, American literature was poised to take an important place on the world cultural stage, as American social and political influence increased and the so-called American century began to take shape. American fiction had a strong tradition on which to draw, with romance writers such as Hawthorne, Melville, and Stowe, realists and naturalists such as Twain, Howells, Frank Norris, and Charles Chesnutt, Stephen Crane and Kate Chopin, and the weighty Henry James all laying a path of succession in the exploration of the underbelly of the American psyche, expressed through everything between thunderous biblical and Shakespearean authority or the autonomy of the vernacular voice in the wilderness. Poets, likewise, found estimable traditions among Emerson, Poe, Whitman, and Crane (with Dickinson in the wings), bridged by E. A. Robinson, Edgar Lee Masters, and Paul Laurence Dunbar. American poets Carl Sandburg, Ezra Pound, T. S. Eliot, William Carlos Williams, Marianne Moore, Langston Hughes, and others, and fiction writers Sherwood Anderson, John Dos Passos, F. Scott Fitzgerald, Ernest Hemingway, Willa Cather, and William Faulkner both drew upon and rebelled against these traditions to find new American voices to speak to a broader audience in a new century, while maintaining a local audience and style that represented America socially, psychologically, and sociopolitically. Whence drama?

American drama is generally understood as coming of age in the twentieth century with little help from past American dramatic successes. Few would suggest that productions by Benjamin Colman, Robert Hunter, John Leacock, Hugh Henry Brackenridge, Robert Rogers, Charlotte Lennox, Royall Tyler, William Dunlap, George Henry Boker, Robert Montgomery Bird, and other earlier dramatists provided sterling example or valuable guidance. The numerous melodramas and romantic comedies, among them numerous versions of *Uncle Tom's Cabin*, as well as the minstrel show tradition, offered little insightful depth unless considered ironically, as many black audiences must have done with the minstrel shows. Even closer contemporaries like David Belasco and William Vaughan Moody, the latter generally considered to be furthering the quality of American drama, were not as daring, deep, and experimental as world drama of the time. Part of the ambition of American dramatists of the twentieth century was to make American drama as relevant, complex, and meaningful as its poetry and fiction, wrestling with similar subject matter, stylistic issues, and sociopolitical implications as their counterparts while dealing with the particular exigencies of the playwrights and their audiences. The oral-performative element that is so crucial to drama, more so than to poetry and fiction, in particular foregrounds the significance of the American voice, physical gesture, and demeanor. The dramatist, then, faces a particular and peculiar call to transgress and transform visually, aurally, and spatially the wilderness of American theatrical tradition without defoliating the trees.

One way to accomplish this was to tend to the same influences and departures as their counterparts in fiction and drama, while keeping abreast of the European drama tradition and contemporary playwrights such as Strindberg, Shaw, Synge, and Ibsen and the realism, naturalism, symbolism, expressionism, and nationalism that informed their work. Freud, Marx, Darwin, Henri Bergson, William James, Jung, and Einstein loomed large in the consciousness of American dramatists, as did the voice of the frontier wanderers such as Natty Bumppo and Huck Finn, the exploited worker of Rebecca Harding Davis's *Life in the Iron Mills* (1861), the blighted small towners of local colorists Mary E. Wilkins Freeman and Sara Orne Jewett, and the victims of urban squalor of Theodore Dreiser and Frank J. Webb's *The Garies and Their Friends* (1857). Employers of dialect such as Twain, George Washington Harris, James Whitcomb Riley, Paul Laurence Dunbar, Daniel Webster Davis, James Edwin Campbell, Bert Williams, and Finley Peter Dunne exemplified a quest, conscious or not, for a unified definition of polyphonic American voices as well, whether the blended black and white voice of Huck, the formularized minstrel voices sometimes sentimentalized by white and black writers, the unbridled bucking of the stallion known as Sut Lovingood, or Mr. Dooley's twinkling brogue. Out of this whirlwind of international and vernacular energy, on largely untested ground with fluid boundaries, emerged some fiery American artists prepared to express America, including those who did so in part through the "celebration, appropriation, development, and contestation of jazz—as style, emblem, inspiration, metaphor, and performance practice," though the use of jazz "was a source of tremendous anxiety for playwrights and critics intent on legitimizing theater as an elite cultural practice"

(Savran, "The Search" 459). However, those whose ambitions did not seek elitist ends, though not without their concerns, negotiated the aesthetic employment of hot music more easily, though not without some sociopolitical consequences for themselves and the theater in America. Through the work of Eugene O'Neill, Paul Green, John Howard Lawson, and Mike Gold, elements of American hot music at last caught the three o'clock stage for theatrical modernism, running on time and in time to become over time a lasting part of a highballing genre that now includes Langston Hughes, Ossie Davis, Edward Albee, James Baldwin, Amiri Baraka, Ntozake Shange, and August Wilson.

The dramatist who led the way to literary maturity, Eugene O'Neill, was a groundbreaking, pivotal figure whose use of racial themes and vernacular language in his work was also extremely controversial at the time. Working with the Provincetown Players, an experimental group he joined after he left a tuberculosis sanitarium with a commitment to playwrighting, O'Neill drew on a wide variety of influences, including the Shakespearian acting past of his father James and his own broad reading in contemporary European classics. His menial jobs in rough neighborhoods such as Hell's Kitchen, with brothels, flophouses, and saloons like Jimmy the Priest's, floors covered with sawdust to soak up the piss, snot, blood, and beer that flowed freely each evening at dusk, exposed him to the slimy underbelly of human consciousness, and the poignant attempts to transcend it. Radical political tracts encouraged by his friend anarchist Benjamin Tucker educated O'Neill in the battlefront brotherhood's sociopolitical agenda. And George Pierce Baker's formative "47 Workshop" drama class at Harvard in 1914 helped him to forge from his experiences a new dramatic tradition of anti-materialistic American themes, European techniques and complexity, and a richness of lower-class American voices that were simple and natural, yet laden with poetry and depth. And musical, at times, with the sounds of African American hot music. As biographers Arthur and Barbara Gelb point out, O'Neill loved jazz and ragtime (*Life* 198, 236), and his letters reveal an O'Neill ecstatic about the Louis Armstrong recording of "St. James Infirmary" (1928), of which he was memorizing the lyrics, and various Bessie Smith recordings including "Sing Sing Blues" (1924), "Soft Pedal Blues" (1925), and "Empty Bed Blues" (1928), all sent to him by Carl Van Vechten (Bogard and Bryer 352). Fifteen years after his early play *The Emperor Jones* (1922) appeared, Charlie Barnet, one of the earliest white jazz bandleaders to feature black performers with his orchestra, recorded a song entitled "The Emperor Jones" (1937), testimony to the reach and importance of O'Neill's work (Rust I: 99).

Predating O'Neill's major plays beginning in 1920 with the Pulitzer Prize–

winning *Beyond the Horizon* were a run-up of poems, a vaudeville sketch, and one-act plays that show O'Neill developing his depth and range from his readings in Emma Goldman, Shaw, Ibsen, Wilde, Nietzsche, Tolstoy, Dostoyevsky, Jack London, Synge, and others. O'Neill also confided around 1903 an interest in popular novels by, among others, Thomas W. Dixon, author of *The Leopard's Spots* (1902), *The Clansman* (1905), and *The Traitor* (1907) trilogy, the second volume of which told the racist stories on which D. W. Griffith's film *Birth of a Nation* (1915) was based. Such an interest seems strange for O'Neill, given the extreme racism of the novels. However, the seething controversy caused by the novels, which reached up to the offices of President Wilson and the chief justic of the Supreme Court, and the very public passions evoked, would have likely appealed to a budding playwright trying to create an explosive and subversive new theater of ideas. O'Neill's work on a vaudeville sketch in 1913 demonstrates his interest both in the stage and popular culture of the type that worked in vaudeville, with its frequent broad humor and racial and sexual stereotypes, though O'Neill was primarily interested in the hack work for money.

The poetry from 1915–1917 O'Neill felt was only of historical interest: "I was trying to write popular humorous journalistic verse for a small town paper and the stuff should be judged—nearly all of it—by that intent" (O'Neill, *Poems* vi). Still, in it we can see bits of O'Neill's interests in some manifestation of African American hot music. Arthur and Barbara Gelb point out that O'Neill appreciated a variety of music, including "chanteys, jazz, show tunes (especially Irving Berlin's), and an indiscriminate smattering of the classical" (*Life with Monte Cristo*, 198), the reference to Berlin reminding us of Berlin's own connection to African American music in tunes such as "Alexander's Ragtime Band." For example, O'Neill's speaker in "Ballad[e] of the Modern Music Lover" (1912) professes to be unable to bring himself to like the classical music of Mozart, Handel, Haydn, Liszt, Chopin, Wagner, and Tschaikowsky [*sic*], because, he says, "The joy of my heart is a ragtime tune" (*Poems* 15)—presumably producing the syncope from which syncopation derives its meaning. For a "modern" music lover, little of this classical material would be considered modern. Perhaps one intention of the poem is to criticize, without even mentioning, contemporary avant-garde music, Wagner coming the closest but still some distance from Debussy, Ives, Bartok, Stravinsky, and Schoenberg's advances. The disconnect serves to throw into question just what "modern music" is, whether in the realm of the classical, the popular, or some hybrid of the two.

Of course, ragtime is itself a hybrid of European and African sources. It is part of the ragginess of the music that it pieces together elements with vaulting syncopation and sometimes mild to crashing dissonances into a virtuoso performance requiring formidable formal technique and a mastery of European genres run through African rhythmic genius. For a racially open-minded artist like O'Neill, ragtime offered the opportunity to push the boundaries socially and aesthetically, while dazzling with the concatenation of language and images that would democratize theatrical productions and combine American vernacular language with advances in European experimentation.

However, the ragtime music to which the speaker refers is all pop or classical sheet music influenced by ragtime—"Mendelssohn Rag" (1909), "Hungarian Rag" (1913), "Oh, You Beautiful Doll" (1911), and "Waiting for the Robert E. Lee" (1912). The Mendelssohn and Liszt "Hungarian Rag" contained strains of Hungarian classical music, and was recorded by black ragtime pianist Eubie Blake in 1917, are of particular note here because, by mentioning them, the speaker acknowledges the existence of such musical hybrids, and finds them to be sometimes, but not always, pleasing. In a similar way, black pianist Blake recognizes, culturally, aesthetically, and financially, the value of such musical hybrids. Donald Gallup notes that Barrett Clark felt this ballad "seems to be an expression of an honest conviction," and O'Neill responded "I did & do like good music—from my childhood—my mother was a fine pianist—exceptionally fine, I believe" (*Poems* 16). Unfortunately, this clarifies nothing. The conviction to which Gallup refers is not necessarily O'Neill's but the speaker's. The "good music" to which O'Neill refers is not specified. The meaning lies in the tone of the poem which, as "apprentice" work, may not be entirely under O'Neill's control.

We do know that the poem was originally printed under the heading "Laconics" in the *New London Telegraph*, which refers to concise, abrupt, or terse speech and, in relation to books such as those by Thomas Brown and Hanford Lennox Gordon with the word in the title, encompasses the pithy and memorable nuggets and truisms offered by respected authors, in the tradition of Franklin's *Poor Richard's Almanack*. Franklin, of course, cast an ironic spectacle on the tradition in "The Way to Wealth," and so well might have O'Neill thought ironically about this heading. As O'Neill also did with the poem "Ballad(e) of Old Girls" (*Poems* 8–9), "ballad" was also rendered in print as "ballard," clearly not a mistake. It seems as if O'Neill uses "ballard" as an obsolete reference to a musical instrument, presumably one used to render the ballad itself. By using this outdated term, O'Neill gives this statement of current taste a veneer of age, as if it has been passed down from some obscure earlier time. The strategy, in a sense, fractures time in the poem, removing the "chronological authority" of classical music over ragtime by expressing ragtime's superiority in the time-honored tradition of the ballad. Thinking of the poem in these terms, it seems a rather ironic reversal by the speaker of the conventional valuing of classical over pop composers, particularly such time-tested, venerated masters as Mozart and Handel. The speaker comments ironically and denigratingly on the pompous protectors of the sacred canon. But is this O'Neill's attitude? The speaker seems rather superficial in his own way, talking about "falling for" classical music as if aesthetic appreciation were a brief infatuation, yet later makes a clever pun about suffering "through concerts by the score" (15), and another about being "a rank barbarian" as he compares (ranks) different kinds of music. The statement itself challenges traditional Western valuations of classical and non-classical music. Certainly some of the rhymes are comical—Mozart–beaux arts (reminding us of Mencken's coming attack on the South in his 1920 essay "Sahara of the Bozart") and vulgarian-American, which makes the conventional wisdom about American values more real and more ironic at the same time.

The speaker also makes a solid artistic point about championing American music, clearly a concern of O'Neill's at the time, though what American values are being championed is a stickier issue. The question becomes how much the speaker is aware of what he is doing. Is the objectification of a woman as a great big beautiful doll an example of "real" American music, and does it replace reality with a fantasy of a woman which conforms to male American ideals and values? Is the use of the name of Robert E. Lee ironic in that Lee was on the "wrong" side of the war for American reunification, and on the slaveholding side of the equation that would have kept in servitude the people who invented ragtime? O'Neill may well be taking a semi-ironic attitude toward the speaker, with whose love of ragtime and American art he identifies but whose blindness to the sinister situations from which ragtime sprung and the commercialization of the idiom O'Neill seeks to recognize and display. Ultimately, it seems as if O'Neill feels the power of ragtime, even in its commercial manifestations, but must question what sacrifices were suffered to create it. The poem, then, simultaneously champions and challenges American values, and with both tragic and comic underpinnings.

Ragtime appears to different purpose in the poem "The Haymarket" (1912). Here it appears to be soundtrack to the illusion of truth, happiness, satisfaction, purpose, and love at a near–Jazz Age dance. The music here is "blaring" something unpleasant, and enters the room as a "chilly blast," an explosion, that promotes motion but not gracefulness, a body but not a soul behind the "set expression." All is "polished," "powdered," "rouged," as the "vulture" male swoops in upon his prey, not suspecting that he is the prey himself, lured through his lechery by the illusion of innocence into the debauched den of deceit. If there is a death of innocence here, whose is it? Not the man's, who doesn't suspect duplicity but certainly does not come to the woman with his hands clean or his gullet dry. Not the woman's, who has played this besotted "innocence" game before, and will again, trading illusion for commodity. Conceived in illusion, the poem ends in "lies," an inevitable result of the desperate dance with hollowness.

A white artist like O'Neill was essential to moving depictions, discussions, and disruptions of race to center stage, where ultimately African Americans might be able to take up such issues with broader audiences once the theaters had been opened up to them. As early as 1918, O'Neill employed an all-black cast in *The Dreamy Kid*, anticipating greater successes, and controversies, in his later plays and productions. O'Neill suffered unbelievable negative publicity over interracial relationships in his play *All God's Chillun Got Wings* (1924), but tolerated it because he believed the play fostered "a more sympathetic understanding between the races, through the sense of mutual tragedy involved" (Diggins 150). Though O'Neill advised Mike Gold that "Art and politics don't mix" (Gelb 359), it was an extremely nuanced line that O'Neill both walked and talked. O'Neill asked actors to boycott a dinner that excluded black actor Charles Gilpin, for example (even though he also later fired Gilpin for being difficult), but did not see controversies raised by his work as political (Gelb, *O'Neill* 448–49). In a May 11, 1924, interview with Louis Kantor of the *New York Times*, O'Neill expounded on his racial and political views: "Spiritually . . . spiritually speaking, there is no superiority between races, any race. We're just a little ahead mentally as a race, though not as individuals . . . But . . . I've no desire to play the exhorter in any racial no-man's land. I am a dramatist. To me every human being is a special case, with his or her own special set of values" (Estrin 46). As for *All God's Chillun Got Wings*, O'Neill defended his play against those who attempted to remake it in their own image: "The persons who have attacked my play have given the impression that I make Jim Harris a symbolic representative of his race and Ella of the white race—that by writing them I urge intermarriage. Now Jim and Ella are special cases and represent no one but themselves . . . Of course, the struggle between them is primarily the result of the difference in their racial heritage. It is their characters, the gap between them and their struggle to bridge it which interests one as a dramatist, nothing else. I didn't create the gap, this cleavage—it exists. Whether they should or not isn't in my play" (46).

Of course, the notion of every black person as a representative of the "black race" was a burden since at least the time of Phillis Wheatley. O'Neill was at a disadvantage in having to deal with the popular notion of the black individual representing the group, and may have anticipated something of this controversy, though as an artist he is not bound to do so. "Life is hard enough,"

O'Neill philosophized, "without, in addition, burdening ourselves with prejudices" (54). He might have said the same thing about art—though ignoring prejudices that exist does not make them nonexistent. Still, O'Neill should be seen, as John Patrick Diggins asserts, as an artist who attempted to "promote racial understanding" (149–50), one human being at a time.

O'Neill also played a role in the Harlem Renaissance as an established artist who encouraged African Americans to present honest portraiture based on the truths of their own experiences. "Be yourselves!" O'Neill advised in *The Messenger*, "Make *your stuff* and *your good!*" (Hutchinson 17). O'Neill was also asked to be a judge in literary contests for *The Crisis*, and Montgomery Gregory, Paul Robeson, Eric Walrond, Alain Locke, and W. E. B. Du Bois all praised O'Neill's dramatic efforts and achievements, despite ambivalence or hostility on the part of other black reviewers. Like Carl Van Vechten, O'Neill suffered criticism from veering too close to controversial subjects and potentially misunderstood social and aesthetic issues, which prompted paranoia about possible slights and racism and produced objections that may or may not stand scrutiny. For example, O'Neill felt it realistic and necessary to use the word "nigger" in his plays from 1913–1920, which he did with infrequency (this was one of Van Vechten's violations of taboo). It particularly dominated, necessarily for many, *The Emperor Jones* (1920), as did issues of brutishness and primitivism, both of which O'Neill was exploring, along with their applications to the consciousness, as O'Neill argued, of one African American male. As Du Bois sympathized, "Eugene O'Neill is bursting through. He has my sympathy, for his soul must be lame with the blows rained upon him. But it is work that must be done" (Musser, 86–87).

A look at O'Neill's drama from 1913–1920 reveals a good many references to the color blue—not, of course, necessarily a reference to the blues tradition, but perhaps an emotional barometer given the content of the plays, with their brutalized brutes and down-and-out characters struggling with the blighted modern landscape. On the other hand, in a number of places, characters refer to having the blues, though again not necessarily a reference to the African American blues tradition. In *Warnings* (1913), lonesome James Knapp, a wireless operator, faded and unshined like his suit and shoes, laments "I guess I've got the blues" (*Complete Plays 1913–1920* 83) in response to an impending trip, and his son Charlie regrets asking for a new suit when he sees how "blue" his father is (*Complete Plays 1913–1920* 85). In *Fog* (1914), passengers in a drifting lifeboat recall the previous day, when the fog obscured the sun and hid them from rescue, and the damp and cold heightened the tragedy of the death of a child relentlessly mourned by his mother. "It was enough to give anyone the blues, that's sure," comments the usually optimistic "First

Voice," indicating the presence and power of tragedy (*Complete Plays 1913–1920* 98). In the four-act play *Bread and Butter* (1914), stenographer Bessie Brown refers to her brother John's family troubles as "just an attack of the Sabbath blues" (*Complete Plays 1913–1920* 177, 180). Mrs. Ashleigh tells Lucy it is "ungrateful to be blue on a beautiful day like this" (*Complete Plays 1913–1920* 427) in *Now I Ask You* (1916). "Some people say these overseas blues ain't bad," Charley Patton sang in "Down the Dirt Road Blues" (1929), answering, "It must not have been them overseas blues I had." So with Mrs. Ashleigh.

Of O'Neill's fifteen plays between 1920 and 1929, there are eighteen instances of the word "nigger," a bit less frequent than in the previous decade, most coming in *All God's Chillun Got Wings* (1924), with two apiece in *Diff'rent* (1920) and *The Hairy Ape* (1921). O'Neill, thus, was not overtly backing away from his use of the word in his work, necessary as it was to his sense of the realism of its current usage. O'Neill does not seem to use the term in his own private correspondence, if the selected letters published are any gauge. In one letter from 1915 he makes an intense reference to "niggers" in Liberia in a love letter (Bryer 58), but only uses it in references to titles by Joseph Conrad and Carl Van Vechten elsewhere. The word seemed too coarse for O'Neill's own usage, and he did not seem to use it even flippantly or bombastically, as Pound, Eliot, or Hemingway might have.

However, there is a slight increase in his references to African American music, likely due at least in part to the advancing popularity of black music in the commercial arena. The word" jazz" occurs in *Diff'rent*, here as the mock-upbeat soundtrack of the withered Emma's fear of aging and Benny's advancing flirtations: says Emma, "I like them jazz tunes myself. They put life and ginger in an old lady like me—not like them slow, old-timey tunes" (28). Suggesting that jazz is the epitome of contemporary music, quick and peppy and spicy in the face of "old-timey" tunes from the past, which seem to place a drag on life and experience, shows how quickly the explosion of jazz as the twenties approached entered literary and popular consciousness. It is another of the many references to the attitude that African American music, especially jazz and blues, is sexually stimulating, an attitude, of course, taken up by many artists, and an attitude that is not outrageous, though likely overemphasized in popular commercial depictions of the genre, as Sterling Brown and Guy B. Johnson lamented.

In *All God's Chillun Got Wings*, O'Neill makes interesting use of the color blue to represent the stress produced by conflicting feelings of utter desperation and desperate hope. In act 1, scene 4, a scene that expressionistically renders both the psychology of the lovers, black Jim and white Ella, and the hypocritically near-spiritual racial divisions in American society, their church door becomes "like wooden lips of an idol that has spat them out." The processional of this scene has been the unrelentingly sad spiritual, as close to the blues as any spiritual comes, an adaptation of "Sometimes I Feel Like a Motherless Child" (recorded by Lois Deppe with Earl Hines on piano in 1923, as well as Paul Robeson, Marian Anderson, and others), sung by a "Negro tenor . . . in a voice of shadowy richness." The idea that the voice partakes both of shadow and richness suggests its ability to evoke a knowledge and strength that transcends (the flying of a dove and an eagle) the obscurity of a racially limited vision where Jim, dressed in black, and Ella, dressed in white, both standing in sunlight, are "shrinking and confused." The person who sings the song brings different interpretations to each stanza, from "a contented, childlike melancholy" of the mourning dove stanza to "the dreamy, boyish exultance" of the eagle stanza, to the "brooding, earthbound sorrow" of the stanza wishing he had never been born (295). That O'Neill refers to the first two stanzas as "childlike" and "boyish" suggests that O'Neill has a somewhat condescending attitude toward spirituals, especially as they express for him docility and illusion, even though a primary hero is a very active Moses, whose migratory exploits were paralleled with the efforts of African Americans to escape from slavery and the migrations of African Americans to Kansas during and after Reconstruction. Some might see spirituals as expressing some kind of dreamy innocence, later undercut by earthly (and earthbound) experience, but in performance these words are anything but innocent, always imbued with a tearful emotion that indicates deep emotion recollected in a worldly, melancholy retrospection. O'Neill's wise choice of a spiritual that combines so intrinsically elements associated with both the blues and spirituals indicates a level of sensitivity to black music's power to combine earthly and heavenly spirit into a song emotionally and intellectually powerful enough to reflect the totality of the experience he describes.

O'Neill does suggest the richness of the tradition, and the vision of the words, as Jim and Ella begin to channel through the two lines of people, past the organ grinder churning out the racist "Old Black Joe," to a curb where no taxi will come. Mrs H. offers, "Dere's one road where de white goes on alone; dere's anudder road where de black goes on alone" (298), and the two roads suggested by the two lines of folks attempt to channel Jim and Ella on those roads. Besides the racist scenario of a black man being unable to get a taxi in certain areas of New York City, the scene also portrays Jim's hapless belief that things will work out for them. Willfully ignoring the song, he looks to the sky, and to the ocean, and interprets the color blue as "hope," even though he has heard the hope of the song turn to despair as it leaves behind childish innocence and takes on its earthbound cast. In stunned desperation, Jim repeats the empty mantra "We're all the same" as he nears the curb on his taxi-less taxi ride, for which he pays so dearly. Meanwhile Ella, whose paranoia about the gazes of the lines of people looking at her and Jim has been averted by Jim to force her to have her face fixed upon the sky, exhibits "trancelike calm and peace" (296) in the wake of Jim's desperate need to escape all that curbs him in his racially blighted life. Interestingly, what O'Neill is describing here is what is termed by biologists as *taxis*. That is, Jim and Ella are exhibiting "the movement of a whole and free-moving cell organism toward or away from some external stimulus" (*Webster's New World Dictionary* 1458), though in this naturalistic world, the movement can take them nowhere where their so-called freedom will save them from the external stimulus of racism.

As Jim and Ella, they return from a sojourn in France still unhappy with their lives because of Ella's continuing sensitivity to what she imagines other people think. Significantly, she grows "paler and paler" as she obsesses about miscegnation, until Jim is affected: he tells his sister Hattie upon their return, "I got to feeling blue." Although Jim professes that he knows Ella loves him—in perhaps an echo of a blues song such as Peg Leg Howell's "Rock and Gravel Blues" (1928) or the traditional "Goodnight Irene," Jim states, "If I didn't know that, I'd have to jump in the river" (300)—his self-doubts begin to get the better of him. His blues make him begin to question his manhood, and motivate him to "have a plain talk, look everything straight in the face, hide nothing, and come out with the exact truth of what we feel" (301). In this, Jim is like the blues singer whose song is an attempt to discuss his blues as a way of overcoming them, of producing a new mood that will actuate a new mode of existence. "Feel like a broke down engine, ain't got no drivin' wheel / If you've ever been down and lonesome you know how a poor man feel," Willie McTell put it in "Broke Down Engine Blues" (1931) using the machine metaphor for his sexuality in the best futurist mode and connecting his interpersonal troubles, poverty, and bad luck to his sexual impotence. When Jim states of himself and Ella, "We were alone together!" (301), he describes not only his relationship with Ella, but the relationship of his own bifurcated mind. His return, to his family, his aspirations for the Bar, and his trials in his private life demonstrate how he tries to pull together his public and private lives despite the vicissitudes of his existence.

As Jim forges ahead with his doomed plans to pass the Bar and help his people and his family, he feels more and more weary and depressed. He "sits down wearily" to talk with Hattie, and gets "crazy mad" with thinking. His euphemism for the social and racial problems he is facing—"There's only so much bad luck allowed to one family, maybe" he says, forcing "a wan smile," laughing to keep from crying—reminds us that blues singers may have used this masking term "bad luck" to express covertly impatience with racism and discrimination. Weariness is ubiquitous in the blues, and Mamie Smith's "Crazy Blues" (1920) established intemperate thoughts and actions as common to blues behavior as well, so it comes as no surprise that Jim's next words are the limp and dejected "I'm tired—and blue—that's all" (307). Indeed, that *WAS* all, *IS* all, and *SHALL BE* all. Hattie points to Jim's bleak future, offering "The doctor said Ella's liable to be sick like this a very long time" (307), meaning a sickness unto death.

A source of Jim's existential angst is his sense that he can do something about his and Ella's situation, and that he can do it by himself. He throws himself into his school work until he is beaten down, and denies Ella's racism, her feeling that "her skin was turning black" and her racial epithets, as when she calls Hattie "a dirty nigger." Jim holds out against his admission of defeat, studying, changing doctors, even proscribing Ella's racist attitudes to something "Deep down in her people—not deep in her" (308). Robert Lockwood sang in "Black Spider Blues" (1941) "If I don't go crazy, I will surely lose my mind," a brilliant and beautifully understated sentiment that captures the near-final resignation of the besieged, and Jim himself welcomes the opportunity to join Ella, committed to an insane asylum with ideas of equality and justice (309). As Ella descends to the position of a "vindictive maniac" (311), Jim "bows his head on his outstretched arms," perhaps to suggest the manner of a crucified Christ, "too stricken for tears" (311). The blues singer will often sing about tears, but as the words often suggest or proclaim, the song reproduces the experience in a creative, meaningful way for an audience ripe for vicarious expression. This is not the same as Jim's lack of tears here—he is drained, beyond grief, wonder, and vision—but O'Neill himself is like the blues ballad singer here, offering his third person portrayal of "Frankie and Johnny" with only the art between the audience and death to motivate us to change a world of such tragic implications.

When the next scene opens, stage directions offer that "[t]he sun has just gone down," and one can almost here Robert Johnson complete the line "dark gon' catch me here" ("Cross Road Blues," 1936), reflecting the terror of a black man caught out after dark in a Mississippi backwoods town that leaves charred black knuckles in a jar at the General Store for a welcome sign. A transformed Ella enters, described by O'Neill in terms many of which seem to portray the figure of Josephine Baker in the twenties: "thin," "eyes glow[ing] with a mad energy," "movements . . . abrupt and spring-like," "arms akimbo," "her attitude one of crazy mockery, fear and bravado" (311). Jim's failure at the Bar exam has revivified her, filled her with hope for the innocuous roles that the two of them will be allowed to play by a society too frightened of race-mixing to allow anything but the transformation of the people into objects of their own innocence or fancies. This, of course, returns us to the use of "Motherless Child" earlier in the play. The innocence, the childish and boyish sound presents not necessarily what is. Perhaps what was in pre-lapsarian times, before the racial Fall; perhaps what seemed to be, or was projected to be. Perhaps what shall be—the sun gonna shine in my back door someday / Big wind's gonna rise and blow my blues away (Son House, "Delta Blues"). Jim seems willing, finally worn down, to "let be be finale of seem," vowing to "play right up to the gates of heaven" with Ella in her little racial caricatures of little boy Jim and Uncle Jim, with no fecund adulthood, no driving wheel to threaten the image of racial superiority and inferiority. And no song to sing through the gray miasma of doom.

Though there are stray references to hot music (ragtime in *Bound East for Cardiff*; being blue in *Strange Interlude*) in O'Neill's plays, these seem to be the most prominent explicit uses of its subject matter, ambience, and form up to 1929. While not, of course, the only dramatist, black or white, to people his plays with African Americans and their music, O'Neill is seminal because he brought to the proscenium the "respectability" of a white, Pulitzer Prize–winning playwright who put his head in the lion's mouth in the circus of twentieth-century depictions of race in art. Praised by some, vilified by others for his racial depictions, O'Neill undoubtedly put African Americans in the searing lights of Broadway, in the literary history books, and writ large in the headlines with his boundary-wrecking gestures that sought to portray all of his characters as *individuals*, not types, and as human beings, not theses (or feces). It is easy to understand what Gilbert Osofsky meant when he wrote, "White literary rebels . . . saw Negroes not as people but as symbols of everything white America was not" (183). All that "newness" of the twenties, really just unrecognized oldness for bourgeois culture, served to heighten the differentiation among so-called races. In the face of that, we understand the difficulties white writers faced overcoming generations of racism and discrimination, their good-hearted badness, stilted portraits, sentimentality, and bald racism. It is difficult, perhaps impossible, to grow hair when the roots are stagnant. Yet a look at O'Neill's poems, plays, and interviews suggests a person with real appreciation of African American culture and considered opinions on race in America. If there is over-emphasis on the primitivistic and tawdry, that also occurs in his plays about whites. His intent is not to create rose-coloured spectacles. So there is also true human emotion, one person at a time, which tends to transcend the categorizations, even as it describes them. O'Neill tends not to be political, but to raise the hackneyed hackles of political necks.

II

There is a difference between being born on Times Square in the Barrett Hotel, a Broadway establishment, and being born and working on a farm employing both black and white tenant farmers in Harnett County in North Carolina. Though of course there are many variables that can influence a life in progress, the ambience of such places is inevitably imbibed by its inhabitants. As O'Neill soaked up the stage life and blaring lights of big city theatrics, so Paul Green breathed in the tumultuous trials and triumphs of the backwoods dramatis personae no less important than O'Neill's city cousins. In fact, as Green saw it, "there is something in the life of 'the people' which seems of deeper significance so far as the nature of the universe goes than the characters who might be termed sophisticated" (Adams 20). In his variant of the wise fool, Green partook of a tradition that showed just how much feeling, how much intelligence, how much beauty was there for the picking in the vernacular culture of the working man.

Indeed, Green acknowledged in the prefatory note to his volume *The House of Connelly and Other Plays* 1931) that elements of the folk speech and folk thought that he encountered profoundly influenced not only elements he reported but the speech he invented as well: "Many bits and snatches of true Southern folksongs and ballads have been used in this volume. For the most part, however, I have found it necessary to create my own words and music as better suiting the mood and continuity of the different situations" (n.p.). Among the songs that he enumerates he wrote for the play are titles that clearly draw from southern folklore generally and African American folklore specifically: "Say my gal laid down her head and cried," "Done sold my soul to the Devil," "I ain't nothin' but a broke down man," "Heard mighty rumbling under the ground," and even a John Henry song, "This heah the hammer killed John Henry," all of which occur in African American music with similar syntax and speech characteristics (n.p.). Bob Coleman's "Sing Song [*sic*] Blues" (1929), Clara Smith's "Done Sold My Soul to the Devil" (1924), Lonnie Clark's "Broke Down Engine" (1929), Blind Willie McTell's "Talkin' to Myself" (1930), and Mississippi John Hurt's "Spike Driver Blues" (1928) respectively all reflect the style of language and syntax in addition to the subject matter of Green's compositions. Though not the sophisticated language of Broadway and Seventh Avenue, it is, as Green recognized, as poetic and significant as the syllables spoken there by Shakespearean actors and sham-polish self-aggrandizers. And like O'Neill, Green had the Pulitzer to prove it.

Not to romanticize Green's upbringing and attitudes with regard to race.

As Agatha Boyd Adams admitted, where Green grew up "[r]ace prejudice undoubtedly pervaded the neighborhood climate;" however, according to her, "it never had conscious expression in the Green house" (4). Born on March 17, 1894, Green grew up during what Rayford Logan termed the nadir of race relations in the United States in reference to the loss of rights, physical violence, and expressions of white supremacy suffered by African Americans (Logan). It would have been difficult for Green not to have at least heard and seen expressions of racial prejudice and violence, as well as paternalistic expressions of pity and condescension. Yet Green might have identified with the "underdog," so to speak, by dint of his illness with osteomyelitis at age ten and the loss of his mother when he was twelve. Broke down and a motherless child, Green determined to overcome his "bad luck": through sheer determination he became "champion cotton-picker of Harnett County" (Adams 8) and star pitcher for the Lillington Cats baseball team. Not long after he became a Lillington leading light, a playwright and then Kenan Fellow in Philosophy at the University of North Carolina. Underdog no longer, he never forgot what it was like to be the runt of the litter, as many of his later activities attest.

The polarized nature of white Americans' responses to race relations at the time certainly made it possible to travel to the two poles of response, the intense and isolating hatred of groups such as the KKK or guilty and condescending worship of African Americans such as one might encounter among some slummers in Harlem. During a stint in the military in World War I, Green revisited some "Negro poems" he had written in the States, revising them from "objective humor to a subjective sense of black bravery and sacrifice" (Roper 42). Green also became much more self-consciously aimed at fighting racial prejudice in America as a result of the segregation and humiliation of troops of different "races" in the war. Indeed, if Adams is right about his upbringing in North Carolina, he was predisposed to respond with loathing to segregation and discrimination, but, as John Herbert Roper points out, it was the military that "liberalized him on the race issue" (42), not his home or university experiences. Green leaned toward the artificially positive pole of the spectrum, though not so mechanically or effusively as to be an imposition or embarrassment. His art was not artificial in the origins of its feelings. Adams, in her admittedly worshipful biography, places Green in attitudinal context: "Paul Green's interest in the Negro is undoubtedly related to a general quickening of appreciation of negro art and life, but his concern goes much deeper than any trend or literary fad; it had been aroused in early childhood, in a region quite remote from the ripples of literary fashion. He likes Negroes as people, likes their music, their humor, their speech, their spontaneous poetry, and he feels deeply the injustice which they have suffered" (Adams 32–33).

Though some people might object to some of the language here, Green's admiration for the positive aspects of African American life and aesthetic, such as the emphasis on improvisation in the "spontaneous poetry," which oversimplifies the nature of improvisation, is clear. And, as Adams continues, "[a]lthough he has frequently been called by that old, unfair Southern tag based on prejudice, 'nigger-lover,' he has not been a blind or even always an enthusiastic admirer of the race" (33).

Green's later role in bringing Langston Hughes to stay at his house after a contribution to *Contempo* in 1931, and his collaboration with Richard Wright on the screenplay for *Native Son* in 1941 certainly upset a large contingent in the South, and his opposition to the cruelty of chain gangs bespoke his sympathy for the man furthest down as well. Both Carl Van Vechten and E. Franklin Frazier praised Green's play *In Abraham's Bosom*, and James Weldon Johnson considered it to be "part of the Harlem Renaissance" (Roper 108). The accessibility of the New York stage to Green, of course, lent him some importance and authority, but clearly Green had an insight into race relations and black folk life that assisted in his success. In his introduction to *The Lord's Will and Other Plays* (1925), Frederick Koch averred that Green's plays "reveal an almost uncanny insight into the character of the negro and a rare feeling for the imagery and the melody of his race life" (xii), and though one wishes that Koch had said "negroes" and "melodies," reading Green gives the all-too-often superficial reference to the "musicality" of the African American strong undercurrents with which to work.

Green made a number of references to "the blues" in an emotional sense in his letters. These were mostly to Elizabeth Atkinson Lay, married to Green on July 6, 1922, whose play "When Witches Ride" was the first performed by the Carolina Playmakers on a double bill with one by Thomas Wolfe (Avery xvii). Green made references to the blues in his private talk frequently enough to suggest that the reference came from more than the popular term for just some incidental state of mind. For example, he refers to the "blue spell" from a 1918 letter from World War I (Avery 12) that accompanies a letter from a mother to the front. Then he was "tired and blue and whipped," "down in the dumps," and overcome by "blueness" (Avery 25) in a 1920 letter about a gathering that included Frederick H. Koch, founder of the Carolian Playmakers, who were cureently featuring one of Green's plays. As Green muses on Job's experience, he exclaims, "one grows so awry, so blue, so funny" (Avery 29), referring to some of the lost-ness, sadness, and ironic humor of the blues. Another 1920 letter cheers him up from a "blue Monday trance" (Avery 32). He laments that "the blue devils have been in my room all day" (Avery 34), that another night "is a blue one" (Avery 72), and that one of his friends "is all blues" (Avery 75). Green's film script for *Cabin in the Cotton* (1932) features a blind black guitarist singing, chorus-like, "in the darkess night, Lawd, wid haid hung down so low" (Avery 211). Surely blues music murmured just beneath the surface of Green's visceral landscape.

Winner of the Belasco Cup, *The No 'Count Boy* (1925) was one of Green's early successes, its wishes, dreams, and wanderlust among the lower-class African Americans an affecting portrait of how a humble harmonica player can aspire to greatness and provide a voice for the voiceless masses. In this case those voiceless masses are represented in the misunderstood Ophelia, surely a Shakespearean reference to the character in *Hamlet* slowly driven crazy by the duplicitous nature of the males she loves. Green uses vernacular pronunciation to elide the name into "Pheelie," emphasizing her romantic nature and her close connection with her feelings, the blues among them: "Pheelie had the blues ag'in" (171). In white dress, shoes, and stockings (145), she is the naïve, innocent young idealist with natural emotions and dreams, a reader of books whose "leaves" take her to other places, far away from her mundane milieu. In late summer, the deterioration of the land is imminent, the well boarded up—perhaps an Eliotic *Waste Land* element—and her boyfriend has straightened his "natural" hair in preparation to meet the faces that he meets (154). Into this setting, with the Devil "Old Scratch"—that itch to transcend, is it really evil?—Faust asks, clearly on the scene (149), a mysterious young, harmonica-playing boy enters. As if a spirit out of the air, he enters with a musical jig fanfare, claiming it "cuts no wood who's boy I is" (160)—setting him in clear opposition to the industry of the wood cutter. Neither will he allow any name to pin him down, saying whom he is called by others, but not who he is himself: "dey calls me de No 'Count Boy" (159). Just who he actually is forms the central question of Green's play.

The boy is clearly a persona to appeal to Pheelie. A self-described wandering hobo (161), he has seen the places, such as New York (179), that Pheelie desires to explore. Although Pheelie's primary interest is the artistry of the writer, she clearly has affinities for the boy's music as well. While Pheelie's book reading helps sustain her in her unsatisfying surroundings, the boy says he plays harp for food (163), much like the wandering Vachel Lindsay, using his "people's art" to keep himself alive. But the art is not merely a commodity. The boy cries while he plays, emphasizing the value and deep feeling of his art, and creating a bridge between himself and Pheelie, whose boyfriend vows to "crucify" the boy (185).

As Pheelie sees the boy as a natural, innocent, and exalted figure, so Enos seems to recognize that the boy represents a spiritual interruption to the comfortable life he plans, and thus Enos must destroy the boy and, through him,

Pheelie's fickle feelings. In fact, the boy is associated in the play with "possibility," "dreams" (160), aesthetic feeling (164), art (168–72), natural expression (166–67), travel (160), literacy (152, 189), and instruction (181–82), all of which give him an exalted status that Enos fears. When the boy offers to teach Pheelie his songs (181–82), he takes on a status similar to that which Tea Cake would later take on with Janie in Hurston's *Their Eyes Were Watching God* (1937), of encouraging self-reliance and the recognition of a power and lifestyle outside the conventional limits of society. This, of course, is one of the functions of African American music—when Pheelie "had de blues" (171), he cheered her up (181–82). Naturally, these realizations can be both exciting and scary at the same time. Pheelie, after all, vacillates between her feelings for Enos and the boy (185–86). She is choosing between innocence and experience, dreams and practicality, books and real life, nature and society, natural and artificial, possibility and limited status quo, "craziness" and "sanity," and "God" and the "Devil."

The boy's harmonica playing is described in some detail in the play, and has affinities with harmonica players of the African American vernacular tradition that Green would have known. The emphasis on his feeling, his crying while he plays, is certainly one of those elements. To say that a harmonica player makes a harmonica cry or wail is to offer great praise, suggesting that the player is emoting from the heart. Louis Myers recorded a humorously misspelled harmonica instrumental, "Just Whaling [*sic*]," that indicates the value of the emotion itself. (And no, this is not evidence that Melville was writing about the blues in *Moby Dick*.) Further, the train imitation is ubiquitous in the blues, and here the harmonica's train imitation is clearly a narrative and lyric event, where the boy's dramatization of the voices of everybody and everything and his sound effects *create* the scene before his listeners' eyes and ears. As an artist and god-like creator, he makes vivid not only Pheelie's temporal desires but her spiritual longings for release in the same way that harmonica train imitations always appealed to audiences in part because the train was a powerful symbol of escape and deliverance from physical and spiritual enslavement, a sexual release, and a seizure of power as the traditional position of porter fades in favor of a black man with a railroad of his own. Countless harmonica recordings such as DeFord Bailey's "Pan American Blues" and Dixie Flyer Blues" (1927), Noah Lewis's "Chickasaw Special" (1929), George "Bullet" Williams's "Frisco Leaving Birmingham" (1928), and William McCoy's "Train Imitations and the Fox Chase" (1927) suggest just how prominently the event resonated with audiences in the 1920s and into the 1930s, when the Depression set many an individual hoboing, taking freight trains to be their friends.

Further, the boy's harmonica playing is also associated with birds as well. Not only does he play a bird song (166), he also communicates with them through his music—an exalted vision of the artist in touch with nature, much like the Aeolian harp, or the Whitmanian bard. Actually, as librarian Dena J. Epstein points out, whistling was one of the "Distinctive Characteristics of Secular Black Folk Music" in the nineteenth century (184). Indeed, there were harmonica players in the African American tradition that incorporated other sound elements, such as whistling, into their performances. One was Pete Hampton, who recorded extensively in London, England, between 1903 and 1911. In fact, his recording of "Dat Mouth Organ Coon" (1904), one of several recordings he made of the tune, features singing, a sentimental interlude, frenetic melodies, a train imitation, a fox chase, and simultaneous whistling and harmonica playing in echoic fashion in the same musical register. The seeming rustic and limited nature of the harmonica belies the possibilities for true artistic performance, and yet in the hands especially of African American harmonica masters the diatonic harmonica became an instrument of great depth and nuance (as did the chromatic harmonica with Larry Adler, Borrah Minovitch, and John Sebastian). In this the diatonic is, perhaps, a symbol of vernacular culture, indeed the "vernacular masses," from which society frequently expects little of aesthetic value, even in a democracy. That the boy's music is so expressive, so creative, on a humble instrument, suggests possibilities for physical, social, and spiritual transcendence for Pheelie and the boy in the face of the oppressive weight of societal taboos and expectations. Is he crazy for dreaming, or visionary? Or both?

This is in part the significance of what he is called in the play. They call him "the no 'count boy." The vernacular is once again here marvelously open to alternative possibilities and meanings beyond the notion that he amounts to nothing. Is the untutored boy unable to count *things* and yet, in his natural state, unbothered by his inability to enumerate things? Is the suggestion that he doesn't count, that is, that he is not important, at least in their eyes of those who cannot value his freedom? Is there simply no accounting for him, how he adopted the values and lifestyle he did, and how he can exist in a world that contradicts his aesthetic? Or is it that he can give no account for himself, cannot explain who he really is? Perhaps, as the vernacular song goes, he doesn't need to give an account at the judgment, being simple and natural himself, and Christ-like in Pheelie's and Enos's eyes. Of course, all of these questions are complicated by the ending, where we find out that the boy is not who he says he is. His mother says he is "not des right in his haid" (189), that his knowledge is from books. It all appears, then, to be an illusion that he has been to these places, and that his experiences represent possibilities for

Pheelie as well. The humble instrument, the train imitation, the bird songs, are all just unimportant, artificial, unnatural fakes, and Pheelie is left with Enos to circumscribe her miserable life. Well, literally, it depends on how you look at it. The boy's music was still inspiring, communicative, entrancing. The hopes and wishes he got from books were real. The art created by his imagination was still real, and moving, to him and to Pheelie, because dreams are real, and can be transformative, in artistic hands attuned to expressing aspirations that resonate in the hearts and minds and cultures close enough to the mainstream to see the fish, but barred from the banks by birth. We cannot account for the boy's genius—or is it perjury?—at representing what he has not physically done, seen, or heard, except that, like Plato's poet, he is a liar, in this case a natural born liar, whose art is of, by, and for the people.

In the minstrel song "Good Old Turnip Greens" (1928), Bo Carter (Chatmon) sang, "When I was a little bird, I always wanted to fly." A metaphor for escape from slavery, political freedom, social accomplishment, perhaps all three? Quite a dream for a no 'count Negro in 1920s Mississippi. And yet as Bo Carter and a member of the Mississippi Sheiks he flew into blues history as a sly lyricist and sophisticated guitarist, and into American history as recording the first version of the standard "Corrine Corrina" (1928), later recorded by Milton Brown, Bob Wills, Big Joe Turner, Ray Peterson, and Dean Martin, among many others. In his 1926 volume *Lonesome Road: Six Plays for the Negro Theater* (1926), Green makes these sympathies clear through his dedication of the book to one of his characters from a 1924 play, a farmer, whose attempts to improve himself and his life are sabotaged by segregation:

> To
> *Abraham McCranie*
> Dreamer and Martyr. (v)

Is the no 'count boy a martyr? Well, that is the way we know him, how we call him. He will always bear that demeaning burden, and have the disapprobation, even of the "stout negro woman" who tracks him down at the end of the play.

Several plays published by Green in 1926 also made references to African American sacred and secular music, frequently in tandem. Barrett Clark goes a bit too far in suggesting in his introduction to *Lonesome Road: Six Plays for the Negro Theater* (1926) that "Mr. Green is doing for our drama what the writers of spirituals have done for Negro music" (xx). Overemphasizing Green's contributions while ascribing the spirituals of the oral tradition to "writers" and thus missing in some ways the importance of Green's ability to recognize the value of the oral tradition in his writing, Clark nonetheless recognizes, as some critics of the time did not, that folk contributions other than spirituals had their beauty and value, even if recognition and exaltation had come to the spirituals through volumes such as *Slave Songs of the United States* and the lucrative popularity of touring groups such as the Fisk Jubilee Singers. The title of the volume may well have some reference to the blues tradition as well. Not only is the idea of the "lonesome road" ubiquitous in a blues tradition spawned in an era of migration for African Americans, but country artist Henry Whitter recorded a "Lonesome Road Blues" in 1923, and Harry A. Yerkes, with vocalist Al Bernard, recorded a "Lonesome Road Blues" in 1919 (incidentally, the same year he recorded a tune entitled "Shake, Rattle, and Roll"). "Lonesome Road Blues" is also another title for "Going Down the Road Feeling Bad."

With Charles Gilpin in the title role, Green took North Carolina farmers from 1885 to Broadway and a Pulitzer Prize in *In Abraham's Bosom* (1926), an expansion and reworking of two earlier one-act plays from 1923 and 1924. Abraham McCranie is a rebellious North Carolina farmer whose existence symbolizes the rapacious nature of black-white relations in the South—what might be termed a "voluntary rape" on the altar of economic necessity, if Abe's mother's rape is anything like Abe's wife Goldie's. Product of a white master and black slave, the tragic mulatto theme finds early expression in the explanation for Abe's bifurcated consciousness: "White and black make bad mixtry" (*The Field God and In Abraham's Bosom* 23). The play begins in the turpentine camps that were one of the primary birthplaces of barrelhouse and boogie woogie piano, where Zora Neale Hurston shot some fieldwork footage in 1928, and where sawdust sopped up watered-down "licker," sweat, blood, snot, and tears in dusty clumps on the barrelhouse floors. One worker, Puny, calls Abe "no' count" (21), like the previous protagonist, and in the tempestuous and rough-hewn racist world of the logging camps, perhaps he is, with his revolutionary notions of freedom, equality, and brotherhood (remembering Green's racial sensitivity developing while he was in Paris in World War I)—he even publicly names old man McCranie as his father, and thus Lonnie as his brother. While others believe that "Nigger's place down de bottom" (22), Abe champions "eddication" as a means of self-improvement, reading books while folks like Lije while away their time playing the harmonica (28, 42, 45, 46), and Abe's own son Douglass becomes, to Abe's mind, a no account guitar player (93–94, 114).

Indeed it is Abe's desire to learn enough to teach school himself, to help others to learn to read and write, that runs head on into the southern racism that will cause his problems and, ultimately, the replication of his life story with his own wife, and his death. That Abe is compared ironically by Puny to Abraham Lincoln (24), the "Great Emancipator," and has a son named Douglass, perhaps with reference to both Frederick Douglass's connections with literacy and freedom and Lincoln foe and pro-slavery advocate Stephen Douglass, representing the continuing slavery debate of American history within Abe's own family, both give historical resonance to their fictional names. That he calls himself "crazy" (39) at one point for standing up for himself connects him to the oral history collected by Alan Lomax from blues singers Big Bill Broonzy, Memphis Slim, and Sonny Boy Williamson I, who told stories of how standing up for yourself frequently sparked the designation "crazy," and a lynching as well (*Blues in the Mississippi Night*). But he persists in his practical craziness because, like Mamie Smith in "Crazy Blues," not only does he suffer from hard times and frustration, but he also needs to strike at the figures that, as Chicago mayor Richard J. Daley commented much later in 1968, "preserve disorder."

Undereducated himself, Abe champions book learning and the written tradition at the expense of what the oral tradition can provide. Harmonica playing, after all, was valuable for the "no 'count boy," and Lije uses it in this play to relax himself as well, while others argue and battle. Lije also sings "Dark Was the Night," best known today for the 1927 version by Blind Willie Johnson placed in a time capsule orbiting the Earth, with ironic reference to the violence of the turpentine camp environment, as well as a reference to crucifixion in light of the sacrifice of Abe in the play. In fact, Puny and Lije, who as workers are a bit behind the others in productivity, use a musical metaphor with relation to African American song to emphasize their abilities: "When he gi' de call we gi' him de 'sponse eve'y time, suh" (33). While such elements are signs of dissipation or acquiescence to Abe, they can in fact produce moments of enlightenment and fellowship, even if they may be misused to reinforce a slavery status quo, as when Bud and Lije accept the "[n]igger's place down de bottom" as, ironically, "gospel" (22). As others around him mouth the mantra of racial inferiority, Abe answers a calling of his own, but with a response that tries to lift but only separates.

After all, Muh Mack and Douglass connect with each other closely when Douglass plays his guitar—two of the few places in the play where some happy communion takes place. Muh Mack is described as having hair "around her head Medusa-like" (49)—lines not spoken in performance—with clear reference to her feminine outrage over the situation of African Americans and women, including her sister, Abe's mother. Her malevolence toward Abe and assistance to Douglass behind Abe's back mark her as a dangerous, though explicably angered, force in Abe's life, one that does little to bring about uplift, and thus an identifiable segment of an 1885 African American community. Her lullaby for Douglass predicts he will be "a champeen sojer" (49)—ironic perhaps when used as a soporific, but certainly a hint that Muh Mack knows that some type of warrior is needed.

Abe wavers in the play between blaspheming and Christian devotion, claiming "ain't no God for the black man, that's a white man's god" (130) but later in the same scene delivering a sermon of praise and devotion to the "God of the poor and of the sinful" (135). Envisioning his son, like Frederick Douglass or Harriet Tubman, a "new Moses" (135), though Muh Mack terms him in scene 5 the proverbial blues "poor boy" (158), he clearly disapproves of the old secular song and dance—the diversions he feels have delayed and prevented real progress—to which Muh Mack and Douglass laugh and caper. They do so even as Douglass sings the old blues murder ballad about the no 'count gambler "Brady," a version of which was recorded for the Library of Congress by Blind Jesse Harris in Alabama in 1937. Remembrance of the "sporting life" and reckless dissipation are not what Abe is about, but Douglass, whose teacher has put him back in the third reader (100), can "make music raght out'n [his] haid" (93), a clear reference to the oral tradition and its different values from the written. Douglass, who has seen the violence and the road gangs and wielded the eight-pound hammers, still knows the songs that the people love, be they murder ballads, work songs, or dance instruction songs like "Jonah's Band" (128–29), with its references to "coonjine" and "Mobile Buck" dances. A pre-gospel Georgia Tom Dorsey, slide master Tampa Red, and female impersonator Frankie "Half-Pint" Jaxon, as "The Black Hillbillies," recorded a "Kunjine Baby" in 1929, mixing corny jokes and rowdy music into a rollicking good time that seems old-fashioned, but in a warmly down-home way. And Douglass can elicit warm responses from Muh Mack when no one else can. Although Abe is right to agitate for rights and freedom, his uncompromising tunnel vision and self-righteous, if understandable, condescension—he beats a student half to death for lying (142)—toward those who resist his call for literacy and uplift alienates those who remain connected to the folk past and only need to be fostered along more carefully to an acceptance of Abe's call for advancement. Abe faces the attitudes in the community that blacks belong subordinated to whites, as stated by his coworkers in scene 1, Muh Mack throughout the play (161), and Douglass in scene 7. They find books to be antithetical to the existence of blacks, and Abe runs headlong into the attitude as expressed by Goldie in scene 4 that "Old Master gwine be good to us now" (157). Abe's belief in a meritocracy (159) and his mantra of education (160) blind him to the complexities and nuances of the situation of the post-slavery African American seeking a path out of the welter of racism, damaged group psychology, and sociopolitical and socioeconomic disadvantages that dominate physical existence. Like the biblical patriarch, Abe is willing to sacrifice his son in obedience to his commitment, but Abe becomes not a father of Israel but fodder for the unreal racist replication of his mother's humiliation, and a Cain to Lonnie's Abel (136, 174)—though Abel did not sleep with Cain's wife.

The play also contains sufficient language that is often, but not necessarily, associated with the blues to give it a bluesy ambience, such as references to "bad luck" (56, 130) and "trouble" (118, 132) and phrases like "ain't no use to cry" (42), which echoes Bessie Smith's "You've Been a Good Old Wagon" (1925) and Barefoot Bill's (Ed Bell's) "My Crime" (1929). In scene 6, after Abe is beaten, he perhaps echoes some blues language when he comments on "de moon looking on it so peaceful lak" (117), as in Lightnin' Hopkins's "Shining Moon," and also sung in variations by Charley Patton and Big Joe Turner—"Don't the moon look pretty shining down through the trees." Abe's answer is to "dig me a hole now and cover me up" (117), suggesting John Lee Hooker's "Build Myself a Cave" (1949), Arthur Crudup's "I'm Gonna Dig Myself a Hole" (1951) ("and move down under the ground"), and Mr. Honey's "Build a Cave" (1951)—and makes one wonder about Sister Morgan's unissued "Dig a Hole Blues," recorded with Will Shade in 1927 (Dixon, Godrich, Rye 662). The decision in scene 4 to return to the McCranie country plantation to live after fifteen grueling, tumultuous years in the big city of Durham resonates with the lyrics of blues songs dealing with a post–Great Migration disillusion with urban life, just as Abe's resolve to "build up on a new foundation" (156) echoes the gospel song "Working on a Building" (Swan Silvertones). Also notable, though never heard in performance, are the ominous stage directions provided by Green just after he kills Lonnie: "The wind groans through the trees like the deep note of some enormous fiddle and then dies away with a muffled boom across the open fields" (121), a most evocative association of the troubles of the moment with music, nature, and the blues, urging Abe from his deepest fears to escape into the expanses of the world. Earlier in the play, Puny uses the epithet "'y God" (17), anticipating Hurston's use of "I God" in Jody's speech in *Their Eyes Were Watching God*, but neither Puny nor Abe are God, neither can control their inexorable fates. Despite Abe's grand gestures, or Mr. McCranie's belated and puny ones, the cycle continues. Abraham, after years of wandering, returns to the plantation to pursue the gospel of education by establishing a school for blacks. Unfortunately, once his plans are disclosed, violence and murder ensue, and Abraham, defiant in the throes of death, foresees freedom in the future of his people, while his wife, Goldie, only foresees rutting "lak hawgs" (124) in a ditch as her only way out.

However, in comparison to the language of Howard W. Odum in his novels, the speech is much less freighted with folk sayings and folk song references. If at times Odum overplayed his hand as folklorist, Green, who is also drawing on folk materials here, neither overdoes the dialect nor the lore. Green steers an economical via media between folk language submersion/asphyxiation and laissez-faire formal elocution that seems satisfactorily appropriate to the characters.

Hailed by many critics at the time, white and black, *In Abraham's Bosom* placed Green as a central catalyst in the Harlem Renaissance aim to raise the profile of literature about African Americans as it exposed issues important in their lives, and indeed the lives of all Americans. While it is probably Green's most famous play, others that he wrote at the time were reasonably successful, and partook of the folk-blues and hot music roots that howl and hum in the grasses and forests of these two plays. From the same 1926 volume, *White Dresses*, for example, employs "Gwine on down the road" (56), "mah time ain't long" (57), and a jailhouse blues (67), all used in a sacred-secular continuum as they occur in the folk tradition, as "my time ain't long" occurs in both spirituals by the Virginia Female Jubilee Singers (1921) and Elmore James's "Dust My Broom" (subtitled "I Believe My Time Ain't Long," 1951). Even more pertinent, the plays "The Prayer-Meeting" and "Your Fiery Furnace," both from *Lonesome Road*, feature appearances by the McCranies, making Green's volume hang together like the short fiction cycles of Sarah Orne Jewett's *The Country of the Pointed Firs* (1896), Sherwood Anderson's *Winesburg, Ohio* (1919), Jean Toomer's multi-genred *Cane* (1923), and Ernest Hemingway's *In Our Time* (1925), with Faulkner's Yoknapatawpha County just around the corner.

"The Prayer-Meeting" is a one-act play that includes Douglass McCranie as a guitar playing "fast nigger" (93) who has designs on Lorina, one of Grandmuh Boling's granddaughters, while a local preacher, Joe Day, straight out of the folk tradition of mocking the randy preacher, pursues (and runs away from), the other granddaughter, Ila. When the four set up a phony "prayer meeting" as a front for a good-time gathering to fool Grandmuh Boling, the stage is set to explore the interactions between sacred and secular musics and actions, and the implications of their presence in the African American community. The implications of the "prayer meeting" in African American culture are reflected in Langston Hughes's poem of the same title, in which an impoverished sister sings three times within the short space of the poem "the dawn's a comin'" (*Collected* 35). As if she is trying to convince herself of some new part or possibility, she hopes for a transformation of the world from night to darkness in language that is general enough to hide whatever might be dangerous to say, but fervent enough to make it heard and understood. If this prayer meeting of Lorina's and Ila's will produce a new day, what kind does Green suggest it will be?

The play starts with a snippet from an African American song, fittingly one that could be either sacred or secular, and certainly one of the most touchingly dramatic depictions of human misery and desire on record:

> *I lie in de grave and stretch out my arms,*
> *And I lay dis body down* . . . . (89)

This lyric was, in fact, published in the *Atlantic Monthly* in 1867 in the reminiscences of Thomas Wentworth Higginson who, as the colonel of an all-black regiment, frequently heard soldiers singing such songs as would provide early examples of spirituals, as well as language that might later translate to the blues as well. Ishmon Bracey sang similarly "Went to the graveyard, fell down on my knees" in "Trouble-Hearted Blues" (1928), and Furry Lewis intoned in "Sweet Papa Moan" (1927) "Ooh, I'd rather be dead and in my grave / Than be here in the world, baby, and be your slave," the reference to enslavement making allusion to historical conditions of chattel slavery as well. Of course, as we have said before, blues and religious traditions are on an overlapping continuum in African American music, sometimes responding to each other in texts that are in the know. Willie Mitchell, for example, recorded a tune entitled "Prayer Meeting" that is a twelve-bar blues; Jimmy Smith chilled on a walking blues entitled "The Sermon." The notion of a bluesman preaching might be alien among some of the faithful in the pews, but blues and jazz performers have been known to preach the gospel truth for many years, and not without a bevy of religious nuggets amongst the hard truths of the countrysides and streets. Green's mix of the two here is set to offer a nuanced view of the interaction between artificially opposing sides.

The heightened sense of life in the throes of the fervid wish for release captures perfectly the sense of entrapment felt by a variety of black characters, for various reasons, in Green's plays. Here the young women are struggling with racism, classism, ageism, and gender discrimination as they walk the courtship plank over shark-infested waters. Each step is fraught with the dangers of racist, classist, and sexist stereotyping, as well as with the surrealistic and satirical dangers that Peetie Wheatstraw conveyed in his lyric:

> When I first met you, baby, you was beat just like a slave.
> You had one foot on a banana peeling and the other foot in the grave.

Lorina complains, "Things is changed. Young folks is going to have pleasure this day and time" (94), echoing the lament of the first blues generation born outside of slavery (and perhaps every other generation in all times!), but despite the changes, elements of institutional discrimination remain firmly entrenched in the cores of the boilers. Saying that Grandmuh acts "as if she was still a slave" (94) and comparing her to the devil ("Old Scratch" 92), she makes her misery her ex-slave grandmother's fault rather than the fault of the enslavers.

Black, poor, young, and female in the South in the late nineteenth century, the illusion that "true womanhood" and "'spectability" (93) might somehow be within their grasps while Jim Crow laws, job discrimination, and misogyny clawed at their heels, the young women experienced the immobile desperation of the deluded masses. The young men, trapped also in their gender roles and facing the same socioeconomic and racial barriers, do their best to live up to their roles as hunters and gatherers and protectors in a world where they are very exposed and conquerable. And Grandmuh fears a world where she is becoming more frequently irrelevant and powerless to exert even a moral suasion over her charges, where the old ways are becoming increasingly anachronistic. And all are living in the pressure cooker of the paradoxical apocalypse, where a world that never existed is about to be destroyed and replaced by the illusion of a world that never will be.

With this lyric firmly in mind, the casual opening and humble setting, with petty arguments only vaguely hinting at more cataclysmic issues, seems ironic unless we keep in mind Green's observation that there is deeper significance to be found in the lives of the "lower" classes. Slivers of song work into the play to provoke the aches that will grow into tragedy. For example, Lorina sings a train song at the outset:

> O mister engineer,
> I'm a-going away from here . . .
> Going down to Alabam',
> Going to see my man.
> And the engineer, he say— (92)

Invoking the notion of travel so important to the blues and the period in which it emerged, and the love relationships that became elective and increasingly important in the era, the song lays out Lorina's loneliness. The power of the machine, the train, to deliver her from her isolation makes her optimistic and suggests that there is a possibility of achieving mobility—not only geographic but socioeconomic—and interpersonal stability. Unfortunately, the suggestion that she must appeal to a male engineer, in an era when women were still restricted in movement by their gender, suggests a barrier to fulfillment, a barrier that is underscored when the song is interrupted before the engineer can respond. The lack of communication here sets us up not only for the misunderstandings of the couples, but for conflicting imperatives and goals of the males and females in the play, and the mystery of how hidden and not-so-hidden forces will be able to derail their plans. When Lorina interrupts her singing to ask whether her "placket" is showing, her intentions to conceal something for which Douglass, a sporting guitarist (102–3), will most certainly be looking—the means to remove her skirt easily—blends smoothly with the engineer's lost communication and sets the couple at loggerheads immediately, playing the gendered game of coy-itus. That is prime territory for the blues, especially those of the whore houses of New Orleans, the juke joints of Mississippi, and the ditches of North Carolina.

We get even further inkling that this will not be a fervent prayer meeting when Lorina cranks up the old graphophone and puts on a traditional and popular minstrel song, "The Preacher and the Bear," to greet the imitation congregation. The song, part of the repertoire of blackface comedienne and singer Rosa Scott in 1906 (Abbott and Seroff 22), was recorded by Arthur Collins in 1905, the Golden Gate Quartet in 1937, and blues singer and songster Virgil Childers in 1938. While the lyrics are not included in the play, Green's allusion evokes the tradition of satirizing preachers as scoundrels just the same as anyone else—a secular element that also occurs in the blues, partricularly from the point of view of surrealists who see blues singers as being on the side of evil (Garon 136). The titular preacher is going out to hunt on the Sabbath, which is strictly forbidden. Later, when he is pursued by a bear, he pulls out a razor—a hallmark of the stereotypical no 'count negro—to protect himself, and then humorously offers a prayer that if the Lord won't help him, "please don't help that bear." The intention both to criticize and mock the preacher is clear. His hypocrisy foreshadows that of preacher Joe Day in the play, whose unsavory character does not go unremarked, described in stage directions with an urbane sauciness that would fit into George Schuyler's later satire *Black No More* (1931) as "a lover of chicken dinners and plump hostesses" (102). Plural, not singular.

Of course, Lorina remains hopeful that Joe *can* be faithful, even though she expresses her cynicism. She breaks out into song with a stanza about true love and faithfulness from the blues ballad "John Henry," describing the way that John Henry's wife said she was "going where [her] man fell dead" (98). Significantly, though, the faithfulness and commitment is on the part of the wife in the story, not the man, and even Lorina "laughs shrilly" (98) at the song's outcome—what would one get by going where a man fell dead? Having just spoken about "going to the devil" for her evil ways, and pinned a rose, symbol of love, into her hair, she snaps, "Oh, hell, what a song," a sign that her own cynicism and lack of sentimentality might just help deliver her to hell, and that her flowery accessories are merely insincere veneer.

Significantly, immediately after she comments negatively on the blues ballad of heroism, strength, and faithfulness, she "starts the graphophone softly playing 'Negro Blues'" (98) as Angie enters the room with a hidden handgun. The blues and their frequently violent environments are often associated with weapons and danger, so the blues song in fact awakens us to that blues element in Angie's actions. Since Green capitalizes the first letters of each word and puts them in parenthesis, it seems he is referring to a specific and not simply some generic blues. In fact, "Nigger Blues," copyrighted in 1912 by Leroy "Lasses" White and recorded for phonograph record four different times and piano rolls four times between 1916 and 1919, was quite popular at the time (Muir 30). Green might have wished to avoid using the epithet in his stage directions, since they are in his own voice, and that may account for the change to "Negro," though the "Lasses" White song was actually first titled "Negro Blues." As Muir points out, the song "is strongly influenced by folk blues" (30) in comparison to other pop-oriented blues of the time, and its seeming authenticity may well be a reason for Green's choice. As the play enters more deeply into interpersonal relationships between black males and black females in the story, the folk-ballad heroism of "John Henry" gives way to a greater cynicism with regard to such issues.

White's song is actually made up of common "floating" verses from the blues tradition, strung together loosely or associatively in the folk-blues style. A "prominent Washington lawyer and businessman" (Evans, *Let's Get Loose* 4) named George O'Connor was among those who recorded the song, in his best "negro" manner. The song consists of an opening section that defines what the blues is, initially in masculinist terms—"a good man feelin' bad" and "the doggone heart disease." More importantly for the play, the song segues into a section that deals with the train, and the reader can track the train motif as it blows through the play. Having moved through the engineer's song and then the railroad ballad "John Henry," Green maintains the motif—even though the lyrics are not included in the play—with his evocation of "Negro Blues." In this case, the first train stanza outlines how men and women respond differently to the blues: the man "takes a train and rides," and the woman "hangs her little head and cries." Not only does the lyric suggest that men and women are fundamentally different in their responses to the blues—and perhaps to life—

the men active and the women passive (and weak with their "little" heads), but it cynically suggests that the rift between them is hopeless, and shows a movement away from communication (the engineer song) and reunification ("John Henry") toward destructive polarities. Is there some truth to the notion that women, with more limited mobility and greater gender-role responsibility for children, might be less likely to be able to catch the train and go away? Indeed. But that does not necessarily mean that they will passively be left behind. Many a blues woman has suggested she merely picked up and moved on to another relationship.

The man may not be as necessary or as mourned as he might think he is. The following stanza says the train "ain't going to bring [him] back." The song doesn't say he was asked. What will bring him back is the notion that she will wear black—will mourn him. If she does, he threatens his ghost will come back to haunt her if she responds sentimentally—or in some cases even practically—to her loss. There is more than a bit of nastiness in this directive, and some arrogance as well. He is going to tell her how to respond? How much control does he think he has? And is that part of their problem?

The transition to the following stanza, however, is abrupt. In the final stanza, the traditional lines about laying his head on a railroad line and letting the train "pacify [his] mind" (used later in Thelma La Vizzo's 1924 version of Richard M. Jones's "Trouble in Mind") present the fatalistic conclusion that the lyrics express about his life—and hers. While he actively destroys himself, she is left behind with the directive to respond unsentimentally to his passing. Of course, the blues is not encouraging suicide here, but charting the graph of human experience and response, much in the manner of the naturalist dissecting the actions of characters under examination. Does a man necessarily catch a train and ride, and a woman simply give way to despondency? Must the story end in horrible, mangling decapitation? Not only don't they or must they, but things frequently didn't play out this way. The song is not an imperative, but a suggestive scenario displaying a blues ur-narrative for consideration. African Americans had been enslaved enough by ur-narratives to simply give in to them. The mix of feelings and responses are meant to be provocative, not controlling, participatory in the manner of the communal orientation of performance in the West African and African American tradition. They are call-and-response, just what that fragile black platter is spinning dizzily on the turntable about.

Just before Angie leaves and Lorina sings another song to herself, Lorina argues with Angie, ending her dismissal of him with "she'll [Grandmuh] be done o' you some o' these days" (100). Green continues with the blues motif here, echoing common southern expressions that made up the title of Shelton Brooks's tune "Some of These Days," recorded in 1911 by white singer Sophie Tucker, and re-recorded by Tucker with Ted Lewis's popular band in 1926, the year the volume of plays was published (Rust II: 1706). The song treats the separation of two lovers and the lament of the one left behind, continuing the foreshadowing of interpersonal difficulties among the couples. In relation to Angie, the other half of the "couple" is Grandmuh, who is not fully aware of Angie's dissipation. The evocation of the song opens up the phrase to broader social interpretations—if you mistreat me now, it is coming back to you, be you son, daughter, partner, preacher, black person, white person, whatever. For example, when John Rucker rewrote Ernest Hogan's popular coon song "All Coons Look Alike to Me" as "All Guns Look Alike to Me" (Abbott and Seroff *Ragged* 15) there is more that a hint of malevolence in the titular parody. Whether the lyrics reflect that or not, as one considers the nature of the coon stereotypes, Rucker's objections might be inferred, but some more explicit lyrical statement would have been considered subversive and dangerous to Rucker's health. The reference to the title of the blues song sets up everyone in the play for some type of separation and loss, whether it be partner, family, tradition, group identity, or goals. In the lyrics are scenarios fraught with exploration and wisdom, not just drunken razor fights, dissipation, and lamentation.

All the more significant, then, is the transition to the song "Raise a Ruckus Tonight." Recorded as early as 1923 by the Norfolk Jazz and Jubilee Quartet as "Raise R-U-K-U-S Tonight," the song has remained popular as a high-spirited party song, and it was recorded as "Gonna Raise a Ruckus Tonight" by jug band veteran Gus Cannon at his session for Stax Records in 1963. However, in the masking tradition of a good many African American songs, it does not hesitate to inject pointed lyrics of protest and complaint in a jovial performance where they might not be noticed or taken as such. One stanza that turns up on various recorded versions dates from the days and memories of slavery:

My old Mistus promised me
Raise a ruckus tonight
'Fore she died she'd set me free
Raise a ruckus tonight
She lived so long 'til her head got bald
Raise a ruckus tonight
She got out the notion of dyin' at all
Raise a ruckus tonight.

With its refrain,

> Come along, little children come along
> While the moon is shinin' bright
> We gonna git on board and down the river flow
> Gonna raise a ruckus tonight . . . (*Field Recordings* vol. 12)

it sounds for all the world like a song of anger at broken promises of freedom, and an invitation to respond in uninhibited fashion under cover of darkness, to escape down the river. Indeed, a song with these sentiments actually occurs in the text (115–6), though, as with certain apocalyptic lyrics (118) that they sing, Lorina offers that it "[a]in't nothin' but a song" (119). Unfortunately, the "prayer meeting" is really only a gathering, and the gathering is only a party, so there will be no appropriate "ruckus" raised in response to the way the white folks still treat Grandmuh and the rest of the blacks in the vicinity.

In fact, immediately following the "rucas" song, the sounding of a whip-poor-will replaces the celebration of an unfettered life with thoughts of death. In folk cultures, whip-poor-wills are frequently associated with the departure of a spirit from the body. Here, its juxtaposition with the "rucas" suggests that whatever the party is to signify, sounds of death are close by to foreshadow Angie's murder of Gus Turner later on, and the terrible swift sword of "justice" that arrives at the end of the play (132–33). When the granddaughters sing their songs of sin and retribution, they laugh away what Grandmuh sees and knows, and thus are unprepared for the climax. Furthermore, the name itself, whip-poor-will, suggests that Grandmuh, who rocks strongly and swiftly at the end of the play, is strong enough to overcome the weak-willed (whip-poor-will), and therefore survives intact, ready to leave her current residence. The signs she sees (128–9), communicated in a song that evokes the oft-recorded folk song "Don't Leave Me Here"/"Don't You Leave Me Here" (to the tune of "I'm Alabama Bound" and, later, "Don't You Feel My Leg") prompt her to this resolution, while Angie's crime ultimately separates the two, as she has been separated from her female grandchildren by their errant ways. While the others are shocked and defeated, Grandmuh offers the benediction, "Boy, you's gut to pay" (131), though what he has to pay for is not merely a personal fault, but one produced by social conditions produced by racism and prejudice as well.

Grandmuh has to *pray*, even as she pays, for the racism that keeps her religion from being a compelling force in the lives of her post-Reconstruction grandchildren. She is herself only partially connected to her folk-heritage, clinging to the religion, but lacking the knowing and rebellious mother-wit, that, combined with her faith, would allow her to function more meaningfully in her community. Mother-wit, a native intelligence or perception that sees through the illusions of race, class, and gender superiority, is a mode of surviving that partakes of observation, reflection, and insight rooted in a particular sense of the need for this certain kind of power from the perspective of multiple powerlessness. It is the black woman who must read her world from the disadvantage of subordinations, and thus develop a peculiar skill at perceiving and interpreting racial and patriarchal power gestures. Because Grandmuh is unable to recognize the deliberate and incidental operations of these gestures in her life and the lives of her grandchildren, she is doomed to live in the ashes of the past.

These plays do not exhaust all of Green's use of African American music in his plays of the 1920s. "White Dresses" (1926) includes a field holler blues song with "road/heavy load" lyrics (*Lonesome Road* 56–57) similar to those used by Langston Hughes in "Bound No'th Blues." Later in the same play, he interpolates a jailhouse blues (67), "Your Fiery Furnace" (1926), with obvious reference to the story of Shadrach, Meshach, and Abednego, references "spo'ting blood" (*Lonesome Road* 185), "a box to play" (192), a "lonesome road" blues, "Duncan and Brady" (196–97, here with the "hacks all dead in line" instead of the train's tracks all out of line, as in Blind Lemon Jefferson's "Rambler's Blues"), and a judgment day song as well (205–06). His "Supper for the Dead," printed in the 1927 release *The American Caravan*, employs several folk-chants in a Cape Fear River swamp in North Carolina (Van Wyck Brooks 1–17). From *In the Valley* (1928), Green's "In the Valley" includes a John Henry character, song (9–10), seer, and prophet, references again to "Duncan and Brady" (3) and perhaps to "Casey Jones" (7–8), a hammer song (28), an engineer song (30), the lyric "somebody's been here since I been gone" (32–33, referenced earlier in Bo Carter and Howlin' Wolf lyrics), and work songs such as "Water Boy" (36, 42–47, referenced earlier in Paul Robeson's version). Clearly, as an aficionado of African American folklore, Green made broad and deep use of the folk and popular traditions current at the time of his compositions, revealing a nuanced understanding of the uses and meanings of African American folk and hot sources to help legitimize his selection of subject matter and dramatize sociopolitical and racial elements in the segregated world of the South. The intersections among the lives of religious and secular African Americans, as well as blacks and whites, steam from out of the songs like a swampy mist, thick with tradition and experience, ghostly as midnight lynchings in the full moonlight, and never quite within the grasp of the lost and dejected characters stumbling through the plays with the hellhounds circling eerily at their heels, ready to spring when the time suits them.

III

Of course, there were a variety of other plays making use of some kind of American hot music at the time. Darwin Turner referenced playwrights John Dos Passos, J. P. McEvoy, and Channing Pollock among those artists using pop culture to express anti-capitalist ideas in the 1920s (111). Two other white playwrights who wrote plays with significant hot music elements are John Howard Lawson (also mentioned by Turner) and Mike Gold. More crucially than John Dos Passos in his expressionistic play about dehumanizing capitalism *The Garbage Man* (1926), Lawson's *Processional: A Jazz Symphony of American Life* (1925) seeks to revitalize the theater by employing the "native" idiom and making use of vaudeville and revues to demonstrate the importance of jazz and its relationship to rebellion against the middle class, while at the same time trying to suggest its inadequacy as a result of co-optation by vulgar capitalistic forces in society. While Dos Passos had certainly employed a variety of African American–based minstrel, ragtime, pop, and jazz songs in *The Garbage Man* (subtitled "A Parade with Shouting"), and mixed realism with burlesque and musical comedy freely, Lawson relates jazz to society in more important and essential ways.

Lawson employs, as critic Ryan Jerving points out, "dance production numbers, ethnic caricatures, hand-made jazz, political cartoonery, media satire, Freudian brooding, and sentimental mother songs" (528) in an outrageous theatrical event in stereo-vision that both championed and challenged the use of jazz in contemporary theatrical productions. Julia Walker reports that this production had perhaps a forerunner in a 1917 ballet production entitled *Parade* (Walker 189–91), the scenario of which was written by Jean Cocteau, the dancing choreographed by Léonide Masssine and performed by Serge Diaghilev's Ballets Russes, with music by Erik Satie conducted by Ernest Ansermet, and sets and costumes by Pablo Picasso. It's one-act scenario included cardboard costumes, typewriters and foghorns as musical instruments, and a ragtime song that achieved separate success later, an addition to a variety of popular entertainments on stage. The technological instruments preceded Antheil's similar use of instruments by several years.

In his Foreword to Lawson's *With a Reckless Preface*, Harold Clurman, a reader for the Theatre Guild and co-editor with Lawson of Lawson's play *Success Story* (1932), writes of Lawson's first play *Roger Bloomer* (1923), where "[p]athos must be 'jazzed up,' the portrait of pain must be high-lighted and glaring as a poster" (xix). *The Pure in Heart* (1928) is dubbed by Clurman "Lawson's swan-song of the jazz-and-racket age" (xxii). In Clurman's eyes, both make use of jazz as rhythm, energy, chutzpah, and machine age spectacle, seriously and ironically, to portray the demands of the age upon its high-lifers and low-lifers. The question is, was this too great of a contradictory burden for jazz, and Lawson, to carry.

Born in New York City on September 25, 1894, Lawson began writing plays during his undergraduate years at Williams College. Opposed to joining the war effort, he got a position in the American Red Cross ambulance corps, where he met John Dos Passos. While in the corps, Lawson worked on his playwriting. He spent time postwar in Rome and France, where he completed his play *Roger Bloomer* (1923), which ran for fifty performances on Broadway in 1923. The socialist Lawson's expressionistic play *Processional* (1925)—featuring calypso singer Sam Manning, who made some recordings with jazz and blues groups, as Rastus—had a dismal run with the Theatre Guild, but Lawson, spurred on in 1926 at the New York International Theatre Exposition by constructivist, cubist, and futurist plays, became even more enthusiastic about drama. He began to work for the Workers Drama League and New Playwrights Theatre (the latter funded by Hart Crane's patron Otto Kahn) with his friends Dos Passos and Michael Gold through 1929, and later the National Executive Committee that attempted to establish the Proletarian Artists and Writers League with Soviet backing in 1926. Continuing his playwriting with such works as *Processional* (1925) and *The International* (1928), Lawson headed for Hollywood in 1928 where five years later he helped to found and became a president of the Screen Writers' Guild. In 1947, along with the rest of the "Hollywood Ten," he refused to testify before the House Un-American Activities Committee. After the blacklist, Lawson taught and continued to write, including the screenplay for *Cry, The Beloved Country* (1951). He died August 11, 1977.

In *Processional*, Lawson deals with a miners' strike in the West Virginia coal fields, portraying an expressionistic mindscape where proletarian workers sort through a confusing and violent world. The subtitle of the play, "*A Jazz Symphony of American Life*," connects the play to the world of European classical music; Gershwin's opera *Blue Monday* (1922), Milhaud's ballet *La Création du Monde* (1923), Gershwin's *Rhapsody in Blue* (1924), and George Antheil's *A Jazz Symphony* (1925) all shortly preceded Lawson's play. There was clearly a sense that versions of jazz were typifying American life in various confusing and contradictory ways, so the duration had to be orchestrated with a tapestry of cantankerous, cacophonous, and downright deadly moods and motives that necessitated, some authors thought, an expansive European canvas to capture its amorphous magnitude, seriousness, and importance. Composer Aaron Copland indicated something like this when, in 1952, he articulated what many classical composers were after in the 1910s: "We wanted to find a music that would speak of universal things in a vernacular of American speech rhythms. We wanted to write music on a level that left popular music far behind—music with a largeness of utterance wholly representative of the country Whitman had envisaged" (Alexander 333). Though one of Whitman's models was the expansiveness of American territories, certainly his use of European operatic techniques in his work provided a model of elevation and legitimacy as well.

As Jerving points out, this forces the play to be "vaudevillesque" (536) rather than plain vaudeville, because it cannot be symphony and vaudeville at the same time: "the symphony implies a normative aesthetic unity; vaudeville, a menacing heterogeneity" (536). However, neither designation negates the possibility of the other: a constantly menacing heterogeneity does imply an aesthetic unity, and aesthetic unity can also be built out of bursts of heterogeneity. It is a difficult concept and form with which Lawson is working, but not one which was foreign to American shores, or unknown in a country where "E Pluribus Unum" cries out from every shred of its dollar bills. It is the American enterprise itself, real as a paper dollar in the pocket of a ghost.

The title *Processional* suggests a formal, perhaps even religious mood, one quite at odds with the author's expressionistic irreverence toward the characters and the setting in the story. In fact, the tensions to which Jerving points, "character/context, vaudeville/symphony tensions" (537) are accompanied by a variety of ancillary tensions in the play. *Processional* also sets up an immediate tension between the long, time-honored extended work and the brief initial processional: is this the whole story, or just the beginning? And when the people process *out* at the end, is it more appropriately a *recessional*, or one more procession to nowhere? Since Lawson describes his "symphony" as being in four movements, it seems he has in mind the standard symphonic form, suggesting an overall conventional endoskeleton on which to drape jazz scintillation, banality, and dissipation. In all, it is a most unsettled and unsettling form, though exactly what the age demanded: a chaotic mosaic of broken images of jazz reflecting the weariness, acedia, and perfectly functioning capitalistic lens that exposed the dysfunctional nature of American society in the 1920s, particularly its battling xenophobia and cultural pluralism (Jerving 538).

Lawson imbues the style and subject matter of the play with the rhythm, pace, and frantic feel of jazz as he conceives it. Stage directions set the political and social parameters for Lawson's broad and loose jam with jazz, or "native technique," as he terms it: "The rhythm is staccato, burlesque, carried out by a formalized arrangement of jazz music" (ix). Burlesque, of course, is key, since Lawson is sending up various aspects of American society through a grandiose, serio-comic symphony, king of the European musical genres. In the play, jazz is a virtual shape-shifting "confidence music," expressing everything from entertainment to politics to strikes to violence to carefree fun. Lawson (ab)uses jazz as he sees it popularly employed, in a commercialized, exploitative, jingoistic, racist, latest rage faddishness that reflects American society unable to come to terms with the realities of its race, class, and aesthetic idiocies. Lawson mixes characters (caricatures) from vaudeville (4), minstrelsy ("Rastus Jolly" 6), and pop-jazz with unions and union busters, pop-parlance, and patriotic appropriations of jazz—"wave the flag an' play a little jazz" (18)—to present a dizzying world where jazz is everything and nothing, a catch-all term that is "Runnin' Wild" (82, 91, 159). The Federal Theatre poster for the 1937 production of the play called it "The First Modern American Play."

There is a procession of bizarre attempts to manipulate a sense of reality toward a contemporary and upbeat attitude about divergent interpretations of American society. The unions are "jazzin' up the big strike" (4), making "jazz today for the glory of the working class" (7) and playing "striker's jazz" (33). In response, the town sheriff asserts, "I make my jazz with a gun, understan'" (66). Back of the serious issues confronted in the strike theme come banjo player and minstrel stereotype "Rastus Jolly," and fast-life slang references: "She's a jazz kid . . . Got a jazz bug" (184) and silly pop-blues such as "Bow Wow Blues" (58–9, 193). Jazz is on the "wrong" side of the tracks—"[t]he jazz melody of a bad woman in a small own"—as well as mixing in middle-class respectability: act 4 is entitled "The Jazz Wedding," which is really just a metaphor for the "illusion of harmony" (Jerving 540–41), a midsummer night's dream where all is not well that (seems to) end well. Nonetheless, when Jerving suggests that positive reviewers such as Fannie Hurst got it wrong by suggesting that the play was "a straight case of the vaudevilles, a 'jumble' as 'mad as we are mad'" (541), he seems to skirt the point that the play has to work as both vaudeville and symphony to represent the American many and one as well, and that, perhaps, that is the problem. Can many and one merge in a capitalistic society ruled by the belittling stereotypes, treacherous cynicism, and unrepentant rapacity that underlie, and undermine, our democracy? When Joseph Wood Krutch suggests that the point of the production is "not the particular story which the play has to tell but the sensation which it gives of the cries of disorganized humanity orchestrated in the form of a nearly formless symphony" (100), he evokes the notion of objective correlative, which places the play in stark relief against Eliot's "Prufrock" as a dizzily orchestrated journey into mayhem. But it is a Whitmanian journey as well, stopping momentarily to wait for us before passing on again; and a Poe-esque journey into the madness of a seemingly sane society which has constructed its own rationalizing voice.

In fact, hybrid jazz and blues, "Jazz March" (yoking jazz with its military ancestor in contemporary times) and "Yankee Doodle Blues," are the soundtrack for the entire play. A "Yankee Doodle Blues" was recorded in 1922 by Jazzbo's Carolina Serenaders, Ladd's Black Aces, and the Virginians, the last, actually "The Yankee Doodle Blues," with Gershwin *Rhapsody in Blue* arranger Ferde Grofé on piano. Gershwin, in fact, composed "The Yankee Doodle Blues," which appeared in *Spice of 1922* using lyrics by Irving Caesar and Buddy De Sylva. While the recordings were all instrumentals, Lawson uses the lyrics for his tune, put in the mouth of the minstrel banjo player Rastus Jolly. However, like many popular conceptions of African American performers at the time, Rastus is a ludicrous figure of amusement, a lugubrious figure howling like a dog and singing

> I got them Bow Wow Blues
> 'Cause they treats me like a dawg . . . (58)

all the while lamenting he is "one lonesome nigger, Boss" in his prescribed role of comic underdog. While, of course, he is an underdog, Lawson makes him howl and "bow wow" like a trained animal in the circus, while Rastus ironically dresses up in Klan clothes to keep himself safe (193), only to find himself about to be killed because, also ironically, he "ain't fit to associate with class-conscious workmen" (193). There is no mistaking the satire on the permutations through which African Americans and the working class must go to survive, and the masquerading and cases of mistaken identity that result from the misconceptions of the enemies that should be allies.

Lawson's "Yankee Doodle Blues" is another "Jolly" song, a patriot corker that brings the men together at the end, crying "make me lose those . . . Yankee Doodle Blues" (215). Jingoistically patriotic, it encourages "treasonous patriotism" that betrays American ideals for a pseudo-jazz march into meaninglessness. Originally, the song "Yankee Doodle" was employed by the British to mock English-speaking colonists who were too illiterate or ill-mannered or ill-bred to recognize their own deficiencies. The colonists embraced the song, and the supposed shortcomings, with a sense of their own superiority, and thus made a strength out of their inability to tell that a feather in a coon-skin cap was not highly fashionable, or that "keeping it up" is not the sign of a worthy moral gentleman. The song's employment here is a brilliant stroke on Lawson's part. Not only does it represent a common characterization of Americans that became a patriotic staple, but it also mixes truth and illusion to become a burlesqued insult of the originator, just as Lawson challenges the illusions and realities of American society. However, although the jazz band that performs throughout the play, The Jazz Miners (white banjoist Harry Reser performed in bands dubbed the "Jazz Pilots," "Seven Rag Pickers," and "Seven Wild Men" in the 1920s), believes it makes "the jazz today for the glory of the working class" (7), it is cut off from its black roots. The only black member, Rastus Jolly, turns out to be burdened with the name of a blackface stereotype, and he is a weak traitor and Klan member who sells out himself and his conspirators, while his music marches away from him. Jazz rhythm becomes, for Lawson, not an African American art form, but the representation of an authentic inner imperative: "The reality of America spiritually and materially, is a movement, a rhythm of which the inner meaning has not been found. Buried under the hokum [that jazz-age term that also described a genre of black music] of advertisements, headlines, radio speeches, there is a genuine inner necessity, a sense of direction" (Lawson xiii). Unfortunately, the hokum is not merely rubbish, not sly *double-entendre* of Tampa Red and Georgia Tom, but nefarious in its twisted omnipresence. Without the inner imperative, without the spirit, it is merely broken wind, speech without substance, mockery music of a society constantly processing without mining anything of real value, and of art that has a notion that the revolutionary elements of jazz can tear down, as well as build up, but doesn't quite know how to do it.

Processional was not Lawson's only play to make use of such elements. Both *Loud Speaker* and *The International* (both 1927) did so as well, as did *The Pure in Heart* (1928). Eventually, Lawson became less involved with avant-garde theatre and more so with film scripts, before his "membership" in the Hollywood Seven sidetracked his career. However, in the mid-twenties, Lawson made some important statements about American society and mythology with the protean and diluted meanings of jazz figuring heavily into his mix, though the African American element had typically been racheted down to minstrel stereotype with a nefarious and misunderstood purpose. This portrayal was not Lawson's invention, but his portrayal of a sad commercial reality.

When Itzok Granich was born in 1893 to Jewish immigrants on Manhattan's Lower East Side, his *nom de plume* as radical Mike Gold was over two decades away. An eighth grade high school dropout who nonetheless spent 1912–1913 in journalism classes at New York University and 1914 at Harvard as a special student, he was familiar with the Wobblies through his brother Manny. He linked to leftist radicalism in early works published in Floyd Dell and Max Eastman's *The Masses* in August 1914—less than half a year after he found the Worker's Revolution at the end of a policeman's billy club—and his plays staged by the Provincetown Players between 1916 and 1920. In 1920–21, he took the name Mike Gold from a Jewish Civil War veteran who had fought on behalf of freeing African American slaves. Gold became co-editor of *The Liberator* in 1921–1922 with African American writer and African Blood Brotherhood member Claude McKay, and a founding editor of the *New Masses* in 1926, two years after writing a volume on the life of John Brown. This cemented his reputation as a radical proletarian figure through his editorship and by attacking such writers as Proust and Gertrude Stein for their intellectualized experimental difficulty in the face of the need for plain-spoken directness, much in the way that the Popular Front would turn away from such musical experimentation to embrace folk song. (Gold himself edited *Proletarian Song Book of Lyrics from the Operetta "The Last Revolution"*). Gold was a champion of the multiplicity of forms and styles he felt proletarian literature could take, including support for the uses to which writers like Langston Hughes could put the blues, or to which he could put them himself.

A supporter of the Communist revolution of 1917 and the party itself until his death, Gold's work as a columnist and polemicist has been outdistanced for many by his novel/fictionalized autobiography and prototypical proletarian work, *Jews Without Money* (1930), a fascinating and moving account of Gold's childhood in a Jewish ghetto and an achievement to stand alongside other such novels as James T. Farrell's *Studs Lonigan* trilogy (though Gold had a few critical words for Farrell). After its huge success, Gold joined *The Daily Worker* as a columnist, remaining with the paper until his death in the San Francisco Bay area in 1967. Though too often forgotten in American literary history now, he was an important artist and polemicist, prodder of literary lions (notably Sherwood Anderson, Hemingway, and the others listed above), and a staunch advocate of the proletariat. In fact, he called for "Letters from hoboes, peddlars, small town atheists, unfrocked clergymen, schoolteachers—/Revelations by rebel chambermaids and night club waiters" among many other contributions from his list of potential "worker-correspondents" (Denning 203). Michael Folsom entitles his introduction to a selection of Gold's literary works "The Pariah of American Letters," but he was important enough for Ernest Hemingway to tell him to "go fuck himself" (Carlos Baker 459) for calling Hemingway a "sentimental storyteller to . . . white collar slaves" (Folsom 159), "heartless as a tabloid" (160), and "a scoundrel" evidencing "enormous self-pity" (160). Gold was fearless, yet as sensitive as his model for proletarian literature, Walt Whitman, about whom Gold said, "Walt feared nothing; nothing shook his powerful serenity; he was unafraid before the bewildering tragedy of life; he was strong enough to watch it steadily, and even to love it without end" (Folsom 68). Ultimately, the Gold who sought "singing and music rising in every American street" (Folsom 70) felt that the "method must be the revolutionary method—from the deepest depth upward" (Folsom 70). From the Jewish slums, from the African American ghettoes, art and life would rise from the depths to the pinnacle in a Gold-en world of people without money.

Gold's *Hoboken Blues, or the Black Rip Van Winkle: A Modern Negro Fantasia on an Old American Theme* (1927) is one of the wildest theatrical rides of the 1920s. Part comedy, part history, part musical, part proletarian drama/political propaganda, Gold's expressionist play whirls an audacious path through social, racial, and artistic issues of 1920s America, making use of the blues as indicating individual trouble and hardship along with societal decay and discrimination, and the musical genre as well. Gold's outrageous dramatis personae includes a circus ringmaster, revival preacher, drunken horse-car philosopher, and chronically jobless banjo player among the fictional characters rubbing elbows with Plato, Spartacus, Christopher Columbus, George Washington, Henry Ford, the Angel of Death, and a 10,000-year-old Hoboken angel. Gold also eschews realism in setting, substituting a "peasant gaudiness" of color and "simultaneous planes of action . . . [of] some futurist paintings" (548). Snatches of music draw from pop songs, hurdy gurdy music, cakewalks, spirituals, ragtime, blues, jazz, and "futurist city music in the style of Edgar Varèse" (604), emphasizing again the anti-bourgeois futurist elements on which Gold regularly draws as a countercurrent to the humanistic elements he wishes to emphasize in the play. It is worthy of note that Varèse years later was a composer that Charlie Parker set out to study with, and that Varèse participated in a 1957 "jam session" workshop with Art Farmer, Charles Mingus, Teo Macero, and others that was on the cutting edge of the "Free Jazz" movement that emerged in the 1950s. Though it is outside the immediate realm of this book, it does suggest interesting affinities between classical music and jazz (*WFMU's Beware of the Blog*).

Works like Alexander Mosolov's "Zavod" (1927), a movement from his ballet *Steel*, imitated the sounds of an iron foundry and glorified the machine, ruler of the brutal urban environment. A year earlier, George Antheil had premiered his *Ballet Mécanique*, employing buzzers and airplane propellers, but unfortunately crashed in his American premiere in 1927. There is an interesting mixture of the mechanization of contemporary life and jazz and blues-like elements in *Ballet Mécanique*. This is particularly true in the second section, where almost boogie woogie–like ostinatos and bluesy runs join the shifting polyrhythms, syncopation, tone coloration such as buzzing and whirring, and percussiveness of the work—all hallmarks of West African music and its influence on African American music, jazz and blues in particular. Antheil, like Russian futurists (and like the early classical composers of the Popular Front who later made concessions to American folk songs to reach their public), hoped and believed his avant-garde music would appeal to the masses. Unfortunately, Randall Thompson's judgment that the *Ballet* represented for the public "the acme of demented modernism" (Cheek 3) dashed his hopes of achieving some kind of mainstream acceptance with his outlandish inventions. Like a number of writers of the 1920s, Gold clearly hears jazz as a cacophonous clanging analogous to the machine in some of its effects on the human beings subjected to the harsh elements of the city. When George Gershwin asserted in 1926 that jazz is an analogue to American life, which he described as "nervous, hurried, syncopated, ever *accelerando*, and slightly vulgar" (Wyatt 93), he too saw it as an appropriate expression of the spirit of American life. Writing for the most part a vigorous African American vernacular associated with the class of people who generated the folk-blues, with occasional "foolosopher" classical elevation and a touch of the Communist Party line from Plato and Spartacus, Gold's realistic language provides the home base from which the shifting times and settings outlandishly depart, and allow us always to return home to the point of view of banjo player Sam—whose language is the authority of the play.

As E. D. Lowry points out, "the most important discovery of the Futurists was the realization that fragmentation, contrast, and the interplay of various discordant materials constituted a direct expression of the speed and diversity of modern life" (1628). Gold exploits this dizzying pastiche of elements to portray negatively contemporary social upheaval and imbalance in contrast to the harmony of Hoboken. Even Gold's transitions from scene to scene rush forward, overlapping, compressing time and phasing through space, lending a nervous energy to its movement that fits F. T. Marinetti's reputation as "the caffeine of Europe" (Rawson 151). The fact that Gold also ignores the unity of time in the play, jumping forward twenty-five years to contrast Hoboken with Harlem, lends further disjunction to the play. Both Hoboken and Harlem appeared in titles of jazz and blues songs during the era, Harlem much more so that Hoboken. In *Jazz Records*, Hoboken appears in the titles "Hoboken Bucket" (323), "Hoboken Prison Blues" (622), and "Hoboken Rock" (478), and seems more of an oddity or jokey location for Gold to use in his play in contrast to a center of jazz and blues in Harlem. While Marinetti proclaimed "a racing motorcar . . . more beautiful than the victory of Samothrace" (Moholy-Nagy 90), Gold's driver Chill McGregor fades into an unhappy stupor without his horse-drawn car, chastised and nearly arrested at the behest of a Henry Ford (605), whose automobiles, like other mechanized elements of society, have gained ascendancy and made Chill an anachronism: "And de past is dead, ole man, it's done; it's absolutely, completely ruined; it wuz run over by a ten-ton auto-truck; it wuz pushed from the sixtieth floor of a skyscraper and got smashed. (Excitedly.) Yes, an aeroplane bombed it to pieces; a dynamo electrocuted it; a flapper and a banker buried it; it's under the daisies; even radio can't reach it no more" (605). Thus, Gold laments a lack of unity much like Henry Adams did in *The Education of Henry Adams* (1907; 1918), seeing a multiverse with which he has not been prepared to deal, and a dynamo that starkly contrasts to Adams's vision of the Virgin and the thirteenth century and Gold's of the angel of Hoboken, which allow for a unified feeling not possible in the blaring cacophony of 1920s city life.

Such lamentations are not uncommon to the blues tradition. In the face of declarations of a northern Promised Land and land of milk and honey by such organs as *The Chicago Defender*, migration from South to North was common following the Civil War into the 1920s. However, any number of poor migrants, faced with the distinct problems posed in the urban environment, heard their miseries expressed in the blues songs that were produced for them. John Lee "Sonny Boy" Williamson sang in "Down South Blues,"

> Lord, I'm goin back down South, man, where the weather suits my clothes.
> Now I done fooled around in Chicago, and I done almost froze.

Other songs recorded during the era are rife with references to going back South or to some southern location such as Georgia, Mississippi, or Memphis, Tennessee, in the face of rampant cold, hunger, northern inhospitality, police brutality, and vice.

The reference to the flight of airplanes here emphasize the importance of flight to Gold's play, as well as its relation to futurism. In the preamble to his first manifesto, Marinetti proclaimed "soon we will see the first angels fly," and in his novel *Mafarka le Futuriste*, the transcendent Gazurmah is said to make "total music" (Rawson 143). Sam's visitation by the Hoboken angel, who tells Sam, "We are alike—we are music" (595), adding "You are music, Sam Pickens. That's why I love you. I hear music coming from you that I can forever dance to, the world's eternal music. You must rise and come with me to Long Island, Sam Pickens, and we will live together and be happy" (596). This vision of music, in particular the banjo music that Sam makes as opposed to the commercial jazz and futurist music of Varèse as part of the Hoboken vision and the workers' paradise, emphasizes the people-based rather than machine- and money-based aesthetic of Harlem in the play. Sam and the angel are, after all, shortly thereafter beaten and arrested for vagrancy and sentenced to work in a factory with the words "I find them guilty of being poor. I find them guilty of being lazy and musical. I find them guilty of every other crime possible to persons who can't afford lawyers. These are two of the worst offenders against morality and Nordic Americanism I have ever had in my court" (598). Singer-guitarist Blind Blake described in song his own encounter with the police, who accosted him on his way home, put him in jail with no explanation or bond, adding, "They beat me and they kicked me, and put me through the third degree" ("Third Degree Blues," 1929). Rosa Henderson sang that policemen in Chicago "can't police at all" ("Chicago Policeman Blues," 1926), while Mamie Smith, in her groundbreaking recording that inaugurated the blues recording boom in 1920, asserted, "[I'm gonna] get myself a gun and shoot myself a cop" ("Crazy Blues," originally titled "Harlem Blues"). Clearly the antipathy between police and African Americans was very real. Sam, in fact, eventually calls the whites who prevent him from getting a job "white devils" (593, 594), just before he is sentenced for "petty happiness during business hours" (597), the devils standing in clear contrast to the angel of Hoboken (594) and the angel of Death (556). Ultimately, Sam is crowned with a barbed-wire crown of thorns in a parody of Christ's crucifixion, meant ironically by the townspeople, but seriously by Gold, who follows in a long tradition of comparing slaves to an innocent or crucified Christ, as in Paul Laurence Dunbar's "The Haunted Oak" (*Collected Poetry* 219–20).

Sam mentions the blues a number of times during the play, from playing the banjo to get rid of the blues (570) to the bum whose conversation gives him the blues (587) to his own ability to make up a "musical blues" that should make him employable (589). Most importantly, he sings a blues lyric to the music of his Hoboken song while playing an imaginary banjo, emphasizing the importance or art, imagination, and the ideal of Hoboken to his life:

> I got de blues, I got de blues,
> I got de job-huntin', nuthin'-to-do blues,
> Noo Yawk and Hoboken jes de bluest towns,
> Never give yo' nawthin— (588)

His straightforward assertion of his emotional condition, as well as the association of that condition with the situation he faces in the external world, is typical of the genre of the blues, which often describes environments as being imbued with the blues—"Harlem Blues," "Chicago Blues," "Fourteenth Street Blues," "St. Louis Blues," "St. James Infirmary Blues"—even "Front Door Blues," "Back Door Blues," and "Graveyard Blues."

Interestingly, his song is interrupted by a "blare of circus music" (588), which produces a ringmaster who announces an opening for a "savage" in the circus (589), indicating the limitations of job roles available to African Americans at the times. In fact, circus sideshow tents did employ African American musicians playing blues, jazz, and ragtime material (Abbott and Seroff, *Ragged* 166). This is significant because later Sam asserts that the city jazz he hears sounds like circus music (619), associating commercialized and, for Gold, co-opted jazz music with part of the racist game run by the white devils in power. When Sam returns to Harlem later in the play and is called on to speak, he is mocked by a person in the crowd, who says, "Dis is a circus" (614), indicating in his mind the joke they are playing on Sam; however, in Gold's mind the joke is on the crowd that has been duped into a money-grabbing, machine-driven gold rush. It is a circus, a canvas of unreality and false values, a dream (623–24). In the end, Sam calls for a world where there is "a place for de poor men, black and white, where birds sing sweet, and every house is full of music, and dere's sunflowers round de factory door. Where no one is hungry, where no one is lynched, where dere's no money or bosses, and men are brudders" (626). Then he breaks into his blues song, "The Hoboken Blues," and the crowd joins in. The "jazzing, singing couples" now place their jazzing at the service of Sam's vision, and transform the jazz into something that serves the people. They are now united with Sam through the music of the folk, not Varèse, to jettison their acquisitive capitalist vision for the values of the "peasant" class, whose wash hung on the lines like "tremendous rainbow symphonies" (548) at the outset of the play. This "black Rip Van Winkle," who, unlike the Rip who has slept through the Revolutionary War, has been unconscious through a counter-revolutionary war for the mechanization and capitalization of American society, wakes up to his responsibility to tell his story, like Rip, but to tell it to a purpose and reclaim American society.

Perhaps Gold chose Hoboken as the city of value because "hobo" is embedded within it. Although there are those who lump bums, tramps, and hoboes together indiscriminately, hoboes do not avoid work, as bums do. Rather, they move from job to job: they are "migratory workers" (Garon and Tomko 1)—in circuses, foundries, coal mines, harvesting, and such like jobs. Sam is misunderstood as a "lazy, no-count, triflin' bum" (551) by his wife Sally; he is in fact closed out of a number of jobs because he is African American, or dismissed from them for that reason, but is quite willing to go where necessary to work in a position that does not ask him to sacrifice his life and identity for money. In fact, out of desperation, he even offers to do that: "But I kin be a savage, mistuh. I'll do anything foh a job" (589). He promises to learn how to dance like a savage—one recalls a highly literate Bert Williams learning to speak dialect—and to forget how to learn to read and write—just what is required of him as an African American to know his place—but he is still rejected for the position.

The vision of Hoboken is one that is made for someone who has been a hobo and would like an easygoing, humanistic lifestyle instead of the contemporary hurtling of the "Twentieth Century Limited," as Hart Crane called it (62). The kinds of lives led by hoboes can be much like the pastiche that Gold concocts for his play—an array of variable positions arrived at by hopping a freight and left in the same manner. But unlike the fragmentation, contrast, and interplay of various discordant materials that defines futurism, this is a choice of freedom, not an imposition of society. The snatches of various songs that make up the soundtrack of the hobo's life are picked up from the folk, transmitted by the folk, to the folk, and the songs reconnect the people to their heritage, or perhaps better for Gold, to their class longing for liberation.

The works discussed in this chapter don't get much, well, play anymore. The canon has hardened, some say ossified, even petrified. Challenges to social mores seem outdated, and the sometimes almost sentimental notions of racial cooperation and understanding, while progressive for their times, smack of an inadequate understanding of the nuances of racism that is uncomfortably embarrassing in current conversation. But at the time the theatre was at times extremely exciting and avant garde, aiming to redirect a hopelessly wandering, shell-shocked, lynch-rocked, machine-locked world by expanding the social, political, and aesthetic boundaries of art. And just as tempers were flaring, the music was often hot as well.

Conclusion

As the 1920s came to a close and the stock market was set to blow its top, the retrospective reader might have looked upon a decade that was permeated by hot music. Popular culture teemed with it, race records sizzled, Broadway titillated, piano rolls and sheet music cranked it out, movies and cartoons concretized images. As American literature became international, so did American culture—by which was often meant African American culture. If with the millennium commentators recently labeled the twentieth century the American century, look how it was dominated by the color line, and the emergence of African American music especially, from ragtime to blues to jazz to swing to bop and rhythm and blues to soul to rap. From New Orleans's ragtime pianist Tony Jackson to Neverland Ranch's Michael Jackson, black music came increasingly to represent popular music in America, and the face of the King of Pop the face of a syncretistic America. While some authors felt pressured to pander to hot music to pay their winter heating bills, more often the remarkable perspectives, challenges, and artistic and social manumission produced by hot music excited authors examining the problems, prejudices, paradoxes, politics, and propriety of the color line.

Years ago, rhythm and blues singer H-Bomb Ferguson told me a story about performing in the segregated South in clubs that admitted both black and white patrons anxious to see the latest popular black performers. The club owners and town officials would meet the band at the outskirts of town, escorting them into town to ensure the black band went *nowhere* other than the club. Then the sheriff showed them around to the back door of the joint, where colored folks could get a sandwich. Upon entering the club to set up their equipment, after driving all night and day with windshields full of dust and sun, from their last gig, where they had been stiffed by an oily, absentee owner, the band would see it. That. That rope. That yellowish rope that ran down the middle of the club's dance floor to maintain the "proper" separation between black and white dancers once the band began to play. The rope, of course, had a special meaning in African American history, threatening symbol now of all the progress that hadn't been made. A Jim Crow slap in the face and grim welcome mat of Mississippi hospitality. It really put you in the mood to play.

But once the playing started! At first, the cordon was taboo, carefully avoided like the Egyptian plagues of skin disease and darkness. And then the touch. The jostle. The trembling of the rope, an ominous swinging. White go right and black go left, unconsciously, uninhibitedly, moved by the music into zones only hot music could produce, and the slender cord tipped and rocked, and loosened and untied the Gordian knot. And then a simple, natural step, a dance move descended from the vaudeville stage and there from the plantation, an expression of joy, and the color line fell to the music of H-Bomb, without a single casualty. A polychromatic field of action that produced a brief shock of recognition while the band played on. Of course, once the dance was over, the black band was escorted by the sheriff to the city limits again, with the admonition not to return for any reason. But for a couple of hours, blue notes and syncopation produced the polyrhythms that generated a call-and-response that moved america a little bit closer to AMERICA. That is the power of hot music.

So when America's writers began to employ the music, each with his or her own strengths and weaknesses, each in his prison, thinking of the key, confirming his prison, as Eliot would say, it was a huge small step, by black and white writers, in the direction of democracy. Of course, there have been backward steps and sidesteps, and times when it appeared we had no feet at all. But somehow the music kept us dancing, and singing, and eventually thinking. The music is better, the literature is better, the life is better, what for all these swapping of juices. Huck was right. Things just go better this way.

The sun *is* gonna shine in our back doors someday.

Hey! Hey!

Small world.

Appendix 1: Discography and Videography

Discography

This project would have been far more onerous without the heroic and indispensable service offered by Austrian Johnny Parth, from his early Roots and Paltram LP reissues, and especially his commitment to his Document CD reissue program, including the Wolf, Matchbox, Earl Archives, Old Tramp, RST, and Story of Blues labels. Making almost all pre-1945 reissued and unreissued blues recordings available was of monumental importance, and these frequently complete recordings of individual artists, as well as compilations of lesser-known recorded artists, have been a boon to the entire music world. These recordings have been constant companions during the process of writing this book (and way before, and I'm sure long after). Not only that, but the catalog of his releases has made my work much easier as well. Johnny is a treasure, and his legacy of releases is now in the capable hands of Gary Atkinson in the UK, at sales@document-records.com. (All references are listed in CD reissues except where noted.)

"Ahanta Chant One." *Ghana: Ancient Ceremonies, Songs, and Dance Music*. Elektra Nonesuch. CD. 9 72082-2.

Alderson, Mozelle. "Leave My Man Alone." *Kansas City Kitty: Complete Recorded Works in Chronological Order*. Document BDCD 6023.

Alexander, Texas. "Corn-Bread Blues." *Complete Recorded Works in Chronological Order, Vol. 1*. Matchbox, 2001. CD.

———. "Levee Camp Moan Blues." *Complete Recorded Works in Chronological Order, Vol. 1*. Matchbox, 2001. CD.

———. "Yellow Girl Blues." *Complete Recorded Works in Chronological Order, Vol. 1*. Matchbox, 2001. CD.

Alpert, Pauline. "Blue Baby." http://www.youtube.com/watch?v=IOH5BHwbDRc&feature=related

———. "Hallelujah." Victor 78 RPM 20786-B.

Anderson, Marian. "My Way's Cloudy." *Softly Awakes My Heart*. Naxos Nostalgia 8.120566.

Antheil, George. *Ballet Mecanique*. Naxos CD 8.559060.

———. "Jazz Sonata." *George Antheil: Bad Boy's Piano Music*. Col Legno 1CD 31880.

———. "Sonata Sauvage." *George Antheil: Bad Boy's Piano Music*. Col Legno 1CD 31880.

Armstrong, Louis. "Big Butter and Egg Man." *Portrait of the Artist as a Young Man 1923–1934*. Columbia Legacy 57176.

———. "Dear Old Southland." *Louis Armstrong: 1929–1930*. Classics 642.

———. "Heebie Jeebies." *The Hot Fives and Sevens*. JSP CD 311-315.

———. "Melancholy Blues." *The Hot Fives and Sevens*. JSP CD 311-315.

———. "Shine." *The Essential Louis Armstrong*. Columbia Legacy 89280.

———. "St. James Infirmary." *Essential Louis Armstrong*. Sony Legacy R 660315.

———. "Twelfth Street Rag." *The Hot Fives and Sevens*. JSP CD 311-315.

Arnold, Kokomo. "Bad Luck Blues." *Complete Recorded Works in Chronological Order, Vol. 4*. Document DOCD 5040.

Ashley, Clarence. "Dark Holler Blues." *Mountain Blues: Blues, Ballads, and String Bands*. JSP 7740.

Austin, Gene. "My Blue Heaven." *A Time to Relax, 1925–1936*. Take Two Records 414.

Bailey, De Ford. "Casey Jones." *Harp Blowers: Complete Recorded Works in Chronological Order, 1925–1936*. Document DOCD 5164.

———. "Dixie Flyer Blues." *Harp Blowers: Complete Recorded Works in Chronological Order, 1925–1936*. Document DOCD 5164.

———. "Pan American Blues." *Harp Blowers: Complete Recorded Works in Chronological Order, 1925–1936*. Document DOCD 5164.

Barbecue Bob. "Barbecue Blues." *Complete Recorded Works in Chronological Order, Vol. 1*. Document DOCD 5046.

———. "Brown-Skin Gal." *Complete Recorded Works in Chronological Order, Vol. 1*. Document DOCD 5046.

———. "Chocolate to the Bone." *Complete Recorded Works in Chronological Order, Vol. 1*. Document DOCD 5046.

———. "Darktown Gamblin'—Pt. 2 (The Skin Game)." *Complete Recorded Works in Chronological Order, Vol. 3*. Document DOCD 5048.

———. "Hurry and Bring It Back Home." *Complete Recorded Works in Chronological Order, Vol. 1*. Document DOCD 5046.

Barefoot Bill. See Ed Bell.

Barnet, Charlie. "Emperor Jones." *The Chronological Charlie Barnet and His Orchestra 1937–1939*. Classics 1194.

Basie, Count, and Jimmy Rushing. "It's the Same Old South." *America's #1 Band: The Columbia Years*. Columbia/Legacy C4K 87110.

Bell, Ed. "Hambone Blues." *Complete Recorded Works in Chronological Order*. Document DOCD 5090.

———. "Mean Conductor Blues." *Complete Recorded Works in Chronological Order*. Document DOCD 5090.

———. "My Crime." *Complete Recorded Works in Chronological Order*. Document DOCD 5090.

Bennett, Will. "Railroad Bill." *Sinners and Saints*. Document DOCD 5106.

Berry, Chuck. "Johnny B. Goode." *The Great Twenty-Eight*. Chess CHD 92500.

Big Boy. "Blues." *Field Recordings, Vol. 1: Virginia*. Document DOCD 5575.

———. "John Henry." *Too Late, Too Late, Vol. 10*. Document DOCD 5601.

Big Maybelle. "Gabbin' Blues." *The Complete OKeh Recording Sessions*. Legacy 53417.

Black Europe. Bear Family. 16095.

Blake, Eubie. "Hungarian Rag." *From Ragtime to Jazz, Vol. 3*. Timeless Records SRD 582070.

Blind Blake. "He's In the Jailhouse Now." *All the Published Sides*. JSP 77109.

———. "Panther Squall Blues." *All the Published Sides*. JSP 77109.

———. "Righteous Blues." *All the Published Sides*. JSP 77109.

———. "Third Degree Blues." *All the Published Sides*. JSP 77109.

———. "Too Tight." *All the Published Sides*. JSP 77109.

———. "Walking Across the Country." *All the Published Sides*. JSP 77109.

Blind Percy and his Blind Band. "Fourteenth Street Blues." *Complete Recorded Works in Chronological Order, Vol. 1*. Document DOCD 5153.

Blues in the Mississippi Night. Rykodisc RD 90155.

Bogan, Lucille. "B. D. Woman's Blues." *Shave 'Em Dry: The Best of Lucille Bogan*. Columbia Legacy CK 65705.

———. "Lonesome Midnight Blues." *Complete Recorded Works in Chronological Order, Vol. 3*. Document BDCD 6038.

———. "Shave 'Em Dry." *Shave 'Em Dry: The Best of Lucille Bogan*. Columbia Legacy CK 65705.

———. "Skin Game Blues." *Complete Recorded Works in Chronological Order, Vol. 3*. Document DOCD 6038.

———. "Sloppy Drunk Blues." *Complete Recorded Works in Chronological Order, Vol. 2*. Document DOCD 6037.

———. "They Ain't Walkin' No More." *Complete Recorded Works in Chronological Order, Vol. 2*. Document DOCD 6037.

Boyd, Eddie. "Five Long Years," "Third Degree." *Five Long Years: The Complete Recordings Vol. 2*. EPM.

Bracey, Ishmon. "Trouble-Hearted Blues." *Legends of Country Blues*. JSP 7715.

Broadway Band. "I've Got the 'Yes, We Have No Bananas' Blues." *Black Europe.* Bear Family 16095.

Brooks, Hadda. "Jump Back Honey." *Complete OKeh Sessions.* Sony 246916.

Broonzy, Big Bill. "Bull Cow Blues." *Complete Recorded Works in Chronological Order, Vol. 2.* Document DOCD 5124.

———. "Eagle Riding Papa." *The Hokum Boys Vol. 1.* Wolf WBCD 011.

———. "House Rent Stomp." *Complete Recorded Works in Chronological Order, Vol. 1.* Document DOCD 5123.

———. "Just a Dream." *Complete Recorded Works in Chronological Order, Vol. 8.* Document DOCD 5130.

———. "Mean Old World." *Complete Recorded Works in Chronological Order, Vol. 6.* Document DOCD 5128.

———. "Mississippi River Blues." *Complete Recorded Works in Chronological Order, Vol. 3.* Document DOCD 5125.

———. "Plow Hand Blues." *Complete Recorded Works in Chronological Order, Vol. 10.* Document DOCD 5132.

———. "State Street Women." *Complete Recorded Works in Chronological Order, Vol. 1.* Document DOCD 5050.

Brown, Ada. "Down Home Dance." *Porter Grainger: Complete Recorded Works in Chronological Order, 1923–1929.* RST JPCD 1521-2.

Brown, Bessie. "Pork Chop Blues." *George Williams and Bessie Brown Vol. 1.* Document DOCD 5527.

Brown, Gabriel. "Education Blues." *Field Recordings Vol. 7: Florida.* Document DOCD 5587.

Brown, Ida G. "Jail House Blues." *Piron's New Orleans Orchestra: Complete Recordings, 1923–1926.* Azure CD 13.

Brown, Lillyn. *Esther Bigeou: Complete Recorded Works in Chronological Order, 1921–1923.* Document 5489.

Brown, Milton. "St. Louis Blues." *The Complete Recordings of the Father of Western Swing.* Texas Rose Records TXRCD 1–5.

Brown, Sweet Georgia. "Rockin' in the Groove." *Sammy Price and the Blues Singers.* Wolf WBJ-007.

Bull City Red. "Black Woman and Poison Blues." *Bull City Red.* Story of Blues CD 3527-2.

Bumble Bee Slim. "The Death of Leroy Carr." *Complete Recorded Works in Chronological Order Vol. 4.* Document DOCD 5264.

———. "If I Make It Over." *Complete Recorded Works in Chronological Order Vol. 8.* Document DOCD 5268.

Bumgarner, Samantha. "The Worried Blues." *Mountain Blues: Blues, Ballads, and String Bands.* JSP7740.

Burks, Pinetop. "Sundown Blues." *San Antonio Blues*. Document DCOD 5232.

Butterbeans and Susie. "Elevator Papa, Switchboard Mama." *Elevator Papa, Switchboard Mama (1927–1930)*. JSP CD 329.

———. "Love Me and the World is Mine." *Complete Recorded Works in Chronological Order, Vol. 2*. Document DOCD 5545.

Byrd, John. "Old Timbrook Blues." *John Byrd and Walter Taylor*. Story of Blues 3517-2.

Byrd, Roy. "(They Call Me) Dr. Professor Long Hair." *Rock 'n' Roll Gumbo*. Sunnyside SCC 3049.

Calloway, Cab. "Savage Rhythm." *Cab Calloway: Vol. 2: 1935–1940*. JSP 914.

Cannon, Gus. "Can You Blame the Colored Man." *Complete Recorded Works in Chronological Order, Vol. 1*. Document DOCD 5032.

———. "Gonna Raise a Ruckus Tonight." *Walk Right In*. Stax 702. Rpt. P-Vine PCD 5184.

Carlisle, Cliff. "Ash Can Blues." *White Country Blues: A Lighter Shade of Blue."* Columbia Roots and Blues C2K 47466.

———. "Crazy Blues." *Vol. 2: When I Feel Froggie I'm Gonna Hop*. JSP 7768.

———. "Mouses' Ear Blues." *A Country Legacy, 1930–1939*. JSP 7732.

———. "That Nasty Swing." *A Country Legacy, 1930–1939*. JSP 7732.

Carr, Leroy. "Blues Before Sunrise." *Complete Recorded Works in Chronological Order, Vol.4*. Document DOCD 5137.

———. "Good Woman Blues." *Complete Recorded Works in Chronological Order, Vol.5*. Document DOCD 5138.

———. "Love is Dead." Vocalion unissued.

———. "Papa's On the House Top." *Complete Recorded Works in Chronological Order, Vol.3*. Document DOCD 5136.

———. "Suicide Blues." *Complete Recorded Works in Chronological Order, Vol. 6*. Document DOCD 5139.

Carson, Fiddlin' John. "Gonna Swing on the Golden Gate." *Complete Recorded Works in Chronological Order, Vol. 4*. Document DOCD 8017.

———. "John Henry Blues." *Complete Recorded Works in Chronological Order, Vol. 1*. Document DOCD 8014.

Carter, Alice Leslie. "I Want My Daddy Now." *Female Blues Singers Vol. 4*. Document DOCD 5508.

Carter, Bo. "Banana in Your Fruit Basket." *Complete Recorded Works in Chronological Order, Vol. 1*. Document DOCD 5078.

———. "Good Old Turnip Greens." *Complete Recorded Works in Chronological Order, Vol. 1*. Document DOCD 5078.

Charles, Ray. "I Believe to My Soul." *Pure Genius: The Complete Atlantic Recordings*. Atlantic R2 74731.

"Child Waters." http://www.ling.hawaii.edu/faculty/stampe/Oral-Lit/English/Child- Ballads/child.html#21.

Childers, Virgil. "The Preacher and the Bear." *Carolina Blues Guitar*. Old Tramp OTCD 03.

Ciro's Club Coon Orchestra. "St. Louis Blues." *That Devilin' Tune*. WHRA 6003.

Clark, Lonnie. "Broke Down Engine." *Rare Paramount Blues*. Document DOCD 5277.

Clay, Sonny. "Chicago Breakdown." *Jazz in California*. Timeless Historical 13791.

Cobb, Junie. "Chicago Buzz." *The Junie C. Cobb Collection, 1926–1929*. Collector's Classics CDCD 14.

Coleman, Bob. "Cincinnati Underworld Woman." *Cincinnati Blues*. Catfish UK KAT CD 186.

———. "Sing Song [*sic*] Blues." *Cincinnati Blues*. Catfish UK KAT CD 186.

———. "Tear It Down." *Cincinnati Blues*. Catfish UK KAT CD 186.

Coleridge-Taylor, Samuel. *24 Negro Melodies*. Orion 7806-2.

Collins, Arthur. "The Preacher and the Bear." Victor 17221-A. 78 RPM.

Collins, Sam. "Graveyard Digger's Blues." *Complete Recorded Works in Chronological Order*. Document DOCD 5034.

———. "The Jail House Blues." *Complete Recorded Works in Chronological Order*. Document DOCD 5034.

———. "My Road is Rough and Rocky (How Long, How Long?)." *Complete Recorded Works in Chronological Order*. Document DOCD 5034.

Confrey, Zez. *Piano Scores and Rolls*. Warner Classics 0927 49309-2.

Copland, Aaron. *Four Piano Blues*. *The Complete Music for Solo Piano*. Sony SM2K 66 345.

———. *Three Moods*. *Four Piano Blues*. *The Complete Music for Solo Piano*. Sony SM2K 66 345.

Cox, Ida. "Chicago Bound Blues (Famous Migration Blues)." *Complete Recorded Works in Chronological Order, Vol. 1*. Document DOCD 5322.

———. "How Can I Miss You When I Got Dead Aim?" *Complete Recorded Works in Chronological Order, Vol. 3*. Document DOCD 5324.

———. "I Ain't Got Nobody." *Complete Recorded Works in Chronological Order, Vol. 3*. Document DOCD 5324.

———. "Lonesome Blues." *Complete Recorded Works in Chronological Order, Vol. 3*. Document DOCD 5324.

———. "Southern Woman's Blues." *Complete Recorded Works in Chronological Order, Vol. 3*. Document DOCD 5324.

———. "Trouble in Mind." *Complete Recorded Works in Chronological Order, Vol. 1*. Document DOCD 5322.

———. "Wild Women Don't Have the Blues." *Complete Recorded Works in Chronological Order, Vol. 2.* Document DOCD 5323.

Cream. "Sunshine of Your Love." Atco 45 6544. 45 RPM.

Crudup, Arthur. "I'm Gonna Dig Myself a Hole." *Atomic Platters.* Bear Family BCD 16065.

Custer, Clay (George Thomas). "The Rocks." *Texas Piano, Vol. 1.* Document DOCD 5224.

Darby and Tarleton. "Sweet Sarah Blues." *White Country Blues: A Lighter Shade of Blue."* Columbia Roots and Blues C2K 47466.

Davenport, Cow Cow. "Jim Crow Blues." *Complete Recorded Works in Chronological Order, Vol. 1.* Document DOCD 5141.

———. "Slow Drag." *Complete Recorded Works in Chronological Order, Vol. 1.* Document DOCD 5141.

Davis, Henryette. "Jazzaphobia Blues." *Female Blues Singers Vol. 5: C/D/E.* Document DOCD 5509.

Davis, Jimmie. "Sewing Machine Blues." *Midnight Blues, 1929–1933.* Acrobat ACMCD 4220.

———. "Tom Cat and Pussy Blues." *Midnight Blues, 1929–1933.* Acrobat ACMCD 4220.

Davis, Madlyn. "Gold Tooth Papa Blues." *Tampa Red: Complete Recorded Works in Chronological Order, Vol. 1.* Document DOCD 5073.

———. "Too Black Bad." *Tampa Red: Complete Recorded Works in Chronological Order, Vol. 1.* Document DOCD 5073.

Davis, Walter. "Love Will Kill You." *Complete Recorded Works in Chronological Order, Vol. 3.* Document DOCD 5283.

Dédé, Edmond. *Orchestral Works.* Naxos 8.559038.

Delaney, Mattie. "Down the Big Road Blues." *Mississippi Girls.* RST BD 2018.

Delta Boys. "Black Gal Swing." *"Brownsville" Son Bonds: Complete Recorded Works in Chronological Order.* Wolf WBCD 003.

Deppe, Lois. "Sometimes I Feel Like a Motherless Child." *Black and White Piano Vol. 3.* Document 5655.

Diawara, Djeli, and Bob Brozman. *Ocean Blues: From Africa to Hawaii.* Celluloid 67022-2.

Dickson, Tom. "Happy Blues." *Memphis Blues: Complete Recorded Works in Chronological Order.* Document DOCD 5014.

———. "Labor Blues." *Memphis Blues: Complete Recorded Works in Chronological Order.* Document DOCD 5014.

Dinwiddie Colored Quartet. "My Way is Cloudy." *The Earliest Negro Vocal Quartets Vol. 2.* Document DOCD 5288.

Dixon, Willie. "That Last Home Run." *Baseball's Greatest Hits Vol. 1.* Rhino 70710.

Donno Drummers. *Ghana: Ancient Ceremonies, Songs, and Dance Music.* Elektra Nonesuch 9 72082-2.

Dorsey, Georgia Tom. "Pig Meat Blues." *Complete Recorded Works in Chronological Order, Vol. 1.* Document BDCD 6021.

———. "Pig Meat Papa." *Complete Recorded Works in Chronological Order, Vol. 1.* Document BDCD 6021.

———. "Suicide Blues." *Complete Recorded Works in Chronological Order, Vol. 1.* Document BDCD 6021.

Easton, Amos. "Blues Blues." *Complete Recorded Works in Chronological Order, Vol. 2.* Document DOCD 5262.

Elizalde, Fred. *The Heart of a Nigger Suite.* Decca GA 4563-4566. 78 RPM.

Ellington, Duke. "Choo Choo." *Duke Ellington 1924–1927.* Classics 539.

———. "Cotton Tail." *Duke Ellington: The Centennial Edition.* RCA Victor 09026-63386-2.

———. "The Dicty Glide." *Duke Ellington: The Centennial Edition.* RCA Victor 09026- 63386-2.

———. "Jazz Convulsions." *The Jungle Band: Brunswick Era, Vol. 2.* Decca MCAD-42348.

Estes, Sleepy John. "Tell Me How About It." *Complete Recorded Works in Chronological Order, Vol. 2.* Document DOCD 5016.

Evans, Joe. "Down in Black Bottom." *Complete Recorded Works in Chronological Order.* Document DOCD 5044.

Everett, Luke Cavendish. "The Prehistoric Cake Walk and Two Step." *Black People: CD to Accompany the Book by Rainer Lotz.* No label, no number, 1997.

Excelsior Quartette. "Jelly Roll Blues." *The Earliest Negro Vocal Quartets. Complete Recorded Works in Chronological Order, Vol. 2.* Document DOCD 5288.

Fleck, Bela. *Throw Down Your Heart: Tales From the Acoustic Planet, Vol. 3—Africa Sessions.* Rounder 011661063426.

Foster, Dessa. "Tell It to the Judge Pt. 1." *J. T. "Funny Paper" Smith: Complete Recorded Works in Chronological Order.* Document BDCD 6016.

Fowler, Lem. "Express Train Blues." *Complete Recorded Works in Chronological Order.* RST JSP 1520–2.

Fra Fra Tribesmen. "Yarum Praise Songs." *The Story of the Blues.* Columbia D 30008. (LP).

Fula Flutist. "Bengsimbe." *The Essential Blues Collection, Volume 10: Blues Roots.* Rhino R2 71135.

Fuller, Blind Boy. "Meat Shakin' Woman." *Complete Recorded Works in Chronological Order, Vol. 4.* Document DOCD 5094.

———. "What's That Smells Like Fish?" *Complete Recorded Works in Chronological Order, Vol. 4.* Document DOCD 5094.

Gaither, Little Bill. "Champ Joe Louis." *Complete Recorded Works in Chronological Order, Vol. 3.* Document DOCD 5253.

Gates, Reverend J. M. *Complete Recorded Works in Chronological Order, Vol. 2.* Document DOCD 5432.

Gershwin, George. *Concerto in F. Music for Moderns.* Nostalgia Naxos 8.120505.

———. *Rhapsody in Blue. Music for Moderns.* Nostalgia Naxos 8.120505. [with Gershwin on piano, recorded 1927]

Gibson, Cleo. "I've Got Ford Movement in My Hips." *Territory Singers: Complete Recorded Works in Chronological Order Vol. 2.* Document DOCD 5471.

Gibson, Clifford. "Whiskey Moan Blues." *Complete Recorded Works in Chronological Order Vol. 2.* Document BDCD 6015.

Gillum, Jazz. "Riley Springs Blues." *Complete Recorded Works in Chronological Order, Vol. 2.* Document DOCD 5198.

Glover, Mae. "Pig Meat Mama." *Complete Recorded Works in Chronological Order.* Document DOCD 5185.

Golden Gate Quartet. "Preacher and the Bear." *Golden Gate Jubilee Quartet, Vol. 1.* Document DOCD 5472.

Goofus Five. "I Had Someone Else Before I Had You." *Goofus Five 1924–1925.* Timeless Historical.

———. "Yes, Sir, That's My Baby." *Goofus Five 1924–1925.* Timeless Historical.

Gottschalk, Louis Moreau. *Piano Music.* Naxos 8.559145.

Grayson and Whitter. "Train 45." *Music from the Lost Provinces: Old-Time String Bands from Ashe County, North Carolina, and Vicinity, 1927–1931.* Old Hat 1001.

Green, Clarence. "Johnson City Blues." *White Country Blues: A Lighter Shade of Blue."* Columbia Roots and Blues C2K 47466.

Guitar Slim. "The Things I Used to Do." *Sufferin' Mind.* Specialty 7007.

Hampton, Pete. "Dat Mouth Organ Blues." *Black People: CD to Accompany the Book by Rainer Lotz.* No label, no number, 1997.

———. "When Sousa Comes to Coon-Town." *Black Europe.* Bear Family 16095.

Hannah, George. "Freakish Man Blues." *Piano Blues: Complete Recorded Works in Chronological Order, Vol. 3.* Document DOCD 5314.

Harris, Jesse. "Brady." *Field Recordings Vol. 4: Mississippi and Alabama.* Document DOCD 5578.

Harris, Joe, and Kid West. "Bully of this Town." *Field Recordings Vol. 5: Louisiana, Texas, Bahamas.* Document DOCD 5579.

Harris, Marion. "After You've Gone." *American Pop: An Audio History. From Minstrel to Mojo, 1893–1946.* West Hill Audio Archives 1017.

———. "I Ain't Got Nobody." *The Complete Victor Releases*. Archeophone 5001A.

———. "My Syncopated Melody Man." *The Complete Victor Releases*. Archeophone 5001A.

———. "Paradise Blues." *The Complete Victor Releases*. Archeophone 5001A.

Hawkins, Buddy Boy. "Raggin' the Blues." *William Harris and Buddy Boy Hawkins*. Document DOCD 5035.

Hegamin, Lucille. "He May Be Your Man But He Comes to See Me Sometimes." *Lucille Hegamin: Complete Recorded Works in Chronological Order, Vol. 1*. Document DOCD 5419.

———. "Jazz Me Blues." *Lucille Hegamin: Complete Recorded Works in Chronological Order, Vol. 1*. Document DOCD 5419.

———. "Syncopatin' Mama." *Lucille Hegamin: Complete Recorded Works in Chronological Order, Vol. 2*. Document DOCD 5420.

Henderson, Edmonia. "Lazy Daddy Blues." *Female Blues Singers Vol. 9*. Document DOCD 5513.

Henderson, Fletcher. "The Dicty Blues." *Fletcher Henderson, Vol. 1*. Neovox Cassette 706A.

Henderson, Rosa. "Back Woods Blues." *Complete Recorded Works in Chronological Order, Vol. 2*. Document DOCD 5402.

———. "Chicago Policeman Blues." *Complete Recorded Works in Chronological Order, Vol. 4*. Document DOCD 5404.

———. "Do That Thing." *Complete Recorded Works in Chronological Order, Vol. 2*. Document DOCD 5402.

———. "He May Be Your Dog But He's Wearing My Collar." *Complete Recorded Works in Chronological Order, Vol. 1*. Document DOCD 5401.

———. "Hey Hey and He He, I'm Charleston Crazy." *Complete Recorded Works in Chronological Order, Vol. 2*. Document DOCD 5402.

———. "I'm a Good Gal (But I'm a Thousan' Miles From Home)." *Complete Recorded Works in Chronological Order, Vol. 2*. Document DOCD 5402.

———. "Poplar Bluff Blues." *Complete Recorded Works in Chronological Order, Vol. 3*. Document DOCD 5403.

———. "Slow Up Papa." *Complete Recorded Works in Chronological Order, Vol. 4*. Document DOCD 5404.

———. "Undertaker's Blues." *Complete Recorded Works in Chronological Order, Vol. 3*. Document DOCD 5403.

Hensely, Larry. "Match Box Blues." *Mountain Blues: Blues, Ballads, and String Bands*. JSP7740.

Hicks, Edna. "Cemetery Blues." *Edna Hicks / Hazel Meters / Laura Smith: Complete Recorded Works in Chronological Order, Vol. 2*. Document DOCD 5431.

———. "The Dicty Blues." *Fletcher Henderson: His Entire Recorded Output for the Vocalion and Brunswick Labels, Vol. 1*. Neovox cassette 706.

Hill, Chippie. "Street Walker Blues." *Complete Recorded Works in Chronological Order*. Document DOCD 5330.

———. "Weary Money Blues." *Complete Recorded Works in Chronological Order*. Document DOCD 5330.

"Hitler Toast." *Roosevelt's Blues: African American Blues and Gospel Songs on FDR*. Agram ABCD 2017.

Hokum Boys. "Pig Meat Strut." *Too Late Too Late, Vol. 4*. DOCD 5321.

Holiday, Billie. "God Bless the Child." *The Lady Billie Holiday: Complete Collection*. CBS Sony OODP 570-577.

Holmes, Wright. "Alley Special." *Alley Special*. Collectables CD-5320.

Honegger, Arthur. "Pacific 231." *Honegger: Pacific 231*. Denon 78831.

Hooker, John Lee. "Build Myself a Cave." *Graveyard Blues*. Fantasy 7018.

Hopkins, Lightnin'. "Bad Luck and Trouble." *Jake Head Boogie*. Ace 697.

———. "The Dirty Dozens." *1954 and 1959*. Document DOCD Private Issue.

———. "Shinin' Moon." *The Complete Prestige-Bluesville Recordings*. 7PCD 4406-2.

House, Son. "Death Letter Blues." *Father of the Delta Blues*. Columbia C2K 48867.

———. "Delta Blues." *Complete Library of Congress Recordings*. Travelin' Man TM 02.

———. "Preachin' the Blues Pt. 1." *Son House and the Great Delta Blues Singers*. Document DOCD 5002.

House, Son, and Willie Brown. "Camp Hollers." *Complete Library of Congress Recordings*. Travelin' Man TM 02.

Howell, Peg Leg. "Beaver Slide Rag." *Peg Leg Howell and Eddie Anthony: Complete Recorded Works in Chronological Order Vol. 1*. Matchbox MBCD 2004.

———. "Rock and Gravel Blues" (1928). *Peg Leg Howell and Eddie Anthony: Complete Recorded Works in Chronological Order Vol. 1*. Document 2004.

———. "Skin Game Blues." *Peg Leg Howell and Eddie Anthony: Complete Recorded Works in Chronological Order Vol. 1*. Document 2004.

———. "Too Tight Blues." *Peg Leg Howell and Eddie Anthony: Complete Recorded Works in Chronological Order Vol. 1*. Matchbox MBCD 2004.

———. "Turtle Dove Blues." *Peg Leg Howell and Eddie Anthony: Complete Recorded Works in Chronological Order Vol. 2*. Matchbox MBCD 2005.

Howlin' Wolf. "Back Door Man." *His Best*. Chess CHD 9375.

———. "Interview." *Screamin' and Hollerin' the Blues: The Worlds of Charley Patton*. Revenant 212.

———. "Smokestack Lightnin'." *His Best*. Chess CHD 9375.

Hughes, Langston. *The Story of Jazz*. Folkways LP FJ 7312.

Hull, Papa Harvey, and Long Cleve Reed. "Hey, Lawdy Mama—The France Blues." *The Songster Tradition*. Document 5045.

Hunter, Alberta. "He's Got a Punch Like Joe Louis." *Complete Recorded Works in Chronological Order Vol. 4*. Document 5425.

———. "My Castle's Rockin'." *Complete Recorded Works in Chronological Order Vol. 4*. Document 5425.

———. "Vamping Brown." *Complete Recorded Works in Chronological Order Vol. 2*. Document 5423.

Hurt, Mississippi John. "Casey Jones." OKeh unissued.

———. "Spike Driver Blues." *The Greatest Songsters*. Document 5003.

Hutchinson, Frank. "Cannon Ball Blues." *White Country Blues: A Lighter Shade of Blue.* Columbia Roots and Blues C2K 47466.

———. "The Train That Carried the Girl From Town." *White Country Blues: A Lighter Shade of Blue.* Columbia Roots and Blues C2K 47466.

Ives, Charles. *Central Park in the Dark. Charles Ives: Symphony No. 2 and others.* Deutsche Grammophone 429 220-2.

———. *The Unanswered Question. Charles Ives: Symphony No. 2 and others.* Deutsche Gramophone 429 220-2.

Jackson, Bo Weavil [sic]. "Poor Boy Blues." *Backwoods Blues*. Document DOCD 5036.

———. "Some Scream High Yellow." *Backwoods Blues*. Document DOCD 5036.

———. "You Can't Keep No Brown." *Backwoods Blues*. Document DOCD 5036.

Jackson, Jim. "Dicty Blues." Vocalion unissued.

———. "He's in the Jailhouse Now." *Complete Recorded Works in Chronological Order, Vol. 1*. Document 5114.

———. "Jim Jackson's Kansas City Blues." *Complete Recorded Works in Chronological Order, Vol. 1*. Document 5114.

———. "Old Dog Blue." *Complete Recorded Works in Chronological Order, Vol. 1*. Document 5114.

———. "St. Louis Blues." *Complete Recorded Works in Chronological Order, Vol. 2*. Document DOCD 5115.

Jackson, New Orleans Willie. "Railroad Man Blues." *Male Blues of the Twenties: Complete Recorded Works in Chronological Order, Vol. 2*. Document 5532.

Jackson, Papa Charlie. "The Faking Blues." *Papa Charlie Jackson: Complete Recorded Works in Chronological Order, Vol. 1*. Document 5087.

———. "Shake That Thing." *Papa Charlie Jackson: Complete Recorded Works in Chronological Order, Vol. 1*. Document 5087.

Jacquet, Illinois. "Flying Home." *Hamp: The Legendary Decca Recordings of Lionel Hampton*. Decca GRD-2-652.

James, Elmore. "Dust My Broom." *The Classic Early Recordings*. Ace ABOXCD 4.

———. "Something Inside Me." *The Complete Fire and Enjoy Recordings*. Collectables 8829.

James, Skip. "Devil Got My Woman." *Complete Recorded Works in Chronological Order*. Document DOCD 5005.

———. "Hard Time Killing Floor Blues." *Complete Recorded Works in Chronological Order*. Document DOCD 5005.

Jefferson, Blind Lemon. "Bed Springs Blues." *The Complete 94 Classic Sides Remastered.* JSP 7706.

———. "Broke and Hungry." *The Complete 94 Classic Sides Remastered.* JSP 7706.

———. "Christmas Eve Blues." *The Complete 94 Classic Sides Remastered.* JSP 7706.

———. "Dry Southern Blues." *The Complete 94 Classic Sides Remastered.* JSP 7706.

———. "Dynamite Blues." *The Complete 94 Classic Sides Remastered.* JSP 7706.

———. "Got the Blues." *The Complete 94 Classic Sides Remastered.* JSP 7706.

———. "Long Lonesome Blues." *The Complete 94 Classic Sides Remastered.* JSP 7706.

———. "Match Box Blues." *The Complete 94 Classic Sides Remastered.* JSP 7706.

———. "Rambler's Blues." *The Complete 94 Classic Sides Remastered.* JSP 7706.

———. "Stocking Feet Blues." *The Complete 94 Classic Sides Remastered.* JSP 7706.

———. "That Black Snake Moan." *The Complete 94 Classic Sides Remastered.* JSP 7706.

Johnson, Buddy. "Did You See Jackie Robinson Hit That Ball?" *Walk 'Em.* Ace 623.

Johnson, Lil. "Rock That Thing." *Complete Recorded Works in Chronological Order Vol. 1.* Document DOCD 5307.

Johnson, Lonnie. "Blue Ghost Blues." *Complete 1937–June 1947, Vol. 1.* Document DOCD. 6024.

———. "Hard Times Ain't Gone No Where." *Complete 1937–June 1947, Vol. 1.* Document DOCD 6024.

———. "Love is a Song." *Complete Recorded Works in Chronological Order, Vol. 7.* Document DOCD 5069.

Johnson, Lonnie, and Eddie Lang. "Blue Room (Blues)." *Complete Recorded Works in Chronological Order, Vol. 5.* Document DOCD 5067.

———. "Hot Fingers." *Complete Recorded Works in Chronological Order, Vol. 5.* Document DOCD 5067.

Johnson, Louise. "On the Wall." *Mississippi Blues, Vol. 1.* Document DOCD 5157.

Johnson, Margaret. "Done Made a Fool Out of Me." *Complete Recorded Works in Chronological Order.* Document DOCD 5436.

———. "Suicide Blues." *Complete Recorded Works in Chronological Order.* Document DOCD 5436.

Johnson, Robert. "Cross Road Blues." *The Complete Recordings.* Columbia C2K 64916.

———. "Me and the Devil." *The Complete Recordings.* Columbia C2K 64916.

———. "32-20 Blues." *The Complete Recordings.* Columbia C2K 64916.

Johnson, Tillie. "Chicago Man Blues." Gennett 6438 (78 RPM).

Johnson, Tommy. "Canned Heat Blues." *Legends of Country Blues.* JSP 7715.

———. "Cool Drink of Water Blues." *Legends of Country Blues*. JSP 7715.

Johnson, Willie. "Dark Was the Night, Cold Was the Ground." *The Complete Blind Willie Johnson*. Columbia C2K 52835.

Jolson, Al. "That Haunting Melody." *Early Years*. Collectable 848.

Jones, Coley. "The Elder He's My Man." *Texas Blues*. Document DOCD 5161.

Jones, Curtis. "Blues in the Alley." *Complete Recorded Works in Chronological Order, Vol. 2*. Document DOCD 5297.

Jones, Jake. "Southern Sea Blues." *Texas: Black Country Dance Music*. Document DOCD 5162.

Jones, Little Hat. "Kentucky Blues." *Texas Blues*. Document DOCD 5161.

Jones, Maggie. "Don't Never Tell Nobody What Your Good Man Can Do." *Complete Recorded Works in Chronological Order, Vol. 1*. Document DOCD 5348.

———. "Suicide Blues." *Complete Recorded Works in Chronological Order, Vol. 1*. Document DOCD 5348.

———. "You May Go But You'll Come Back Some Day." *Complete Recorded Works in Chronological Order, Vol. 1*. Document DOCD 5348.

Jordan, Charley. "Keep It Clean." *Complete Recorded Works in Chronological Order, Vol. 1*. Document DOCD 5097.

———. "Tight Haired Mama Blues." *Complete Recorded Works in Chronological Order, Vol. 1*. Document DOCD 5097.

Jordan, Luke. "Traveling Coon." *The Songster Tradition*. Document DOCD 5045.

Jubilee Gospel Team. "These Bones Goin' Rise Again." *Jubilee Gospel Team—Deep River Plantation Singers*. Document DOCD 5519.

Justice, Dick. "Brown Skin Blues." *Mountain Blues: Blues, Ballads, and String Bands*. JSP7740.

Kansas Joe. "Dresser Drawer Blues." *Too Late, Too Late, Vol. 2*. Document DOCD 5216.

Keghouse. "Sock It Blues." *Piano Blues*. Document DOCD 5336.

Kid Coley. "War Dream Blues." *Cincinnati Blues*. Catfish KATCD 186.

King Solomon Hill. "The Gone Dead Train." *Backwoods Blues*. Document DOCD 5036.

———. "Whoopee Blues." *Backwoods Blues*. Document DOCD 5036.

King, B. B. "Gambler's Blues." *King of the Blues*. MCA MCAD4-10677.

———. "Sweet Sixteen." *King of the Blues*. MCA MCAD4-10677.

Kit-Kat Band. "If You Hadn't Gone Away." HMV B-2197 (78 RPM).

Krenek, Ernst. *Jonny spielt auf. The Music Survives!* London CD 452 664-2.

Kru Tribe. "Battle Signals, War Horn." *African Music: Rhythm in the Jungle*. Victor Records P-10 (87B). (78 RPM).

Leadbelly. "Poor Howard." *The Remaining Library of Congress Recordings Vol. 2.* Document DOCD 5592.

———. "Stewball." *Leadbelly: Take This Hammer.* Bluebird 82876-50957-2.

Lee, Bertha. "Mind Reader Blues." *Charley Patton: Complete Recorded Works in Chronological Order, Vol. 3.* Document DOCD 5011.

Lenoir, J. B. "Eisenhower Blues." *The Truman and Eisenhower Blues.* Agram 2018.

Lewis, Furry. "Dry Land Blues." *Complete Recorded Works in Chronological Order.* Document DOCD 5004.

———. "Furry's Blues." *Complete Recorded Works in Chronological Order.* Document DOCD 5004.

———. "I Will Turn Your Money Green." *Complete Recorded Works in Chronological Order.* Document DOCD 5004.

———. "John Henry, Pt. 1." *Complete Recorded Works in Chronological Order.* Document DOCD 5004.

———. "Sweet Papa Moan." *Complete Recorded Works in Chronological Order.* Document DOCD 5004.

Lewis, Meade Lux. "Honky Tonk Train Blues." *The Chronological, 1927–1939.* Classics 722.

Lewis, Noah. "Chickasaw Special." *Gus Cannon and Noah Lewis, Vol. 2.* Document DOCD 5033.

Lil Johnson. "Black and Evil Blues." *Complete Recorded Works in Chronological Order, Vol. 2.* Document DOCD 5308.

Lillie Mae. "Wise Like That." *Georgia Blues and Gospel.* Document DOCD 5160.

Liston, Virginia. "House Rent Stomp." *Complete Recorded Works in Chronological Order, Vol. 1.* Document DOCD 5446.

———. "I Ain't Got Nobody." *Virginia Liston and Lavinia Turner.* Document DOCD 5447.

———. "Jail House Blues." *Complete Recorded Works in Chronological Order, Vol. 1.* Document DOCD 5446.

Little Esther. "Mainliner." *Bad Bad Girl.* Charly CD 47.

Little Milton. "I Play Dirty." *Greatest Hits.* Chess CHD 9386.

Little Walter. "Blue and Lonesome." *The Essential Little Walter.* MCA 9342.

———. "Mean Old World." *His Best: The Chess 50th Anniversary Collection.* MCA Chess CHE93842.

Lockwood Jr., Robert. "Black Spider Blues." *Mississippi Blues: Complete Recorded Works, 1935–1951.* Wolf WBCD 005.

———. "Little Boy Blues." *Mississippi Blues: Complete Recorded Works, 1935–1951.* Wolf WBCD 005.

Lomax, Alan, interviewer. *Blues in the Mississippi Night*. 1947. Rpt. Rounder 82161-1860-2.

"Lord Rendal." http://www.ling.hawaii.edu/faculty/stampe/Oral-Lit/English/Child-Ballads/child.html#21.

Louisiana Johnny. "Razor Cuttin' Man." *Rare 1930s Blues: Complete Recorded Works in Chronological Order, Vol.1*. Document DOCD 5331.

Mahal, Taj. "Mahini Me." On Ali Farka Touré. *The Source*. Hannibal HNCD 1375.

———. "Roucky." On Ali Farka Touré. *The Source*. Hannibal HNCD 1375.

Manson, Charlie. "Nineteen Women Blues." *Charley Jordan: Complete Recorded Works in Chronological Order, Vol. 3*. Document DOCD 5099.

Martin, Daisy, and Ozie McPherson. *Complete Recorded Works and Remaining Titles in Chronological Order, 1921–1926*. Document 5522.

Martin, Sara. "Blue Gum Blues." *Complete Recorded Works in Chronological Order, Vol. 2*. Document DOCD 5396.

———. "Death Sting Me Blues." *Complete Recorded Works in Chronological Order, Vol. 4*. Document DOCD 5398.

———. "New Orleans Hop Scop Blues." *Complete Recorded Works in Chronological Order, Vol. 2*. Document DOCD 5396.

———. "Sobbin' Hearted Blues." *Complete Recorded Works in Chronological Order, Vol. 3*. Document DOCD 5397.

Martinu, Bohuslav. "Jazz-Suite for Small Orchestra." *Works Inspired by Jazz and Sport*. Supraphon SU 3058-2 011.

Mayfield, Percy. "The River's Invitation." *Poet of the Blues*. Specialty SPCD 7001.

McClennan, Tommy. "Bluebird Blues." *The Bluebird Recordings, 1939–1942*. RCA 07863 67430-2.

McClennon, George. "Brown Skin Girl." *The Bluebird Recordings, 1939–1942*. RCA 07863 67430-2.

———. "While You're Sneakin' Out." *George McClennon / Wilton Crawley*. Jazz Oracle BDW 8022.

McCoy, Charlie. "Last Time Blues." *Complete 1928–1932 Recordings*. Document DOCD 6018.

———. "The Northern Starvers Are Returning Home." *Complete 1928–1932 Recordings*. Document DOCD 6018.

McCoy, William. "Mama Blues." *Texas: Black Country Dance Music*. Document DOCD 5162.

———. "Train Imitation and Fox Chase." *Texas: Black Country Dance Music*. Document DOCD 5162.

McCurdy, Ed. *The Best of Dalliance*. Elektra LP EKL 213.

McGhee, Brownie. "Born For Bad Luck." *The Complete*. Columbia 475700 2.

McKay, George Frederick. *Epoch: An American Dance Symphony.* Naxos 8.559330.

McKinney's Cotton Pickers. "There's a Rainbow Round My Shoulder." *Put It There, 1928–1929.* Frog DGF 25.

McTell, Blind Willie. "Broke Down Engine Blues." *Complete Recorded Works in Chronological Order, Vol. 1.* Document DOCD 5006.

———. "Come On Around to My House Mama." *Complete Recorded Works in Chronological Order, Vol. 1.* Document DOCD 5006.

———. "Dark Night Blues." *Complete Recorded Works in Chronological Order, Vol. 1.* Document DOCD 5006.

———. "Monologue on History of the Blues." *Complete Library of Congress Recordings in Chronological Order (1940).* Document BDCD 6001.

———. "Searching the Desert for the Blues." *The Victor Recordings, 1927–1934.* RCA 66718.

———. "Southern Can is Mine." *Complete Recorded Works in Chronological Order, Vol. 1.* Document DOCD 5006.

———. "Talking to Myself." *Complete Recorded Works in Chronological Order, Vol. 1.* Document DOCD 5006.

Memphis Jug Band. "Everybody's Talking About Sadie Green." *Complete Recorded Works in Chronological Order, Vol.3.* Document DOCD 5023.

———. "K. C. Moan." *Complete Recorded Works in Chronological Order, Vol. 2.* Document DOCD 5022.

Memphis Minnie. "Blues Everywhere." *Complete Recorded Works in Chronological Order, 1935–1941, Vol. 3.* Document BDCD 6010.

———. "In My Girlish Days." *Complete Recorded Works in Chronological Order, 1935–1941, Vol. 5.* Document BDCD 6012.

———. "Ma Rainey." *Complete Recorded Works in Chronological Order, 1935–1941, Vol. 5.* Document BDCD 6012.

———. "New Dirty Dozen." *Memphis Minnie and Kansas Joe: Complete Recorded Works in Chronological Order, Vol. 2.* Document DOCD 5029.

———. "Reachin' Pete." *Complete Recorded Works in Chronological Order, 1935–1941, Vol. 1.* Document BDCD 6008.

———. "Shake Mattie." *Complete Recorded Works in Chronological Order, 1929–1934, Vol. 2.* Document DOCD 5029.

Meyers, Hazel. "The Man Ain't Born Who Can Treat Me Like You Do." *Female Blues: The Remaining Titles.* Document DOCD 1005.

———. "Soldier Boy Blues." *Edna Hicks / Hazel Meyers / Laura Smith Complete Recorded Works in Chronological Order, Vol. 2.* Document DOCD 5431.

Miles, Josie. "A to Z Blues." *Complete Recorded Works in Chronological Order, Vol. 1.* Document DOCD 5466.

———. "Freight Train Blues." *Complete Recorded Works in Chronological Order, Vol. 1.* Document DOCD 5466.

Miller, Emmett. "Love Sick Blues." *The Minstrel Man from Georgia.* Columbia Roots and Blues CK 66999.

Miller, Sodarisa. "Don't Dog Me 'Round Blues." *Barrel House Women.* Document DOCD 5497.

Mills Blue Rhythm Band. "Futuristic Jungleism." *Harlem Heat, 1931–36.* ASV Living Era 5634.

Mississippi Sheiks. "He Calls That Religion." *Complete Recorded Works in Chronological Order, Vol. 3.* Document DOCD 5085.

Mitchell, Louis. "The Montmartre Rag." *Black Europe.* Bear Family 16095.

Monkey Joe. "Wise to the Jive." *Complete Recorded Works in Chronological Order, Vol. 1.* Document DOCD 5412.

Monroe, Bill. "John Henry." *The Music of Bill Monroe, 1936–1994.* MCAD4 11048.

Moody, Julia. "He'll Do You Wrong." *Viola McCoy / Julia Moody: Complete Recorded Works in Chronological Order*. Document DOCD 5418.

Moore, Alice. "Black and Evil Blues." *St. Louis Bessie and Alice Moore, Vol. 1.* Document DOCD 5290.

———. "Lonesome Dream Blues." *St. Louis Bessie and Alice Moore, Vol. 1.* Document DOCD 5290.

Morton, Jelly Roll. "Winin' Boy." *Jelly Roll Morton: The Complete Library of Congress Recordings by Alan Lomax.* Rounder 11611-1888-2.

Mosolov, Alexander. *Russian Futurism, Vol. 1. Alexander Mosolov: Piano Works.* Arte Nova 277930.

Moss, Buddy. "Gravy Server." *Complete Recorded Works in Chronological Order, Vol. 3.* Document DOCD 5125.

———. "No Money Blues." ARC unissued.

Mound City Blue Blowers. "Arkansaw [*sic*] Blues." *Hot Comb and Tin Can.* Vintage Music Productions 0151.

———. "Blue Blues." *Hot Comb and Tin Can.* Vintage Music Productions 0151.

Mr. Honey. "Build a Cave." *Juke Joint Blues.* Blues Classics LP 23.

Nelson, Romeo. "Gettin' Dirty Just Shakin' That Thing." *Boogie Woogie and Barrelhouse Piano: Complete Recorded Works in Chronological Order, Vol. 2.* Document DOCD 5103.

Norfolk Jazz and Jubilee Quartet. "Monday Morning Blues." *Complete Recorded Works in Chronological Order, Vol. 1.* Document DOCD 5381.

———. "Raise R-U-K-U-S Tonight." *Complete Recorded Works in Chronological Order, Vol. 2.* Document DOCD 5382.

Norsingle, Ben. "Motherless Blues." *Territory Singers: Complete Recorded Works in Chronological Order, Vol. 1.* Document DOCD 5470.

O'Connor, George. "Nigger Blues." *Let's Get Loose: Folk and Popular Blues Styles From the Beginnings to the Early 1940s*. New World Records NW 290 (LP).

One Arm Slim. "Howling Man Blues." *Country Blues Collector's Items Vol. 2*. Document DOCD 5426.

Original Dixieland Jazz Band. "Crazy Blues." *Complete Original Dixieland Jazz Band, 1917–1936*. RCA Black and White 2 CD No. 70.

———. "Livery Stable Blues." *Stomp and Swerve*. Archeophone 1003.

Otis, Johnny. "The Dirty Dozens." *Snatch and the Poontangs / Cold Shot*. Ace CDCHD 855.

———. "One O'Clock Jump." *The Big Tenor: The Complete Ben Webster on EmArcy*. EmArcy 824 836-2 (1).

Parham, Florence. "He May Be Your Good Man on Friday." Victor unissued trial recording.

Patton, Charlie. "34 Blues." *Complete Recorded Works in Chronological Order, Vol. 3*. Document DOCD 5011.

———. "Down the Dirt Road Blues." *Complete Recorded Works in Chronological Order, Vol. 1*. Document DOCD 5009.

———. "Going to Move to Alabama." *Complete Recorded Works in Chronological Order, Vol. 1*. Document DOCD 5009.

———. "High Sheriff Blues." *Complete Recorded Works in Chronological Order, Vol. 3*. Document DOCD 5011.

———. "Mississippi Bo Weavil Blues." *Complete Recorded Works in Chronological Order, Vol. 1*. Document DOCD 5009.

———. "Pony Blues." *Screamin' and Hollerin' the Blues: The Worlds of Charley Patton*. Revenant 212.

———. "Some Happy Day." *Complete Recorded Works in Chronological Order, Vol. 2*. Document DOCD 5010.

———. "Some Summer Day Part. 1." *Complete Recorded Works in Chronological Order, Vol. 3*. Document DOCD 5011.

Peanut the Kidnapper. "Suicide Blues." *Alabama and the East Coast*. Document DOCD 5450.

Peg Leg Sam. *The Last Medicine Show*. Flyright LP 507-508.

Phillips' Louisville Jug Band. "Soldier Boy Blues." *Clifford Hayes and the Louisville Jug Band, Vol. 4*. RST JPCD 1504-2.

Platt, Moses ("Clear Rock"). "Run, Nigger, Run." *Field Recordings Vol. 6: Texas*. Document DOCD 5580.

Poole, Charlie. "If the River Was Whiskey." *You Ain't Talkin' to Me: Charlie Poole and the Roots of Country Music*. Columbia 92780.

Pound, Ezra. *Ego Scriptor Cantilenae: The Music of Ezra Pound*. Other Minds CD 1005-2.

———. *Ezra Pound's Opera: Le Testament de Villon*. Fantasy LP 12001.

———. *The World's Great Poets Vol. III: Ezra Pound Reads His Cantos*. CMS LP 619.

Prysock, Red. "Hand Clappin'." *Swingsation*. Polygram 339195.

Pullum, Joe. "Blues With Class." *Complete Recorded Works in Chronological Order, Vol. 1*. Document DOCD 5393.

Quillian, Rufus and Ben. "Ragged But Right." *Hokum, Blues, and Rags*. Document DOCD 5392.

Rafferty, Carl. "Dresser with the Drawers." *Roosevelt Sykes: Complete Recorded Works in Chronological Order, Vol. 3*. Document DOCD 5118.

Rainey, Ma. "Bad Luck Blues." *Complete Recorded Works in Chronological Order, Vol. 1*. Document DOCD 5581.

———. "Black Cat Hoot Owl Blues." *Complete Recorded Works in Chronological Order, Vol. 5*. Document DOCD 5585.

———. "Dead Drunk Blues." *Complete Recorded Works in Chronological Order, Vol. 4*. Document DOCD 5584.

———. "Down in the Basement." *Complete Recorded Works in Chronological Order, Vol. 3*. Document DOCD 5583.

———. "Last Minute Blues." *Complete Recorded Works in Chronological Order, Vol. 1*. Document DOCD 5581.

———. "Lost Wandering Blues." *Complete Recorded Works in Chronological Order, Vol. 1*. Document DOCD 5581.

———. "Lucky Rock Blues." *Complete Recorded Works in Chronological Order, Vol. 1*. Document DOCD 5581.

———. "See See Rider Blues." *Complete Recorded Works in Chronological Order, Vol. 2*. Document DOCD 5582.

———. "Slave to the Blues." *Complete Recorded Works in Chronological Order, Vol. 3*. Document DOCD 5583.

———. "Southern Blues." *Complete Recorded Works in Chronological Order, Vol. 1*. Document DOCD 5581.

———. "Walking Blues." *Complete Recorded Works in Chronological Order, Vol. 1*. Document DOCD 5581.

"Raise a Ruckus Tonight." *Field Recordings Vol. 12*." Document DOCD 5614.

Red Onion Jazz Babies. "Nobody Knows the Way I Feel This Morning." *Louis Armstrong and King Oliver*. Milestone CD.

Reinhardt, Django. "Blues Primitif." *Jazz in Paris: Django's Blues*. Gitanes

———. "Mystery Pacific." *Djangology*. Coffret 7806602-7806692.

Rey, Alvino. "Mama's Blues." *The Big Band Steel Guitar of Alvino Rey*. Steel Guitar Record Club number 13.

Reynolds, Blind Joe. "Outside Woman Blues." *Son House and the Great Delta Blues Singers*. Document DOCD 5002.

Richmond Jazz Quartette. "Gone Jazz Crazy." *Black Secular Vocal Groups In Chronological Order, Vol. 1*. Document DOCD 5546.

Robeson, Paul. "Water Boy." *Songs of Free Men*. Sony MHK 63223.

———. "Were You There?" *Ol' Man River: His 56 Finest, 1925–1945*. Nimbus Records.

Robeson, Paul, with Count Basie. "King Joe Pt. 1" and "King Joe Pt. 2." *My Old Flame*. Centurion Jazz IECJ315.

Rockmore, Clara. "Summertime." *Clara Rockmore's Lost Theremin Album*. Bridge 9208.

———. "Water Boy." *Clara Rockmore's Lost Theremin Album*. Bridge 9208.

Rodgers, Jimmie. "Blue Yodel No. 9." *The Singing Brakeman*. Bear Family BCD 15540.

———. "Brakeman's Blues." *The Singing Brakeman*. Bear Family BCD 15540.

———. "Let Me Be Your Sidetrack." *The Singing Brakeman*. Bear Family BCD 15540.

Rollini, Adrian. "Savage Serenade." *Tap Room Swing*. ASV Living Era ASY 5424.

Rushing, Jimmy. "Boogie Woogie Blues." *America's #1 Band: Count Basie and His Orchestra*. C4K 87110.

Russell, Luis. *Luis Russell & His Orchestra—1930–1934*. Classics 606.

Samuels, Joseph. "Crazy Blues." OKeh 4250 (78 RPM).

Sandburg, Carl. "The Boll Weevil" (1926). *Songs For Political Action*. Bear Family BCD 15720 JL.

———. *Carl Sandburg Reading His Poetry*. Caedmon CDL 51150.

———. "Five Poems." *100 Modern American Poets Reading Their Poems*. Spoken Arts SAC 1040.

———. *The Great Carl Sandburg: Songs of America*. Lyrichord LYRCD 6003.

Sapps, Booker T. "Mule on the Mountain." *Field Recordings, Vol. 7: Florida*. Document DOCD 5587.

Satie, Erik. "Ragtime Dada." *Dada Works and Entr' Actes*. LTM CD 2474.

Schoenberg, Arnold. *Suite, op. 29. Boulez Conducts Arnold Schoenberg I*. Sony 88697562522.

Schulhoff, Erwin. "Double Concerto for Flute and Piano." *Concertos alla Jazz*. London D 113435.

Schweinfest, George. "Nigger Fever." Berliner 0945 (78 RPM).

Shankar, Ravi. *The Essential Ravi Shankar*. Columbia/Private Music/Legacy 82876 71610 2

Shaw, Allen. "I Couldn't Help It." *Memphis Blues*. Document DOCD 5014.

Shepard, Ollie. "Shepard Blues." *Complete Recorded Works in Chronological Order, Vol. 2*. Document 5435.

Sissle, Noble, and Eubie Blake. "Crazy Blues." Paramount 12007 (78 RPM).

Six Brown Brothers. *Broadway's Favorite Clowns.* Archeophone 6007

———. "The Bullfrog and the Coon." *Those Moaning Saxophones*. Archeophone 6002.

Slim Harpo. "I'm a King Bee." *Hip Shakin'*. Excello 2001.

Smith, Bessie. "Alexander's Ragtime Band." *The Complete Recordings, Vol. 3*. Columbia 2CD 472189-2.

———. "Back Water Blues." *The Complete Recordings, Vol. 3*. Columbia 2CD 472189-2.

———. "Blue Blues." *The Complete Recordings, Vol. 4*. Columbia 2CD 52838.

———. "Cemetery Blues." *The Complete Recordings, Vol. 1*. Columbia 2CD 467895-2.

———. "Dirty No-Gooder Blues." *The Complete Recordings, Vol. 4*. Columbia 2CD 52838.

———. "Empty Bed Blues." *The Complete Recordings, Vol. 4*. Columbia 2CD 52838.

———. "Homeless Blues." *The Complete Recordings, Vol. 3*. Columbia 2CD 472189-2.

———. "I Ain't Got Nobody." *The Complete Recordings, Vol. 2*. Columbia 2CD 468767.

———. "Jail-House Blues." *The Complete Recordings, Vol. 1*. Columbia 2CD 467895-2.

———. "Jazzbo Brown From Memphis Town." *The Complete Recordings, Vol. 3*. Columbia 2CD 472189-2.

———. "New Orleans Hop Scop Blues." *The Complete Recordings, Vol. 4*. Columbia 2CD 52838.

———. "Nobody In Town Can Bake a Sweet Jelly Roll Like Mine." *The Complete Recordings, Vol. 1*. Columbia 2CD 467895-2.

———. "Sing Sing Blues." *Volume 3*. Frog DGF 42.

———. "Soft Pedal Blues." *Volume 4*. Frog DGF 43.

———. "The St. Louis Blues." *The Complete Recordings, Vol. 2*. Columbia 2CD 468767.

———. "Wasted Life Blues." *The Complete Recordings, Vol. 4*. Columbia 2CD 52838.

———. "Young Woman Blues." *The Complete Recordings, Vol. 3*. Columbia 2CD 472189-2.

———. "You've Been a Good Old Wagon." *Volume 4*. Frog DGF 43.

Smith, Clara. "Done Sold My Soul to the Devil." *Complete Recorded Works in Chronological Order, Vol. 2*. Document DOCD 5365.

———. "Don't Advertise Your Man." *Complete Recorded Works in Chronological Order, Vol. 2*. Document DOCD 5365.

———. "Down Home Bound Blues." *Complete Recorded Works in Chronological Order, Vol. 3*. Document DOCD 5366.

———. "Every Woman's Blues." *Complete Recorded Works in Chronological Order, Vol. 1*. Document DOCD 5364.

———. "Jelly Look What You Done." *Complete Recorded Works in Chronological Order, Vol. 5.* Document DOCD 5368.

———. "My John Blues." *Complete Recorded Works in Chronological Order, Vol. 3.* Document DOCD 5366.

———. "Prescription for the Blues." *Complete Recorded Works in Chronological Order, Vol. 2.* Document DOCD 5365.

———. "War Horse Mama." *Complete Recorded Works in Chronological Order, Vol. 2.* Document DOCD 5365.

———. "Whip it to a Jelly." *Complete Recorded Works in Chronological Order, Vol. 4.* Document DOCD 5367.

———. "You Don't Know My Mind." *Complete Recorded Works in Chronological Order, Vol. 1.* Document DOCD 5364.

Smith, Jabbo. "Croonin' the Blues." *Jabbo Smith's Rhythm Aces, Vol. 1.* Hallmark.

Smith, Mamie. "Crazy Blues." *Complete Recorded Works in Chronological Order, Vol. 1.* Document 5357.

———. "Goin' Crazy with the Blues." *Complete Recorded Works in Chronological Order, Vol. 4.* Document DOCD 5360.

———. "I Want a Jazzy Kiss." *Complete Recorded Works in Chronological Order, Vol. 1.* Document DOCD 5357.

———. "That Thing Called Love." *Complete Recorded Works in Chronological Order, Vol. 1.* Document DOCD 5357.

———. "You Can't Keep a Good Man Down." *Complete Recorded Works in Chronological Order, Vol. 1.* Document DOCD 5357.

Smith, Ruby. "Interview with Chris Albertson." *Besssie Smith: The Complete Recordings Volume 5.* Columbia 57546.

Smith, Trixie. "Black Bottom Hop." *Complete Recorded Works in Chronological Order, Vol. 2.* Document 5333.

———. "Sorrowful Blues." *Complete Recorded Works in Chronological Order, Vol. 1.* Document DOCD 5332.

———. "The World's Jazz Crazy, and So Am I." *Complete Recorded Works in Chronological Order, Vol. 2.* Document 5333.

Spaulding, Henry. "Cairo Blues." *St. Louis Country Blues.* Document DOCD 5147.

Spivey, Victoria. "Black Snake Blues." *Complete Recorded Works in Chronological Order, Vol. 1.* Document 5316.

———. "Jelly Look What You Done Done." *Complete Recorded Works in Chronological Order, Vol. 2.* Document 5317.

———. "New Black Snake Blues." *Complete Recorded Works in Chronological Order, Vol. 2.* Document 5317.

Stafford, Mary. "Ain't Got Nobody to Grind My Coffee in the Morning." *"Ain't*

Gonna Settle Down": The Pioneering Blues of Mary Stafford and Edith Wilson. Archeophone 6006.

———. "Crazy Blues." *"Ain't Gonna Settle Down": The Pioneering Blues of Mary Stafford and Edith Wilson*. Archeophone 6006.

State Street Swingers. "Chicago Rhythm." *State Street Swingers*. RST JPCD 1507-2.

Stein, Gertrude, and Virgil Thomson. *Four Saints in Three Acts*. Elektra Nonesuch 9 79035-2. 2CD.

Still, William Grant. "Africa." *William Grant Still*. Naxos 8.559174.

Stokes, Frank. "T'Ain't Nobody's Business If I Do." *The Victor Recordings in Chronological Order*. Document DOCD 5013.

———. "You Shall." *The Beale Street Sheiks*. Document DOCD 5012.

Stone, Joe. "It's Hard Time." *St. Louis Country Blues*. Document DOCD 5147.

Straun's Pullman Porters. "Casey Jones." Gennett 3005. (78 RPM).

Stravinsky, Igor. "Piano-Rag Music" and "Ragtime for 11 Instruments." *Works of Igor Stravinsky* Sony BMG. 22CD.

Streamline Mae. "Blues Blues." *St. Louis Women, Vol. 2*. Document DOCD 5291.

Street Incredibles. "When Ragtime Rosie Ragged the Rosary." *Encore*. No label information.

Suesse, Dana. "Ivory Tips." *Jazz Nocturne: The Collected Piano Music of Dana Suesse*. Sara Davis Buechner, piano. E1 KIC-CD-7770.

———. *Jazz Nocturne: The Collected Piano Music of Dana Suesse*. E1 KIC-CD-7770.

Swan Silvertones. "Working on a Building." *The Swan Silvertones, 1946–1951*.

Sweatman, Wilbur. *Jazzin' Straight Thru Paradise*. Archeophone CD 6004.

Sweet Georgia Brown. "Rock Me in the Groove." Wolf WBJCD-007-4.

Swing Tanzen Verboten: Swing Music & Nazi Propaganda Swing During World War II. Proper UK Box 56.

Sykes, Roosevelt. "Dirty Mother For You." *Complete Recorded Works in Chronological Order, Vol. 4*. Document DOCD 5119.

———. "Love Will Wear You Down." *Complete Recorded Works in Chronological Order, Vol. 6*. Document DOCD 5121.

Tampa Red. "It Hurts Me Too." *Complete Recorded Works in Chronological Order, Vol. 11*. Document DOCD 5211.

———. "It's Tight Like That." *Complete Recorded Works in Chronological Order, Vol. 1*. Document DOCD 5073.

———. "Rock It in Rhythm." *Complete Recorded Works in Chronological Order, Vol. 9*. Document DOCD 5209.

Tanner, Gid, and His Skillet Lickers. "Casey Jones." *People Take Warning! Murder Ballads and Disaster Songs, 1913–1938*. Tompkins Square TSQ 1875.

Taylor, Eva. "Jazzin' Babies Blues." *Complete Recorded Works in Chronological Order, Vol. 2*. Document DOCD 5409.

Thomas, Elvie. "Motherless Child Blues." *Mississippi Blues: Complete Recorded Works in Chronological Order, Vol. 1*. Document DOCD 5157.

Thomas, Henry. "Bull Doze Blues." *Texas Worried Blues*. Yazoo CD 1080 / 1081.

———. "Fishing Blues." *Texas Worried Blues*. Yazoo CD 1080 / 1081.

———. "Texas Worried Blues." *Texas Worried Blues*. Yazoo CD 1080 / 1081.

Terry, Sonny. "Fox Chase." *Complete Recorded Works in Chronological Order, 1938–1945*. Document DOCD 5230.

Thomas, Ramblin'. "No Job Blues." *Ramblin' Thomas and the Dallas Blues Singers*. Document DOCD 5107.

Tibbs, Andrew. "Bilbo is Dead." *Chess Blues*. MCA/Chess CHD4-9340.

Touré, Ali Farka. *Savane: The King of the Desert Blues Singers*. Nonesuch 79965-2.

———. *The Source*. Hannibal HNCD 1375.

Tuareg Tribesmen. "War Song." *African Music: Rhythm in the Jungle*. Victor Records P-10 (86A). (78 RPM)

Tucker, Bessie. "Key to the Bushes." *Complete Recorded Works in Chronological Order*. Document DOCD 5070.

———. "Mean Old Master Blues." *Complete Recorded Works in Chronological Order*. Document DOCD 5070.

———. "Penitentiary." *Complete Recorded Works in Chronological Order*. Document DOCD 5070.

Tucker, Sophie. "Some of These Days." *Origins of the Red Hot Mama, 1910–1922*. Archeophone CD 5010.

Turner, Big Joe. "Roll 'Em Pete." *Boogie Woogie Stomp!* ASV AJA 5101.

Turner, Lavinia. *Virginia Liston Vol. 2 and Lavinia Turner: Complete Recorded Works in Chronological Order, 1921–1926*. Document 5447.

Two Black Crows. "In the Jailhouse." *American Sound Archives Presents Moran and Mack: "The Two Black Crows."* American Sound Archives ASA 5007.

Tyus, Charles and Effie. "Jazz Crazy." *Vocal Duets: Complete Recorded Works in Chronological Order, 1924–1931*.

Various. *Actionable Offenses: Indecent Phonograph Recordings from the 1890s*. Archeophone CD 1007.

———. *Africa and the Blues*. Neatwork AB 101.

———. *American Pop: An Audio History. From Minstrel to Mojo, 1893–1946*. West Hill Audio Archives 1017. [Includes "Memphis Blues" by the Victor Military Band, "Memphis Blues" by James Reese Europe, "After You've Gone" by Marion Harris, and other performers from the early days of the recording industry].

———. *Cap'n, You're So Mean: Negro Songs of Protest, Vol. 2*. Rounder LP 4013 [Lawrence Gellert recordings].

———. *Country Blues Collector's Items: Complete Recorded Works in Chronological Order, 1924–1928*. Document 5169 [two recordings by Barrelhouse Ed Andrews].

———. *Fiddling in West Africa*. UCLA Ethnomusicology Archive Series, Vol. 2, 88251 70007 2 4.

———. *Field Recordings, Vol. 9*. Document 5599 [Lawrence Gellert recordings].

———. *God's Trombones*. Penguin HighBridge Audio HBP 22773 [James Weldon Johnson sermons].

———. *The Influence of Jimmie Rodgers*. Bear Family 6 CD 16863.

———. *Jali Kunda: Griots of West Africa and Beyond*. Ellipsis Arts CD3510.

———. *Lost Sounds: Blacks and the Birth of the Recording Industry, 1891–1922*. Archeophone 1005. [Williams and Walker, W. C. Handy, Wilbur Sweatman, Booker T. Washington, and others].

———. *Monarchs of Minstrelsy: Historical Recordings by the Stars of the Minstrel Stage*. Archeophone 1006 [includes Golden and Hughes, Al Bernard, Al Jolson, and the Cohan and Harris Minstrels, among others].

———. *Negro Songs of Protest*. Rounder LP 4004 [Lawrence Gellert recordings].

———. *Nobody Knows My Name: Blues from South Carolina and Georgia*. Heritage LP HT 304 [Lawrence Gellert recordings].

———. *Piano Music Without Limits: Compositions of the 1920s*. MDG 645 1404-2. [pianola compositions].

———. *Roosevelt's Blues*. Agram Blues AB 2017. [Dealing with events during FDR's presidency].

———. *The Rough Guide to Africa Blues*. RGNET1186CD.

———. *Songs For Political Action*. Bear Family BCD 15720 JL [includes recordings by Josh White, Carl Sandburg, the Almanac Singers, Sonny Terry, Brownie McGhee, Paul Robeson, Charles Seeger, Pete Seeger, and others associated with the Popular Front].

———. *Stomp and Swerve*. Archeophone 1003 ["Nobody" by Bert Williams, "Some of These Days" by Sophie Tucker, "Livery Stable Blues" by the Original Dixieland Band, and "Crazy Blues" by Mamie Smith].

———. *That Devilin' Tune*. WHRA 6003. ["Some of These Days" by Sophie Tucker, "Country Club Blues" by Gus Haenschen, "Homesickness Blues" by Nora Bayes, "Paradise Blues" by Marion Harris, "St. Louis Blues" by Ciro's Coon Club Orchestra, and "Unlucky Blues" by Bert Williams, plus Wilbur Sweatman and others].

———. *The Truman and Eisenhower Blues*. Agram ABCD 2018.

———. *The Unexpurgated Folk Songs of Men*. Collected by Mack McCormack. Raglan label, R 51.

———. *Violin, Sing the Blues for Me: African American Fiddlers, 1926–1949*. Old Hat 1002.

The Versatile Three. "I Want a Doll." *The Earliest Black String Bands Vol. 3*. Document DOCD 5624.

Virginia Female Jubilee Singers. "My Time Ain't Long." *The Earliest Negro Vocal Groups, Vol. 4*. Document DOCD 5531.

Wagner, Richard. *Wagner - Parsifal / Knappertsbusch*. Philips 464 756-2.

Walker, Ruby. "Interview." *Bessie Smith The Complete Recordings, Vol. 5: The Final Chapter*. Columbia Legacy 2 CD.

Walker, T-Bone. "Mean Old World." *The Complete T-Bone Walker, 1940–1954*. Mosaic MD6 130.

Wallace, Minnie. "The Cockeyed World." *Memphis Harp and Jug Blowers: Complete Recorded Works in Chronological Order*. Document BDCD 6028.

Wallace, Sippie. "The Flood Blues." *Complete Recorded Works in Chronological Order Vol.2*. Document DOCD 5400.

Waters, Ethel. "At the New Jump Steady Ball." *Ethel Waters, Vol. 1*. Classics 796.

———. "Down Home Blues." *Ethel Waters, Vol. 1*. Classics 796.

———. "Shake That Thing." *Ethel Waters, Vol. 1*. Classics 796.

———. "That Da Da Strain." *Ethel Waters, Vol. 1*. Classics 796.

Weldon, Casey Bill. "Red Hot Blues." *Complete Recorded Works in Chronological Order, Vol. 3*. Document DOCD 5219.

———. "W.P.A. Blues." *Complete Recorded Works in Chronological Order, Vol. 1*. Document DOCD 5217.

Welk, Lawrence. "Doin' the New Lowdown." *In Concert*. Ranwood R 6001.

Welsh, Nolan. "Chicago Women Blues." *Piano Blues: Complete Recorded Works in Chronological Order, Vol. 3*. Document DOCD 5314.

Wheatstraw, Peetie. "Chicago Mill Blues." *Complete Recorded Works in Chronological Order, Vol. 6*. Document DOCD 5246.

———. "Cut Out Blues." *Complete Recorded Works in Chronological Order, Vol 4*. Document DOCD 5244.

———. "The Last Shall Be First and the First Shall Be Last." *Complete Recorded Works in Chronological Order, Vol. 3*. Document DOCD 5243.

———. "No 'Count Woman." *Complete Recorded Works in Chronological Order, Vol. 7*. Document DOCD 5247.

———. "Pete Wheatstraw." *Complete Recorded Works in Chronological Order, Vol. 1*. Document DOCD 5241.

———. "Suicide Blues." *Complete Recorded Works in Chronological Order, Vol. 7*. Document DOCD 5247.

White, Georgia. "I'll Keep Sittin' On It." *Complete Recorded Works in Chronological Order, Vol.2*. Document DOCD 5302.

White, Josh. "Black and Evil Blues." *Complete Recorded Works in Chronological Order, Vol. 1*. Document DOCD 5194.

———. *Chain Gang Songs*. Collectables Records COL 7789.

———. *Complete Recorded Works in Chronological Order, Vol. 3.* Document 5196.

———. *Complete Recorded Works in Chronological Order, Vol. 4.* Document 5405.

———. *Free and Equal Blues.* Smithsonian Folkways SFW 40081.

White, Leroy "Lasses." "Nigger Blues." *Let's Get Loose: Folk and Popular Blues Styles From the Beginnings to the Early 1940s.* New World LP NW 290.

Whitter, Henry. "Lonesome Road Blues." OKeh 40015. (78 RPM).

Wiley, Arnold and Irene. "You'd Better Not Go Down To 35th and State No More." *Blues Obscurities.* Document DOCD 5481.

Wilkins, Robert. "Falling Down Blues." *Memphis Blues: Complete Recorded Works in Chronological Order.* Document DOCD 5014.

Williams, Annie. "Don't Grieve After Me." LC, 1942.

Williams, Bert. All in, Out and Down." *His Final Releases.* Archeophone 5002.

Williams, George. "Bullet." "Frisco Leaving Birmingham." *Great Harp Players.* Document DOCD 5100.

Williams, Hank. *Low-down Blues.* Mercury Nashville 731453273726.

Williams, Henry, and Eddie Anthony. "Georgia Crawl." *Peg Leg Howell and Eddie Anthony: Complete Recorded Works in Chronological Order Vol. 1.* Matchbox MBCD 2004.

Williams, Joe. "Mean Stepfather Blues." *Complete Recorded Works in Chronological Order Vol. 1.* Document BDCD 6003.

Williams, William Carlos. *William Carlos Williams Reads His Poetry.* Caedmon SWC 51047.

Williamson I, John Lee "Sonny Boy." "Blue Bird Blues Pt. 1." *The Bluebird Recordings, 1937–1938.* RCA 07863 66723-2.

———. "Down South." *The Bluebird Recordings, 1937–1938.* RCA 07863 66723-2.

———. "Sloppy Drunk Blues." *Complete Recorded Works in Chronological Order, Vol. 4.* Document DOCD 5058.

———. "Win the War Blues." *Complete Recorded Works in Chronological Order, Vol. 4.* Document DOCD 5058.

Williamson II, "Sonny Boy." "Don't Start Me to Talkin'." *His Best.* Chess CHD 9377.

Wilson, Edith. "Rules and Regulations 'Signed Razor Jim.'" *Johnny Dunn: Complete Recorded Works in Chronological Order, Vol. 1.* RST JPCD 1522.

———. "Vampin' Liza Jane." *Johnny Dunn: Complete Recorded Works in Chronological Order, Vol. 1.* RST JPCD 1522.

Wilson, Leola B., and Kid Wesley Wilson. "Have Your Chill, I'll Be There When Your Fever Rises." *Grant and Wilson: Complete Recorded Works in Chronological Order, Vol. 1.* DOCD 5563.

———. "Rock, Aunt Dinah, Rock." *Grant and Wilson: Complete Recorded Works in Chronological Order, Vol. 1.* DOCD 5563.

Wood, Smokey. "Everybody's Truckin'." *Kings of Western Swing: Smile and Jive.* Charly CDGR 182-2.

Woods, Ruby Lee. "Love'll Make You Drink." LC.

Xenakis, Iannis. *Chamber Music.* Naive CD 14.

Yates, Richard. "Bunion Blues." *Male Blues of the Twenties, Vol. 1.* Document DOCD 5482.

Yerkes, Harry A. "Lonesome Road Blues." AV 12135 (78 RPM).

Videography

Chaplin, Charles. *Modern Times.* Warner M2K éditions DVD 37943.

———. *A Woman of Paris/The King in New York.* Warner MK2 éditions DVD 37653.

Frank, Ron, and Paul D. Lehrman. *Bad Boy Made Good.* EMF DVD 060.

Jolson, Al. *The Jazz Singer.* Warner Brothers DVD 79889.

———. "A Plantation Act." In *The Jazz Singer.* Warner Brothers DVD 79889.

Lincoln, Elmo. *Tarzan of the Apes.* Alpha Video ALP 5867D.

Martin, Steven M. *Theremin: An Electronic Odyssey.* MGM 4002442.

Times Ain't Like They Used to Be. Yazoo DVD 512.

Appendix 2: Chronology

Blues	Ragtime, Pop, Jazz, Country, Classical	Literature and Folklore	Stage, Screen, Events
1902 Jelly Roll Morton hears blues in New Orleans Ma Rainey hears the blues in Missouri	Hager's Orchestra, "Loop the Loop (Cake Walk)" Ralph Vaughan Williams calls for "real music"	Dunbar, *The Sport of the Gods*	Jane Addams, *Democracy and Social Ethics* Enrico Caruso's first recordings Cecil Rhodes dies
1903 W. C. Handy hears the blues in Tutwiler, Mississippi	Bert Williams, "The Cake Walk" London Production of *In Dahomey*	W. E. B. Du Bois, *The Souls of Black Folk* Gertrude Stein likes "primitive things to be more savage" Van Vechten begins familiarity with black entertainers	Eighty-four African Americans reported lynched Henry Ford founds the Ford Motor Co. Wright Brothers flight at Kitty Hawk
1904	Pete Hampton, "Dat Mouth Organ Coon"	Abbey Theater founded	Seventy-six African Americans reported lynched AME Church calls for a New Negro Renaissance
1905 Odum hears the blues in Mississippi and Georgia (1905–1908)	Arthur Collins, "The Preacher and the Bear"	Henry Adams confronts New York City of the Nunc Age	First issue of the *Chicago Defender* published IWW founding in Chicago Niagara Movement founded
1906	Bert Williams, "All In, Out, and Down" Charles Ives, *Central Park in the Dark* Ives, *The Unanswered Question*	Upton Sinclair, *The Jungle*	Sixty-two African Americans reported lynched

Blues	Ragtime, Pop, Jazz, Country, Classical	Literature and Folklore	Stage, Screen, Events
1907		Henry Adams, *The Education of Henry Adams* Sandburg involved in Wisconsin Social-Democratic politics John Jacob Niles begins collecting folklore	First cubist exhibition in Paris Alain Locke named first African American Rhodes scholar
1908 Antonio Maggio, "I Got the Blues" sheet music composition Jelly Roll Morton claims that boogie woogie has its beginnings in Chicago in 1908 John Jacob Niles reports hearing the blues in Kentucky Ophelia Simpson, "Black Alfalfa's Jail-House Shouting Blues"	Albert Gumble, "Bolo Rag" Bartok studies Magyar folk melodies Debussy, "Golliwog's Cakewalk" Henry Gilbert, *Dance in Place Congo*	Remy de Gourmont anticipates the Imagist Movement Langston Hughes hears the blues on Independence Avenue in Kansas City Lindsay lectures on African Americans Odum researching the lives of African American performers around Clark University	Eighty-nine African Americans reported lynched Jack Johnson wins heavyweight championship Booker T. Washington records the Atlanta Exposition address
1909 Robert Hoffman, "I'm Alabama Bound" sheet music E. C. Perrow reports hearing music similar to the blues in Mississippi	Gene Green scat singing	Pound "Sestina: Alataforte" Stein, *Three Lives* Odum, "Religious Folk-Songs of the Southern Negro"	Sixty-nine African Americans reported lynched Founding of NAACP Taft inaugurated president
1910 Reports of blues singing in southern vaudeville theaters	"An Operatic Rag" Stravinsky, *L'Oiseau de Feu*	*Opportunity* journal established Pound telegraphs coming anti-Semitism Pound, *The Spirit of Romance* Odum, *Social and Mental Traits of the Negro*	Sixty-seven African Americans reported lynched Roughly the beginning of the Great Migration Jack Johnson defeats Jim Jeffries Piet Mondrian's Parisian grids

1911	Six Brown Brothers, "The Bullfrog and the Coon" George Van Eps, "Rag Pickings" Scott Joplin, *Treemonisha* Al Jolson, "That Haunting Melody" Sophie Tucker, "Some of These Days" "When Ragtime Rosie Ragged the Rosary" sheet music	Ambrose Bierce, *The Devil's Dictionary* Poetry magazine established Pound, *Canzoni* Pound, "Redondillas" Odum, "Folk-Song and Folk-Poetry as Found in the Secular Songs of Southern Negroes"	Sixty African Americans reported lynched Arnold Schonberg, *Manual of Harmony*
1912 W. C. Handy's "Memphis Blues" sheet music H. Franklin "Baby" Seals's "Baby Seals Blues" sheet music Will Thomas collects blues in Texas Hart A. Wand's "Dallas Blues" sheet music G. W. Warford, "The Blues and the Dream" Leroy "Lasses" White's "Nigger Blues" sheet music	Clef Club Concert Gene Buck and Herman Ruby, "That Shakespearian Rag" Melville Gideon, "Ragtime Improvisation on Rubenstein's Melody in F" John Alden Carpenter, "A Plea"	J. W. Johnson, *Autobiography of an Ex-Colored Man*	Sixty-one African Americans reported lynched Jane Addams, *A New Conscience and an Ancient Evil* Edison Diamond Discs introduced Titanic sinks
1913 W. C. Handy, "The Jogo Blues"	Luckey Roberts, "The Junk Man Rag" Debussy declares "a century of aeroplanes deserves its own music" Stravinsky, *The Rite of Spring*	Braithwaite, *Anthology of Magazine Verse* first published (-1929) O'Neill, *Warnings* Vorticist manifestoes 1913–1914	Fifty-one African Americans reported lynched The Armory Show in New York Ford establishes the assembly line for the Model T

Blues	Ragtime, Pop, Jazz, Country, Classical	Literature and Folklore	Stage, Screen, Events
1914 W. C. Handy, "The St. Louis Blues" W. C. Handy, "Yellow Dog Blues" Anna Kranz Odum collects religious and secular songs in Tennessee	"The Castles in Europe" sheet music Morton Harvey makes first blues vocal recording "Operatic Rag" Paul Biese and F. Henri Klickmann, "Hysterics Rag" Important New Orleans jazz figures migrate to Chicago	Edgar Rice Burroughs, *Tarzan* Lindsay's "The Congo" Mina Loy and Van Vechten meet O'Neill, *Fog* Sandburg's Socialist Party Membership expires Williams's "Sick African"	"African Savage Art," America's first major exhibition of "primitive" art Dil Pickle club established in Chicago The Great Migration, 1914–1919 Outbreak of World War I
1915 Artie Mathews, "The Weary Blues" W. Prescott Webb collects blues in Texas Spencer Williams composition "I Ain't Got Nobody"	John Alden Carpenter, *Concertino for Piano and Orchestra*	Bodenheim moves from Chicago to New York Eliot's "Prufrock" takes second place to Lindsay's "The Chinese Nightingale" for Harriet Monroe's *Poetry* prize *Others* journal established Dorothy Scarborough president of the Texas Folklore Society	Fifty-six African Americans reported lynched Duchamp's first dadaist works D. W. Griffith's *Birth of a Nation* KKK charted Fulton County, GA Carter G. Woodson establishes the ASNLH and the *Journal of Negro History* Oscar DePriest elected Chicago's first African American alderman
1916 Kay Swift hears "The Railroad Blues" in the Adirondacks	Charles Luckyeth Roberts records for Columbia Wilbur Sweatman segues from ragtime to jazz The American Republic Band recording of Spencer Williams's "Shim-Me-Sha-Wobble" Marion Harris, "Paradise Blues"; "My Syncopated Melody Man"; "I Ain't Got Nobody"	Henri Barbusse, *Le Feu* Robert Coady's journal *The Soil* Lindsay's "The Apple Blossom Snow Blues" Mina Loy comes to NY O'Neill, *Now I Ask You* Sandburg, "Nigger" Cecil Sharp arrives from England to collect folklore	Fifty African Americans reported lynched First birth control clinic opens in the US Marcus Garvey arrives in New York and establishes the Universal Negro Improvement Association

	Manuel Romain, "Hippodrome Minstrel Medley" Gus Haendschen, "Country Club Medley"		
1917 Ciro's Club Coon Orchestra records "St. Louis Blues" in London John A. Lomax collects blues in Texas	Original Dixieland Jazz Band, "Livery Stable Blues" "Some Jazz Blues"	Cocteau, *Parade* Hart Crane first visits New York Eliot, "Ballade pour la Grosse Lulu" Lindsay, "Booker T. Washington Trilogy" *New York Evening Sun* calls Mina Loy an exemplar of the modern woman Loy, *Songs to Joannes* Gertrude Stein meets Van Vechten Van Vechten begins practice of championing African American writers William Carlos Williams, "Danse Russe," "Ballet," "Canthara," "Apology," and "Divertimiento" John Jacob Niles hears experiences of black soldiers in France	Thirty-six African Americans reported lynched C. G. Jung, *Psychology of the Unconscious* US enters World War I Woodrow Wilson inaugurated as president
1918	Scrap Iron Jazz Band, "The Ragtime Volunteers Are Off to War" Gershwin, "The Real American Folk Song is a Rag"	Henry Adams, *The Education of Henry Adams* Hurston goes to Washington, DC Mina Loy leaves New York	Sixty African Americans reported lynched Elmo Lincoln, *Tarzan of the Apes* Race riots continue to break out Emmett Scott's *Birth of a Race*

Blues	Ragtime, Pop, Jazz, Country, Classical	Literature and Folklore	Stage, Screen, Events
	Gilda Gray performs "St. Louis Blues" on Broadway Original Dixieland Jazz Band, "Bluin' the Blues" Wilbur Sweatman, "Bluin' the Blues" Stravinsky, *Ragtime for Eleven Instruments* Thomas Griselle ragtime composition "Cubist" Henry Gilbert, *The Dance in Place Congo* John Powell, *Rhapsodie Negre*	Pound essay on Imagism Pound edits Fenollosa's *The Chinese Written Character as a Medium for Poetry* Sandburg, "Band Concert" Spengler, *Decline of the West*	
1919 Will Marion Cook's band plays at Buckingham Palace and Royal Albert Hall	Joseph Lamb, "Bohemia Rag" Al Bernard, "Bluin' the Blues" Sophie Tucker, "Everybody Shimmies Now" Versatile Three, "I Want a Doll" Bert Williams, "I'm Sorry You Ain't Got It You Could Have It If I Had It Blues" Louisiana Five, "Weary Blues" Ansermet writes glowing review of Sidney Bechet performance Antheil, *The Profane Waltzes* Stravinsky, *Piano-Rag Music*	Malcolm Cowley arrives in New York Hart Crane visiting cabarets in New York Cummings, *Tulips and Chimneys* ms. Du Bois, "Returning Soldiers" Pound begins work as composer Dorothy Scarborough, *From a Southern Porch*	Eighty-three Africans reported lynched Prohibition ratified January 16 "Red Summer" race riots Socialist Party convention in Chicago

1920 Lucille Hegamin, "Jazz Me Blues" Noble Sissle, "Crazy Blues" Mamie Smith, "Crazy Blues" Mamie Smith, "That Thing Called Love" Mamie Smith, "You Can't Keep a Good Man Down" Windy City Trio, "Weary Blues"	Pauline Alpert, "Blue Baby" Anita Patti Brown records Copland, *Three Moods* (1920–1921) Theremin invented Varèse, *Ameriques* (1920–21)	Dos Passos, *Three Soldiers* Lindsay, *The Daniel Jazz* Lindsay, *The Golden Whales of California* Amy Lowell, "Some Musical Analogies" Mencken, "Sahara of the Bozart" O'Neill, *Beyond the Horizon* O'Neill, *Diff'rent* O'Neill, *The Emperor Jones* Pound, *Hugh Selwyn Mauberley* Sandburg, "Vaudeville Dancer" W. C. Williams, *Kora in Hell* Sandburg, "Honky Tonk in Cleveland, Ohio"	Fifty-three African Americans reported lynched Nineteenth Amendment grants Women's Suffrage Gandhi becomes leader in India's struggle for independence
1921 Alice Carter, "I Want My Daddy Now" Alberta Hunter, "How Long, Sweet Daddy, How Long" Joseph Samuels, "Crazy Blues" Mamie Smith, "I Want a Jazzy Kiss" Mary Stafford, "Crazy Blues" Ethel Waters, "Down Home Blues" Edith Wilson, "Frankie" Edith Wilson, "Vampin' Liza Jane" Norfolk Jazz and Jubilee Quartet, "Monday Morning Blues" Virginia Female Jubilee Singers, "My Time Ain't Long"	*Shuffle Along* Original Dixieland Jazz Band, "Crazy Blues" Carpenter, *Krazy Kat*	Clive Bell places Eliot in the "jazz school" of poetry Gold and McKay become co-editors of *The Liberator* Hughes submits "The Negro Speaks of Rivers" to Jessie Fauset for publication in *The Crisis* Johnson, *Autobiography of an Ex-Colored Man* O'Neill, *The Hairy Ape*	Fifty-nine African Americans reported lynched Warren G. Harding inaugurated president Ku Klux Klan activities become brazenly violent across the South

Blues	Ragtime, Pop, Jazz, Country, Classical	Literature and Folklore	Stage, Screen, Events
1922 Lucille Hegamin, "He May Be Your Man But He Comes to See Me Sometimes" Alberta Hunter, "Jazzin' Babies Blues" Trixie Smith, "My Man Rocks Me" Ethel Waters, "At the New Jump Steady Ball" Ethel Waters, "That Da Da Strain" Edith Wilson, "Rules and Regulations" Excelsior Quartette, "Jelly Roll Blues"	Avery Robinson, "Water Boy" The Georgians, The Caroling Serenaders, Bailey's Lucky Seven, "Chicago" Jazzbo's Carolina Serenaders, "The Yankee Doodle Blues" Ladd's Black Aces, "The Yankee Doodle Blues" The Virginians, "The Yankee Doodle Blues" Carpenter, *Skyscrapers* (–1923) Gershwin, *Blue Monday* Milhaud visits Harlem	Bodenheim, *Introducing Irony* Cummings, manuscript of *Tulips and Chimneys* Eliot, *The Waste Land* Field, "Carlsbad" and "Sabine Farm" Hughes, "Laughers" Hughes, "Song for a Banjo Dance" J. W. Johnson, *The Book of American Negro Poetry* Joyce, *Ulysses* W.C. Williams, *Spring and All* Fitzgerald, *The Beautiful and Damned*	Fifty-one African Americans reported lynched Death of Bert Williams Discovery of tomb of King Tut Dyer Anti-Lynching Bill passed in House but filibustered in Senate Meta Vaux Warrick Fuller's "Ethiopia Awakening" exhibited in New York
1923 Ida Cox, "Any Woman's Blues" Ida Cox, "Chicago Bound Blues" Clay Custer, "The Rocks" Lucille Hegamin, "Syncopatin' Mama" Rosa Henderson, "He May Be Your Dog But He's Wearing My Collar" Edna Hicks, "Cemetery Blues" Edna Hicks, "The Dicty Blues" Edna Hicks, "Uncle Sam Blues" Alberta Hunter, "Stingaree Blues" Alberta Hunter, "Vamping Brown" Maggie Jones, "Don't Never Tell Nobody What Your Good Man Can Do"	Miller and Lyles's *Runnin' Wild* California Ramblers, "Lady of the Evening" The Original Capitol Orchestra, "Lady of the Evening" Connie's Inn established Fletcher Henderson, "Chime Blues" New Orleans Rhythm Kings, "Weary Blues" Clarence Williams, "The Weary Blues" Pound, *Le Testament de Villon* Lois Deppe and Earl Hines, "Sometimes I Feel Like a Motherless Child"	Cullen, "Heritage" Hughes, "Jazzonia," "Cabaret" Lawson, *Roger Bloomer* Mina Loy moves to Paris O'Neill, *All God's Chillun Got Wings* Stevens, *Harmonium* Toomer, *Cane* Williams, *Spring and All* Sterling Brown graduates from Harvard and goes to teach at Lynchburg, Virginia, where he meets Big Boy Davis John W. Work ranks Stephen Foster melodies above African American secular songs	Twenty-nine African Americans reported lynched Calvin Coolidge succeeds Harding as president Garvey sentenced to five years in prison for mail fraud Murnau, *Nosferatu*

Virginia Liston, "House Rent Stomp" Sara Martin, "Blind Man Blues" Sara Martin, "Blue Gum Blues" Florence Parham, "He May Be Your Good Man on Friday" Peach Tree Payne, "Peachtree Man Blues" Ma Rainey, "Bad Luck Blues" Ma Rainey, "Last Minute Blues" Ma Rainey, "Southern Blues" Ma Rainey, "Walking Blues" Bessie Smith, "Cemetery Blues" Bessie Smith, "Jail House Blues" Bessie Smith, "Nobody In Town Can Bake a Sweet Jelly Roll Like Mine" Clara Smith, "Every Woman's Blues" Eva Taylor, "Jazzin' Babies' Blues" Elkins-Payne Jubilee Singers, "Down by the Riverside" Norfolk Jazz and Jubilee Quartet, "Raise R-U-K-U-S Tonight"			
1924 Bessie Brown, "Pork Chop" Ida Brown, "Jail House Blues" Ida Cox, "Wild Women Don't Have the Blues" Edmonia Henderson, "Lazy Daddy Blues" Rosa Henderson, "Back Woods Blues"	Emmett Miller first records Duke Ellington, "Choo Choo" Fletcher Henderson at the Club Alabama Vic Meyers, "Weary Blues" Jelly Roll Morton, "Weary Blues" Mound City Blue Blowers, "Arkansaw [*sic*] Blues" and "Blue Blues"	Breton, *Introduction to the Discourse on the Paucity of Reality* Jessie Fauset, *There is Confusion* Langston Hughes works in Montmartre at Le Grand Duc Walter White, *Fire in the Flint*	Vladimir Lenin dies James Van Der Zee begins a photographic series on Marcus Garvey and the Universal Negro Improvement Association

Blues	Ragtime, Pop, Jazz, Country, Classical	Literature and Folklore	Stage, Screen, Events
Rosa Henderson, "Do That Thing"	The Original Capitol City Orchestra, "Gigolette"		
Rosa Henderson, "Hey Hey and He He, I'm Charleston Crazy"	Red Onion Jazz Babies, "Nobody Knows the Way I Feel This Morning"		
Rosa Henderson, "I'm a Good Gal"	Gershwin premieres *Rhapsody in Blue* at Aeolian Hall		
Rosa Henderson, "Undertaker's Blues"	Honegger, *Pacific 231*		
First recordings of Papa Charlie Jackson, Barrelhouse Ed Andrews			
Maggie Jones, "You May Go But You'll Be Back Some Day"			
Virginia Liston, "Jail House Blues"			
Sara Martin, "Sobbin' Hearted Blues"			
Hazel Meyers, "The Man Ain't Born Who Can Treat Me Like You Do"			
Hazel Meyers, "War Horse Mama"			
Josie Miles, "A to Z Blues"			
Josie Miles, "Freight Train Blues"			
Sodarisa Miller, "Don't Dog Me 'Round Blues"			
Ma Rainey, "Lost Wandering Blues"			
Ma Rainey, "Lucky Rock Blues"			
Ma Rainey, "Ma Rainey's Mystery Record"			
Ma Rainey, "See See Rider Blues"			
Clara Smith, "Don't Advertise Your Man"			

Clara Smith, "Prescription for the Blues" Clara Smith, "You Don't Know My Mind" Trixie Smith, "Sorrowful Blues" Whistler and His Jug Band, "Chicago Flip"			
1925 Ida Cox, "How Can I miss You When I Got Dead Aim?" Ida Cox, "I Ain't Got Nobody" Ida Cox, "Lonesome Blues" Ida Cox, "Southern Woman's Blues" Papa Charlie Jackson, "Coffee Pot Blues" Papa Charlie Jackson, "The Faking Blues" Papa Charlie Jackson, "Shave 'Em Dry" Virginia Liston, "I Ain't Got Nobody" Julia Moody, "He'll Do You Wrong" Bessie Smith and Louis Armstrong, "The St. Louis Blues" Bessie Smith, "I Ain't Got Nobody" Bessie Smith, "You've Been a Good Old Wagon" Clara Smith, "Down Home Bound Blues" Clara Smith, "My John Blues" Trixie Smith, "Black Bottom Hop"	Straun's Pullman Porters, "Casey Jones" Lem Fowler, "Express Train Blues" Lem Fowler, "Hoochy Coochy Blues" Goofus Five, "I Had Someone Else Before I had You" Goofus Five, "Yes, Sir, That's My Baby" Antheil, *A Jazz Symphony* Gershwin, *Concerto in F*	Anderson, *Dark Laughter* Dos Passos, *Manhattan Transfer* Green, "The No 'Count Boy" Hemingway, "Soldier's Home" Hughes, "Negro Dancers," "The Weary Blues" Lawson, *Processional* Lindsay, *Collected Poems* Locke, *The New Negro* Williams contributes to surrealist magazine *Aesthete* Niles, *Impressions of a Negro Camp Meeting* Odum and Johnson, *The Negro and His Songs*	Brotherhood Of Sleeping Car Porters organized Lon Chaney, *Phantom of the Opera* Calvin Coolidge inaugurated president *Exposition Internationale des Artes Decoratifs et Industriels Modernes* Adolf Hitler, *Mein Kampf* Malcolm X born Robeson visits Paris Scopes "Monkey Trial" takes place

Blues	Ragtime, Pop, Jazz, Country, Classical	Literature and Folklore	Stage, Screen, Events
Trixie Smith, "The World's Jazz Crazy and So Am I" Charles and Effie Tyus, "Jazz Crazy" Ethel Waters, "Loud Speakin' Papa (You'd Better Speak Easy to Me)" Leola B. and Kid Wesley Wilson, "Rock, Aunt Dinah, Rock"			
1926 DeFord Bailey performs regularly on Barn Dance/ Grand Ole Opry Blind Blake, "Too Tight" Butterbeans and Susie, "Love Me and the World is Mine (Hit Me and the Jail is Yours)" Margaret Carter, "I Want Plenty Grease in My Frying Pan" Ida Cox, "Trouble in Mind" Rosa Henderson, "Chicago Policeman Blues" Bertha "Chippie" Hill, "Street Walker Blues" Bo Weavil Jackson, "Poor Boy Long Way From Home" Bo Weavil Jackson, "Some Scream High Yellow" Blind Lemon Jefferson, "Broke and Hungry"	Sonny Clay, "Chicago Breakdown" Junie Cobb, "Chicago Buzz" George McClennon, "While You're Sneakin' Out" Frank Hutchison, "The Train That Carried My Girl from Town" Antheil premieres *Ballet Mecanique* Carpenter sets Hughes poems to music Copland, *Four Piano Blues* (1926–1948) Gershwin, *Three Preludes for Piano* Schoenberg, *Suite, op. 29* Schulhoff, *Blues (pour) Paul Whiteman*	Gold a founding editor of *New Masses* Green, *Lonesome Road: Six Plays for the Negro Theater* Green, *In Abraham's Bosom* wins Pulitzer Hemingway, *The Sun Also Rises* Hughes, "The Negro Artist and the Racial Mountain" Lindsay, *Going to the Stars* *Palms* African American poetry issue in October Sandburg records for Victor Records Van Vechten, *Nigger Heaven* Eric Walrond, *Tropic Death* Handy, *Blues: An Anthology* Odum, *Negro Workaday Songs*	Twenty-three African Americans reported lynched Ralph Barton shoots film *Camille* Aaron Douglas embarks on the "Emperor Jones" series of illustrations Jolson, "A Plantation Act" Woodson introduces Negro History Week

Blind Lemon Jefferson, "Dry Southern Blues"
Blind Lemon Jefferson, "Stocking Feet Blues"
Ma Rainey, "Down in the Basement"
Bessie Smith, "Jazzbo Brown from Memphis Town"
Bessie Smith, "Young Woman Blues"
Clara Smith, "Whip it to a Jelly"
Mamie Smith, "Goin' Crazy with the Blues"
Mary Stafford, "Ain't Got Nobody to Grind My Coffee in the Morning"
Rev. J. M. Gates, "Death's Black Train is Coming"

1927 Texas Alexander, "Corn Bread Blues"
Texas Alexander, "Levee Camp Moan Blues"
DeFord Bailey, "Pan American Blues"
DeFord Bailey, "Dixie Flyer Blues"
Barbecue Bob, "Barbecue Blues"
Barbecue Bob, "Brown Skin Gal"
Ed Bell, "Hambone Blues"
Ed Bell, "Mean Conductor Blues"
Booker Orchestra, "Salty Dog"
Big Bill Broonzy, "House Rent Stomp"

Hammerstein's *Show Boat*
Moran and Mack, "The Two Black Crows"
Louis Armstrong, "Melancholy Blues"
Ellington takes up residence at the Cotton Club
Porter Grainger, "Homeless Blues"
California Ramblers, "Casey Jones"
California Ramblers, "Steamboat Bill"
Fiddlin' John Carson, "Gonna Swing on the Golden Gate"

The American Caravan
Bodenheim, *Returning Emotion*
Sterling Brown, "When De Saints Go Ma'ching Home" in *Opportunity*
Countee Cullen, ed. *Caroling Dusk*, includes Brown's "Odyssey of Big Boy"
Countee Cullen, *Copper Sun*
Faulkner, *Mosquitoes*
Rudolph Fisher, "The Promised Land"
Mike Gold, *Hoboken Blues*
Hesse, *Steppenwolf*

Cullen gets MA at Harvard
The Jazz Singer premieres
Marcus Garvey's sentence commuted, and he is deported
Hurston goes South on a folklore collecting trip
Fritz Lang, *Metropolis*
Charles Lindberg flies the Spirit of St. Louis non-stop from New York to Paris
Ann Pennington teaches Fritz the Cat the Black Bottom
Sacco and Vanzetti executed

Blues	Ragtime, Pop, Jazz, Country, Classical	Literature and Folklore	Stage, Screen, Events
Gus Cannon, "Can You Blame the Colored Man"	Grayson and Whitter, "Train 45"	Langston Hughes, *Fine Clothes to the Jew*	
Jaybird Coleman, "Boll Weevil"	Jimmie Rodgers, "Brakeman Blues"	Langston Hughes called "poet low-rate of Harlem" for his blues poems	
Sam Collins, "Jail House Blues"	Gid Tanner, "Casey Jones"	J. W. Johnson, reissue of *Autobiography of an Ex-Colored Man*	
Cow Cow Davenport, "Jim Crow Blues"	Antheil's New York premiere of *Ballet Mecanique*	J. W. Johnson, *God's Trombones*	
William Harris, "I'm Leavin' Town"	Diaghilev produces Elizalde's *The Heart of a Nigger Suite*	Lawson, *The Loudspeaker*	
Rosa Henderson, "Slow Up Papa"	Krenek, *Jonny Spielt Auf*	Lawson, *The International*	
Bertha "Chippie" Hill, "Weary Money Blues"	Mosolov, "Zavod"	Niles, *Singing Soldiers*	
Buddy Boy Hawkins, "Raggin' the Blues"	Ravel, *Violin Sonata in C: Blues*	Pound, *Antheil and the Treatise on Harmony*	
Peg Leg Howell's Gang, "Beaver Slide Rag"	Stein and Thomson, *Four Saints in Three Acts* (–1928)	Sandburg, *American Songbag*	
Peg Leg Howell, "Skin Game Blues"		Sandburg, "Baby Song of the Four Winds"	
Jim Jackson, "Jim Jackson's Kansas City Blues"		Sandburg collects "Frankie and Johnny"	
Blind Lemon Jefferson, "Match Box Blues"		Edward C. L. Adams, *Congaree Sketches*	
Blind Lemon Jefferson, "Right of Way Blues"			
Blind Lemon Jefferson, "See That My Grave is Kept Clean"			
Furry Lewis, "Casey Jones"			
Furry Lewis, "Sweet Papa Moan"			
Meade Lux Lewis, "Honky Tonk Train Blues"			

William McCoy, "Mama Blues" William McCoy, "Train Imitations and Fox Chase" Ma Rainey, "Dead Drunk Blues" Bessie Smith, "Back Water Blues" Sippie Wallace, "The Flood Blues" Sippie Wallace, "Lazy Man Blues" Richard Yates, "Sore Bunion Blues" Arnold and Irene Wiley, "You Better Not Go to 35th and State No More"			
1928 DeFord Bailey, "Casey Jones" Barbecue Bob, "Hurry and Bring It Back Home" Blind Blake, "He's In the Jail House Now" Blind Blake, "Panther Squall Blues" Blind Blake, "Walkin' Across the Country" Ishmon Bracey, "Trouble-Hearted Blues" Leroy Carr, "How Long—How Long Blues" Leroy Carr, "Low-down Dirty Blues" Bo Carter, "Good Old Turnip Greens"	Gene Austin, "My Blue Heaven" Emmett Miller, "I Ain't Got Nobody" Paul Robeson and Paul Whiteman, "Ol' Man River" Lawrence Welk, "Doin' the New Low-down" Louis Armstrong, "St. James Infirmary" Duke Ellington Orchestra and Marty Malneck Orchestra, "The St. Louis Blues" McKinney's Cotton Pickers, *Rainbow Round My Shoulder* King Oliver, "Speakeasy Blues" Martinu, *Jazz-Suite for Small Orchestra*	Stephen Vincent Benet, *John Brown's Body* Bodenheim, *Georgie May* Bodenheim, *The King of Spain* Sterling Brown, "Strange Legacies" in *The Crisis* Paul Green, *In the Valley* Nella Larsen, *Quicksand* John Howard Lawson, *The Pure in Heart* Claude McKay, *Home to Harlem* Carl Sandburg, *Good Morning, America* Edward C.L. Adams, *Nigger to Nigger* Archive of American Folk Song established	Cullen marries Yolande Du Bois Oscar DePriest elected first African American congressman from a northern state "Jazz Frightens Bears" *New York Times* headline Film *Jazz Mad* featuring Jean Hersholt *Keep Shufflin'* Ravel's *Bolero* premieres WGY broadcasts first scheduled television programs

Blues	Ragtime, Pop, Jazz, Country, Classical	Literature and Folklore	Stage, Screen, Events
Bob Coleman, "Tear It Down" Blind Bogus Ben Covington, "Adam and Eve" Blind Bogus Ben Covington, "I Heard the Voice of a Pork Chop" Ida Cox, "Fogyism" Madlyn Davis, "Gold Tooth Papa Blues" Tom Dickson, "Labor Blues" William Harris, "Hot Time Blues" Rosa Henderson, "Poplar Bluff Blues" Peg Leg Howell, "Rock and Gravel Blues" Peg Leg Howell, "Turtle Dove Blues" Mississippi John Hurt, "Casey Jones" Jim Jackson, "He's In the Jail House Now" Jim Jackson, "Old Dog Blue" Blind Lemon Jefferson, "Christmas Eve Blues" Lonnie Johnson and Eddie Lang duets Tillie Johnson, "Chicago Man Blues"	William Grant Still, *Africa*	John Jacob Niles and Doris Ullmann make four collecting trips to the Appalachians Howard W. Odum, *Rainbow Round My Shoulder*	

Tommy Johnson, "Canned Heat Blues"
Tommy Johnson, "Cool Drink of Water Blues"
Keghouse, "Sock It Blues"
Furry Lewis, "Dry Land Blues"
Furry Lewis, "I Will Turn Your Money Green"
Blind Willie McTell, "Dark Night Blues"
Ben Norsingle, "Motherless Blues"
Ma Rainey, "Black Cat Hoot Owl Blues"
Pine Top Smith, "Pine Top's Boogie Woogie"
Victoria Spivey, "My Handy Man"
Victoria Spivey, "New Black Snake Blues"
Freddie Spruell, "Low-down Mississippi Bottom Man"
Frank Stokes, "T'Ain't Nobody's Business"
Tampa Red and Georgia Tom, "It's Tight Like That"
Henry Thomas, "Bull Doze Blues"
Ramblin' Thomas, "No Job Blues"
Bessie Tucker, "Penitentiary"
Nolan Welsh, "Chicago Women Blues"

Blues	Ragtime, Pop, Jazz, Country, Classical	Literature and Folklore	Stage, Screen, Events
Robert Wilkins, "Jail House Blues" George "Bullet "Williams, "Frisco Leaving Birmingham" Jubilee Gospel Team, "These Bones Goin' Rise Again" Novelty Four Quartet, "The Blood Done Signed My Name" Richmond Jazz Quartette, "Gone Jazz Crazy" Utica Institute Singers, "Swingin' on the Golden Gate"			
1929 Willie Baker, "No No Blues" Ed Bell, "My Crime" Will Bennett, "Railroad Bill" The Black Hillbillies, "Kunjine Baby" Blind Blake, "Third Degree Blues" Ada Brown, "Down Home Dance" Leroy Carr, "Love is Dead" Lonnie Clark, "Broke Down Engine" Bob Coleman, "Cincinnati Underworld Woman" Georgia Tom Dorsey, "Pig Meat Blues"	Bob Miller, "Missouri Joe" Duke Ellington, "Jazz Convulsions" James P. Johnson, "You've Got to Be Modernistic" Lonnie Johnson and Eddie Lang, "Blue Room (Blues)" Jabbo Smith, "Croonin' the Blues"	Maxwell Bodenheim, *Sixty Seconds* Sterling Brown, "Riverbank Blues" in May *Opportunity* Witter Bynner, "Gotham" William Faulkner, *Sartoris* William Faulkner, *The Sound and the Fury* Jessie Fauset, *Plum Bun* Wallace Thurman, *The Blacker the Berry* Walter White, *Rope and Faggot* Virginia Woolf, *A Room of One's Own* Howard W. Odum, *Wings on My Feet*	Einstein propounds the "Unified Field Theory" Herbert Hoover inaugurated president *Connie's Hot Chocolates* moves to Broadway Archibald Motley paints *Blues* Stock market crash

Georgia Tom Dorsey, "Pig Meat Papa"
Cleo Gibson, "I've Got Ford Movement in My Hips"
Clifford Gibson, "Whiskey Moan Blues"
Mae Glover, "Pig Meat Mama"
Jim Jackson, "Dicty Blues"
Blind Lemon Jefferson, "Dynamite Blues"
Lil Johnson, "Rock That Thing"
Coley Jones, "The Elder He's My Man"
Jake Jones, "Southern Sea Blues"
Furry Lewis, "John Henry"
Sara Martin, "Death Sting Me Blues"
Romeo Nelson, "Gettin' Dirty Just Shakin' That Thing"
Nick Nichols, "Frankie and Johnny"
Charley Patton, "Going to Move to Alabama"
Charley Patton, "Mississippi Boweavil Blues"
Charley Patton, "Pony Blues"
Charley Patton, "Some Happy Day"
Rufus and Ben Quillian, "Ragged But Right"
Bessie Smith, "Dirty No-Gooder's Blues"

Blues	Ragtime, Pop, Jazz, Country, Classical	Literature and Folklore	Stage, Screen, Events
Bessie Smith, "Nobody Knows You When You're Down and Out"			
Bessie Smith, "Wasted Life Blues"			
Henry Spaulding, "Cairo Blues"			
Speckled Red, "The Dirty Dozens"			
Henry Thomas, "Don't Leave Me Here"			
Bessie Tucker, "Key to the Bushes Blues"			
Bessie Tucker, "Mean Old Master Blues"			
Robert Wilkins, "Falling Down Blues"			
1930		Hart Crane, *The Bridge* Mike Gold, *Jews Without Money*	

Works Cited

There have been several constant companions for my work on this volume. I single them out here as reference works that allowed me to take information I remembered and or titles I sought and bring greater specificity to my discussions. Scholars have long owed debts to these pioneers for the outstanding work they have done:

Dixon, Robert, John Godrich, and Howard Rye. *Blues and Gospel Records, 1890–1943*. 4th ed. Oxford: Oxford University Press, 1997.

Russell, Tony. *Country Music Records: A Discography, 1921–1942*. Oxford: Oxford University Press, 2004.

Rust, Brian. *Jazz and Ragtime Records, 1897–1942*. Vol. 1. Highlands Ranch, CO: Mainspring Press, 2002.

———. *Jazz and Ragtime Records, 1897–1942*. Vol. 2. Highlands Ranch, CO: Mainspring Press, 2002.

———. *Song Title Index*. Denver: Mainspring Press, 2003.

Sutton, Allan. *Cakewalks, Rags, and Novelties: The International Ragtime Discography, 1894–1930*. Denver: Mainspring Press, 2003.

Abbott, Lynn, and Doug Seroff. *Ragged But Right*. Jackson: University Press of Mississippi, 2007.

Adams, Agatha Boyd. *Paul Green of Chapel Hill*. Chapel Hill: University of North Carolina Library, 1951.

Adams, E. C. L. *Tales of the Congaree*. Originally published as *Congaree Sketches* (1927) and *Nigger to Nigger* (1928). Rpt. Edited and with an Introduction by Robert G. O'Meally. Chapel Hill: University of North Carolina Press, 1987.

Adams, Henry. *The Education of Henry Adams*. Boston: Massachusetts Historical Society, 1918.

Aiello, Thomas, ed. *Dan Burley's Jive*. DeKalb: Northern Illinois University Press, 2009.

Aiello, Thomas, ed. *Dan Burley's Jive*. DeKalb: Northern Illinois University Press, 2009.

Alexander, J. Heywood, ed. *To Stretch Our Ears: A Documentary History of America's Music*. New York: W. W. Norton and Co, 2002.

Alfonso, Barry. "John Jacob Niles: Dean of American Balladeers." http://john-jacob-niles.com/

American Treasures of the Library of Congress. Website. http://www.loc.gov/exhibits/treasures/tri049.html.

Amirkhanian, Charles. Notes. *Ego Scriptor Cantilenae: The Music of Ezra Pound*. Other Minds 1005–2: 10–13.

Anderson, Martin. "Nikolai Kapustin, Ukrainian Composer of Classical Jazz." *Fanfare* (Sept/Oct 2000): 93–97.

Anonymous. Notes. *William Carlos Williams Reads His Poetry*. Caedmon Cassette SWC 51047.

Ansermet, Ernest. "Sur Un Orchestre Négre." (1919). Rpt. *Keeping Time: Readings in Jazz History*. Ed. Robert Walser. New York: Oxford, 1999. 9–11.

Appel, Alfred. *Jazz Modernism: From Ellington and Armstrong to Matisse and Joyce*. New Haven: Yale University Press, 2004.

Arthur, Anthony. *Radical Innocent: Upton Sinclair*. New York: Random House, 2006.

Asante, Molefi Kete. "African Elements in African American English." In *Africanisms in American Culture*. Ed. Joseph E. Holloway. Bloomington: Indiana University Press, 2005.

Avery, Lawrence. *A Southern Life: Letters of Paul Green, 1916–1981*. Durham: University of North Carolina Press, 1994.

Axelrod, Alan, and Harry Oster. *The Penguin Dictionary of American Folklore*. New York: Penguin, 2000.

Babb, Valerie. "'The Joyous Circle': The Vernacular Presence in Frederick Douglass's Narratives." *College English* 67.4 (March 2005): 365–77.

Badger, Reid. *A Life in Ragtime: A Biography of James Reese Europe*. New York: Oxford University Press, 1995.

Bailey, Peter. *Popular Culture and Performance in the Victorian City*. Cambridge: Cambridge University Press, 1998.

Baker, David. "Jazz and Black Elements in Art Music." Liner Notes. *Krazy Kat*. New World NW 228.

Balaji, Murali. *The Professor and the Pupil: The Politics of W. E. B. Du Bois and Paul Robeson*. New York: Nation Books, 2007.

Balakian, Anna. *André Breton*. New York: Oxford University Press, 1971.

Baldwin, James. "Sonny's Blues." In *Write Me a Few of Your Lines: A Blues Reader. Amherst: University of Massachusetts Press*, 1999. 394–415.

———. "The Uses of the Blues." In *Playboy* (January 1964): 131–32, 240–41.

"Ballet: Diaghilev." *Grove's Dictionary of Music and Musicians, 5th ed.* Ed. Eric Blom. New York: St. Martin's Press, Inc., 1954. 383–92.

Barney, Natalie Clifford. *Aventures de L'esprit.* Paris: Emile Paul Freres, 1929. Rpt. New York: Ayer Co., 1975.

Bastin, Bruce. "Notes." *The Last Medicine Show.* Flyright LP 07–508: 1–28.

Bek, Josef. "Erwin Schulhoff: Concertos." *Schulhoff: Concertos alla Jazz.* London D 113435.

Benfey, Christopher. *The Double Life of Stephen Crane.* New York: Knopf, 1992.

Berlin, Edward A. *King of Ragtime: Scott Joplin and His Era.* New York: Oxford University Press, 1994.

Bierce, Ambrose. *The Devil's Dictionary.* 1911. Rpt. New York: Dover Books, 1958.

Blair, Sara. "Modernism and the Politics of Culture." *The Cambridge Companion to Modernism*, ed. Michael Levenson. Cambridge: Cambridge University Press, 1999.

Blues: A Magazine of New Rhythms. 1929–1930. Rpt. New York: Johnson Reprint Co., 1967.

Bodenheim, Maxwell. *60 Seconds.* New York: Liveright, 1929.

———. *Bringing Jazz.* New York: Liveright, 1930.

———. *Introducing Irony.* New York: Boni and Liveright, 1922.

———. *The King of Spain and Other Poems.* New York: Boni and Liveright, 1928.

———. *Ninth Avenue.* New York: Boni and Liveright, 1926.

———. *Returning to Emotion.* New York: Boni and Liveright, 1927.

———. *Selected Poems of Maxwell Bodenheim, 1914–1944.* New York: The Beechhurst Press, 1946.

Bogard, Travis R., and Jackson Bryer, eds. *Selected Letters of Eugene O'Neill.* 1988. Rpt. New York: Limelight Editions, 1994.

Bogardus, Emory S. "Odum and Folk Sociology." *Sociology and Social Research* 42.2 (July–August 1957): 441–48.

Bolden, Tony. *Afro-Blue: Improvisations in African American Poetry and Culture.* Urbana: University of Illinois Press, 2004.

Boone, Graeme M. "Twelve Key Recordings." *Cambridge Companion to Blues and Gospel Music.* Ed. Allan Moore. Cambridge: Cambridge University Press, 2002. 61–88.

Borshuk, Michael. "A Synthesis of Racial Caress. Hybrid Modernism in the Jazz Poems of Williams and Mina Loy." *Rigor of Beauty: Essays in Commemoration of William Carlos Williams.* Ed. Ian D. Copestake. Bern: Peter Lang AG, 2004. 255–71.

Boulton, Laura C. Liner Notes. *African Music: Rhythm in the Jungle.* Victor P-10 78 RPM Records. CD 84–89.

Bradbury, Malcolm. "The Non-Homemade World: Europeanized American Modernism." *American Quarterly* 39.1 (Spring 1987): 27–36.

Brennan, Juan Arturo. Liner Notes. *Villa-Lobos: The Complete String Quartets*. Dorian DSL 90904. CD. 1–14.

Brooker, Jewel Spears, and Joseph Bentley. *Reading the Waste Land: Modernism and the Limits of Interpretation*. Amherst: University of Massachusetts Press, 1990.

Brooks, Van Wyck, Alfred Kreymborg, Lewis Mumford, and Paul Rosenfeld, eds. *The American Caravan: A Yearbook of American Literature*. New York: The Macaulay Company, 1927.

Brown, Claudette. "Rudoplh Fisher." *Dictionary of American Negro Biography*. Eds. Rayford Logan and Michael R. Winston. New York: Norton, 1982. 55.

Brown, Sterling. "An American Epoch." *Opportunity* 9 (June 1931): 187.

———. "Black Ulysses at War." *Opportunity* (December 1929): 383–84.

———. "The Blues as Folk Poetry." In *Folk-Say 1*. Ed. Benjamin A. Botkin. Norman: University of Oklahoma Press, 1930. 324–39.

———. *The Collected Poems of Sterling A. Brown*. New York: Harper Colophon, 1980.

———. "Negro Character as Seen by White Authors." 1933. Rpt. *The New Cavalcade Vol. 1*. Eds. Arthur P. Davis, J. Saunders Redding, and Joyce A. Joyce. Washington, DC: Howard University Press, 1991. 607–39.

———. *Negro Poetry and Drama and the Negro in American Fiction*. 1937. Rpt. New York: Atheneum Press, 1972.

Burke, Carolyn. *Becoming Modern: The Life of Mina Loy*. New York: Farrar, Straus, and Giroux, 1996.

Bynner, Witter. "Gotham." *Blues: A Magazine of New Rhythms* 1 (March 1929): 45–6.

Calt, Stephen. *Barrelhouse Words: A Blues Dialect Dictionary*. Urbana: University of Illinois Press, 2009.

Carroll, Alice Elizabeth. *Word, Image, and the New Negro*. Bloomington: Indiana University Press, 2005.

Carson, Warren C. "Manhood, Masculinity, and Male Bonding." *Reviewing James Baldwin's Things Not Seen*. Ed. D. Quentin Miller. Philadelphia: Temple University Press, 2000. 12–32.

Caws, Mary Ann. *André Breton*. New York: Twayne 1971.

Charles, John. "Eugene O'Neill." *Encyclopedia of the Harlem Renaissance, Vol. 2*. Ed. Cary D. Wintz and Paul Finkelman. New York: Routledge, 2004. 927–29.

Charters, Samuel. *The Bluesmen*. New York: Oak Publications, 1967.

———. *The Roots of the Blues: An African Search*. New York: Perigree, 1981.

Childs, Donald J. *Modernism and Eugenics*. Cambridge: Cambridge University Press, 2001.

Chinitz, David. "A Jazz-Banjorine, Not a Lute: Eliot and Popular Music Before *The Waste Land*." In *T.S. Eliot's Orchestra*. Ed. John Xiros Cooper. New York: Garland, 2000: 3-24.

Christensen, Paul. "William Carlos Williams in the Forties: Prelude to Postmodernism." *Ezra Pound and William Carlos Williams*. Ed. Daniel Hoffman. Philadelphia: University of Pennsylvania Press, 1983. 149–63.

Clark, Barrett H. "Introduction." *Lonesome Road: Six Plays for the Negro Theatre*. New York: Robert M. McBride and Co., 1926. vii–xviii.

Clayton, Jay, and Eric Rothstein. "Figures in the Corpus: Theories of Influence and Intertextuality." *Influence and Intertextuality in Literary History*. Ed. Clayton and Rothstein. Madison: University of Wisconsin Press, 1991. 3–36.

Clemens, Samuel. *The Annotated Huckleberry Finn*. Ed. with an Introduction and Notes by Michael Patrick Hearn. New York: Norton, 2001.

Clurman, Harold. "Foreword." *With a Reckless Preface*. John Howard Lawson. New York: Farrar and Rinehart, 1934.

Collier, Eugenia. "The Phrase Unbearably Repeated." *James Baldwin: A Critical Evaluation*. Ed. Therman B. O'Daniel. Washington, DC: Howard University Press, 1977. 38–46.

Collier, James Lincoln. *Louis Armstrong: An American Genius*. New York: Oxford University Press, 1983.

Copeland, Carolyn Faunce. *Language & Time & Gertrude Stein*. Iowa City: University of Iowa Press, 1975.

Cowley, Malcolm. *Blue Juniata: A Life*. New York: Penguin, 1985.

———. *The Exile's Return*. New York: Norton, 1934.

Coyle, Michael, ed. *Ezra Pound and African American Modernism*. Orono: The National Poetry Foundation, 2001.

Crane, Hart. *Complete Poems and Selected Letters*. Ed. Langdon Hammer. New York: Library of America, 2006.

———. *The Complete Poems and Selected Letters and Prose of Hart Crane*. Ed. Brom Weber. New York: Liveright, 1966.

Crane, Stephen. *Maggie: A Girl of the Streets*. Ed. Thomas A. Gullason. New York: Norton, 1979.

Cullen, Countee. "Review of Langston Hughes's *The Weary Blues*." *Opportunity* 4 (Feb. 1926): 73–74.

Cummings, David. "Improvisation." *Random House Encyclopedic Dictionary of Classical Music*. New York: Random House, 1997.

cummings, e.e. *Complete Poems, 1904–1962*. Ed. George James Firmage. New York: Liveright, 1991.

———. *Tulips and Chimneys: The Original 1922 Manuscript*. Ed. George James Firmage. New York: Liveright, 1976.

Dandridge, Raymond. *Zalka Peetruza and Other Poems*. Cincinnati: The McDonald Press, 1928.

Darrell, R. D. "The Music of Henry F. Gilbert, John Powell, John Alden Carpenter, and Adolph Weiss." *Krazy Cat/Dance in Place/American Life/Rhapsodie Négre.* New World Records 80228–2, 7–17.

Davis, Angela Y. Blues Legacies and Black Feminism. New York: Pantheon, 1998.

Davis, Arthur P. From the Dark Tower. Washington, D.C.: Howard University Press, 1982.

Davis, Sheila. The Craft of Lyric Writing. Writer's Digest, 1984.

Davis, Thadious M. *Nella Larsen: Novelist of the Harlem Renaissance.* Baton Rouge: Louisiana State University Press, 1994.

Debus, Allen G., with Richard Martin. Liner Notes. *Monarchs of Minstrelsy: Historic Recordings by Stars of the Minstrel Stage.* Archeophone CD 1006.

Delany, Martin R. *Blake, or, The Huts of America.* Rpt. Boston: Beacon Press, 1971.

Dempsey, Peter. Liner Notes. *Music for Moderns.* Nostalgia Naxos 8.120505. CD.

Denning, Michael. *The Cultural Front: The Laboring of American Culture in the Twentieth Century.* London: Verso, 1996.

Desalvo, Debra. *The Language of the Blues from Alcorub to Zuzu.* New York: Billboard Books, 2006.

Dickinson, Donald C. *A Bio-Bibliography of Langston Hughes.* Hamden, CT: Archon Books, 1967.

Dickinson, Emily. *The Complete Poems of Emily Dickinson.* Ed. Thomas H. Johnson. Boston: Little, Brown and Co., 1960.

Diggins, John Patrick. *Eugene O'Neill's America: Desire Under Democracy.* Chicago: University of Chicago Press, 2007.

Dixon, Robert, and John Godrich. *Recording the Blues.* New York: Stein and Day, 1970.

Dixon, Robert, John Godrich, and Howard Rye. *Blues and Gospel Records, 1890–1943.* 4th ed. Oxford: Oxford University Press, 1997.

Doob, Leonard, ed. *Ezra Pound Speaking.* Westport, CT: Greenwood Press, 1978.

Dos Passos, John. *The Garbage Man.* New York: Harper and Brothers, 1926.

Douglas, Ann. *Terrible Honesty: Mongrel Manhattan in the 1920s.* New York: Farrar, Straus, Giroux: 1996.

Drew, Elizabeth. *T. S. Eliot: The Design of His Poetry.* New York: Scribner's, 1949.

Driggs, Frank, and Harris Lewine. *Black Beauty, White Heat: A Pictorial History of Classic Jazz.* New York: Da Capo Press, 1996.

Du Bois, W. E. B. "Close Ranks." *The Crisis* (July 1915). In *Let Nobody Turn Us Around: Voices of Resistance, Reform, and Renewal; An African American Anthology.* Eds. Manning Marable and Leith Mullings. New York: Bowman & Littlefield Publishers, Inc., 2000. 242–43.

———. "Returning Soldiers." *The Crisis* XVIII (May 1919), 13.

———. *The Illustrated Souls of Black Folk*. Ed. and annotated by Eugene F. Provenzo Jr. Boulder: Paradigm Publishers, 2005.

Dunbar, Paul Laurence. *Lyrics of Lowly Life*. 1895. Rpt. New York: Citadel Press, 1984.

———. *The Collected Poetry of Paul Laurence Dunbar*. Joanne M. Braxton, ed. Charlottesville: University Press of Virginia, 1993.

Early, Gerald, ed. *My Soul's High Song: The Collected Writings of Countee Cullen*. New York: Anchor Books, 1991.

Edelman, Lee. *Transmemberment of Song: Hart Crane's Anatomies of Rhetoric and Desire*. Stanford University Press, 1987.

Eliot, T. S. *The Complete Poems and Plays*. New York: Harcourt, Brace & World, 1971.

———. *Inventions of the March Hare: Poems 1903–1917*. Ed. Christopher Ricks. 1996. Rpt. New York: Harvest Books, 1998.

———. *The Letters of T. S. Eliot*. Ed. Valerie Eliot. Vol. 1. New York: Harcourt, Brace, and Jovanovich, 1988.

———. *Selected Prose of T. S. Eliot*. New York: Harcourt, 1975.

———. *The Use of Poetry and Use of Criticism: Studies in the Relation of Criticism to Poetry in England (Charles Eliot Norton Lectures for 1932–33)*. Cambridge: Harvard University Press, 1986.

———. *The Waste Land: A Facsimile and Transcript of the Original Drafts Including the Annotations of Ezra Pound*. Ed. Valerie Eliot. New York: Harcourt Brace Jovanovich, Inc., 1971.

Eliot, William G. *The Story of Archer Alexander*. Boston: Cupples, Upham, and Company, 1885.

Ellison, Ralph. *The Collected Essays of Ralph Ellison*. New York: Modern Library, 2004.

———. *Invisible Man*. 1952. Rpt. New York: Vintage, 1989.

———. *Shadow and Act*. New York: Random House, 1964.

Emerson, Ralph Waldo. "Nature." *Essays and Lectures*. New York: Library of America, 1983.

Epstein, Daniel Mark. "Condensing Eternity." *The New York Times* July 14, 2002, sec. 7, col. 1: 12.

Epstein, Dena J. *Sinful Tunes and Spirituals*. Urbana: University of Illinois Press, 1977.

Esterhammer, Angela. *Romanticism and Improvisation, 1750–1850*. Cambridge: Cambridge University Press, 2009.

Estrin, Mark W. *Conversations with Eugene O'Neill*. Oxford: University Press of Mississippi, 1990.

Evans, David. "African Elements in the Blues." *L'Oceano dei Suoni: Migrazioni, Musica, e Razze nella Formazion edelle Societa Eurotelantiche*. Ed. Pierangelo Castagneto. Torino: Otto Editore, 3–16.

———. *Big Road Blues: Tradition and Creativity in the Folk Blues*. Berkeley: University of California Press, 1982.

———."The Development of the Blues." *The Cambridge Companion to Blues and Gospel Music*. Ed. Allan Moore. Cambridge: Cambridge University Press, 2002. 20–43.

———. "Formulaic Composition in the Blues: A View from the Field." *Journal of American Folklore* 120 (478): 482–99.

———. Liner Notes. *Let's Get Loose: Folk and Popular Blues Styles from the Beginnings to the Early 1940s*. New World NW 290 (LP).

———. "Patterns of Reinterpretation in African-American Music of the United States." *African Perspectives: Pre-colonial History, Anthropology, and Ethno-Musicology*. Eds. Regine Allgayer-Kaufmann and Michael Weber. Frankfurt: Peter Lang, 2008. 206–14.

———. "The Reinterpretation of African Musical Instruments in the United States. *The African Diaspora: African Origins and New World Identities*. Eds. Isidore Okpewho, Carol Boyce Davies, and Ali A. Mazrui. Bloomington: Indiana University Press, 1999.

———. "Traditional Blues Lyrics and Myth: Some Correspondences." *The Lyrics in AfricanAmerican Popular Music. Proceedings of Metz (September 29th–30th 2000)*. Ed. Robert Springer. Bern: Peter Lang, 2001. 17–40.

Faulkner, William. *Mosquitoes*. 1927. Rpt. New York: Dell, 1962.

———. *Sartoris*. 1929. Rpt. New York: Signet Classic, 1964.

———. *Soldier's Pay*. 1926.

Fauset, Arthur Huff. "The Negro's Cycle of Song: A Review." *Opportunity* 3 (November 1925): 333–35, 348.

Filreis, Alan. *Counter-revolution of the Word: The Conservative Attack on Modern Poetry, 1945–1960*. Chapel Hill: University of North Carolina Press, 2007.

Fisher, Rudolph. "The Promised Land." *The City of Refuge: The Collected Stories of Rudolph Fisher*. Columbia: University of Missouri Press, 1987. 48–59.

Fitzgerald, F. Scott. *The Beautiful and Damned*. 1922. Rpt. New York: Charles Scribner's Sons, 1950.

———. *The Great Gatsby*. 1925. Rpt. New York: Scribner's, 1953.

Floyd, Samuel A., Jr. *The Power of Black Music*. New York: Oxford University Press, 1995.

Folsom. Michael, ed. *Mike Gold: A Literary Anthology*. New York: International Publishers, 1972.

Ford, Charles Henri. *The Garden of Disorder and Other Poems*. Introd. William Carlos Williams. London:Europa Press, 1938.

Garabedian, Steven. "Reds, Whites, and the Blues: Lawrence Gellert, 'Negro Songs of Protest,' and the Left-Wing Folk-Song Revival of the 1930s and 1940s." *American Quarterly* 57 (March 2005): 179–206.

Gardner, Helen. *The Art of T. S. Eliot*. New York: Dutton, 1950.

Garon, Paul. *Blues and the Poetic Spirit*. London: Eddison Press, 1975.

Gelb, Arthur, and Barbara Gelb. *O'Neill*. Enlarged Edition. New York: Harper and Row, 1973.

———. *O'Neill: Life with Monte Cristo*. New York: Applause Books, 2000.

Gelfant, Blanche. *The American City Novel*. Norman: University of Oklahoma Press, 1954.

Gellert, Lawrence. *Me and My Captain: Negro Songs of Protest, Volume 2*. New York: Hours Press, 1939.

———. *Negro Songs of Protest*. New York: American Music League, 1936.

Giles, Paul. *The Contexts of "The Bridge."* Cambridge: Cambridge University Press, 2009.

Gill, Jonathan. "Protective Coloring: Modernism and Blackface Minstrelsy in the Bolo Poems." *T. S. Eliot's Orchestra*. Ed. John Xiros Cooper. New York: Garland, 2000: 65-84.

Ginell, Cary, et al. "Notes." *The Influence of Jimmie Rodgers*. Bear Family BCD 16863.

Ginsberg, Allan. *Howl and Other Poems*. The Pocket Poets Series. San Francisco: City Lights, 1959.

———. Letter to the Author. 28 July 1988.

Gioia, Ted. *The Imperfect Art*. New York: Oxford University Press, 1988.

Gold, Mike. *Hoboken Blues*. In *The American Caravan*. Eds. Van Wyck Brooks, et al. New York: Macaulay Co., 1927.

———, ed. *Proletarian Song Book of Lyrics from the Operetta "The Last Revolution."* With J. Ramirez and Rudolph Liebich. Chicago: Local Chicago, Workers Party of America, 1925.

Goldberg, Isaac. *Tin Pan Alley: A Chronicle of American Popular Music*. New York: John Day Co., 1930.

Gordon, Lyndall. *Eliot's Early Years*. New York: Noonday Press, 1977.

Green, Paul. "In Abraham's Bosom." *Lonesome Road: Six Plays for the Negro Theatre*. New York: Robert M. McBride and Co., 1926.

———. "In the Valley." *In the Valley and Other Carolina Plays*. New York: Samuel French, 1928.

———. "The No 'Count Boy." *The Lord's Will and Other Plays*. New York: Henry Holt, 1925.

Green, Thomas A., ed. *Folklore: An Encyclopedia of Beliefs, Customs, Tales, Music, and Art*. Santa Barbara: ABC-CLIO, 1997.

Grove, Robin. "Pereira and After: The Cures of Eliot's Theater." *The Cambridge Companion to T. S. Eliot*: New York: Cambridge University Press, 1994. 158–75.

Gruver, Rod. "The Blues as Secular Religion." *Write Me a Few of Your Lines: A Blues Reader*. Amherst: University of Massachusetts Press, 1999. 222–30.

Halbreich, Harry. "Chamber Music for Strings, Piano Solo, and Piano and Strings." *Iannis Xenakis: Chamber Music, 1955–1990.* Naive CD 14.

Hale, Thomas D. *Griots and Griottes.* Bloomington, Indiana University Press, 1999.

Handy, W. C., ed. *Blues: An Anthology.* 1926. Rpt. Bedford, MA: Applewood Books, n.d.

Hanscombe, Gillian, and Virginia L. Smyers. "Mina Loy's Life." *Women Writing Their Lives: The Modernist Women, 1910–1940.* Boston: Northeastern University Press, 1987112-28.

Hardy, Clarence E., III. *James Baldwin's God: Sex, Hope, and Crisis in Black Holiness Culture.* Knoxville: University of Tennessee Press, 2003.

Harker, Brian. *Louis Armstrong's Hot Five and Hot Seven Recordings.* New York: Oxford University Press, 2011.

Harris, Mark. *City of Discontent.* 1952. Rpt. Urbana: University of Illinois Press, 1992.

Harris, Trudier. "Watchers Watching Watchers: Positioning Characters and Readers in Baldwin's 'Sonny's Blues' and Morrison's 'Recitatif.'" *James Baldwin and Toni Morrison: Comparative Critical and Theoretical Essays.* Eds. Lovalerie King and Lynn Orilla Scott. New York: Palgrave, 2006. 103–120.

Harvilahti, Lauri. "The Production of Finnish Epic Poetry: Fixed Wholes or Creative Compositions?" *Oral Tradition* 7.1 (1992): 87–101.

Hasse, John Edward, ed. *Ragtime: Its History, Composers, and Music.* New York: Schirmer, 1985.

Hawkes, Terence. *That Shakespeherian Rag: Essays on a Critical Process.* London: Methuen, 1986.

Haymes, Max. *Railroadin' Some: Railroads in the Early Blues.* York, England: Mentor Books, 2006.

Hemenway, Robert. *Zora Neale Hurston: A Literary Biography.* Urbana: University of Illinois Press, 1977.

Hemingway, Ernest. "A Clean, Well-Lighted Place." *The Short Stories of Ernest Hemingway.* 1938. Rpt. New York: Chas. Scribner's Sons, 1966.

Herskovits, Melville. *The Myth of the Negro Past.* 1941. Rpt.. New York: Beacon, 1958.

Higginson, Thomas Wentworth. *Army Life in a Black Regiment.* 1870. Rpt. New York: Penguin, 1997.

———. "Negro Spirituals." *Atlantic Monthly* 19: 116 (June 1867): 685–94.

Hill, Robert A., and Barbara Bair, eds. *Marcus Garvey: Life and Lessons.* Berkeley: University of California Press, 1987.

Hinton, David, trans. and ed. *Classical Chinese Poetry: An Anthology.* New York: Farrar, Straus, and Giroux, 2008.

Holbrook, Susan, and Thomas Dilworth, eds. *The Letters of Gertrude Stein and Virgil Thomson: Composition as Conversation.* New York: Oxford University Press, 2010.

Horowitz, Joseph. *Artists in Exile: How Refugees From Twentieth-Century War and*

Revolution Transformed the American Performing Arts. New York: HarperCollins, 2008.

Huggins, Nathan I., ed. *Voices From the Harlem Renaissance*. New York: Oxford, 1976.

Hughes, Langston. *The Big Sea*. New York: Knopf, 1940.

———. *The Collected Poems of Langston Hughes*. Eds. Arnold Rampersad and David Roessel. New York: Random House, 1995.

———. *The Collected Works of Langston Hughes, Vol. 1*. Gen. Eds. Arnold Rampersad, Dolan Hubbard, Leslie Sanders, and Steven C. Tracy. Columbia: University of Missouri Press, 2001.

———. *The Collected Works of Langston Hughes, Vol. 9*. Gen. Eds. Arnold Rampersad, Dolan Hubbard, Leslie Sanders, and Steven C. Tracy. Columbia: University of Missouri Press, 2001.

———. *I Wonder As I Wander*. 1956. Rpt. Columbia: University of Missouri Press, 2003.

———. "The Negro Artist and the Racial Mountain." *Nation* 122 (1926): 692–94. In *Voices from the Harlem Renaissance*. Ed. Nathan I. Huggins. New York: Oxford University Press, 1976: 305–09.

———. *Not Without Laughter*. 1930. Rpt. New York: Scribner, 1969.

———. "Review of *Rainbow Round My Shoulder*." *Opportunity* (May 1928): 149.

———. "Songs Called the Blues." *Phylon* 2.2 (1941): 143–45.

———. "Who's Passing for Who." *Langston Hughes: Short Stories*. Ed. Akiba Sullivan Harper. New York: Hill and Wang, 1996. 170–74.

Hughes, Langston, and Milton Meltzer. *Black Magic: A Pictorial History of the Negro in American Entertainment*. Englewood Cliffs: Prentice-Hall, 1967.

Hulme, T. E. *Speculations: Essays on Humanism and the Philosophy of Art*. Ed. Herbert Read. London: Routledge and Kegan Paul, 1924.

Hunter, Tera. *To 'Joy My Freedom: Southern Black Women's Lives and Labors After the Civil War*. Cambridge: Harvard University Press, 1997.

Hurston, Zora Neale. "Characteristics of Negro Expression." 1934. Rpt. in *The Sanctified Church*. Berkeley: Turtle Island, 1983. 49–68.

———. *The Complete Stories*. New York: HarperCollins, 1995.

———. "Letter to Alain Locke." May 1, 1928. *Zora Neale Hurston: A Life in Letters*. Ed. Carla Kaplan. New York: Double Day, 2002. 118.

———. *Mules and Men*. 1935. Rpt. New York: Harper Perennial, 1990.

———. *Their Eyes Were Watching God*. 1937. Rpt. New York: Harper and Row, 1990.

Hutchinson, George. *The Harlem Renaissance in Black and White*. Cambridge, MA: Belknap Press of Harvard University Press, 1995.

Hutchison, Percy. "Review of *Rainbow Round My Shoulder*." *New York Times Book Review* (March 4, 1928): 5.

Hyland, William. *Gershwin: A New Biography*. Westport, CT: Praeger Publishers, 2003.

Jackson, Jeffrey H. "Music-Halls and the Assimilation of Jazz in 1920s Paris." *Journal of Popular Culture* 32.4 (Fall 2000): 69–82.

Jahn, Janheinz. *A History of Neo-African Literature*. New York: Grove Press, 1968.

———. *Muntu*. London: Faber and Faber, 1961.

James, Henry. *Hawthorne*. 1879. Rpt. New York: Dolphin Books, 1965.

Januzzi, Marisa. "Mongrel Rose: The Unerring Esperanto of Loy's Poetry." *Mina Loy: Woman and Poet*. Eds. Maeera Shreiber and Keith Tuma. New York: National Poetry Foundation, 1989: 403-42.

"Jazz Frightens Bears." *New York Times* (Nov. 24, 1928): 16: 5.

Jerving, Ryan. "An Experiment in Modern Vaudeville: Archiving the Wretched Refuse in John Howard Lawson's *Processional*." *Modern Drama* 51.4 (Winter 2008): 528-51.

Johnson, Charles S. "Jazz." *Opportunity* 3.29 (1925): 133.

Johnson, James Weldon, ed. *The Book of American Negro Poetry*. 1922; 1931. Rpt. New York: Harcourt Brace and Co., 1969.

———, ed. *The Book of American Negro Spirituals*. 1925. Rpt. New York: Da Capo, 1989.

———, ed. *The Second Book of American Negro Spirituals*. 1926. Rpt. New York: Da Capo, 1989.

Jolson, Al. *The Jazz Singer*. Three Disc Deluxe Edition. Warner Brothers DVD 79889.

Jones, Gene, and David Jasen. *Spreadin' Rhythm Around: Black Popular Songwriters, 1880–1930*. New York: Routledge, 2005.

Kaplan, Carla, ed. *Zora Neale Hurston: A Life in Letters*. New York: Doubleday, 2002.

Kellner, Bruce. "Langston Hughes's *Nigger Heaven Blues*." *Langston Hughes: The Man, His Art, and His Continuing Influence*. Ed. C. James Trotman. New York: Garland, 1995. 87–96.

Kennedy, J. Gerald. "Average Racism: Poe, Slavery, and the Wages of Literary Nationalism." *Edgar Allan Poe and the Masses*. Ed. Terence Whalen. New Brunswick: Princeton University Press, 1999: 11-46.

Kenny, Vincent S. *Paul Green*. New York: Twayne, 1971.

Kostelanetz, Richard, ed. *Aaron Copland: A Reader*. London: Routledge, 2004.

Kouidis, Virginia M. *Mina Loy: American Modernist Poet*. Baton Rouge: Louisiana State University Press, 1980.

Krutch, Joseph Wood. "Jazz of the Spirit." *Nation* 28 (Jan. 1925): 99–100.

Kubik, Gerhard. *Africa and the Blues*. Jackson: University Press of Mississippi, 1999.

Laki, Peter. *Bartok and His World*. Princeton: Princeton University Press, 1995.

Larsen, Nella. *Quicksand*. Rpt. *Quicksand and Passing*. Ed. Deborah E. McDowell. New Brunswick: Rutgers University Press, 1986. xxxix–135

Lawson, John Howard. *The International*. New York: Macaulay Co., 1927.

———. *Processional: A Jazz Symphony of Negro Life*. New York: Thomas Seltzer, 1925.

———. *With a Reckless Preface*. New York: Farrar and Rinehart, 1934.

Lawson, Rob. *Jim Crow's Counterculture: The Blues and Black Southerners, 1890–1945*. Baton Rouge: Louisiana State University Press, 2010.

Levet, Jean-Paul. *Talkin' That Talk: Le langage du blues et du jazz*. Editions du Kargo, 2003.

Lewis, Wyndham. "Early London Environment." 1948. Rpt. in *T. S. Eliot: A Collection of Critical Essays*. Ed. Hugh Kenner. Englewood Cliffs, NJ: Prentice Hall, 1962.

Lincoln, Abraham. *Speeches and Writings: 1859–1865*. New York: Library of America, 1989.

Lindsay, Vachel. *The Poetry of Vachel Lindsay*. Vol. 1. Ed. Dennis Camp. Peoria: Spoon River Poetry Press, 1984. 1–410.

———. *The Poetry of Vachel Lindsay*. Vol. 2. Ed. Dennis Camp. Peoria: Spoon River Poetry Press, 1984. 411–817.

Locke, Alain, ed. *The New Negro*. 1925. Rpt. New York: Atheneum, 1970.

Logan, Rayford. *The Negro in American Life and Thought: The Nadir, 1877–1901*. New York: Dial Press, 1954.

Lohf, Kenneth A. *The Literary Manuscripts of Hart Crane*. Columbus: Ohio State University Press, 1967.

Lomax, Alan. "The Homogeneity of African-Afro-American Musical Style." *Afro-American Anthropology*. Eds. Norman E. Whitten Jr. and John F Szwed. New York: Free Press, 1970. 181–201.

Lornell, Kip. Liner Notes. *Virginia Traditions: Tidewater Blues*. BRI 006, 1–17.

———. Song Structure and Social Structure." *Ethnology* 1.4 (October 1962): 425–51.

Lotz, Rainer E. *Black People: Entertainers of African Descent in Europe, and Germany*. Bonn: Lotz, 1997.

Lowell, Amy. "Some Musical Analogies in Modern Poetry." *The Musical Quarterly* 6.1 (January 1920): 127–57.

Mahar, William J. *Behind the Burnt Cork Mask: Early Black Face Minstrelsy and Antebellum American Popular Culture*. Urbana: University of Illinois Press, 1998.

Mariani, Paul. *William Carlos Williams: A New World Naked*. New York: McGraw-Hill, 1982.

Marshall, Cynthia. "Man of Steel Done Got the Blues: Melancholic Subversion of Presence in *Antony and Cleopatra.*" *Shakespeare Quarterly* 44.4 (1993): 385–408.

Massa, Ann. *Vachel Lindsay: Fieldworker for the American Dream*. Bloomington: Indiana University Press, 1970.

Masters, Edgar Lee. *Vachel Lindsay*. 1935. Rpt. New York: Biblo and Tannen, 1969.

Mazor, Barry. *Meeting Jimmie Rodgers: How America's Original Roots Music Hero Changed the Pop Sounds of a Century*. New York: Oxford University Press, 2009.

McBride, Katharine Winters. *A Concordance to the Complete Poems of E. E. Cummings*. Ithaca: Cornell University Press, 1989.

McCann, Paul. *Race, Music, and National Identity: Images of Jazz in American Fiction, 1920–1960.* Madison: Fairleigh Dickinson University Press, 2008.

McCleery, David. Notes. *Discover the Music of the 20th Century.* Naxos CD 8.558168-69.

McCluskey, John, ed. *The Collected Stories of Rudolph Fisher.* Columbia: University of Missouri Press, 1987.

———. "Healing Songs." *CLA* Journal 26.2 (December 1982): 191–203.

McDowell, Deborah E. Introduction. *Quicksand and Passing.* Ed. Deborah E. McDowell. New Brunswick: Rutgers University Press, 1986.

McElderry, B. R., Jr. "Eliot's 'Shakespeherian Rag.'" *American Quarterly* 9 (1957): 185–86.

McIntire, Gabrielle. *Modernism, Memory, and Desire: T. S. Eliot and Virginia Woolf.* Cambridge: Cambridge University Press, 2007.

McKay, Claude. *The Passion of Claude McKay.* Ed. Wayne Cooper. New York: Schocken, 1973.

McNeilly, Kevin. "Culture, Race, Rhythm: *Sweeney Agonistes and the Live Jazz Break.*" *T. S. Eliot's Orchestra.* Ed. John Xiros Cooper. New York: Garland, 2000: 25-48.

Meade, Guthrie T., Jr., with Dick Spottswood and Douglas S. Meade. *Country Music Sources: a Biblio-Discography of Commercially Recorded Traditional Music.* Chapel Hill: Southern Folklife Collection, 2002.

Mellow, James R. *Invented Lives.* Boston: Houghton Mifflin, 1984.

Melville, Herman. *Clarel: A Poem and Pilgrimage in the Holy Land.* 2 vols. 1876. Rpt. New York: Russell & Russell, Inc., 1963.

Mencken, H. L. *Prejudices: The Complete Series.* 2 vols. Ed. Marion Elizabeth Rodgers. New York: Library of America, 2010.

Miller, James E., Jr. *T. S. Eliot: The Making of an American Poet.* University Park: Pennsylvania State University Press, 2005.

Mishkin, Tracy. *The Irish and Harlem Renaissances: Language, Identity, and Representation.* Gainesville: University Press of Florida, 1997.

Moholy-Nagy, L. "Literature." *The Avant-Garde Tradition in Literature.* Ed. Richard Kostelanetz. Buffalo, New York: Prometheus Books, 1982. 78–141.

Moody, A. David. *Ezra Pound: Poet, A Portrait of the Man and His Work, Vol. 1.* New York: Oxford University Press, 2007.

Moore, Jack B. *Maxwell Bodenheim.* New York: Twayne, 1970.

Morris, Ronald L. *Wait Until Dark: Jazz and the Underworld, 1880–1940.* Bowling Green: Bowling Green University Popular Press, 1980.

Muir, Peter. *Long Lost Blues: Popular Blues in America, 1850–1920.* Urbana: University of Illinois Press, 2010.

Murray, Albert. *Stomping the Blues.* New York: McGraw Hill, 1976.

Musser, Charles. "Troubled Relations: Paul Robeson, Eugene O'Neill, and Oscar

Micheaux." *Paul Robeson, Artist and Citizen*. New Brunswick: Rutgers University Press, 1998. 81–102.

Nadeau, Maurice. *The History of Surrealism*. Trans. Richard Howard. New York: Macmillan, 1965.

Needham, Maureen, ed. *I See America Dancing: Selected Readings 1685–2000*. Urbana: University of Illinois Press, 2002.

Nikiprowetzky, Toila. Liner Notes. Ocora OCR 15 and OCR 20. Quoted in *Jali Kunda*. Liner Notes by Robert Palmer. Ellipsis Arts CD 3510.

Niles, Abbe. "Introduction." *Blues: An Anthology*. Ed. W. C. Handy. 1926. Rpt. Bedford, MA: Applewood Books, n.d. 1–40.

———. "New Books Overflowing with Vitality." *New York World*. (March 11, 1928): 11.

Niles, John Jacob. *Impressions of a Negro Camp Meeting; Eight Traditional Songs*. Carl Fischer, 1925.

———. *Singing Soldiers*. New York: Charles Scribner, 1927.

Niven, Penelope. *Carl Sandburg: A Biography*. New York: Scribner's, 1991.

Nketia, J. H. Kwabena. *Ethnomusicology and African Music*. Accra, Ghana: Afram Publications, 2005.

North, Michael. *The Dialect of Modernism: Race, Language, and Twentieth-Century Literature*. New York: Oxford University Press, 1994.

North, Michael, ed. *The Waste Land: Authoritative Text, Contexts, Criticism*. New York: W. W. Norton & Company, 2001.

Northup, Solomon. *Twelve Years a Slave*. 1853. Rpt. Mineola: Dover, 1970.

Notes. *Ravi Shankar: A Journey Through his Music*. Membran CD 223970-326.

O'Connor, Patrick. "Minstrel and Medicine Shows: Creating a Market for the Blues." *Overland Review* 32.1/2 (2005): 57–68.

Odum, Howard W. *Cold Blue Moon: Black Ulysses Afar Off*. Indianapolis: Bobbs-Merrill, 1931.

———. *Rainbow Round My Shoulder: The Blue Trail of Black Ulysses*. Indianapolis: Bobbs-Merrill, 1928. Rpt. Bloomington: Indiana University Press, 2006.

———. *Wings on My Feet: Black Ulysses at the Wars*. Indianapolis: Bobbs-Merrill, 1929. Rpt. Bloomington: Indiana University Press, 2007.

Odum, Howard W., and Guy B. Johnson. *The Negro and His Songs*. 1925. Rpt. Hatboro, PA: Folklore Associates, 1964.

Ogren, Kathy J. *The Jazz Revolution: Twenties America and the Meaning of Jazz*. New York: Oxford University Press, 1992.

Oliver, Paul. *Conversation with the Blues*. 1965. Rpt. Cambridge: Cambridge University Press, 1997.

———. *Savannah Syncopators: African Retentions in the Blues*. New York: Stein and Day, 1970.

———. *Songsters and Saints: Vocal Traditions on Race Records*. Cambridge: Cambridge University Press, 1984.

———. *The Story of the Blues*. Philadelphia, Chilton, 1969.

O'Meally, Robert. "Introduction." *Seeing Jazz: Artists and Writers on Jazz*. Ed. Elizabeth Goldson. San Francisco: Chronicle Books, 1997.

O'Neill, Eugene. *Complete Plays, 1913–1920*. New York: Library of America, 1988.

———. *Complete Plays, 1920–1931*. New York: Library of America, 1988.

Osofsky, Gilbert. *Harlem: The Making of a Ghetto, Negro New York, 1890–1930*. New York: Harper, 1968.

The Compact Edition of Oxford English Dictionary. New York: Oxford University Press, 1971.

Patton, Sharon F. *African American Art*. New York: Oxford University Press, 1998.

Pen, Ron. *I Wonder As I Wander: The Life of John Jacob Niles*. University Press of Kentucky, 2010.

Perkins, David. *A History of Modern Poetry: Modernism and After*. Cambridge: Harvard University Press, 1987.

Perloff, Marjorie. *Poetry On and Off the Page: Essays for Emergent Occasions*. Evanston, IL: Northwestern University Press, 1998.

———. "'To Give a Design': Williams and the Visualization of Poetry." *William Carlos Williams: Man and Poet*. Ed. Carroll F. Terrell. Ororno, Maine: National Poetry Foundation, 1983: 159-86.

Peterson, Bernard L., Jr. *A Century of Musicals in Black and White: An Encyclopedia of Musical Stage Works By, About, or Involving African Americans*. Westport, CT: Greenwood Press, 1993.

Pfeiffer, Kathleen. Introduction. *Nigger Heaven*. Urbana: University of Illinois Press, 2000. ix–xxxix.

Pinkerton, Jan, and Randolph H. Hudson. *Encyclopedia of the Chicago Literary Renaissance*. New York: Facts on File, Inc., 2004.

Pollack, Howard. *John Alden Carpenter: A Chicago Composer*. Urbana: University of Illinois Press, 2001.

———. *Skyscraper Lullaby: The Life and Music of John Alden Carpenter*. Washington: Smithsonian Institution Press, 1995.

Pound, Ezra. *The ABC of Reading*. 1934. Rpt. New York: New Directions, 1960.

———. *Antheil and the Treatise on harmony, with supplementary notes*. Chicago: P. Covici, Inc., 1927.

———. *The Cantos of Ezra Pound*. New York: New Directions, 1972.

———. *Guide to Kulchur*. 1936. Rpt. New York: New Directions, 1968.

———. *The Literary Essays of Ezra Pound*. 1935. Rpt. New York: New Directions, 1968.

———. *Poems and Translations*. New York: Literary Classics of the United States, 2003.

———. *Pound/Joyce: The Letters of Ezra Pound to James Joyce, With Pound's Critical Essays and Articles About Joyce*. New York: New Directions, 1970.

———. *The Selected Letters of Ezra Pound, 1907–1941*. 1950. Rpt. New York: New Directions, 1971.

———. *Selected Prose, 1909–1965*. New York: New Directions, 1973.

———. *The Spirit of Romance*. 1910. Rpt. New York: New Directions, 2005.

Radano, Ronald. *Lying Up a Nation*. Chicago: University of Chicago Press, 2003.

Raine, Craig. *T. S. Eliot*. New York: Oxford University Press, 2006.

Read, Herbert. "T. S. Eliot—A Memoir." *T. S. Eliot: The Man and His Work*. Ed. Allen Tate. New York: Delacorte Press, 1966. 11–37.

Reilly, John M. "'Sonny's Blues:' James Baldwin's Image of Black Community." *James Baldwin: A Collection of Critical Essays*. Ed. Keneth Kinnamon. Englewood Cliffs, N.J.: Prentice Hall, 1974. 139–46.

Richardson, John. *A Life of Picasso, Vol. 1, 1881–1906*. New York: Random House, 1991.

———. *A Life of Picasso, Vol. 2, 1907–1917*. New York: Random House, 1996.

Robinson, Alan. *Symbol to Vortex: Poetry, Painting, and Ideas, 1885–1914*. New York: St. Martin's, 1985.

Rood, Karen. "Charles Henri Ford." *DLB Vol. 48,* Second Series. Ed. Peter Quartermain. Detroit: Gale Research Co., 1986. 191–210.

Roper, John Herbert. *Paul Green: Playwright of the Real South*. Athens: University of Georgia Press, 2003.

Rosemont, Franklin. "A Revolutionary Poetic Tradition." *Living Blues*. (January-February 1976): 20–23.

———. "Surrealism and Blues: Introduction." *Living Blues*. (January-February 1976): 19.

Rosemont, Franklin, ed. *The Rise and Fall of the Dil Pickle*. Chicago: Charles H. Kerr Publishing Company, 2004.

Rosemont, Franklin, and Robin D. G. Kelley, eds. *Black, Brown, and Beige: Surrealist Writings from Africa and the Diaspora*. Austin: University of Texas Press, 2009.

Russell, Tony. *Blacks, Whites, and Blues*. New York: Stein and Day, 1970.

———. *Country Music Records: A Discography, 1921–1942*. Oxford: Oxford University Press, 2004.

———. Liner Notes. *Field Recordings, Vol. 1: Virginia*. Document DOCD 5575: 1–2.

Rust, Brian. *Jazz and Ragtime Records, 1897–1942*. Vol. 1. Highlands Ranch, CO: Mainspring Press, 2002.

———. *Jazz and Ragtime Records, 1897–1942*. Vol. 2. Highlands Ranch, CO: Mainspring Press, 2002.

———. *Song Title Index*. Denver: Mainspring Press, 2003.

Sandburg, Carl. *Always the Young Strangers*. New York: Harcourt, Brace, and Co., 1952.

———. *The American Songbag*. New York: Harcourt, Brace & World, 1927.

———. *The Complete Poems of Carl Sandburg*. Revised and Expanded Edition. San Diego: Harcourt Brace Jovanovich, 1970.

Sanders, Lynn Moss. *Howard W. Odum's Folklore Odyssey: Transformation to Tolerance through African American Folk Studies*. Athens: University of Georgia Press, 2003.

Savran, David. "The Search for America's Soul: Theatre in the Jazz Age." *Theatre Journal* 58.3 (October 2006): 459–78.

Schaefer, William J., and Johannes Riedel. *The Art of Ragtime*. Baton Rouge: Louisiana State University Press, 1973.

Schreiber, Maeera, and Keith Tuma, eds. *Mina Loy: Woman and Poet*. Orono, ME: National Poetry Foundation, 1998.

Schultz, Elizabeth. "To Be Black and Blue: The Blues Genre in Black American Autobiography." *Kansas Quarterly* 7.3 (1975): 81–96.

Scott, Lynn Orilla. *Witness to the Journey: James Baldwin's Later Fiction*. East Lansing: Michigan State University Press, 2002.

Shusterman, Richard. "Eliot as Philosopher." *The Cambridge Companion to T. S. Eliot*. Ed. A. David Moody. Cambridge: Cambridge University Press, 1994.

Silvester, Peter. *A Left Hand Like God: A Study of Boogie-Woogie*. London: Quartet Books, 1988.

Simawe, Saadi A. "What Is In a Sound? The Metaphysics and Politics of Music in *The Amen Corner*." *Reviewing James Baldwin's Things Not Seen*. Ed. D. Quentin Miller. Philadelphia: Temple University Press, 2000. 12–32.

Singal, Daniel Joseph. "Towards a Definition of American Modernism." *American Quarterly* 39.1 (Spring 1987): 7–26.

Soitos, Stephen F. *The Blues Detective: A Study of African American Detective Fiction*. Amherst: University of Massachusetts Press, 1996.

Speer, Albert. *Inside the Third Reich*. 1970. Rpt. New York: Simon and Schuster, 1997.

Spencer, Jon Michael. *Blues and Evil*. Knoxville: University of Tennessee Press, 1993.

Stauffer, John, ed. *The Works of James McCune Smith*. New York: Oxford University Press, 2006.

Stein, Gertrude. *Writings, 1903–1932*. New York: Library of America, 1998.

Stevens, Wallace. *The Collected Poems of Wallace Stevens*. New York: Knopf, 1978.

Stock, Noel. *The Life of Ezra Pound*. San Francisco: North Point Press, 1982.

Stovall, Tyler. *Paris Noir: African Americans in the City of Light*. New York: Houghton Mifflin, 1996.

"Stravinsky for Jazz Ensemble." http://stravinskyforjazzensemble.blogspot.com/2009/11/rite-of-spring-as-work-or-jazz.html

Stuckey, Sterling. *African Culture and Melville's Art: The Creative Process in Benito Cereno and Moby Dick*. New York: Oxford University Press, 2009.

Sudhalter, Richard M. *Lost Chords: White Musicians and Their Contribution to Jazz, 1915–1945*. New York: Oxford University Press, 1999.

Sullivan, Jack. *New World Symphonies*. New Haven: Yale University Press, 1999.

Sutton, Allan. *Cakewalks, Rags, and Novelties: The International Ragtime Discography, 1894–1930*. Denver: Mainspring Press, 2003.

Sutton, Walter. "A Visit with William Carlos Williams." *Interviews with William Carlos Williams*. Ed. Linda Welsheimer Wagner. New York: New Directions, 1976. 38–76.

Taft, Michael. *The Blues Lyric Formula*. New York: Routledge, 2006.

———. *Talkin' to Myself: Blues Lyrics, 1921–1942*. 1983. Rpt. New York: Routledge, 2005.

Thompson, Lawrance. *Robert Frost: A One-Volume Edition of the Acclaimed Authorized Biography*. New York: Holt, Rinehart and Winston, 1982.

Thompson, Robert Farris. "An Aesthetic of the Cool: West African Dance." *African Forum* 2.2 (Fall 1966): 87.

Thomson, Virgil. Notes. *Four Saints in Three Acts*. Nonesuch 2 CD 9 79035-2.

Thurman, Wallace. *The Blacker the Berry*. 1929. Excerpted in *The Collected Writings of Wallace Thurman*. Eds. Amritjit Singh and Daniel M. Scott III. New Brunswick: Rutgers University Press, 2003: 449-62.

———. "Negro Poets and Their Poetry." 1928. Rpt. *The Collected Writings of Wallace Thurman*. Eds. Amritjit Singh and Daniel M. Scott III. New Brunswick: Rutgers University Press, 2003: 205-16.

———. "Review of *Blues: An Anthology*." 1926. Rpt. *The Collected Writings of Wallace Thurman*. Eds. Amritjit Singh and Daniel M. Scott III. New Brunswick: Rutgers University Press, 2003: 185-86.

Thurman, Wallace, and William Jourdan Rapp. "Harlem: A Melodrama of Negro Life." 1928. *The Collected Writings of Wallace Thurman*. Eds. Amritjit Singh and Daniel M. Scott III. New Brunswick: Rutgers University Press, 2003: 313-69.

Tick, Judith, ed. *Music in the USA: A Documentary Companion*. New York: Oxford University Press, 2008.

Tidwell, John Edgar. *Livin' the Blues*. Madison: University of Wisconson Press, 1992.

Tignor, Eleanor. "Rudolph Fisher." *Dictionary of Literary Biography, Vol. 51*. Ed. Trudier Harris. Detroit: Gale, 1987. 86–95.

Tipaldi, Art. *Children of the Blues: 49 Musicians Shaping a New Blues Tradition*. New York: Backbeat, 2002.

Toelken, Barre. *The Dynamics of Folklore*. Boston: Houghton Mifflin, 1979.

Toomer, Jean. *Cane*. 1923. Rpt. Ed. Darwin T. Turner. New York: Norton, 1988.

Tosches, Nick. *Where Dead Voices Gather*. Boston: Little, Brown and Co., 2001.

Townley, Eric. *Tell Your Story*. Chigwell, Essex: Storyville, 1976.

Tracy, Steven C., "Introduction." *John Henry: Roark Bradford's Novel and Play*. New York: Oxford University Press, 2008: 3-53.

———. *Langston Hughes and the Blues*. Urbana: University of Illinois Press, 1988.

———, ed. *Write Me a Few of Your Lines: A Blues Reader*. Amherst: University of Massachusetts Press, 1999.

———. *Writers of the Black Chicago Renaissance*. Urbana: University of Illinois, 2011.

Truth, Sojourner. *The Narrative of Sojourner Truth*. 1878. Rpt. New York: Oxford University Press, 1991.

Turner, Darwin T. "Jazz-Vaudeville Drama in the Twenties." *Educational Theatre Journal* 11.2 (May 1959): 110–16.

Twain, Mark. *The Adventures of Huckleberry Finn*. Berkeley: University of California Press, 1985.

Tytell, John. *Ezra Pound: The Solitary Volcano*. New York: Anchor Press, 1987.

van Rijn, Guido. Liner Notes. *Too Late, Too Late, Vol. 10*. Document DOCD 5601: 1–6.

———. *Roosevelt's Blues: African-American Blues and Gospel Songs on FDR*. Jackson: University Press of Mississippi, 1997.

———. *The Truman and Eisenhower Blues: African-American Blues and Gospel Songs, 1945–1960*. London: Continuum, 2004.

Van Vechten, Carl. *Nigger Heaven*. 1926. Rpt. Urbana: University of Illinois Press, 2000.

WFMU's Beware of the Blog. http://blog.wfmu.org/freeform/2009/06/edgar-varèse-and-the-jazzmen-mp3s.html.

Wagner, Bryan. *Disturbing the Peace*. Cambridge: Harvard University Press, 2009.

Wald, Elijah. "Louis Armstrong Loves Guy Lombardo! Acknowledging the Smoother Roots of Jazz." *Jazz Research Journal* 1 (2007): 129–45.

Walker, Julia. *Expressionism and Modernism in the American Theatre: Bodies, Voices, Words*. Cambridge: Cambridge University Press, 2005.

Walser, Robert, ed. *Keeping Time: Readings in Jazz History*. New York: Oxford, 1999.

Waterman, Richard Alan. "African Influence on the Music of the Americas." *Acculturation in the Americas*. Ed. Sol Tax. Chicago: University of Chicago Press, 1952: 201-18.

Watson, Steven. *The Harlem Renaissance: Hub of African-American Culture, 1920–1930*. New York: Pantheon, 1995.

———. *Strange Bedfellows: The First American Avant-Garde*. New York: Abbeville Press, n.d.

Whipple, Leon. "War Blues." *The Survey* 63.2 (November 1, 1929): 162–63.

White, Shane, and Graham White. *The Sounds of Slavery*. Boston: Beacon Press, 2005.

Whitman, Walt. "Edgar Poe's Significance." *Specimen Days*. Ed. Floyd Stovall. New York: New York University Press, 1963: 230-33.

———. *Notes Left Over*. "British Literature." *Poetry and Prose*. Ed. Justin Kaplan. New York: Library of America, 1996. 1082–84.

———. *Poetry and Prose*. Ed. Justin Kaplan. New York: Library of America, 1996.

Wier, Albert E. *Dance Music the Whole World Plays*. New York: Broadcast Music, Inc., 1917.

Williams, Sherley Anne. "The Black Musician: The Black Hero As Light Bearer." *James Baldwin: A Collection of Critical Essays*. Ed. Keneth Kinnamon. Englewood Cliffs, NJ: Prentice Hall, 1974. 139–46.

———. "The Blues Roots of Contemporary Afro-American Poetry." 1979. Rpt. *Write Me a Few of Your Lines: A Blues Reader*. Ed. Steven C. Tracy. Amherst: University of Massachusetts Press, 1999. 445–55.

Williams, William Carlos. *Collected Poems of William Carlos Williams, Vol. 1*. New York: New Directions, 1986.

———. "For a New Magazine." *Blues* 1.2 (1929): 30–32.

———. "Introduction." *The Garden of Disorder and Other Poems*. By Charles Henri Ford. London: Europa Press, 1938. 9–11.

———. *Kora in Hell: Improvisations*. Boston: The Four Seas Company, 1920.

Wilson, Edmund. *The Twenties*. New York: Farrar, Straus, and Giroux, 1975.

Wondrich, David, and Richard Martin. Liner Notes. *Stomp and Swerve: American Music Gets Hot*. Archeophone Arch 1003.

Work, John W. "Negro Folk Song." *The Opportunity Reader*. Ed. Sondra Kathryn Wilson. New York: Modern Library, 1999. 336–42.

Wright, Richard. "Big Boy Leaves Home." *Uncle Tom's Children*. 1938. Rpt. New York: Harper and Row, 1965.

Wyatt, Robert, and John Andrew Johnson, eds. *The George Gershwin Reader*. New York: Oxford University Press, 2004.

Yannella, Philip R. *The Other Carl Sandburg*. Jackson: University Press of Mississippi, 1996.

Yeomans, W. E. "T. S. Eliot, Ragtime, and the Blues." *University Review—Kansas City* 34 (1968): 267–75.

Yoseloff, Thomas, ed. *Seven Poets in Search of an Answer*. New York: B. Ackerman, 1944.

Zukovsky, Louis. *A*. Berkeley: University of California Press, 1978.

Index